Readings in Managerial Economics

Readings in Managerial Economics

Edited by

Thomas Joseph Coyne
The University of Akron

W. Warren Haynes
Late of the State University of New York, Albany

Dale K. Osborne
Federal Reserve Bank of Dallas

1977

Revised Edition

BUSINESS PUBLICATIONS, INC. Dallas, Texas 75243
Irwin-Dorsey Limited Georgetown, Ontario L7G 4B3

Revised Edition

4 5 6 7 8 9 0 MP 5 4 3 2 1 0 9

ISBN 0-256-01904-5
Library of Congress Catalog Card No. 76-62633
Printed in the United States of America

Preface

Producing an anthology may be similar to adopting a baby. It cannot be accomplished until and unless someone else conceives the child, bears the pain, and delivers the package. Production of a collection of readings in managerial economics is accomplished by adopting a few of the hundreds of articles reviewed. These papers are ones conceived by "academic scribblers," submitted by them to critical and exhaustive investigations and/or experimentation, and delivered for publication after painful inquiry. This particular combination, or mix, of articles approximates closely a package which the editors hope will facilitate better student understanding of the subject.

An anthology is intended to improve student access to journal articles while allowing authors an outlet for somewhat wider dissemination of their views. Hopefully, this publication does not differ in that respect. This Revised Edition retains those articles which reportedly appeal to economics scholars; in addition, it contains research of interest to skills-oriented business students, to the B.B.A.'s and the M.B.A.'s who must learn when, how, and why certain tools and techniques of the economist are applicable.

A few articles in the original version of this publication were too complicated for some students. An attempt is made here to alter this condition. Professors wanting to minimize pure economic theory may welcome this slight change of emphasis.

The writings of the classical and socialistic economic theorists, which have contributed significantly to the literature, were not found in the original version and are *not* found in this edition. Likewise, the unmistakable brilliance of the many economists who concerned themselves with the study and explanation of how an economy works and whether certain desirable goals such as full employment and price stability could be achieved are unnecessary in this kind of book. For the most part, those writers did not address themselves specifically to the price and output decisions that must be made daily by corporate executives, many of the tools for which *are* explained in this publication.

The purpose of this edition is to demonstrate that economic theory need not be confined to some ivory tower. Its objective is to supplement the reader's understanding of economic theory with enough knowledge of procedural technique(s) that he or she will become a more effective decision maker, a more useful member of the management team.

One hesitates to guess at the number of articles that were reviewed in the selection process for this edition. Suffice it to say that many were called but few were chosen. And the probability is high that some mistakes were made. Naturally, the editors assume full responsibility for these errors, judgmental or otherwise.

Suggestions received from several colleagues almost caused adoption of a more uniform level of abstraction throughout the volume. The temptation was overcome; consequently, the user has abstract articles that develop important principles mixed with elementary ones that illustrate those principles clearly.

Constraints common to the practice continue with this edition; namely space, coverage, and balance. A self-imposed limitation of not reprinting materials from books is retained.

Whenever possible, footnotes are removed and, at times, textual material that does not contribute significantly to the overall aims of the book is omitted. To the greatest possible extent, editorial changes are minimal.

A matrix of cross references between several leading textbooks and specific articles in this publication is provided for the user. In addition, these chapters are cross-referenced with specific articles in the Table of Contents.

Very sincere thanks is expressed to the authors and publishers who provided permission to reprint these articles.

We have benefited from helpful comments and suggestions received from a number of students and colleagues. We are particularly grateful to students for feedback concerning many of the articles considered.

February 1977

T. J. Coyne
D. K. Osborne

Table of Contents and Text Cross-References*

PART ONE
The Scope and Method of Managerial Economics

* Textbooks referenced include:

Brigham, Eugene, and Pappas, James, *Managerial Economics,* 2d ed. (Hinsdale, Ill.: Dryden Press, 1976).

Christenson, Charles J., Vancil, Richard F., and Marshall, Paul W., *Managerial Economics: Text and Cases,* rev. ed. (Homewood, Ill.: Irwin, 1973).

Colberg, Marshall G., Forbush, Dascomb R., and Whitaker, Gilbert R., *Business Economics* (Homewood, Ill.: Irwin, 1970).

Haynes, Warren W., and Henry, William R., *Managerial Economics* (Dallas, Tex.: Business Publications, 1974).

McGuigan, James R., and Moyer, R. Charles, *Managerial Economics* (Hinsdale, Ill.: Dryden Press, 1975).

Spencer, Milton H., Seo, K. K., and Simkin, Mark G., *Managerial Economics: Text, Problems, and Short Cases* (Homewood, Ill.: Irwin, 1975).

PART TWO
Demand

PART THREE
Forecasting

PART FOUR
Costs

PART FIVE
Pricing

PART SIX
Capital Budgeting

TEXT CROSS-REFERENCES

Readings in This Book	Part and Chapter Numbers					
	Part I Scope and Method of Managerial Decisions	*Part II Demand*	*Part III Fore-casting*	*Part IV Costs*	*Part V Pricing*	*Part VI Capital Budgeting*
Brigham and Pappas	1, 3	4, 5	App. B, 5	8, 9, 11, 13	2, 10, 11	13
Christenson, Vancil and Marshall	Introd., 4	7	6	1, 11	7	5, 11
Colberg, Forbush and Whitaker ...	1	3, 4, 12	2	5, 6, 7	12	7
Haynes and Henry	1	3, 4	4, 10	6, 10	8, 9	2, 11
McGuigan and Moyer	1, 2	6, 8	7	10, 14	4, 12, 13	15, 16
Spencer, Seo and Simkin	2, 3	5, 6	4, 6	8, 12, 14	12	11, 14

part ONE

The Scope and Method of Managerial Economics

INTRODUCTION

Managerial economics is economics applied to managerial decision making. It is a branch of economics bridging the gap between abstract theory and managerial practice. Its stress is on the use of the tools of economic analysis in clarifying problems, in organizing and evaluating information, and in comparing alternative courses of action. Though it is sometimes known as business economics, its methods and point of view are applicable not only in business but also in other institutions, such as government, universities, nonprofit foundations, etc., which allocate resources.

Economics is defined sometimes as the study of the allocation of scarce resources among unlimited wants. It follows that *managerial* economics is the study of the allocation of resources available to a firm or other decision-making institution. Thus, like all economics, managerial economics is concerned with choice; but, among the various branches of economics, it is supremely pragmatic. It cuts through many of the refinements of theory. While it seems to avoid some of the most difficult issues of abstract economic theory, it inevitably faces complications that are ignored in pure theory, for it must deal with the total situation in which decisions are made.

Managerial economics is therefore manifestly different from microeconomic theory; but it is somehow related. Just what this relation is has been a lively topic of debate. The extreme positions are, on the one hand, a naive belief that the most abstract economic theories are applicable to the most complex of managerial problems and, on the other, an equally repugnant belief that no part of economic theory is applicable to even the simplest of them. From a large and admirable literature covering the question from one extreme to the other, articles have been selected that express some of the more tenable views.

The well-known paper by William Baumol establishes a point of view for managerial economics; namely, that a managerial economist can make significant contributions as a member of the management group simply because he is an effective model builder. The economist's analytic tools and techniques help him to deal with the problems of the firm in a very rigorous and revealing manner.

Herbert Simon argues for the recognition of the numerous instances where applied price theory overlaps with areas of psychology and sociology. It must be realized that economic man—the consumer as well as the entrepreneur—is a compassionate person hoping to attain and then maintain a variety of objectives, only one of which happens to be profit maximization.

Different issues are addressed by Rex V. Brown who wants to know if decision theory is worthwhile and, if so, who uses it. Executives find various decision methods useful and Brown concludes that future users can learn important lessons from past experiences.

1. What Can Economic Theory Contribute to Managerial Economics?*

WILLIAM J. BAUMOL

What to me is one of the most significant aspects of economic theory for management science was brought out very clearly in a talk I had some time ago with a biologist friend of mine. This biologist is an eminent authority on clock mechanisms in animals. There is a remarkable and well-known periodicity in the behavior of a large variety of animal species—in fact, probably among all of them. To illustrate the point, the emergence of adult fruit flies from their pupae usually occurs shortly after dawn. Even if the flies are placed in a darkened room whose temperature, humidity, and other evidences of passage of time are carefully controlled, they will continue to emerge from the pupae at just about the same time day after day. However, if after being kept under these controlled laboratory conditions they are suddenly shown some light in order to produce the effect of a false dawn, there is a permanent shift of phase and, after some transient behavior, they will change the time at which they emerge from the pupae to that corresponding to the dawn which they were last shown. This suggests that there is a very definite way in which these animals can tell the time; that is to say, in which they can recognize when twenty-four hours are over, even though there is nothing conscious about it.

Of course a clock mechanism suggests periodicity, and periodicity, to any good cycle theorist, suggests difference or differential equations. And in fact, after this biologist had been working on the subject for some time, he became aware of this possibility and set out to find a mathematician who could help him to determine an appropriate equation. This was done, a relationship was fitted by statistical methods, and it turned out that it was appropriate to use a nonlinear differential equation. It was found that one such equation could fit a great variety of the data which this man had available. Not only could it do that,

* *American Economic Review,* vol. 51, no. 2 (May 1961), pp. 142–46.

but with the aid of the equation he was able to make a number of interesting predictions which were subsequently very closely confirmed by data which he was able to collect.

Here is where we come to the point of the story—the contrast between the situation of the biologist and that of the economic theorist—for the biologist who had obtained a very nice relationship on the basis of empirical data was totally unable to give any sort of analytical explanation of what he had. He had absolutely no model on which he could base a derivation of his mathematical relationship. We may, perhaps, generalize by remarking that biologists, with some notable exceptions, have data without models, whereas we in economic theory have models which usually are created without data. And in this way we have summarized one of the economic theorist's greatest weaknesses and one of his greatest strengths.

I would now like to emphasize the latter, the more pleasant, side: the fact that the economist is an expert model builder. Indeed, there are very few disciplines which produce model builders with such practice and such skill. This, I think, is one of the most important things which the economic theorist can contribute to the work of management science. In management science it is important—in fact, absolutely essential—to be able to recognize the structure of a managerial problem. In order to be able to analyze it at all and to be able to do so systematically, it is necessary to do several things: first of all, to undertake a judicious simplification—an elimination of minor details which are peripheral to the problem and which, if included in the model, would prevent any successful and systematic analysis. Second, it is important to capture in a formal statement the essence of all the interrelationships which characterize the situation, because it is only after stating these interrelationships so explicitly that we can hope to use the powerful techniques of rigorous analysis in the investigation of a managerial problem. It is the model which incorporates both these features; it is the central focus of the entire analysis which must capture the essence of the situation which is being investigated.

Thus, in any of the complex situations which are encountered in the systematic analysis of management problems, model building is a critical part of the investigation. Problems as diverse as the optimal size and composition of a department store product line or the location of a company's warehouses have one thing in common: their complexity—which arises to a large extent out of the network of interrelationships among their elements. An increase in the number of items carried in a store reduces the capacity for carrying stocks of other items: on the one hand it makes it more likely that the customer will find what she wants when she enters the store; on the other she may find more often that although the store usually carries what she desires, it happens to be out of it temporarily. The length of time a customer must search for an item is affected by a change in product line; the likelihood of "impulse" purchases is also affected, etc. The drawing together of such a diversity of strands is the major function of the model, without which most of our tools will not function. Moreover, in my experience it is not atypical that nearly half of the time spent in the investigation of such a problem is devoted to model building—to capturing the essence of the situation in a set of explicit relationships. For there are no cut and dried rules in model building. It is essentially a matter of discovery, involving all of the intangibles of discovery—hunch, insight, and intuition, and no holds are barred. Only after the model has been built can the problem sometimes be reduced to a routine by use of standard rules of calculation.

To my knowledge there are few classroom courses in this critical skill of model building, and, because it has no rules, it cannot be taught like trigonometry or chemistry. But apparently it can be learned by experience. And, as I have said, the economic theorist has had a great deal of experience in the construction and use of such models. When he employs some differential equations, you can almost be certain that he has derived them from a model which he built, not, like the biologist, from some data which he has collected.

This, then, is one of the major contributions which the economic theorist can, in my opinion, make to managerial analysis. It is, however, a skill and a predisposition that he brings with him, not a series of specific results.

This takes me to the second major point that I wish to make: the other way in which I think economic theory can be helpful to management science. I believe the most important thing a managerial economics student can get out of a course in economic analysis is not a series of theorems but rather a set of analytical methods. And for that reason I think it is far more important for him to learn the basis of these theorems, their assumption and their methods of derivation, than to end up with a group of conclusions. I can say quite categorically that I have never encountered a business problem in which my investigation was helped by any specific economic theorem, nor, may I add, have I ever met a practical problem in which I failed to be helped by the method of reasoning involved in the derivation of some economic theorem.

One of the major reasons that the propositions of economic theory are not directly applicable to management problems is that the theory does not deal with the major concerns of the businessman. Product line, advertising, budgeting, sales force allocation, inventory levels, new product introduction are all relative strangers to the idealized firm of value theory whose major concern is price-output policy. Certainly there is little in the theoretical literature which refers directly to the warehouse location or the department store product line problems which were mentioned previously.

Even where more familiar theoretical matters, such as pricing problems, arise in practice, the results of the theory provide only limited help. This is because theorems in economic analysis deal with rather general abstract entities, with firms which have the peculiar and most interesting characteristics of actual companies eliminated from them in order to enable the analyst to draw conclusions which apply to the entire economy and not just to one or several particular firms. As a result, when attempting to apply these theorems, one finds that they have abstracted some of the features it is most essential to retain in order to analyze the specific situation with which one is faced in the market. The theory offers us fairly general admonitions, like the one which tells us that marginal cost must equal marginal revenue if we are to maximize profits—surely a statement which is not very much of a guide in application. I repeat that in my applied work I have never found any occasion to use either this theorem or any other such specific proposition of economic analysis.

But I have often found it absolutely essential to use the techniques of marginal analysis as it occurs in the theory of the firm, the theory of production, and in welfare economics. Several times I have even found it helpful to use the techniques and derivations of some of the elasticity theorems. This last illustration perhaps merits a little expansion. It may appear extraordinary that the elasticity theorems were of any use in application at all for they would seem to provide the ultimate illustration of tools whose use requires the availability of extensive data. However, the point I am making is that it was not the theorems but the methods of analysis and derivation which were employed. For example, an analogue of the elementary proposition that unit elasticity is the borderline between increasing and decreasing total revenue in response to a decrease in price can be applied in other situations. In fact, it is precisely because of the lack of data that it often becomes necessary to decide just where such break-even points occur, and in a number of cases I have found that the ability to prove that this critical point is sufficiently beyond what may reasonably be expected is an adequate substitute for the availability of data. Thus knowledge of the method of derivation of the theorems—and, indeed, of the spirit of the theorems themselves—often enables one to do things without data which otherwise would be pretty much out of the question.

But this is not the major point. If it is true—and it certainly has been true in my experience—that every firm and every managerial situation requires a model which is more or less unique, none of the standard theorems is going to fit in with it. It will be necessary, in effect, to derive special theorems which enable one to deal with that specific situation. Here one is helped, then, not by the generalized propositions which have been developed by the theorist, but by the methods which have enabled him to achieve his results which show us how analogous conclusions or analogous analyses can be conducted for the problems at hand. It is for this reason that I make my plea about the teaching of economics and economic theory to the managerial economist. This plea is not only that economic theory should be taught to the business student but that it should be presented to him pretty much as it is taught to the liberal arts student, with the emphasis not on a series of canned conclusions but on the methods of investigation on the derivations behind the results—on the analytic tools and methods.

There is a third way in which economic theory can help in managerial analysis—and, perhaps strangely, here the more elementary concepts of economics are primarily involved or, rather, concepts which though relatively sophisticated are used in a very elementary way. These elementary concepts can imbue the economist with habits of thought which enable him to avoid some significant pitfalls. For example, consider the case of external economies and diseconomies. How much can familiarity with this concept tell us about the dangers involved in directing one branch of an enterprise to maximize its profits in disregard of the effects of its actions on other parts of the firm! Similarly, we economists are made very sensitive by marginal analysis to the perils of resource allocation by average cost and profit—resource allocation rules of thumb which are so frequently encountered in business practice. Such bits of reasoning once led one of my colleagues, who was reviewing some of the cases cited in the literature of managerial analysis, to remark that he was amazed at how often this reading had forced him to recall his sophomore economics!

To summarize, then, I have suggested very little by way of concrete contribution from economic theory to managerial economics. With some exceptions, I have not said that this particular result or that particular body of discussion is essential or even particularly helpful for the managerial economist. I have been able to offer no illustrations of managerial problems in which I was able to use very specific pieces of the body of economic analysis. But this is right in line with the very nature of my major point: the assertion that a managerial economist can become a far more helpful member of a management group by virtue of his studies of economic analysis, primarily because there he learns to become an effective model builder and because there he acquires a very rich body of tools and techniques which can help him to deal with the problems of the firm in a far more rigorous, a far more probing, and a far deeper manner.

2. Theories of Decision Making in Economics and Behavioral Science*

HERBERT A. SIMON

Recent years have seen important new explorations along the boundaries between economics and psychology. For the economist, the immediate question about these developments is whether they include new advances in psychology that can fruitfully be applied to economics. But the psychologist will also raise the converse question—whether there are developments in economic theory and observation that have implications for the central core of psychology. If economics is able to find verifiable and verified generalizations about human economic behavior, then these generalizations must have a place in the more general theories of human behavior to which psychology and sociology aspire. Influence will run both ways.

I. HOW MUCH PSYCHOLOGY DOES ECONOMICS NEED?

How have psychology and economics gotten along with little relation in the past? The explanation rests on an understanding of the goals toward which economics, viewed as a science and a discipline, has usually aimed.

Broadly speaking, economics can be defined as the science that describes and predicts the behavior of several kinds of economic man—notably the consumer and the entrepreneur. While perhaps literally correct, this definition does not reflect the principal focus in the literature of economics. We usually classify work in economics along two dimensions: (a) whether it is concerned with industries and the whole economy (macroeconomics) or with individual economic actors (microeconomics); and (b) whether it strives to describe and explain economic behavior (descriptive economics), or to guide decisions either at the level of public policy (normative macroeconomics) or at the level of the individual consumer or businessman (normative microeconomics).

The profession and literature of economics have been largely preoc-

* *American Economic Review,* vol. 49, no. 3 (June 1959), pp. 253–80.

cupied with normative macroeconomics. Although descriptive macroeconomics provides the scientific base for policy prescription, research emphases have been determined in large part by relevance to policy (e.g., business cycle theory). Normative microeconomics, carried forward under such labels as "management science," "engineering economics," and "operations research," is now a flourishing area of work having an uneasy and ill-defined relation with the profession of economics, traditionally defined. Much of the work is being done by mathematicians, statisticians, engineers, and physical scientists (although many mathematical economists have also been active in it).

This new area, like the old, is normative in orientation. Economists have been relatively uninterested in descriptive microeconomics—understanding the behavior of individual economic agents—except as this is necessary to provide a foundation for macroeconomics. The normative microeconomist "obviously" doesn't need a theory of human behavior: he wants to know how people *ought* to behave, not how they *do* behave. On the other hand, the macroeconomist's lack of concern with individual behavior stems from different considerations. First, he assumes that the economic actor is rational, and hence he makes strong predictions about human behavior without performing the hard work of observing people. Second, he often assumes competition, which carries with it the implication that only the rational survive. Thus, the classical economic theory of markets with perfect competition and rational agents is deductive theory that requires almost no contact with empirical data once its assumptions are accepted.

Undoubtedly there is an area of human behavior that fits these assumptions to a reasonable approximation, where the classical theory with its assumptions of rationality is a powerful and useful tool. Without denying the existence of this area, or its importance, I may observe that it fails to include some of the central problems of conflict and dynamics with which economics has become more and more concerned. A metaphor will help to show the reason for this failure.

Suppose we were pouring some viscous liquid—molasses—into a bowl of very irregular shape. What would we need in order to make a theory of the form the molasses would take in the bowl? How much would we have to know about the properties of molasses to predict its behavior under the circumstances? If the bowl were held motionless, and if we wanted only to predict behavior in equilibrium, we would have to know little, indeed, about molasses. The single essential assumption would be that the molasses, under the force of gravity, would minimize the height of its center of gravity. With this assumption, which would apply as well to any other liquid, and a complete knowledge of the environment—in this case the shape of the bowl—the equilibrium is completely determined. Just so, the equilibrium behavior of a perfectly adapting organism depends only on its goal and its environment; it is otherwise completely independent of the internal properties of the organism.

If the bowl into which we were pouring the molasses were jiggled rapidly, or if we wanted to know about the behavior before equilibrium was reached, prediction would require much more information. It would require, in particular, more information about the properties of molasses: its viscosity, the rapidity with which it "adapted" itself to the containing vessel and moved towards its "goal" of lowering its center of gravity. Likewise, to predict the short-run behavior of an adaptive organism, or its behavior in a complex and rapidly changing environment, it is not enough to know its goals. We must know also a great deal about its internal structure and particularly its mechanisms of adaptation.

If, to carry the metaphor a step farther, new forces, in addition to gravitational force, were brought to bear on the liquid, we would have to know still more about it even to predict behavior in equilibrium. Now its tendency to lower its center of gravity might be countered by a force to minimize an electrical or magnetic potential operating in some lateral direction. We would have to know its relative susceptibility to gravitational and electrical or magnetic force to determine its equilibrium position. Similarly, in an organism having a multiplicity of goals, or afflicted with some kind of internal goal conflict, behavior could be predicted only from information about the relative strengths of the several goals and the ways in which the adaptive processes responded to them.

Economics has been moving steadily into new areas where the power of the classical equilibrium model has never been demonstrated, and where its adequacy must be considered anew. Labor economics is such an area, oligopoly or imperfect competition theory another, decision making under uncertainty a third, and the theory of economic development a fourth. In all of these areas the complexity and instability of his environment becomes a central feature of the choices that economic man faces. To explain his behavior in the face of this complexity, the theory must describe him as something more than a featureless, adaptive organism; it must incorporate at least some description of the processes and mechanisms through which the adaptation takes place. Let us list a little more concretely some specific problems of this kind:

(a) The classical theory postulates that the consumer maximizes utility. Recent advances in the theory of rational consumer choice have shown that the existence of a utility function, and its characteristics, if it exists, can be studied empirically.

(b) The growing separation between ownership and management has directed attention to the motivations of managers and the adequacy of the profit-maximization assumption for business firms. So-called human relations research has raised a variety of issues about the motivation of both executives and employees.

(c) When, in extending the classical theory, the assumptions of perfect competition were removed, even the definition of rationality became ambiguous. New definitions had to be constructed, by no means as "obvious" intuitively as simple maximization, to extend the theory of rational behavior to bilateral monopoly and to other bargaining and outguessing situations.

(d) When the assumptions of perfect foresight were removed, to handle uncertainty about the environment, the definition of rationality had to be extended in another direction to take into account prediction and the formation of expectations.

(e) Broadening the definition of rationality to encompass goal conflict and uncertainty made it hard to ignore the distinction between the objective environment in which the economic actor "really" lives and the subjective environment that he perceives and to which he responds. When this distinction is made, we can no longer predict his behavior—even if he behaves rationally—from the characteristics of the objective environment; we also need to know something about his perceptual and cognitive processes.

We shall use these five problem areas as a basis for sorting out some recent explorations in theory, model building, and empirical testing. In section II, we will examine developments in the theory of utility and consumer choice. In section III, we will consider somewhat parallel issues relating to the motivation of managers. In section IV, we will deal with conflict of goals and the phenomena of bargaining. In section V, we will survey some of the work that has been done on uncertainty and the formation of expectations. In section VI, we will explore recent developments in the theory of human problem solving and other higher mental processes, and see what implications these have for economic decision making.

II. THE UTILITY FUNCTION

The story of the reestablishment of cardinal utility, as a consequence of the introduction of uncertainty into the theory of choice, is well known. When Pareto and Slutsky had shown that the theory of consumer demand could be derived from the properties of indifference curves, without postulating a cardinal utility function underlying these curves, it became fashionable to regard utility as an ordinal measure—a ranking of alternatives by preference. Indeed, it could be shown that only ordinal utility had operational status—that the experiments that had been proposed, and even tried in a couple of instances, to measure an individual's utilities by asking him to choose among alternatives could never distinguish between two cardinal utility functions that were ordinally equivalent—that differed only by stretchings and contractions of the unit of measurement.

It was shown by von Neumann and Morgenstern, as a by-product of their development of the theory of games, that if the choice situation were extended to include choices among uncertain prospects—among lottery tickets, say—cardinal utilities could be assigned to the outcomes in an unequivocal way. Under these conditions, if the subject's behavior was consistent, it was possible to measure cardinally the utilities that different outcomes had for him.

A person who behaved in a manner consistent with the axioms of choice of von Neumann and Morgenstern would act so as to maximize the expected value—the average, weighted by the probabilities of the alternative outcomes of a choice—of his utility. The theory could be tested empirically, however, only on the assumption that the probabilities assigned to the alternatives by the subject were identical with the "objective" probabilities of these events as known to the experimenter. For example, if a subject believed in the gamblers' fallacy, that after a run of heads an unbiased coin would be more likely to fall tails, his choices might appear inconsistent with his utility function, while the real difficulty would lie in his method of assigning probabilities. This difficulty of "subjective" versus "objective" probability soon came to light when attempts were made to test experimentally whether people behaved in accordance with the predictions of the new utility theory. At the same time, it was discovered that the problem had been raised and solved thirty years earlier by the English philosopher and mathematician Frank Ramsey. Ramsey had shown that, by an appropriate series of experiments, the utilities and subjective probabilities assigned by a subject to a set of uncertain alternatives could be measured simultaneously.

Empirical Studies

The new axiomatic foundations of the theory of utility, which show that it is possible, at least in principle, to determine empirically whether people "have" utility functions of the appropriate kind, have led to a rash of choice experiments. An experimenter who wants to measure utilities, not merely in principle but in fact, faces innumerable difficulties. Because of these difficulties, most experiments have been limited to confronting the subjects with alternative lottery tickets, at various odds, for small amounts of money. The weight of evidence is that, under these conditions, most persons choose in a way that is reasonably consistent with the axioms of the theory—they behave as though they were maximizing the expected value of utility and as though the utilities of the several alternatives can be measured.

When these experiments are extended to more "realistic" choices—choices that are more obviously relevant to real-life situations—difficulties multiply. In the few extensions that have been made, it is not at all clear that the subjects behave in accordance with the utility axioms. There is some indication that when the situation is very simple and transparent, so that the subject can easily see and remember when he is being consistent, he behaves like a utility maximizer. But as the choices become a little more complicated—choices, for example, among phonograph records instead of sums of money—he becomes much less consistent.

We can interpret these results in either of two ways. We can say that consumers "want" to maximize utility, and that if we present them with clear and simple choices that they understand they will do so. Or we can say that the real world is so complicated that the theory of utility maximization has little relevance to real choices. The former interpretation has generally appeared more attractive to economists trained in classical utility theory and to management scientists seeking rules of behavior for normative microeconomics; the latter to behavioral scientists interested in the description of behavior.

Normative Applications

The new utility theory has provided the formal framework for much recent work in mathematical statistics—i.e., statistical decision theory. Similarly (it would be accurate to say "synonymously"), this framework provides the basis for most of the normative models of management science and operations research designed for actual application to the decision-making problems of the firm.[1] Except for some very recent developments, linear programming has been limited to decision making under certainty, but there have been far-reaching developments of dynamic programming dealing with the maximization of expected values of outcomes (usually monetary outcomes) in situations where future events can be predicted only in terms of probability distributions.

Again, there are at least two distinct interpretations that can be placed on these developments. On the one hand, it can be argued: "Firms would like to maximize profits if they could. They have been limited in doing so by the conceptual and computational difficulties of finding the optimal courses of action. By providing powerful new mathematical tools and computing machines, we now enable them to behave in the manner predicted by Alfred Marshall, even if they haven't been able to in the

[1] This work relates, of course, to profit maximization and cost minimization rather than utility maximization, but it is convenient to mention it at this point.

past." Nature will imitate art and economic man will become as real (and as artificial) as radios and atomic piles.

The alternative interpretation rests on the observation that, even with the powerful new tools and machines, most real-life choices still lie beyond the reach of maximizing techniques—unless the situations are heroically simplified by drastic approximations. If man, according to this interpretation, makes decisions and choices that have some appearance of rationality, rationality in real life must involve something simpler than maximization of utility or profit. In section VI, we will see where this alternative interpretation leads.

The Binary Choice Experiment

Much recent discussion about utility has centered around a particularly simple choice experiment. This experiment, in numerous variants, has been used by both economists and psychologists to test the most diverse kinds of hypotheses. We will describe it so that we can use it as a common standard of comparison for a whole range of theories and empirical studies.

We will call the situation we are about to describe the *binary choice* experiment. It is better known to most game theorists—particularly those located not far from Nevada—as a two-armed bandit; and to most psychologists as a partial reinforcement experiment. The subject is required, in each of a series of trials, to choose one or the other of two symbols—say, plus or minus. When he has chosen, he is told whether his choice was "right" or "wrong," and he may also receive a reward (in psychologist's language, a reinforcement) for "right" choices. The experimenter can arrange the schedule of correct responses in a variety of ways. There may be a definite pattern, or they may be randomized. It is not essential that one and only one response be correct on a given trial: the experimenter may determine that both or neither will be correct. In the latter case the subject may or may not be informed whether the response he did not choose would have been correct.

How would a utility-maximizing subject behave in the binary choice experiment? Suppose that the experimenter rewarded "plus" on one third of the trials, determined at random, and "minus" on the remaining two thirds. Then a subject, provided that he believed the sequence was random and observed that minus was rewarded twice as often as plus, should always, rationally, choose minus. He would find the correct answer two thirds of the time, and more often than with any other strategy.

Unfortunately for the classical theory of utility in its simplest form, few subjects behave in this way. The most commonly observed behavior is what is called *event matching*. The subject chooses the two alternatives (not necessarily at random) with relative frequencies roughly proportional to the relative frequencies with which they are rewarded. Thus, in the example given, two thirds of the time he would choose minus, and as a result would make a correct response, on the average, in five trials out of nine (on two thirds of the trials in which he chooses minus, and one third of those in which he chooses plus).[2]

All sorts of explanations have been offered for the event-matching behavior. The simplest is that the subject just doesn't understand what strategy would maximize his expected utility; but with adult subjects in a situation as transparent as this one, this explanation seems far-fetched. The alternative explanations imply either that the subject regards himself as being engaged in a competitive game with the experimenter (or with "nature" if he accepts the experimenter's explanation that the stimulus is random), or that his responses are the outcome of certain kinds of learning processes. We will examine these two types of explanation further in sections IV and V respectively. The important conclusion at this point is that even in an extremely simple situation, subjects do not behave in the way predicted by a straightforward application of utility theory.

Probabilistic Preferences

Before we leave the subject of utility, we should mention one recent important development. In the formalizations mentioned up to this point, probabilities enter only into the estimation of the consequences that will follow one alternative or another. Given any two alternatives, the first is definitely preferable to the second (in terms of expected utility), or the second to the first, or they are strictly indifferent. If the same pair of alternatives is presented to the subject more than once, he should always prefer the same member of the pair.

One might think this requirement too strict—that, particularly if the utility attached to one alternative were only slightly greater or less than that attached to the other, the subject might vacillate in his choice. An empirical precedent for such vacillation comes not only from casual observation of indecision but from analogous phenomena in the psychophysical laboratory. When subjects are asked to decide which of two weights is heavier, the objectively heavier one is chosen more often than the lighter one, but the relative frequency of choosing the heaviest approaches one half as the two weights approach equality. The probability that a subject will choose the objectively heavier weight depends, in general, on the ratio of the two weights.

Following several earlier attempts, a rigorous and complete axiom

[2] Subjects tend to choose the more highly rewarded alternative slightly more frequently than is called for by event matching. Hence, the actual behavior tends to be some kind of average between event matching and the optimal behavior.

system for a utility theory incorporating probabilistic preferences has been constructed recently by Duncan Luce. Although the theory weakens the requirements of consistency in preference, it is empirically testable, at least in principle. Conceptually, it provides a more plausible interpretation of the notion of "indifference" than does the classical theory.

III. THE GOALS OF FIRMS

Just as the central assumption in the theory of consumption is that the consumer strives to maximize his utility, so the crucial assumption in the theory of the firm is that the entrepreneur strives to maximize his residual share—his profit. Attacks on this hypothesis have been frequent. We may classify the most important of these as follows:

(a) The theory leaves ambiguous whether it is short-run or long-run profit that is to be maximized.

(b) The entrepreneur may obtain all kinds of "psychic income" from the firm, quite apart from monetary rewards. If he is to maximize his utility, then he will sometimes balance a loss of profits against an increase in psychic income. But if we allow "psychic income," the criterion of profit maximization loses all of its definiteness.

(c) The entrepreneur may not care to maximize, but may simply want to earn a return that he regards as satisfactory. By sophistry and adept use of the concept of psychic income, the notion of seeking a satisfactory return can be translated into utility maximizing, but not in any operational way. We shall see in a moment that "satisfactory profits" is a concept more meaningfully related to the psychological notion of aspiration levels than to maximization.

(d) It is often observed that under modern conditions the equity owners and the active managers of an enterprise are separate and distinct groups of people, so that the latter may not be motivated to maximize profits.

(e) Where there is imperfect competition among firms, maximizing is an ambiguous goal, for what action is optimal for one firm depends on the actions of the other firms.

In the present section we shall deal only with the third of these five issues. The fifth will be treated in the following section; the first, second, and fourth are purely empirical questions that have been discussed at length in the literature; they will be considered here only for their bearing on the question of satisfactory profits.

Satisficing versus Maximizing

The notion of satiation plays no role in classical economic theory, while it enters rather prominently into the treatment of motivation in psychology. In most psychological theories the motive to act stems from *drives,* and action terminates when the drive is satisfied. Moreover, the conditions for satisfying a drive are not necessarily fixed, but may be specified by an aspiration level that itself adjusts upward or downward on the basis of experience.

If we seek to explain business behavior in the terms of this theory, we must expect the firm's goals to be not maximizing profit, but attaining a certain level or rate of profit, holding a certain share of the market or a certain level of sales. Firms would try to "satisfice" rather than to maximize.

It has sometimes been argued that the distinction between satisficing and maximizing is not important to economic theory. For in the first place, the psychological evidence on individual behavior shows that aspirations tend to adjust to the attainable. Hence in the long run, the argument runs, the level of aspiration and the attainable maximum will be very close together. Second, even if some firms satisficed, they would gradually lose out to the maximizing firms, which would make larger profits and grow more rapidly than the others.

These are, of course, precisely the arguments of our molasses metaphor, and we may answer them in the same way that we answered them earlier. The economic environment of the firm is complex, and it changes rapidly; there is no a priori reason to assume the attainment of long-run equilibrium. Indeed, the empirical evidence on the distribution of firms by size suggests that the observed regularities in size distribution stem from the statistical equilibrium of a population of adaptive systems rather than the static equilibrium of a population of maximizers.

Models of satisficing behavior are richer than models of maximizing behavior, because they treat not only of equilibrium but of the method of reaching it as well. Psychological studies of the formation and change of aspiration levels support propositions of the following kinds: (a) When performance falls short of the level of aspiration, search behavior (particularly search for new alternatives of action) is induced. (b) At the same time, the level of aspiration begins to adjust itself downward until goals reach levels that are practically attainable. (c) If the two mechanisms just listed operate too slowly to adapt aspirations to performance, emotional behavior—apathy or aggression, for example—will replace rational adaptive behavior.

The aspiration level defines a natural zero point in the scale of utility—whereas in most classical theories the zero point is arbitrary. When the firm has alternatives open to it that are at or above its aspiration level, the theory predicts that it will choose the best of those known to be available. When none of the available alternatives satisfies current aspirations, the theory predicts qualitatively different behavior: in the short run, search behavior and the revision of targets; in the longer run, what we have called above emotional behavior, and what the psychologist would be inclined to call neurosis.[3]

Studies of Business Behavior

There is some empirical evidence that business goals are, in fact, stated in satisficing terms. First, there is the series of studies stemming from the pioneering work of Hall and Hitch that indicates that businessmen often set prices by applying a standard markup to costs. Some economists have sought to refute this fact, others to reconcile it—if it is a fact—with marginalist principles. The study of Earley belongs to the former category, but its evidence is suspect because the questions asked of businessmen are leading ones—no one likes to admit that he would accept less profit if he could have more. Earley did not ask his respondents how they determined marginal cost and marginal revenue, how, for example, they estimated demand elasticities.

Another series of studies derived from the debate over the Keynesian doctrine that the amount of investment was insensitive to changes in the rate of interest. The general finding in these studies has been that the rate of interest is not an important factor in investment decisions.

More recently, my colleagues Cyert and March have attempted to test the satisficing model in a more direct way. They found in one industry some evidence that firms with a declining share of market strove more vigorously to increase their sales than firms whose shares of the market were steady or increasing.

Aspirations in the Binary Choice Experiment

Although to my knowledge this has not been done, it would be easy to look for aspiration-level phenomena in the binary choice experiment. By changing the probabilities of reward in different ways for different groups of subjects, we could measure the effects of these changes on search behavior—where amount of search would be measured by changes in the pattern of responses.

Economic Implications

It has sometimes been argued that, however realistic the classical theory of the firm as a profit maximizer, it is an adequate theory for

[3] Lest this last term appear fanciful, I should like to call attention to the phenomena of panic and broken morale, which are well known to observers of the stock market and of organizations but which have no reasonable interpretation in classical utility theory. I may also mention that psychologists use the theory described here in a straightforward way to produce experimental neurosis in animal and human subjects.

purposes of normative macroeconomics. Mason, for example, in commenting on Papandreou's essay on "Problems in the Theory of the Firm" says, "The writer of this critique must confess a lack of confidence in the marked superiority, *for purposes of economic analysis,* of this newer concept of the firm over the older conception of the entrepreneur." The italics are Mason's.

The theory of the firm is important for welfare economics—e.g., for determining under what circumstances the behavior of the firm will lead to efficient allocation of resources. The satisficing model vitiates all the conclusions about resource allocation that are derivable from the maximizing model when perfect competition is assumed. Similarly, a dynamic theory of firm sizes, like that mentioned above, has quite different implications for public policies dealing with concentration than a theory that assumes firms to be in static equilibrium. Hence, welfare economists are justified in adhering to the classical theory only if: (a) the theory is empirically correct as a description of the decision-making process; or (b) it is safe to assume that the system operates in the neighborhood of the static equilibrium. What evidence we have mostly contradicts both assumptions.

IV. CONFLICT OF INTEREST

Leaving aside the problem of the motivations of hired managers, conflict of interest among economic actors creates no difficulty for classical economic theory—indeed, it lies at the very core of the theory—so long as each actor treats the other actors as parts of his "given" environment, and doesn't try to predict their behavior and anticipate it. But when this restriction is removed, when it is assumed that a seller takes into account the reactions of buyers to his actions, or that each manufacturer predicts the behaviors of his competitors—all the familiar difficulties of imperfect competition and oligopoly arise.[4]

The very assumptions of omniscient rationality that provide the basis for deductive prediction in economics when competition is present lead to ambiguity when they are applied to competition among the few. The central difficulty is that rationality requires one to outguess one's opponents, but not to be outguessed by them, and this is clearly not a consistent requirement if applied to all the actors.

Game Theory

Modern game theory is a vigorous and extensive exploration of ways of extending the concept of rational behavior to situations involving

[4] There is by now a voluminous literature on the problem.

struggle, outguessing, and bargaining. Since Luce and Raiffa have recently provided us with an excellent survey and evaluation of game theory, I shall not cover the same ground here. I concur in their general evaluation that, while game theory has greatly clarified the issues involved, it has not provided satisfactory solutions. Not only does it leave the definition of rational conduct ambiguous in all cases save the zero-sum two-person game, but it requires of economic man even more fantastic reasoning powers than does classical economic theory.

Power and Bargaining

A number of exploratory proposals have been put forth as alternatives to game theory—among them Galbraith's notion of countervailing power and Schelling's bargaining theory. These analyses draw at least as heavily upon theories of power and bargaining developed initially to explain political phenomena as upon economic theory. They do not lead to any more specific predictions of behavior than do game-theoretic approaches, but place a greater emphasis upon description and actual observation, and are modest in their attempt to derive predictions by deductive reasoning from a few "plausible" premises about human behavior.

At least four important areas of social science and social policy, two of them in economics and two more closely related to political science, have as their central concern the phenomena of power and the processes of bargaining: the theory of political parties, labor-management relations, international politics, and oligopoly theory. Any progress in the basic theory applicable to one of these is certain to be of almost equal importance to the others. A growing recognition of their common concern is evidenced by the initiation of a new cross-disciplinary journal, *Journal of Conflict Resolution.*

Games against Nature

While the binary choice experiment is basically a one-person game, it is possible to interpret it as a "game against nature," and hence to try to explain it in game-theoretic terms. According to game theory, the subject, if he believes in a malevolent nature that manipulates the dice against him, should "minimax" his expected utility instead of maximizing it. That is, he should adopt the course of action that will maximize his expected utility under the assumption that nature will do her worst to him.

Minimaxing expected utility would lead the subject to call plus or minus at random and with equal probability, regardless of what the history of rewards has been. This is something that subjects demonstrably do not do.

However, it has been suggested by Savage and others that people are not as interested in maximizing utility as they are in minimizing regret. "Regret" means the difference between the reward actually obtained and the reward that could have been obtained with perfect foresight (actually, with perfect hindsight!). It turns out that minimaxing regret in the binary choice experiment leads to event-matching behavior. Hence, the empirical evidence is at least crudely consistent with the hypothesis that people play against nature by minimaxing regret. We shall see, however, that event matching is also consistent with a number of other rules of behavior that seem more plausible on their face; hence we need not take the present explanation too seriously—at least I am not inclined to do so.

V. THE FORMATION OF EXPECTATIONS

While the future cannot enter into the determination of the present, expectations about the future can and do. In trying to gain an understanding of the saving, spending, and investment behavior of both consumers and firms, and to make short-term predictions of this behavior for purposes of policy making, economists have done substantial empirical work as well as theorizing on the formation of expectations.

Empirical Studies

A considerable body of data has been accumulated on consumers' plans and expectations from the Survey of Consumer Finances, conducted for the Board of Governors of the Federal Reserve System by the Survey Research Center of the University of Michigan. These data, and similar data obtained by others, begin to give us some information on the expectations of consumers about their own incomes, and the predictive value of their expenditure plans for their actual subsequent behavior. Some large-scale attempts have been made, notably by Modigliani and Brumberg and, a little later, by Friedman to relate these empirical findings to classical utility theory. The current empirical research on businessmen's expectations is of two main kinds:

1. Surveys of businessmen's own forecasts of business and business conditions in the economy and in their own industries. These are obtained by straightforward questionnaire methods that assume, implicitly, that businessmen can and do make such forecasts. In some uses to which the data are put, it is also assumed that the forecasts are used as one basis for businessmen's actions.

2. Studies of business decisions and the role of expectations in these decisions—particularly investment and pricing decisions. We have already referred to studies of business decisions in our discussion of the goals of the firm.

Expectations and Probability

The classical way to incorporate expectations into economic theory is to assume that the decision maker estimates the joint probability distribution of future events. He can then act so as to maximize the expected value of utility or profit, as the case may be. However satisfying this approach may be conceptually, it poses awkward problems when we ask how the decision maker actually estimates the parameters of the joint probability distribution. Common sense tells us that people don't make such estimates, nor can we find evidence that they do by examining actual business forecasting methods. The surveys of businessmen's expectations have never attempted to secure such estimates, but have contended themselves with asking for point predictions—which, at best, might be interpreted as predictions of the means of the distributions.

It has been shown that under certain special circumstances the mean of the probability distribution is the only parameter that is relevant for decision—that even if the variance and higher moments were known to the rational decision maker, he would have no use for them. In these cases, the arithmetic mean is actually a certainty equivalent, the optimal decision turns out to be the same as if the future were known with certainty. But the situations where the mean is a certainty equivalent are, as we have said, very special ones, and there is no indication that businessmen ever ask whether the necessary conditions for this equivalence are actually met in practice. They somehow make forecasts in the form of point predictions and act upon them in one way or another.

The "somehow" poses questions that are important for business cycle theory, and perhaps for other problems in economics. The way in which expectations are formed may affect the dynamic stability of the economy, and the extent to which cycles will be amplified or damped. Some light, both empirical and theoretical, has recently been cast on these questions. On the empirical side, attempts have been made: (a) to compare businessmen's forecasts with various "naïve" models that assume the future will be some simple function of the recent past, and (b) to use such naïve models themselves as forecasting devices.

The simplest naïve model is one that assumes the next period will be exactly like the present. Another assumes that the change from present to next period will equal the change from last period to present; a third, somewhat more general, assumes that the next period will be a weighted average of recent past periods. The term "naïve model" has been applied loosely to various forecasting formulae of these general kinds. There is some affirmative evidence that business forecasts fit such models. There is also evidence that elaboration of the models beyond the first few steps of refinement does not much improve prediction. Arrow and his colleagues have explored some of the conditions under which forecasting formulae will, and will not, introduce dynamic instability into an economic system that is otherwise stable. They have shown, for example, that if a system of multiple markets is stable under static expectations, it is stable when expectations are based on a moving average of past values.

The work on the formation of expectations represents a significant extension of classical theory. For, instead of taking the environment as a "given," known to the economic decision maker, it incorporates in the theory the processes of acquiring knowledge about that environment. In doing so, it forces us to include in our model of economic man some of his properties as a learning, estimating, searching, information-processing organism.

The Cost of Information

There is one way in which the formation of expectations might be reincorporated in the body of economic theory: by treating information gathering as one of the processes of production, so to speak, and applying to it the usual rules of marginal analysis. Information, says price theory, should be gathered up to the point where the incremental cost of additional information is equal to the incremental profit that can be earned by having it. Such an approach can lead to propositions about optimal amounts of information-gathering activity and about the relative merits of alternative information-gathering and estimating schemes.

This line of investigation has, in fact, been followed in statistical decision theory. In sampling theory we are concerned with the optimal size of sample (and in the special and ingenious case of sequential sampling theory, with knowing when to stop sampling), and we wish to evaluate the efficiencies of alternative sampling procedures. The latter problem is the simpler, since it is possible to compare the relative costs of alternative schemes that have the same sampling error, and hence to avoid estimating the value of the information. However, some progress has been made also toward estimating the value of improved forecast accuracy in situations where the forecasts are to be used in applying formal decision rules to choice situations.

The theory of teams developed by Marschak and Radner is concerned with the same problem. It considers situations involving decentralized and interdependent decision making by two or more persons who share a common goal and who, at a cost, can transmit information to each other about their own actions or about the parts of the environment with which they are in contact. The problem then is to discover the optimal communication strategy under specified assumptions about communication costs and payoffs.

The cost of communication in the theory of teams, like the cost of observations in sampling theory, is a parameter that characterizes the economic actor, or the relation of the actor to his environment. Hence, while these theories retain, in one sense, a classical picture of economic man as a maximizer, they clearly require considerable information about the characteristics of the actor, and not merely about his environment. They take a long stride toward bridging the gap between the traditional concerns of economics and the concern of psychology.

Expectations in the Binary Choice Experiment

I should like to return again to the binary choice experiment, to see what light it casts on the formation of expectations. If the subject is told by the experimenter that the rewards are assigned at random, if he is told what the odds are for each alternative, *and if he believes the experimenter,* the situation poses no forecasting problem. We have seen, however, that the behavior of most subjects is not consistent with these assumptions.

How would sequential sampling theory handle the problem? Each choice the subject makes now has two consequences: the immediate reward he obtains from it, and the increment of information it provides for predicting the future rewards. If he thinks only of the latter consequences, he is faced with the classical problem of induction: to estimate the probability that an event will occur in the future on the basis of its frequency of occurrence in the past. Almost any rule of induction would require a rational (maximizing) subject to behave in the following general manner: to sample the two alternatives in some proportion to estimate the probability of reward associated with each; after the error of estimate had been reduced below some bound, always to choose the alternative with the higher probability of reward. Unfortunately, this does not appear to be what most subjects do.

If we give up the idea of maximization, we can make the weaker assumption that the subject is adaptive—or learns—but not necessarily in any optimal fashion. What do we mean by adaptation or learning? We mean, gradually and on the basis of experience responding more frequently with the choice that, in the past, has been most frequently rewarded. There is a whole host of rules of behavior possessing this characteristic. Postulate, for example, that at each trial the subject has a certain probability of responding "plus," and the complementary probability of responding "minus." Postulate further that when he makes a particular response the probability of making the same response on the next trial is increased if the response is rewarded and decreased if the response is not rewarded. The amount of increment in the response probability is a parameter characterizing the learning rate of the particular subject. Almost all schemes of this kind produce asymptotic behaviors, as the number of trials increases, that are approximately event matching in character.

Stochastic learning models, as the processes just described are usually called, were introduced into psychology in the early 1950s by W. K. Estes and Bush and Mosteller and have been investigated extensively since that time. The models fit some of the gross features of the observed behaviors—most strikingly the asymptotic probabilities—but do not explain very satisfactorily the fine structure of the observations.

Observation of subjects in the binary choice experiment reveals that usually they not only refuse to believe that (or even to act as if) the reward series were random, but in fact persist over many trials in searching for systematic patterns in the series. To account for such behavior, we might again postulate a learning model, but in this case a model in which the subject does not react probabilistically to his environment, but forms and tests definite hypotheses about systematic patterns in it. Man, in this view, is not only a learning animal; he is a pattern-finding and concept-forming animal. Julian Feldman has constructed theories of this kind to explain the behavior of subjects in the binary choice experiment, and while the tests of the theories are not yet completed, his findings look exceedingly promising.

As we move from maximizing theories, through simple stochastic learning theories, to theories involving pattern recognition, our model of the expectation-forming processes and the organism that performs it increases in complexity. If we follow this route, we reach a point where a theory of behavior requires a rather elaborate and detailed picture of the rational actor's cognitive processes.

VI. HUMAN COGNITION AND ECONOMICS

All the developments we have examined in the preceding four sections have a common theme: they all involve important modifications in the concept of economic man and, for the reasons we have stated, modifications in the direction of providing a fuller description of his characteristics. The classical theory is a theory of a man choosing among fixed and known alternatives, to each of which is attached known consequences. But when perception and cognition intervene between the decision maker and his objective environment, this model no longer proves adequate. We need a description of the choice process that recognizes that alternatives are not given but must be sought; and a description that takes into account the arduous task of determining what consequences will follow on each alternative.

The decision maker's information about his environment is much less than an approximation to the real environment. The term "approximation" implies that the subjective world of the decision maker resembles the external environment closely, but lacks, perhaps, some fineness of detail. In actual fact the perceived world is fantastically different from the "real" world. The differences involve both omissions and distortions, and arise in both perception and inference. The sins of omission in perception are more important than the sins of commission. The decision maker's model of the world encompasses only a minute fraction of all the relevant characteristics of the real environment, and his inferences extract only a minute fraction of all the information that is present even in his model.

Perception is sometimes referred to as a "filter." This term is as misleading as "approximation," and for the same reason: it implies that what comes through into the central nervous system is really quite a bit like what is "out there." In fact, the filtering is not merely a passive selection of some part of a presented whole, but an active process involving attention to a very small part of the whole and exclusion, from the outset, of almost all that is not within the scope of attention.

Every human organism lives in an environment that generates millions of bits of new information each second, but the bottleneck of the perceptual apparatus certainly does not admit more than 1,000 bits per second, and probably much less. Equally significant omissions occur in the processing that takes place when information reaches the brain. As every mathematician knows, it is one thing to have a set of differential equations, and another thing to have their solutions. Yet the solutions are logically implied by the equations—they are "all there," if we only knew how to get to them! By the same token, there are hosts of inferences that *might* be drawn from the information stored in the brain that are not in fact drawn. The consequences implied by information in the memory become known only through active information processing, and hence through active selection of particular problem-solving paths from the myriad that might have been followed.

In this section we shall examine some theories of decision making that take the limitations of the decision maker and the complexity of the environment as central concerns. These theories incorporate some mechanisms we have already discussed—for example, aspiration levels and forecasting processes—but go beyond them in providing a detailed picture of the choice process.

A real-life decision involves some goals or values, some facts about the environment, and some inferences drawn from the values and facts. The goals and values may be simple or complex, consistent or contradictory; the facts may be real or supposed, based on observation or the reports of others; the inferences may be valid or spurious. The whole process may be viewed, metaphorically, as a process of "reasoning," where the values and facts serve as premises, and the decision that is finally reached is inferred from these premises. The resemblance of decision making to logical reasoning is only metaphorical, because there are quite different rules in the two cases to determine what constitute "valid" premises and admissible modes of inference. The metaphor is useful because it leads us to take the individual *decision premise* as the unit of description, hence to deal with the whole interwoven fabric of influences that bear on a single decision—but without being bound by the assumptions of rationality that limit the classical theory of choice.

Rational Behavior and Role Theory

We can find common ground to relate the economist's theory of decision making with that of the social psychologist. The latter is particularly interested, of course, in social influences on choice, which determine the *role* of the actor. In our present terms, a role is a social prescription of some, but not all, of the premises that enter into an individual's choices of behavior. Any particular concrete behavior is the resultant of a large number of premises, only some of which are prescribed by the role. In addition to role premises there will be premises about the state of the environment based directly on perception, premises representing beliefs and knowledge, and idiosyncratic premises that characterize the personality. Within this framework we can accommodate both the rational elements in choice, so much emphasized by economics, and the nonrational elements to which psychologists and sociologists often prefer to call attention.

Decision Premises and Computer Programs

The analysis of choice in terms of decision premises gives us a conceptual framework for describing and explaining the process of deciding. But so complex is the process that our explanations of it would have remained schematic and hypothetical for a long time to come had not the modern digital computer appeared on the scene. The notion of decision premise can be translated into computer terminology, and when this translation has been accomplished, the digital computer provides us with an instrument for stimulating human decision processes—even very complex ones—and hence for testing empirically our explanations of those processes.

A fanciful (but only slightly fanciful) example will illustrate how this might be done. Some actual examples will be cited presently. Suppose we were to construct a robot incorporating a modern digital computer, and to program (i.e., to instruct) the robot to take the role of a business executive in a specified company. What would the program look like? Since no one has yet done this, we cannot say with certainty, but several points are fairly clear. The program would not consist of a list of prescribed and proscribed behaviors, since what an executive does is highly contingent on information about a wide variety of circumstances. Instead, the program would consist of a large number of *criteria* to be applied to possible and proposed courses of action, of routines for *generating* possible courses of action, of computational procedures for *assessing* the state of the environment and its implications for action, and the like. Hence, the program—in fact, a role prescription—would interact with information to produce concrete behavior adapted to the situation. The elements of such a program take the form of what we have called decision premises, and what the computer specialists would call instructions.

The promise of constructing actual detailed descriptions of concrete roles and decision processes is no longer, with the computer, a mere prospectus to be realized at some undefined future date. We can already provide actual examples, some of them in the area of economics.

1. *Management Science.* In the paragraphs on normative applications in section II, we have already referred to the use of such mathematical techniques as linear programming and dynamic programming to construct formal decision processes for actual situations. The relevance of these decision models to the present discussion is that they are not merely abstract "theories" of the firm, but actual decision-making devices. We can think of any such device as a simulation of the corresponding human decision maker, in which the equations and other assumptions that enter into the formal decision-making procedure correspond to the decision premises—including the role prescription—of the decision maker.

The actual application of such models to concrete business situations brings to light the information-processing tasks that are concealed in the assumptions of the more abstract classical models.

(1) The models must be formulated so as to require for their application only data that are obtainable. If one of the penalties, for example, of holding too small inventories is the loss of sales, a decision model that proposes to determine optimal inventory levels must incorporate a procedure for putting a dollar value on this loss.

(2) The models must call only for practicable computations. For example, several proposals for applying linear programming to certain factory scheduling problems have been shown to be impracticable because, even with computers, the computation time is too great. The task of decision theory (whether normative or descriptive) is to find alterna-

tive techniques—probably only approximate—that demand much less computation.

(3) The models must not demand unobtainable forecast information. A procedure that would require a sales department to estimate the third moment of next month's sales distribution would not have wide application, as either description or prescription, to business decision making.

These models, then, provide us with concrete examples of roles for a decision maker described in terms of the premises he is expected to apply to the decision—the data and the rules of computation.

2. *Engineering Design.* Computers have been used for some years to carry out some of the analytic computations required in engineering design—computing the stresses, for example, in a proposed bridge design. Within the past two years, ways have been found to program computers to carry out synthesis as well as analysis—to evolve the design itself. A number of companies in the electrical industry now use computers to design electric motors, transformers, and generators, going from customer specifications to factory design without human intervention. The significance of this for our purpose here is that the synthesis programs appear to simulate rather closely the processes that had previously been used by college-trained engineers in the same design work. It has proved possible to write down the engineers' decision premises and inference processes in sufficient detail to produce workable computer programs.

3. *Human Problem Solving.* The management science and engineering design programs already provide examples of simulation of human decision making by computer. It may be thought that, since in both instances the processes are highly arithmetical, these examples are relevant to only a very narrow range of human problem-solving activity. We generally think of a digital computer as a device which, if instructed in painful detail by its operator, can be induced to perform rather complicated and tedious arithmetical operations. More recent developments require us to revise these conceptions of the computer, for they enable it to carry out tasks that, if performed by humans, we would certainly call "thinking" and "learning."

Discovering the proof of a theorem of Euclid—a task we all remember from our high school geometry course—requires thinking and usually insight and imagination. A computer is now being programmed to perform this task (in a manner closely simulating the human geometer), and another computer has been successfully performing a highly similar task in symbolic logic for the past two years. The latter computer is programmed to learn—that is to improve its performance on the basis of successful problem-solving experience—to use something akin to imagery or metaphor in planning its proofs, and to transfer some of its skills to other tasks—for example, solving trigonometric identities—involving completely distinct subject matter. These programs, it should be observed, do not involve the computer in rapid arithmetic—or any arithmetic for that matter. They are basically nonnumerical, involving the manipulation of all kinds of symbolic material, including words.

Still other computer programs have been written to enable a computer to play chess. Not all of these programs, or those previously mentioned, are close simulations of the processes humans use. However, in some direct attempts to investigate the human processes by thinking-aloud techniques and to reproduce in computer programs the processes observed in human subjects, several striking simulations have been achieved. These experiments have been described elsewhere and can't be reviewed here in detail.

4. *Business Games.* Business games, like those developed by the American Management Association, International Business Machines Corporation, and several universities, represent a parallel development. In the business game, the decisions of the business firms are still made by the human players, but the economic environment of these firms, including their markets, are represented by computer programs that calculate the environment's responses to the actions of the players. As the games develop in detail and realism, their programs will represent more and more concrete descriptions of the decision processes of various economic actors—for example, consumers.

The games that have been developed so far are restricted to numerical magnitudes like prices and quantities of goods, and hence resemble the management science and engineering design programs more closely than they do those we have described under the heading of human problem solving. There is no reason, however, to expect this restriction to remain very long.

Implications for Economics

Apart from normative applications (e.g., substituting computers for humans in certain decision-making tasks) we are not interested so much in the detailed descriptions of roles as in broader questions: (1) What general characteristics do the roles of economic actors have? (2) How do roles come to be structured in the particular ways they do? (3) What bearing does this version of role theory have for macroeconomics and other large-scale social phenomena?

Characterizing Role Structure. Here we are concerned with generalizations about thought processes, particularly those generalizations that are relatively independent of the substantive content of the role. A classical example is Dewey's description of stages in the problem-solving process. Another example, of particular interest to economics, is the hypothesis we have already discussed at length: that economic man is a *satisficing* animal whose problem solving is based on search activity to meet certain aspiration levels rather than a *maximizing* animal whose problem solving involves finding the best alternatives in terms of specified criteria. A third hypothesis is that operative goals (those associated with an observable criterion of success, and relatively definite means of attainment) play a much larger part in governing choice than nonoperative goals (those lacking a concrete measure of success or a program for attainment).

Understanding How Roles Emerge. Within almost any single business firm, certain characteristic types of roles will be represented: selling roles, production roles, accounting roles, and so on. Partly, this consistency may be explained in functional terms—that a model that views the firm as producing a product, selling it, and accounting for its assets and liabilities is an effective simplification of the real world, and provides the members of the organization with a workable frame of reference. Imitation within the culture provides an alternative explanation. It is exceedingly difficult to test hypotheses as to the origins and causal conditions for roles as universal in the society as these, but the underlying mechanisms could probably be explored effectively by the study of less common roles—safety director, quality control inspector, or the like—that are to be found in some firms, but not in all.

With our present definition of role, we can also speak meaningfully of the role of an entire business firm—of decision premises that underlie its basic policies. In a particular industry we find some firms that specialize in adapting the product to individual customers' specifications; others that specialize in product innovation. The common interest of economics and psychology includes not only the study of individual roles, but also the explanation of organizational roles of these sorts.

Tracing the Implications for Macroeconomics. If basic professional goals remain as they are, the interest of the psychologist and the economist in role theory will stem from somewhat different ultimate aims. The former will use various economic and organizational phenomena as data for the study of the structure and determinants of roles; the latter will be primarily interested in the implications of role theory for the model of economic man, and indirectly, for macroeconomics.

The first applications will be to those topics in economics where the assumption of static equilibrium is least tenable. Innovation, technological change, and economic development are examples of areas to which a good empirically tested theory of the processes of human adaptation and problem solving could make a major contribution. For instance, we know very little at present about how the rate of innovation depends on the amounts of resources allocated to various kinds of research and development activity. Nor do we understand very well the nature of "know-how," the costs of transferring technology from one firm or economy to another, or the effects of various kinds and amounts of education upon national product. These are difficult questions to answer from aggregative data and gross observation, with the result that our views have been formed more by armchair theorizing than by testing hypotheses with solid facts.

VII. CONCLUSION

In exploring the areas in which economics has common interests with the other behavioral sciences, we have been guided by the metaphor we elaborated in section I. In simple, slow-moving situations, where the actor has a single, operational goal, the assumption of maximization relieves us of any need to construct a detailed picture of economic man or his processes of adaptation. As the complexity of the environment increases, or its speed of change, we need to know more and more about the mechanisms and processes that economic man uses to relate himself to that environment and achieve his goals.

How closely we wish to interweave economics with psychology depends, then, both on the range of questions we wish to answer and on our assessment of how far we may trust the assumptions of static equilibrium as approximations. In considerable part, the demand for a fuller picture of economic man has been coming from the profession of economics itself, as new areas of theory and application have emerged in which complexity and change are central facts. The revived interest in the theory of utility, and its application to choice under uncertainty, and to consumer saving and spending is one such area. The needs of normative macroeconomics and management science for a fuller theory of the firm have led to a number of attempts to understand the actual processes of making business decisions. In both these areas, notions of adaptive and satisficing behavior, drawn largely from psychology, are challenging sharply the classical picture of the maximizing entrepreneur.

The area of imperfect competition and oligopoly has been equally active, although the activity has thus far perhaps raised more problems than it has solved. On the positive side, it has revealed a community of interest among a variety of social scientists concerned with bargaining as a part of political and economic processes. Prediction of the future is another element common to many decision processes, and particularly important to explaining business cycle phenomena. Psychologists and economists have been applying a wide variety of approaches, empirical and theoretical, to the study of the formation of expectations. Surveys of consumer and business behavior, theories of statistical induction, stochastic learning theories, and theories of concept formation have all been converging on this problem area.

The very complexity that has made a theory of the decision-making process essential has made its construction exceedingly difficult. Most approaches have been piecemeal—now focused on the criteria of choice, now on conflict of interest, now on the formation of expectations. It seemed almost utopian to suppose that we could put together a model of adaptive man that would compare in completeness with the simple model of classical economic man. The sketchiness and incompleteness of the newer proposals has been urged as a compelling reason for clinging to the older theories, however inadequate they are admitted to be.

The modern digital computer has changed the situation radically. It provides us with a tool of research—for formulating and testing theories—whose power is commensurate with the complexity of the phenomena we seek to understand. Although the use of computers to build theories of human behavior is very recent, it has already led to concrete results in the simulation of higher mental processes. As economics finds it more and more necessary to understand and explain disequilibrium as well as equilibrium, it will find an increasing use for this new tool and for communication with its sister sciences of psychology and sociology.

3. Do Managers Find Decision Theory Useful?*

REX V. BROWN

For thousands of years, businessmen have been making decisions in the face of uncertainty about the future. Such decisions have often served to separate "the men from the boys" in business—and perhaps always will. In recent years, however, the problem executives face has been altered by the introduction of a set of techniques of quantitative analysis which I shall refer to here as Decision Theory Analysis (DTA). These methods have stimulated widespread attention, both critical and laudatory, in the business world.

As might be expected when a radically new approach is used, business executives have often found DTA methods frustrating and unrewarding. Nevertheless, there is a steadily growing conviction in the management community that DTA should and will occupy a very important place in an executive's arsenal of problem-solving techniques. Only time can tell if, as some enthusiasts claim, decision theory will be to the executive of tomorrow what the slide rule is to the engineer of today. But clearly, in my opinion, the *potential* impact of DTA is great.

The primary purpose of this article, which is based on a survey of 20 companies made in 1969, is to present some of the experiences of practitioners who have been exploring various applications of DTA techniques to management decision making. These experiences should help would-be users to identify particular situations in their own companies where the new technology might greatly benefit them, and to build on the lessons learned the hard way by earlier users.

Executives and staff specialists in the companies provided the bulk of the material. The companies included three organizations with several years of active experience with DTA (Du Pont, Pillsbury, and General Electric); a sampling of corporations that have taken up DTA in the past two or three years and are now quite active in employing it (e.g., General Mills and Inmont Corporation); one or two organizations whose experience with DTA has been disappointing; a few companies (such as

* *Harvard Business Review*, vol. 48, no. 3 (May–June 1970), pp. 78–89.

Ford Motor and Time, Inc.) where there is a definite interest in DTA but—at least, as of 1969—little application; and a couple of consulting firms with well-known expertise in the area (notably Arthur D. Little, Inc. and McKinsey & Company).

During the course of the survey, particular attention was focused on such questions as the following, which will be discussed in this article:

What tangible impact does DTA have on how businesses are run and on how individual decisions are made?

What areas of decision making is DTA best suited for?

What practical benefits result?

What trends in usage are apparent?

What obstacles and pitfalls lie in the way of more effective usage?

What organization steps should management take to use DTA more effectively?

What remains to be done in developing and expanding the usefulness of DTA?

DTA IN REVIEW

Before turning to the findings of the survey, let us review some of the elements of DTA. (The theory does not, by the way, always go under this name. Sometimes it is called "Personalist Decision Theory" or "Bayesian Decision Theory.")

First, what information does DTA demand of the executive? It requires such inputs as executive judgment, experience, and attitudes, along with any "hard data," such as historical records. In particular, the executive is asked to:

1. Stipulate what decision alternatives are to be considered in the analysis of a problem.
2. Make a probabilistic statement of his assessment of critical uncertainties.
3. Quantify some possible consequences of various actions and his attitudes toward these consequences.

The logically preferred decision can then be derived routinely according to the highly developed statistical theory that underlies DTA, using decision trees, computer programs, and/or other computational devices.

The use of DTA is not restricted to investment, marketing, or other types of business decisions. Potential and actual applications are also to be found in the area of medical, military, engineering, and government decisions. The most ambitious application of decision theory yet reported apparently was employed in the hypothetical problem of whether to push the nuclear button if the President receives different kinds of ambiguous evidence of an impending Russian attack on the United States.

The analyst does not need to keep in his head all the considerations that are taken into account, and, indeed, all the considerations do not need to be evaluated by the same person (although whoever makes the decision must *accept* the evaluations). For instance:

The company president might determine the company's attitude toward risk in new product planning.

The vice president of marketing might choose the business decisions to be compared.

The director of research might provide information on development times, likely success in solving technical problems, and so on.

The probable costs might come from the controller's office.

The probable sales might come from a sales manager or forecasting specialist.

Contentious elements in the analysis can be lifted out, and revised assessments substituted for them, without the analyst's having to reconsider every issue.

How DTA Works

One version of DTA—the "decision tree" approach—lends itself readily to simple manual computations, and can be used to illustrate the general ideas involved in this subject.

All elements which an executive considers important to a decision, however subjective, can be represented on a decision tree. To show how the process of common-sense decision making can be expressed in the necessary manner, let us take an example involving a hypothetical, but realistic, business decision.

Suppose that a New York metal broker has an option to buy 100,000 tons of iron ore from a Far Eastern government at an advantageous price, of, say, $5 a ton. Other brokers have received the same offer, and so our man in New York feels that an immediate decision must be made. He knows he can get $8 a ton for this ore, but he believes there is a 50-50 chance that the U.S. government will refuse to grant an import license. In such an event, the contract would be annulled at a penalty of $1 a ton.

A decision tree, representing what I shall call the initial problem, is shown in Part A of Figure 1. Note that both the "act forks" (labeled in capitals) and the "event forks" (lower case) are represented by branches on the decision tree, and that at each fork there are as many branches as there are alternatives.

The choice between alternative acts (in this case, the decision whether or not to buy the ore) is under the control of the decision maker. On the other hand, the occurrence of a particular event (the approval or refusal of the import

FIGURE 1
An Example of Decision Tree Analysis ($000 consequences or expected consequences)

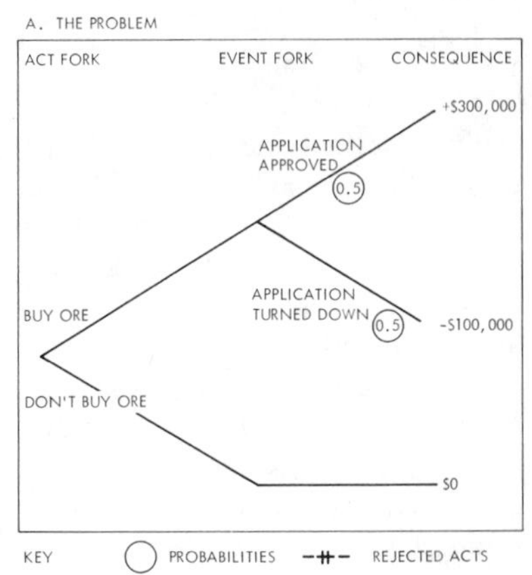

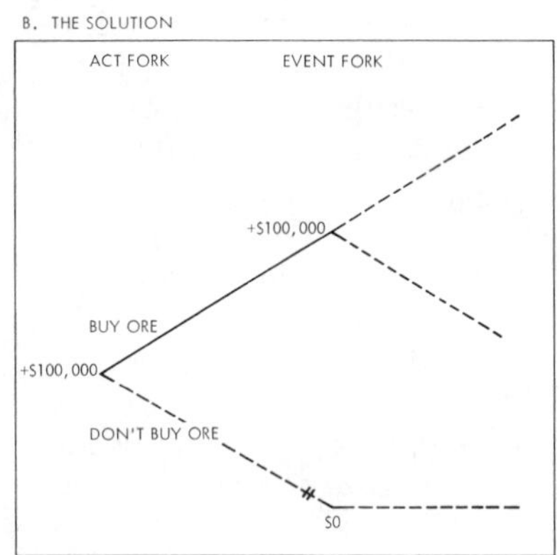

KEY ◯ PROBABILITIES —╫— REJECTED ACTS

license) is beyond his control. He estimates a 50-50 chance of approval. The probabilities are noted in parentheses.

The uncertainty about the license makes it impossible to know in advance what the "best" decision would be. Every path through the tree corresponds to a possible sequence of acts and events, each with its own unique consequence. For example, if our broker decides to buy ore, but his license application is rejected, he stands to lose (assuming a penalty of $1 a ton) $100,000.

In order to reach a good decision, the broker clearly has to take into account the probabilities, as he sees them, of each of the two events, approval or refusal of the import license. Intuitively, it is easy to see that if the broker assesses a high probability of approval, he would be wise to go ahead and buy the ore; but since he actually thinks there is only a 50-50 chance of approval, he is faced with 50% chance of obtaining $300,000 (his best estimate now of the potential profit) against an equal chance of losing $100,000. His estimates of the gains and losses are shown to the right of the decision tree, in Figure I-A.

Which act should he prefer? His attitude toward possible consequences must be noted. Suppose he has a general policy of "playing the averages" and is not at all averse to taking risks. This can be restated formally as maximizing the "expected" monetary consequences. (By contrast, other people "play it safe" or, conversely, are "gamblers," indicating they like to deviate from the averages.)

Formal analysis begins by computing an "expected" consequence for all event forks at the right-hand edge of the decision tree. This value is treated as if it were the certain consequence of reaching the base of the event fork. Its value is then substituted for the actual event fork and its consequences, as shown in

Figure 1-B. In this case, there is only one event fork (approval or rejection of the application) on the tree; it is therefore replaced by \$100,000—that is, .5(\$300,000) + .5(−\$100,000). If there were several event forks on the right, each would be replaced by an expected consequence.

Since the event fork is now eliminated, only the act fork is left. The branch which has the highest expected consequence is now selected. That is the "Buy ore" branch with a consequence of \$100,000. The analysis of this problem is now complete. With such a simple problem, it may hardly seem worth going to the trouble of a formal analysis. The real pay-off is likely to occur when the problem has more separable elements than the decision maker can comfortably take account of in his head. Typically, in such cases, there will be more than two "echelons" of forks in a decision tree, and more than one fork at each echelon. By alternating the two methods described for eliminating event and act forks respectively, the origin at the left-hand side of the tree will eventually be reached, and both the optimum strategy and its expected consequence will be determined.

Although the analysis depicted in Figure 1 could be perfectly adequate in representing our New York broker's first thoughts about his problem, a little reflection may lead him to take into account new considerations whose action implications are less easy to think through informally. For instance, it may occur to him that the acts "Buy ore" and "Don't buy ore" are not the only ones immediately available for consideration. As in most business problems, he may have the option of delaying his decision while he gathers more information. If so, the additional options and the consequences of every set of act-event sequences could be shown on the decision tree, and an optimum strategy determined in essentially the same way. Similarly, he might want to take into account some aversion to risk that he may possess in certain circumstances, the possibility of nonmonetary side effects (like goodwill), or uncertainty about quantities he had previously treated as certain (such as the price he can get for the ore).

These considerations, too, can be handled in the same format and with very little in the way of additional technique. However, more ambitious forms of DTA, such as computer simulations, often prove to be more convenient when there is a technical specialist available.

While, in principle, any decision problem *can* be analyzed by DTA methods, this is a very far cry from arguing that it always *should* be. In various instances, traditional decision making may be more economical, practical, and sound than modern methods of quantitative analysis.

GROWING USE

Only a few U.S. companies appear to have used DTA in operations for any length of time. Two of these companies are Du Pont, which got started with the approach in the late 1950s, and Pillsbury, which got started in the early 1960s. However, there has been a dramatic increase in DTA activity since about 1964. That is when executive interest began to be stimulated through executive orientation seminars, reports of successful applications on the part of pioneering companies, and, perhaps most important of all, a steady stream of DTA-trained MBAs who began to enter managerial ranks in substantial numbers.

Stimulated by such developments, executives in a number of companies began to explore the potential applications of DTA to their own operations. For example:

General Electric set up an intensive study of DTA by a high-level committee that led to major changes in plant appropriation methods.

Ford Motor and other companies put literally hundreds of their middle and senior managers through training programs varying in length from a few days to several weeks.

Other companies, including General Mills, began to introduce DTA on a project-by-project basis.

IMPACT ON DECISION MAKING

Since the companies in the survey were selected on the basis of their actual or imputed use of DTA, no special significance can be attached to the fact that most of them do indeed use the tools. What is significant, in my opinion, is that even these companies, leaders though they are, do not show drastic changes in their general decision-making procedures as a result of DTA. However, *individual* decisions are often profoundly affected. Examples from the experience of the most active companies interviewed—Du Pont, Pillsbury, GE, and Inmont—give some measure of how DTA is being used by managers.

Application at Du Pont

Substantial DTA activity is going on throughout the Du Pont organization, stimulated by staff groups in the Development Department and elsewhere. Managers in the various departments have shown increasing interest in the staff groups' services (which are supplied for a fee) during the past ten years. Yet, even after all this time, Dr. Sig Andersen, manager of one of the consulting groups and perhaps the most prominent figure in the application of DTA, says he feels that DTA has not yet reached the point where it really has a major impact at the general manager level in Du Pont. J. T. Axon, Manager of the Management Sciences Division, says:

"I think [Andersen and his colleagues] have indeed been pioneers and missionaries on behalf of DTA within Du Pont, and I share with them the conviction that their work has improved the quality of numerous decisions around the company. Their impact has been seriously limited, however, by the absence of appropriate educational efforts aimed at the decision makers. Even at this date, we have in Du Pont, in my judgment, very few key decision makers who are 'alive' to the possibilities of DTA and comfortable in its use. It is this lack that has dragged down the Du Pont effort."

At Du Pont middle and even senior managers increasingly will take action or submit recommendations that include DTA along with more conventional analyses, but the presentation to top management is likely to be supported by more informal reasoning, not DTA. Thus:

In the case of a new product which had just reached the prototype stage at Du Pont, the question before management was: On what scale should initial pilot production be carried out? Critical uncertainties involved the reliability of the military demand for which the prototype had been originally designed, and the amount of supplementary commercial business that would be generated.

DTA was performed on a computer to produce "risk profiles" of return on investment for various plant sizes and pricing strategies. The inputs included probability assessments of demand for each possible end-use of the product (based on market research), as well as assessments of cost and timing. The analysis indicated that, on the basis of the assessments used, a certain price was optimal, and a $3 million pilot plant would have the highest expected rate of return.

When this conclusion was transmitted to top management, it was couched in the language of informal reasoning, not of DTA. Management opted for a smaller, $1-million plant, but adopted—unchanged—the pricing recommendation of the study. It appears that top management, without explicitly disagreeing with the assumptions underlying the analysis, possessed an aversion to risk which was not assumed in the analysis.

Pillsbury's Approach

James R. Petersen, Vice President of The Pillsbury Company and General Manager of the Grocery Products Company, uses decision trees regularly in evaluating major recommendations submitted to him. More than a dozen marketing decisions a year are approved by him on the basis of the findings of detailed DTA. (Many more decisions in his divisions are rendered after first using a skeletal decision tree to clarify the key problem issues.)

Typically, a middle manager in the Grocery Products Company will spend a week or so developing a DTA approach, often with the help of a staff specialist. When the middle manager's recommendation comes to be considered by Petersen, this analysis is the vehicle for discussion. For instance:

In one case, the issue before management was whether to switch from a box to a bag as a package for a certain grocery product. Petersen and his sales manager had been disposed to retain the box on the grounds of greater customer appeal. The brand manager, however, favored the bag on cost considerations. He supported his recommendation with a DTA based on his own best assessments of probable economic, marketing, and other consequences. Even when the sales manager's more pessimistic assessments of the market impact of a bag were substituted for the brand manager's, the bag still looked more profitable. Petersen adopted the recommendation, the bag was introduced, and the profits on the product climbed substantially.

During the course of discussions, some Pillsbury executives urged that the bag be test-marketed before management made a firm decision. The original DTA showed, however, only a one-in-ten chance that the bag would prove unprofitable—and if that occurred, it would probably be not too unprofitable. A simple, supplementary DTA showed that the value of making a market test could not remotely approach its cost. Accordingly, no test marketing was undertaken. Management's confidence in the analysis was later confirmed by the bag's success.

Uses at GE

At General Electric there has recently been a formal head office requirement that all investment requests of more than $500,000 be supported by a probabilistic assessment of rate of return and other key measures. In the wake of this requirement, and largely in the area of plant appropriations, more than 500 instances of computerized DTA have been recorded over the past four years.

Heavy use is made of a library of special DTA programs developed largely by Robert Newman, Manager of Planning Services, who works with managers in other GE operations on a consulting basis. The consulting relationship, no doubt enhanced by Newman's own experience in line management, often has an impact on issues beyond the scope of the originating inquiry, as this example shows:

One GE division was faced with a shortage of manufacturing capacity for a mature industrial product. Using the information and assessments supplied by the division manager (including a suspicion that the product was obsolescent), Newman spent a few hours on a DTA which suggested that the division should not increase capacity, but raise prices. Both the consultant and the manager felt uneasy about this conclusion.

Further discussion yielded new but confidential information that the division was developing a product which promised to supplant the old one. This intelligence, plus various estimates of the probability of success and related matters, led to a new DTA (which employed GE's prepackaged computer programs). This study pointed to the conclusion that research and development expenditures on the new product should be increased by a factor of 20. The recommendation was adopted, the new product went into production two years later, and it achieved highly profitable sales of some $20 million a year.

Inmont's Programs

Although Inmont Corporation's usage of DTA is less extensive than that of the three companies just discussed, James T. Hill, President, comments that he often uses computer simulations in evaluating potential acquisition candidates. Preliminary information available on such candidates is programmed into a model by his assistant. This model is part of a prepackaged DTA simulation program which merges Inmont and the acquisition candidate according to the specific purchase strategy that Inmont is contemplating. The computer prints out detailed information as to the cost to Inmont and the return to the individual shareholders of the acquired company, including a pro forma balance sheet and income statement both before and after conversion of convertible securities.

Once the results are reviewed by Hill and his top executives, any alternative financing schemes that have been suggested can be explored in a matter of minutes in order to determine the best financial plan. Computer terminals are available at strategic decision-making locations in the head office, and the program is designed so as to enable any executive's secretary to put in data for different possible modes of acquisition. It is an easy matter, therefore, for alternative strategies to be evaluated quickly at any stage in the decision-making process.

When the most desirable financial approach has been determined, a second program can be utilized to run projected pro forma balance sheets and income statements for any period into the future. This program uses probability theory to arrive at the "best guess" as to the outcome of various operating strategies. It also enables executives to determine the factors most crucial to the future return on investment of a proposed merger. This "sensitivity analysis" thus focuses on the critical questions with which Inmont's management would have to deal if it were to undertake the acquisition.

This is what Hill says about Inmont's use of the procedure:

"The two programs, together, help ensure that the decision as to a potential acquisition is made after a comprehensive analysis of alternatives. It is not necessary to choose only one method of financing or one method of operation, for example. Rather, it is possible to explore, in a very short period of time, numerous strategies to discover that which will maximize the benefits to the merged companies. It is understood that the decision is no better than the reliability of the inputs, including the assigned probabilities."

Various other companies responding to my survey report that they are using DTA on a more-or-less systematic basis for marketing and allied decisions, most frequently in the area of new product selection and development, but also in promotion, pricing, test marketing, and other activities. In fact, about 50 specific applications of DTA to marketing problems are noted—and some of these will be mentioned subsequently in this article.

OBSTACLES AND PITFALLS

Enthusiasm for DTA is very great in many quarters. For example, Robert Newman of General Electric predicts:

"Within 10 years, decision theory, conversational computers, and library programs should occupy the same role for the manager as calculus, slide rules, and mathematical tables do for the engineer today. The engineer of Roman times had none of these, but he could make perfectly good bridges. However, he could not compete today, even in bridge building, let alone astro-engineering. Management is today at the stage of Roman engineering. Needless to say, managers will still use specialists, just as engineers use heat transfer experts."

While Newman's time schedule may be optimistic, my survey findings in no way contradict the substance of his view. However, a number of more or less serious obstacles—many no doubt attributable to inexperience in using DTA—lie in the path of a major revolution such as Newman envisages.

Personal Competence

It is clear that companies will experience only limited success with a new analytical approach like DTA unless they have executives who are alive to its possibilities and use it effectively. While there is a substantial and rapidly expanding number of DTA-oriented executives in positions to influence management decisions, they represent a tiny fraction of the total managerial pool. The momentum of educational processes will remedy this problem in time—but it will take time.

Much the same can be said about the current scarcity of trained technical specialists needed to carry out or advise managers on DTA. After all, the first comprehensive handbook on applied DTA was published only recently.

However, even if there were no manpower shortage, serious obstacles to successful and expanding use of DTA would still exist. Removing them may require more deliberate initiative and research on management's part than will correcting the lack of line and staff training.

Uncertainty over Return

For one thing, no substantial personal or corporate benefits of using the technique may be apparent to the potential user. Many effective managers have a "show me" attitude toward new decision-making techniques, and as yet there is little to show. Indeed, no firm evidence is available to prove that DTA *does* have widespread practical value. The evidence from my survey is encouraging, but far from conclusive; enough disappointments have been reported to sustain the doubts harbored by many businessmen. For example:

A central staff team for an international manufacturer of industrial components carried out a sophisticated and competent DTA designed to help a regional subsidiary choose which of several alternative markets to compete in. When the DTA part of the study was presented to the subsidiary's president, however, he perceived it as having little relevance to him in his decision making. He told me that the market forecast and other input data gathered for the analysis were certainly of substantial value to him, but he could not see that the DTA itself added much that was useful. Indeed, while the market data provided a basis for much of the subsidiary's subsequent strategy, no specific action appeared to be traceable to the DTA part of the study (though some people diffuse influence on several decisions).

The managers of the subsidiary are seeking to adapt the DTA to meet their needs, and the prospects look encouraging. Moreover, the staff team from the head office has since introduced DTA to *other* subsidiaries with, it seems, substantial success.

Note that this experience was the first the company had had with DTA. Almost all of the most successful users of DTA have started out with one or more disappointing experiences. What accounts for such disappointments? Let us take the international manufacturer again as a case example. Its experience is typical of that of several other companies I know about:

1. The logic and language of DTA was unfamiliar to the president and his senior executives, and they could not readily and comfortably incorporate it into their normal mode of thinking. A more gradual introduction of the complex technology would surely have been more digestible.

2. The decision options addressed by the DTA turned out *not* to be the ones the president was concerned about. (For example, he was more interested in deciding *how* to develop a particular market sector than in *whether* to be in it at all.) Fuller and earlier communication between

executive and staff analysts helps to counter this very common problem experienced in applying DTA.

3. The DTA was initiated and performed by "head office" people over whom the subsidiary had no direct control, and the subsidiary president may have felt some threat to his autonomy. Having such an analysis performed or commissioned by his own people would have removed the threat.

4. The subsidiary president told me that the way to make money in his business was to get good data and implement decisions effectively. He had little interest in improved ways of *processing* data to make decisions, which is, of course, the special province of DTA.

Diffused Decision Making

At Ford Motor Company, some 200 senior executives have passed through a brief DTA-oriented program during the past five years; the program has been followed up in some divisions by intensive workshops for junior executives. And yet, according to George H. Brown, former Director of Marketing Research at Ford headquarters, usage of DTA at Ford has been negligible in the marketing area, and the prospects unpromising, at least as of the time of this survey. In his opinion, large organizations with diffuse decision-making processes (like Ford) are not as well suited to the effective use of DTA as, say, the small or one-man organization is.

John J. Nevin, now Vice President of Marketing for Ford, adds the following observations:

"I am not sure that there is any reason to be discouraged by the fact that, in many companies, DTA may be far more accepted and far more utilized by middle management. Maybe all analytical tools sneak into general usage through the back door. It does not seem to me to be improbable that the middle management people, who are more comfortable with these techniques and are using them on very specific technical problems today, will, as they grow to top management positions, feel as uncomfortable switching to some new decision-making process as many of today's managers feel in switching to a more disciplined analysis."

He also notes that the average executive has difficulty picking up all of the variables in a complex decision-making problem. He attributes this in large part to the executive's inability to discipline himself to use a new technique.

Nevertheless, several Ford divisions are now exploring DTA applications at their most senior executive levels. Since my survey began, early in 1969, there have been some cases of successful implementation. For instance:

At Ford Tractor, a product policy decision was recently required. In a regional market suffering from competitive inroads, the main options were to reduce prices or to introduce one of several possible new models; a modest DTA was carried out on these choices. Several runs incorporating assessments and modifications advanced by the marketing manager, the assistant general manager, and the general manager were made. The somewhat controversial conclusion to introduce a certain model was presented in DTA form to the general manager, who adopted it and initiated the necessary engineering studies.

Organizational Obstacles

If there is one dominant feature that distinguishes the successful from the less successful applications of DTA, judging from the findings of this survey, it is the organizational arrangements for offering DTA. The most successful appears to be the "vest pocket" approach, where the analyst works intimately with the executive and typically reports directly to him (Pillsbury's Grocery Products Company and Inmont Corporation provide excellent examples of this approach).

At the other end of the spectrum is the arms'-length approach, which is characteristic of much operations research. In this approach the analysis is performed by a staff group which is organizationally distant from the executive being served. In such instances, the executive may feel threatened rather than supported by DTA, and critical weaknesses may thus develop in the communication of the problem and its analyses.

Relation with Consultants

The epitome of the arms'-length arrangement appears in the role of the outside consultant. The survey suggests that consulting firms are doing relatively little DTA work for their clients. (One exception is McKinsey & Company, which reports substantial DTA work in nonmarketing areas.) I find this significant, in view of the facts that potentially, at least, consulting firms are a major resource for companies that want to use DTA, and that leading consultants have done much to explain DTA to businessmen.

It seems that clients often insist on holding some of their cards close to their chests—and effective DTA depends critically on incorporating in the analysis *all* of the elements that the decision maker sees as important. Many clients prefer to limit consultants to performing clearly specified technical or data-gathering tasks with a minimum of two-way communication; executives worry about jeopardizing company security and giving the consultant too much say in their business.

Dr. Harlan Meal, a departmental manager for Arthur D. Little, makes a telling observation concerning the role of consultants and general obstacles to the adoption of DTA:

"Many of the executives who hire consultants or who employ expert technical staff do so in order to reduce the uncertainty in their decision making, rather than to improve their ability to deal with uncertain situations. Many of the clients we have want to buy from us information which will make the outcome of a particular course of action more certain than it would otherwise have been. If all we can do for them is reduce the chance of making an incorrect decision or improve the expected performance of the decision they do make in the face of uncertainty, they are not very interested.

"It is on this point that I think the application of decision theory analysis gets stuck nearly every time. Very few executives think of themselves as gamblers or of making the best kind of decisions in a gambling situation. They want, instead, to think of themselves as individuals whose greater grasp of the available information and whose greater insight remove the uncertainty from the situation.

"When the information quality is so poor that the assignment of probabilities to outcomes seems an exercise in futility, decision theory analysis can be most useful. Yet most executives in such a situation say that the only thing which really can be useful is their own experienced intuition. The executive is going to behave as though he has information about the situation, whether he has it or not."

Technical Questions

A further obstacle to the widespread use of DTA has to do with the logical underpinnings of DTA. Some potential users, especially in staff positions, take the position that where information about an uncertain quantity is weak, there is no point in *attempting* to measure that uncertainty. This amounts to a rejection of a basic tenet of DTA, viz., that subjective judgment, however tenuous, must be taken into account *somehow* by the decision maker, and that a DTA approach may do the job more effectively than unaided intuition.

In addition, increase in the effectiveness of DTA is to some extent dependent on the state of the art. The development and propagation of economical and quick routines utilizing inputs and outputs that can be readily communicated will no doubt be a major factor. Such routines affect the practicality and appeal of DTA in a management setting. However, it seems clear that purely theoretical developments are not holding up further application of DTA; the frontiers of the technology are way ahead of the applications, in most cases.

REALIZING THE POTENTIALS

How beneficial is a DTA to a company? Does it lead to "better" decisions than other approaches to decision making? Logic alone cannot give us the answer. However, it seems clear that DTA may *not* be the best approach if:

1. The subjective inputs required for the analysis are inaccurately measured and recorded. (Executives, as Meal suggests in the comment quoted earlier in this article, may not explicitly admit to uncertainty about some critical variable, whereas they may take it into account in their informal reasoning.)

2. The DTA does not incorporate all the considerations which the executive would informally take into account—for example, some non-monetary side effect like goodwill. (Where there is good communication between executive and analyst, the executive often can and does make "eyeball" adjustments for anything that has been left out of the analysis. Sometimes, though, such adjustments are so substantial that they swamp and thereby invalidate the entire DTA.)

Considering all the angles and factors that bear on a good DTA (or any other analysis) is time-consuming and sometimes quite frustrating. Clearly, though, it is one of the prerequisites of making this approach. The following experience should suffice to make the point:

A corporate staff team at General Mills evaluated an acquisition opportunity by means of a DTA computer program that took four months to develop and another two months to run with successively modified inputs corresponding to new assessments and assumptions made by the researchers and executives. In all, 140 computer runs were made before arriving at a recommendation to make the acquisition and to adopt a specific marketing and production strategy. The recommendation was rejected by top management, however, when the company's legal counsel advised against the acquisition on certain legal grounds. The lawyers discovered that a critical consideration had been omitted from the analysis which rendered it unusable for the purpose at hand.

It should be noted that this was the company's first major attempt at applying DTA, and the experience performed a valuable function in exposing line and staff to the scope and pitfalls of DTA. The company's record with DTA since then has been quite successful.

Costs versus Benefits

The cost of applying DTA are by no means inconsequential. It is true that the out-of-pocket costs for technicians and computers, even for a large-scale analysis, may be relatively trivial. Moreover, these costs can be expected to decline as DTA technology becomes more streamlined. Other, less obvious costs, however, are not trivial and are unlikely to become so. For example:

Critical decisions may be unacceptably delayed while an analysis is being completed. (When General Mills does not use DTA for market planning decisions, this is cited as the most common reason.) A busy executive needs to devote some of his valuable time to making sure that all of the relevant judgments he can make have been fed into the analysis.

Even more serious a "cost" is the discomfort an executive feels as he forces his traditional way of thinking into an unfamiliar mold and lays bare to the discretion of a DTA specialist the most delicate considerations that enter into his decision making. These considerations sometimes include confidential information (as in the GE new product example previously noted), admissions of uncertainty (which often run counter to the prevailing managerial culture), and embarrassing motivations. In one instance of an elaborate analysis of possible locations for a European subsidiary, the actual decision was dominated by the fact that key personnel wanted to be near the International School in Geneva. Somehow, that consideration seemed too noneconomic and nonrational to be fed into the analysis.

However, such costs are by no means prohibitive if management's approach to DTA is sound and thorough. When that is the case, the advantages claimed by users of DTA are material and persuasive:

It focuses informal thinking on the critical elements of a decision.

It forces into the open hidden assumptions behind a decision and makes clear their logical implication.

It provides an effective vehicle for communicating the reasoning which underlies a recommendation.

Many of the executives most satisfied with DTA value it as a vehicle for communicating decision-making reasoning as well as for improving it. My own feeling is that DTA's contribution to the quality of decision making often seems to come more from forcing meaningful structure on informal reasoning than from supplementing it by formal analysis. For instance, in the Pillsbury Grocery Products Company, for every DTA pushed to its numerical conclusion, there are half a dozen cases where only a conceptual decision tree has been drawn. Such a tree is used to focus attention on the critical options and uncertainties, and is then dropped in favor of informal reasoning.

Suggestions for Starting

After reflecting on the experiences of successful and unsuccessful users of DTA, I want to offer some suggestions for the executive intent on trying out DTA in his organization:

Ensure the sympathetic involvement of the chief executive of the company (or operating unit).

Make sure that at least a few key executives have a minimal appreciation of what DTA can do for them and what it requires of them. (This might be done by means of one of the short DTA orientation courses currently available.)

Make at least one trial run on a decision problem—preferably a live one—with the help of a DTA specialist. Use the exercise as a training vehicle for your executives and staffers, without expecting immediate pay-offs.

Plan on recruiting or developing in-house staff specialists to do the detail on subsequent analyses. The specialists should report directly to you, not to part of an organizationally distant operations research group.

Wean yourself and your staff from outside specialists as soon as possible, using them only as residual technical resources.

On any particular DTA, follow the analysis closely enough to make sure that the problem which gets solved is the problem you have, and that you accept *all* of the underlying assumptions. This will probably mean a less sophisticated analysis than would gladden the heart of the typical technician. It will also probably mean you spend more time with the analysis than you think you can afford.

CONCLUSION

What efforts are needed to make DTA a more effective tool for the executive? It may be helpful to think of DTA as in some way analogous to an industrial product and to ask ourselves: What aspects of its "manufacture" or "marketing" stand most in need of attention?

The "fundamental research" and "product design" aspects (corresponding to statistical decision theory and the development of special analytical devices) appear to be in rather good shape. Rare are the instances in which successful use of DTA is held up through shortcomings in the purely technical state of the art. Of course, there are areas where improved DTA techniques need to be developed, such as the extraction of probability assessments, handling risk aversion and nonmonetary criteria for action, and accommodating group decision making. But, even so, it is clear that greater use of DTA does not depend on such refinements. The tools that exist are well in advance of the capacity of most companies to use them.

Improvements in "production technique"—i.e., in the ability to deliver competent DTA at an acceptable cost—appear to be somewhat harder to achieve. In one major analysis of a pricing problem, the only reason that subjective probabilities were not introduced explicitly was that the computer cost would have been too high. However, we can be confident that within a few years progress in computer technology will largely eliminate this deterrent.

The manpower costs and delays involved in performing a reasonably complete analysis are usually more intractable. With the emergence and propagation of generalized computer programs of the type developed independently by each of the leaders (notably General Electric) in the DTA field, such costs can also be expected to decline—but the improvement will be gradual during the next five to ten years.

The inadequacy of "production facilities"—that is, the ability of DTA analysts to use available methods and concepts—is another temporary obstacle. Solving this problem will take more formal education and increased awareness of the issues and techniques that others have learned. Certainly help to this end will come from university programs and professional publications. Need for access to physical facilities, such as computer services, does not seem to be a serious limiting factor.

"Promotion" and "packaging" are areas requiring serious attention because they have been more neglected. It is true that the "product awareness" needed to stimulate management demand has been created by publications and executive development programs. But willingness to *try* the product (DTA) requires communicating to a potential user the benefits he can expect. These benefits need to be ascertained and documented in a far more effective way than by incomplete testimonials from satisfied—and not so satisfied—users (as in a survey like the present one).

"Repeat buying" on the part of experimental users requires an attractive and convenient "package" so that an executive can contribute judgments and estimates with less pain and confusion, and also so that the conclusions of a DTA can be presented in a more effective, appealing manner. Confusing computer print-outs and technical reports account for many indifferent receptions to what are otherwise very adequate DTAs.

Somewhat allied to the packaging problem, and still more critical, is the question of how DTA should be *used* in the context of a company's operation. This raises the whole issue of how to organize the DTA function, how to implement recommendations, and how to identify suitable applications. Kent Quisel, a senior analyst at Du Pont, comments that he spends a third of his time on what he calls "user engineering," and that this amount is still not enough. At companies less experienced in DTA than Du Pont is, the proportion of time spent in this way is generally much less than a third, to the almost invariable detriment of DTA's effectiveness.

Possibly the most important area of all for study is "product evaluation." Just how good a product *is* DTA? How deserving is it of intensive development and promotion? The survey findings leave no doubt in my mind that many users are pleased with DTA, and with good cause. What is much less clear is just how important its impact can be on business as a whole. After all, only a very minute fraction of companies have so much as experimented with DTA. Can it really revolutionize management as mathematics has revolutionized engineering? Or will it forever be an occasionally helpful side calculation in a decision-making process that remains essentially unchanged?

The answers are clearly of major importance to businessmen and, indeed, depend in large measure on the businessmen themselves. How eager are they to improve the quality of their decision making? What scope for improvement is there? The answers to these questions are the key to many of the issues raised in this article.

part TWO
Demand

INTRODUCTION

An understanding of demand for a firm's product requires identification of those factors which determine or influence existing sales volume. After a firm or industry defines as precisely as possible *why* its product is selling at current levels, it may be in a better position to consider certain changes; consequently, this chapter dealing with Demand is a necessary prelude to the one on Forecasting, Part III.

Demand analysis is important to decision making in two ways: (1) it provides the basis for analyzing market influences on the firm's products and thus helps the firm to adapt to the influences; and (2) it provides guidance in the manipulation of demand itself. Some decisions require a passive adaptation to market forces while others require the active shifting of those forces.

If the theoretical foundations of demand analysis are useful to the managerial economist, it would seem that empirical studies of demand are, too. Unfortunately, however, the results of very few empirical demand studies have stood up. The classic article by E. J. Working tells why.

To provide reliable estimates of elasticities, an empirical study must follow a simultaneous equations approach, and deal with such well-known econometric problems as identification and multicollinearity; but even all the trimmings of grand econometric method are only necessary, not sufficient, conditions for reliable demand estimates, as experience sadly shows. Nevertheless, the subject is important. The brief note by Hogarty and Elzinga estimates price and income elasticities for a rather popular beverage: beer. Careful reading and understanding of their article may allow inclusion of its methodology in the student's tool kit.

A much broader study of demand is undertaken by Daniel B. Suits. Expressed in terms of annual retail sales, Suits studies the final formulation of the demand function for new passenger automobiles. His estimate uses least-squares linear regression with variables expressed in first differences, a method which represents another fine addition to the student's tool kit. The beer and automobile articles are good companion pieces.

Because of the problems that hinder demand estimation by statistical techniques, economists are always looking for alternative methods. "Quasi-experimental techniques are feasible for some products. If enough other variables can be held constant, observations on prices and purchases can give quite a lot of information about price elasticities." An application of this method to liquor is reported on in the article by Julian Simon.

L. J. Atkinson's article is a good example of the cross-sectional approach to demand analysis, using many social and personal as well as economic variables. It may perhaps be read more for its exemplary use of a particular method than for its substantive results. There is no particular reason to doubt the results. But even good results can become dated; good methods do not.

Good methods of estimating demand are mandatory if demand studies are to be useful in predicting the effects of changes in the independent variables. But a frequently used alternative to the statistical approches surveyed here is one of the traditional forecasting methods. The material in Part III, therefore, is pertinent to this section as well.

4. What Do Statistical "Demand Curves" Show?*

E. J. WORKING

Many questions of practical importance hinge upon the elasticity of demand, or of demand and supply. The economist can answer them only in a vague and indefinite manner, because he does not know the nature of the demand curve. What will be the effect of a five-million-bushel increase in the corn crop upon the price of corn and of hogs? What will be the effect of a tariff on imports and prices; on the protected industry; on the balance of international payments? How large an indemnity can Germany pay? The answers all depend in greater or less measure upon the elasticity of demand of the various commodities in question.

Such are the needs of the theorist, and in recent years a great deal of attention has been turned to the construction of statistical demand curves. Beef, corn, cotton, hay, hogs, pig iron, oats, potatoes, sweet potatoes, sugar, and wheat are on the list of commodities for which we have statements of the "law of demand." Many economists have been skeptical, while others have been enthusiastic, on the significance of such demand curves. In consequence of this divergence of opinion, it may be well to consider some of the theoretical aspects of what the demand curves constructed by our statistical experts may be expected to show. Do they correspond to the demand curves of economic theory? If so, it would seem that they represent something tangible by which our theories may be tested and turned to better account.

Among the statistical studies of demand that have been made, there are cases in which the same commodity has been studied by more than one investigator, and their results indicate varying degrees of elasticity of demand. But despite this, in all but one of the cases the demand curves have been negatively inclined—they have been in accord with Marshall's "one general *law of demand.*"

In the case of pig iron, however, Professor H. L. Moore finds a "law

---

* *The Quarterly Journal of Economics,* vol. 41, no. 2 (February 1927), pp. 212–35.

of demand" which is not in accord with Marshall's universal rule. He finds that the greater the quantity of pig iron sold, the higher will be the prices. If this is the nature of the statistical demand curve for pig iron, surely statistical demand curves must be of a very different sort from the demand curves of traditional economic theory!

Professor Moore holds that the statistical "law of demand" at which he arrives is a *dynamic* law, while that of theory is a *static* law. He says in part: "The doctrine of the uniformity of the demand function is an idol of the static state—the method of *cœteris paribus*—which has stood in the way of the successful treatment of dynamic problems." If it be true that statistical demand curves and the demand curves of theory differ so utterly from each other, of what value is statistical analysis to the theorist—of what value is economic theory to the statistical analyst? It would seem that so far as the study of demand is concerned, the statistical analyst and the economic theorist are on paths so divergent as to be wholly out of touch with each other. Before we accede to such a discouraging thought, let us examine a little more closely the nature of statistical demand curves as they may be viewed in the light of economic theory.

Let us first consider in what way statistical demand curves are constructed. While both the nature of the data used and the technique of analysis vary, the basic data consist of corresponding prices and quantities. That is, if a given quantity refers to the amount of a commodity sold, produced, or consumed in the year 1910, the corresponding price is the price which is taken to be typical of the year 1910. These corresponding quantities and prices may be for a period of a month, a year, or any other length of time which is feasible; and, as has already been indicated, the quantities may refer to amounts produced, sold, or consumed. The technique of analysis consists of such operations as fitting the demand curve, and adjusting the original data to remove, in so far as is possible, the effect of disturbing influences. For a preliminary understanding of the way in which curves are constructed, we need not be concerned with the differences in technique; but whether the quantities used are the amounts produced, sold, or consumed is a matter of greater significance, which must be kept in mind.

For the present, let us confine our attention to the type of study which uses for its data the quantities which have been sold in the market. In general, the method of constructing demand curves of this sort is to take corresponding prices and quantities, plot them, and draw a curve which will fit as nearly as possible all the plotted points. Suppose, for example, we wish to determine the demand curve for beef. First, we find out how many pounds of beef were sold in a given month and what was the average price. We do the same for all the other months of the period over which our study is to extend, and plot our data with quantities as abscissas and corresponding prices as ordinates. Next we draw a curve to fit the points. This is our demand curve.

In the actual construction of demand curves, certain refinements necessary in order to get satisfactory results are introduced. The purpose of these is to correct the data so as to remove the effect of various extraneous and complicating factors. For example, adjustments are usually made for changes in the purchasing power of money, and for changes in population and in consumption habits. Corrections may be made directly by such means as dividing all original price data by "an index of the general level of prices." They may be made indirectly by correction for trends of the two time series of prices and of quantities. Whatever the corrections and refinements, however, the essence of the method is that certain prices are taken as representing the prices at which certain quantities of the product in question were sold.

With this in mind, we may now turn to the theory of the demand-and-supply curve analysis of market prices. The conventional theory runs in terms substantially as follows. At any given time, all individuals within the scope of the market may be considered as being within two groups—potential buyers and potential sellers. The higher the price, the more the sellers will be ready to sell and the less the buyers will be willing to take. We may assume a demand schedule of the potential buyers and a supply schedule of the potential sellers which express the amounts that these groups are ready to buy and sell at different prices. From these schedules supply and demand curves may be made. Thus we have our supply and demand curves showing the market situation at any given time, and the price which results from this situation will be represented by the height of the point where the curves intersect.

This, however, represents the situation as it obtains at any given moment only. It may change; indeed, it is almost certain to change. The supply and demand curves which accurately represent the market situation of today will not represent that of a week hence. The curves which represent the average or aggregate of conditions this month will not hold true for the corresponding month of next year. In the case of the wheat market, for example, the effect of news that wheat which is growing in Kansas has been damaged by rust will cause a shift in both demand and supply schedules of the traders in the grain markets. The same amount of wheat, or a greater, will command a higher price than would have been the case if the news had failed to reach the traders. Since much of the buying and selling is speculative, changes in the market price itself may result in shifts of the demand and supply schedules.

If, then, our market demand-and-supply curves are to indicate conditions which extend over a period of time, we must represent them as shifting. A diagram such as the following, Figure 1, may be used to indicate them. The demand and supply curves may meet at any point within the area *a*, *b*, *c*, *d*, and over a period of time points of equilibrium will occur at many different places within it.

FIGURE 1
Utility and Demands

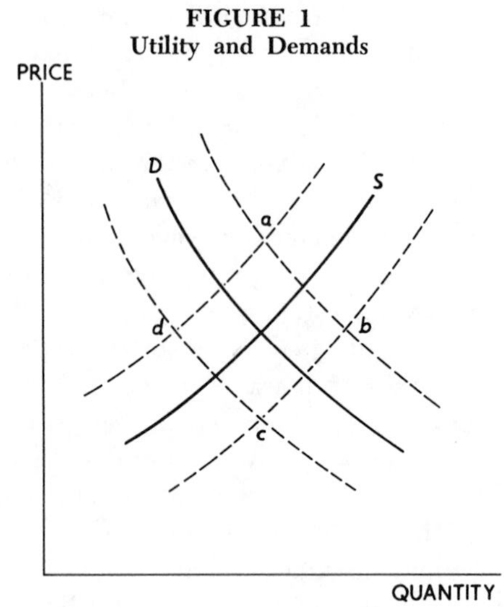

But what of statistical demand curves in the light of this analysis? If we construct a statistical demand curve from data of quantities sold and corresponding prices, our original data consist, in effect, of observations of points at which the demand and supply curves have met. Although we may wish to reduce our data to static conditions, we must remember that they originate in the market itself. The market is dynamic and our data extend over a period of time; consequently our data are of changing conditions and must be considered as the result of shifting demand and supply schedules.

Let us assume that conditions are such as those illustrated in Figure 2, the demand curve shifting from D_1 to D_2 and the supply curve shifting in similar manner from S_1 to S_2. It is to be noted that the chart shows approximately equal shifting of the demand and supply curves.

Under such conditions there will result a series of prices which may be graphically represented in Figure 3. It is from data such as those represented by the dots that we are to construct a demand curve, but evidently no satisfactory fit can be obtained. A line of one slope will give substantially as good a fit as will a line of any other slope.

But what happens if we alter our assumptions as to the relative shift-

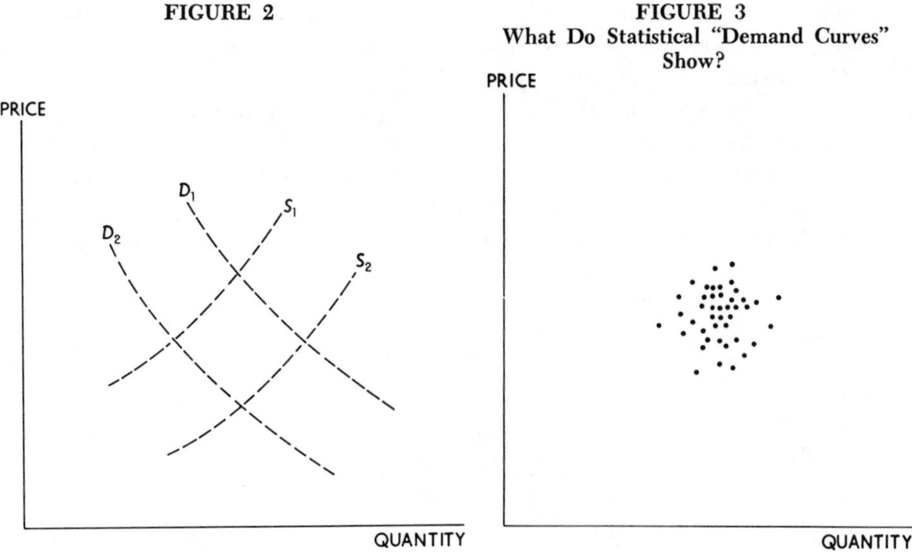

FIGURE 2

FIGURE 3
What Do Statistical "Demand Curves" Show?

ing of the demand and supply curves? Suppose the supply curve shifts in some such manner as is indicated by Figure 4, that is, so that the shifting of the supply curve is greater than the shifting of the demand

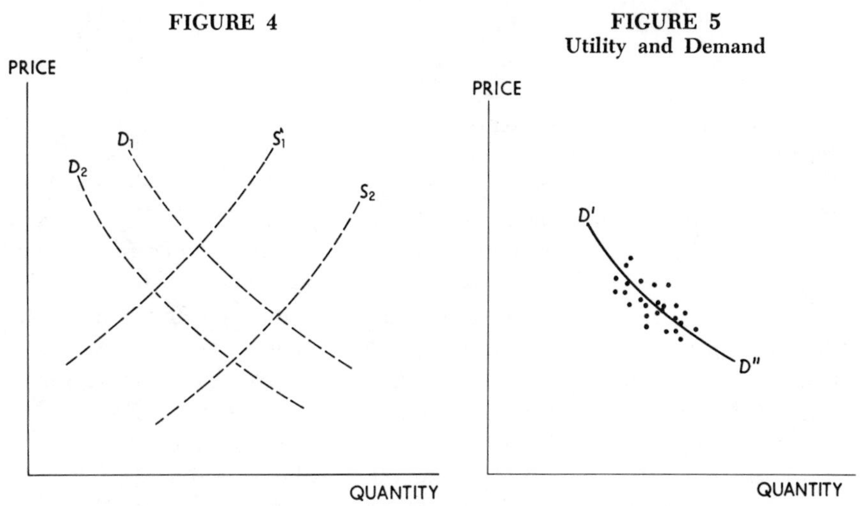

FIGURE 4

FIGURE 5
Utility and Demand

curve. We shall then obtain a very different set of observations—a set which may be represented by the dots of Figure 5. To these points we may fit a curve which will have the elasticity of the demand curve that we originally assumed, and whose position will approximate the central position about which the demand curve shifted. We may consider this to be a sort of typical demand curve, and from it we may determine the elasticity of demand.

If, on the other hand, the demand schedules of buyers fluctuate more than do the supply schedules of sellers, we shall obtain a different result. This situation is illustrated by Figure 6. The resulting array of prices and quantities is of a very different sort from the previous case, and its nature is indicated by Figure 7. A line drawn so as most nearly

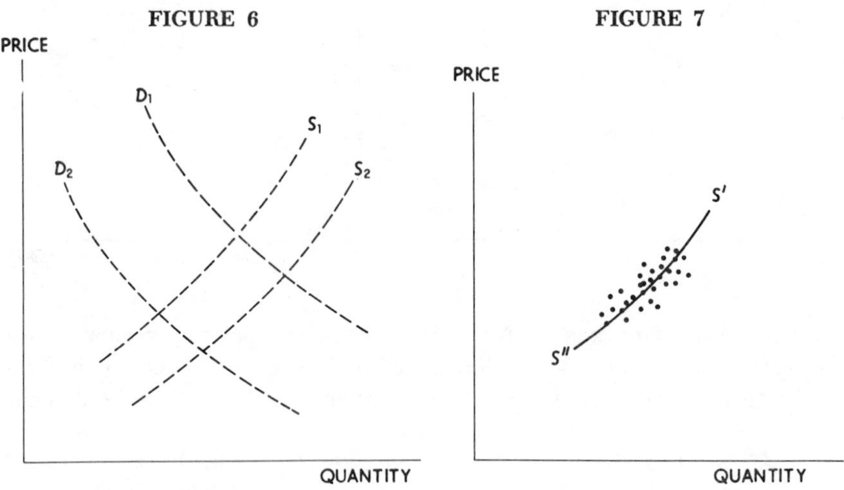

to fit these points will approximate a supply curve instead of a demand curve.

If this analysis is in accord with the facts, is it not evident that Professor Moore's "law of demand" for pig iron is in reality a "law of supply" instead? The original observations of prices and corresponding quantities are the resultant of both supply and demand. Consequently, they do not necessarily reflect the influence of demand any more than that of supply. The methods used in constructing demand curves (particularly if the quantity data are of quantities sold) may, under some conditions, yield a demand curve, under others, a supply curve, and, under still different conditions, no satisfactory result may be obtained.

In the case of agricultural commodities, where production for any given year is largely influenced by weather conditions, and where farmers sell practically their entire crop regardless of price, there is likely to be a much greater shifting of the supply schedules of sellers than of the demand schedules of buyers. This is particularly true of perishable commodities, which cannot be withheld from the market without spoilage, and in any case the farmers themselves can under no conditions use more than a very small proportion of their entire production. Such a condition results in the supply curve shifting within very wide limits. The demand curve, on the other hand, may shift but little. The quantities which are consumed may be dependent almost entirely upon price, so that the only way to have a much larger amount taken off the market is to reduce the price, and any considerable curtailment of supply is sure to result in a higher price.

With other commodities, the situation may be entirely different. Where a manufacturer has complete control over the supply of the article which he produces, the price at which he sells may be quite definitely fixed, and the amount of his production will vary, depending upon how large an amount of the article is bought at the fixed price. The extent to which there is a similar tendency to adjust sales to the shifts of demand varies with different commodities, depending upon how large overhead costs are and upon the extent to which trade agreements or other means are used to limit competition between different manufacturers. In general, however, there is a marked tendency for the prices of manufactured articles to conform to their expenses of production, the amount of articles sold varying with the intensity of demand at that price which equals the expenses of production. Under such conditions, the supply curve does not shift greatly, but rather approximates an expenses-of-production curve, which does not vary much from month to month or from year to year. If this condition is combined with a fluctuating demand for the product, we shall have a situation such as that shown in Figures 6 and 7, where the demand curves shift widely and the supply curves only a little.

From this, it would seem that, whether we obtain a demand curve or a supply curve, by fitting a curve to a series of points which represent the quantities of an article sold at various prices, depends upon the fundamental nature of the supply and demand conditions. It implies the need of some term in addition to that of elasticity in order to describe the nature of supply and demand. The term "variability" may be used for this purpose. For example, the demand for an article may be said to be "elastic" if, at a given time a small reduction in price would result in a much greater quantity being sold, while it may be said to be "variable" if the demand curve shows a tendency to shift markedly. To be called variable, the demand curve should have the tendency to shift back and forth, and not merely to shift gradually and consistently to the right or left because of changes of population or consuming habits.

Whether a demand or a supply curve is obtained may also be affected by the nature of the corrections applied to the original data. The corrections may be such as to reduce the effect of the shifting of the demand schedules without reducing the effect of the shifting of the supply schedules. In such a case the curve obtained will approximate a demand curve, even though the original demand schedules fluctuated fully as much as did the supply schedules.

By intelligently applying proper refinements, and making corrections to eliminate separately those factors which cause demand curves to shift and those factors which cause supply curves to shift, it may be possible even to obtain both a demand curve and a supply curve for the same product and from the same original data. Certainly it may be possible, in many cases where satisfactory demand curves have not been obtained, to find instead the supply curves of the articles in question. The supply curve obtained by such methods, it is to be noted, would be a market supply curve rather than a normal supply curve.

Thus far it has been assumed that the supply and demand curves shift quite independently and at random; but such need not be the case. It is altogether possible that a shift of the demand curve to the right may, as a rule, be accompanied by a shift of the supply curve to the left, and vice versa. Let us see what result is to be expected under such conditions. If successive positions of the demand curve are represented by the curves D_1, D_2 D_3, D_4, and D_5 of Figure 8, while

FIGURE 8
Utility and Demand

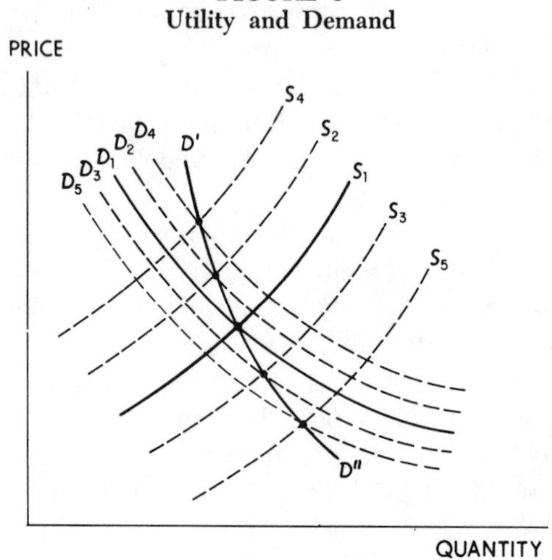

the curves S_1, S_2, S_3, S_4, and S_5 represent corresponding positions of the supply curves, then a series of prices will result from the intersection of D_1 with S_1, D_2 with S_2, and so on. If a curve be fitted to these points, it will not conform to the theoretical demand curve. It will have a smaller elasticity, as is shown by D′D″ of Figure 8. If, on the other hand, a shift of the demand curve to the right is accompanied by a shift of the supply curve to the right, we shall obtain a result such as that indicated by D′D″ in Figure 9. The fitted curve again fails to conform to the theoretical one, but in this case it is more elastic.

Without carrying the illustrations further, it will be apparent that similar reasoning applies to the fitted "supply curve" in case conditions are such that the demand curve shifts more than does the supply curve.

FIGURE 9

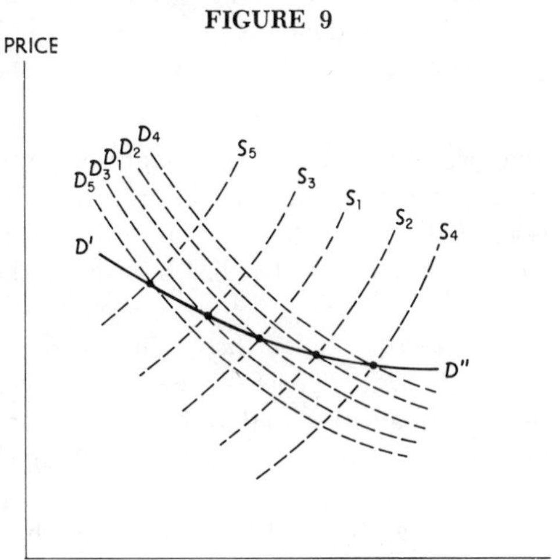

If there is a change in the range through which the supply curve shifts, as might occur through the imposition of a tariff on an imported good, a new fitted curve will result, which will not be a continuation of the former one—this because the fitted curve does not correspond to the true demand curve. In case, then, of correlated shifts of the demand and supply curves, a fitted curve cannot be considered to be the demand curve for the article. It cannot be used, for example, to estimate what change in price would result from the levying of a tariff upon the commodity.

Perhaps a word of caution is needed here. It does not follow from the foregoing analysis that, when conditions are such that shifts of the supply and demand curves are correlated, an attempt to construct a demand curve will give a result which will be useless. Even though shifts of the supply and demand curves are correlated, a curve which is fitted to the points of intersection will be useful for purposes of price forecasting, provided no new factors are introduced which did not affect the price during the period of the study. Thus, so long as the shifts of the supply and demand curves remain correlated in the same way, and so long as they shift through approximately the same range, the curve of regression of price upon quantity can be used as a means of estimating price from quantity.

In cases where it is impossible to show that the shifts of the demand and supply curves are not correlated, much confusion would probably be avoided if the fitted curves were not called demand curves (or supply curves), but if, instead, they were called merely lines of regression. Such curves may be useful, but we must be extremely careful in our interpretation of them. We must also make every effort to discover whether the shifts of the supply and demand curves are correlated before interpreting the results of any fitted curve.

. . . . .

In assuming that we are dealing with quantities actually sold in the market, and in disregarding the fact that for many commodities there is a whole series of markets at various points in the marketing chain, we have simplified our problem. But it has been more than mere simplification, for the interpretation which is to be placed on statistical demand curves depends in large measure upon these matters. Whether the demand curve is a "particular" or a "general" demand curve, depends upon whether or not we use quantities sold. Whether it represents consumer or dealer demand, depends upon the point in the marketing chain to which the quantities sold refer.

Most theorists are acquainted with the concept of the general demand curve as it is presented by Wicksteed and Davenport. Briefly, the idea is that demand should be considered as including not merely the quantities that are bought, but rather all those in existence. The general demand curve, then, includes the possessors of a commodity as having a demand for it at any price below their reservation price, even if they are prospective sellers. Instead of showing the amounts that will be bought at various prices, it shows the marginal money valuation which will be placed upon varying quantities of an existing supply.

Wicksteed even indicates that the supply curve ought not to be considered at all. The following gives an intimation of his viewpoint:

> But what about the "supply curve" that usually figures as a determinant of price, coördinate with the demand curve? I say it boldly and baldly: There is no such thing. When we are speaking of a marketable commodity, what is usually called a supply curve is in reality a demand curve of those who possess the commodity; for it shows the exact place which every successive unit of the commodity holds in their relative scale of estimates. The so-called supply curve, therefore, is simply a part of the total demand curve.[1]

Thus the general demand curve is an expression of the relation between the supply of a commodity and its valuation.

. . . . .

[1] P. H. Wicksteed, "The Scope and Method of Political Economy in the Light of the 'Marginal Theory of Value,'" *Economic Journal* (March, 1914) p. 1.

The amount of a commodity sold at one point in the marketing chain may differ from that sold at another in much the same way that the amount produced may differ from the amount sold. This is particularly true if monthly data are used. A case in point would be the demand for eggs. The amount of eggs sold by farmers in the spring of the year is greatly in excess of the amount sold by retail dealers, while in the winter months it is much less. Since differentials between the prices received by farmers and those received by retail dealers remain fairly constant, very different demand curves would be obtained. The consumers' demand curve would be very much less elastic than that of the dealers who buy from farmers.

Differences between dealer demand and consumer demand are largely dependent upon whether we are considering short or long periods. Over long periods of time, dealer demand tends to conform to consumer demand. This difference, however, is not a thing which depends upon the length of period over which the data extend, but of the length of period to which the individual observations of prices and quantities refer. In the case of eggs, if yearly data were used, the principal difference which would be found between the elasticity of consumer and dealer demands would be due to price differentials alone.

The question whether statistical demand curves are static or dynamic is a perplexing one and rather difficult to deal with. This is largely due to uncertainty as to just what is meant by the terms "static" and "dynamic." Moore holds that his "laws of demand" are dynamic, and that this is an eminently desirable feature. Schultz, while considering it most desirable to obtain both a static and a dynamic law by means of multiple correlation, holds that the statistical devices of relative changes and of trend ratios give a static "law of demand."

Conditions are often defined as being static or dynamic on two different grounds. They may be called static if they refer to a point of time; or else they may be said to be static if all other things are held equal. Statements such as these, however, lack much in clarity and accuracy. How can a statement be made as to prices at which different quantities of a commodity will sell at a *point* of time? Is it really supposed that *all* other things must be held equal in order to study the demand of the commodity? Rather, the real supposition, though it may not be accurately expressed, is that the relationships between the various economic factors should be the same as those which exist at a given point of time, or that the relationships between these factors should remain constant.

The data used in a statistical study of demand must, of course, extend over a period of time, but they may in effect conform to conditions at a point of time if trend is removed and if there is no other change in the relationship between quantity and price. Of course, the shifting of the demand and supply curves constitutes a change in the relationship between the quantity and price, but the process of curve fitting corresponds to that of averaging. Consequently, the fitted curve may be considered to depict the average relationship between quantity and price. This amounts to the same thing as representing the relationship at a point of time which is typical for the period studied. In this sense, then, of relating to a point of time, Moore's "laws of demand" are static instead of dynamic.

Holding "all other things equal," however, is a different matter. Schultz states the difficulty in the following manner:

> In *theory* the law of demand for any one commodity is given only on the assumption that the prices of all other commodities remain constant (the old *ceteris paribus* assumption). This postulate fails in the case of commodities for which substitutes are available. Thus when the price of beef is changed markedly, the prices of such rival commodities as mutton, veal, and pork cannot be supposed to remain constant. Likewise, the price of sugar cannot be increased beyond a certain point without affecting the prices of glucose, corn sugar, and honey.[2]

Marshall makes similar restrictions as to the need for other things to be held equal, and suggests that in some cases it may be best to "group together commodities as distinct as beef and mutton," in order to obtain a demand curve which will not be too restricted because of other things being equal.

The question arises, however, whether it is desirable to hold all other things equal in any case. Is it not better to have a demand curve for beef which expresses the relation between the price and quantity of beef while the prices of pork, mutton, and veal, vary as they normally do, with different prices of beef? Furthermore, may not this be called a static condition? The point can perhaps be made clearer if we take an extreme example. If we are studying the demand for wheat, it would be almost meaningless to get the demand curve for No. 2 Winter wheat while holding the price of all other grades of wheat constant. Other grades of wheat can be so readily substituted that the demand would be almost completely elastic. The difference between this and holding the prices of pork, mutton, and veal constant, while the price of beef varies, is only one of degree—a difference which depends upon the ease with which substitutes can be used in place of the article whose demand is being studied.

All other things being held equal is not a condition represented by a statistical law of demand or, strictly interpreted, of any useful demand curve theory. Some of the things that are correlated with the price of the commodity in question may be held equal, but it is impossible for

---

[2] Henry Schultz, "The Statistical Law of Demand," *The Journal of Political Economy* (October and December 1925). See pp. 498–502 of October issue.

all things to be held equal. However, a statistical law of demand represents a condition under which the relationships between factors may be considered to have remained the same, or, to put it more accurately, a condition which is an average of the relationships during the period studied.

In conclusion, then, it is evident that the mere statement that the demand for a commodity has a given elasticity is meaningless. As with the results of all other statistical analysis, statistical demand curves must be interpreted in the light of the nature of the original data and of the methods of analysis used. There are four questions, the answers to which it is particularly important to know. They concern (1) whether the supply or demand curve is more variable, (2) the market to which the price and quantity data refer, (3) the extent to which "other things are held equal," and (4) whether the shifting of the supply and demand curves is correlated or random.

For precision, it is preferable that the data of price and quantity should refer to the same market. Yet this may be out of the question. In a study of the demand for wheat, for example, if we want to obtain a demand curve of the quantity demanded by the entire country, we cannot use prices for all different points and for all different grades. Instead, the price at one market and for one grade may be used as representative, and the demand of the entire country determined for various prices at the one marketplace. If the price at any other market or for any other grade were used, the elasticity of demand might be different.

Furthermore, the point in the market chain must be specified and the results interpreted accordingly. As is the case with geographical points, it is preferable that the quantities and prices should refer to the same stage in the marketing process. If this is not the case, the interpretation should be made with the situation in view.

It is to be expected that the methods used in constructing statistical demand curves should be such as to give a demand curve which represents a point of time, that is, that trends in both quantities and prices are removed, or else multiple correlation is used to effect the same result. If, in addition to this, other things are held constant, the fact should be noted and the elasticity of demand should be stated as referring to a condition where these other things are held constant.

The matter of correlation between shifts of the demand and supply curves is a more difficult problem to deal with. Every effort should be made to discover whether there is a tendency for the shifting of these to be interdependent. In case it is impossible to determine this, it should be carefully noted that the demand curve which is obtained is quite likely not to hold true for periods other than the one studied, and cannot be treated as corresponding to the demand curve of economic theory.

5. The Demand for Beer*

THOMAS F. HOGARTY and KENNETH G. ELZINGA

I. INTRODUCTION

This note presents estimates of the price and income elasticities of beer. Aside from the usual academic and commercial interest in learning of demand characteristics, knowledge of the demand for beer also has public policy implications due to the heavy taxation of the product. About 35 percent of the price of a glass of beer represents tax revenue with federal and state taxes on beer currently generating more than 1.5 billion dollars in revenue.

In what follows, we first summarize available knowledge on the demand for beer. Then we discuss the methodology and data employed in the present study. Finally, we present our findings and their implications.

II. PREVIOUS STUDIES

William Niskanen analyzed the markets for alcoholic beverages with aggregate time series data for the 22 years 1934–1941 and 1947–1960. Wholesale price indexes (including taxes) for spirits and wine were prepared specially for his study from data provided by the Washington State Liquor Control Board. The beer price indexes were derived from a (now discontinued) Census series by Niskanen on total expenditures for beer. The results of his study, as they apply to the demand for beer, were that: (1) the price elasticity of beer was about —0.7; (2) the income elasticity of beer was about —0.4; (3) spirits and beer were weak substitutes while the relations between the beer and wine markets were highly unstable.

Ira and Ann Horowitz, as part of their overall study of the beer industry, estimated the price and income elasticity of demand for beer with combined cross-section and time series data. Lacking specific data on beer prices, they used state excise tax levels as proxies. They found a weak, negative correlation between beer consumption and excise taxes on beer for 9 of the 13 years (1949–1961) studied. Their estimates of

* *The Review of Economics and Statistics*, vol. 54, no. 2 (May 1972), pp. 195–198.

income elasticity were uniformly positive, but not significantly different from zero after 1956.

III. THE PRESENT STUDY

Sample Data

The price indexes used in this study are based primarily on the FOB mill prices of "Blatz Pilsner" and "Pabst Blue Ribbon" beers for 48 states and the District of Columbia for the years 1956–1959. In raw form these price data consisted of FOB mill prices for cases of twenty-four 12-ounce returnable bottles, exclusive of state excise taxes and bottle deposits. We made the following adjustments:

1. Where prices changed during the year, we computed an average price, weighted in terms of the relative number of months the new price was in effect.

2. States very enormously in terms of consumption of packaged and draft beer, e.g., in Alabama in 1956–1959 virtually all beer consumed was packaged beer; while in Wisconsin draught beer comprised some 40 percent of consumption. Niskanen calculated from 1947, 1954, and 1958 Census of Manufactures data that the average wholesale value of packaged beer, exclusive of all excise taxes, was about 1.8 times the average value of draught beer in each year. We used this relation to calculate approximate FOB prices (in case equivalents) for draught beer. After adding appropriate federal and state excise taxes to both the packaged and draught FOB prices, we computed for each state a weighted average price for each brand of beer, the weights then consisting of the relative proportions of packaged and draught beer consumed in the various states (U.S. Brewers Association).

3. These first three adjustments produced approximate retail prices for each of the two brands of beer. Our price index was then calculated as a simple average of these two brand prices.

4. Data on transport rates from Milwaukee for 1957 only were used in conjunction with the 1957 Blatz price data to estimate the impact of excluding transport rates from other years. These and other data on distances show this source of bias to be relatively minor.

5. A final insoluble problem was lack of reliable data on retail markups. Fortunately, in view of our results (see Section IV below), this defect causes modest concern.

6. As a final adjustment, the price indexes were expressed in real terms by means of the Bureau of Labor Statistics Consumer Price Index for 1956–1959.

Data on quantity (U.S. Brewers Association (USBA)), consisted of apparent consumption (in cases) per adult. Estimates of the *adult* population in each state consisted of interpolated Census data (1950, 1960). Estimates of state *per capita* income, also expressed in real terms, were derived from a special Census estimate (1966).

Methodological Issues and Data Problems

Two potential difficulties confront our attempt to estimate demand elasticities for beer. The first is the standard identification problem; the second results from our use of individual brand prices.

The first problem appears inconsequential. The period 1956–1959 was one of excess capacity in the beer industry.[1] Hence, the assumption of perfectly elastic supply appears appropriate.

The second problem appears almost as minor. To begin with, the brand structure of prices in the beer industry is (or at least was) relatively stable:

"Anheuser-Busch once conducted a survey involving 113,305 price comparisons in 78 areas. In over 100,000 comparisons, a differential of 5 cents per can or per 12-ounce bottle existed between Budweiser and the popular priced beers. In over 90 percent of the comparisons a 10 cent differential existed over local beers."

In addition, the nationwide market shares of Pabst and Blatz were relatively stable during 1956–1959, as were the shares of premium, popular, and local beers in three states during 1957–1960.[2] Finally, the prices of Pabst and Blatz can be considered representative of premium and popular priced beers, respectively. Unfortunately, price data for local beers are unavailable.

Ideally, of course, we should like to use a weighted index of prices, with the weights corresponding to the relative market shares of premium, popular, and local beers in the various states. Fortunately, however, our lack of data on prices of local beers and relative market shares does not seriously distort our price elasticity estimates.

[1] During 1956–1959, United States breweries, on the average, operated at about 64 percent of capacity.

[2] For Blatz, the correlations between market share in 1956 and market shares in 1957–1959 were 0.97, 0.87, and 0.81, respectively; for Pabst, the corresponding correlations were 0.99, 0.95, and 0.90, respectively.

For the three-state area comprised of Illinois, Michigan, and Wisconsin, the following market shares prevailed during 1957–1960.

Year	*Premium Beers*	*Popular Priced Beers*	*Local Beers*
1957	27.86	51.80	20.34
1958	28.54	50.13	21.33
1959	29.05	51.02	19.93
1960	29.51	50.22	20.27

Procedure

Our mode of analysis consisted of ordinary least squares with, at least initially, all variables expressed in logarithmic form, as in

$$\ln Q_{it} = b_0 + b_1 \ln P_{it} + b_2 \ln Y_{it} \tag{1}$$

where

Q_i = apparent consumption (in cases) of beer *per adult* in i^{th} state in year t
P_i = real price of case of beer in i^{th} state in year t
Y_i = real, *per capita* income in i^{th} state in year t
$i = 1, 2, \ldots, 45$
$t = 1, 2, 3, 4$

Estimates of the coefficients of equation (1) were made for each of the years 1956–1959 individually ($n = 45$) and for a combined sample consisting of data for the entire period ($n = 180$). A test for overall homogeneity indicated that all four cross-sections could be regarded as coming from the same population and hence only estimates for the entire period are presented.[3]

IV. RESULTS

As indicated in equation (1), our initial estimates presumed constant price and income elasticities. The estimates obtained are presented in table 1 (line 1).

With respect to price elasticity, our estimate of unity plus accords approximately with those of Niskanen in that neither Niskanen's esti-

[3] The test for overall homogeneity is:

$$F = \frac{\left[S_d^2 - \sum_{t-6} S_{at}^2\right] \Big/ (T-1)(K+1)}{\sum_{t-6} S_{at}^2 \Big/ [N - T(K+1)]}$$

where

S_d^2 = residual sums of squares from grand regression (n = 180)
S_{at}^2 = residual sums of squares from cross-section regression t (t = 1956, 57, 58, 59) ($n = 45$)
T = number of years (sub-samples)
K = number of independent variables.

For our sample

$$F = \frac{[7.715 - 7.309]/9}{(7.309)/168} = 1.025$$

which is not statistically significant at the 0.05 level.

TABLE 1
Estimates of Price and Income Elasticity[a] of Beer Based on Sample Excluding States with Substantial Local Excise Taxation of Beer[b] (n = 180)

	b_0	b_1	b_2	b_3[c]	b_4	$\bar{R}2$
(1)	−2.935	−1.128	0.926			.666
(2)	4.823	−0.992		0.942		.687
(3)	3.539	−0.889		0.430[d]	0.174[d]	.759

Entry identification:

b_0 = intercept.
b_1 = price elasticity.
b_2 = (constant) income elasticity.
b_3 = (median) income elasticity.
b_4 = elasticity of beer consumption with respect to national origin.

[a] Unless otherwise indicated, all coefficients are significantly different from zero at the 0.01 level or better; however, unless otherwise indicated, none of the coefficients are significantly different from unity at the 0.10 level or better.

[b] These states were Alabama, Georgia, Louisiana, and Tennessee.

[c] The income elasticities in this column were calculated at the income level prevailing in the median income state.

[d] Significantly different from unity at 0.01 level.

mates nor ours differed significantly from unity. The estimate of income elasticity was more surprising inasmuch as the Horowitzes found beer consumption to be unrelated to income while Niskanen found beer to be an inferior good. Experimentation with subsamples of high and low income states[4] demonstrated a tendency for the income elasticity of beer to vary inversely with the level of income.

Accordingly, we reformulated equation (1) to read:[5]

$$\ln Q_{it} = b_0 + b_1 \ln P_{it} - b_3 (1/Y_{it}) \qquad (2)$$

The results of fitting equation (2) to our data are contained in table 1 (line 2). The estimate of income elasticity presented is calculated at the median level of real, *per capita* income.

Our next step consisted of adding as independent variables indexes of

[4] The states were classified as high or low income according to whether or not their *per capita* income for 1956–1959 was above or below that for the *median* state.

[5] The income elasticity for equation (2) is

$$I_E = e^{b_0 - b_3/Y} \cdot \frac{b_3}{QY}$$
$$= \frac{b_3}{Y} \text{ since } Q = \frac{e^{b_0 - b_3}}{Y}$$
$$= 2 \text{ when } Y = \frac{b_3}{2}.$$

Hence, income elasticity varies inversely with income and asymptotically approaches zero as income increases.

spirits and wine prices.[6] Unfortunately, these attempts were unsuccessful.[7] On the other hand, we were able to account, at least in part, for differences in taste. On the presumption that immigrants were more prone to beer drinking than native Anglo-Saxons, we introduced as a proxy variable the percent of each state's population that was foreign born. The results are presented in table 1 (line 3).

Thus, our final estimates of price and income elasticity for beer are —0.9 and 0.4, respectively. In addition, we estimate the beer-drinking capacity of the United States as a little more than two cans (12 ounces per adult per day.)[8]

V. CONCLUDING REMARKS

Although lack of price data on beer for the past decade makes prediction impossible, we note that from 1962 to 1969 per adult beer consumption increased by 16 percent while real, *per capita* income rose by 27 percent. Assuming stable real prices for beer, the implied income elasticity is 0.59. Average *per capita* income (1958 dollars) during 1962–1969 was approximately $2,250. At this level we estimate income elasticity as 0.37. Since average state taxes on beer increased about 7 percent in real terms during 1962–1969 our estimate appears sufficiently close to warrant confidence in its reliability.

Regarding implications for the future, it appears that the beer industry can anticipate moderate increases in consumption, assuming the price of beer remains relatively stable. Moreover, it further appears that excise taxes on beer could be reduced considerably with only modest losses in tax revenues. The desirability of such reductions might be questioned on noneconomic grounds; however, there appears little doubt that beer excise taxes are regressive.

[6] Our initial step consisted of using excise taxes on spirits and wine as proxies for price. This procedure produced cross elasticity estimates of zero for both spirits and wine. Our second attempt consisted of using the retail price of Seagram's 7 Crown (fifth) as an index of retail prices in general (Simon, 1966).

[7] The estimates of cross elasticity between beer consumption and the price of spirits were statistically significant, but negative. These results persisted despite use of subsamples which excluded dry, moonshine, and transient liquor traffic states. We rejected these results on the grounds that beer and spirits were unlikely complements. Nonetheless, these results, insofar as they applied to the estimates of price and income elasticity for beer, were roughly in accord with those presented in table 1.

[8] Ignoring price effects, the drinking capacity of the United States is that level of consumption which would prevail at infinitely high levels of income. In our formulation this is e^{b_0} cases per adult per year or, as noted, approximately two cans per adult per day.

6. The Demand for New Automobiles in the United States 1929–1956*

DANIEL B. SUITS

In this paper we present the results of a new study of the demand for passenger automobiles, embodying a number of improvements over the attempts of previous investigators. In particular: (a) some account is taken of the influence of credit conditions on demand; (b) the dynamics of the market derive primarily from the accumulation of a stock of cars rather than from the rate of change of income; (c) the statistical work is carried out in terms of first differences to facilitate testing the influence of the variables.

In the final formulation of the demand function, annual retail sales of new passenger automobiles are explained by: (1) real disposable income; (2) the stock of passenger cars on the road, January 1; and (3) the average real retail price of new passenger automobiles divided by the average number of months' duration of automobile credit contracts. The price variable is, thus, an index of the monthly payment associated with the purchase of passenger automobiles. Use of this variable involved an estimate of a retail price index and of the number of months' duration of credit contracts. The source and nature of these estimates is taken up in the Appendix. Finally (4), we use a dummy shift variable to account for the special conditions of the automobile market in years of severe production shortage.

The demand was estimated by least-squares linear regression with the variables expressed in first differences. For purposes of summary the results are expressed in table 1 as elasticities computed by reference to mean values.

The statistical demand schedule fits the observed behavior of the market very well. When the equation is expressed in first differences, the coefficient of multiple correlation is .93. When calculated changes are added to sales of the preceding year, the correlation between ac-

* *The Review of Economics and Statistics,* vol. 40, no. 3 (August, 1958), pp. 273–280.

TABLE 1
Elasticities of Demand for New Passenger Automobiles

Variable	*Demand Elasticity*
Real disposable income	4.16
Stock of cars, January 1	−3.65
Index of real monthly payment	− .58

tual and predicted levels is .98. It is particularly notable that the sensational rise in demand in 1955 and the sharp drop in 1956 are well represented. Moreover when applied to 1957, the demand equation predicts a level of sales of slightly less than 6.0 million. This compares favorably with a preliminary estimate of 6.1 million actual sales for the year and stands in sharp contrast with sales forecasts of 6.5 million and over which were common in the industry at the start of the year.

The detailed discussion of the nature of the demand function and its setting in the model of the automobile market is given in the first section. The second section contains the statistical results when alternative formulations of the demand function are evaluated. The third section is devoted to comparison of the results with those of some earlier studies of automobile demand. Problems of data are discussed in the Appendix; particular attention is called to the procedure used in estimating the average duration of automobile credit contracts.

MATHEMATICAL FORMULATION OF NEW CAR DEMAND

The automobile market may be approximately represented as a system of four equations representing: (1.1) the demand for new cars by the public, (1.2) the supply of new cars by retail dealers, (1.3) the supply of used cars by retail dealers, and (1.4) the demand for used cars by the public. The variables employed in this formulation with the symbols used are as follows:

1. Retail sales of new cars (R).
2. Real disposable income (Y).
3. The real retail price of new cars (P).

This variable requires some explanation. In payment for a new car the retailer generally receives cash (or a debt instrument of cash value) and a used car trade-in. In order to obtain the full retail cash price of the new car the dealer must then dispose of the used car, perhaps taking another in trade which in turn must be sold, etc. The net effect of these operations is to render the retail value of the new car to the dealer, although in general no single buyer pays the entire price in cash or its equivalent. The statistical problems which arise in measuring this retail price are discussed in the Appendix. Conceptually, however, it may be thought of as the total receipts of new car dealers from sale of new and used cars alike, divided by the number of *new* cars sold. This retail price is then converted to real terms by dividing by the consumer price index.

4. The average real price of used cars (U).
5. Average credit terms (M). This is the number of months the average automobile installment contract runs.
6. The stock of used cars (S). This is the number of automobiles in existence on January 1 of the year.
7. The real wholesale price of new cars (W).
8. Retailers' operating costs (T).
9. The supply of used cars to the public (R').
10. Influence of omitted factors (u_1, u_2, u_3, u_4).

The four equations then become:

Demand for New Cars:

$$R = a_1 \frac{(P - U)}{M} + a_2 Y + a_3 \Delta Y + a_0 + u_1. \tag{1.1}$$

The annual demand for new cars is related to the level and rate of increase in real disposable income and to the net real monthly outlay the buyer must make $(P - U)/M$. The term u_1 includes the remaining demand factors.

Supply of New Cars at Retail:

$$R = b_1 P + b_2 W + b_3 T + b_0 + u_2. \tag{1.2}$$

The willingness of new car dealers to sell depends on the price they obtain, the wholesale price of the car, and on dealers' costs of operations; u_2 includes the remaining factors.

Supply of Used Cars:

$$R' = c_1 R + c_0 + u_3. \tag{1.3}$$

This is a simple approximation equation, the supply of used cars being assumed to derive from the sale of new cars.

Demand for Used Cars:

$$R' = d_1 U/M + d_2 Y + d_3 \Delta Y + d_4 S = d_0 + u_4. \tag{1.4}$$

The demand for used cars depends on the monthly price of used cars (U/M) and the number of used cars in existence. Moreover it is influenced by the other factors in a way analogous to the demand for new cars.

It will be noted that we have included the existing stock of cars as a part of the used car demand equation, but not directly as a part of new car demand as such. This reflects the well known fact that new car buyers are, by and large, those who already own relatively new cars. Individuals without cars, or with old used cars, rarely go directly into the new car market. On the other hand, the "new" supply of used cars must compete with the already existing stock. The existing stock of cars thus exercises a strong *indirect* influence on the new car market via its influence on the price of used cars and hence on the net outlay required of new car buyers.

Ideally, the next step in our analysis would be to confront the mathematical model with historical market data and use the appropriate statistical procedures to estimate the parameters of the equations, particularly equation (1.1). Unfortunately, however, the data are not adequate for this purpose. Available series of used car prices extend back only to 1935, while reliable net outlay figures $(P - U)$ are available only since World War II. But while we cannot estimate the several equations as such, we can merge the new and used car demands together to obtain a *composite* new car demand relation from which the unavailable variables have been eliminated. This is done by solving (1.3) and (1.4) simultaneously to obtain an expression for U/M in terms of R, Y, ΔY, and S; used car sales, R', being eliminated in the process. Substituting this value of U/M into equation (1.1) and simplifying gives us an expression of the form:

$$R = c_1 P/M + c_2 Y + c_3 \Delta Y + c_4 S + c_0 + u_5 \qquad (1.5)$$

where u_5 is a linear combination of u_1, u_3, and u_4.

Equation (1.5) is now an expression of the demand for new cars as a function of the total retail price (no matter how many trades are required to realize it), real disposable income, the total stock of existing cars, average credit terms, and the rate of increase in income. Put another way, (1.5) is an expression for the demand for new cars, the influence of the used car market being implicitly taken into account.

STATISTICAL ESTIMATION OF DEMAND

The period covered by this analysis extends from 1929 through 1956, but not all years could be given equal treatment. The war years 1942–45 clearly had to be omitted outright, and the postwar price disequilibrium exerted such a distorting influence on the market that the years 1946–48 were likewise discarded. The remaining years represent approximately normal operation of the market with the exception of 1941 (conversion) and 1952 (during which new automobile production was under government allocation and price control, and suffered from a severe steel strike). During both these years the behavior of the automobile market was distorted, but not so seriously as during 1946–48. It was decided to include these years in the study but to identify them by a dummy variable (X); X has the value 0 except in 1941 and 1952 when it takes on the value 1; it is intended to act as something of a "shock absorber" and take up at least the average influence of the abnormality of these years, allowing the remaining variables to play something like their normal roles.

Like most economic functions estimated from time series, the demand for automobiles may be expected to exhibit auto-correlation of the residuals. To avoid the complications presented by this fact it was decided to conduct all analysis in terms of first differences of the variables. This also has the great advantage of suppressing the relative influence of such slowly changing factors as consumer tastes, population, etc., thus permitting a better measurement of the effect of the factors represented in the equation. The combined secular influence of the sticky factors is embodied in the constant term of the equation which represents the secular trend. The general formulation of the demand equation was thus:

$$\Delta R = a_1\,\Delta Y + a_2\,\Delta\frac{P}{M} + a_3\,\Delta S + a_4\,\Delta X + a_0. \qquad (2.0)$$

The result of fitting (2.0) by least squares[1] was:

$$\Delta R = \underset{(.011)}{.106}\,\Delta Y - \underset{(.088)}{.234}\,\Delta\left(\frac{P}{M}\right) - \underset{(.086)}{.507}\,\Delta S - \underset{(.261)}{.827}\,\Delta X + .115 \qquad (2.1)$$

Figures in parentheses are standard errors of the parameter estimates. In this regression, retail sales (R) and the existing stock of cars (S) are in millions of cars; real disposable income (Y) is in billions of 1947–49 dollars; and the average monthly price (P/M) is an "index," whose units are indicated in the appendix; ΔX is the first difference in the dummy shift variable X: $\Delta X = +1$ in 1941 and 1952; $\Delta X = -1$ in 1953; in all other years $\Delta X = 0$.

It will be noted that all variables enter the regression with parameter estimates which compare very favorably with their standard errors; the omission of the rate of increase of income from the equation is due to its failure to enter significantly (see below). The coefficient of correlation, adjusted for degrees of freedom, is .93.

The close agreement between actual and calculated new car demand

[1] It may be argued that since, in our model, both the retail price of new passenger cars and the number sold are endogenous variables, the estimate of (2.0) by least squares leads to biased results. This is so, but it is our contention that in view of the very rough data we are employing, any such bias is surely negligible in comparison with errors in the data and that the use of an elaborate technique in an attempt to avoid this bias is uneconomical, if not presumptuous.

is shown in charts 1 and 2. In chart 1 the first differences are compared; in chart 2 the calculated difference has been added to sales of the preceding year to calculate total sales for the year. The real interest in form (2.1), however, lies in the fact that it includes some account of

CHART 1
Annual Changes in Automobile Sales, Actual and Calculated, 1930–1956

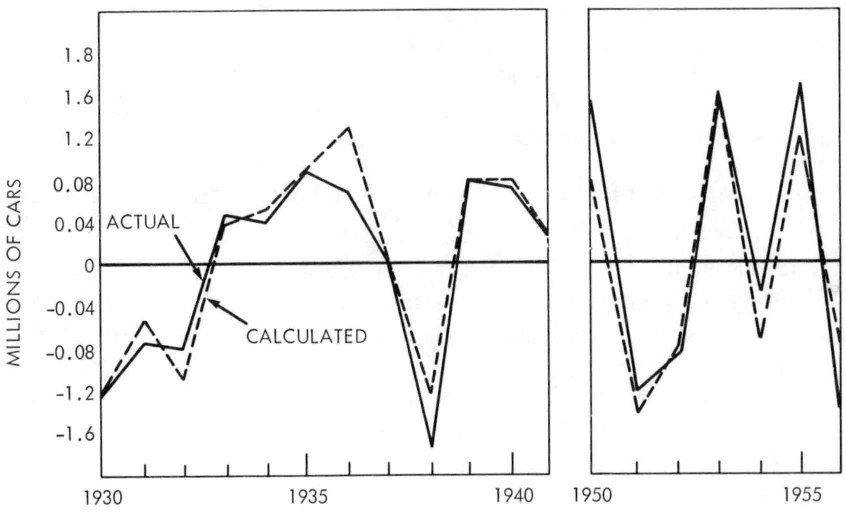

CHART 2
Retail Sales of New Passenger Automobiles, Actual and Calculated, 1930–1956

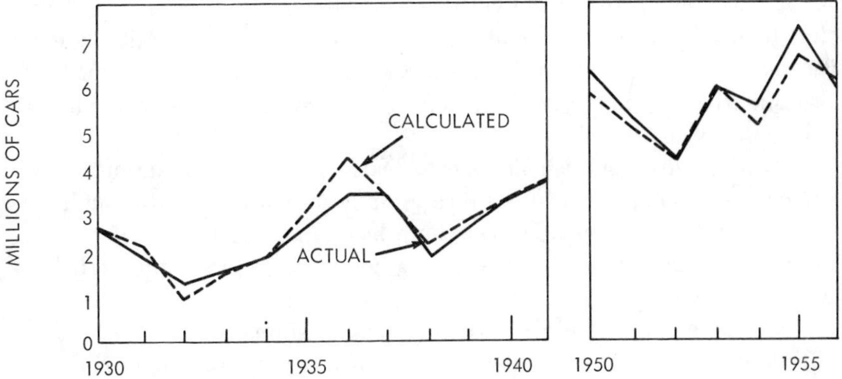

credit conditions and that the rate of change of income fails to attain significance as an explanatory variable. The statistical implications of this may de demonstrated by contrasting (2.1) with alternative formulations. To facilitate these comparisons, the regression coefficients are transformed into beta-coefficients which are readily compared from equation to equation, and which, within a given equation, reflect the relative importance of the several variables. Thus transformed, (2.1) becomes:

$$\Delta R = \underset{(.094)}{.919\,\Delta Y} - \underset{(.098)}{.578\,\Delta S} - \underset{(.101)}{.268\,\Delta}\left(\frac{P}{M}\right) - \underset{(.100)}{.317\,\Delta X}. \tag{2.1t}$$

The coefficient of determination for this equation is $R^2 = .87$. It is readily seen that disposable income is, as would be expected, the variable of greatest importance, followed by the stock of cars on the road, and the real monthly price index.

We may contrast (2.1t) with the somewhat poorer result ($R^2 = .80$) obtained when no account is taken of crédit terms:

$$\Delta R = \underset{(.132)}{1.018\,\Delta Y} - \underset{(.119)}{.568\,\Delta S'} + \underset{(.146)}{.100\,\Delta P} - \underset{(.167)}{.513\,\Delta X}. \tag{2.2t}$$

In (2.2t) monthly payment, P/M, is replaced by retail price P alone. When reference to credit terms is thus omitted the price variable no longer enters the relationship significantly, and in fact assumes the incorrect sign.

Finally we may compare (2.1t) with the result obtained when the rate of increase in income is included along with the other variables. Where $\Delta^2 Y$ represents the second difference in income, we have:

$$\Delta R = \underset{(.176)}{.843\,\Delta Y} - \underset{(.105)}{.525\,\Delta S} - \underset{(.106)}{.252\,\Delta P/M} - \underset{(.103)}{.324\,\Delta X} + \underset{(.157)}{.089\,\Delta^2 Y}. \tag{2.3t}$$

Inspection of (2.3t) clearly shows that the rate of increase in income is the least important of the variables in the equation, falling well below the stock of cars on the road on this score. Moreover it fails to enter the relationships significantly. Its presence causes all standard errors to rise slightly, but not enough to impugn any of the other variables. In this equation $R^2 = .86$.

It will hardly astonish anyone to learn that the explanation of new car demand is improved by even so crude a measure of credit conditions as we have introduced here. On the other hand, the failure of the rate of change of income strikes many as a complete surprise, but we believe it is easily explained.

The automobile, like all durable goods, is subject to an acceleration effect caused by the fact that the service *desired* is a function of income, while the service *supplied* is a function of the existing stock. Therefore, as an approximation, where S^* is desired level of stock:

$$S^* = kY, \text{ so} \tag{2.4}$$

$$\Delta S^* = k\,\Delta Y, \text{ and, neglecting other variables} \tag{2.5}$$

$$R = a\,\Delta S^* + b = ak\,\Delta Y + b. \tag{2.6}$$

That is, we expect the rate of change in *actual* stock to correlate with the rate of change in the desired level, and since the rate of change in actual stock results from variation in the level of retail sales, we should surely expect the level of retail sales to be significantly related to the rate of change of desired stock—as represented by the rate of change of income. This line of reasoning is certainly valid, and, in the absence of information about the actual level of stocks, will serve as a useful approximation in the analysis of market behavior. But where we have actual information, we may formulate a superior approximation to the accelerator mechanism: retail sales respond, not directly to the desired level of stocks, but to the *gap* between the desired level and the actual level. Thus, again neglecting other variables:

$$R = a(S^* - S) + b = akY - aS + b. \tag{2.7}$$

That is, the level of retail sales should be directly correlated with the level of income and inversely with the existing level of stock. The use of formulation (2.7) is clearly superior dynamic theory, and the fact that it leads to improved statistical results is less surprising than might at first appear.

CHART 3
Regression of Error in Estimated Credit Duration (*e*) on Trend in Outstanding Credit (*T*), 1929–1939

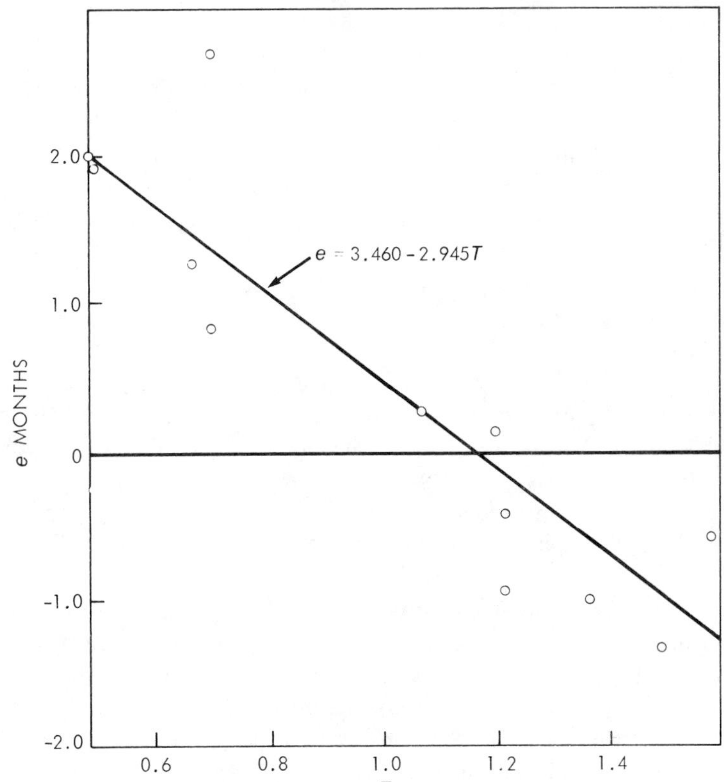

All this is not to say that the demand for new automobiles is necessarily unrelated to the rate of increase in income. Indeed there is some evidence from cross-section data that such a relationship exists. But this aspect of automobile demand arises from such factors as the status significance of a new car to upwardly mobile income groups, which is hardly the same thing as an acceleration effect in the usual sense of the term. Use of the rate of change of income as an empirical expedient, without taking account of the existing stock of cars, unfortunately confuses the durability of the automobile with its other characteristics.

COMPARISON WITH OTHER RESULTS

In conclusion it is interesting to compare so far as possible the results of the previous section with those of other researchers. Three previous studies in this area are now generally familiar: (1) the work of Roos and von Szeliski, (2) the demand equation computed by L. Jay Atkinson as part of the Department of Commerce study of the demand for durable goods, and (3) the equation estimated by Morris Cohen for the National Industrial Conference Board. Differences in technique preclude elaborate comparisons, a fact which is particularly unfortunate in the case of the complex Roos-von Szeliski study, since it is the only one of the three in which the dynamics of demand were directly related to the stock of automobiles rather than accounted for in proxy fashion by the rate of change of income. The Atkinson and the Cohen formulations are both in terms of sales, income, and change in income per household and include a time trend. The Atkinson equation also includes real retail price. In both cases the demand equations were fitted in logarithmic form, the regression parameters reading directly as elasticities. To facilitate comparison, our results are presented in the upper part of Table 2 as elasticities computed at the mean levels of the variables and are thus readily compared with results derived from other studies shown in the lower portion.

Table 2 indicates systematic differences in results. Our estimates of income elasticity of demand are uniformly higher, and those of price elasticity lower than those given in the earlier work. To some extent, of course, these comparisons arise out of our use of first differences rather than the actual magnitudes of the variables, and out of the use of different sample periods, but an important contribution derives from other sources.

There may be some suspicion that the striking contrasts arise out of our use of the dummy variable X to identify years of severe production shortages. This was tested by deleting the variable X and the years in question (1941, 1952, 1953) from the data. The resulting regression hardly differed at all from (2.1) above, indicating that this aspect of our method was not a cause of the divergence.

TABLE 2
Comparison of Elasticities Calculated from Several Equations for New Passenger Automobile Demand

		Elasticity with respect to:		
Equation	*Income*	*Price per Month*	*Retail Price*	*Stock of Cars*
(2.1t)	4.16	−.59	—	−3.65
(2.2t)	4.59	—	+ .40	−3.59
(2.3t)	3.80	−.55	—	−3.31
Roos and von Szeliski	1.5–2.5	—	−1.5	[a]
Atkinson	2.455	—	−1.31	—
Cohen	2.283	—	—	—

[a] Although the stock of cars is included in this equation, no elasticity figure is given in the text, and there is insufficient information about magnitudes of the required variables to permit its calculation.

On the other hand, a considerable part of the difference can be shown to derive from our use of the stock of cars. When the stock of cars is dropped from (2.3t), the estimate of income elasticity of demand falls to about 3, while the price elasticity becomes almost unity. This would account for most of the difference between the Atkinson and Cohen estimates and ours, but it cannot explain the Roos-von Szeliski estimates since the stock of cars was included in their calculations.

Interestingly enough, however, the difference between the Roos-von Szeliski estimates and ours are largely a matter of judgment and definition rather than measurement. In the first place their price elasticity figure of —1.5 was adapted by judgment from an actually calculated estimate of —.65, a value much closer to ours. In the second place their income elasticity was related to "supernumerary" income—essentially income over and above the cost of subsistence—rather than total income. According to their calculations, supernumerary income amounted to roughly two thirds of total. Thus a 10 percent increase in total income is equivalent to a 15 percent increase in supernumerary income. This being so, their supernumerary income elasticity figures may be converted to disposable income elasticities by multiplying by one and a half, and their figures then cover the range 2.5 to 3.8. These are again much more nearly comparable to our estimates.

APPENDIX

The series used in the regressions are shown in table A–1. As will be noted several of these are estimates prepared for the purpose. The methods used to estimate the stock of cars on the road and the retail price index require only brief exposition. Special interest attaches to the

TABLE A–1
Basic Data Employed

Year	Credit Terms (months)	Real Retail Price Index, Passenger Automobiles	Real Disposable Income (billions of 1947–49 dollars)	Stock of Cars Jan. 1 (millions)	Retail Sales, New Automobiles (millions)
1929	12.5	118.0	113.4	18.7	3.91
1930	12.6	113.8	104.2	19.7	2.65
1931	13.0	120.2	98.2	19.6	1.90
1932	13.1	126.5	83.4	18.7	1.10
1933	13.3	128.5	82.6	17.9	1.53
1934	13.8	128.5	90.9	18.9	1.93
1935	14.3	120.5	99.3	19.4	2.87
1936	16.2	117.0	111.6	20.1	3.51
1937	17.4	121.0	115.6	21.5	3.51
1938	16.8	133.8	109.0	22.3	1.96
1939	15.5	131.0	118.5	22.7	2.72
1940	16.1	134.3	127.0	23.2	3.46
1941	13.5	144.9	147.9	24.5	3.76
1949	15.5	186.6	184.9	30.6	4.87
1950	18.6	186.6	200.5	33.1	6.37
1951	14.4	181.5	203.7	35.7	5.09
1952	16.4	195.7	209.2	37.6	4.19
1953	18.8	188.2	218.7	39.3	5.78
1954	18.6	190.2	221.6	41.6	5.47
1955	21.6	196.6	236.3	43.0	7.20
1956	23.2	193.4	247.2	47.0	5.90

somewhat more elaborate procedure used to estimate credit contract duration.

Stock of Cars on the Road, January 1 was estimated by subtracting new registrations for the first six months from R. L. Polk figures for total registration, July 1.

Retail Price Index was obtained by multiplying the BLS wholesale price index for new passenger automobiles by an index of dealers' gross margins. The latter was obtained as the ratio of the average retail expenditure per new car to average wholesale value. The resulting price index was deflated by the Consumer Price Index. The derivation is shown in table A–2.

Average Duration of Credit Contracts was estimated from data on credit outstanding and monthly repayments by a two-stage procedure. The basis of the technique is the fact that when credit extensions are stable, the number of months duration of the average credit contract is given by the formula

$$M^* = \frac{2C - r}{r}$$

TABLE A–2
Derivation of Retail Price of Passenger Automobiles

	(1) B.L.S. Wholesale Price, Passenger Automobiles (1947–49 = 100)	(2) B.L.S. Consumer Price Index (1947–49 = 100)	(3) Retail Expenditure Automobiles ($ billion)	(4) Average Retail Value per Car (dollars)	(5) Average Wholesale Value per Car (dollars)	(6) Retailers' Margin Factor	(7) Real Retail Price Index, Passenger Automobiles (1947–49 dollars)
1929	57.3	73.3	3.693	945	626	1.509	118.0
1930	54.1	71.4	2.343	884	589	1.501	113.8
1931	51.7	65.0	1.632	859	568	1.512	120.2
1932	50.3	58.4	.906	824	561	1.469	126.5
1933	48.5	55.3	1.110	725	495	1.465	128.5
1934	51.3	57.2	1.460	756	528	1.432	128.5
1935	49.3	58.7	2.151	749	522	1.435	120.5
1936	48.7	59.3	2.743	781	548	1.425	117.0
1937	52.4	61.4	2.837	808	570	1.418	121.0
1938	55.4	60.3	1.752	894	614	1.456	133.8
1939	54.1	59.4	2.394	880	612	1.438	131.0
1940	56.0	59.9	3.165	915	637	1.436	134.3
1941	60.2	62.9	3.864	1,028	679	1.514	144.9
1949	108.9	101.8	11.037	2,266	1,299	1.744	186.6
1950	108.3	102.8	14.315	2,247	1,270	1.770	186.6
1951	113.0	111.0	12.306	2,417	1,356	1.783	181.5
1952	121.3	113.5	11.465	2,736	1,494	1.831	195.7
1953	120.7	114.4	15.173	2,625	1,471	1.784	188.2
1954	121.7	114.8	14.507	2,652	1,478	1.794	190.2
1955	125.4	114.5	20.341	2,825	1,573	1.795	196.6
1956	132.2	116.2	16.840	2,854	1,677	1.70	193.4

Sources: Col. (1): Passenger automobile component of B.L.S. wholesale price of motor vehicles, 1947–49 = 100.
(2): B.L.S. consumer price index, 1947–49 = 100.
(3): Department of Commerce: Estimated consumer expenditure on new and net used automobiles, plus estimated investment expenditure on new passenger automobiles.
(4): Col. 3 ÷ Retail sales, new passenger automobiles (Table 1, Col. 5).
(5): Automobile Manufacturers Association reported value of wholesale passenger car sales ÷ reported number sold at wholesale.
(6): Col. (4) ÷ Col. (5).
(7): [Col. (1) ÷ Col. (2)] × Col. (6).

where M^* is estimated duration in months, C is credit outstanding at the end of the month, and r is repayments during the month.[2] Unfortunately, however, credit extensions are rarely stable, and the formula yields biased results when the volume of outstanding credit is changing. If outstanding credit is growing, the disproportionate amount of younger contracts included increases C relatively to r and causes M^* to overestimate contract duration. Conversely, during a period of contraction M^* is underestimated. Thus while M^* was used as a first approximation,

[2] A discussion of this formula can be found in any good textbook in the mathematics of finance.

TABLE A–3
Estimated Credit Contract Duration: Derivation of Correction for Extensions Trend

Year	(1) Credit Outstanding December 31 (C) ($ million)	(2) Repayments (r) December ($ million)	(3) Actual Contract Average Duration (months)	(4) Preliminary Estimate of Duration (M*)	(5) Error (e)	(6) Credit Trend Index (T)
1928	1,078	152	12.4	13.2	– .8	—
1929	1,318	196	12.5	12.4	.1	1.223
1930	928	146	12.6	11.7	.9	.704
1931	637	100	13.0	11.7	1.3	.686
1932	322	53	13.1	11.2	1.9	.505
1933	459	60	13.3	14.3	–1.0	1.255
1934	576	76	13.8	14.2	– .4	1.255
1935	940	113	14.3	15.6	–1.3	1.632
1936	1,289	148	16.2	17.2	–1.0	1.371
1937	1,384	171	17.4	17.1	.3	1.047
1938	970	127	16.8	14.3	2.5	.701
1939	1,267	n.a.	15.5	n.a.	n.a.	n.a.
1940	2,071	233	16.1	16.8	– .7	1.635

Sources: (1), (2): Federal Reserve Bulletin, *passim*.
(3): 1928–1938: D. M. Holthausen and others, *The Volume of Consumer Credit, 1929–1938*, National Bureau of Economic Research, Studies in Consumer Installment Financing no. 7, p. 45, Table A–4. 1940: Gottfried Haberler, *Consumer Installment Credit and Economic Fluctuations*, National Bureau of Economic Research, Studies in Consumer Installment Financing no. 9, Chart IX, p. 93.
(4): Calculated from (1) and (2) by: $M^* = \frac{2C - r}{r}$.
(5): (3)—(4).
(6): Calculated from (1): C_t/C_{t-1}. See text.

TABLE A–4
Estimated Automobile Credit Contract Duration 1941; 1949–56

Year	(1) Credit Outstanding (c) Dec. 31 ($ million)	(2) Repayments (r) December ($ million)	(3) M*	(4) T	(5) M
1940	2,071	—	—	—	—
1941	2,458	340	13.5	1.187	13.5
1948	2,966	—	—	—	—
1949	4,555	517	16.6	1.536	15.5
1950	6,074	604	19.1	1.333	18.6
1951	5,972	806	13.8	.983	14.4
1952	7,733	870	16.8	1.294	16.4
1953	9,835	977	19.1	1.271	18.8
1954	9,809	1,029	18.1	.997	18.6
1955	13,468	1,161	22.2	1.373	21.6
1956	14,436	1,208	22.0	1.072	23.2

Sources: (*1*) and (*2*): *Federal Reserve Bulletin*.
(*3*): Calculated from (*1*) and (*2*): $M^* = \frac{2C - r}{r}$.
(*4*): Calculated from (*1*): C_t/C_{t-1}.
(*5*): $M = M^* + 3.460 - 2.945\,T$. See text.

an attempt was made to adjust it for bias. For the period 1929–40 actual average duration is available. By comparing these actual durations with M^* it was possible to calculate the error in the estimate (e), which could then be compared with the link relative of outstanding credit ($C_t/C_{t-1} = T$). For this purpose the linear regression of e on T was employed:

$$e = 3.460 - 2.945T.$$

For the years following 1940, then, the estimate M^* was adjusted by the calculated value of e to provide some refinement of the estimate by:

$$M = M^* + e$$

The data employed will be found in table A–3 and A–4.

7. The Price Elasticity of Liquor in the U.S. and a Simple Method of Determination*

JULIAN L. SIMON

1. INTRODUCTION AND LITERATURE SURVEY

The price elasticity of demand for liquor is of considerable practical importance to the American community because it is the basis for calculations of the effect of liquor taxes upon total tax revenue and upon liquor industry sales and profits. Estimates of liquor elasticity affect the judgments of legislators when they consider tax bills and, hence, the estimates affect the levels of taxes.

At this time we do not have a satisfactory elasticity estimate for the United States. These are the studies that bear on the matter.

(1) Richard Stone developed estimates from time series in England covering the period 1920–38. His best estimates were —0.57 for price and 0.60 for income. Stone's work is sufficiently well known so that we need not evaluate it here. The major drawback for our purposes is that the elasticity in the United States may differ from that in England for a host of cultural and economic reasons.

(2) A. R. Prest developed price elasticity estimates from time series in England, 1870–1938, using a method similar to Stone's. He obtained —0.57 using a logarithmic function and —0.031 using a linear function.

(3) Using a time-series technique for the years 1923–39 in Sweden, S. Malmquist estimated a price elasticity of —0.2 to —0.4. Liquor was rationed in Sweden during that period, which introduced great complexities into Malmquist's analysis, and thus reduces the comparability to the United States. Also, the price of liquor was extremely stable over the measured period.

(4) As part of an exhaustive institutional study of the liquor industry, Harold Wattell regressed sales linearly on price and income in Pennsylvania from 1935 to 1951. His estimate was that price was decidedly inelastic.

* *Econometrica,* vol. 34, no. 1 (January 1966), pp. 193–205.

(5) William A. Niskanen developed a structural equation system of linear demand and supply functions for the U.S. beer, wine, and liquor markets. His endogenous variables were total consumption of each beverage type and price indices for each beverage type. His exogenous variables were demand deposits, time trend (last two digits of year), and average tax revenues for beverage types. Prices and taxes were deflated to 1947. He estimated the structural parameters indirectly by least squares from the reduced form equations.

For the period 1934–54, Niskanen estimated the price elasticity of liquor to be —1.74. In a longer and later work, he estimates that for 1934–41 and 1947–60 the "price elasticity is around —2.0 . . . ," and this was the estimate on which he relied. Before further adjustment, however, the elasticity estimate of his most-relied-on regression is —1.420.

2. RELEVANT PROBLEMS OF CONVENTIONAL METHODS

There are two basic methods of evaluating elasticities: time-series and cross-sectional analysis. The two methods are sometimes used in combination, cross section for income and time series for price.

The difficulties in *time-series* analysis pertinent to liquor-elasticity determination are:

(1) Over time, changes in taste occur with a vengeance in liquor consumption. Per capita consumption in the United States has been as high as 3.25 gallons in 1860, compared to 1.14 gallons in 1949. And there is considerable fluctuation from year to year even when income and price are held constant. The year-to-year changes are more than large enough to obscure the effect of even a very large price change, as is the case with the federal excise increase in 1951.

It should not surprise us that liquor consumption is more variable and more subject to general cultural influences in the short run than is food, say. Liquor's major psychological function is to reduce fear and inhibition, and the tension level of our society varies with various external stimuli. And in the long run, shifts in religious beliefs and general style of life also affect drinking behavior.

(2) Changes in relative income, relative price, price levels, and other variables also cause trouble.

(3) Price indices are hard to create.

(4) Typically, the current price of liquor changes very infrequently; and it changes only slightly when it changes at all, because of government regulation and the nature of the commodity. This means that the time series has few observations to work with, scattered over long periods of time during which other variables can change radically. None of the studies mentioned above had data meeting the requirement of a time-series sample that has a wide representation of experiences.

These difficulties with time-series analysis are sufficiently great that investigators of liquor price elasticity have indicated little confidence in their estimates.

The main difficulty with *cross-sectional* analysis is that the population of the various states—which would be the appropriate price-change units for a U.S. study—have very different tastes for liquor. Nor are the differences explained by income. Compare the four states in which the price of Seagrams 7 Crown was $4.85 in January 1962 as shown in table I.

TABLE I

State	*January 1962 Price of Seagrams 7 Crown*	*Per Capita Liquor Consumption in 1961*	*Gallons of Liquor Consumed per $1 Million of Income*
Indiana	4.85	1.26	350
Massachusetts	4.85	2.76	681
Minnesota	4.85	2.22	613
New Mexico	4.85	1.75	506

Source: *Liquor Handbook*, 1962.

These variations in taste render useless a simple cross-sectional correlation of consumption and price in the various states. Furthermore, even if states were far more numerous than they are, we probably could not expect random differences in state tastes to wash out because of the likely association between state price and state taste.

3. DESCRIPTION OF METHOD

This investigation uses a method that has features of both the cross section and the time series. Though it has not been used by economists, to my knowledge, it is very similar to designs used for experiments in psychology and the natural sciences and to sociological paradigms. Because this method is not an experiment, though similar to one, I call it the "quasi-experimental" method.

. . . . . .

The essence of the method is to examine the "before" and "after" sales of a given state, sandwiched around a price change and standardized with the sales figures of states that did not have a price change. The standardizing removes year-to-year fluctuations and the trend. We then pool the results of as many quasi-experimental "trial" events as are available.

When it can be used, this method avoids the important difficulties of time series and cross section and introduces no major new difficulties. Moreover, it has some special advantages which we shall discuss later.

This is the procedure:

1. Select as quasi-experimental events each state price increase of 2 percent or more from 1950 to 1961. Exclude states where moonshine is an important part of liquor consumption. Exclude price change events that occur within 18 months before or after a federal tax change.

2. Notation: "—1" is the month preceding a state price change, "+1" is the month following a price change.

3. Compute the per capita consumption for the 12-month periods, —14 to —3 and +5 to +16. Find the percent of change in consumption between "before" and "after." The periods before and after the tax change are timed to avoid the stock-up that occurs before a price change and the liquidation of stock-up.

4. Compare each monopoly-state trial with other monopoly states, private license states with other private license states. (The two groups differ in consumption measurements and in the structure of liquor retailing.) Compare each trial state against other states in its group, excluding (a) states that themselves had price changes between —18 and +18, (b) states that had sales tax changes, (c) moonshine states, (d) the District of Columbia and two anomalous states. Data for the comparison states were combined (i) by simple averaging of the per capita consumption figures of the individual states, (ii) by totaling the consumption and population figures and computing per capita estimates from the totals, and (iii) where applicable, computing total estimates with and without Pennsylvania. Elasticity estimates were generated for all three sets of data.

The index used for comparison is:

$$\frac{\text{Trial state, per capita consumption "after"} - \text{Trial state, per capita consumption "before"}}{\text{Trial states, per capita consumption "before"}}$$

minus

$$\frac{\text{Comparison states, p.c. consumption "after"} - \text{Comparison states, p.c. consumption "before"}}{\text{Comparison states, per capita consumption "before"}}$$

5. Estimate the percent price change in the test state. In most monopoly state tax changes in our sample, the price increase actually is a change in the markup percentage, perfectly appropriate for our purposes. In a few monopoly state cases, there was the complication that part of the state's pricing formula included flat per gallon taxes. In those cases the writer made *ad hoc* adjustments somewhat similar to the license state situation below, in order to arrive at a point estimate.

The usual form of a tax change in license states is a change in the flat gallonage excise tax. This causes the same *absolute* change in the wholesale, and subsequently the retail, prices of all brands of liquor. The percent price change for low-priced liquors is therefore greater than for high-priced liquors. A percentage estimate of price change for the state as a whole therefore depends implicitly upon the distribution of liquor in each price range sold in the state, data which are not available.

The license state estimate was made in this fashion. Assuming customary retail markups, the increase in the retail price of a fifth was calculated. This price change was then expressed as a percent of the retail price of a fifth of a medium-priced liquor before the tax change. The calculated change was then compared against the actual change in Seagrams 7 Crown and other large selling brands, to the extent that these data were available.[1]

6. Divide the index in paragraph 4 by the percent price change in paragraph 5 to get an estimate of price elasticity.

7. As in all statistical investigations, there were exceptions that required special handling. For example, one state changed its price structure in two steps spaced three months apart. The "before" and "after" periods therefore required special adjustment.

4. PROBLEMS WITH THIS METHOD

Most of the difficulties that arise in this investigation also plague other techniques. They include.

1. Consumption figures in private license states refer to wholesale rather than retail purchases. The wholesale purchases lead retail purchases by weeks or months. Wholesale purchases are also subject to greater fluctuation from period to period than are retail sales, one cause of which is changes in brand prices not associated with general price changes and business anticipations. Monopoly state consumption, on the other hand, is measured by actual retail sales.

2. The accuracy of population figures is unexpectedly crucial. We used interpolated yearly adjusted census figures, but they are far from perfect. This is a major source of variability in the elasticity estimates.

3. As discussed above, there are flaws in the estimates of price changes. Individual brand price changes during the before and after

---

[1] Seagrams 7 Crown was used as an index of a medium-priced brand, based on *Liquor Handbook* estimates of quantities sold at various prices in the U.S. Seagrams 7 Crown is by far the largest selling brand in the United States, selling 2.5 times as much as the next biggest seller, and accounting for more than 7 percent of total U.S. liquor consumption. Its price is commonly used as a standard in the liquor industry and its price to the retailer practically never changes except in response to tax level changes.

We may gain some reassurance from the fact, inherent in the relative sizes of the quantities with which we are working, that the percent estimate of price change is quite insensitive to errors in the choice of index of the central tendency of the distribution.

periods will also affect consumption. But the remarkable stability of most liquor prices, in large part a result of fair trade and state control, renders this source of error very minor.

4. Bar and carry-out sales are differentially affected by price changes. Carry-out sales account for 70–75 percent of the total, and we used carry-out prices as an index of all prices. Different states have different laws controlling or limiting bar sales.

5. Price changes can affect interstate purchase traffic.

5. RESULTS: AN ESTIMATE OF PRICE ELASTICITY

The median of the elasticity estimates for the nonmoonshine trial states shown in column 6 of table II is —0.79. This median, adjusted upwards somewhat to take account of the moonshine states but still closer to —0.79 than to —1.0, is perhaps our best estimate of elasticity for the United States as a whole, subject to the following considerations:

1. The median was chosen as an estimate of the central tendency of the data because (a) it is not affected by the extremity of the extreme observations, and (b) it has no conceptual difficulty with positive elasticity estimates. If we were to compute a mean it would be reasonable, but theoretically uncomfortable, to include the positive estimates as being positive.

2. We may say with .965 probability that the mean of the population from which this sample of elasticity estimates was drawn is between —0.03 and —0.97.

3. The variation among elasticity estimates for the various states in the sample may be due to true variation among the states as well as to random error. Variation among the states may result from different states' elasticities, or from different trends in consumption, or both.

If there is true variation among the states, the accuracy of our overall elasticity estimate depends upon how fair a sample of the states (with respect to the characteristic under consideration) we actually obtained. We can only hope that the states that fell into our sample were not self-selected in some biased fashion.

. . . . . .

In light of the extremely small price changes with which we worked, the amount of variation in the elasticity estimates is not surprising.

4. Inclusion of two observations for some states is a questionable practice. It is done because of the fewness of observations. The paired observations are in the center of the distribution, however, which suggests that they do not cause a serious bias.

5. The extreme states are small states, which increases our confidence in the median estimate. Nevada might well be eliminated from the sam-

TABLE II

State	Date of Price Change (1)	Price of Seagram 7 Crown Fifth Before Price Change (2)	Relative Price Change (Price "After" Minus Price "Before" Divided by Price "Before") (3)	For the Trial State: Per Capita Consumption "After" Minus Per Capita Consumption "Before" Divided by Per Capita Consumption "Before" (4)	For the Comparison States Totaled: Per Capita Consumption "After" Minus Per Capita Consumption "Before" Divided by Per Capita "Before" (5)
Rhode Island	6/1/58	4.60	.033	+.073	+.041
Idaho	5/1/61	4.45	.020	+.035	+.018
Ohio	6/6/55	3.46	.061	+.083	+.033
Washington	4/15/61	4.80	.052	+.031	+.018
Oregon	5/11/59	4.35	.035	+.053	+.051
Washington	4/1/59	4.58	.048	+.059	+.058
Oregon	7/1/61	4.60	.033	+.017	+.018
Maine	7/1/61	4.15	.024	+.015	+.018
Montana	12/1/58	4.25	.071	+.036	+.047
Nevada	5/1/61	4.55	.039	+.041	+.047
Vermont	8/1/57	(3.60) est.	.143	−.046	+.034
Missouri	5/1/61	(4.70) est.	.028	+.025	+.047
Idaho	3/16/55	4.05	.086	−.047	+.025
Maine	1/2/59	4.05	.025	+.040	+.061
California	7/1/55	4.38	.048	+.039	+.085
Oregon	5/2/55	4.10	.061	−.025	+.036
Iowa	7/1/61 & 4/1/59	4.03	.030	−.013	+.018
Connecticut	7/1/61	(4.50) est.	.066	−.031	+.054
Ohio	7/1/59	3.67	.100	−.081	+.051
Iowa	4/2/55	(3.78) est.	.050	−.070	+.025
Illinois	8/1/59	4.19	.036	−.018	+.053
Montana	7/1/57	(4.09) est.	.040	−.182	−.033
Alaska	7/1/61	5.85	.026	−.059	+.054

ple on the same ground that the District of Columbia was, namely, that its liquor clientele is heavily transient, which would induce an artificially high elasticity estimate. And Idaho's price change was only 2 percent which makes the elasticity estimate unduly sensitive to random error.

6. Some liquor traffic among states is possible. The estimate for the United States as a whole therefore must be less elastic than for the individual states, just as an industry elasticity must be lower than the mean elasticity for the firms in the industry.

7. The states in table II do not include those states in which important quantities of moonshine are made. table III shows estimates for price changes in moonshine states. We had hypothesized that estimates of elasticity would be higher in moonshine states. There is an indication in

TABLE II
(Continued)

Price Elasticity (Comparison States Totaled): Col. 4 – Col. 5 / Col. 3 (6)	*For the Comparison States Totaled without Pennsylvania 1959 Tax Change: Per Capita Consumption "After" Minus Per Capita Consumption "Before" Divided by Per Capita "Before"* (7)	*Price Elasticity (Comparison States Totaled without Pennsylvania): Col. 4 – Col. 7 / Col. 3* (8)	*For the Means of the Comparison States: Per Capita Consumption "After" Minus Per Capita Consumption "Before" Divided by Per Capita "Before"* (9)	*Price Elasticity (Means of Comparison States): Col. 4 – Col. 9 / Col. 3* (10)	*Price Elasticity Using Total Comparison States, and as the "After" Period the Six Months from +11 to +16* (11)
+0.97		+0.97	+.051	+0.67	−0.24
+0.85	+.009	+1.30	+.020	+0.75	+1.65
+0.82		+0.82	+.029	+0.88	+0.28
+0.25	+.009	+0.42	+.020	+0.21	+1.02
+0.06	+.063	−0.29	+.060	−0.20	−0.20
+0.02		+0.02	+.061	−0.04	+0.04
−0.03	+.009	+0.24	+.036	−0.58	+0.51
−0.12	+.009	+0.25	+.036	−0.88	+4.63
−0.15		+0.15	+.049	−0.18	−0.48
−0.15		−0.15	+.038	+0.08	+2.95
−0.56		−0.56	+.014	−0.42	−5.38
−0.79 [median]		−0.72 [median]	+.038	−0.46	−2.07
−0.84		−0.84	+.023	−0.81	−0.98
−0.84	+.071	−1.24	+.065	−1.00	−5.72
−0.96		−0.96	+.077	−0.79 [median]	−2.00
−1.00		−1.00	+.029	−0.88	−0.92
−1.03	+.009	−0.73	+.036	−1.63	−1.30
−1.29		−1.29	+.046	−1.17	−1.02
−1.32	+.063	−1.44	+.059	−1.40	−1.39
−1.90		−1.90	+.024	−1.88	−1.94
−1.97		−1.97	+.039	−1.58	−2.39
−3.73		−3.73	−.025	−3.93	−3.23
−4.35		−4.35	+.046	−4.04	−0.08

the skimpy data of a somewhat higher elasticity. However, more than 90 percent of moonshine production takes place in states that consume less than 9 percent of legal U.S. consumption.

8. This method ignores substitution effects of beer and wine. In some cases, wine prices are changed along with liquor prices; in other cases they are not. The amount of wine sold (measured in alcohol) is small compared to liquor consumption. Therefore, the shift to wine will not be very important in affecting liquor consumption even if wine is very elastic with respect to liquor prices. . . .

9. This method estimates price elasticity by way of estimating the change in quantity sold, and assuming the mean price-paid-per-bottle changes as the price index changes. This estimate must be more elastic

TABLE III

State	*Date of Price Change (1)*	*Price of Seagram 7 Crown Fifth Before Price Change (2)*	*Relative Price Change (Price "After" Minus Price "Before" Divided by Price Before) (3)*	*For the Trial State: Per Capita Consumption "After" Minus Per Capita Consumption "Before" Divided by Per Capita Consumption "Before" (4)*	*For the Comparison States Totaled: Per Capita Consumption "After" Minus Per Capita Consumption "Before" Divided by Per Capita "Before" (5)*
Georgia	6/6/55	(4.80) est.	.069	+.127	+.085
Alabama	12/1/59	4.20	.101	−.075	+.019
Virginia	7/1/60	3.65	.100	−.140	0
West Virginia	7/1/57	3.85	.065	−.086	+.021
Virginia	7/1/58	3.55	.028	−.013	+.050

than an estimate based upon the total revenue before and after the price change, because the price change will shift some purchases to relatively cheaper brands. Investigation shows, however, that the switch to cheaper brands as a result of product price changes is slight, even when the trend to higher priced brands is taken into account.

10. It is not immediately clear what the length-of-run nature of these elasticities is. Because the "after" time period begins four months after the price change, the estimate is certainly not a very-short-run elasticity of the usual type. . . .

After an initial unsettled period, theory would lead us to expect that demand would become progressively less elastic as liquor drinkers retool their tastes and stomachs and switch to beer, wine, and other liquor substitutes. To test for this effect, I broke the "after" period into two six-month segments and developed elasticity estimates for the second six-month segments, as shown in column 11.

The signs of the differences between the 6-month period and the 12-month period are thoroughly mixed. In 13 cases the late-period estimate is higher, and in 10 cases it is lower. There is no reason to think that the elasticity was falling during the "after" period, or that the longer run estimate should be less elastic.

It is worth noting, however, that if there *had* been differences between long- and short-run elasticities, this method could have detected the differences. The time-series method alone cannot compare long- and

TABLE III
(Continued)

Price Elasticity (Comparison States Totaled) Col. 4 – Col. 5 / Col. 3 (6)	*For the Comparison States Totaled without Pennsylvania 1959 Tax Change: Per Capita Consumption "After" Minus Per Capita Consumption "Before" Divided by Per Capita "Before"* (7)	*Price Elasticity (Comparison States Totaled without Pennsylvania): Col. 4 – Col. 7 / Col. 3* (8)	*For the Means of the Comparison States: Per Capita Consumption "After" Minus Per Capita Consumption "Before" Divided by Per Capita "Before"* (9)	*Price Elasticity (Means of Comparison States): Col. 4 – Col. 9 / Col. 3* (10)	*Price Elasticity Using Total Comparison States, and as "After" Period the Six Months from 11 to 16* (11)
+0.61		+0.61	+.077	+0.72	+1.17
–0.93	+.049	–1.23	+.042	–1.16	–0.77
–1.40	–.023	–1.17	+.012	–1.52	–1.36
–1.65	+.032	–1.82	+.020	–1.63	–1.66
–2.25	+.061	–1.71	+.053	–2.36	–2.14

short-run elasticities. Indeed, the interpretation of the length-of-run nature of elasticities derived from cross-section methods, and from time series, including the various transformations of time series, is far from clear-cut. Nor can we claim a perfectly straightforward interpretation for quasi-experimental elasticities either, because the world in which the price changes play out their effect is not an otherwise static world, even after we standardize with the comparison states. Nevertheless, the interpretation would seem to be less difficult than for other methods, the biggest advantage being that the periods during which we examine the effect of particular price changes are exactly defined in length and are the same in each case, which is not true of the time-series method.

Elasticities may not be the same for a price decrease as for a price increase. Though we have not done so here, the quasi-experimental method would make possible the comparison of down-side and up-side elasticities, as time series and cross-sectional methods will not.

11. Informal inspection suggests no relationship between elasticity estimates and (a) amount of price change, (b) absolute price of liquor, or (c) secular date of price change. But if such relationships did exist, this method could reveal them. This is an important advantage over time series, which can estimate only *an* elasticity, whether or not it is constant over the range of prices.

. . . . . .

6. EVALUATION OF METHOD

1. All the cited time-series studies take explicit account of income changes, and some take account of taste trends and changes in general price level, as devices to reduce the variability in the universe and to isolate the effect of price changes. By comparison, the method used in this study not only takes out the long-term trends, but also the period-to-period variability, to the extent that income and taste changes affect the various states in the same way. Furthermore, the use of a sample of trial states must help wash out the idiosyncratic movements of given states with reference to all other states. On balance, I think this method has vast advantages over the time series in accounting for variations and trends in income, price level, and taste.

2. The method of this study is limited by the paucity of data. There are only 25 price changes to be considered. But no other method can develop *more* information than is provided by this number of price changes. And, in fact, the regression method tends to *lose* information where there are changes in consumption when prices do not change, if the consumption changes are not completely explained by the other variables—as, of course, they cannot be. It is true that a regression approach using a composite price index gains some information from brand price changes that take place in addition to tax-induced price changes. But prices are remarkably sticky, so this is not a great advantage.

Furthermore, composite indices of liquor prices must be extremely crude, because of the multiplicity of brands and the lack of knowledge about individual brand sales, especially if the regression is for the United States as a whole.

3. The quasi-experimental method has in common with true experimental methods that causation is clearly established, because we can be reasonably sure which is the exogenous variable. This is a great advantage over time series.

4. A major advantage of this method is that it permits the critical reader to test it with his intuition at every step of the way to see if the method and results are reasonable. Complex econometric techniques are too often black boxes even to adepts; their complexity makes it impossible to *understand* the relationships, and consequently they leave one with a sense of unease. Such is not the case with the quasi-experiment. It does not demand faith for one to have belief in its results.

5. The method used in this study would seem to be useful in investigations where there are several divisible and independent economic units *within* which prices (or other sales-influencing variables) move together, but *among* which prices change independently. As an example, this author is presently using the same method in an investigation of the elasticities of retail and local advertisers with respect to newspaper advertising rates.

8. Factors Affecting the Purchase Value of New Houses*

L. JAY ATKINSON

SECTION I—INTRODUCTION AND SUMMARY

Why do some families pay more than others for their new homes? Income is obviously an important reason but what other factors are also important? Are the age, occupation, and education of the household head—to cite a few characteristics—of any significance? If so, how are they related to the amount a family pays for a new home? And how do changes over time in relative prices and credit conditions affect the amount paid?

. . . . . .

Given the number of units that may be demanded in the future, it becomes necessary to determine average value per unit if projections of aggregate value are required. Although projections of average unit value were obtained by extending past trends, this technique did not provide much in the way of analytical content. This report analyzes unpublished data and yields a number of insights into the demand factors that give rise to variations in the purchase price of new houses. No projections are shown.

Cross-Section Data

Except in the last section, which is concerned with a time series analysis, most of the data for the present report are cross-sectional and are from the 1960 Census of Housing. The data, which are based on a large sample of buyers of new homes, include an extensive list of characteristics pertaining to the structure and to the household.

The article provides several cross-tabulations that show how the value of a newly built house varies by income class and by other characteristics of the household. Although the sample is a good-sized one, with many

* *The Survey of Current Business,* vol. 46, no. 8 (August 1966), pp. 20–34.

cells containing a fairly large number of observations, there are obvious limits to the number of cross-classifications that can be shown and readily interpreted. In order to lay bare the net relationships—that is, the relationship between house value and each of several characteristics of the household, with all other factors held constant—the individual household data have been analyzed by means of multiple regression. The regression analysis is the heart of this report. The basic regression took this general form: The value of a newly built house acquired by a family or individual depends upon the current income of the household; the age, sex, race, education, occupation, and marital status or length of time married of the household head; and the location of the housing unit. Some modifications of this regression were also explored.

A feature of this study is its treatment of a large number of nonincome variables, for which data have not ordinarily been available until recently. The use of such data in statistical analysis had been limited not only because they were scarce but also because many of the variables were nonnumerical. The development in the last few years of new statistical techniques involving the use of "dummy" variables and the availability of large computers have overcome these obstacles.

In addition to the analysis of nonincome influences, this article puts considerable emphasis on the estimation of income elasticity—the percentage change in purchase price or value associated with that in income. Tests were made to determine if income elasticity is constant throughout the full range of income.

Limitations of Cross-Section Estimates

Although the analysis is based on a rich body of statistical data, the cross-section study has certain limitations:

(1) It applies to a single period. The stability of the relationships shown can be tested only with observations for other periods.

(2) The analysis omits a number of variables that on a priori grounds would appear to be significant in accounting for variation in house value. Some of these omitted variables, such as changes over time in prices and financing terms (including downpayments, amortization period, and interest rates), are for all practical purposes inherent limitations of a single-period cross-sectional approach. For others, such as assets held by the household and the prices of comparable accommodations afforded by used houses, the data were not available.

(3) Although the estimated regression coefficients are statistically significant at the 1 percent level, they have sizable errors; this reflects both sampling variability and intercorrelation among the independent variables.

(4) Certain biases are characteristic of regression computations from

cross-section data, as has been widely noted. One type of bias is related to the concept of income that is appropriate for calculating elasticity.[1]

Time Series Analysis

The final section of this paper uses time series data to analyze the factors influencing house value. Ideally, the results of time series analysis could serve as a check on the cross-section results and would permit the introduction of variables such as price and credit terms that were necessarily excluded in the cross-section approach.

In practice, the time series analysis has serious shortcomings. The various nonincome factors (age, education, etc.) used in the cross-section analysis are not available in usable time series. The few series that are available—on house value, price, income, and credit terms—are deficient in many respects. Moreover, there is a high degree of correlation among the independent variables, so that it is difficult to isolate and appraise their separate relationship to house value. An important characteristic of the available time series is that they are highly aggregative—annual averages for the United States—in contrast to the cross-section data, which are on a household basis.

In the analysis of many other types of problems—consumption functions, for example—estimates based on aggregated time series have usually been considerably different from those derived from cross-section data, and the two types of estimates have seldom been reconciled. In this study, such differences are encountered, and no reconciliation has been achieved.

Principal Findings

Points 1 through 5 apply to the cross-section analysis.

(1) All of the independent variables accounted for about half of the total variation in the price paid for new homes.

(2) As was expected, income was the single most important variable, accounting for almost 50 percent of the explained variation in house value.

(3) With all of the other explanatory variables held constant and with the highest and lowest income groups excluded, the cross-section estimates of income elasticity ranged from 0.41 to 0.47. This means

[1] Such possible biases have been discussed in numerous publications. Many of these are cited by Margaret G. Reid in *Income and Housing* (University of Chicago Press, 1963). This study and others suggest that estimates of income elasticity for housing derived from cross-section data may be too low. See also R. F. Muth, "The Demand for Nonfarm Housing," in A. C. Harberger (ed.), *The Demand for Durable Goods* (University of Chicago Press, 1960).

that a difference of 10 percent in income was associated with a difference of around 4.1 to 4.7 percent in the value of a newly purchased house. These net regression results were not much different from the simple regression estimate of income elasticity when only income was related to the value of a new house.

(4) The income elasticity estimate was found to be constant over an extremely wide range of income. Other investigations of income elasticity have often found that elasticity declined as income increased.

(5) Several nonincome variables had an important influence upon the variation in house values in the cross-section analysis. For example, with all other factors held constant, an increase in age, years married, or amount of education of the household head raises the value of new homes acquired. Again, with all other factors held constant, homes acquired by white household heads have a higher value than those acquired by nonwhites, and homes in the North and West have a higher value than those in the South.

The following points are from the time series analysis:

(6) When house value was related to family income in a simple relationship based on aggregated data, the estimate of income elasticity was around 0.8. The (net) income elasticity rose to approximately 1.0 when variables for credit terms and prices were added to the estimating equation.

(7) The price elasticity for new houses was estimated to be less than unity, with the usual inverse relationship between price and real value of house purchased. An inverse relationship was also found between house value and a credit variable in the form of monthly mortgage payments, i.e., the lower the monthly payments, the higher the value of house acquired.

The remainder of this article is organized as follows: Section II presents the cross-section data and some preliminary cross-section relationships. In the third and longest section, the data are analyzed by means of multiple regression to show how the value of new houses is related to the income of the household and a series of nonincome characteristics. The fourth section deals with the constancy of the estimated income elasticity throughout the income range and also modifies the cross-section estimate of income elasticity. The fifth and final section is an analysis, based on time series, of income elasticity and the effect of changes in prices and credit on house value.

SECTION II—THE DATA AND THEIR TREATMENT

Most of the basic data used in this study were part of a systematic 1-in-1,000 sample of the 53 million U.S. households enumerated in the 1960 Census. For each sample household, the Census Bureau made available on magnetic tapes about 100 characteristics, of which 15 were selected as the most relevant for this analysis. Information from Census tabulations and housing studies was utilized in selecting the most appropriate characteristics.

For most of the characteristics except house value and income (e.g., age, education, years married), the Census designations are self-explanatory. The value of the house is that reported to the Census Bureau in answer to the question "What is the current [spring 1960] market value of your house?" Although a householder's appraisal of value may be rather imprecise, especially for older houses, it seemed reasonable to suppose that for newly acquired houses the respondent would give the purchase price. An independent check confirmed this assumption.

Income is measured as the total money income of all members of the household in the preceding year (1959) as reported to the Census Bureau.

As the first step in this study, the entire Census sample of 53,000 households was classified according to "tenure type." Tenure type designates certain features of the housing unit—whether it is owner-occupied or rented, when it was built, and the number of units in the structure. The various tenure-type classifications, which were derived from the 1960 Census data, are shown in table 1. The portion of the sample that had recently bought new homes constitutes the main set of (cross-

TABLE 1
Number of Households Classified by Tenure Type, April 1960
(thousands)

	Number	*Percent distribution*
Total households	**52,875**	**100.0**
Owners	**32,742**	**61.9**
Buyers, 1955–60:		
Houses built 1959–60	1,398	2.6
Houses built 1955–58	4,677	8.9
Houses built before 1955	6,457	12.2
Other owners	20,210	38.2
Renters	**20,133**	**38.1**
In one-to-two-family houses	12,458	23.6
Built 1955–60	883	1.7
Built before 1955	11,575	21.9
In three-or-more-family structures	7,675	14.5
Built 1959–60	159	.3
Built 1955–58	392	.7
Built before 1955	7,124	13.5

Source: U.S. Department of Commerce, Office of Business Economics. Universe estimates based on tabulations from 1-in-1,000 sample of households, U.S. Census of Housing, 1960.

section) data analyzed in this article. There were 1,398 observations in this group, of which 1,155 had complete records.

. . . . . .

Some Characteristics of New House Buyers

Although this paper does not analyze the factors that influence the decision to buy (or not to buy) a new house, some background information on this subject may be of interest. Chart 1 illustrates the relationship between the purchase of a new home and a few of the characteristics considered here. It shows a percentage distribution of buyers of new houses according to each of three characteristics—age, education, and region. For comparison, similar data are presented for all households in the United States as of April 1960.

Among those households that had recently bought new homes, the 10-year age brackets 25 to 34 and 35 to 44 accounted for 70 percent of the total. Those under 25 and those 55 or older accounted for only a small portion of buyers. The age distribution of buyers was quite different from the age distribution of all households. Relative to all household heads (male), buyers were more common for each of the age groups under 45 and less common for each of the older groups.

The amount of education of the household head was directly related to the probability that he would buy a new house. Those whose education did not exceed seven years were only half as likely to be new buyers as all household heads; those who graduated from college were twice as likely to be new buyers.

As of 1960, the South and the West had higher-than-average proportions of new house buyers relative to all households; the North Central region was a little below average and the Northeast considerably below average.

Some Preliminary Relationships

Chart 2 suggests some of the ways that house value is related to income and nonincome factors. The top panel shows the relationship between house value and income for three broad age classifications. It indicates three main points: There is a direct relationship between value and income for each of the three classifications; the slopes of the three lines are about the same; and for any given income, there is some difference in the average house value for the different age groups.

The middle panel, in which households are classified by educational attainment of the household head, also illustrates the direct relationship between house value and income. There is less uniformity in the slopes of the lines than there was for the age classifications. Finally, at any

CHART 1

Percent Distribution of Buyers of New Houses Built 1959—First Quarter 1960 Compared with All Households

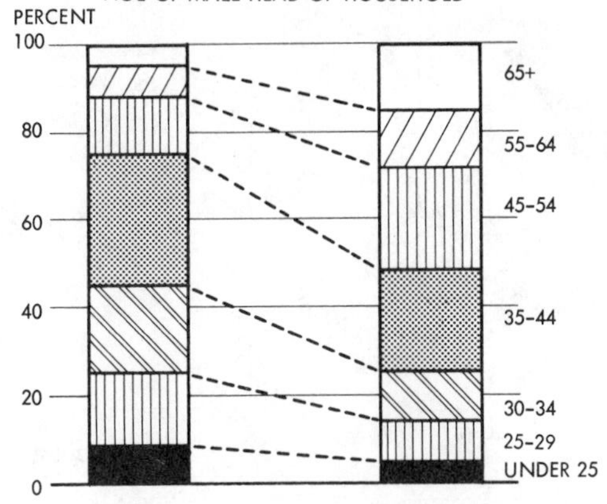

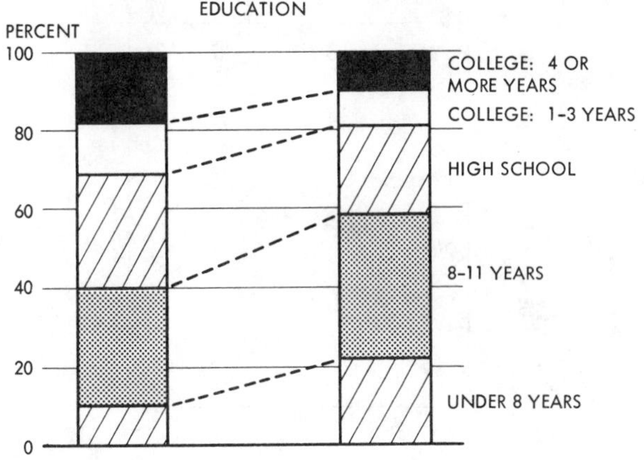

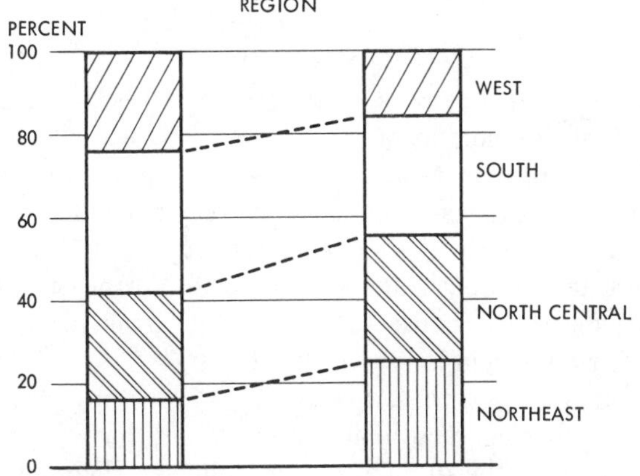

Source: U.S. Department of Commerce, Office of Business Economics; Basic Data: Census 66-8-7.

CHART 2

Relationship between House Value and Income, Buyers of New Houses Built 1959—First Quarter 1960

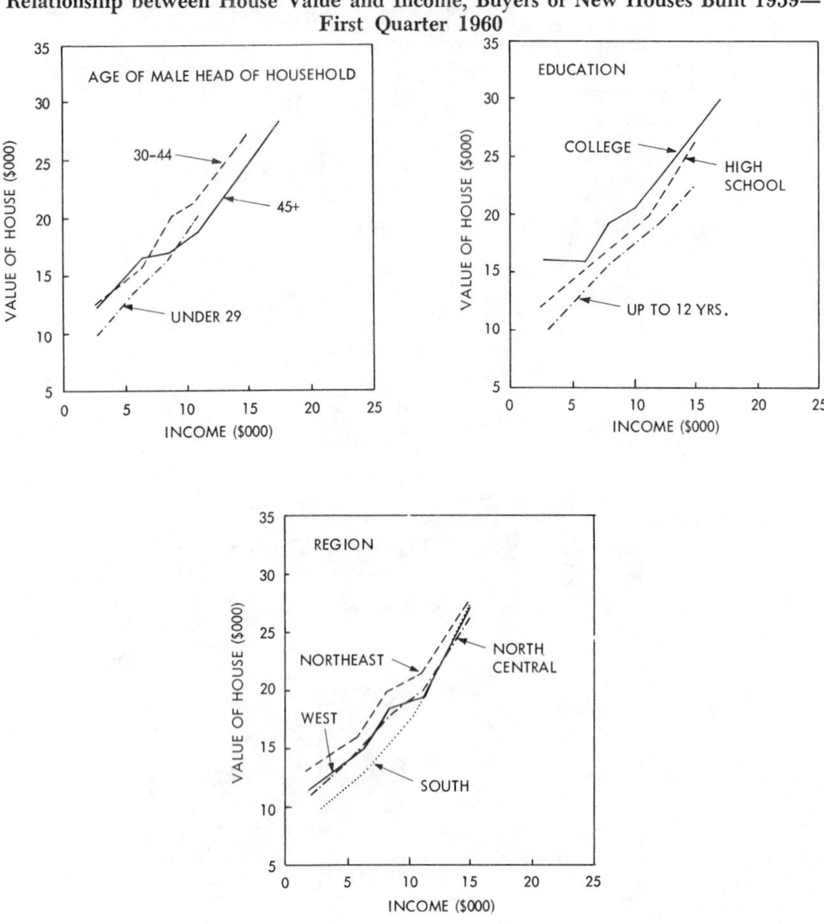

Source: U.S. Department of Commerce, Office of Business Economics; Basic Data: Census 66-8-8.

given income level, house value appears to vary directly with the level of education of the household head.

The direct value-income relation also shows up when the data are classified by region. However, some clearcut regional differences are apparent with respect to both the slope of the lines and their level. The slope is greatest in the South and least in the Northeast. Throughout most of the income range, house values for any given income level are highest in the Northeast and lowest in the South.

As was indicated earlier, these relationships between house value and income, with one other characteristic held constant, have been presented only to give a taste of the discussion that follows. Their interpretation is deferred to the section dealing with the comprehensive regression analysis, in which both gross and net relationships are considered.

SECTION III—REGRESSION ANALYSIS

. . . . .

Form of Relationship

In the general form of the regression, the value of the house (dependent variable) is a function of income and eight other characteristics of the household or the household head: region, size of place, size of Standard Metropolitan Statistical Area (SMSA) and location within the area, age and sex, length of time married, race, education, and finally, occupation.

In the regression equation shown in this section, the value of the house and income are numerical variables. All the other variables are classified in nonnumerical categories and are treated in the regressions as "dummy" variables, even though some, such as years of education, were originally reported by the household in numerical form.

As would be expected, there was a question as to the appropriate form of the relationship between house value and income. On the basis of past studies, there seemed to be some preference for a log form—i.e., relative differences in income are related to relative difference in house value. However, four forms were calculated: log-log, linear-linear, log-linear, and linear-log. The two mixed forms yielded no improvement in fit and are not shown in the article. There was little difference between the results calculated by the log form and those calculated by the linear form, although the log form accounted for somewhat more of the variation in house value (significant at the 1 percent level).

Summary results of the log equation (#3) are presented first. Then, for the sake of simplicity, a systematic explanation will be made for the linear equation (#1).

Summary of Results: Log Equation (#3)

Table 2 gives summary results for the log equation (#3) and shows the relative importance of each of the nine characteristics in explaining the variation in house value. Together, the nine independent variables in the equation accounted for 47 percent of the relative variation in the value of new house acquired. ($R^2 = 0.47$). For time series correlations of highly aggregated data, an R^2 with this value would be unacceptable, but for cross-section data in which the unit of observation

TABLE 2
Analysis of Variation in Value of New Houses
Log Equation (#3)

	Sum of squares	*Percent of total*	*Percent of total explained*
Total	**56.480**	**100**	...
Variation explained by regression	26.683	47	100
Variation attributable to:			
Location	(6.570)	(12)	(25)
Region	4.511	8	17
Size of place	.141	(*)	1
Size of SMSA	1.918	3	7
Age and sex	2.124	4	8
Marital status	.842	1	3
Race	.495	1	2
Education	4.304	8	16
Occupation	.966	2	4
Income	11.382	20	43
Variation not explained by regression	29.797	53	...

* Less than ½ of 1 percent.
Note: Detail may not add to totals because of rounding.

is the household, these results appear to be very satisfactory by the usual standard of generally comparable analyses.

Income was by far the most important variable and accounted for 20 percent of the total variation. Each of the other characteristics also made a significant contribution (at the 1 percent level). Large influences upon variation in house value were exerted by two of the three location variables—region and size of SMSA—as well as by education and age and sex of the head. Smaller but important effects were associated with occupation, length of time married, and race. However, the size of the urban area in which the home was located was not very important. As a group, the nonincome variables accounted for 27 percent of the total variation in the value of new houses or over half of that explained by the regression. On the basis of results obtained from similar studies, it is surprising that the nonincome variables accounted for so much variation.

Income Effects

As has already been indicated, income was the most important explanatory variable. In the simple regression between value and income, income accounted for 30 percent of the variation in the value of new houses. As the nonincome variables were introduced into the regression equation, they lowered the net variation explained by income because of the correlation between income and the other "independent" variables. When all the variables were included in the regression equation, the contribution of income was reduced by one third, from 30 to 20 percent. Although the correlation among the independent variables is substantial, as was expected, the explanatory influence of income still remaining is considerable.

In the log form of the equation, the regression coefficient for income is an estimate of the income elasticity for new house value. In the gross or simple regression, the income coefficient was 0.42; that is, differences of 10 percent in income were associated with differences of 4.2 percent in house value. This result is consistent with a large number of estimates that have been made in similar analyses of cross-section data. As each of the other significant variables was introduced into the equation, all previously calculated regression coefficients were affected to some extent. The regression coefficient on income declined (with only an insignificant exception), reaching a terminal value of 0.28 when all the variables had been included. A modification of the regression calculation, which is discussed in section IV, results in an increase in the estimate of the net income elasticity to the 0.41–0.47 range mentioned in the introduction.

The Linear Multiple Regression (#1)

The preceding discussion has shown the relative importance of each of the nine independent variables in accounting for the variation in the value of new houses, and has given one estimate of the income elasticity coefficient. The next step is the consideration of the regression coefficients for the nonincome characteristics, using the results of the linear equation.[2] Each of the variables is discussed in turn. For each characteristic or variable, the coefficients are shown as deviations from the mean, so that for a characteristic as a whole the weighted sum of the deviations is zero. Chart 3 provides a general view of the results. It shows gross differences in house value (expressed as deviations from the mean) for each of several nonincome variables and then gives the corresponding net differences obtained from equation #1. These gross and net differences are discussed in detail in the rest of this section.

Location

Data from the cross-classifications suggest that region may have an important influence on the average value of new houses. For each region, column 1 of the summary table shows the gross difference from the U.S. average house value. Average value is least in the South and highest

[2] In the linear equation, the independent variables account for 42 percent of the variation in the dependent variable.

CHART 3
Gross and Net Difference in House Value from U.S. Average New Houses Built 1959-First Quarter 1960

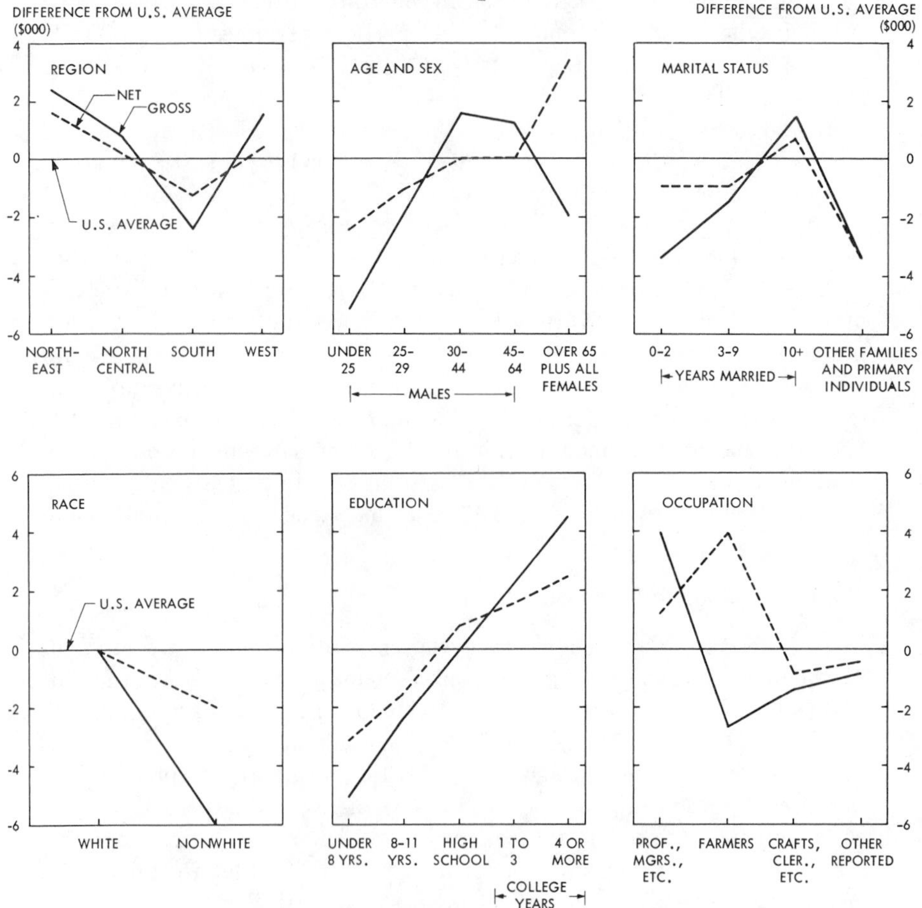

Note: Net based on linear regression equation (#1).
Source: U.S. Department of Commerce, Office of Business Economics; Basic Data: Census 66-8-9.

in the Northeast and West, with the North Central not far above the U.S. average. However, these gross differences in value may reflect not only purely regional differences but also differences associated with regional variations in income, size of city, and age, race, education, and occupation of the household head, as well as factors not included in the regression equation. The net differences among regions, with the influence of all other characteristics included in the regression equation held constant, are shown in column 4. Because income has an important influence on house value and because there are major regional differences in income, the adjustment for income is shown separately in column 2; gross differences adjusted for income are shown in column 3.

Influence of Region on Variation in Average Value of New Houses

Region	*Gross Differences from U.S. Average*	*Adjustment for Differences Attributable to Income*	*Gross Differences Adjusted for Differences in Income*	*Net Differences from U.S. Average*
	Col. 1	*Col. 2*	*Col. 3 = Col. 1 + Col. 2*	*Col. 4*
Northeast	$2,336	−$166	$2,170	$1,790
North Central	596	−77	519	565
South	−2,384	510	−1,874	−1,406
West	1,726	−664	1,062	486

Part of the gross variation in each of the four regions is obviously attributable to regional differences in income. The adjustment for income difference is largest for the West, where incomes are well above the national average, and nearly as large (in the opposite direction) for the South, where incomes are below average; for the other two regions, the income adjustment is small. When adjustment is made for the differences among regions in all of the other characteristics, there remain fairly sizable net differences in house value that are associated with region. On a net basis, average value is also least in the South and highest in the Northeast; however, the West, like the North Central region, is only moderately above the U.S. average.

There may be several reasons for the large net differences in house value in the South and Northeast. In the South, they may reflect lower construction costs for a house of specified characteristics, less elaborate heating systems needed because of the milder climate, and lower land values. The opposite conditions may give rise to deviations in the opposite direction in the Northeast.

Two other locational factors were considered in the regression equation and are mentioned very briefly here. First, classification was made according to "size of place"—into rural nonfarm areas, small urban areas, and large urban areas. The net differences in house value for these classifications were rather small, although the variance of the three as a group was statistically significant (at the 1 percent level). A more elaborate classification pertaining to Standard Metropolitan Statistical Areas (SMSAs) was more successful. For households located outside SMSAs, net values were considerably below average (—$1,443). Net differences above the U.S. average were largest for central cities in SMSAs of over 1 million population ($4,273) and well above the U.S. average in suburban (noncentral city) locations in such SMSAs ($1,488).

They were only a little above average in SMSAs of less than 1 million, both in the central city ($171) and in the suburbs ($206).

Age and Sex

It was apparent from the cross-tabulations that the value of new houses purchased by households with male heads increased directly with age in the younger age groups (under age 35), reached a maximum in the intermediate age groups, and declined for the oldest age groups. A similar pattern prevailed for income in relation to age. Therefore, the question posed was whether there was a net association between age and value of house, that is, one not attributable to differences in income or in other nonincome variables.

The adjustment for income (column 2) is fairly sizable (on a relative basis) for the first three age groups in the table and very large for the two oldest groups. Still, the broad pattern that can be seen in column 1 is evident after the income adjustment (column 3). When allowance is made for all of the other explanatory variables, appreciable net differences in house value associated with age remain only for the two youngest groups and the oldest age group, which also includes all female household heads. On a net basis, the gross differences virtually disappear for the two intermediate age groups, 30–44 and 45–64, and are considerably reduced for the two youngest age groups. For the remaining group (males 65 and over and all females), house value is substantially above

Influence of Age and Sex on Variation in Average Value of New Houses

Age and Sex of Household Head	*Gross Differences from U.S. Average*	*Adjustment for Differences Attributable to Income*	*Gross Differences Adjusted for Differences in Income*	*Net Differences from U.S. Average*
	Col. 1	*Col 2*	*Col. 3 = Col. 1 + Col. 2*	*Col. 4*
Male under 25 years	–$5,194	$1,340	–$3,854	–$2,361
25–29 years	–2,094	673	–1,421	–1,139
30–44 years	1,367	–349	1,018	–4
45–64 years	1,047	–995	52	138
65 years and older and all females	–2,053	1,729	–324	3,373

average on a net basis—just the reverse of the pattern evident on a gross basis.

Why, after allowance is made for income and other factors, do young household heads buy houses that are less expensive than average while the oldest heads acquire more expensive houses? If it were mainly a question of anticipated family needs and income expectations, one might have looked for just the opposite results: relatively high house values for the young and relatively low values for the old. An influence more powerful than income prospects and anticipated family needs appears to be at work here. Net asset holdings may explain the net results observable in the table. Recent studies have shown a strong positive correlation between net asset holdings and age. Thus, the effect of asset holdings, a variable that could not be directly measured in the present study, may be indirectly reflected in the net variation associated with age.

Marital Status

In the consideration of marital status, comparisons were made for couples married for various lengths of time and for the small number of other households (families with only one spouse present and primary individuals) that had acquired new homes. These "other households" are not discussed because they are a rather small group and contain several different household types.

For married couples, the gross data show a positive association be-

Influence of Marital Status on Variation in Average Value of New Houses

Marital Status of Household Head	*Gross Differences from U.S. Average*	*Adjustment for Differences Attributable to Income*	*Gross Differences Adjusted for Differences in Income*	*Net Differences from U.S. Average*
	Col. 1	*Col. 2*	*Col. 3 = Col. 1 + Col. 2*	*Col. 4*
Husband-wife married:				
0–2 years	–$3,244	$975	–$2,269	–$983
3–9 years	–1,374	526	–848	–948
10 years and over	1,473	–595	878	994
Other families and primary individuals.	–3,201	1,733	–1,468	–3,165

tween years married and purchase price. Differences in income account for roughly one third of the differences in house value. When all other factors are allowed for, a further sizable reduction is made in the large negative deviation for the group married two years or less, but little change occurs for the other two groups. On a net basis, those married less than 10 years buy houses about $1,000 below average and those married longer about $1,000 above average.

It was recognized that the length of time married would be correlated with the age of the household head. Nevertheless, a significant reduction in the variation in house value was accounted for by the length of time married, although the reduction was considerably smaller than that associated with age and sex of the head. It may well be that the years-married variable, like the age variable, reflects the influence of asset holdings on the purchase price of a house.

Race

Nonwhites acquired homes that were valued at $5,000 less than the U.S. average. Of this difference, one fourth was associated with lower income, and nearly one half (in addition) with other nonincome factors in the equation; the remaining portion was associated with race, as is shown below. The net difference may reflect the effects of the less advantageous financing terms available to Negro house buyers or the other difficulties Negroes face in buying houses in line with their incomes and assets.

Influences of Race on Variations in Average Value of New Houses

Race	*Gross Differences from U.S. Average*	*Adjustment for Differences Attributable to Income*	*Gross Differences Adjusted for Differences in Income*	*Net Differences from U.S. Average*
	Col. 1	*Col. 2*	*Col. 3 = Col. 1 + Col. 2*	*Col. 4*
White	$246	$11	$257	$75
Nonwhite	-5,824	1,453	-4,371	-1,804

Education

The education of the household head was an important influence on value. The net variation associated with education accounted for one sixth of the variance explained by all the variables.

As the table shows, gross differences in value varied directly and widely with differences in education. The corresponding variation in income accounted for about one fourth of the gross variation. The other nonincome variables brought about a similar reduction in variation for those with the least and the most education but were not important for those who had some high school or one to three years of college education.

Influence of Education on Variations in Average Value of New Houses

Education of Household Head	*Gross Differences from U.S. Average*	*Adjustment for Differences Attributable to Income*	*Gross Differences Adjusted for Differences in Income*	*Net Differences from U.S. Average*
	Col. 1	*Col. 2*	*Col. 3 = Col. 1 + Col. 2*	*Col. 4*
Under 8 years	–$4,944	$1,113	–$3,831	–$3,092
8–11 years	–2,124	623	–1,501	–1,503
High school	246	–96	150	628
College, 1–3 years	2,216	–586	1,630	1,455
College, 4 or more years	4,646	–1,154	3,492	2,352

The net differences in house value associated with education may well reflect different income prospects. As compared with the less educated, household heads who have graduated from college are likely to acquire homes that are more expensive in relation to their incomes because they have better prospects for rising income throughout their working lives. Lending institutions are likely to take account of such different prospects.

Occupation

Two general points may be made regarding occupation: First, this variable is obviously related to education; second, the classification system leaves something to be desired. It includes two small and poorly identified groups: Those not reporting occupation and "farmers" living in nonfarm areas. In addition, it includes a heterogeneous "other reported" group, which contains laborers, service workers, and salesmen.

The findings for the three groups will not be discussed, mainly because they are not significant.

Influence of Occupation on Variation in Average Value of New Houses

Occupation of Household Head	*Gross Differences from U.S. Average*	*Adjustment for Differences Attributable to Income*	*Gross Differences Adjusted for Differences in Income*	*Net Differences from U.S. Average*
	Col. 1	*Col. 2*	*Col. 3 = Col. 1 + Col. 2*	*Col. 4*
Professional, managerial, etc.	$3,960	-$1,423	$2,537	$1,064
Craftsmen, operatives, clerical	-1,442	333	-1,109	-805
Farmers.	-2,635	780	-1,855	4,039
Other reported	-983	517	-466	-356
Not reported	-1,283	-136	-1,147	-808

The highest skilled group, which embraces professionals, managers, officials, and proprietors, acquired new houses valued at nearly $4,000 above the average; one third of the gross deviation was associated with higher income, and one third was attributable to other nonincome factors in the regression. The group classified as craftsmen, operatives, and clerical workers acquired houses valued below the national average; a little less than one fourth of this deviation was attributable to below-average income. The nonincome influences brought about a similar reduction, and the net deviation for this class was still below the average (—$800).

The prospect of rising income is probably one factor that explains the above-average house value for the professional and managerial group. Another is that lenders may be favorably disposed toward persons in this occupational group because they experience little unemployment.

Use of Regression Coefficients: An Example

The preceding discussion of net regression coefficients has indicated how house value would vary if all explanatory variables (income, region, age and sex, education, etc.) except the one under consideration were held constant. This section is a digression that illustrates an interesting use of the coefficients.

Suppose one wished to estimate house value for a hypothetical household with a series of specified characteristics. The regression coefficients can be thought of as building blocks to be combined in various ways to yield an estimate of house value. Subject to certain limitations, table 3, which is based on data for 1959 and the first quarter of 1960, illustrates the procedure to be followed.

TABLE 3
Calculated House Value for a Hypothetical Household

Average, based on households reporting house value		**$17,662**
Income	$7,000	
As deviation from mean	−$1,340	−614
Region	South	−1,406
Location	Suburb of small SMSA	206
Age and sex	25–29, male	−1,139
Years married	3–9	−948
Race	White	75
Education	High school	628
Occupation	Craftsman	−805
Equals: calculated total		**13,659**

Source: Equation #1.

The left-hand column of table 3 gives the general characteristics and the next column the specific values assumed for the household. The third column gives the regression coefficient taken from the tables just discussed.

It should be remembered that the net coefficients have been shown as deviations from the mean; thus, the calculated house value will be the net result of additions to and subtractions from the grand average house value for the entire sample—$17,662.

In the example, it is assumed that the household has an income of $7,000. Since the average for all households in the sample was $8,340, the income coefficient (.4584) is multiplied by the difference ($7,000 — $8,340) to yield the adjustment in value (—$614) corresponding to the assumed income. The rest of the adjustments in the illustration are taken directly from the tables. The example chosen yields a house value of $13,659. Similar computations may be made for any set of specified characteristics.

Such a calculation makes use of the assumption that the variables are independent in their influence upon the dependent variable and that their effects are additive in the manner shown. However, this is unlikely to be strictly true, as was indicated earlier. Age and number of years married are obviously related, as are other independent variables. In addition, all of the coefficients are subject to error. Because of these limitations, the results shown must be used with caution; however, they should be of some value to those interested in analyzing housing markets.

SECTION IV—MODIFICATION OF ESTIMATED INCOME ELASTICITY

The importance of income in the preceding regression analysis has already been made clear. In the four equations that were calculated (two of which have been shown), income accounted for 40 to 45 percent of the explained variation in house value—more than any other single variable.

The next step involves a more intensive analysis of the net regression coefficient on income and an analysis of the constancy of the income coefficient throughout the income range. A straight line fitted to the logs of house value on the logs of income, as in equation #3, assumes that the income elasticity is constant for all income levels.[3] Although it could be ascertained in advance by simple graphic methods that the gross value-income relationship was approximately logarithmic, no such simple expedient permitted the establishment of the net relationship after the influence of the other variables (age and sex, education, etc.) had been accounted for. The usual supposition is that the elasticity would be higher in the lower part of the income range and would decline at upper income levels, as has been reported for many consumption goods in family budget studies.

This section produces a modification of the estimate of income elasticity and tests for constancy in a broad range of income. The test is made possible by extending the dummy variable technique—previously employed only with nonincome characteristics—to the income variable. The modification of the estimated income elasticity comes about chiefly through the omission of the two open-end income classes.

Initially, equations #1 and #3 were recalculated (and designated 1A and 3A); for the specific income of each household, 1 of 12 dummy variables representing the 12 income classes was substituted. An advantage of this technique is that it does not require the analyst to specify in advance the form of the relationship between house value and income. As is indicated below, with the dummy variable technique, each income class has its own regression coefficient. Once these have been calculated, it can then be determined whether they show constant, decreasing, or increasing elasticity.

[3] Each of the other equations involves a specific implication concerning income elasticity. Equation #1 (linear) implies that elasticity rises with rising income; one linear-log combination implies increasing elasticity as income rises and the other implies decreasing elasticity.

The results of the recalculations are shown in chart 4. The 12 points connected by the heavy black line represent calculated house value based on equation 3A. If a least squares straight line is now fitted through these calculated values, the slope of this line (0.31) turns out to be

CHART 4

House Value-Income Net Regression, Buyers of New Houses Built 1959—First Quarter 1960

(when open-end income classes are included, the slope of the net regression line is reduced)

RATIO SCALE

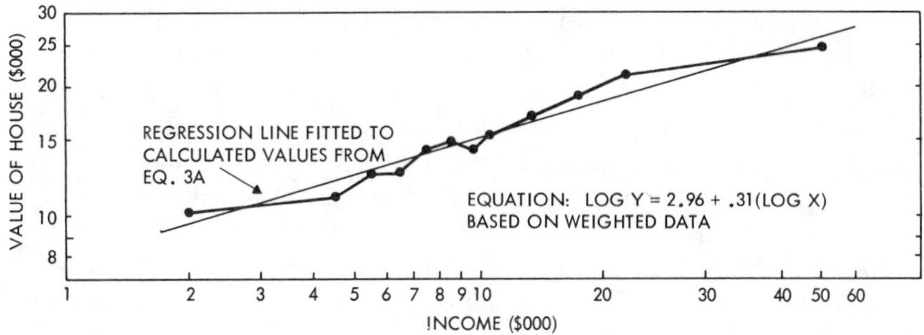

(when open-end classes are excluded, the slope is increased—the equation shows constant elasticity throughout the income range from $4,000 to $25,000)

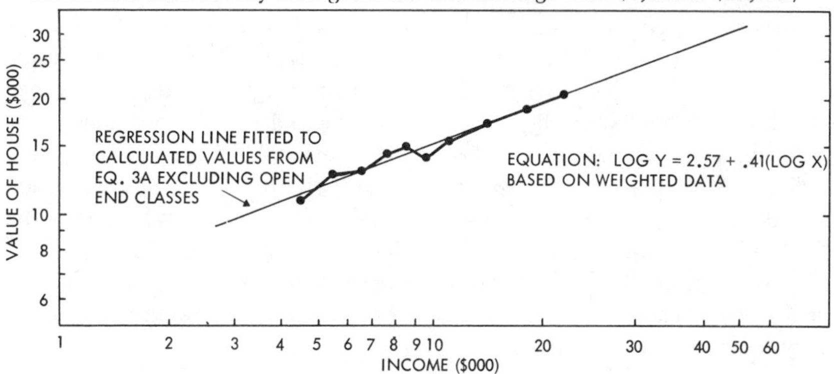

Source: U.S. Department of Commerce, Office of Business Economics; Basic Data: Census 66-8-10.

only a little larger than that of the line of net regression on income from equation #3 (0.28). The points for the lowest and highest income classes appear out of line; the inclusion of these two extreme points reduces the slope of the line, as may be seen in the chart.

There seemed to be some merit in establishing a relationship between house value and income with the two extreme income groups omitted. The lowest income group accounted for about 15 percent of the new house sample; the highest group, about 2 percent. The principal reason for excluding the $25,000-and-over income group is that the data do not have a solid basis, since specific income and value data were not available for income above $25,000 and house values above $35,000.

For households with incomes under $4,000, influences other than current income appear to be much more important in affecting the price paid for new housing. This group is unusual in many respects. One fourth of these household heads did not work at all in the preceding year; it seems very likely that most of these were retired persons, since one sixth of the group were 65 years of age or older. Such households draw upon accumulated saving from past incomes for house purchases. About one-sixth were female household heads, a much higher proportion than in the total sample; many of these were widows using the proceeds from insurance or inheritance to purchase a house. The group was also probably overweighted with household heads whose incomes were too low to obtain funds through ordinary financial channels and who obtained family loans or gifts.

In the bottom part of chart 4, a least squares line has been fitted to the results (logarithms) of equation 3A, excluding the two open-end classes; it yields an income elasticity of 0.41, as compared with 0.31 based on all the income classes. It can be seen, moreover, that the line fits the points well, so that it is fair to conclude that the income elasticity is constant through the income range of $4,000 to $25,000.

Results based on equation 1A (which is like equation #1, except for the substitution of dummy variables) also tend to confirm the finding that income elasticity is essentially constant throughout the income range of $4,000 to $25,000. The slope of the line based on equation 1A is 0.47, somewhat above the slope based on equation 3A.[4]

These adjusted estimates of income elasticity based on net regression are about the same as the simple regression estimates derived from the relationship between house value and income for all income classes. They are also within the fairly narrow range reported by other investigators using cross-section data of fairly recent vintage and only one or a very few independent variables.

SECTION V—TIME-SERIES ANALYSIS

If time-series data on income and nonincome characteristics of house buyers were available, it would be possible, through the use of the coefficients obtained in the cross-section analysis, to make estimates of house value over time. This approach would permit one to take account

[4] The Durbin-Watson values for the two equations are 2.54 for equation 3A and 1.44 for equation 1A. These are nonsignificant values at the 5 percent level, and (for a cross-section regression) they indicate no significant departure from linearity for the log variables fitted.

of shifts in the various characteristics that were shown to be important in influencing the value of new house acquisitions. For example, there have been trends toward increased education and a higher degree of occupational skills of employed persons. To the extent that these trends exist among new home buyers, the average unit value of new house purchases would tend to rise.

In principle, such estimates would also reflect the inherent deficiencies of the cross-section analysis. For example, they would ignore changes in average unit value that were due to changes in relative prices, credit terms, or asset holdings. At any particular point in time, the variations observed in average unit value among households may reflect the influence of the prevailing structure of prices, credit terms, and asset holdings, as well as other unspecified factors. Changes in such factors over time could give rise to changes in average house value from one period to another.

In practice, time series are not available for the nonincome characteristics of house buyers, so that an estimating procedure like the one outlined cannot be employed. Nevertheless, a time-series analysis was made, using aggregative data on prices, credit, and income. Such an analysis does not explicitly provide for variables that, according to the cross-section analysis, affect average unit value. However, it may shed some light on the effect of variables previously ignored in this study.

The available time-series data have serious shortcomings. Our main interest is in changes in the average U.S. value of all new nonfarm houses in real terms, but a suitable series is not available even on a current dollar basis, much less on a constant dollar basis. The available price series (for deflation purposes) have major deficiencies. Moreover, there are no credit data applicable to all purchasers of new houses in the nation as a whole.

The only consistent set of time series available for new single-family houses is the group insured by FHA, and it was decided to use these in an attempt to explain changes over time in the average value of new houses. Consistency of data is a considerable advantage in any statistical analysis; it may yield results that are biased with respect to the entire nation but provide analytical insights that might otherwise be obscured by faulty data. The following discussion will therefore be in terms of new houses insured by FHA. Afterwards, an attempt will be made to explain the variation over time in the construction cost of all new single-family houses in the United States, using data from a variety of sources.

FHA Data

Annual data on average acquisition price for new single-family homes with mortgages insured by FHA under section 203 are available from

1947 to 1964. The data are broken down into value of site and value of house. To deflate value of house excluding site, a special cost index, based mainly on FHA cost estimates of a standardized house, was used. This index rose about half as fast as the Boeckh index over the postwar period. No price series was available to deflate the market value of the site. It was assumed that the change in market value reflected price change only. The addition of the site value for a single year (1958) to each of the annual estimates of deflated construction cost for the house itself (in 1958 dollars) yields a deflated series on average value including site. It should be noted that this deflated series, following a general rise throughout the earlier postwar period, declined slightly after 1957 and then edged upward.

The income series used is the "effective income" of purchasers of new FHA houses. This is estimated by FHA to be the mortgagor's earning capacity (before deduction for Federal income taxes) that is likely to prevail during approximately the first third of the mortgage term. Current earnings are adjusted by FHA if they are considered to be partly of a nonpermanent character. Ordinarly, future increases that may be anticipated by the mortgagor are not included in the FHA estimate of effective income. The income series was deflated by OBE's implicit price deflator for personal consumption expenditures to obtain real income in 1958 dollars.

The price index is derived by combining the separate indexes for house and site. Since the values of residential building lots have shown a considerably larger relative rise than construction costs over the postwar period, it may be noted that their inclusion results in a more rapid rise for the combined cost of a house and lot in the years 1957–64 than for the construction cost of a house exclusive of lot. The combined price index was divided by the deflator for personal consumption expenditures to yield a series on the relative price of new houses of fixed specifications.

In general, it was thought that credit would influence house value in two main ways: by its effect on the downpayment and by its effect on the monthly payment on interest and principal. The monthly payment is a composite that reflects the size of the mortgage, the rate of interest, and the length of the amortization period. Other things being equal, the lower the downpayment or monthly payment, the more expensive the house the purchaser may be expected to buy. There are complications, however. In some cases, a given change in credit conditions may affect both monthly payments and downpayment, and in opposite directions. For example, a change in the downpayment requirement will change the size of the mortgage and thus the monthly payments. In other cases, a change in credit conditions—e.g., a change in interest rates—will affect monthly payments but not the downpayment.

Considerable information on downpayment, length of mortgage term, and mortgage interest rates is available from FHA. An attempt was made to introduce these factors explicitly as separate independent variables; because of intercorrelations, the results were not satisfactory. In particular, the coefficients for the downpayment ratio and for the mortgage interest rate usually had the wrong sign. Accordingly, it was decided to combine the separate credit elements into a composite credit factor that would reflect changes in monthly payments.[5]

Several ordinary least squares equations were fitted to the data for the years 1947–64, using deflated average annual acquisition price as the dependent variable and real income, relative price, credit terms, and a time trend as independent variables. All variables were expressed in logs. Generally speaking, the results yielded high coefficients of determination. Results of the equation with income, price, and the composite credit variable just cited are shown immediately below.

$$\begin{aligned} {}^{\bar{v}}FHA = \; & \underset{(.002)}{1.63} + \underset{(.09)}{1.15}\,\text{Inc.} - \underset{(.40)}{.74}P - \underset{(.07).}{.34}\;CCF \\ & \bar{R}^2 = .982;\ \text{D.W.} = 1.38. \end{aligned}$$

where

${}^{\bar{v}}FHA$ = log of deflated value ("acquisition cost") of FHA new one-family houses in 1958 dollars.

Inc. = log of deflated "effective income" (in 1958 dollars) of FHA home buyers.

P = log of deflated price index for a standardized FHA house (1958 = 100).

CCF = log of composite credit factor.

As can be seen from the $\bar{R}^2$, the fit was quite good. The intercorrelation between the independent variables was high, as is usually the case in such regressions, and the Durbin-Watson test (D.W.) indicates that serial correlation was significant at the 5 percent level. Coefficients of the three independent variables all have the expected signs. The coefficients for income and credit are several times their respective standard errors, and the price coefficient is 1.85 times its standard error.

[5] The composite credit factor is based on an index of monthly payments on interest and principal. It was derived by multiplying an index of the amount of the mortgage by an index of cost per dollar of mortgage. Cost per dollar of mortgage was computed from the standard formula for level (equal) monthly payments, based in the interest rate and the length of the amortization period.

At any given time, downpayment ratios vary directly with house value. A shift over time toward more expensive houses would therefore tend to raise downpayment ratios in the absence of any change in credit conditions. In the derivation of the composite credit factor, it was necessary to exclude the influence of such shifts in order that the credit factor might reflect only changes in credit over time.

For interest rate, mortgage yield rather than nominal interest rate was used in all calculations.

The income elasticity coefficient is above unity (1.15). This estimate based on annual averages of new FHA houses is substantially higher than the cross-section elasticity estimate based on the household data in section II.

The price-elasticity coefficient of —0.74 is about midway in the range of estimates reported by others.[6] The price index data for houses, however, are of such limited quality that comparisons are not completely valid. The standard error for the price coefficient is relatively larger than the errors associated with the two other coefficients, and as is illustrated below, the price elasticity coefficient was rather unstable. The standard error at 0.4 means that a range of one standard error about the coefficient extends from —0.34 to —1.14.

The final variable in the equation is the composite credit factor, which reflects the combined influence of shifts in downpayment and mortgage ratios, mortgage yield, and length of amortization period on monthly payments. According to the equation, a 10 percent reduction in monthly payments as a result of a change in credit terms is associated with a 3.4 percent increase in the value of house acquired.

When a time trend was added to the equation, it was not statistically significant and had little effect on the value of the other coefficients; it is omitted in the equation shown. Other options were also tried. For example, the use of the Boeckh index as a deflator for house value in place of the FHA series for the cost of a standardized house resulted in little change in the coefficients, except that the income elasticity estimate was reduced to less than unity. The equation in logs is:

$$\bar{V}_{bk} = \underset{(.002)}{1.97} + \underset{(.12)}{.90}\ \text{Inc.} - \underset{(.30)}{.73P_{bk}} - \underset{(.10)}{.46}\ \text{CCF}$$

$$\bar{R}^2 = .933 \quad \text{D.W.} = 1.42$$

The symbols are the same as above, with the subscripts bk referring to the Boeckh index. The equation containing the Boeckh index did have a time trend, which was not quite significant at the 5 percent level. The inclusion of the time trend in the Boeckh equation reduced the price elasticity coefficient so that it was no longer statistically significant. Finally, an equation was also fitted using the previous year's house value as an independent variable. The results were similar to

[6] The range of estimates of price elasticity for housing is extremely wide, varying from —0.08 by James S. Duesenberry and Helen Kistin ("The Role of Demand in the Economic Structure," in Wassily Leontieff [ed.], *Studies in the Structure of the American Economy* [Oxford University Press, 1953], p. 467), to more than —1.0 by R. F. Muth ("The Demand for Nonfarm Housing," in A. C. Harberger [ed.], *The Demand for Durable Goods* [University of Chicago Press, 1960], pp. 72–3), and —1.4 by Tong Hun Lee ("The Stock Demand Elasticities for Nonfarm Housing," *Review of Economics and Statistics*, February 1964, pp. 82–9).

those shown in the equation above, with an insignificant contribution of the lagged variable.

Other Time-Series Regressions

Since one would like to know how the value of all new houses—rather than FHA houses only—is related to income, price, and credit influences, a similar set of time-series regressions was attempted for all single-family houses in the nation. The series on house value was based on the regular Census series on the construction cost of one-family nonfarm houses. The income series is the OBE personal income data divided by number of households; this average for all households is used rather than a series on the income of buyers of new houses. The deflations were carried out in the way described earlier. For the deflated house price series, alternatives based on FHA and Boeckh cost indexes were employed. The credit series was the same as that used in the FHA regression.

The results were less satisfactory than those obtained in the FHA equations. The income elasticity estimate was about the same, i.e., around unity. The credit term variable taken from the FHA data had a coefficient about the same size as in the FHA regression, but the standard error was much larger than before and not quite significant at the 5 percent level. For the price elasticity coefficient, no meaningful results were obtained with either the FHA cost for a standardized house or the Boeckh series. Finally, the use of lagged variables resulted in little change in the estimates of elasticity.

Evaluation of Results

A major contribution of the time-series analysis is the fact that credit terms appear to have significant and important effects on house value and that relative prices are important in some formulations. The extent to which the various net regression coefficients derived from the 1960 cross-section household data were affected by the particular pattern of prices and credit terms prevailing at that time cannot be determined, as was already indicated.

The net coefficient on income from the FHA time-series data (after the introduction of price and credit variables) turned out to be considerably greater than the cross-section estimates based on individual household data. The two sets of data are, of course, not comparable in terms of coverage. Conceivably, the use of "effective income" in the FHA data rather than actual income could account for some of the difference in the two estimates of income elasticity, but a limited test suggests otherwise. For six years—1958–64—both "effective" and actual income data were available from FHA reports. For the years 1959–63, the ratio of actual to effective income varied by only 1 percent; only in 1964 did actual income increase much more sharply than effective income.

There may be nonincome influences that are not included in the time-series regression and that partially account for the difference in the two estimates of income elasticity. One such influence may be education, as was suggested in the introduction to this section. Differences of this kind are by no means unique to this study. More comprehensive data are clearly needed before a start can be made in resolving the differences between the two basic approaches.

part THREE
Forecasting

INTRODUCTION

The general subject of forecasting may be divided in two ways: (1) according to the forecast period, whether short-run or long, and (2) according to the forecasting method, whether "subjective" (judgmental) or "objective" (based on economic relationships and statistical techniques). The article by John Lewis cuts across this classification, concerning itself with method in short-run forecasts. Lewis argues that many of the short-run methods are complementary, that a good combination of subjective and objective methods can achieve better forecasts than either when used alone.

The "economic indicators" approach to forecasting is an objective method discussed briefly by Geoffrey H. Moore. Subtle relationships exist between and among specific measures of economic activity such as employment, output, income, capital investment, and so on. If perceived properly, Moore says, these relationships are useful to one attempting to forecast economic developments.

An econometric method of forecasting is explained by Suits. "The compilation of an econometric model requires a certain degree of technical specialization, but once constructed any competent economist can apply it to policy analysis and economic forecasting." Suits demonstrates the statistical model to be one of the more useful and flexible devices available for economic forecasting.

American economic history is replete with dramatic ups and downs in economic activity. Periods of rapid growth have been followed often by uncomfortably long periods of decline in employment, output, and income. In an effort to plan for these downturns and perhaps to be able to guard against them via implementation of certain policy changes, academic, government, business, and labor economists attempt to forecast the future using one or more of the generally accepted forecasting methods. The question that begs itself becomes: How good are these forecasts? Stephan K. McNees interprets the forecasting performance of the early 1970s.

Input-output analysis as a tool in economic forecasting is available to us primarily because of the pioneering effort of Nobel prize-winning laureate, Wassily Leontief. His work relates the production of each industry to its consumption from every other industry.

Input-output tables are provided for the entire economy by the U.S. government. These tables differ in a statistical sense from those provided initially by Leontief; yet they are based on ideas revealed by Leontief in *Scientific American*.

9. Short-Term General Business Conditions Forecasting: Some Comments on Method*

JOHN P. LEWIS

The assignment that gave rise to this paper stipulated that I should first establish some kind of classification of general short-term forecasting techniques and then evaluate the several techniques on the basis of their showings during the past two or three years. What follows, however, does not really attempt the second of these tasks. One's impulse to construct batting averages is forestalled, for one thing, by the near impossibility of defining the universe from which a sample of representative forecasts might be drawn. Moreover, it is far harder to classify forecasters than forecasting techniques; few of us in practice are willing to stick exclusively to a particular technique, no matter how partisan to it we may be (and in this habit of mixed practice, I shall be saying, we are very wise.) Furthermore, insofar as one *can* associate particular forecasters or forecasting groups or exercises with particular techniques, the variance in recent performance is much greater between the best and worst records within particular categories than it is among the best performances in the several categories. Finally, as one who must sometimes practice the art himself, I feel, in any event, that there is a certain basic indecency about displaying forecasters' comparative batting average publicly. To do so is too much like reading a paper to an open meeting of a county medical society in which one undertakes to spell out which local doctors lost the most patients last year.

Accordingly, my purpose here will be to dwell, rather than upon batting averages, upon the potentialities for complementarity among the several major forecasting approaches. In doing so, I hope largely to avoid contentiousness, of which we have already had altogether too much with respect to short-term forecasting methodology. The central, if pious, thesis of the paper is that all of us who find ourselves engaged in the

* *Journal of Business,* vol. 35, no. 4 (October 1962), pp. 343–56.

forecasting enterprise rather urgently need every bit of quasi-respectable help we can get from one another.

I. SOME GROUND CLEARING

I propose to focus my discussion on five varieties of forecasting techniques that currently constitute the professional economic core of the activity—(1) leading indicators of the National Bureau of Economic Research (NBER) variety, (2) the leading monetary indicators that have been pioneered by Professor Milton Friedman and his associates, (3) use of those surveys of spenders' intentions and of other compilations of advance plans and commitments that, I believe, Martin Gainsbrugh was the first to label collectively as "foreshadowing indicators," (4) econometric model building, and (5) that looser, less elegant, but more comprehensive variety of model building that has been called many things, which I prefer to label "opportunistic."

These techniques have certain common characteristics. They share a certain professional respectability and orthodoxy; they are not, within the trade, regarded as crackpot approaches (although this, if one looks at the history of the art, is not necessarily a cause for reassurance). They all invite some use of the economists' trained skills; thereby they implicitly assume that a systematic marshalling of such skills can yield insights into the near-term economic future that an intelligent layman would be likely to miss. In this sense they are not diffident techniques. Finally, they all are genuinely professional techniques in that they are regimens for arriving by mainly dispassionate, quasi-objective procedures at technically honest answers to the question of what the unfolding condition of the economy is likely to be. They are not the best techniques, in other words, for telling bosses, Presidents, congressmen, and other decision makers what they want to hear. All of these techniques, to be sure, can be twisted to yield preconceived answers, but at least they create tensions—they set up conflicts of loyalties—in any conscientious professional when he is called upon to abuse them in this fashion.

By concentrating on these five varieties of technique—the two kinds of leading-indicator analysis, the foreshadowing indicators, and the two kinds of model building—we shall be leaving out of account a fair part of the total methodological terrain. We shall pass over, for example, those analytical cults whose basic forecasting hypothesis is that inexorable, rhythmical cycles in activity are so deeply rooted in the laws of the economy that all the forecaster needs to do is, first, identify the relevant cycles by penetrating the cunning veil which nature seems to cast over them; second, locate the present position of the economy in the identified cycle or cycles; and then, third, proceed to read future business conditions right off the calendar. It would be presumptuous to say that the rhythmical cycle hypothesis has no place at all in sensible forecasting practice—it has certain, although limited, uses, for example, in the inventory field—but those who retain it as their principal general forecasting doctrine have, by now, been consigned to the crackpot category, and I think deservedly so.

We also shall be passing over a rather mixed bag of forecasting practices that I have labeled elsewhere as the "agnostic techniques"—meaning by that those more or less self-evidently weak methods for probing the future to which people resort when they doubt their capacity to do anything better. They may, for example, adopt a no-change hypothesis, projecting the latest period's level to the coming period, or, if they want to be a bit more sophisticated, they may extrapolate the recent trend to future periods. In the very best contemporary forecasting, of course, there are a number of points at which practitioners still fall back on precisely this procedure. However, if no-change extrapolations were the craft's universal methodology, it would be professionally bankrupt.

General expectations surveys also belong in the "agnostic" category. I am referring now to surveys, not of respondents' spending intentions or even of their own sales expectations, but of their anticipations of general business conditions. Such general expectations surveys may provide the forecaster with some useful data of a psychological sort, but if they are viewed as producing self-contained forecasts in their own right, their use rests on the hypothesis that the blind can lead the blind—if they do it collectively, that is. Then there is that variety of forecaster whom we might call "the parasitical agnostic"—the fellow who relies, via the Joe Livingston type of survey, upon the consensus of the experts. This, of course, is a fairly sensible, if unambitious, procedure, and, in fact, such surveys are of great utility to the experts themselves. For if there is any quality that ill suits a practicing forecaster it is arrogant indifference to what others in the trade are saying. All the same, the surveying of expert expectations obviously is a derivative forecasting methodology at best; it would cease to exist if the only experts were those who were expert in surveying experts' expectations.

Gerhard Colm has suggested to me one other methodological category that ought to be included in the list, but it too I shall largely pass over here. Colm's suggestion is the "cynical" forecast, and his example is the curious inability of the Council of Economic Advisers late in the Eisenhower Administration to detect the approach or even the start of the recession of 1960–61. I would prefer a slightly less harsh label—say, the "contrived" or "ulterior-motive" forecast—and, to balance things up politically, suggest as another example the present Administration's forecast of a $570 billion GNP for 1962. This last has not entailed any violent wrenching of professional standards, but Administration economists rather plainly have been looking on the bright side for a reason.

Having brought the matter up, I want to make a couple of quick comments on central-government forecasting, particularly that done within the executive office of the president. Two separable problems are involved. One is simply the feedback problem that besets any highly influential forecaster, public or private: Shall he allow himself to be deflected by the fact that his prognostications are likely, themselves, to have some impact upon business conditions in the forecast period? The accepted answer to this question, it seems to me, is "No." An agency like the Council of Economic Advisers should do the most accurate job it can of identifying the prospects likely to emerge under existing policies. But then when, by following this no-nonsense procedure, it finds itself about to release a pessimistic forecast, it also should do what it can to see that there comes, packaged with the forecast, a program of policies whose adoption would tend to make the disappointing forecast become untrue.

The other, and much stickier, problem under which official forecasters labor is that of occasional but stubborn direct political constraints. At least two economic-policy changes presently under discussion in Washington would relax the political inhibitions under which government forecasters lately have been working. One is the proposed delegation of increased standby stabilization powers to the president. This would weaken the presently inhibiting assumption that the tempo of adjustments in fiscal policy directed by business conditions necessarily should match the tempo of our congressional and electoral calendars. The second—and, in this context, the more important—reform may occur in the field of budgeting practice. Moves are under way to deflate further the traditional administrative budget concept and, in particular, to inject some sort of business-style distinction between capital and current outlays into federal accounting. Such a change, which would parallel the standard practice in most West European countries, could, as one of its by-products, greatly ease the constraint that the balanced-budget fetish has been imposing on responsible forecasters.

But I stray too far afield. For the ulterior-motive type, like the agnostic and rhythmical-cycle types, of forecasting lies beyond the boundaries to which I want to confine the burden of this discussion.

II. SOME LIMITATIONS OF THE TECHNIQUES USED SINGLY

As for the central core of professional short-term forecasting techniques, a commentator at this juncture, I think, must deliberately choose what the mood of his commentary is going to be. One could readily take a very bullish view of things, for the state of the art plainly is greatly improved from its condition a generation or even a decade ago. It would be equally legitimate, however, to adopt a thoroughly bearish stance and enlarge on the theme that, when you come right down to it, we are still practicing alchemy, not chemistry. So long as two intelligent persons or groups practicing the "same" techniques can come out with radically different forecasting answers, our scientific pretensions do not become us very well.

As indicated already, however, my own choice of a theme is neither gloom nor buoyancy but, rather, synthesis. I want to emphasize the complementarity of the several techniques we have under inspection, and this can best be done in two stages. First, I want to suggest some of the weaknesses that each of the five conventionally respectable techniques exhibits as a self-sufficient, go-it-alone device. But then, second, I want to underscore the contribution that each of these techniques can make to a properly comprehensive and synthesized forecasting exercise.

A. NBER Leading Indicators

The point has been rather widely made by now that the National Bureau of Economic Research type of leading indicator analysis constitutes a good bit less than a complete set of forecasting tools. This comes as no shock to the more responsible users and proponents of leads-and-lags analysis. However, a brief summary of the limitations of the method may still be in order. They seem to me to be these:

In the first place, the NBER leading indicators are inherently weak devices for detecting the *magnitude* of coming changes in business conditions. Their purpose is the detection of coming turning points, but, despite the improvements that Julius Shiskin lately has attempted in this regard, they have little capacity for disclosing how sharp the turn will be or how high or deep the upswing or downswing will go.

In the second place, the leading indicators as a group are quite short-range devices. Even if there were no problem of garbled signals, they would, as a group, give us no more than six months' advance notice of a coming downturn in the economy—and far less than that in the case of upturns.

In the third place, there *is* a problem of garbled signals. Looked at individually the leading indicators series run jagged courses. When any given wiggle occurs it usually takes two or three months to tell whether the leading indicator really has turned a significant corner or not, and by then, of course, much of its lead has been eaten up. Moreover, the leads of the particular indicators are not consistent from cycle to cycle, making it difficult to guess how soon a signaled change may occur. More important, the several leading indicators almost never all point in the same direction, especially in months just prior to general turns in business conditions. And while the "diffusion indexes" represent a natural and probably necessary attempt to cope with this last problem, they suppress most of the illuminating detail in the series that underlie them; typically they give no weight to the magnitudes of the expansions and contractions in the component series; they weight all of the components together as if they were of equal intrinsic importance; and, despite all of this, the diffusion indexes themselves are highly irregular in their movements.

Finally, as a self-sufficient technique, the leads-and-lags approach has this major limitation: it implicitly assumes a very high degree of structural rigidity in the economy. It has no adequate way of coping, for example, with major changes in the structure of demand. It is in such terms, I think, that one must explain the few past occasions—in 1951, 1956, and in 1959—on which the leading indicators have given concerted and prolonged false signals.

B. The Leading Monetary Indicators

The rest of us are much indebted to Friedman and his colleagues for emphasizing in recent years the degree to which the rate of change in the money supply tends to lead changes in general business activity, and changes in monetary reserves lead the money supply, and changes in central bank policy lead monetary reserves. The efforts to marshal the evidence underlying these assertions, to establish a format for the presentation of pertinent indicators, and to interest some of our reserve banks and other financial institutions in their publication have been all to the good.

Despite my reading of some of Friedman's writings on the subject and several lucid papers by Beryl Sprinkel, however, I confess to some confusion as to how far the proponents of the leading monetary indicators mean to go in claiming self-sufficiency for them as forecast devices. This confusion is rooted, in turn, in my confusion about the theoretical debate from which advocacy of the leading monetary indicators seems to emerge.

I am rather puzzled by the alleged contest between so-called modern quantity theory and the better contemporary versions of what is called income and expenditure theory. It seems to me just as evident that early Keynesian theory went much too far in underrating the role of money as a determinant of general economic activity even as the quantity theorists of the twenties went too far in overrating it. Surely it was a mistake to believe that the frail stem of the money rate of interest could bear the full burden of the impact of finance and financial institutions on investment activity, just as it was a mistake to talk as if monetary and credit conditions had a direct impact only on investment and not also upon such other sectors as consumer buying of durables and state and local government outlays. I should have supposed that today just about any journeyman analyst of the so-called income and expenditure persuasion, and certainly any sensible forecaster working in that tradition, is, therefore, vitally concerned with monetary prospects. That, indeed, is precisely why such analysts are very *much* interested in the current posture of the Federal Reserve and are sometimes critical of it. And that is why they prize the help Friedman et al. are giving us in identifying the time linkages that seem to relate changes in monetary policy to changes in the availability and cost of finance.

But to go beyond this to the opposite extreme and accept the leading monetary indicators as *sufficient* tools for predicting general business conditions would seem to me a most bizarre procedure. It would rest on the hypothesis that, for predictive purposes, the economy could be treated as if central bank decision making were the only significant independent variable in the system. For better or worse, things are more complicated than this. The capacity for influential autonomous decision making is far more widely dispersed. Considerable quantities of it lodge also, for example, in the Congress, in the White House, in the Finance Committee of the United States Steel Corporation, in Detroit, in all the great industrial houses and major labor organizations in the country and, even, in fifty million households. The responsible general forecaster must, somehow or other, directly concern himself with all of this pivotal decision making, not just with a particular slice of it. Academically, it is an interesting exercise to imagine that one had to settle for a single, go-it-alone set of predictive indicators and then debate the question of which would be the more reliable—the monetary set or some other? But this is a good deal like the question with which good book would you most like to be cast on a desert isle? Neither question has much practical relevance. As a practical matter, there seems to be no reason for the general forecaster to confine himself to so spare and oversimplified a predictive hypothesis as sole reliance upon the leading monetary indicators would imply.

I do not mean to accuse Friedman and his associates of actually advocating exclusive reliance upon their wares, but some of their arguments have seemed to me susceptible to such a misinterpretation. The leading monetary indicators also have two more specific limitations.

First, the series on changes in monetary reserves and in the money supply, even after seasonal adjustment, are, like many of the NBER leading indicators, subject to rather violent gyrations. Thus it is much harder to detect, from the current data, a change of direction in the smoothed trends of these series than might first appear when one looks at the dramatic shifts in the ex post multimonth averages that the published charts of these series typically display.

Second, I would make the strange-sounding complaint that the average lead that the rate of change in the money supply is alleged to have over general cyclical downturns—namely, some twenty months since the mid-twenties, is really too *long* to be very useful for forecasting purposes. Recent cyclical fluctuations in the American economy have appeared more or less to have followed a three-phase format. In a recession phase activity falls away from its long-term growth trend. In a second, recovery phase, it moves back up toward the long-term trend. But then, in a third, normal-growth or normal-prosperity phase, it moves *along* the trend. And this is the key point: most of us would say that it is impossible to predict at the time it starts how long this third, along-the-trend phase of the cycle is likely to be. There are certain internal dynamics within the system that may tend roughly to govern the durations of most recession and recovery phases. But the duration of the prosperity phase probably is another matter; it appears to depend upon the particular sequence of demands—first, in autos, for example, then in plant and equipment or national defense, and then perhaps in state and local government—that happens to emerge as a result of the particular combination of decision making that occurs in a particular field.

Thus to tell me—as in effect the monetary change indicator does—that these prosperity, along-the-trend phases of cycles since the 20s have *averaged* about 20 months really does not help very much. It gives me no confidence at all that such will be the case this particular time. Especially it gives me no such confidence if I believe, as I do, that there is nothing inevitable or immutable about cyclical rhythms and that deliberate discretionary changes in federal fiscal and monetary policies often decisively affect the duration of prosperity periods.

C. Foreshadowing Data

If it is jousting with a straw man to disprove the self-sufficiency of the leading indicators as forecast devices, it would be still worse to belabor the point that foreshadowing data—the spenders' intentions surveys, the federal budget, contract construction awards, new orders of durable goods manufacturers, and so on—do not in themselves constitute a full kit of forecasting tools. For I know of no serious developer or advocate of such data who has ever hinted that they can single-handedly generate a forecast. On the contrary, there has from the beginning been an alliance between the assemblers of foreshadowing data and model builders, especially of the less elegant, looser persuasion, with the former, of course, supplying much of the latter's inputs. For the sake of the present record, however, and because one still does occasionally encounter people who seem to think that if we could only finish the job of blanketing the GNP with intentions surveys, we would have the forecasting problem licked, let me venture just a few comments on the limitations of the foreshadowing series.

In the past the approach has been constrained by sheer problems of technique—for one thing, in the area of sampling and survey methods, and for another thing, with respect to the interpretation of the sequences of decreasingly tentative expectations and decreasingly conditional decisions into which the surveys from time to time dip. Franco Modigliani, however, has made sense of this latter matter, and certainly our better sampling and survey technology has become highly sophisticated. It is my layman's impression, therefore, that technical problems no longer are the real roadblocks in the area.

However, the coverage of the foreshadowing series is not yet all that it might be. There are some gaps—notably in the case of state and local government outlays—where spenders do indeed make advance plans, commitments, or conditional spending decisions (in the case of state and local governments they are a matter of public record) but where we simply have no agency yet that has assumed the task of systematically collecting or sampling and collating them.

But there are major segments of the GNP—notably in the area of consumer soft goods and services—that are destined, I should think, to remain effectively immune to intentions surveys, no matter how willing the surveyors may be, for the simple reason that buyers in these fields do not do enough coherent advance planning so that they themselves can recognize and report it.

Finally, there is the familiar but important point that the existence of plans, even strongly intentioned plans, offers no assurance that they will be carried out. The forecaster must convert the finding of an intentions survey into a forecast at his own peril. In particular when he makes such a conversion he must assume that the general economic developments that the expenditure planner does *not* foresee are not going to thwart his spending intentions. Modigliani has supplied us with a very intriguing refinement of this point—namely, that if the survey can canvass a respondent's sales or income expectations at the same time it canvasses his spending intentions and if it can be shown that past discrepancies between intended and actual outlays have been related to the discrepancies between expected and actual sales or incomes, it may be possible systematically to "correct" the intentions figure for forecasting purposes—*if* the forecaster is in a position to second-guess respondents' reported sales or income expectations. This approach seems to me to have considerable promise: perhaps even more in the fields of consumer intentions and of business inventory intentions, than in the plant and equipment sector where Modigliani first experimented with it. But as he emphasizes it must be used within the framework of a general model-building exercise. For only in such a context would the forecaster have any real basis for judging that spenders' expectations of future sales or incomes are unlikely to be realized. Modigliani's point, in other words, only underscores the conclusion that foreshadowing series are not go-it-alone devices.

D. Econometric Models

I shall focus my remarks about the limitations of general short-term econometric forecasting upon the single example of the present version of the original Klein-Goldberger model over which Daniel Suits now presides at the University of Michigan. This is one of the oldest econometric forecasting exercises with a continuous work record. It would appear to be fairly representative of its genus. And, for our purposes, it has the overwhelming advantage of just having been laid out for all of us to see in Suits's lucid article in the March 1962 *American Economic Review.*

Judging from this sample of one, we can draw the happy conclusion that econometric forecasting has been in process recently of getting constructively corrupted. In the course of drafting my book on *Business Conditions Analysis* about five years ago, I was casting about for a sharp distinction to be drawn between econometric model building and the less rigorous varieties that I call "opportunistic." I hit on these propositions. A true econometrician was a man, first, who insisted on cranking his forecast out of his explicit simultaneous-equation model without hedging or judgmental adjustment. He insisted, second, upon selecting all of the independent variables in his equations and deriving all of their parameters from an analysis of historical time series. By this definition, Suits no longer is an econometrician—which is to say, the definition is out of date.

There are two striking concessions that Suits's present methodology makes to the "practical" considerations espoused by opportunistic model builders. First, he now freely plugs in—instead of a rather lame investment function that makes business fixed capital spending wholly dependent on last year's profits and last year's growth in plant-and-equipment stock—an intentions-survey result (in this case, the McGraw-Hill) as his business fixed-investment input. (Incidentally, he has not yet, so far as I can tell, adopted the Modigliani proposal for making a systematic correction in the intentions figure to compensate for the "error" in investors' sales expectations.) Second, the Michigan team now evidently feels free to tinker with the "*a*" constants in any or all of its linear equations to make allowance for judgmental considerations regarding the particular year at hand that it feels the formal model does not adequately encompass. In short, you might say that the Michigan group has become nothing but a bunch of elegant opportunists—and with good results. Its forecast record since it began corrupting its model in this considered fashion is a good bit better than it was in the early and middle fifties.

As it is represented by the present Michigan exercise, therefore, econometric model building already has gone a long way toward overcoming limitations with which I would have charged it a few years ago. But it is still far short of having surmounted its basic problem of excessive rigidity—that is, in effect, excessive simplification. To attempt to cram the myriad complexity of the economy into even a thirty-two-equation model entails, as Suits is careful to emphasize, an heroic abstraction. This is evident if one considers the model's lack of nimbleness in adjusting to the sort of temporary and significant but unusual development that is forever cropping up and of which the looser model builder routinely takes account. For example, most opportunistic model builders, I should suppose, added a bit extra to their inventory investment estimates for the first quarter of 1962 to allow for some steel stockpiling and then shaved their second and/or third quarter estimates a compensating amount. The Suits model has no explicit, untinkered-with capacity for handling such refinements. Its limitations become most evident if one considers the stark simplicity of the theories of sector-demand determination that underlie some of its expenditure equations.

Indeed, I would urge sector-demand specialists who have not already done so to look carefully in Suits' March 1962 article in the *American Economic Review* at the demand functions for their own particular sectors—at the equations, for example, for automobiles, for other consumer durables, and for housing starts. They are apt to find themselves a bit amazed that a forecasting technique that indulges in such gross oversimplifications with respect to the particular sectors in which they are expert can produce such generally good GNP forecasts as the Michigan model has done in recent years. That it can, of course, is dramatic testimony to the importance in general forecasting of that quality which is econometric model building's particular strength—namely, the quality of internal consistency. Even when many of its sector legs rest on quite mushy foundations, a model of the economy whose income-distribution and receipts, expenditures, and savings relationships all are internally consistent, judged by past experience, has a pretty fair chance of hitting the aggregates. But this does not mean that mushy sector forecasting and an incapacity for encompassing the idiosyncrasies of a particular period are admirable qualities in their own right.

E. Opportunistic Model Building

It is almost a contradiction in terms to imagine the looser forms of model building as being self-sufficient with respect to the other techniques. For the very essence of this approach—the reason I call it "opportunistic"—is its scavenging quality. Opportunistic model building is a procedure for gathering data, information, and insights of just about any conceivably relevant kind and for assembling them, in some orderly manner, into a coherent and quantified statement of prospects. I already have mentioned this approach's particularly heavy dependence upon inputs of foreshadowing data; in addition, sensible practitioners have ravenous appetites for help of other kinds.

Nevertheless, as a kind of horrible example, one can conjure up an imaginary forecaster who might take some pleasure in thinking of himself as a model builder and would indeed express his outlook judgments in the form of a GNP breakdown. But his would be strictly a laundry-list style of forecasting. He would simply go down the sector list, making up forward estimates, one by one, by some intuitive process out of whatever mix of past data, current gossip, and recent comments in the business press he happened to have at hand. He would not even bother to avail himself of the foreshadowing data systematically. He would ignore the insights that the NBER leading indicators might give him into the timing of coming changes in general activity and the help that the leading monetary indicators could supply as to prospective money and credit conditions. He would simply put down his sector forecasts, tot them up, and call the sum his forecast. The entire theory of aggregate demand determination underlying his analysis would consist of the national-income accounting identity that the GNP equals the sum of its parts. His analysis would contemplate no intersectoral, no income-expenditure, and no asset-expenditure interactions. The only internal-consistency test to which it would submit would be one to make sure that the GNP components did, indeed, add up to the total. And his mathematical requirements would be limited, not just to arithmetic, but to addition and subtraction.

Although I have called the foregoing an imaginary horrible example, a good bit of the actual short-term forecasting being done today comes uncomfortably close to fitting this description. This serves only to prove that something fairly close to go-it-alone opportunistic model building is, indeed, possible. But it also, it seems to me, is almost self-evidently foolish.

III. THE OPPORTUNITY FOR SYNTHESIS

So much for my argument that none of our five major short-term forecasting techniques is an island—at least not a very successful island when a consolidation of the five is perfectly feasible. The case for consolidation already has been anticipated considerably in the case against separatism. Thus I propose to enlarge on it only briefly, and shall do so in a moment.

A. A Few Substantive Comments on Opportunistic Model Building

First, by way of an aside, I want to get in a few somewhat more explicit licks on the craft of opportunistic model building. These are intended mainly as discussion provokers; I shall put my points very sketchily and, in a couple of cases, vulnerably.

The Usefulness of a Capacity Concept. The most controversial of the points I want to make about model-building practice is that such analysis can be greatly assisted by the incorporation of an explicit capacity concept. One must grant, of course, that capacity is a fuzzy, ambiguous, imprecise, not directly measured variable. But it generalizes about characteristics of the economy that are objective, dated, and vitally important. In one guise or another it is an essential concept for the general forecaster if he is going to discharge his ultimate function, which is to predict the basic healthiness of economic activity in a coming period. For that healthiness will depend most pivotally not on the absolute level of output but on the relationship between output and normal productive capacity. Such is plainly the crucial consideration, for one thing, in the case of general price prospects. For it is quite impossible to formulate any working hypothesis about the price-output relationships that changes in demand will encounter during a forecast period without formulating, at least implicitly, some assumption about the level and growth rate of capacity during the period.

The prospective relationship of capacity to output, adjusted for cyclical variations in output per man-hour, in the labor force, and in average working hours, likewise is the pivotal consideration for unemployment forecasting. Thus, although a model-building group may keep its capacity estimates invisible to the naked eye, as, for example, Suits's group does at Michigan, implicitly they are present in one form or another if the group is attempting to do a comprehensive forecasting job. The best procedure, I think, is to bring the capacity estimates out into the open where they can be seen and be argued about.

The Need for Explicit Sector Income Estimates. A second practice that I would urge upon opportunistic model builders is the construction of a model that forces the analyst to make explicit the breakdown of the gross national income into net receipts of governments, net foreign transfers by government, gross retained earnings of business, and disposable personal income that he is setting over against his final-demand breakdown. For only by this means does one have a framework that facilitates allowance for the impacts of expenditures in one sector upon those in others and that permits very much of the internal-consistency testing that is model building's greatest potential advantage.

If I read him rightly, Friedman may raise an eyebrow at this suggestion on the ground that I am asking for models with built-in multipliers, and that it can be shown that in this economy during the past several decades "investment multipliers," or "autonomous sector" multipliers have in fact been highly unreliable phenomena. With Friedman's findings of fact I heartily agree; indeed, they are what I would expect since I believe that the stability characteristics of the economy have been considerably improved during the past generation, with most of that improvement taking the form of just such a weakening of the intersectoral cumulative mechanisms as Friedman's findings suggest. In particular, we beneficently have managed, partly thanks to the so-called built-in stabilizers, greatly to reduce the sensitivity of disposable personal income (DPI) to declines in the GNP.

However, the inference for forecasting practice that I draw from all this is not that multiplier effects therefore should be banned from outlook models but rather than they require considerably more elaborate treatment than our simplified textbook theories of a few years back seemed to suggest. In a little semiannual forecast exercise that we run at Indiana, for example, we do three things. First, we separate consumer durables from the rest of consumption and treat them as a quasi-autonomous sector of the same sort as housing or plant and equipment. This is on the thesis that the aggregate of consumer soft goods and services is a much more stable function of DPI than is total consumption. Second (and this is the newest wrinkle of the three in our practice) we nevertheless treat the relation between soft goods and services consumption as being cyclically variable within fairly narrow limits. Third, and most important, we explicitly forecast the ratios of DPI to personal income and of personal income to GNP, treating both of these also as being cyclically variable.

Thus, in effect, we systematically incorporate into the model a rather highly variable multiplier that, in particular, takes explicit account of the tax-less-transfers and retained-earnings leakages between GNP and DPI. Rightly or wrongly, we attribute most of the very good luck that we have had with the exercise the last two or three times around to the more careful efforts we have been making along these lines.

Inventories and Net Exports. My other two substantive comments are far narrower in scope, and I shall no more than mention them. Both concern matters rather urgently in need of further investigation. First, it appears to me that our forecasting doctrines for inventory investment presently are in a state of some theoretical disarray. Having become rather thoroughly disenchanted with the practical usefulness of inventory-sales ratios as guides for inventory forecasting, many of us have become rather excited about the greater utility of new orders and order backlogs as indicators of prospective changes in manufacturers' inventories. In this we have followed the lead, for example, of the Duesenberry-Eckstein-Fromm model of a few years ago. The trouble, however, is that this new doctrine really makes sense only for those industries that produce to order, not to stock, and have little or no finished-goods inventory. Consequently, for improved inventory forecasting I suspect that we need a considerably more disaggregated approach than is now customary; we need to know a good bit more than published data presently reveal of the differing degrees to which different manufacturing sectors rely, on the one hand, upon order backlogs and, on the other, upon finished-goods inventories for cushioning the lags of their output behind their demand; knowing this, we need to forecast changes in manufacturing inventories by fabrication stages; and, I suspect, in the case of manufacturers' finished stocks as well as trade inventories we need to hark back to inventory-sales ratios but with renewed attention to inventory-cycle models.

The other point is simply that net-export forecasting is in a bad way because of the average forecaster's or forecasting group's inability to make any closely reasoned prediction of exports. With the passing of the dollar shortage it no longer is legitimate to assume that the volume of United States exports will be determined simply by the volume of dollars that the United States supplies to the rest of the world through its imports and its transfers abroad of public and private capital. But lacking this short cut, the general forecaster is left with an apparent but impossible need to predict demand developments the world over if he is to make a considered estimate of United States exports. Because of the comparatively narrow limits with which net exports move, the problem is not a particularly serious one for the aggregate domestic forecast. But if anyone can come up with a new legitimate short cut to export prediction, he certainly at least will ease the consciences of many of us.

B. Joining the Techniques Together

By way of conclusion, let me indicate how the five forecasting techniques upon which we have been focusing can sensibly complement one another. Perhaps this can be conveyed most succinctly by describing what I would regard as an ideal short-term forecasting exercise.

In the first place, this would be a group exercise. Outlook analysis is an activity, I think, in which the group has an inherent advantage over the lone wolf, partly because it benefits from a division of labor, partly because it must be considerably judgmental and gains from an effort to achieve a consensus. Second, it would be a continuing exercise.

I frankly would become bored as a member of a staff that gave its uninterrupted attention to the business outlook, and there are comparatively few organizations that could afford a fairly elaborate staff that had this single function. However, we are conjuring up an ideal, and there is no denying the expertise that comes with daily immersion in the outlook problem. Third, it would be a rather highly structured exercise. The free-wheeling virtuosity of gifted seat-of-the-pants analysts always is impressive, but it also is commonly overrated, and it has very little transferability. One quality of an ideal forecasting organization would be a considerable ability to maintain continuity despite changes in personnel. Well-defined tasks, procedures, and analytical doctrines would all contribute to this end.

I would place at the head of such a staff a seasoned opportunistic model-builder with a good measure of forecasting experience, theoretical sophistication, and executive ability. I would associate with him three deputy directors, each of whom would have cognizance of the whole operation. One Friedman would be asked to nominate; one Geoffrey Moore or Arthur F. Burns would nominate; and the third would be a first-class econometrician whose professional sensibilities, however, did not bruise too easily. The balance of the staff would be composed mainly of specialists who were immersed in the lore and data of particular demand and/or industry sectors.

The format of my idealized exercise would be a simultaneous equation model—indeed, a far more elaborate model than that presently employed at Michigan—and all members of the staff would require the limited command of mathematics necessary for translating their views into the terminology of such a model and for comprehending its manipulation. The point here would be for the exercise to avail itself of the maximum internal-consistency insurance, and its feasibility would depend upon ready and continuing access to adequate electronic computer services.

The equations in the model, however, would be subject to constant tending. Variables (and, as necessary, equations) would be added or subtracted and parameters would be altered as fast as, and for whatever reason, the staff judged such changes appropriate. In fact, each equation would constitute a summary statement of the staff's presently operative forecasting doctrine for the particular demand sector or the particular income relationship involved. It would be the responsibility of each sector forecaster to keep his equation(s) in a continuing state of repair so that at any given moment the most accurate forecast of which the staff currently was collectively capable, with the help of a computer, could be cranked out of the model with minimum delay.

Foreshadowing data with built-in adjustments, where appropriate, along the lines that Modigliani suggests would figure very prominently as inputs into the model. Monetary and credit variables would be more explicitly knit into the model than has been customary with econometric models to date, with the leading monetary indicators being incorporated as lead devices for signaling later changes in the money supply and credit availability. Moreover, despite the realistic complexity that would be built into the model, the forecasting staff would not consider its findings to be inexorably bound to the model results. In particular, the NBER leading indicators would be used as an independent aid for timing prospective changes of course in the economy, a feat at which opportunistic model building is notoriously clumsy.

This, perhaps, is enough to convey the gist of what I have in mind. Few of us, probably, ever will work in circumstances that closely parallel the conditions just sketched. But at least we can strive for whatever intertechnique collaboration fits our particular scale of operations. We can recognize that not merely should the several respectable short-term forecasting techniques be able to coexist; they have far more to gain from outright alliance than they do from internecine bickering.

10. The Analysis of Economic Indicators*

GEOFFREY H. MOORE

Business cycles, large and small, appear to be a continuing feature of the economic landscape. A turn up or down in the economy is clearly an event of major social significance. Considerable interest therefore attaches to the means whereby an economic turn can be forecast and its extent can be estimated. That is the role of economic indicators, which rest on the numerous measurements of the pulse of the economy made by government agencies, private organizations and individual economists. The analysis of economic indicators (a subject in which my colleagues and I at the National Bureau of Economic Research have been much interested) is a well-developed technique for ascertaining what the many pulse readings are saying about the state of the economy.

Economic indicators are often likened to a barometer because they register some significant aspect of the performance of the economy, are sensitive to changes in the economic climate and may portend further changes. A barometer, however, measures only one characteristic of the atmosphere. Moreover, the barometer itself does not cause a change in the weather. Hence it is frequently in a disparaging sense that the term barometer is applied to an economic indicator; the implication is that the indicator is only a barometer, having no real causal significance and covering only a small part of what one should know about economic change.

Such characterizations may apply to many individual economic indicators, but they do not apply to indicators as a class. Economic indicators have come to embrace virtually all the quantitative measures of economic change that are continuously available. One can find daily, weekly, monthly and quarterly indicators; they measure production, prices, incomes, employment, investment, inventories, sales, and so on, and they record plans, commitments, and anticipations as well as recent transactions. Some of the indicators, such as the unemployment rate or the consumer price index, are calculated by the federal government on

* *Scientific American*, vol. 232, no. 1 (January 1975), pp. 17–23.

the basis of elaborate sampling surveys conducted each month. Others, such as the indexes of stockmarket prices and the surveys by purchasing agents of prices, orders, and inventories, are constructed by private organizations on the basis of information they collect or obtain as a by-product.

As a result the economist or businessman interested in forecasting change is faced, like the weather forecaster, with a mass of factual information that pours in constantly. He must assess in some systematic way what the information says about the present and the future. The technique of indicator analysis embraces various systematic ways of looking at this information with a view to discerning significant developments in the business cycle.

One of the earliest systems of the kind, which was devised shortly before World War I, came to be known as the Harvard ABC curves. The A curve was an index representing speculation, more specifically stock prices. The B curve represented business activity, measured by the dollar volume of checks drawn on bank deposits. The C curve represented the money market, measured by the rate of interest on short-term commercial loans. Historical studies, particularly those carried out by Warren Persons of Harvard University, showed that these three curves typically moved in sequence: stock prices first, bank debits next, and interest rates last, with the lagging turns in interest rates preceding the opposite turns in stock prices. The economic logic of the sequence was that tight money and high interest rates led to a decline in business prospects and a drop in stock prices, which led to cutbacks in investment and a recession in business. The recession in turn led to easier money and lower interest rates, which eventually improved business prospects, lifted stock prices, and generated a new expansion of economic activity.

The system came to grief in the Great Depression of 1929 because the interpreters of the curves took too optimistic a view and failed to foresee the debacle. Economists generally regard the episode as one of the great forecasting failures of all time. Curiously, however, the timing of the sequence of events on which the system was originally based has in large measure persisted. This is not to say, however, that the ABC curves would still suffice if they were revised; since 1929 much more comprehensive systems of indicators have been developed, and the empirical and theoretical base on which they stand has been far more thoroughly studied, documented, and tested.

The sharp recession of 1937–1938, which occurred before the economy had fully recovered from the Great Depression, helped to spur that development. In the fall of 1937 Henry Morgenthau, Jr., the Secretary of the Treasury, asked the National Bureau of Economic Research (which is a private, nonprofit research agency) to devise a system of indicators that would signal when the recession was nearing an end. At that time the quantitative analysis of economic performance in the U.S. did not approach today's standards. The government's national income and product accounts, which form the foundation of much modern economic analysis, were just being established. Other vital economic statistics, including unemployment rates, were being developed or refined by public agencies trying to provide information that would be useful in fighting the depression. Few statistical series were issued in seasonally adjusted form, as they are now. Comprehensive econometric models (systems of equations expressing quantitative relations among economic variables), which are widely employed now to forecast the economy and to evaluate economic policies, were virtually unknown then.

Under the leadership of Wesley C. Mitchell and Arthur F. Burns the National Bureau of Economic Research had since the 1920s assembled and analyzed a vast amount of monthly, quarterly, and annual data on prices, employment, production, and other factors as part of a major research effort aimed at gaining a better understanding of business cycles. This project enabled Mitchell and Burns to select a number of series that, on the basis of past performance and of relevance in the business cycle, promised to be fairly reliable indicators of business revival. The list was given to the Treasury Department late in 1937 in response to Morgenthau's request and was published in May 1938. Thus originated the system of leading, coincident, and lagging indicators widely employed today in analyzing the economic situation, determining what factors are favorable or unfavorable, and forecasting short-term developments.

Since 1938 the availability, the study, and the use of economic indicators have been greatly expanded under the leadership of the National Bureau of Economic Research, the U.S. Bureau of the Census, and other public and private agencies. The list of indicators assembled in 1937 was revised in 1950, 1960, and 1966 to take account of the availability of new economic series, new research findings, and changes in the structure of the economy. A new evaluation is currently in progress under the auspices of the U.S. Department of Commerce. With each revision the performance of the indicators both before and after the date of their selection has been carefully examined and exposed to public scrutiny.

In 1957 Raymond J. Saulnier, who was then chairman of the President's Council of Economic Advisers, asked the Bureau of the Census to develop methods whereby the appraisal of current business fluctuations could take advantage of the large-scale electronic data processing that was becoming available at the time, with the results to be issued in a monthly report. Experimental work done over the next few years under the leadership of Julius Shiskin, who was the chief economic statistician of the Bureau of the Census, resulted (in 1961) in the publication by the Department of Commerce of *Business Cycle Develop-*

ments. (It is now called *Business Conditions Digest;* under both names economists have referred to it as *BCD,* and those initials appear on its cover in larger type than the full name does.) This monthly publication has greatly increased the accessibility of current indicator data and of various statistical devices that aid in their interpretation. As a result the analysis of the indicators has become a major tool of economic forecasting among the economists whose interest is in the current and future performance of the economy.

As I have noted, the analysis of economic indicators rests on an empirical footing and a theoretical one. Both the selection of particular indicators and the emphasis given to them have been guided by what is understood of the causes of business cycles. Obviously one would wish to examine recent changes in any economic process that is believed to play a significant role in any widely accepted explanation of cyclical fluctuations.

Many different explanations have been advanced for these fluctuations. Some of them lay primary stress on the swings in investment in inventory and fixed capital that both determine and are determined by movements in final demand. Others assign a central role to the supply of money and credit or to government spending and tax policies or to relations among prices, costs, and profits.

All these factors undoubtedly influence the course of business activity. Some of them may be more important at a given time than others. No consensus exists, however, on which is the most important or even on how they all interact. Hence it is prudent to work with a variety of indicators representing a broad range of influences. Ready access to a wide range of indicator data enables one to test competing or complementary hypotheses about current economic fluctuations.

With this principle in mind the National Bureau of Economic Research has classified economic activities into a few broad categories of closely related processes that are significant from the business-cycle point of view. Indicators have been selected from each group. The principal categories now included in *Business Conditions Digest* are employment and unemployment; production, income, consumption, and trade; fixed capital investment; inventories and inventory investment; prices, costs, and profits; money and credit; foreign trade and payments, and federal government activities (table 1).

The reader will note that these categories do not include all aspects of the economy. For example, statistics on agriculture, state and local government, population and wealth are omitted. Nevertheless, the categories do provide a framework of factors that enter into theories of the business cycle and are important in assessing the performance of the economy.

Within each category research on business cycles has uncovered sta-

TABLE 1

Economic Process	Relation to Business Cycle			
	Leading	*Roughly Coincident*	*Lagging*	*Unclassified*
	Average workweek and overtime	Job vacancies		
Employment and unemployment	Hiring and layoff rates	Total employment and unemployment	Long-duration unemployment	
	New unemployment insurance claims			
Production, income, consumption, and trade		Total production, income, and sales		
Fixed capital investment	New investment commitments	Backlog of investment commitments	Investment expenditures	
	Formation of business enterprises			
Inventories and inventory investment	Inventory investment and purchasing		Inventories	

Prices, costs, and profits	Sensitive commodity prices Stock prices Profits and profit margins Cash flow	Wholesale price index for industrial commodities	Labor costs per unit of output	Consumer price index
	Money and credit flows	Bank reserves	Outstanding debt	
Money and credit	Credit delinquencies and business failures	Interest rates on money market	Mortgage and bank-loan rates	
Foreign trade and payments				Imports, exports, and export orders Balance of payments
Activities of federal government				Receipts and expenditures Defense orders, contracts, and purchases

Classification of indicators is done in two ways. One is by major economic process, such as employment and unemployment. The other is according to the relation the indicators have to turns in the business cycle. The leading, roughly coincident, and lagging indicators shown in the table represent only a small portion of the many indicators that are normally classified in this way.

tistical series that behave in a systematic way. These findings have provided a basis for selecting particular indicators and classifying them according to their characteristic cyclical behavior (see figure 1). Two of the chief characteristics one looks for are the regularity with which the indicator conforms to business cycles and the consistency with which it leads or lags at turning points in the cycles. Other relevant considerations are the statistical adequacy of the data (since the statistical underpinning of an indicator has a bearing on how well the indicator represents the process it is supposed to reflect), the smoothness of the data (since highly erratic series are difficult to interpret at a given point in time), and the promptness with which the figures are published (since out-of-date figures have a limited bearing on the current situation).

Empirical measures of these characteristics have been drawn up for large numbers of indicators in the categories listed above. Such measures have been employed in the attempt to obtain data capable of conveying an adequate picture of the changes in the economy as it moves through stages of prosperity and recession. In addition the behavior of the indicators after they have been selected has been monitored closely. Many of the indicators have survived several successive evaluations. For example, the indexes of the average workweek, construction contracts, and stock prices were on both the 1937 and 1966 lists of the National Bureau of Economic Research.

The same lists of indicators have also been tested by their performance in other countries, notably Canada, Japan, and the United Kingdom. Every new recession or slowdown provides additional evidence against which the indicators can be assessed, as does every upturn. All this examination and reexamination has accumulated a large amount of empirical evidence that demonstrates both the value of the indicators and their limitations.

A sampling of this evidence is contained in the accompanying illustrations. Let us consider the indicator called the quit rate, which measures the number of people in manufacturing industries (per 100 employed) who voluntarily leave their jobs (see figures 2 and 3). The raw data are statistically decomposed in order to measure and eliminate regular seasonal variations and irregular movements. With factors that are unrelated to the business cycle thus removed, the indicator reveals the tendency for quits to diminish during a recession as new jobs become harder to find and to increase when more prosperous conditions return. The seasonally adjusted quit rate therefore reflects the view that workers have of the labor market and of economic prospects generally.

Most economic indicators today are available in seasonally adjusted form. Some of them are seldom reported in any other way. Examples of indicators that are invariably adjusted for seasonal factors include the gross national product, the unemployment rate, and the index of industrial production.

FIGURE 1

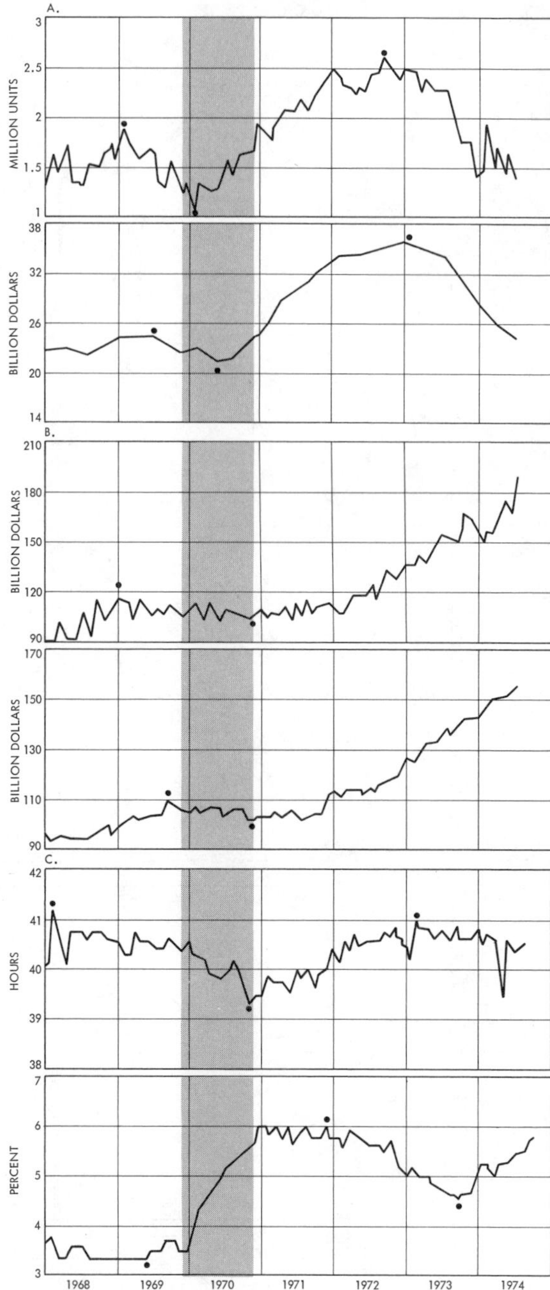

Relations among indicators are traced through the business-cycle contraction of 1969–1970. The three pairs of curves represent leading indicators (top) and the activities they led (bottom), namely housing starts and expenditures on residential structures (a), orders for plant and equipment and corresponding expenditures (b), and average workweek in manufacturing industries against unemployment rate (c). Dots show peaks and troughs.

FIGURE 2

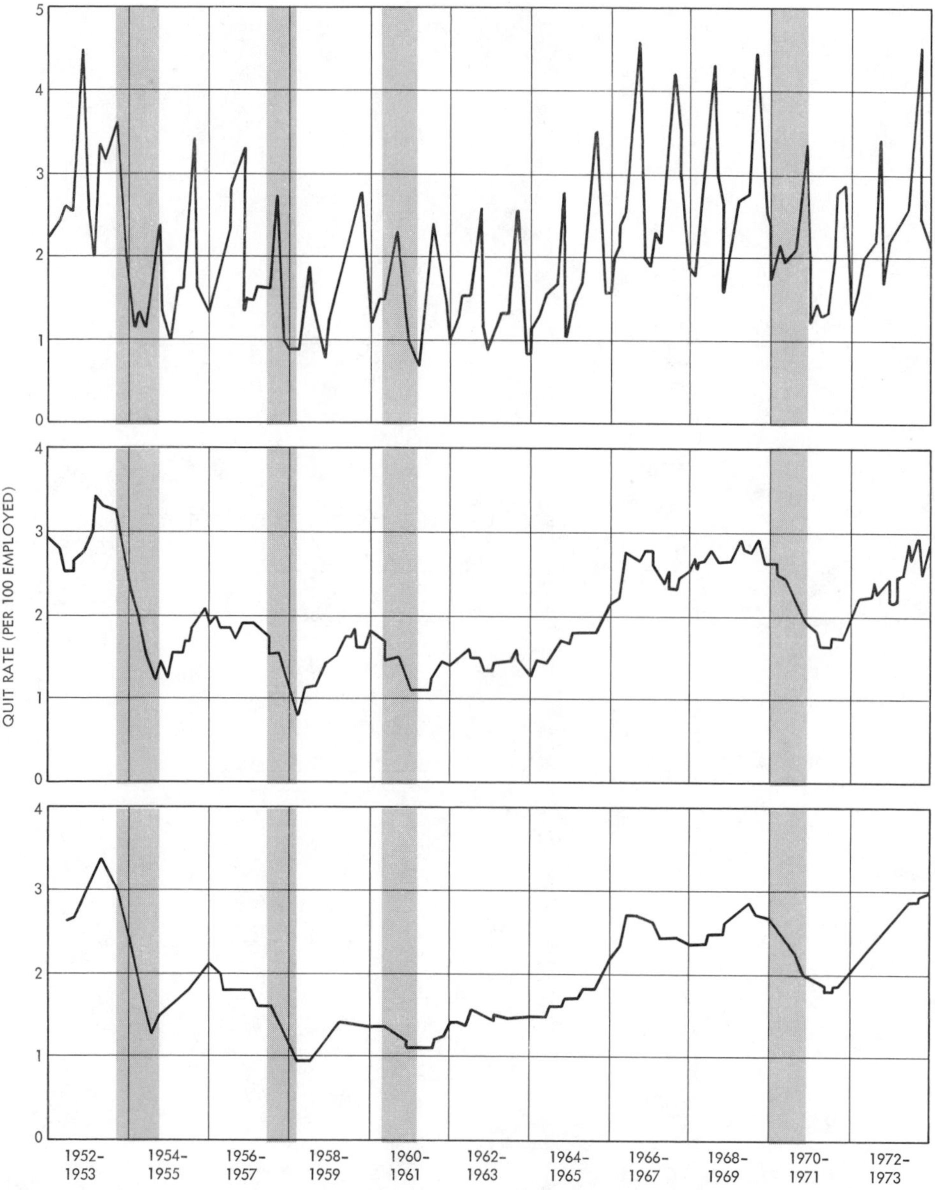

Construction of an, indicator involves the removal of factors that are unrelated to the business cycle. Here the indicator is the quit rate, meaning the number of people per 100 employed who voluntarily leave their jobs. At top is the curve reflecting the raw data, with shaded areas showing four periods of recession. Below it is the seasonally adjusted curve. Bottom curve shows the cyclical movement and the long-term trend of the quit rate.

FIGURE 3

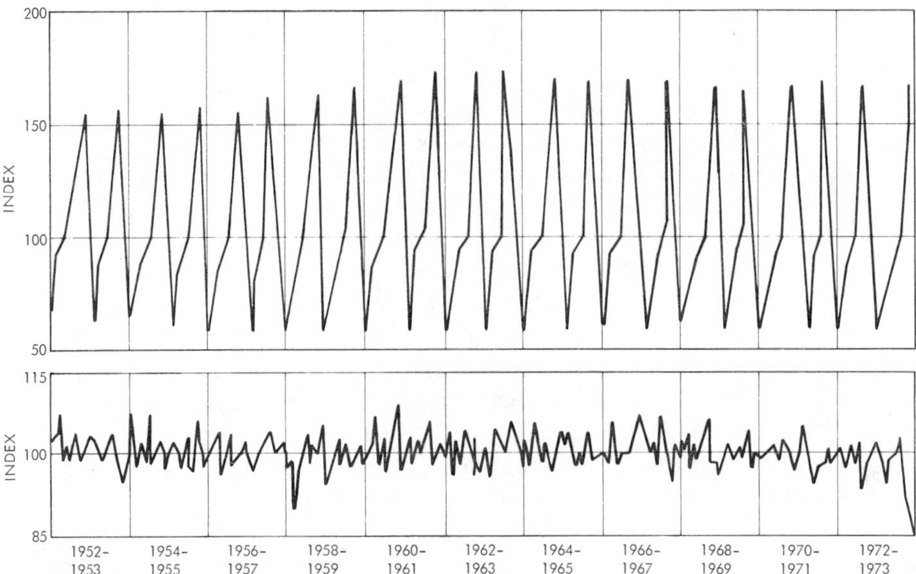

Elements removed from the quit-rate curve are a seasonal component (top) and an irregular component (bottom), which includes such factors as strikes and errors in sampling.

The smoothing of irregular factors is less commonly practiced because the techniques are somewhat less routine. Certain statistical series, however, are subject to much wider irregular movements than others are because of differences in sampling error or in the effects of such factors as the weather and strikes. It is therefore useful in interpreting current changes to have a standard measure of the size of these irregular factors compared with the size of the movements reflecting long-term trends and the events of the business cycle. (In economic discussions these latter factors are often called trendcycle movements.)

Two measures of this kind are provided for all the indicators carried in *Business Conditions Digest*. One shows how large the average monthly change in the irregular component is with respect to the average monthly change in the trend-cycle component. The other shows how many months must elapse on the average before the change in the trend-cycle component, which builds up over a period of time, exceeds the irregular component, which does not. For example, the measures show that monthly changes in housing starts are likely to be dominated by "noise," but that when these changes are measured over spans of four months, the trend-cycle "signal" becomes dominant. On the other hand, the index of industrial production is much less affected by noise, so that monthly movements are more significant.

The most important characteristic of an indicator from the point of view of forecasting is of course the evidence it provides concerning future changes in economic activity. Indicators differ in this respect for numerous reasons. Certain types, such as housing starts, contracts for construction, and new orders for machinery and equipment, represent an early stage in the process of making decisions on investment. Since it takes time to build a house or a factory or a turbine, the actual production (or completion or shipping) usually lags behind the orders and contracts. The lag depends on, among other things, the volume of unfilled orders or contracts still to be completed; where goods are made for stock rather than to order there may be no lag because orders are filled as they are received.

Another kind of lead-lag relation exists between changes in the workweek on the one hand and employment on the other. In many enterprises employers can increase or decrease hours of work more quickly, more cheaply, and with less of a commitment than they can hire or fire workers. Hence in most manufacturing industries the average length of the workweek usually begins to increase or decrease before a corresponding change in the level of employment. The workweek is therefore a leading indicator with respect to the unemployment rate.

Many bilateral relations of this kind have been traced. The matter obviously becomes more complex, however, when the relations are multilateral. Indexes of stock-market prices, for example, have exhibited a longstanding tendency to lead changes in business activity (the Harvard ABC curves relied in part on this tendency), but the explanation seems to require the interaction of movements in profits and in interest rates, and other factors as well. A cyclical decline in profits often starts before a business expansion comes to an end; the proximate cause is usually a rapid rise in the costs of production. Interest rates also are likely to rise sharply. Both factors operate to reduce the attractiveness of common stocks and depress their prices, even though the volume of business activity is still rising. Near the end of a recession the opposite tendencies come into play and lift stock prices before business begins to improve.

One way to cut through such complexities instead of pursuing each bilateral or multilateral relation separately is to measure leads and lags against a common standard. For this purpose a chronology of business cycles has proved useful. The National Bureau of Economic Research has defined business cycles in such a way that peaks and troughs can be dated with reasonable objectivity. (Indeed, much of the dating procedure can now be carried out by computer.) Since the vast majority of indicators that are of interest show cyclical movements conforming to these general business cycles, the peaks and troughs in each indicator can be matched with those of the business cycle to determine characteristic leads and lags.

Following this plan, groups of indicator series that typically lead, coincide with or lag behind turns in the business cycle have been identified (see figure 4). Summary indexes of these groups can be employed (as individual indicators can) to measure the relative severity of an economic downturn as it progresses from month to month. For example, indications

FIGURE 4

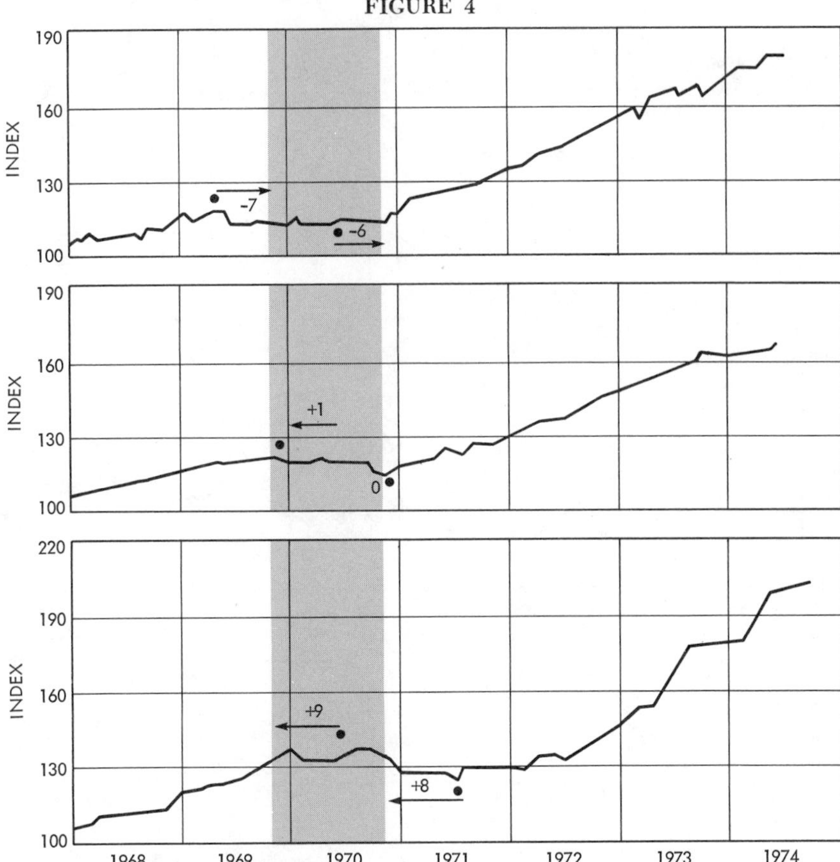

U.S. indicators behaved differently in the recession of 1969–1970 according to whether they were leading (top), coincident (middle) or lagging indicators (bottom). Each curve represents an index of several indicators in its class. Negative numbers with arrows mean the curve was that number of months ahead of the corresponding peak or trough in the business cycle. Positive numbers mean the curve was that number of months behind the cycle.

of a slowdown in the U.S. economy began to accumulate during 1973. Early in 1974 it was possible to conclude that if a recession was under way, a reasonable choice for the date of the business peak from which it started was November 1973. Percentage changes from then to successive months in 1973 and 1974 were calculated for a number of indicators month by month as new data became available and were compared with changes over corresponding intervals in earlier recessions, which had exhibited varying degrees of severity (figure 5).

With such a monitoring scheme one could observe the relative severity of the current decline and draw certain inferences based on the fact that

FIGURE 5

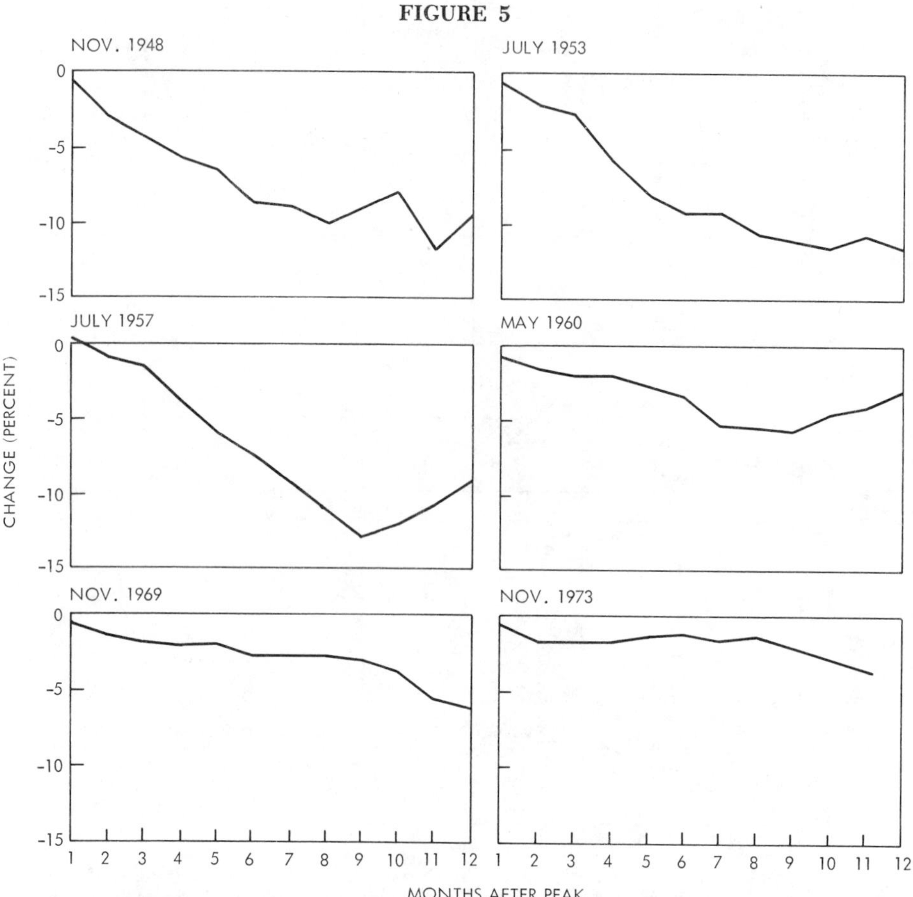

Coincident indicators are traced through six recessions, starting with the data of the business peak preceding the recession. Each curve represents the percentage change in the index of five indicators, namely industrial production, nonfarm employment, unemployment rate, personal income in constant dollars, and total sales in constant dollars. Through October 1974 the current decline most nearly resembled the ones in 1969–1970 and 1960–1961.

the rankings among different recessions have usually not changed a great deal after the first few months. The figures show that the decline of 1974 was relatively sharp early in the year as the effect of the oil crisis began to be felt. According to the latest data available (for October 1974) as of this writing, however, the decline in most indicators appeared moderate compared with the declines in earlier recessions over corresponding intervals. The major exceptions were the sharp declines in housing starts and in prices of common stocks, both of which reflected the sharp rise in interest rates and rapid inflation.

It is of course essential in any appraisal of the economic outlook to take into account actual and prospective policy actions by the government. Such actions include tax reductions or increases, changes in required bank reserves, changes in military expenditures and the establishment of a program of public employment. They often do not fit readily into the framework of indicators, although their effects, together with other influences, may be registered promptly in orders, contracts, housing starts, stock prices, and so on. Still, certain indicators do provide a nearly continuous reading on government activities (figure 6).

Government moves are often countercyclical. In a recession, for example, the government can exert a stimulative effect on the economy by making bank deposits or currency more readily available or by spending more than tax revenues are bringing in. The impact of such measures is a matter of debate. Indeed, it is possible to argue from the figures that policy shifts by the government have sometimes contributed with a lag, to the cyclical movements in the economy that they were designed to offset.

The analysis of economic indicators is one way of assessing the behavior of the economy. Econometric models of the business-cycle process are another. Although the two techniques have developed along independent lines for many years, they have come together at a number of points. The mathematical equations that characterize econometric models can handle elegantly and systematically such matters as multilateral relations among indicators, the distinction between seasonal movement and other types of movement, the influence of changes in government policy, and the plausibility of alternative theoretical explanations of the cycle.

The econometric models focus their explanatory power on such roughly coincident indicators as the gross national product, unemployment, and the rate of inflation. Often they include such cycle-leading indicators as housing starts, the average workweek, stock prices, and changes in business inventories, together with such lagging indicators as mortgage interest rates and investment in plant and equipment. Although the models have so far had a mixed record in representing and forecasting developments in the business cycle, with the result that the competition among alternative models is keen and changes in the specifications of each model are frequent, no user of indicators can afford to ignore the insights that econometric models bring to economic analysis. By the same token, people working with models can benefit from the empirical findings of indicator analysis and from the additional information that indicators often provide from outside the boundaries of a particular econometric model.

FIGURE 6

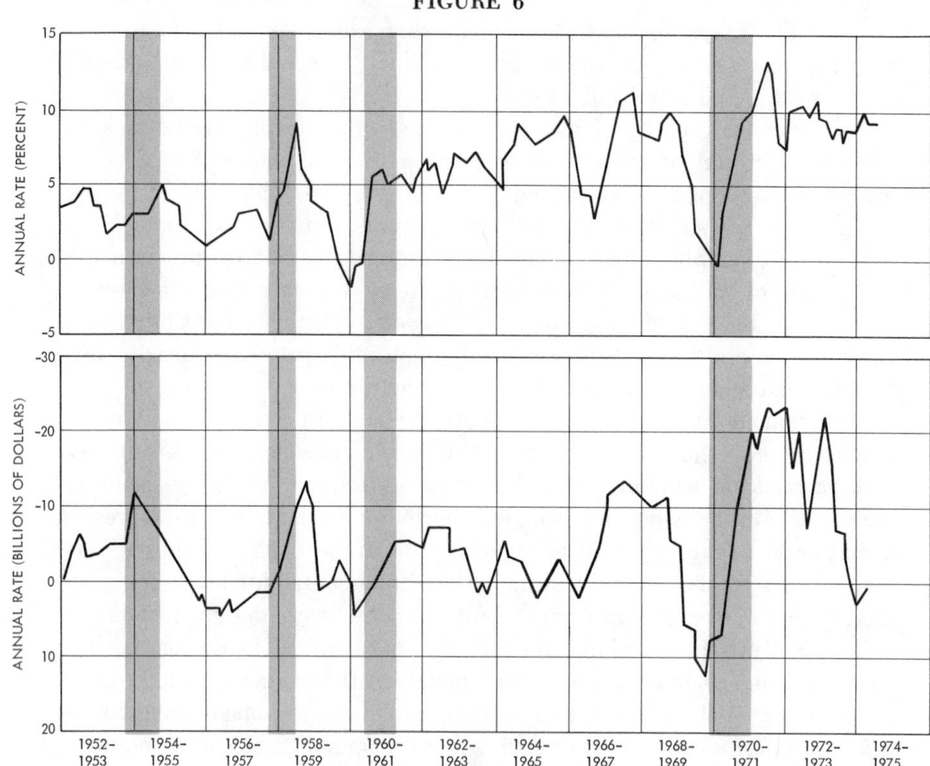

The role of government through four recessions is indicated by curves that portray rates of change in money supply (top) and federal surplus or deficit (bottom). On the bottom curve a rise indicates a shift toward a smaller surplus or larger deficit, a fall the opposite. The behavior of curves in recessions indicates the interaction of government policy with the business cycle.

Economic indicators of all types are followed more widely in the U.S. than in most other countries. The growth of trade, travel, and international finance, however, has increased the demand for promptly available statistics and readily accessible analytical records. In 1974 the National Bureau of Economic Research began a program of assembling and analyzing indicators for a dozen industrial countries.

Fortunately the indicator approach is sufficiently flexible to be adapted readily to situations where, as in many countries since World War II, economic recessions have taken the form of retardations in the growth of aggregate activity rather than absolute declines, and where such retardations may have been deliberately induced by government policies in order to cool off inflation or restore a deteriorating trade balance. Moreover, the approach is flexible enough to accommodate differences among countries in the types of indicator data that are available or are most revealing. For example, in Europe statistics on job vacancies are relied on more than in the U.S. and data on the international migration of workers are more significant because they have larger effects on the size of the work force.

Futhermore, since many economic indicators are available in physical units (such as man-hours of employment or tonnage shipped) or can be expressed in constant prices, a system of indicators can be adapted to conditions where a high rate of inflation dominates the behavior of data that are expressed in current prices. Many countries have recently experienced such conditions. Physical indicators of demand, such as housing starts, hiring rates, and orders for materials, can be expected to throw light not only on subsequent changes in output and employment but also on changes in prices and wages.

FIGURE 7

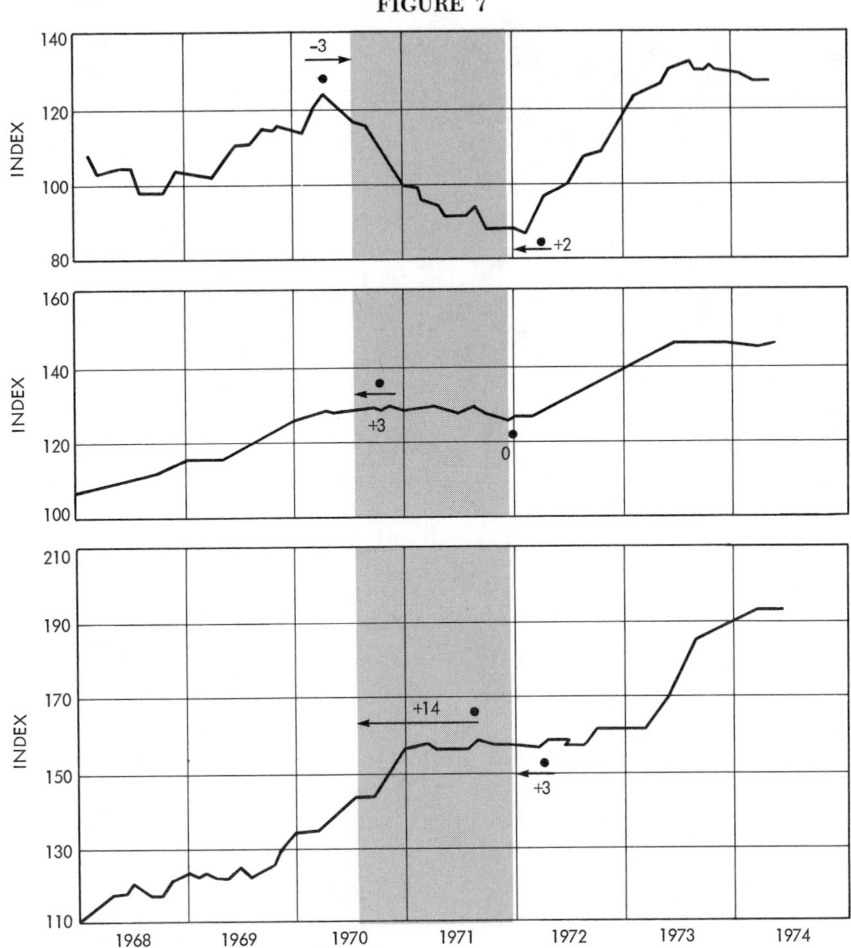

Japanese indicators are portrayed for a recession that ran from July 1970 to December 1971. The method of presentation is the same as for figure 4.

Our study is exploring these paths. Results already in hand for Canada, Japan (figure 7), the United Kingdom, and West Germany demonstrate the feasibility of the approach and its potential value in observing and appraising international fluctuations in economic growth rates and the accompanying trends in price levels, foreign trade, capital investment, and employment. One can envision the evolution of a worldwide system of indicators, built on the plan originally developed for the United States, to support the analysis of economic indicators on a global scale.

11. Forecasting and Analysis with an Econometric Model*

DANIEL B. SUITS

Although an econometric model is the statistical embodiment of theoretical relationships that are every economist's stock in trade, its discussion has largely been kept on a specialized level and confined to the more mathematical journals. Models are rarely explored from the point of view of their usefulness to the profession at large, yet there is nothing about their nature or their application—aside, again, from a solid grasp of economic theory—that requires anything more than an elementary knowledge of school algebra. The compilation of an econometric model requires a certain degree of technical specialization, but once constructed, any competent economist can apply it to policy analysis and economic forecasting.

The purpose of this article is to present an actual econometric model of the U.S. economy, to demonstrate its use as a forecasting instrument, and to explore its implications for policy analysis. To minimize the technical background required, the presentation is divided into two main parts. Part I deals with the general nature of econometric models, and, using a highly simplified schematic example, illustrates how forecasts are made with a model, how a model can be modified to permit the introduction of additional information and judgment, and how short-run and long-run policy multipliers are derived from the inverse of the model. Part II presents the 32-equation econometric model of the U.S. economy compiled by the Research Seminar in Quantitative Economics. This model is the most recent product of a research project whose initial output was the well-known Klein-Goldberger model. In part III the outlook for 1962, as calculated and published in November 1961, is studied as an example of an actual forecast; and earlier forecasts of this kind that have been prepared by the Research Seminar annually since 1953 are compared with actual events as a demonstration of the potential of the method.

In part III the inverse of the model is also presented and its application to policy evaluation is reviewed. Short-run and long-run multipliers

* *American Economic Review,* vol. 52, no. 1, (March 1962), pp. 104–32.

are calculated for selected policy variables. Part III also includes a digression on deficit financing, covering an interesting and important theoretical implication of the model.

I. ECONOMETRIC MODELS AND THEIR APPLICATIONS

The science of economics can be variously defined, but for the present purpose it is useful to think of it as the study of the relationships among a system of observable and essentially measurable variables: prices, costs, outputs, incomes, savings, employment, etc. These relationships derive from the complex behavior and interaction of millions of households, millions of firms, and thousands of governmental units, producing and exchanging millions of products. The relationships can be represented by a system of mathematical equations, but unfortunately a theoretically complete representation (e.g. a Walrasian system) would involve trillions of equations—surely millions for each household and firm. Moreover these equations would be individually as complex as human behavior, and involve the elaborate interaction of numberless variables.

We have neither the time nor the resources to deal with such a vast system of equations; to proceed at all we must simplify and condense. Millions of individual households become a single "household sector," millions of products become a single item of expenditure, e.g., "durable goods." Moreover, complex mathematical relationships among thousands of variables become simple linear approximations involving two or three aggregates. An econometric model of the economy is obtained by confronting these highly simplified equations with data arising from the historical operation of the economic system and, by appropriate statistical techniques, obtaining numerical estimates for their parameters.

The minimum number of equations necessary for an adequate representation of the economic system depends on a number of considerations, but clearly the fewer the equations the greater must be the level of aggregation and the less accurate and useful the result. On the other hand, the larger the number of equations and the greater the detail shown in the variables, the more complicated it is to derive the individual equations, to manipulate the resulting system, and to see the implications of the model. Where modern computing facilities can be used the mere size of the model is no longer a serious barrier to its effective application, but for purposes of exposition the smaller and simpler the model the better.

A. A Simple Illustrative Example

To illustrate the principles of application, let us suppose that the statistical procedure gave rise to the following, purely schematic, model of four equations.

$$C = 20 + .7(Y - T) \tag{1}$$
$$I = 2 + .1Y_{-1} \tag{2}$$
$$T = .2Y \tag{3}$$
$$Y = C + I + G \tag{4}$$

According to equation (1), consumption (C) depends on current disposable income ($Y - T$). In equation (2), investment (I) depends on income lagged one period. The third equation relates taxes (T) to income, while the last defines income as the sum of consumption, investment and government expenditure G.

While this model is small, it illustrates most of the properties of the larger model. The single consumption function in equation (1) corresponds to the set of four equations (01), (02), (03), and (04) that describe the behavior of the consumer sector in part II. The investment behavior represented in (2) corresponds to equations (05) through (10). The single tax equation (3) corresponds to a combination of the eleven tax and transfer equations, while the relationship of production to income embodied in equation (4) is indicated in much greater detail by equations (11) through (20).

This econometric model approximates the economy by a system of equations in which the unknowns are those variables—income, consumption, investment, and tax yield—whose behavior is to be analyzed. The "knowns" are government expenditure and lagged income. When projected values for the "knowns" are inserted in the equations, the system can be solved to forecast the values of the unknowns.

Quotation marks are used advisedly in the word "knowns." For, while some economic variables move so slowly along secular trends that their future values can be projected with considerable accuracy, others—for example new government expenditures—are unknown in advance of their occurrence, even in principle. Moreover, even the values of lagged variables are unknown at the time of the forecast, since a useful forecast must be made some months before the end of the preceding year. For example, each of the forecasts shown in table 3 was made during the first week of November of the preceding year. To make such forecasts, lagged variables are estimated from data for the first three quarters of the year, with the third quarter given double weight.

At any rate, suppose we expect next year's government expenditure to be 20, and the preliminary estimate of this year's income is, say, 100. Substituting $G = 20$ and $Y_{-1} = 100$ into the equations above and solving gives $C = 86.2$, $I = 12$, $T = 23.7$, $Y = 118.2$.

B. Introducing Outside Information

It may appear from the foregoing that this kind of forecasting is a blind, automatic procedure; but while an econometric model looks like a rigid analytical tool, it is actually a highly flexible device, readily modifiable to bring to bear additional information and judgment. For example, the investment equation in our little model is surely an unreliable predictor of capital formation. If no other information were available the equation would have to serve the purpose. But suppose we have available a survey of investment intentions reported by business. An estimate derived from such a survey is clearly superior to any that equation (2) could produce. To introduce the information into the forecast we simply remove equation (2) from the model and, in the remaining equations, set I equal to the survey value. Forecasts made from the Research Seminar model have frequently involved use of a figure for gross investment in plant and equipment derived from the McGraw-Hill Survey of Investment Intentions rather than from equation (05) of the model.

Information can also be used to modify individual relationships short of replacing them entirely. For example a prospective improvement in consumer credit terms—a variable that does not appear in our schematic model—would be expected to stimulate consumption expenditure. It is often possible to set an upper limit to this stimulating effect, and by increasing the constant term in the consumption function by this amount, to set an upper limit to the forecast economic outlook. An adjustment of this kind was applied to equation (01) to allow for the probable influence of the compact car on the outlook for automobile sales during 1960. For the same forecast, a similar modification of the housing starts equation (06) was made in anticipation of activity of the Federal National Mortgage Association.

Using the flexibility to full advantage permits the forecaster to explore any desired number of alternative sets of projections and modifications, and to bring to bear all information and judgment he possesses. The econometric model is not, therefore, a substitute for judgment, but rather serves to focus attention on the factors about which judgment must be exercised, and to impose an objective discipline whereby judgment about these factors is translated into an economic outlook that is consistent both internally, and with the past observed behavior of the economic system.

C. The Inverse Matrix

In principle, the exploration of a range of alternative projections and other modifications of the model consists of inserting each set of alternatives in turn as "knowns" in the equations and solving for the resulting forecast. The process is greatly expedited by further simplifying the model and by the use of the inverse matrix. Simplification of the model is made possible by the fact that one of the unknowns, I, depends only on knowns. I helps to determine the current values of C, T, and Y, but the latter do not, in turn, feed back into the determination of the current value of I. As a result, once the knowns are given, I can be directly calculated from (2) without reference to any other part of the model, and hence, as far as the remaining equations are concerned, I can be treated as a known in the sense used above. (Indeed it is this fact that enables us to replace equation (2) with survey values for I.)

The process of solving the system of equations can then be divided into two parts. First: using the values of the knowns, calculate the value of I. Second: substitute the knowns (now including I) into the remaining equations, and solve for the other unknowns.

The inverse matrix facilitates the second step. For those unfamiliar with matrix manipulations the following will help clarify the nature and use of this table. Since I is now considered as known, the model is reduced to the system of three equations (1), (3), and (4) above. By transferring all unknowns to the left side, and representing the right sides by P_1, P_3, and P_4, these equations can be expressed as:

$$C - 0.7Y + 0.7T = 20 = P_1 \qquad (1)$$
$$-.2Y + 1.0T = 0 = P_3 \qquad (3)$$
$$-C + Y = I + G = P_4 \qquad (4)$$

Now using any convenient method to solve this system for C, Y, and T in terms of P_1, P_3, and P_4 will yield:

$$C = 2.273P_1 - 1.591P_3 + 1.273P_4$$
$$T = .445P_1 + .682P_3 + .455P_4$$
$$Y = 2.273P_1 - 1.591P_3 + 2.273P_4$$

That is, the value of each unknown is obtained as a specified weighted total of P_1, P_3, and P_4. Where a large number of equations is used, and a lot of calculating is to be done, it is convenient to display the weights used for each unknown as a column of numbers in a table, with the detail of the P's shown in a separate column at the right:

C	T	Y	P	
2.273	.455	2.273	20	(1)
−1.591	.682	−1.591	0	(3)
1.273	.455	2.273	$I + G$	(4)

To make a forecast we first substitute Y_{-1} into equation (2) and solve for I. Then I and G are substituted in the P column of the table and the values of P_1, P_3 and P_4 calculated. These values, weighted by the numbers shown in the C column of the inverse and summed, give the forecast value of consumption; use of the weights of column Y gives the forecast for income, etc.[1] For example if we set $Y_{-1} = 100$ and $G = 20$, we first find from (2) $I = 12$. Substituting these values in column P of the table gives the forecast values: $C = 86.2$, $T = 23.7$, $Y = 118.2$.

D. Short-Run Policy Multipliers

It is an obvious step from economic forecasting to short-run policy analysis. To investigate any specified set of prospective government actions, we insert them in the proper place in column P and solve for the forecast implied by these assumptions. The analysis is expedited if we first calculate short-run multipliers for the individual components of government action. These can then be applied in any desired policy mixture.

Short-run multipliers for any policy variable are readily calculated by inserting +1 for the variable everywhere it appears in column P, and then (ignoring all terms that do not contain the variable in question) extending a forecast using the columns of the inverse. For example, to calculate the government expenditure multiplier, set $G = 1$ in row (4) of column P. This makes $P_4 = 1$. To find the effect of this value of G on, say, income, multiply this value of P_4 by the weight in row (4) of the Y column to get $Y = 1 \times 2.273 = 2.273$. That is, the income multiplier on government expenditure is 2.273. Likewise, $T = 1 \times .455 = .455$. That is, the tax-yield multiplier on government expenditure is .455. In other words, for every dollar of additional government expenditure, tax receipts rise by nearly 46 cents. A corollary is that—according to our schematic model—an increase in government expenditure of 1 with no change in tax legislation will generate an increase in deficit of only:

$$G - T = 1 - .46 = .54$$

In addition to changing the value of exogenous variables like government expenditure, government policy can produce changes in the equations themselves. An extensive change—e.g. a substantial alteration in tax rates—can only be studied by replacing the old tax equation by a new one, but less extensive changes can be studied as shifts in the levels of existing equations, the coefficients being unaltered.

Multipliers for such shifts are easily determined by placing +1 in the row of column P that corresponds to the equation being shifted.

---

[1] As those familiar with matrix algebra will recognize, the inverse matrix is tabulated here in its transposed form, and goes into the P vector at the right column by column.

The extensions are then made as before. For example, to calculate the multipliers on a +1 shift in the level of the tax equation, we put +1 in the row marked (3) of column P, since the tax equation is (3). The multiplier effect of this shift is then calculated by multiplying this 1 by the weight in the corresponding row of the appropriate column, as shown above. For example for income:

$$Y = 1 \times (-1.591) = -1.591$$

For consumption:

$$C = 1 \times (-1.591) = -1.591$$

In other words, the multipliers associated with the shift of an equation are merely the weights in the row of the inverse corresponding to that equation.

Note that according to our simplified model, the tax-yield multiplier is .682. That is, an upward shift of $1 billion in the tax *schedule* actually increases *yield* by only $682 million. The difference is due to the decline in income arising from the shift in the tax schedule.

The small size of our illustrative model limits the policy variables to government expenditure and the level of taxes. In the more extensive model below, policy is given considerably more scope; a number of individual tax and transfer equations can be shifted, and a number of different kinds of expenditure altered. The number of possible combinations of action is correspondingly very large; but one important advantage to a linear system lies in the fact that once multipliers for the individual components have been calculated, the economic implications of a complete policy "package" can be estimated by summing the effects of the individual components.

For example, an increase of $1 in government expenditure coupled with an upward shift of $1 in the tax schedule would generate a change in income given by the sum of the two individual multipliers:

$$Y = 2.273 - 1.591 = .682$$

This is what might be called an "*ex ante*-balanced" government expenditure multiplier. That is, the change in the law is such as to increase tax yield at the *existing* level of income by enough to balance the planned expenditure, but the budget will not necessarily be balanced *ex post*. The tax and expenditure program will alter income, and hence will change tax yields. Analysis of the complete fiscal impact of the operation requires the examination of all revenue and outlay items combined.

Adding together the two tax-yield multipliers we find that the additional expenditure of $1 is offset by a tax yield of:

$$.682 + .455 = 1.137$$

That is, the *ex ante*-balanced expenditure of $1 billion would, in our example, be accompanied by an increase of $1.137 billion in tax yield and give rise to an *ex post* surplus of $137 million.

E. Dynamics and Long-Run Multipliers

An increase in government expenditure of 1.0 will increase income by 2.273 the same year. But the long-run effect of expenditure sustained at this level will differ from this. According to equation (2), an increase in income this year will generate an increase in investment next year. This will again raise income and add further stimulus the following year, etc. Once the inverse has been tabulated, however, the sequence can easily be calculated by inserting the forecast values of one year as the "knowns" of the next. Thus an initial increase in G of 1 will raise Y by 2.273. This will raise I by $.2 \times 2.773 = .455$ the following year. The value of P_4 is then $G + I = 1.455$ and the second year income rises to 3.307 above its initial value, etc. The five-year sequence of values would be:

Year	1	2	3	4	5
Income	2.273	3.307	3.775	3.989	4.078

This means, for example, that if government expenditure is increased by 1 in 1961, and sustained at that new level, the level of income in 1965 will—other things equal—be 4.087 higher than it was in 1960.

Similar sequences can be worked out for other policy variables. For example a shift of 1 in the tax schedule in year 1 would imply the following sequence of annual income values:

Year	1	2	3	4	5
Income	−1.591	−2.314	−2.643	−2.793	−2.862

Like short-run multipliers, these long-run multipliers can be combined by simple addition. For example, a permanent rise of 1 in government expenditure coupled with an *ex-ante* shift of 1 in the tax schedule would raise income by $2.273 - 1.591 = .682$ the first year. After five years, however, income would be $4.087 - 2.862 = 1.225$ higher than its initial level.

Although the discussion has been focused on a highly simplified example, the principles developed apply equally to any linear econometric model. The presentation of the actual Research Seminar model in part II will follow the same pattern as the illustration of part I.

II. THE MODEL OF THE U.S. ECONOMY

The model developed by the Research Seminar in Quantitative Economics consists of 32 equations, most of them least-squares linear regressions fitted to annual first differences in the variables.[2]

Five advantages are gained by the use of first differences. In the first place, the autocorrelation of residuals from time series regressions causes a downward bias in calculated standard errors, giving an exaggerated appearance of precision to the result. The use of first differences serves to reduce this bias. Secondly, many of the equations—e.g. the demand for consumer durables—involve stocks for which data are not currently available. The increase in a stock is composed of current acquisitions less retirements. Since the latter tends to be a smooth series, exhibiting little year-to-year variation, the first difference in stock is well represented by acquisitions, a figure readily available on a current basis. Thirdly, in short-run analysis and forecasting, the present position is known, and *ceteris paribus* will continue. The important question is what change from that position will result from projected changes in other factors. The use of first differences serves to focus the power of the analysis on these changes. Fourthly, the use of first differences minimizes the effect of slowly moving variables such as population, tastes, technical change, etc., without explicitly introducing them into the analysis. The net effect of changes in these factors is represented in the constant term of the equation. Finally, use of first differences minimizes the complications produced by data revision when the model is applied. Revisions usually alter the level at which variables are measured, rather than their year-to-year variation.

In calculating the equations, the prewar and postwar periods were explored separately to determine whether there was any indication of a change in the coefficients. Except for institutional relationships—tax laws, transfers, etc.—no important shifts were discovered. Nevertheless the final equations are fitted only to data drawn from the period 1947–1960 to maximize their applicability to current problems.

The equations of the model are presented and discussed below by sectors, and the symbol for each variable is explained the first time it appears. In general the variables correspond to the magnitudes as given in the national accounts, measured in billions of 1954 dollars. In calculat-

[2] The exceptions are definitional equations, and those approximating tax laws. Use of least squares is unnecessary for the former, and inappropriate to the latter. The frequency of change in tax laws makes past data irrelevant to their current analysis. Tax equations were fitted by eye through a few relevant points.

ing the equations, however, all imputations were removed from the Department of Commerce figures for consumer expenditure and disposable income. These imputations, mainly associated with services rendered by financial institutions and by owner-occupied dwellings, are added back in after a forecast is made to maintain comparability with the national accounts. First differences are indicated throughout by prefixing Δ to the symbol of the variable. Note, however, that lagged undifferenced values of certain variables appear at some points (e.g. in the automobile demand equation [01] below). These undifferenced values serve as proxy variables for first differences in stocks as explained above. Figures in parentheses are the standard errors of the regression coefficients.

A. Aggregate Demand

1. *Consumption.*

Automobiles and Parts:

$$\begin{aligned}\Delta A = &\underset{(.086)}{.177}\,\Delta(Y - X_u - X_f - X_s) - \underset{(.168)}{.495}\,A_{-1} \\ &+ \underset{(.082)}{.260}\,\Delta L_{-1} + 4.710\end{aligned} \tag{01}$$

Consumer expenditure for new and net used automobiles and parts (ΔA) depends on disposable income (Y), net of transfers for unemployment compensation (X_a), and other federal (X_f) and state (X_s) transfers. These transfers are deducted on the ground that they are unlikely to find their way into the automobile market. Servicemen's insurance dividends (X_{GI}) are not deducted from disposable income. In addition, automobile demand depends on the stock of cars on the road (A_{-1}) and on the real value of consumer liquid assets at the end of the preceding year (ΔL_{-1}). For this purpose liquid assets are defined as household holdings of currency and demand deposits plus fixed-value redeemable claims as estimated by the Federal Reserve Board. The sizeable constant term in the equation probably reflects replacement demand.

Demand for Other Durables:

$$\Delta D = \underset{(.015)}{.176}\,\Delta Y - \underset{(.029)}{.0694}D_{-1} + \underset{(.016)}{.0784}\,\Delta L_{-1} + .262 \tag{02}$$

This equation relates ΔD, consumer expenditure for durables (other than automobiles and parts) to disposable income (ΔY), the accumulating stock of durables (D_{-1}) and liquid assets.

Demand for Nondurable Goods:

$$\Delta ND = \underset{(.060)}{.224}\,\Delta Y + \underset{(.135)}{.205}\,\Delta ND_{-1} + \underset{(.059)}{.143}\,\Delta L_{-1} - .149 \tag{03}$$

Nondurable expenditure depends on disposable income, liquid assets, and last year's nondurable expenditure (ΔND_{-1}). Notice the difference between this and the foregoing equations. In (01) and (02) the lagged values were undifferenced representing accumulation of stock. In this equation the difference itself is lagged, representing a dynamic adjustment in nondurable expenditure: an initial rise in level is followed by a subsequent secondary rise.

Demand for Services:

$$\Delta S = \underset{(.029)}{.0906}\, \Delta Y + \underset{(.170)}{.530}\, \Delta S_{-1} + \underset{(.029)}{.0381}\, \Delta L_{-1} + .363 \qquad (04)$$

This equation is similar to (03) and relates expenditure for services (ΔS) to disposable income, liquid assets, and lagged service expenditure. It should be remembered that service expenditure is here defined to exclude imputed items.

These four equations constitute the demand sector. Note that the aggregate marginal propensity to consume can be estimated by summing the income coefficients in the four equations. The sum, .67, is an estimate of the marginal propensity to consume, at least as an initial impact. The lagged terms in the individual equations, however, generate a dynamic response of consumption to income. As the equations show, the long-run response of nondurables and services tends to be greater, and that of automobiles and durables less, than the initial impact. The implications of this fact for the calculation of multipliers will appear below.

2. *Gross Capital Expenditure.*

Plant and Equipment Expenditure:

$$\Delta PE = \underset{(.238)}{.605}\, \Delta(P^*_{-1} - T_{fc-1} - T_{sc-1}) - \underset{(.216)}{.124}\, PE_{-1} + 4.509 \qquad (05)$$

ΔPE, expenditure for new plant and equipment, includes producers' durables, nonfarm nonresidential construction, and all farm construction. It is related to the preceding year's corporate profits (P^*_{-1}) after federal (T_{fc}) and state (T_{sc}) corporate income taxes and to its own lagged, undifferenced value (PE_{-1}). The latter represents growth in the stock of plant and equipment. As in (01) above, the large constant term probably represents replacement.

Housing Starts:

$$\Delta HS = \underset{(17.0)}{19.636}\, \Delta \left(\frac{FHA + VA}{2} - Aaa \right) - \underset{(.312)}{.702}\, HS_{-1} + 66.147 \qquad (06)$$

This equation, which applies only to the postwar period, relates the number of nonfarm residential housing starts (ΔHS), measured in thousand of units per month, to the gap between the simple average of the FHA and VA ceiling interest rates on the one hand, and the *Aaa* bond yield on the other (both expressed in percentage points). This interest rate differential reflects the substantial influence of credit availability on the volume of FHA and VA financed residential construction. It can function, however, only in the presence of a strong underlying housing demand. With the accumulation of a large stock as a consequence of construction in recent years, this interest rate differential may lose its role in the model. The term HS_{-1}, the lagged undifferenced value of housing starts, only partially represents the effect of this accumulation, and equation (06) is probably due for revision.

Housing Expenditure:

$$\Delta H = \underset{(.013)}{.125}\,\Delta HS + \underset{(.012)}{.024}\,\Delta HS_{-1} + \underset{(5.42)}{6.580}\,\Delta C + .083 \qquad (07)$$

Expenditure on housing, ΔH, depends on the rate at which residential construction is carried forward, and thus on current and lagged starts. In addition it depends on construction costs. The term ΔC is the ratio of the index of construction costs to the *GNP* deflator.

Durable Goods Inventory:

$$\Delta ID = \underset{(.100)}{.291}\,\Delta(A + D) + \underset{(.157)}{.591}\,\Delta PD + \underset{(.085)}{.305}\,\Delta M_{+1} - \underset{(.109)}{.669}\,ID_{-1} \qquad (08)$$

Accumulation of durable inventories, ΔID, depends on sales of consumer durables, producers durables ΔPD, and the stock of inventory already accumulated ID_{-1}. In addition an important component of inventory is associated with government military orders. Production on such orders appears in the national accounts as goods in process, and exerts a strong impact on the economy long before delivery of the finished product materializes as government expenditure. A wide variety of arrangements and lead times are involved in this process. As a proxy for such orders in any given year, we use ΔM_{+1}, federal military purchases from private industry the following year.

The equilibrium sales-inventory ratio implied by this equation compares favorably with that observed from other data.

Nondurable Goods Inventory:

$$\Delta IND = \underset{(.111)}{.427}\,\Delta ND - \underset{(.248)}{1.121}\,IND_{-1} \qquad (09)$$

Accumulation of nondurable inventory, ΔIND, depends on consumer sales of nondurables and the stock already on hand, IND_{-1}.

Imports:

$$\Delta R = \underset{(.03)}{.0602}\,\Delta G^* + .369 \qquad (10)$$

This relates the aggregate level of imports to the private GNP(G^*).

3. *Private Gross National Product*

$$\Delta G^* = \Delta(A + D + ND + S) + (\Delta F - \Delta R) + \Delta ID + \Delta IND + \Delta PE + \Delta H + \Delta g \quad (11)$$

Private GNP is defined as the sum of its parts including net exports $(\Delta F - \Delta R)$ and government purchases from private firms (Δg).

B. Income and Employment

Wage and Salary Workers, Private Sector:

$$\Delta E = .068\ \Delta G^* \quad (12)$$

This production function, relating ΔE, the number of full-time equivalent employees in the private sector (measured in millions of persons) to the private GNP, applies specifically to the forecast of 1962 and is based on the first three quarters recovery experience during 1961.

Unemployment:

$$\Delta U = \Delta LF - \Delta E_0 - \Delta E_G - \Delta E \quad (13)$$

Unemployment is the difference between labor force (ΔLF) on the one hand, and the number of self-employed and unpaid family workers (ΔE_0), government workers, including armed services (ΔE_G), and employees of private industry (ΔE).

Average Annual Earnings:

$$\Delta w = -\underset{(.0076)}{.0216}\ \Delta U + \underset{(.0025)}{.00436} P^*_{-1} - .0743 \quad (14)$$

Δw, average annual earnings (including wages and salaries plus "other labor income," and measured in thousands of dollars) is related to unemployment and last year's profits. This relationship reflects two facts. First and probably more important, annual earnings are heavily influenced by overtime pay which varies inversely with the level of unemployment. Secondly, pressure of union demands varies directly with profits and inversely with the level of unemployment. The undifferenced level of profits is used since the *existence* of profits acts as a target for wage demands.

Private Wage Bill:

$$\Delta W = \Delta(wE) = w_{-1}\ \Delta E + E_{-1}\ \Delta w \quad (15)$$

By definition the wage bill is the product of average earnings and employment. To keep the model linear, this nonlinear relationship is replaced by the linear approximation shown.

Depreciation:

$$\Delta Dep = .0456\ \Delta G^* + .763 \quad (16)$$

Property Income:

$$\Delta P = \Delta G^* - \Delta W - \Delta Dep - \Delta T_{fe} - \Delta T_{cd} - \Delta T_{bp} - \Delta T_{ss} - \Delta T_{os} - \Delta SI_r \tag{17}$$

Property income (ΔP) is a residual from the GNP after deducting wage costs, depreciation (ΔDep), employer contributions for social insurance (ΔSI_r), and indirect business taxes: federal excises (ΔT_{fe}), customs duties (ΔT_{cd}), business property (ΔT_{bp}), state sales (ΔT_{ss}), and other state taxes on business (ΔT_{os}).

Corporate Profits:

$$\Delta P^* = .902(\Delta P - \Delta P_f) - 1.027 \tag{18}$$

This relates profits (ΔP^*) to total property income net of farm income (ΔP_f). There is, of course, no strong theoretical basis for the particular distribution of corporate business found in the U.S. economy. This equation is an empirical representation of the distribution of property income under existing institutional arrangements.

Dividends:

$$\begin{aligned} \Delta Div = {} & \underset{(.064)}{.229}\ \Delta(P^* - T_{fc} - T_{sc}) \\ & + \underset{(.052)}{.0198}(P^* - T_{fc} - T_{sc} - Div)_{-1} - .0191 \end{aligned} \tag{19}$$

Current dividends (ΔDiv) depend on current profits after federal (T_{fc}) and state (T_{sc}) corporate profits taxes, and on last year's level of undistributed profits.

Disposable Income:

$$\begin{aligned} \Delta Y = {} & \Delta W + \Delta W_G + (\Delta P - \Delta P^*) + \Delta Div + \Delta i_G + \Delta X_u + \Delta X_f + \Delta X_s \\ & + \Delta X_{GI} - \Delta T_{fy} - \Delta T_{sy} - \Delta T_{eg} - \Delta T_{op} - \Delta SI_e + \Delta T_{ref} \end{aligned} \tag{20}$$

Diposable income. is the sum of wages, including government wages (W_G), noncorporate property income ($\Delta P - \Delta P^*$), dividends, government interest payments (i_G), plus transfers, less personal taxes; federal (ΔT_{fy}) and state (ΔT_{sy}) income, estate and gift (ΔT_{eg}), other personal taxes (ΔT_{op}) and personal contributions for social insurance ΔSI_e, all net of tax refunds ΔT_{ref}.

C. Taxes and Government Transfers

1. *Federal Taxes*

Federal Corporate Profits Tax:

$$\Delta T_{fc} = .500\ \Delta P^* \tag{21}$$

Federal Personal Income Tax Receipts:

$$\Delta T_{fy} = .111(\Delta W + \Delta W_G) + .150(\Delta P - \Delta P^* + \Delta i_G) + .195\,\Delta Div \quad (22)$$

This equation relates income tax receipts in the form of withholding, quarterly payments on estimated tax, and final tax payment to the several income components. The coefficients reflect both variation in income shares by tax bracket and the effect of the dividend tax credit.

Federal Personal Income Tax Liability:

$$\Delta T^*_{fy} = .100(\Delta W + \Delta W_G) + .114(\Delta P - \Delta P^* + \Delta i_G) + .154\,\Delta Div \quad (23)$$

Tax receipts commonly exceed liability. The difference (ΔT_{ref}) appears as a tax refund the following year.

Federal Excise Taxes:

$$\Delta T_{fe} = .099\,\Delta A + .011\,\Delta D + .003\,\Delta ND + .010\,\Delta G^* + .015\,\Delta Y \quad (24)$$

Customs Duties:

$$\Delta T_{cd} = .083\,\Delta R + .012 \quad (25)$$

2. *State and Local Taxes*

State Corporate Income Taxes:

$$\Delta T_{sc} = .019\,\Delta P^* \quad (26)$$

State and Local Sales Taxes:

$$\Delta T_{ss} = .033(\Delta A + \Delta D + \Delta ND + \Delta S) \quad (27)$$

State and Local Personal Income Taxes:

$$\Delta T_{sy} = .010(\Delta W + \Delta W_G + \Delta P - \Delta P^* + \Delta Div + \Delta i_G) \quad (28)$$

3. *Social Insurance Programs*

Private Employer Contributions for Social Insurance:

$$\Delta SI_r = .149\,\Delta E \quad (29)$$

Personal Contributions for Social Insurance:

$$\Delta SI_c = .129(\Delta E + \Delta E_G) + .050(\Delta P - \Delta P^*) \quad (30)$$

Covered Unemployment:

$$\Delta U_c = .675\,\Delta U - .140(\Delta LF - \Delta LF_{-1}) \quad (31)$$

The relationship of unemployment covered by compensation programs (ΔU_c) to total unemployment varies with the rate of increase in the labor force. When the labor force is growing rapidly, new entrants, not yet covered, make up a larger proportion of total unemployment.

Unemployment Compensation:

$$\Delta X_u = 1.77\,\Delta U_c + .101 \tag{32}$$

III. THE MODEL AS A FORECASTING INSTRUMENT

A. The Forecast of 1962

The unknowns of the model are the 32 variables like automobile demand, disposable income, private GNP, etc. that stand on the left side of the equations. The knowns are variables like government purchases from private firms, labor force, household liquid assets, etc. that appear only on the right side of the equations, and whose values must be projected or assigned before the unknowns can be forecast.

The forecast of 1962, calculated and presented in November 1961, employed the projected values shown in table 1. The most important single item was the $16.9 billion increase in consumer holdings of liquid assets. A few of the other key items were: a $6.9 billion projected increase in government purchases from private firms; an increase of .6 million in government employment; increase in government wage payments of $1.5 billion; and a $1 billion rise in military orders. Note that investment in plant and equipment is projected directly on the basis of the McGraw-Hill survey rather than from equation (05). All monetary values are in 1954 dollars.

When the projections of table 1 were inserted in the equations, the solution gave the outlook for 1962 shown in table 2. The first two columns contain a detailed comparison of the forecast of 1961 with the preliminary actual values. The middle column contains the solutions obtained from the equations. These are in first differences and are expressed as increases over 1961. When the forecast increase is added to the preliminary actual level for 1961 the result is the forecast level of 1962 shown in the fourth column. In the last column this forecast has been translated into approximate 1962 prices.[3]

The forecast entails substantial increases in consumption expenditure, especially for automobiles. The forecast level of $18.8 billion for this sector constitutes a record level of automobile sales, exceeding the $17.9 billion reached in 1955. This large increase derives primarily from the high level of consumer liquidity and the small addition to stocks of cars during 1961.

[3] To convert the values from 1954 to 1962 prices they were multiplied by deflators obtained by raising 1961 deflators 1.5 percent across the board. The result serves to put the forecast in proper perspective, but should not be thought of as part of the forecast itself.

TABLE 1
Projections Underlying Forecast of 1962

Equation	
(01)	$A_{-1} = 14.3 \quad \Delta L_{-1} = 16.9 \quad X_f = \Delta X_s = 0$
(02)	$D_{-1} = 27.3 \quad \Delta L_{-1} = 16.9$
(03)	$\Delta ND_{-1} = 1.2 \quad \Delta L_{-1} = 16.9$
(04)	$\Delta S_{-1} = 3.4 \quad \Delta L_{-1} = 16.9$
(05)	$\Delta PE = 1.3$[a]
(06)	$\Delta Aaa = +.02 \quad \Delta\left(\frac{FHA + VA}{2}\right) = -.06$[b] $\quad HS_{-1} = 93.1$
(07)	$\Delta HS_{-1} = 3.2 \quad \Delta C = 0$
(08)	$\Delta \mathrm{PD} = .7$[a] $\quad \Delta M_{+1} = 1.0 \quad ID_{-1} = 0.0$
(09)	$IND_{-1} = 1.7$
(10)	—
(11)	$\Delta F = 0 \quad \Delta PE = 1.3$[a] $\quad \Delta g = 6.9$
(12)	—
(13)	$\Delta LF = 1.2 \quad \Delta E_0 = .2 \quad \Delta E_G = .6$
(14)	$P^*_{-1} = 39.6$
(15)	$w_{-1} = 4.38 \quad E_{-1} = 46.9$
(16)	—
(17)	$\Delta T_{bp} = .730 \quad \Delta T_{os} = .087$
(18)	$\Delta P_f = 0$
(19)	—
(20)	$\Delta X_f = \Delta X_s = \Delta X_{GI} = 0 \quad \Delta W_G = 1.5 \quad \Delta i_G = .1 \quad \Delta T_{op} = .35 \quad \Delta T_{ey} = .08$ $\Delta T_{ref} = 0$
(21)	—
(22)	$\Delta W_G = 1.5 \quad \Delta i_G = .1$
(23)	$\Delta W_G = 1.5 \quad \Delta i_G = .1$
(24)	—
(25)	—
(26)	—
(27)	—
(28)	$\Delta W_G = 1.5 \quad \Delta i_G = .1$
(29)	—
(30)	$\Delta E_G = .6$
(31)	$\Delta LF = 1.2 \quad \Delta LF_{-1} = 1.0$
(32)	—
(Addendum)	Δ Imputed Services = 1.5

[a] Based on McGraw-Hill survey showing 4 percent increase in plant and equipment expenditure.
[b] FHA ceiling rates projected at their present level throughout 1962. The projected decline reflects the fact that they were above this level in early 1961.

Aside from the consumer sector the main stimulus to the economy derives from projected increases in government outlays, associated with the trend of state and local expenditures and federal defense expenditure. In preparing the forecast no allowance was made for the possible effect of a steel strike during 1962. Inventory accumulation in anticipation of interruption of steel supplies will probably accelerate inventory accumulation in the first half of the year and depress it in the second half. There is no indication that this will alter the overall level for the year.

TABLE 2
Review of 1961 and Outlook for 1962
(monetary figures, except column 5, are billions of 1954 dollars)

	1961		Forecast Increase	Forecast 1962	
	Forecast	Actual[p]		(1954 prices)	(1962 prices)
Gross National Product	450.1	446.8	27.5[a]	474.3	559.9
Consumption Expenditures					
Automobiles and Parts	14.6	14.3	4.5	18.8	21.2
Other Durables	25.1	24.8	1.9	26.7	28.7
Nondurables	144.7	142.7	5.3	148.0	163.6
Services	119.9	119.6	5.5[a]	125.1	147.9
Private Gross Capital Expenditure					
Plant and Equipment	39.0	37.3	1.3	38.6	48.1
Residential Construction	19.9	17.7	0.1	17.8	21.4
Inventory Investment					
Durables	} 2.4	0.0	2.6	2.6	2.8
Nondurables		1.7	0.4	2.1	2.3
Imports	24.8	22.2	1.9	24.1	24.8
Exports	24.6	26.4	....	26.4	28.7
Government Expenditure on Goods and Services	84.7	84.5	7.8	92.3	120.0
Corporate Profits	40.3	39.6	5.1	44.7	52.5
Dividends	12.4	12.3	0.7	13.0	15.3
Civilian Labor Force[b] (millions of persons)	71.3	71.6	0.9	72.5	
Private Wage and Salary Workers		46.9	1.7	48.6	
Govt. Employees (Civilian)	67.0	8.8	0.3	9.1	
Self-employed		11.0	0.2	11.2	
Unemployed[b]					
Number (millions)	4.3	4.9	- 1.3	3.6	
Percent of Civilian Labor Force	6.0	6.8	....	5.0	

[p] Preliminary.
[a] Includes imputed services.
[b] Annual average.

The forecast increase in production is adequate to absorb more than the growth of the labor force, and the outlook concludes by showing a reduction of 1.3 million in unemployment, reducing the average for the year to 3.6 million or 5 percent of the civilian labor force.

B. Review of Past Forecasts

The Research Seminar in Quantitative Economics has been making annual forecasts since 1953, each a matter of record published in advance of the year forecast. The econometric model has been revised and improved several times over this period (the version presented here was first used for the 1962 forecast), but the review of past forecasting performance in table 3 will illustrate the general reliability of the method.[4] Each forecast is shown as it was presented, and compared with the

[4] The review of the 1961 forecast, compared with the actual outcome, is provided in table 2.

TABLE 3
Review of Past Forecasts

	1953[a]		1954[a]		1955[a]		1956[a]		1957[b]	
	Fore-cast	*Actual*	*Fore-cast*	*Actual*	*Fore-cast*	*Actual*	*Fore-cast*	*Actual*	*Fore-cast*	*Actual*
Gross National Product	177.4	178.6	174.8	173.9	176.4	188.5	191.6	191.2	337.0	335.2
Consumption Expenditure	114.4	115.9	117.3	116.7	118.6	125.1	127.4	128.5	226.2	226.1
Private Gross Capital Formation	24.2	24.9	22.7	23.6	25.2	25.9	28.7	26.3	47.2	44.4
Employee Compensation	80.4[f]	79.8[f]	82.3[f]	83.0[f]	81.2[f]	89.5[f]	107.1	104.3	196.5	196.3

	1958[c]		1959[d]		1960[e]	
	Forecast	*Actual*	*Forecast*	*Actual*	*Forecast*	*Actual*
Gross National Product	432.7	432.5	456.7	475.7	432.0	439.2
Consumption Expenditure	282.1	287.3	295.4	310.7	287.1	296.8
Automobiles	.....	.....	.....	.....	16.7	15.6
Other Durables	.....	.....	.....	.....	25.2	25.2
Nondurables	.....	.....	.....	.....	138.9	141.9
Services	.....	.....	.....	.....	106.3	113.7
Private Gross Capital Expenditure	61.9	53.7	61.2	70.4	62.4	60.5
Plant and Equipment	.....	.....	44.0	43.0	40.5	39.3
Residual Construction	.....	.....	17.8	21.6	19.7	18.0
Inventory	.....	.....	-.6	5.8	2.2	3.2
Government Purchase of Goods and Services } Net Exports }	88.8	90.5	100.1	94.6	83.7	80.3
Net Exports					-1.3	1.6
Employee Compensation	254.3	251.8	261.0	273.4	236.3	257.1
Corporate Profits	39.5	36.5	47.7	45.8	42.7	38.7
Dividends	.....	.....	.....	.....	12.2	12.2
Civilian Employment	66.4	66.5	66.0	65.6	65.5[g]	66.7[h]
Unemployment	4.8	4.7	3.4	3.8	4.4[g]	3.9[h]

[a] 1939 prices [b] 1947 prices [c] 1957 prices [d] 1958 prices [e] 1954 prices [f] private sector only [g] excludes Alaska and Hawaii [h] includes Alaska and Hawaii

actual outcome.[5] Note that from 1953 to 1956 the figures are given in 1939 dollars; thereafter the price level employed was changed almost every year. The increasing elaboration of the model is evident in the table.

As plotted in figure 1, the general accuracy of these forecasts speaks for itself. The direction of movement was correctly forecast each year, and the levels were generally well predicted. The recession of 1954 was forecast with considerable precision. The recovery of 1955 was likewise

FIGURE 1
Comparison of Forecast with Actual Changes in GNP (1953–61)
(billions of 1954 dollars)

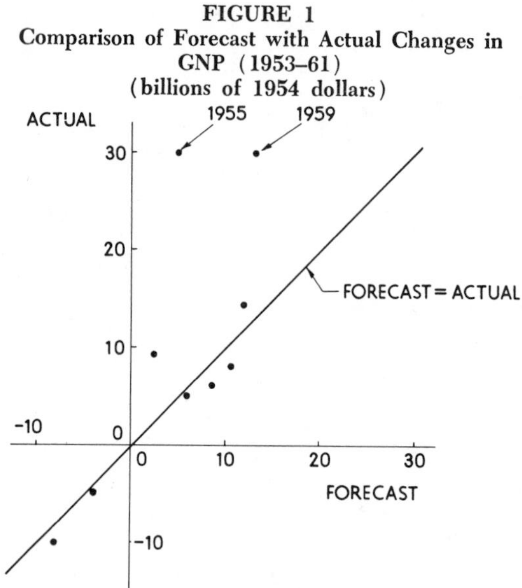

forecast, but the magnitude of the boom that developed was grossly underestimated. The fact that the error of the 1955 forecast is concentrated in the consumer sector lends support to the idea that this was a consumer-generated movement. The recession of 1958 was well predicted. The recovery of 1959 was somewhat underestimated.

In many respects the forecast of 1960 was the most interesting of all. Made in November 1959 at the height of business optimism, and amidst general anticipation of the "soaring sixties," its pessimistic outlook for 1960 was greeted with almost complete skepticism, but it proved to be more exact than any other forecast placed on record in advance.

[5] Since data revisions occur frequently, there is some question as to what figures should be taken as "actual." Since we want the "actual" figures as close as possible in definition and economic context to the data on which the forecast was based, they are taken from the issue of the *Survey of Current Business* appearing in the February following the forecast year. E.g., the "actual" GNP for 1954 is the value for 1954 published February 1955.

C. Short-Run Policy Multipliers

Simplification of the model is carried out as illustrated in part I. Inspection shows that in equation (05), plant and equipment expenditure (ΔPE) depends only on "known" values: last year's profits after taxes, and the stock of plant and equipment available at the beginning of the year. Similarly in equations (06) and (07), housing starts (ΔHS) and expenditure for nonfarm residential construction (ΔH) depend only on credit availability, construction costs, last year's starts, and the stock of houses at the beginning of the year. To make a forecast, therefore, we use the knowns to estimate ΔPE, ΔHS, and ΔH via equations (05), (06), and (07), and then use these values, together with the other knowns, to solve the remaining equations. The inverse of the model is shown in table 4. This is merely an enlarged version of the little table shown earlier for the illustrative model of part I, and is used in the same way. For example, if the projected values of table 1 are inserted in column P of table 4, multiplied by the weights in the automobile column and summed, the result is 4.5, the forecast increase in automobile demand shown in table 2.[6] Short-run multipliers for any policy variable are readily calculated as before by inserting 1 for the variable everywhere it appears in column P and then (ignoring all terms that do not contain the variable in question) extending a forecast using the columns of table 4.

For example, to find the multiplier on government purchases from private firms, set $\Delta g = +1$ everywhere it appears in column P. The term Δg is found in only one place: in row (11) it is multiplied by 1. To find the effect of $\Delta g = \$1$ on, say, private GNP, we multiply the weight in row (11) of the GNP column by 1:

$$\Delta G^* = 1 \times 1.304 = 1.304$$

That is to say, the short-run multiplier on government purchases is about 1.3. Similarly, the effect on, say, automobile demand is given by

$$\Delta A = 1 \times .092 = .092$$

i.e. the short-run "automobile demand multiplier" on government purchases from the private sector is .092.

In working out a policy multiplier, care must be taken to include changes in *all* exogenous variables affected by the policy action. For

[6] To save space some of the less interesting columns of the matrix have been omitted from table 4. Moreover the tax and transfer equations have been consolidated to show only totals for federal taxes, state and local taxes, and social insurance contributions. If values of any omitted variable are required, they can be calculated from the others. For example, to calculate the federal corporate profits tax yield, use the inverse to calculate ΔP^* and substitute this value in equation (21).

TABLE 4
Inverse Matrix

Equation No.	ΔA	ΔD	ΔND	ΔS	ΔID	ΔIND	ΔR	ΔG^*	ΔE
01	1.113	.089	.113	.046	.350	.048	.100	1.660	.113
02	.117	1.092	.118	.048	.351	.050	.101	1.676	.114
03	.130	.103	1.130	.053	.068	.483	.112	1.854	.126
04	.091	.072	.091	1.037	.047	.039	.078	1.298	.088
08	.092	.073	.093	.037	1.048	.040	.078	1.304	.089
09	.092	.073	.093	.037	.048	1.040	.078	1.304	.089
10	−.095	−.076	−.097	−.040	−.050	−.041	.921	−1.318	−.089
11	.092	.073	.093	.037	.048	.042	.078	1.304	.089
12	.884	.623	.793	.321	.439	.339	.192	3.205	1.218
13	−.118	.091	.116	.047	−.008	.049	.010	.167	.011
14	8.621	8.030	10.220	4.133	4.845	4.364	2.283	37.929	2.579
15	.184	.171	.218	.088	.103	.093	.049	.809	.055
16	−.040	−.037	−.047	−.019	−.022	−.020	−.012	−.175	−.012
17	.040	.037	.047	.019	.022	.020	.012	.175	.012
18	−.179	−.166	−.212	−.086	−.100	−.090	−.047	−.786	−.053
19	.202	.188	.240	.097	.114	.102	.054	.890	.061
20	.254	.237	.302	.122	.143	.129	.067	1.119	.076
21	−.046	−.043	−.055	−.022	−.026	−.024	−.012	−.204	−.014
22	−.254	−.237	−.302	−.122	−.143	−.129	−.067	−1.119	−.076
24	−.040	−.037	−.047	−.019	−.022	−.020	−.012	−.175	−.012
25	−.040	−.037	−.047	−.019	−.022	−.020	−.012	−.175	−.012
26	−.046	−.043	−.055	−.022	−.026	−.024	−.012	−.204	−.014
27	−.040	−.037	−.047	−.019	−.022	−.020	−.012	−.175	−.012
28	−.254	−.237	−.302	−.122	−.143	−.129	−.067	−1.119	−.076
29	−.040	−.037	−.047	−.019	−.022	−.020	−.012	−.175	−.012
30	−.254	−.237	−.302	−.122	−.143	−.129	−.067	−1.119	−.076
31	.101	.391	.498	.201	.143	.213	.088	1.461	.099
32	.058	.221	.281	.114	.081	.120	.050	.825	.056

Projections

01	$4.710 - .495A_{-1} + .260\Delta L_{-1} - .177\Delta X_f - .177\Delta X_s$
02	$.262 - .0694D_{-1} + .0784\Delta L_{-1}$
03	$-.149 + .205\Delta ND_{-1} + .143\Delta L_{-1}$
04	$.363 + .530\Delta S_{-1} + .0381\Delta L_{-1}$
08	$0 + .591\Delta PD + .305\Delta M_{+1} - .669ID_{-1}$
09	$0 - 1.121IND_{-1}$
10	$.369$
11	$0 + \Delta F + \Delta PE + \Delta H + \Delta g$
12	0
13	$0 + \Delta LF - \Delta E_0 - \Delta E_G$
14	$-.0743 + .00436P^*_{-1}$
15	0
16	$.763$
17	$0 - \Delta T_{bp} - \Delta T_{os}$

TABLE 4
(*continued*)

Equation No.	ΔW	ΔP^*	ΔDw	$\Delta(P - P^*)$	*Federal Tax Receipts*	*State and Local Tax Receipts*	*Social Ins. Contr.*	ΔX_u	ΔY
01	.609	.694	.076	.076	.585	.066	.035	−.135	.506
02	.615	.780	.085	.084	.545	.068	.036	−.136	.525
03	.680	.875	.096	.096	.600	.072	.040	−.151	.583
04	.476	.606	.066	.066	.414	.060	.028	−.105	.407
08	.478	.638	.070	.069	.432	.028	.028	−.106	.414
09	.478	.638	.070	.069	.432	.028	.028	−.106	.414
10	−.483	−.719	−.079	−.078	−.546	−.030	−.029	.107	−.431
11	.478	.638	.074	.069	.458	.030	.030	−.106	.438
12	6.568	−3.586	−.395	−.390	−1.002	.076	.319	−1.455	3.539
13	−.952	.997	.109	.109	.430	.016	.009	1.181	.516
14	60.808	−25.478	−2.806	−2.767	−4.726	1.091	.579	−3.082	45.619
15	1.297	−.543	−.059	−.060	−.101	.023	.012	−.066	.973
16	−.064	−.980	−.107	−.107	−.544	−.026	−.009	.014	−.211
17	−.064	.980	.107	.107	.544	.026	.009	−.014	.211
18	−.288	.651	.075	−1.038	.106	−.021	−.067	.064	−.946
19	.326	.395	1.040	.043	.497	.045	.019	−.072	1.070
20	.410	.496	.040	.054	.378	.045	.024	−.091	1.346
21	−.075	−.090	−.238	−.010	.886	−.010	−.004	.017	−.245
22	−.410	−.496	−.040	−.054	.622	−.045	−.024	.091	−1.346
24	−.064	−.980	−.107	−.107	.456	−.026	−.009	.014	−.211
25	−.064	−.980	−.107	−.107	.456	−.026	−.009	.014	−.211
26	−.075	−.090	−.238	−.010	−.114	.990	−.004	.017	−.245
27	−.064	−.980	−.107	−.107	−.544	.974	−.009	.014	−.211
28	−.410	−.497	−.040	−.054	−.378	.955	−.024	.091	−1.346
29	−.064	−.980	−.107	−.107	−.544	−.026	.991	.014	−.211
30	−.410	−.497	−.040	−.054	−.378	−.045	.976	.091	−1.346
31	.535	.661	.072	.072	.486	.059	.031	1.651	2.224
32	.303	.374	.041	.041	.274	.033	.018	.932	1.256

Projections
(continued)

18	$-1.027 - .902\Delta P_f$
19	$-.0191 + .0198(P^* - T_{fc} - T_{sc} - Div)_{-1}$
20	$0 + \Delta W_G + \Delta i_G + \Delta X_f + \Delta X_s + \Delta X_{GI} - \Delta T_{op} - \Delta T_{eg} + \Delta T_{ref}$
21	0
22	$0 + .111\Delta W_G + .150\Delta i_G$
24	0
25	.012
26	0
27	0
28	$0 + .010(\Delta W_G + \Delta i_G)$
29	0
30	$0 + .129\Delta E_G$
31	$0 - .140(\Delta LF - \Delta LF_{-1})$
32	.101

example, an increase in government employment involves hiring additional people [ΔE_G in rows (13) and (30)] and paying them wages [ΔW_G in rows (20), (22), and (28)]. At an average annual wage of $5000, an addition of $1 billion to the government wage bill will hire .2 million additional employees. To find the multipliers on government wages, therefore, we set $\Delta E_G = .2$. This gives —.2 in row (13) and .0258 in row (30) of column P. We also set $\Delta W_G = \$1$ to get 1 in row (20), .111 in (22) and .010 in row (28) of column P. The impact of additional government employment on private GNP is then found by extending these figures by the weights in the corresponding rows of the GNP column:

$$\begin{aligned}\Delta G^* &= -.2 \times .167 + 1 \times 1.119 - .111 \times 1.119 - .010 \times 1.119 \\ &\quad -.0258 \times 1.119 \\ &= .692\end{aligned}$$

To find the effect of the action on total GNP, we must add in the additional value added by government (i.e. government wages and salaries). Thus:

$$\text{Total GNP} = .692 + 1 = 1.692$$

We also recall that government tax policy can be expressed by shifts in the equations themselves. As shown in part I, these shift multipliers are equal to the weights found in the row of the inverse matrix that corresponds to the equation being shifted. Thus we see from the —1.119 in row (22) of the GNP column that a $1 billion shift in the federal personal tax function will reduce private GNP by $1.1 billion, etc. Note again [row (22) of the federal tax column] that an upward shift of $1 billion in the federal income tax *schedule* increases federal·tax *yield* by only $622 million due to the decline in personal income and expenditure associated with the rise in taxes.

Some multiplier effects of a selection of government actions are given in table 5. As before, once the multipliers are worked out they can be combined in any desired proportions. Thus an increase in government purchases of $2 billion coupled with additional government wages of $.5 billion and an upward shift of the personal tax schedule of $1.3 billion would produce a total change in GNP of $(2 \times 1.304) + (.5 \times 1.692) + (1.3 \times -1.119) = \$2$ billion. The same program would raise total employment by .211 million, and add $.67 billion to the federal deficit.

D. A Digression on Deficit Financing

An interesting and important conclusion to be drawn from table 5 is that the impact of a government action cannot be measured by merely the existence, or even the size, of a surplus or deficit. In the first place

TABLE 5
Selected Multipliers

Multiplicand	*Multiplier for Impact on:*											
	GNP		*Employment*		*Tax Receipts*		*Social Insurance*		*Government Surplus or Deficit (–)*			
	Private	*Total*	*Private*	*Total*	*Federal*	*State and Local*	*Contributions*	*Transfers*	*Federal*	*State and Local*	*Social Insurance*	*Total*
Plant and Equipment[a]	1.690	1.690	.115	.115	.586	.058	.038	–.137	.586	.058	.175	.819
Federal Purchases from Firms	1.304	1.304	.089	.089	.458	.030	.030	–.106	–.542	.030	.136	–.376
Federal Employment[b]	.692	1.692	.063	.263	.209	.016	.044	–.314	–.791	.016	.358	–.417
Federal Personal Income Tax Shift	–1.119	–1.119	–.076	–.076	.622	–.045	–.024	.091	.622	–.045	–.115	.462

[a] Additional expenditure of $1 billion of which half is spent for producers' durable equipment.
[b] Additional expenditure of $1 billion in government wages to hire .2 million workers.

it makes a great deal of difference whose deficit is under discussion, and it is not always clear whether deficit "multipliers" are supposed to be applied to the federal deficit or to the consolidated government sector. In what follows we confine ourselves to the latter. In the second place, surpluses and deficits result from courses of action; they are the difference between certain expenditures and receipts. While it is elementary that expenditures promote and taxes retard economic activity, the net result depends not only on the amounts of expenditures and tax yields, but also on the kinds, and we cannot speak unqualifiedly of a deficit multiplier.

Although this point can be made from purely theoretical considerations, the econometric model shows the substantial order of magnitudes involved. We see from table 5, for example, that a $1 billion consolidated deficit will result from either $1 ÷ .376 = $2.66 billion of federal government purchases or, say a cut of $1 ÷ 462 = $2.16 billion in the federal income tax schedule. Yet the former action raises total GNP by 1.304 × 2.66 = $3.47 billion, while the latter generates an increase of only 1.119 × $2.16 = $2.42 billion.

This result can be generalized. According to the multipliers in the last column of table 5, the consolidated balance (surplus or deficit) is given by

$$\Delta b = -.376\,\Delta g + .462\,\Delta a$$

where Δb is the change in the balance and Δa is the shift in the federal income tax schedule. A wide range of combinations of expenditures and taxes will produce the same budgetary balance. In fact, if we set Δb at some fixed value, say $\Delta b = 2$, then

$$2 = -.376\,\Delta g + .462\,\Delta a$$

is the equation of an "isobalance" locus. That is, every combination of expenditures and taxation that satisfies this equation produces a $2 billion increase in consolidated surplus. Three isobalance lines—corresponding to a $1 billion surplus, a balanced budget and a $1 billion deficit—are plotted as solid lines in figure 2.

By the same token, the increase in total GNP is given by:

$$\Delta GNP = 1.304\,\Delta g - 1.119\,\Delta a,$$

and if we assign, say $\Delta \text{GNP} = 5$, then

$$5 = 1.304\,\Delta g - 1.119\,\Delta a$$

is the equation of an "iso-GNP" locus. Three of these are plotted as broken lines in figure 2.

FIGURE 2
Relationship of GNP and Deficit to Government Purchases and Level of Personal Taxes

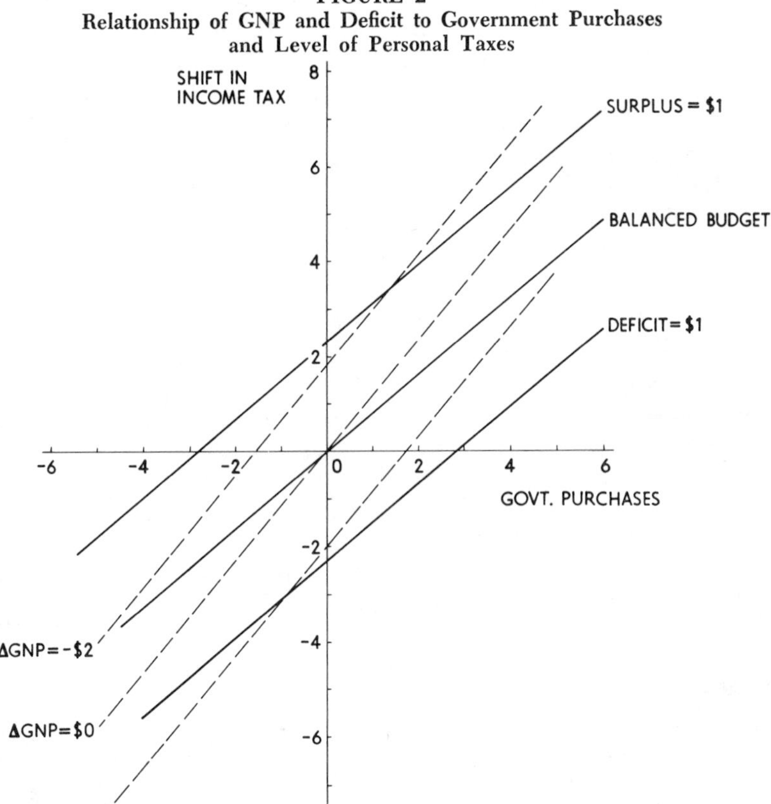

Inspection of the figure immediately shows that any specified increase in GNP can be attained in association with a wide range of balances and that any deficit or surplus may be associated with a wide range of impacts on GNP. In fact, a government program can simultaneously generate a substantial deficit and a sharp deflation, or a substantial surplus and general expansion. Since transfers, corporate profits taxes, defense orders, and government employment will have still other isobalance and iso-GNP lines, this merely scratches the surface of the possibilities.

E. Dynamic Responses and Long-Run Multipliers

As shown in part I, dynamic responses are studied by iteration. Among the initial impacts of any program, we must find the effects on automobile demand, inventory accumulation, plant and equipment, and other variables whose values reenter the system with a lag. These form a set of additional knowns for the next year. Using these values, in turn, gives rise to another set, etc. Repeating this operation enables us to follow the implications of a given program over as long a period as desired. It appears, however, that the dynamic elements stabilize by the end of the fifth year, and the system can be treated as in equilibrium after five iterations.

A complete study of the dynamic behavior of each variable in response to each possible policy action cannot be presented here, but table 6

TABLE 6
Dynamic Responses to a Permanent Increase of $1 Billion in Government Expenditure
(tabulated figures are deviations from initial levels)

	Year				
	1	*2*	*3*	*4*	*5*
Gross National Product[a]	1.304	1.619	1.582	1.545	1.335
Automobiles and Parts	.092	.088	.050	.042	.014
Other Durables	.073	.104	.113	.117	.104
Nondurables	.093	.159	.193	.215	.213
Services	.037	.075	.104	.126	.134
Plant and Equipment	0.	.186	.173	.133	.082
Inventory					
Durable Goods	.048	.079	.017	–.010	–.031
Nondurable Goods	.040	.023	.012	.008	–.002
Net Foreign Investment	–.078	–.101	–.103	–.103	–.098
Government Purchases	1.	1.	1.	1.	1.

[a] Detail may not add to total because of rounding.

shows the response of the GNP and its components to a permanent increase of $1 billion in government expenditure. The tabulated figures are the values of the variables measured as deviations from their levels as of year 0 before the shift in expenditure policy.

In response to increased government expenditure, the GNP rises by $1.3 billion the first year and under the stimulation of the dynamic factors climbs to a maximum of $1.6 billion over its initial level. It declines thereafter under the back-pressure of accumulating stocks. The behavior of the individual components is in keeping with their respective natures. Automobile demand rises immediately to its maximum and declines slowly as the stock of cars on the road accumulates. Consumer expenditure for durables rises sharply and levels off, while outlays on nondurable goods and services continue to rise throughout the period, although at declining rates.

Investment in plant and equipment spurts in response to the immediate improvement in the corporate profits and tapers off as the new plant becomes available. Inventory accumulation occurs at a high rate, but durable inventory overshoots and the rate of accumulation is forced somewhat below the year 0 level.

IV. CONCLUSION

To approximate the behavior of a complex economy by a set of 32 linear approximations is a heroic simplification. Yet experience has shown the statistical model to be a useful and flexible device for economic forecasting. Moreover, while the system of equations is small in relation to the vast structure of pure theory, it is considerably more elaborate than other devices that can be brought to bear on a practical level. Indeed, if an econometric model is nothing else, it is a highly sophisticated method of observing the past operation of the economy and systematizing the information obtained.

Yet, once the technical work of constructing the model is completed, a competent economist needs little more than a knowledge of elementary algebra to understand its nature, or to apply it to a wide range of analytical problems. Properly used, the model provides quantitative estimates of economic responses to specified changes in conditions. It goes without saying that the accuracy of these estimates is below the level that might be inferred from the precision of their statement in the text. But they show the proper order of magnitude involved and fall well within the practical tolerances required for effective policy evaluation.

12. The Forecasting Performance in the Early 1970s*

STEPHEN K. McNEES

Economic forecasters have come under a barrage of criticism for their performance for the 1974-75 recession. Their record over the early 1970s shows that those errors were unprecedented in magnitude, far larger than those before or since. The record also shows that forecasting errors have fallen into fairly distinct patterns over different forecast periods. The most recent information suggests that forecasting errors may return, at least temporarily, to more normal magnitudes.

Forecasts are often evaluated by comparing the latest actual data with the most recent forecast. This comparison encompasses a very short forecast horizon because forecasts are issued so frequently (typically quarterly or even monthly). Forecasts of such short horizons are largely irrelevant for planning decisions because the time lag between actions and their impact is usually significantly longer. This study deals with one-year-ahead forecasts. Given the conventional rule-of-thumb of 6- to 9-month lags, this horizon is sufficiently long that policy actions can effect policy goals. It also minimizes certain technical problems such as seasonal adjustment.

This study is based on the forecasts of five of the most widely known and influential forecasters.[1] Because the objective is to describe the variation in errors over different forecast periods rather than among different forecasters, the individual forecasts are treated anonymously, designating only the high, median, and low forecasts' errors.

The analysis focuses on eight "episodes" during the first half of the 1970s. These episodes were selected (somewhat arbitrarily) as periods in which the pace of economic activity changed considerably and/or in which the outlook was particularly controversial due to a major exogenous shock. The eight episodes selected are:

---

* *New England Economic Review*, (July/August 1976), pp. 29–40.

[1] The forecasts selected are those by the Bureau of Economic Analysis of the U.S. Department of Commerce. Chase Econometric Associates, Inc., Data Resources, Inc., Wharton Econometric Forecasting Associates, Inc., and the median forecast from the Economic Research Survey by the American Statistical Association and the National Bureau of Economic Research.

I. The severity of the 1970 recession, 1970:I to 1971:I.
II. The strength of the early recovery, 1970:IV to 1971:IV.
III. The impact of the New Economic Policies, 1971:III to 1972:III.
IV. Sustained expansion, 1972:II to 1973:II.
V. Soft landing turned stagflation, 1972:IV to 1973:IV.
VI. The impact of the oil embargo, 1973:III to 1974:III.
VII. The recession of 1974-75, 1974:I to 1975:I.
VIII. The strength of the early recovery, 1974:IV to 1975:IV.

In tables 1 through 8, the forecasts prevailing at the start of the episode are compared to the last actual data before the benchmark revisions of the National Income Accounts.

I. THE SEVERITY OF THE 1970 RECESSION, 1970:I TO 1971:I

In their forecasts based on the preliminary actual data for 1970:I, forecasters expected the recession to be very mild. They knew that the economy was in a recession according to the simple definition that two consecutive quarterly declines in real GNP constitute a recession. The unemployment rate was only 4.4 percent in March, but rising rapidly, reaching 5.0 percent in May.

In this recessionary environment, forecasters expected that real GNP would increase 2.2 to 3.6 percent over the next year and the unemployment rate would remain below 5.2 percent. The economic slowdown was expected to reduce the rate of inflation (as measured by the implicit GNP price deflator) to from 3.0 to 4.0 percent in comparison with the 5.0 percent rate registered in 1970:I.

TABLE 1
The 1970 Recession: 1970:I–1971:I

Growth Rate of (percent)	*Forecasts*			
	High	*Median*	*Low*	*Actual*
Real GNP	3.6	2.5	2.2	2.1
GNP deflator	4.0	3.8	3.0	5.0
GNP	7.7	6.2	5.3	7.2
Unemployment rate	5.2	4.6	4.2	6.0

The expectation of resumed real growth proved highly accurate—the actual rate was 2.1 percent compared with the median forecast of 2.5 percent.

The accompanying rise in the unemployment rate to 6.0 percent was substantially underestimated, however, due largely perhaps to the unexpectedly strong growth in the civilian labor force. Moreover, inflation did not decelerate as expected; the rate over the next year held at the 5.0 percent pace of 1970:I. The errors in the inflation forecasts (which ranged from 1 to 2 percent) must be considered large for those times, when the actual rate of inflation varied little between 4 and 6 percent. In summary, the forecasts fairly accurately gauged the mildness of the 1970 recession as measured by output but were far too optimistic about the consequent "Phillips curve."

II. THE STRENGTH OF THE EARLY RECOVERY, 1970:IV TO 1971:IV

When the early 1971 forecasts were issued, it was known that real output had declined in 1970:IV and that the General Motors strike had ended in late November. The unemployment rate had risen steadily to 6.0 percent in December, and the GNP deflator was rising at an annual rate of just over 5.5 percent in 1970:IV. The relevant forecasting issues were the strength of the 1971 recovery and the path of inflation.

TABLE 2
1971 Recovery: 1970:IV–1971:IV

Growth Rate of (percent)	*Forecasts*			
	High	*Median*	*Low*	*Actual*
Real GNP	5.2	4.6	4.3	5.5
GNP deflator	4.4	3.6	3.3	3.5
GNP	9.8	8.3	8.2	9.2
Unemployment rate	6.2	5.8	5.5	5.9

The forecasters expected GNP to grow by 8.2 to 9.8 percent, although the median forecast was only 8.3 percent. The actual figure of 9.2 percent was near the high end of the forecast range. The 5.5 percent real growth during the year was also slightly underpredicted—the median forecast being 4.6 percent—but the general picture of a modest recovery was in fact realized. The median 5.8 percent unemployment rate forecast was very close to the actual, as most of the forecasts accurately showed the unemployment rate as essentially flat during the year.

The inflation forecast is more complex to evaluate. The range of forecasts for the year was very narrow—3.3 to 4.4 percent—and centered on the actual figure of 3.5 percent. The actual figure, of course, reflects the Phase I 90-day wage-price freeze and one month of Phase II controls. The accuracy of the entire year forecasts reflects a general underestimation of the rate of inflation over the first half of the year—the median forecast of 3.5 percent was 1.1 percent below the actual—and an offsetting overestimation of the rate during the period when controls were in effect. Due in part to the imposition of controls, the economic forecasts of early 1971 gave a generally accurate picture of that year's moderate recovery.

III. THE IMPACT OF THE NEW ECONOMIC POLICIES, 1971:III TO 1972:III

During 1971:II, real GNP rose at a 3.6 percent annual rate, the unemployment rate inched up to 6.0 percent, and the rate of inflation de-

TABLE 3
A. Pre-New Economic Policies: 1971:III–1972:III

Growth Rate of (percent)	*Forecasts*			
	High	*Median*	*Low*	*Actual*
Real GNP	6.4	4.9	4.5	6.8
GNP deflator	4.3	3.9	3.5	3.2
GNP	10.1	9.1	8.6	10.2
Unemployment rate	6.0	5.8	5.2	5.6

B. Post-New Economic Policies: 1971:III–1972:III

Growth Rate of (percent)	*High*	*Median*	*Low*	*Actual*
Real GNP	7.7	7.0	6.1	6.8
GNP deflator	3.2	2.5	2.1	3.2
GNP	10.5	9.8	9.0	10.2
Unemployment rate	5.4	5.3	5.0	5.6

clined to 4.2 percent, the lowest since mid-1968. Against this backdrop, forecasters expected a continued modest recovery, with the rate of inflation declining moderately and an unemployment rate between 5.2 and 6.0 percent in 1972:III. In retrospect, the median GNP forecast proved to be 1.1 percent too low, the real growth forecast was 1.9 percent too low, the unemployment rate forecast for 1972:III was .2 percent too high, and the inflation forecast was .7 percent too high.

One source of these errors was the unforeseen introduction of the New Economic Policies (NEP) on August 15, 1971. In the first set of forecasts following the announcement of the NEP, the median GNP forecast was raised .7 percent to 9.8 percent, only .4 percent below the actual outcome. The median real growth forecast was raised by 2.1 percent to 7.0 percent, which was exceedingly close to the actual 6.8 percent. The inflation forecasts were lowered from the 3.5 to 4.3 percent pre-NEP range to a 2.1 to 3.2 percent post-NEP range. While this downward revision was clearly in the correct direction, all but one of the forecasts were scaled down too far.

The unemployment rate forecasts were also lowered in accordance with the revised expectation of more rapid growth in output. However, this revision took the forecasts away from the mark since the pre-NEP forecasts had been quite accurate.

Nevertheless, despite the tendency to be overly optimistic about the reduction in unemployment and, to a lesser extent, the inflation rate, the post-NEP forecasts must be regarded as an overwhelming success. They were devised in a period of considerable uncertainty following several simultaneous and unprecedented policy shifts but proved to be highly accurate.

IV. SUSTAINED EXPANSION, 1972:II TO 1973:II

By mid-1972, there was no doubt that a strong economic recovery was under way. Real GNP in the second quarter grew at an 8.9 percent rate and employment was rising rapidly, although the unemployment rate held at a plateau just under 6.0 percent. Phase II held the rate of inflation to 2.1 percent in the second quarter, down from the 5.1 percent bulge which followed the end of Phase I.

TABLE 4
Sustained Expansion: 1972:II–1973:II

Growth Rate of (percent)	*Forecasts*			
	High	*Median*	*Low*	*Actual*
Real GNP	7.3	6.0	5.7	6.5
GNP deflator	3.7	3.6	3.0	5.0
GNP	10.5	9.8	9.5	11.8
Unemployment rate	5.2	5.1	4.8	4.9

The mid-1972 forecasts slightly underestimated the strength of the economy in late 1972 and early 1973. Most forecasters underestimated the 6.5 percent real growth rate, although the median error was only —.5 percent and the maximum only —.8 percent. This accompanied a similarly minor overestimate of the 4.9 percent unemployment rate in 1973:II, the median error being only .2 and the maximum .3 percent. The nominal variable forecasts that appeared along with these highly accurate real variable forecasts were particularly inaccurate by the standards of the time. The median inflation forecast was 1.4 percent too optimistic. The 5.0 percent rate of inflation was underestimated due to the inability to foresee the acceleration of inflation which occurred in the first half of 1973, after the Phase II controls had been relaxed and reformulated into Phase III (on January 11, 1973). The inflation errors swamped the negligible real growth errors, producing underestimates of GNP growth of from 1.3 to 2.3 percent.

V. SOFT LANDING TURNED STAGFLATION, 1972:IV TO 1973:IV

In early 1973, forecasters knew that real GNP had grown at an 8.5 percent annual rate in 1972:IV, the unemployment rate had held at 5.2 percent in December, and the rate of inflation had been held under 3 percent for three consecutive quarters by the Phase II controls. Before the new forecasts were made, the Phase II controls had been replaced by the more voluntary Phase III system, but there had not been enough time to see how well the new program would work.

TABLE 5
Soft Landing Turned Stagflation: 1972:IV–1973:IV

Growth Rate of (percent)	*Forecasts*			
	High	*Median*	*Low*	*Actual*
Real GNP	4.9	4.8	4.5	3.9
GNP deflator	4.5	3.8	3.5	7.4
GNP	9.2	8.9	8.6	11.6
Unemployment rate	5.0	4.9	4.8	4.7

Forecasters anticipated that inflation in 1973 would exceed the 1972 rate, but even the pessimists far underestimated the actual 7.4 percent which was in store. Similarly, the highest nominal GNP growth forecast was 2.4 percent below the actual 11.6 percent.

In contrast to the underestimates of nominal variables the consensus forecast of a "soft landing," with real growth decelerating in the first half and slowing more substantially to below-trend rates in the second half, was closely realized. Over the year as a whole, fourth quarter to fourth quarter, real growth forecasts ranged narrowly from 4.5 percent to 4.9 percent. Even the narrow "soft landing" consensus slightly overestimated the actual 3.9 percent real growth which occurred, but by an unusually small amount. The corresponding unemployment rate forecasts for 1973:IV were also highly accurate, the median 4.9 percent falling only .2 percent above the actual outcome.

VI. THE IMPACT OF THE OIL EMBARGO, 1973:III TO 1974:III

As of late October 1973, the forecasters knew that real growth had slowed to about 3.5 percent in 1973:III, that the unemployment rate held level in August and September at 4.8 percent, and that their previous forecasts had seriously underestimated the 6.7 percent increase in prices in 1973:III. More importantly perhaps, they knew that the Middle East War had erupted on October 6 and that the posted price of crude oil had been raised by 70 percent on October 16 before their forecasts were made. But they did not yet know that the price of imported oil would soon quadruple. It was not until the November round of forecasts that the "energy crisis" was regarded as a serious threat to the prevailing "soft landing" view.

TABLE 6a
Pre-Embargo: 1973:III–1974:III

Growth Rate of (percent)	*Forecasts*			
	High	*Median*	*Low*	*Actual*
Real GNP	3.4	2.4	2.1	−2.1
GNP deflator	5.4	4.6	4.4	10.5
GNP	8.1	7.4	6.7	8.2
Unemployment rate	5.5	5.2	5.2	5.0

The pre-embargo real growth forecasts for the period 1973:III to 1974:III ranged from 2.1 to 3.4 percent. None foresaw the 2.1 percent decline which was to occur. Inflation forecasts had been raised from the early 1973 levels, but only to about half of the actual 10.5 percent rate. Given an optimistic real growth outlook, the expectation of a modest rise in the unemployment rate by 1974:III to from 5.2 to 5.5 percent somewhat surprisingly overstated the 5.0 percent actual figure.

These misses—real growth was overestimated by from 4.2 to 5.5 percent and the inflation rate was underestimated by from 5.1 to 6.1 percent—were unprecedented in magnitude. These forecasts provided a very poor indication of where the economy was headed.

One of the primary reasons, or at least rationales, for the extraordinarily large errors was the unanticipated oil embargo, announced on October 17, and the consequent "energy crisis." This unique external supply-side shock provided a severe challenge to the conventional, demand-oriented forecasting techniques.

To examine how well the forecasts were adapted to the oil embargo, consider the post-embargo forecasts of the same "energy spasm" period. In contrast to the pre-embargo forecasts, these forecasts are *three-*

TABLE 6b
Post-Embargo: 1973:III–1974:III

Growth Rate of (percent)	*Forecasts*			
	High	*Median*	*Low*	*Actual*
Real GNP	1.8	.6	−.1	−2.1
GNP deflator	8.3	6.6	5.6	10.5
GNP	8.3	7.6	6.4	8.2
Unemployment rate	6.2	5.9	5.7	5.0

quarter-ahead forecasts that combine embargo adjustments with the actual data for 1973:IV.

The post-embargo set of nominal GNP forecasts changed little from the pre-embargo set, slightly underestimating the actual rate of 8.2 percent. The price-output mix was somewhat improved but remained far off the mark. The January forecasts of real growth over this period were flat—the median forecast was .6 percent and the low —.1 percent. These forecasts lent credence to the view that the economy was suffering from a short-lived energy spasm, which would be followed by a resumption of real growth. This mistaken prognosis set the stage for the subsequent disputes about whether the economy was in a recession in early 1974, when employment, industrial production, and new orders for capital orders were holding up fairly well. Due perhaps to labor hoarding based on the expectation of an upturn, employment held up well. Productivity unexpectedly collapsed. Despite the substantial *overestimation* of real output, there was an unusually large *overestimation* of the unemployment rate in 1974:III. After the oil embargo, most forecasters raised their estimates of third-quarter unemployment from about 5.2 percent (compared to the actual of 5.0 percent) to about 6.0, producing errors 3 times larger than the average error for the preceding 3 years. The unexpected stability in employment produced a variety of novel theories, indicating the need for an entirely new approach to the short-term demand for employment.

But time showed that the new theories were not needed. The failure instead had been in the timing, or lag structure, in the simple output-unemployment relationship. The unemployment rate, which had drifted up 1 percentage point between the start of the second and start of the fourth quarters, rose another full percentage point in the last 2 months of the year. Thus, the same post-embargo forecasts, which had seriously overestimated the unemployment rate for 1974:III, turned out to be extremely accurate for the fourth quarter of the year.

Just the opposite conclusion is true of the real GNP forecasts. All the post-embargo forecasts showed an economic recovery or rebound in the second half of the year. Projections of real growth in 1974:IV ranged from 2.5 to 5.9 percent, a far cry from the actual —9.1 percent figure. The inability to foresee the collapse in demand which was to occur in 1974:IV may overstate the misinformation in the forecasts. A fairer statement is that the forecasters were predicting a year (fourth quarter to fourth quarter) of essentially flat economic growth in contrast to the actual outcome of a 4.0 percent decline in real GNP. The resulting error was 4 to 6 times larger than the average error of real GNP forecasts over the previous 3 years.

In sum, the first set of forecasts after the oil embargo were generally correct in leaving the nominal GNP forecasts unchanged from pre-embargo predictions. However, adjustments to show more inflation and lower levels of output, while in the right direction, were not large enough. The upward pressure on prices and downward pressure on output were far stronger than the post-embargo forecasts anticipated. The forecasters were unable to capture the timing of the rise in the unemployment rate.

VII. THE RECESSION OF 1974–1975, 1974:I TO 1975:I

The next episode is one of even greater forecasting failure. In the late April 1974 forecasts made after the embargo had ended, there was still no appreciation of the severity of the 1974-75 recession. It was known that in this first quarter real GNP had declined by 5.8 percent and inflation had moved into the double-digit area, 10.8 percent in 1974:I

In a wave of post-embargo euphoria, the forecasters predicted real GNP growth over the next four-quarter period to be as large as 3.8 percent, and inflation to recede to as low as 6.6 percent. The unemployment rate was projected to level off between 5.7 and 6.1 percent in 1975:I. None of the figures proved to be even a remote representation of the future reality.

TABLE 7
The Recession: 1974:I–1975:I

Growth Rate of (percent)	*Forecasts*			Actual
	High	*Median*	*Low*	
Real GNP	3.8	2.2	1.6	−6.1
GNP deflator	8.5	7.0	6.6	11.0
GNP	11.6	10.3	8.9	4.3
Unemployment rate	6.1	5.9	5.7	8.3

Unlike the 1973–74 forecasts which were quite accurate for nominal GNP but missed the mix between prices and output, the April 1974 forecasts seriously overestimated the growth of nominal GNP. GNP forecasts ranged from 8.9 to 11.6 percent, which, compared with the actual rate of 4.3 percent, produced the largest GNP errors in the first half of the 1970s. The error occurred despite a sizable, but far from record, underestimation of the inflation rate—the median forecast underestimated the 11.0 percent rate of inflation by 4.0 percent; the minimum error was 2.5 percent.

Relative to past performance, the most serious error occurred in the underestimation of the rise in the unemployment rate. The closest one-year-ahead forecast put the unemployment rate 2.2 percent below the actual 8.3 percent figure for 1975:I, an error about 7 times larger than the average error in the previous 4 years. Much of this error stemmed from overestimation of real GNP. The most pessimistic real growth forecast in April 1974, 1.6 percent, gave no indication of the actual 6.1 percent decline.

TABLE 8
Errors and Error Distribution
Low, Median, and High Real GNP Forecasts, 1974:I–1975:I

	Actual Change	Forecast Errors (billions, 1958 $)			Percent of Δ GNP Actual	Percent of GNP Error		
		Low	Median	High		Low	Median	High
	(1)	(2)	(3)	(4)	(5)	(6)	(7)	(8)
(1) Real GNP	−50.5	63.5	68.5	82.5	100.0	100.0	100.0	100.0
(2) Consumer expenditures	−8.2	21.2	19.3	25.4	16.2	33.4	28.2	30.8
(3) Durables	−10.0	15.8	12.7	15.3	19.8	24.9	18.5	18.5
(4) Nondurables and services	1.7	5.5	6.7	10.2	−3.4	8.7	9.8	12.4
(5) Fixed investment	−21.7	24.7	31.3	29.0	43.0	38.9	45.7	35.2
(6) Business	−12.5	16.7	16.6	19.5	24.8	26.3	24.2	23.6
(7) Residential	−9.1	8.0	14.7	9.5	18.0	12.6	21.5	11.5
(8) Inventory investment	−22.3	22.4	19.9	26.3	44.2	35.3	29.1	31.9
(9) Net exports	.1	−5.4	−5.0	−2.4	−0.2	−8.5	−7.3	−2.9
(10) Government purchases	1.7	0.5	2.9	4.0	−3.4	0.8	4.2	4.8

Note: Components may not add to totals because of rounding.

Table 8 gives a detailed breakdown of the errors of the high, median, and low real GNP forecasts of 1974–75 along with the percentage distribution of the total errors among components. The error distributions are similar for each of the three forecasts. As expected, the errors are disproportionately concentrated in the cyclical components: the largest proportion, about one third, was in the change in business inventory investment; the second largest, about one quarter of the total, was in business fixed investment; the next largest, generally of roughly 20 to 25 percent, was in expenditures on consumer durables; and the other sizable error component was investment in residential structures. Net exports, government purchases of goods and services, and consumer purchases of nondurable goods and services were the only components that increased in real terms over this time span. Net exports was the only major demand component whose strength was generally underestimated, partially offsetting some of the large overestimates in other areas. The underestimates of consumer purchases of nondurable goods and services and of government purchases of goods and services were of relatively minor importance.

It is impossible to analyze fully the causes of these errors. Although no final accounting can be given, it is possible to speculate about some of the factors underlying these errors.

Part of the explanation for the overestimation of inventory investment, i.e., the underestimation of the swing to inventory liquidation, arises from the fact that these forecasts were based on preliminary GNP estimates which were subsequently revised to show substantially more inventory investment. Even after the July 1974 National Income and Product Account historical revisions, however, "The forecasters were betting against a regularity of postwar history in expecting no inventory liquidation." This inability to forecast real final sales, particularly the collapse which occurred in 1974:IV, centered around the gross auto product final sales. This failure, in turn, must be attributable to factors peculiar to the 1975 models such as the substantial price increases and the introduction of new pollution control and safety equipment, as well as to more usual factors such as the low level of real disposable income and the erosion of real household wealth positions. The resulting substantial overhang of auto dealers' inventories by yearend, which in turn resulted in heavy liquidation in 1975:I accounted for about 45 percent of the total inventory liquidation for the quarter.

Aside from auto sales, the major error in forecasting final sales comes from the inaccuracy of forecasts of fixed investment. Explanation of the fixed investment error leads to the question of monetary policy assumptions in the April 1974 forecasts. Evaluation of the monetary policy assumptions behind the forecasting errors is particularly difficult because of the lack of general agreement on: the appropriate targets and indicators of monetary policy, the lag structure of the impact of monetary policy, and the size of monetary policy multipliers. The first issue can be partially avoided by examining the behavior of both aggregates and interest rates. Table 9 shows April 1974 forecasts of two of the more commonly watched indicators of monetary policy: the growth in the narrowly defined money stock and the interest rate on four- to six-month commercial paper.[2] The rate of money growth over the entire period was

TABLE 9
Monetary and Financial Forecasts Issued April 1974

Forecaster	*Actual 1974:I*	*Forecast*			
		1974:II	*1974:III*	*1974:IV*	*1975:I*
Money stock growth					
A	5.8	7.4	7.3	7.5	7.5
B	5.6	3.4	5.9	7.1	6.9
C	5.8	6.9	5.3	6.3	6.6
D	5.8	6.0	6.0	6.3	6.2
Actual	5.8	7.3	3.9	3.7	1.4
Yield on 4- to 6-month commercial paper					
A	9.73	9.7	10.0	9.5	8.9
B	9.73	9.2	7.3	6.6	6.7
C	9.73	9.2	8.5	7.8	7.3
D	10.13	10.1	10.0	9.7	9.4
Actual	8.3	10.5	11.5	9.1	6.6

[2] Only four of the five forecasts provide detailed financial-monetary information. Money and the commercial paper rate are the only two financial variables common to all four forecasts.

significantly overestimated and the level of commercial paper rates was generally underestimated. Monetary policy was "tighter" (and/or the demand for money was stronger) than the forecasters anticipated in their April forecasts.

However, because of the lag between financial variables and their impact on spending, production, and employment, the long-term financial variable assumptions had a negligible impact in the forecast period. With the conventional six- to nine-month lag assumption, only the monetary policy assumptions for 1974:II and 1974:III would be relevant for the outcome through 1975:I. Over that period, money growth was 1.75 percent lower than the highest growth forecast but only about 0.5 percent lower than the median forecast. Growth in the second quarter was actually higher than generally anticipated. Taking instead the commercial paper rate in the middle quarters of 1974, it was generally expected that rates would decline throughout the remainder of the period. However, the actual rate continued to climb, reaching a level of nearly 12 percent in mid-July, and did not fall below 10 percent again until October.

It would be interesting to conduct an ex post simulation of the forecast period to examine the impact of underestimating financial stringency on the forecast in this period. In the absence of such a test, one can only speculate on its importance. One guess is that significant underestimation of the declines would have occurred despite foreknowledge of the degree of financial stringency which was to prevail in the middle quarters of 1974 although forecasts of fixed investment, particularly in residential structures, would certainly have improved. For econometric forecasters, most models' coefficients for aggregates or rates are too small and the distributed lags too long to capture the severity and rapidity of the decline. For judgmental forecasters, the memory of shortages, capacity problems, and the need to restructure the capital stock in accordance with the new higher price of energy were too fresh in mind to anticipate the collapse which was in store. Only if appropriate assumptions on the degree of financial stringency had been combined with knowledge of the magnitude of excess inventory holding, the fourth-quarter collapse in consumer demand (especially in auto demand), and the consequent year-end inventory overhang, could the record errors for the period have been reduced to more normal magnitudes.

VIII. THE STRENGTH OF THE EARLY RECOVERY, 1974:IV TO 1975:IV

When the early 1975 forecasts were issued, it was known that in 1974:IV, GNP grew by an annual rate of 3.3 percent, real growth declined at a 9.4 percent rate, the inflation rate reached 13.7 percent, and the unemployment rate had climbed to 7.1 percent in December. It was generally agreed that 1975 would be a year of little real growth, but forecasters could not agree on whether the trough would be in the first or second quarter.

The forecasters expected real GNP to rise during 1975 by less than 1 percent, a relatively small underestimate of the actual increase of 1.8

TABLE 10
The Recovery: 1974:IV–1975:IV

Growth Rate of (percent)	*Forecasts*			
	High	*Median*	*Low*	*Actual*
Real GNP	0.9	0.4	0.1	1.8
GNP deflator	9.2	8.3	7.4	6.3
GNP	9.7	8.7	8.3	8.2
Unemployment rate	8.9	8.1	7.6	8.5

percent. The recession was expected to help cut the rate of inflation to from 7.4 to 9.2 percent. This proved to be unduly pessimistic as the actual rate fell to 6.3 percent. Reflecting the larger overestimates of inflation and the small underestimates of output growth, all of the nominal GNP forecasts were too high, although the median forecast was only .5 percent above the actual. Although the estimates of the fourth quarter unemployment rate ranged from as high as 8.9 percent to as low as 7.6 percent, the median forecast of 8.1 percent was a reasonably close approximation of the actual 8.5 percent rate.

A SUMMARY OF FORECASTING ERRORS IN THE EARLY 1970s

Table 11 summarizes the accuracy of the median one-year-ahead forecasts in the early 1970s. The errors fall into six fairly distinct patterns.

The early-1970 forecasts correctly foresaw that the 1970 recession would be one of the mildest in the post-World War II period. They were, however, overly optimistic about the rise in the unemployment rate and the deceleration of inflation that would accompany the recession.

The forecasts made from mid-1970 through 1971 gave a highly accurate picture of the future path of all major economic variables. This performance is particularly notable because of both the atypical profile of that recovery—sluggish in 1971 and exuberant in 1972—and the dramatic, simultaneous major policy shifts which were embodied in the New Economic Policies. The forecasts in this period provided about as much information about future developments as decision makers can ever hope to obtain.

The forecasts issued in 1972 failed to foresee the acceleration in inflation which occurred in 1973. This was the major cause of the substantial underestimation of nominal GNP. Real variable forecasts, on the other hand, continued to be highly accurate: both the second-half slowdown and the leveling off in the unemployment rate were anticipated well in advance.

Underestimation of the acceleration of inflation in 1974 did not result in an underestimation of current dollar GNP as it had for 1973, however. The failure in the forecasts of 1974 was the inability to apportion GNP growth between price and output increases—the underestimation of inflation was accompanied by roughly equal overestimation of real growth. Despite this, however, the forecasts of unemployment were on track.

The forecasts made in early 1974 produced by far the largest errors of the period for GNP, real GNP, and the unemployment rate—errors 3.75, 4 and 6 times larger respectively than the "normal"errors for the early 1970s. These forecasts failed miserably in warning of the severity of the impending recession. The sources of the errors in real GNP, discussed earlier, were spread fairly evenly among its individual components. Because of the failure to account for a combination of adverse economic forces, these forecasts contributed to the mistaken impression, so widely

TABLE 11
Errors on Median One-Year-Ahead Forecasts, 1971:I–1975:IV
(based on five forecasters)

Four Quarters Ending in	*GNP*	*Percent Change in Real GNP*	*Deflator*	*Change in Unemployment Rate*
71:I	−1.0	0.4	−1.2	−1.0
71:II	−1.0	0.3	−1.4	−0.9
71:III	−0.6	0.4	−0.9	−0.4
71:IV	−0.9	−1.0	0.2	−0.1
72:I	−0.0	0.1	0.2	−0.1
72:II	−0.4	−1.5	1.0	0.2
72:III	−0.6	−0.6	0.1	−0.2
72:IV	−1.2	−1.2	0.1	0.1
73:I	−2.1	−1.6	−0.2	0.4
73:II	−2.0	−0.4	−1.4	0.1
73:III	−2.5	0.4	−2.8	0.4
73:IV	−2.7	0.9	−3.6	0.2
74:I	−0.8	4.1	−5.0	0.4
74:II	−0.5	3.8	−4.4	0.0
74:III	−0.8	4.3	−5.7	−0.3
74:IV	1.0	5.8	−5.5	−0.6
75:I	6.1	8.3	−4.0	−2.4
75:II	5.4	7.0	−2.2	−2.7
75:III	3.3	1.3	1.2	−1.6
75:IV	0.5	−1.4	2.0	−0.2
Mean absolute one-year-ahead median error	1.7	−2.2	2.2	0.6

prevalent even in mid-1974, that inflation was the only major policy problem and that an upturn was imminent.

The forecasts of 1975:IV, the last period for which actual data are available, were significantly more accurate. By late 1974, the forecasters expected an economic recovery and a deceleration of inflation. The median nominal GNP forecast was only 0.5 percent above the actual 8.2 percent growth rate. For the first time in 10 quarters, growth in real GNP was underestimated, and for the second consecutive time inflation slowed by more than expected.

13. Input–Output Economics*

WASSILY W. LEONTIEF

If the great 19th-century physicist James Clerk Maxwell were to attend a current meeting of the American Physical Society, he might have serious difficulty in keeping track of what was going on. In the field of economics, on the other hand, his contemporary John Stuart Mill would easily pick up the thread of the most advanced arguments among his 20th-century successors. Physics, applying the method of inductive reasoning from quantitatively observed, events, has moved on to entirely new premises. The science of economics, in contrast, remains largely a deductive system resting upon a static set of premises, most of which were familiar to Mill and some of which date back to Adam Smith's *The Wealth of Nations*.

Present-day economists are not universally content with this state of affairs. Some of the greatest recent names in economics–Léon Walras, Vilfredo Pareto, Irving Fisher–are associated with the effort to develop quantitative methods for grappling with the enormous volume of empirical data that is involved in every real economic situation. Yet such methods have so far failed to find favor with the majority of professional economists. It is not only the forbidding rigor of mathematics; the truth is that such methods have seldom produced results significantly superior to those achieved by the traditional procedure. In an empirical science, after all, nothing ultimately counts but results. Most economists therefore continue to rely upon their "professional intuition" and "sound judgment" to establish the connection between the facts and the theory of economics.

In recent years, however, the output of economic facts and figures by various public and private agencies has increased by leaps and bounds. Most of this information is published for reference purposes, and is unrelated to any particular method of analysis. As a result we have in economics today a high concentration of theory without fact on the one hand, and a mounting accumulation of fact without theory on the other. The task of filling the "empty boxes of economic theory" with relevant empirical content becomes every day more urgent and challenging.

* *Scientific American*, vol. 185, no. 4 (October 1951), pp. 15–21.

This article is concerned with a new effort to combine economic facts and theory known as "interindustry" or "input-output" analysis. Essentially it is a method of analysis that takes advantage of the relatively stable pattern of the flow of goods and services among the elements of our economy to bring a much more detailed statistical picture of the system into the range of manipulation by economic theory. As such, the method has had to await the modern high-speed computing machine as well as the present propensity of government and private agencies to accumulate mountains of data. It is now advancing from the phase of academic investigation and experimental trial to a broadening sphere of application in grand-scale problems of national economic policy. The practical possibilities of the method are being carried forward as a cooperative venture of the Bureau of Labor Statistics, the Bureau of Mines, the Department of Commerce, the Bureau of the Budget, the Council of Economic Advisers and, with particular reference to procurement and logistics, the Air Force. Meanwhile the development of the technique of input-output analysis continues to interest academic investigators here and abroad. They are hopeful that this method of bringing the facts of economics into closer association with theory may induce some fruitful advances in both.

Economic theory seeks to explain the material aspects and operations of our society in terms of interactions among such variables as supply and demand or wages and prices. Economists have generally based their analyses on relatively simple data—such quantities as the gross national product, the interest rate, price and wage levels. But in the real world things are not so simple. Between a shift in wages and the ultimate working out of its impact upon prices there is a complex series of transactions in which actual goods and services are exchanged among real people. These intervening steps are scarcely suggested by the classical formulation of the relationship between the two variables. It is true, of course, that the individual transactions, like individual atoms and molecules, are far too numerous for observation and description in detail. But it is possible, as with physical particles, to reduce them to some kind of order by classifying and aggregating them into groups. This is the procedure employed by input-output analysis in improving the grasp of economic theory upon the facts with which it is concerned in every real situation.

The essential principles of the method may be most easily comprehended by consulting the input-output table in figure 1. This table summarizes the transactions which characterized the U.S. economy during the year 1947. The transactions are grouped into 42 major departments of production, distribution, transportation, and consumption, set up on a matrix of horizontal rows and vertical columns. The horizontal rows of figures show how the output of each sector of the economy is distributed among the others. Conversely, the vertical columns show how each sector obtains from the others its needed inputs of goods and services. Since each figure in any horizontal row is also a figure in a vertical column, the output of each sector is shown to be an input in some other. The double-entry bookkeeping of the input-output table thus reveals the fabric of our economy, woven together by the flow of trade which ultimately links each branch and industry to all others. Such a table may of course be developed in as fine or as coarse detail as the available data permit and the purpose requires. The present table summarizes a much more detailed 500-sector master table which has just been completed after two years of intensive work by the Interindustry Economics Division of the Bureau of Labor Statistics.

For purposes of illustration let us look at the input-output structure of a single sector—the one labeled "primary metals" (sector 14). The vertical column states the inputs of each of the various goods and services that are required for the production of metals, and the sum of the figures in this column represents the total outlay of the economy for the year's production. Most of the entries in this column are self-explanatory. Thus it is no surprise to find a substantial figure entered against the item "products of petroleum and coal" (sector 10). The design of the table, however, gives a special meaning to some of the sectors. The outlay for "railroad transportation" (sector 23), for example, covers only the cost of hauling raw materials to the mills; the cost of delivering primary metal products to their markets is borne by the industries purchasing them. Another outlay requiring explanation is entered in the trade sector (sector 26). The figures in this sector represent the cost of distribution, stated in terms of the trade margin. The entries against trade in the primary metals column, therefore, cover the middleman's markup on the industry's purchases; trade margins on the sale of primary metal products are charged against the consuming industries. Taxes paid by the industry are entered in the row labeled "government" (sector 40), and all payments to individuals, including wages, salaries and dividends, are summed up in the row labeled "households" (sector 42). How the output of the metals industry is distributed among the other sectors is shown in row 14. The figures indicate that the industry's principal customers are other industries. "Households" and "government" turn up as direct customers for only a minor portion of the total output, although these two sectors are of course the principal consumers of metals after they have been converted into end products by other industries.

Coming out of the interior of the table to the outer row and columns, the reader may soon recognize many of the familiar total figures by which we are accustomed to visualize the condition of the economy. The total outputs at the end of each industry row, for example, are the figures we use to measure the size or the health of an industry. The gross national product which is designed to state the total of productive activity and is the most commonly cited index for the economy as a whole, may be

FIGURE 1
The Exchange of Goods and Services in the U.S. for the Year 1947

INDUSTRY

19 OTHER TRANSPORTATION EQUIPMENT · 20 PROFESSIONAL AND SCIENTIFIC · 21 MISCELLANEOUS · 22 COAL · 23

INDUSTRY PRODUCING	1 AGRICULTURE AND FISHERIES	2 FOOD AND KINDRED PRODUCTS	3 TEXTILE MILL PRODUCTS	4 APPAREL	5 LUMBER AND WOOD PRODUCTS	6 FURNITURE AND FIXTURES	7 PAPER AND ALLIED PRODUCTS	8 PRINTING AND PUBLISHING	9 CHEMICALS	10 PRODUCTS OF PETROLEUM AND COAL	11 RUBBER PRODUCTS	12 LEATHER AND LEATHER PRODUCTS	13 STONE, CLAY AND GLASS PRODUCTS	14 PRIMARY METALS	15 FABRICATED METAL PRODUCTS	16 MACHINERY (EXCEPT ELECTRIC)	17 ELECTRICAL MACHINERY	18 MOTOR VEHICLES
1 AGRICULTURE AND FISHERIES	10.86	15.70	2.16	0.02	0.19	—	0.01	—	1.21	—	—	0.05	*	0.01	—	—	—	—
2 FOOD AND KINDRED PRODUCTS	2.38	5.75	0.06	0.01	*	*	0.03	*	0.79	*	—	0.44	*	*	*	*	*	—
3 TEXTILE MILL PRODUCTS	0.06	*	1.30	3.88	*	0.29	0.04	0.03	0.01	*	0.44	0.09	0.03	—	0.01	0.02	0.05	0.15
4 APPAREL	0.04	0.20	—	1.96	—	0.01	0.02	—	0.03	—	—	*	*	—	*	*	*	0.10
5 LUMBER AND WOOD PRODUCTS	0.15	0.10	0.02	*	1.09	0.39	0.27	*	0.04	0.01	—	0.02	0.02	0.06	0.06	0.09	0.05	0.05
6 FURNITURE AND FIXTURES	—	—	0.01	—	—	0.01	0.01	—	—	—	—	—	—	—	*	0.01	0.10	0.03
7 PAPER AND ALLIED PRODUCTS	*	0.52	0.08	0.02	*	0.02	2.60	1.08	0.33	0.11	0.02	0.05	0.18	*	0.09	0.04	0.07	0.03
8 PRINTING AND PUBLISHING	—	0.04	*	—	—	—	—	0.77	0.02	—	—	—	—	—	0.01	0.01	0.01	—
9 CHEMICALS	0.83	1.48	0.80	0.14	0.03	0.06	0.18	0.10	2.58	0.21	0.60	0.13	0.12	0.18	0.13	0.08	0.20	0.11
10 PRODUCTS OF PETROLEUM AND COAL	0.46	0.06	0.03	*	0.07	*	0.06	*	0.32	4.83	0.01	*	0.05	0.90	0.02	0.04	0.02	0.03
11 RUBBER PRODUCTS	0.12	0.01	0.01	0.02	0.01	0.01	0.01	*	*	*	0.04	0.05	0.01	*	0.01	0.13	0.03	0.50
12 LEATHER AND LEATHER PRODUCTS	—	—	*	0.05	*	0.01	—	*	—	—	—	1.04	—	—	*	0.02	*	0.01
13 STONE, CLAY AND GLASS PRODUCTS	0.06	0.25	*	*	0.01	0.03	0.03	—	0.26	0.05	0.01	0.01	0.43	0.21	0.07	0.07	0.12	0.19
14 PRIMARY METALS	0.01	*	—	*	0.01	0.11	—	0.01	0.19	0.01	0.01	*	0.04	6.90	2.53	2.02	1.05	1.28
15 FABRICATED METAL PRODUCTS	0.08	0.61	*	0.01	0.04	0.14	0.02	*	0.13	0.08	0.01	0.02	*	0.05	0.43	0.62	0.34	0.97
16 MACHINERY (EXCEPT ELECTRIC)	0.06	0.01	0.04	0.02	0.01	0.01	0.01	0.04	*	0.01	—	—	0.01	0.07	0.28	1.15	0.17	0.63
17 ELECTRICAL MACHINERY	—	—	—	—	—	—	—	—	*	—	—	—	0.01	0.05	0.24	0.58	0.86	0.62
18 MOTOR VEHICLES	0.11	*	—	—	*	—	—	—	—	*	—	—	*	*	0.03	0.03	0.01	4.40
19 OTHER TRANSPORTATION EQUIPMENT	0.01	—	—	—	—	—	*	—	*	*	*	—	*	*	—	—	*	0.01
20 PROFESSIONAL AND SCIENTIFIC EQUIPMENT	—	—	—	—	—	*	0.01	0.03	0.01	—	—	—	*	*	0.04	0.04	0.01	0.07
21 MISCELLANEOUS MANUFACTURING INDUSTRIES	*	0.01	*	0.26	*	0.02	0.01	—	0.03	—	*	0.02	0.01	*	0.02	0.05	0.11	0.02
22 COAL, GAS AND ELECTRIC POWER	0.06	0.20	0.11	0.04	0.02	0.02	0.12	0.03	0.19	0.56	0.04	0.02	0.20	0.35	0.08	0.10	0.05	0.06
23 RAILROAD TRANSPORTATION	0.44	0.57	0.09	0.06	0.14	0.05	0.22	0.07	0.29	0.27	0.04	0.04	0.15	0.52	0.13	0.16	0.07	0.23
24 OCEAN TRANSPORTATION	0.07	0.13	0.01	0.01	0.01	*	0.02	*	0.04	0.09	*	*	0.01	0.08	*	*	*	*
25 OTHER TRANSPORTATION	0.55	0.38	0.08	0.03	0.14	0.04	0.12	0.03	0.10	0.47	0.01	0.02	0.07	0.16	0.03	0.04	0.03	0.07
26 TRADE	1.36	0.46	0.23	0.37	0.06	0.06	0.18	0.03	0.17	0.02	0.05	0.06	0.05	0.36	0.20	0.26	0.14	0.06
27 COMMUNICATIONS	*	0.04	0.01	0.02	0.01	0.01	0.01	0.04	0.02	0.01	0.01	*	0.01	0.02	0.02	0.03	0.02	0.02
28 FINANCE AND INSURANCE	0.24	0.15	0.02	0.02	0.08	0.02	0.02	0.02	0.02	0.13	0.01	0.01	0.05	0.06	0.04	0.05	0.04	0.02
29 REAL ESTATE AND RENTALS	2.39	0.09	0.03	0.10	0.02	0.02	0.03	0.06	0.03	—	0.01	0.02	0.02	0.06	0.03	0.04	0.03	0.02
30 BUSINESS SERVICES	0.01	0.63	0.07	0.10	0.02	0.06	0.02	0.06	0.42	0.04	0.02	0.05	0.01	0.03	0.05	0.09	0.06	0.08
31 PERSONAL AND REPAIR SERVICES	0.37	0.12	*	*	0.04	*	*	0.02	0.01	0.01	*	*	0.03	0.01	0.01	0.01	*	*
32 NON-PROFIT ORGANIZATIONS	—	—	—	—	—	—	—	—	—	—	—	—	—	—	—	—	—	—
33 AMUSEMENTS	—	—	—	—	—	—	—	—	—	—	—	—	—	—	—	—	—	—
34 SCRAP AND MISCELLANEOUS INDUSTRIES	—	—	0.02	—	—	—	0.25	—	0.01	—	0.01	—	0.01	1.11	0.02	0.05	*	—
35 EATING AND DRINKING PLACES	—	—	—	—	—	—	—	*	—	—	—	—	—	—	—	—	—	—
36 NEW CONSTRUCTION AND MAINTENANCE	0.20	0.12	0.04	0.02	0.01	0.01	0.04	0.01	0.04	0.03	0.01	0.02	0.03	0.10	0.03	0.05	0.02	0.04
37 UNDISTRIBUTED	—	1.87	0.30	1.08	0.73	0.27	0.17	0.50	1.49	0.65	0.27	0.27	0.47	0.32	1.14	1.71	0.89	0.41
38 INVENTORY CHANGE (DEPLETIONS)	2.66	0.40	0.12	0.19	*	0.01	0.09	0.03	0.14	0.01	*	0.03	*	0.11	*	*	*	0.01
39 FOREIGN COUNTRIES (IMPORTS FROM)	0.69	2.11	0.21	0.28	0.18	0.01	0.62	0.01	0.59	0.26	*	0.04	0.14	0.62	0.01	0.05	*	0.02
40 GOVERNMENT	0.81	1.24	0.64	0.38	0.34	0.11	0.50	0.34	0.76	0.78	0.11	0.14	0.32	0.82	0.48	0.77	0.40	0.66
41 PRIVATE CAPITAL FORMATION (GROSS)	DEPRECIATION AND OTHER CAPITAL CONSUMPTION ALLOWANCES ARE INCLUDED IN HOUSEHOLD ROW																	
42 HOUSEHOLDS	19.17	7.05	3.34	4.24	2.72	1.12	2.20	3.14	3.75	5.04	1.08	1.20	2.35	5.53	4.14	6.80	3.41	3.39
TOTAL GROSS OUTLAYS	44.26	40.30	9.84	13.32	6.00	2.89	7.90	6.45	14.05	13.67	2.82	3.81	4.84	18.69	10.40	15.22	8.38	14.27

This interindustry table summarizes the transactions of the U.S. economy in 1947, for which preliminary data have just been compiled by the Bureau of Labor Statistics. Each number in the body of the table represents billions of 1947 dollars. In the vertical column at left the entire economy is broken down into sectors; in the horizontal row at the top the same breakdown is repeated.

PURCHASING

FINAL DEMAND

MANUFACTURING INDUSTRIES EQUIPMENT · GAS AND ELECTRIC POWER · RAILROAD TRANSPORTATION · OCEAN TRANSPORTATION · OTHER TRANSPORTATION · TRADE · COMMUNICATIONS · FINANCE AND INSURANCE · REAL ESTATE AND RENTALS · BUSINESS SERVICES · PERSONAL AND REPAIR SERVICES · NON-PROFIT ORGANIZATIONS · AMUSEMENTS · SCRAP AND MISCELLANEOUS INDUSTRIES · EATING AND DRINKING PLACES · NEW CONSTRUCTION AND MAINTENANCE · UNDISTRIBUTED

24	25	26	27	28	29	30	31	32	33	34	35	36	37	38	39	40	41	42	INVENTORY CHANGE (ADDITIONS)	FOREIGN COUNTRIES (EXPORTS TO)	GOVERNMENT	PRIVATE CAPITAL FORMATION (GROSS)	HOUSEHOLDS	TOTAL GROSS OUTPUT
—	*	*	—	*	*	0.01	—	*	—	—	—	—	0.12	—	—	0.87	0.09	0.17	1.01	1.28	0.57	0.02	9.92	44.26
—	0.01	0.02	*	0.08	0.01	0.03	0.07	0.01	—	—	—	*	0.25	*	0.02	3.47	*	0.42	0.88	1.80	0.73	—	23.03	40.30
0.01	0.05	0.08	0.07	—	0.01	0.01	0.03	*	—	—	*	0.03	*	—	0.01	—	0.05	0.52	0.06	0.92	0.10	0.02	1.47	9.84
0.01	*	*	*	*	*	*	0.02	*	—	—	—	0.02	0.02	*	0.01	0.02	*	0.15	0.21	0.30	0.28	*	9.90	13.32
0.03	*	0.06	0.06	—	0.01	*	0.03	*	—	0.14	*	*	*	—	0.11	0.01	2.33	0.35	0.17	0.17	0.01	0.04	0.07	6.00
0.02	*	—	*	—	—	*	—	*	0.04	0.08	—	—	*	—	—	—	0.20	0.20	0.08	0.03	0.05	0.57	1.46	2.89
0.02	0.08	0.07	*	*	—	*	0.57	*	*	—	*	0.06	0.03	—	0.68	0.06	0.17	0.31	0.04	0.15	0.06	—	0.34	7.90
—	*	—	*	0.04	*	0.02	0.10	0.03	0.21	—	2.45	0.03	0.17	0.01	0.01	0.03	—	0.68	*	0.07	0.16	0.09	1.49	6.45
0.02	0.05	0.17	0.06	0.03	0.01	0.02	0.07	*	*	—	0.01	0.20	0.22	*	0.03	0.04	0.64	1.25	0.30	0.81	0.19	—	1.96	14.05
0.01	*	0.01	0.47	0.27	0.09	0.45	0.20	*	0.01	0.78	*	0.06	0.06	*	0.01	0.01	0.62	0.36	0.06	0.68	0.18	*	2.44	13.67
0.01	*	0.04	*	*	—	0.13	0.06	*	0.01	*	—	0.07	*	—	*	*	0.06	0.47	0.09	0.17	0.02	0.01	0.71	2.82
*	0.01	0.01	*	—	—	*	*	—	—	—	—	0.03	0.01	—	0.01	—	*	0.29	0.11	0.08	0.03	0.02	2.03	3.81
0.01	0.03	0.06	0.02	0.01	*	*	0.04	*	—	—	—	0.02	0.01	—	*	0.06	1.74	0.36	0.10	0.21	0.02	0.01	0.34	4.84
0.43	0.07	0.20	0.05	0.20	—	0.01	—	*	—	—	—	—	*	—	0.15	*	1.19	1.24	0.16	0.77	0.02	—	0.02	18.69
0.10	0.07	0.04	*	0.03	*	0.01	0.06	*	—	—	*	0.03	0.01	—	0.06	0.02	3.09	1.44	0.21	0.39	0.05	0.28	0.95	10.40
0.22	0.03	*	0.03	0.06	—	0.01	0.01	—	0.02	—	—	0.15	*	—	0.07	—	0.51	2.24	0.37	1.76	0.18	5.82	1.22	15.22
0.12	0.03	0.02	0.02	0.04	—	0.01	0.01	0.05	—	—	0.01	0.09	*	—	0.04	—	0.77	1.27	0.25	0.44	0.17	1.75	0.93	8.38
*	—	—	0.01	*	—	0.13	0.02	*	—	*	—	1.05	*	—	0.07	*	0.04	0.67	0.40	1.02	0.15	2.98	3.13	14.27
0.30	—	—	*	0.04	0.08	0.13	—	—	—	—	—	*	—	—	0.01	—	*	0.46	0.02	0.32	1.25	1.20	0.17	4.00
0.02	0.18	0.02	*	—	—	*	—	*	—	—	0.01	0.05	0.18	—	0.01	—	0.02	0.24	0.03	0.18	0.08	0.26	0.62	2.12
*	0.03	0.16	*	*	*	*	0.01	*	—	—	0.15	0.16	0.05	0.05	0.11	0.02	0.03	0.68	0.04	0.19	0.08	0.51	1.89	4.76
0.03	0.01	0.03	1.27	0.44	*	0.09	0.49	0.01	0.06	3.15	*	0.31	0.16	0.05	—	0.22	0.03	0.02	0.03	0.35	0.20	—	—	9.21
0.04	0.01	0.03	0.15	0.41	*	0.06	0.08	*	0.01	0.42	0.03	0.03	0.05	*	0.03	0.25	0.71	0.30	0.08	0.59	0.33	0.27	2.53	9.95
*	*	0.01	*	—	0.22	—	—	—	—	—	—	—	—	—	*	—	—	*	—	1.16	0.31	—	0.10	2.29
0.01	0.01	0.01	0.03	0.19	0.04	0.25	0.31	*	*	0.13	0.03	0.01	0.02	*	0.02	0.10	0.57	0.17	0.04	0.32	0.35	0.10	4.77	9.86
0.07	0.04	0.05	0.05	0.03	0.01	0.42	0.20	0.01	0.04	0.75	0.14	0.37	0.29	0.01	0.09	1.06	2.52	1.01	0.20	1.00	0.05	2.34	26.82	41.66
0.01	0.01	0.01	0.02	0.02	*	0.04	0.33	0.06	0.09	0.06	0.43	0.12	0.07	0.01	—	0.01	0.04	0.08	—	0.04	0.15	—	1.27	3.17
0.02	0.01	0.02	0.05	0.02	0.12	0.30	1.00	*	1.85	0.56	0.02	0.12	0.09	0.03	—	0.07	0.40	—	—	0.14	0.03	—	6.99	12.81
0.02	0.01	0.03	0.05	0.02	0.01	0.15	1.96	0.05	0.21	0.21	0.06	0.71	0.40	0.18	—	0.39	0.08	—	—	—	0.22	0.80	20.29	28.86
0.01	0.05	0.06	0.01	0.02	*	0.03	1.71	0.09	0.14	0.04	0.06	0.12	0.02	0.10	—	0.06	0.13	0.42	—	*	0.04	—	0.18	5.10
*	*	*	0.02	0.11	0.01	0.26	1.42	0.02	0.11	0.03	0.07	0.56	0.08	0.02	0.03	0.23	0.82	1.17	—	—	0.08	0.27	8.35	14.30
—	—	—	—	—	*	*	—	—	0.02	—	—	—	0.09	—	—	—	—	0.16	—	—	5.08	—	8.04	13.39
—	—	—	—	—	—	—	—	—	—	—	—	—	0.01	0.39	—	—	—	0.01	—	0.13	—	—	2.40	2.94
—	*	—	—	—	—	0.04	0.39	0.01	0.11	0.03	0.02	*	*	0.01	—	—	*	0.01	—	0.03	*	—	—	2.13
—	—	—	—	—	—	0.01	—	—	—	—	—	—	0.15	—	—	—	—	—	—	—	—	—	13.11	13.27
0.02	0.01	0.02	0.27	1.12	*	0.13	0.18	0.18	0.03	4.08	*	0.06	0.34	0.02	—	0.07	0.01	—	—	—	5.26	15.70	0.15	28.49
0.34	0.19	0.87	0.25	0.10	0.04	0.03	2.59	0.01	0.71	0.36	0.31	1.13	0.91	0.22	—	0.59	0.43	—	—	—	—	—	—	21.60
0.01	0.05	0.16	*	—	—	—	—	—	—	—	—	—	—	—	0.40	—	—	—	—	0.02	—	—	—	4.43
0.01	0.05	0.14	0.01	0.04	0.50	0.08	—	0.03	0.10	—	—	—	—	*	0.07	—	—	0.01	—	—	1.31	—	1.32	9.52
0.12	0.13	0.19	1.14	0.91	0.26	0.77	3.30	0.44	1.11	4.00	0.21	0.50	0.17	0.32	0.07	1.41	0.47	2.19	0.34	0.83	3.46	0.22	31.55	63.69
1.95	0.90	2.17	5.11	5.70	0.90	6.20	26.42	2.15	7.93	14.06	1.08	8.20	9.41	1.50	—	4.20	10.73	2.27	—	0.85	30.06	—	2.12	223.58
4.00	2.12	4.76	9.21	9.95	2.29	9.86	41.66	3.17	12.81	28.86	5.10	14.30	13.39	2.94	2.13	13.27	28.49	21.60	5.28	17.21	51.29	33.29	194.12	

When a sector is read horizontally, the numbers indicate what it ships to other sectors. When a sector is read vertically, the numbers show what it consumes from other sectors. The asterisks stand for sums less than $5 million. Totals may not check due to rounding.

derived as the grand total of the five columns grouped under the heading of final demand, but with some adjustments necessary to eliminate the duplication of transactions between the sectors represented by these columns. For example, the total payment to households, at the far right end of row 42, includes salaries paid by government, a figure which duplicates in part the payment of taxes by households included in the total payment to government.

With this brief introduction the lay economist is now qualified to turn around and trace his way back into the table via whatever chain of interindustry relationships engages his interest. He will not go far before he finds himself working intuitively with the central concept of input-output analysis. This is the idea that there is a fundamental relationship between the volume of the output of an industry and the size of the inputs going into it. It is obvious, for example, that the purchases of the auto industry (column 18) from the glass industry (row 13) in 1947 were strongly determined by the number of motor vehicles produced that year. Closer inspection will lead to the further realization that every single figure in the chart is dependent upon every other. To take an extreme example, the appropriate series of inputs and outputs will show that the auto industry's purchases of glass are dependent in part upon the demand for motor vehicles arising out of the glass industry's purchases from the fuel industries.

These relationships reflect the structure of our technology. They are expressed in input-output analysis as the ratios or coefficients of each input to the total output of which it becomes a part. A table of such ratios (figure 2) computed from a table for the economy as of 1939, shows how much had to be purchased from the steel, glass, paint, rubber and other industries to produce $1,000 worth of automobile that year. Since such expenditures are determined by relatively inflexible engineering considerations or by equally inflexible customs and institutional arrangements, these ratios might be used to estimate the demand for materials induced by auto production in other years. With a table of ratios for the economy as a whole, it is possible in turn to calculate the secondary demand on the output of the industries which supply the auto industry's suppliers and so on through successive outputs and inputs until the effect of the final demand for automobiles has been traced to its last reverberation in the farthest corner of the economy. In this fashion input-output analysis should prove useful to the auto industry as a means for dealing with cost and supply problems.

The table of steel consumption ratios (figure 3) suggests, incidentally, how the input-output matrix might be used for the contrasting purpose of market analysis. Since the ultimate markets for steel are ordinarily buried in the cycle of secondary transactions among the metal-fabricating industries, it is useful to learn from this table how many tons of steel at

FIGURE 2

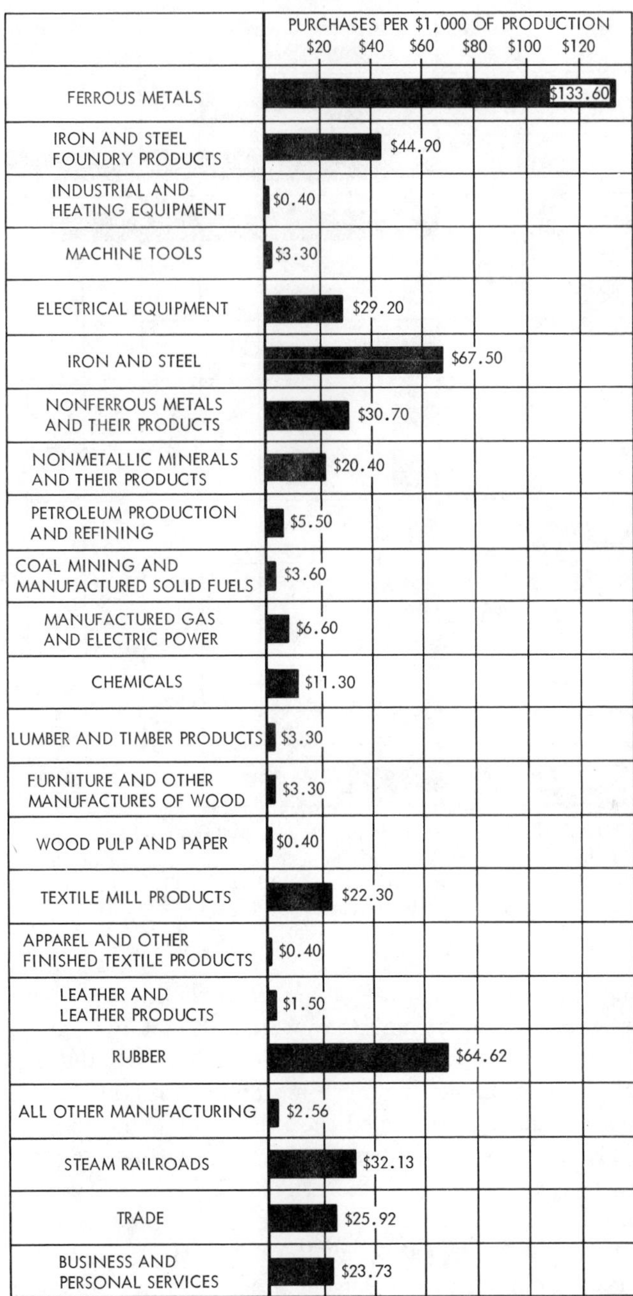

Input to the auto industry from other industries per $1,000 of auto production was derived from the 1939 interindustry table. Comparing these figures with those for the auto industry in the 1947 table would show changes in the input structure of the industry due to changes in prices and technology.

FIGURE 3

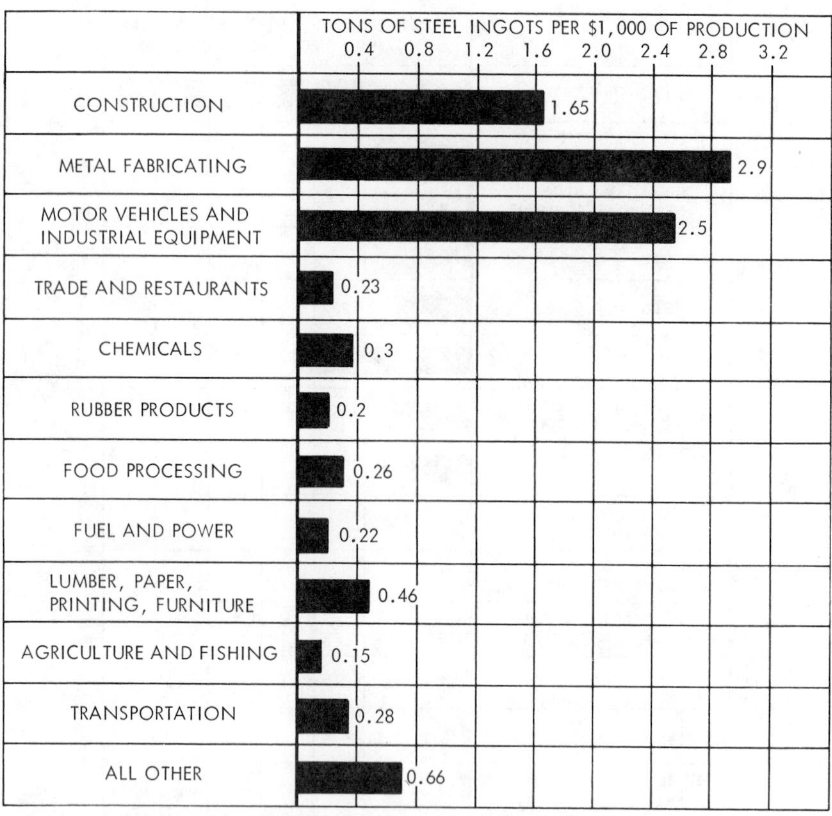

The output of the steel industry depends heavily on what kinds of goods are demanded in the ultimate market. This table shows the amount of steel required to meet each $1,000 of the demand for other goods in 1939. The current demand for the top three items is responsible for the steel shortage.

the mill were needed in 1939 to satisfy each thousand dollars worth of demand for the products of industries which ultimately place steel products at the disposal of the consumer. This table shows the impressively high ratio of the demand for steel in the construction and consumer durable-goods industries which led the Bureau of Labor Statistics to declare in 1945 that a flourishing postwar economy would require even more steel than the peak of the war effort. Though some industry spokesmen took a contrary position at that time, steel production recently has been exceeding World War II peaks, and the major steel companies are now engaged in a 16-million-ton expansion program which was started even before the outbreak of the war in Korea and the current rearmament.

The ratios shown in these two tables are largely fixed by technology Others in the complete matrix of the economy, especially in the trade and services and households sectors, are established by custom and other institutional factors. All, of course, are subject to modification by such forces as progress in technology and changes in public taste. But whether they vary more or less rapidly over the years, these relationships are subject to dependable measurement at any given time.

Here we have our bridge between theory and facts in economics. It is a bridge in a very literal sense. Action at a distance does not happen in economics any more than it does in physics. The effect of an event at any one point is transmitted to the rest of the economy step by step via the chain of transactions that ties the whole system together. A table of ratios for the entire economy gives us, in as much detail as we require, a quantitatively determined picture of the internal structure of the system. This makes it possible to calculate in detail the consequences that result from the introduction into the system of changes suggested by the theoretical or practical problem at hand.

In the case of a particular industry we can easily compute the complete table of its input requirements at any given level of output, provided we know its input ratios. By the same token, with somewhat more involved computation, we can construct synthetically a complete input-output table for the entire economy. We need only a known "bill of final demand" to convert the table of ratios into a table of magnitudes. The 1945 estimate of postwar steel requirements, for example, was incidental to a study of the complete economy based upon a bill of demand which assumed full employment in 1950. This bill of demand was inserted into the total columns of a table of ratios based on the year 1939. By arithmetical procedures the ratios were then translated into dollar figures, among which was the figure for steel, which showed a need for an absolute minimum of 98 million ingot tons. Actual production in 1950, at the limit of capacity, was 96.8 million tons.

Though its application is simple, the construction of an input-output table is a highly complex and laborious operation. The first step, and one that has little appeal to the theoretical imagination, is the gathering and ordering of an immense volume of quantitative information. Given the inevitable lag between the accumulation and collation of data for any given year, the input-output table will always be an historical document. The first input-output tables, prepared by the author and his associates at Harvard University in the early 1930s, were based upon 1919 and 1929 figures. The 1939 table was not completed until 1944. Looking to the future, a table for 1953 which is now under consideration could not be made available until 1957. For practical purposes the original figures in the table must be regarded as a base, subject to refinement and correction in accord with subsequent trends. For example, the 1945 projection of the 1950 economy on the basis of the 1939 table made suitable adjustments in the coal and oil input ratios of the transportation industries on the assumption that the trend from steam to diesel locomotives would continue throughout the period.

The basic information for the table and its continuing revision comes from the Bureau of the Census and other specialized statistical agencies. As the industrial breakdown becomes more detailed, however, engineering and technical information plays a more important part in determining the data. A perfectly good way to determine how much coke is needed to produce a ton of pig iron, in addition to dividing the output of the blast furnace industry into its input of coke, is to ask an ironmaster. In principle there is no reason why the input-output coefficients should not be entirely derived from "below," from engineering data on process design and operating practice. Thus in certain studies of the German economy made by the Bureau of Labor Statistics following World War II the input structures of key industries were set up on the basis of U.S. experience. The model of a disarmed but self-supporting Germany developed in these studies showed a steel requirement of 11 million ingot tons, toward which actual output is now moving. Completely hypothetical input structures, representing industries not now operating, have been introduced into tables of the existing U.S. economy in studies conducted by Air Force economists.

This brings us to the problem of computation. Since the production level required of each industry is ultimately dependent upon levels in all others, it is clear that we have a problem involving simultaneous equations. Though the solution of such equations may involve no very high order of mathematics, the sheer labor of computation can be immense. The number of equations to be solved is always equal to the number of sectors into which the system is divided. Depending upon whether a specific or a general solution of the system is desired, the volume of computation will vary as the square or the cube of the number of sectors involved. A typical general solution of a 42-sector table for 1939 required 56 hours on the Harvard Mark II computer. Thanks to this investment in computation, the conversion of any stipulated bill of demand into the various industrial production levels involves nothing more than simple arithmetic. The method cannot be used, however, in the solution of problems which call for changes in the input-output ratios, since each change requires a whole new solution of the matrix. For the larger number of more interesting problems which require such changes, special solutions are the rule. However, even a special solution on a reasonably detailed 200-sector table might require some 200,000 multiplications and a greater number of additions. For this reason it is likely that the typical nongovernmental user will be limited to condensed general solutions periodically computed and published by special-purpose groups working in the field. With these the average industrial analyst will be able to enjoy many

FIGURE 4

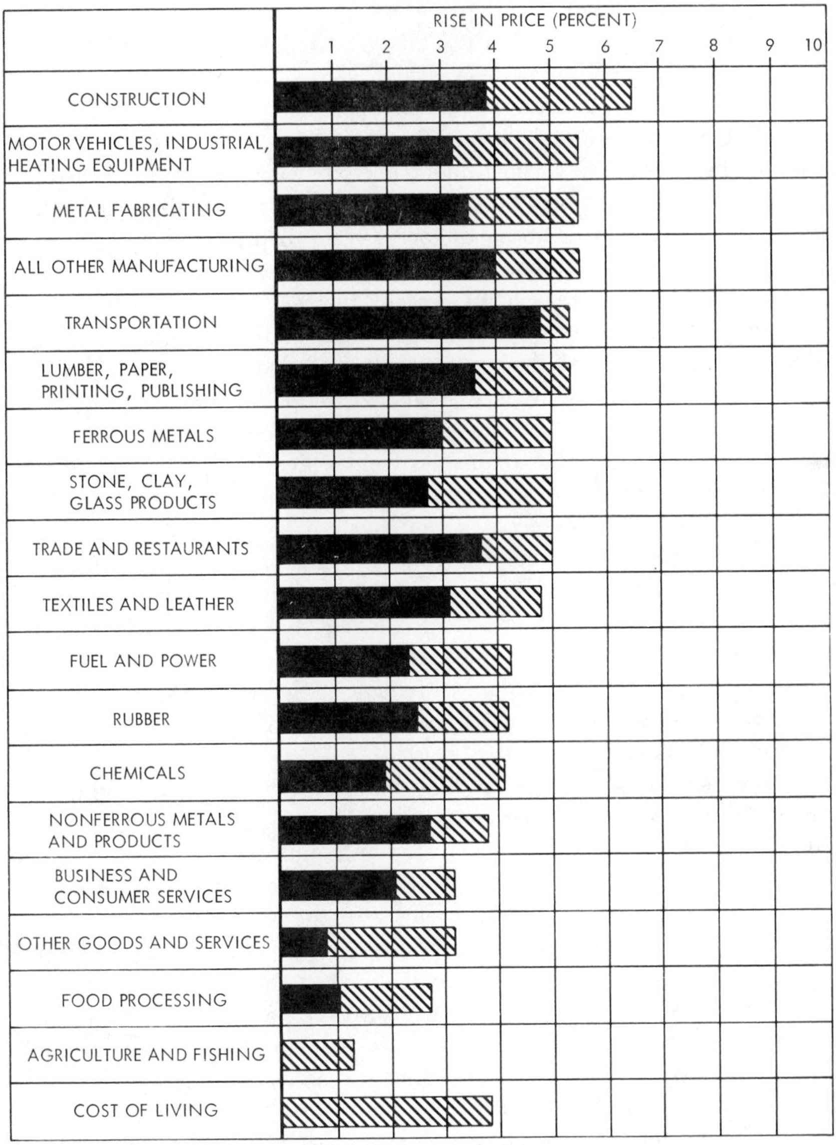

Price increases that would be caused by a 10 percent increase in wages were computed from the 1939 interindustry table. The increases include the direct effect of the rise in each industry's own wage bill (dark bars) and the indirect effect of price increases on purchase from others (striped bars).

of the advantages of the large and flexible machinery required for government analyses relating to the entire economy.

A demonstration of input-output analysis applied to a typical economic problem is presented in figure 4, which shows the price increases that would result from a general 10 percent increase in the wage scale of industry. Here the value of the matrix distinguishing between direct and indirect effects is of the utmost importance. If wages constituted the only ultimate cost in the economy, a general 10 percent rise in all money wages would obviously lead to an equal increase in all prices. Since wages are only one cost and since labor costs vary from industry to industry, it can be seen in the chart that a 10 percent increase in wages would have decidedly different effects upon various parts of the economy. The construction industry shows the greatest upward price change, as it actually did in recent decades. For each industry group the chart separates the direct effect of increases in its own wage bill from the indirect effects of the wage increases in other industries from which it purchases its inputs. Giving effect to both direct and indirect increases, the average increase in the cost of living is shown in the chart to be only 3.7 percent. The 10 percent money-wage increase thus yields a 6.3 percent increase in real wage rates. It should be noted, however, that the economic forces which bring increases in wages tend to bring increases in other costs as well. The advantage of the input-output analysis is that it permits the disentanglement and accurate measurement of the indirect effects. Analyses similar to this one for wages can be carried through for profits, taxes, and other ultimate components of prices.

In such examples changes in the economy over periods of time are measured by comparing before-and-after pictures. Each is a static model, a cross-section in time. The next step in input-output analysis is the development of dynamic models of the economy to bring the approximations of the method that much closer to the actual processes of economics. This requires accounting for stocks as well as flows of goods, for inventories of goods in process and in finished form, for capital equipment, buildings, and, last but not least, for dwellings and household stocks of durable consumer goods. The dynamic input-output analysis requires more advanced mathematical methods; instead of ordinary linear equations it leads to systems of linear differential equations.

Among the questions the dynamic system should make it possible to answer, one could mention the determination of the changing pattern of outputs and inventories or investments and capacities which would attend a given pattern of growth in final demand projected over a five- or ten-year period. Within such broad projections, for example, we would be able to estimate approximately not only how much aluminum should be produced, but how much additional aluminum-producing capacity would be required, and the rate at which such capacity should be installed. The computational task becomes more formidable, but it does not seem to exceed the capacity of the latest electronic computers. Here, as in the case of the static system, the most laborious problem is the assembly of the necessary factual information. However, a complete set of stock or capital ratios, paralleling the flow ratios of all of the productive sectors of the U.S. economy for the year 1939, has now been completed.

This table of capital ratios shows that in addition to the flow of raw pig-iron, scrap, coal, labor and so on, the steel works and rolling mills industry—when operating to full capacity—required $1,800 of fixed investment for each $1,000 worth of output. This would include $336 worth of tools, $331 worth of iron and steel foundry production, and so on down to $26 worth of electrical equipment. This means that in order to expand its capacity so as to be able to increase its output by one million dollars worth of finished products annually, the steel works and rolling mills industry would have to install $336,000 worth of tools and spend corresponding amounts on all other types of new fixed installations. This investment demand constitutes of course additional input requirements for the product of the corresponding capital goods industries, input requirements which are automatically taken into account in the solution of an appropriate system of dynamic input-output equations.

Active experimental work with the dynamic system is under way. Meanwhile the demonstrated power of input-output analysis has thoroughly convinced many workers in the field of its practical possibilities. Of wider consequence is the expectation of theoretical investigators that this new grasp on the facts of the subject will further liberate economics from the confines of its traditionally simplified postulates.

part FOUR
Costs

INTRODUCTION

The literature on empirical cost studies has become increasingly technical. Severe data and econometric problems have forced investigators into ever more sophisticated methods, and armed their critics with ever more powerful weapons. But what is "cost" and how do we know? Robert N. Anthony tells why the word is confusing; moreover, he suggests certain definitions, standards, and approaches necessary for better cost measurement.

Statistical cost functions are useful devices (1) for describing the relationships which exist currently between various measurable variables, and (2) for forecasting the effects of changes in one or more of these variables. Using the Federal Reserve System's functional cost analysis data, William A. Longbrake applies this technique to the commercial banking industry.

Classical methods of statistical estimation are not used by all cost analysts. George J. Stigler applies the "survivor" principle to the investigation of economies of scale; fundamental to problems associated with this approach is acquisition of reliable raw data with which to work.

A primary reason for owning and/or operating a business may be to generate a profit. If profit is measured on an incremental basis, by function, very detailed pieces of information are necessary regarding costs by function. Using commercial banks as an example, the article by Thomas J. Coyne reveals a method of cost of funds calculation and utilization that may be useful in analyzing costs for nonfinancial as well as financial corporations.

Somewhat less abstract than the piece by Stigler is the short-run cost function for multiproduct firms presented by Koot and Walker. They argue that marginal cost curves are constant in the short run as opposed to being U-shaped and subject to the laws of diminishing returns as explained in most textbook presentations of the subject.

14. What Should "Cost" Mean?*

ROBERT N. ANTHONY

Suppose the president of a widget company says, "Last year our cost of manufacturing widgets was $1.80 each." The ordinary person may think he has learned a concrete piece of information from this statement.

Anyone who understands the vagaries of cost accounting knows differently. He knows that "cost" in this context has no generally accepted meaning, that two manufacturers of physically identical widgets who use different, but acceptable, methods of measuring cost could differ in their reported costs of making widgets by 100 percent or more. The informed person therefore realizes that he cannot understand a number that purports to be the cost of a widget unless he knows a great deal about the particular cost accounting system from which it was derived.

Some persons say this situation is inevitable, in view of the complicated nature of business. Others say it is desirable: manufacturers should be encouraged to exercise their own best judgment in measuring cost. Still others, including me, find it neither inevitable nor desirable. They find it deplorable.

The increasing number of responsible persons who find it deplorable has generated activity on several fronts to develop cost standards. The activity involves accounting groups, the General Accounting Office, and the Senate Banking and Currency Committee, which plans hearings on the subject. (Later, I shall offer some ideas as to how cost concepts can best be formulated.)

CORRECTION OF INADEQUACIES

For reasons discussed in the next section, I shall limit myself here to the meaning of "cost" in this situation:

Two parties facing each other across a table are negotiating a contract. Mr. A has agreed to manufacture some articles or perform some services for Mr. B. They have agreed on the specifications and delivery schedule of the articles or services. They also have agreed that the purchaser (B) will pay the supplier (A) for the cost of manufacturing

* *Harvard Business Review,* vol. 48, no. 3 (June 1970), pp. 121–131.

the articles or providing the services, plus a profit. The problem is: What should "cost" mean in this situation?

There are several conceivable ways of answering this question, but in most situations only one way is both fair and practical. Let us look at the possibilities:

1. The parties could leave "cost" undefined, in the belief that there exists a body of generally accepted cost accounting principles defining it. They would be wrong.

2. At the opposite extreme, they could try to imagine all the cost accounting problems that might arise in the course of manufacturing the articles or providing the services, and agree on how each of them is to be resolved. The end product of such an approach would be a cost accounting manual.

But it is not generally practical to write a manual for a specific contract, except for a very simple job; the circumstances, and the possible ways of treating each circumstance, are too numerous. Moreover, the negotiations would be extraordinarily time-consuming.

3. The buyer could permit the manufacturer to define cost to mean what the manufacturer says it means, no more and no less. Even Alice would not accept this White Queen approach, and it is preposterous to expect that a hardheaded buyer would agree to it.

It is, nevertheless, an approach advocated by a number of people for contracts in which they sit on one side of the negotiating table and a government representative sits on the other side, as indicated by this excerpt from a letter written to the General Accounting Office by a trade association representative: "We do not believe that the adoption of Uniform Cost Accounting Standards would be practical for government or industry. Each industry already has developed, and is utiliziing, the most appropriate accounting systems and procedures for its needs."

4. They could negotiate *de novo* a set of standards that would provide at least the general direction of solutions that arose in measuring the cost of the contract. This would be very inefficient. Since most problems that arise in measuring costs have arisen thousands of times before, working out solutions from scratch for each new contract is a waste of everyone's time.

5. They could agree to use a set of standards that has been developed by someone else for contracts of the type being negotiated, or perhaps a set of standards for contracts in general. This is the only fair and practical solution. Neither the first nor the third alternative is fair to the purchaser, and neither the second nor the fourth is practical.

An agreed-on definition of cost that is applicable to a number of situations is what is meant by the term "cost standards." (Incidentally, the phrase "cost standards" should not be confused with "standard costs." Standard costs are a device used for internal control, which is intended to express what costs *should be,* not what they *are.*)

Several such definitions already exist. Section XV of the Armed Services Procurement Regulations (ASPR) is one; it helps to define cost in negotiations when one of the participants is the government. Many trade associations have developed standards for defining costs applicable to their industries.

But these existing sets of standards have serious deficiencies, and the time has come to attempt the construction of a set of standards that will define cost whenever one party to a contract agrees to pay to the other party an amount based on the cost of performing the contract.

The time is propitious because of the interest in this problem that has been generated by a study conducted by the General Accounting Office (GAO) as required by Public Law 370 of the 90th Congress. This law only required the GAO to report on the "feasibility" of applying "uniform cost accounting standards" to negotiated defense contracts. (In the quoted phrase, "uniform" is clearly redundant, and I shall omit it henceforth. Can anyone give an example of a nonuniform cost standard?)

The comptroller general made his report on January 19, 1970. He stated that it is feasible to develop and use cost standards for defense contracts. He could scarcely have concluded otherwise, for it is inconceivable that the two parties to a contract could communicate with one another in the absence of such standards. They communicate now, and have for years, using the previously mentioned ASPR standards.

These standards are inadequate, however. The comptroller general summarized their inadequacies this way: (*a*) in some crucial matters, ASPR instructs the parties to use "generally accepted accounting principles," whereas relevant principles do not exist; (*b*) in other matters, ASPR is silent or vague as to which of several possible cost constructions may be used in a given set of circumstances.

Admittedly, some persons oppose any effort to develop better cost standards. Analysis of their arguments shows that they are not questioning the desirability of standards per se. What they are really worried about is that the standards may be *bad* standards; that is, that the group responsible for developing them will not do a good job.

This, it seems to me, is an untenable position, for such a possibility exists in any proposal to change the status quo. Instead of merely expressing opposition, these critics could make a constructive contribution if they focused their energies on ensuring that the effort to develop standards is well conceived, well organized, and well manned.

HOW BROAD THE STANDARDS?

The first question to be resolved is how broad the standards should be. There are two extremes:

They could define "cost" in whatever context it is used.

They could define cost as used in "all negotiated prime contract and subcontract defense procurements of $100,000 or more," which is the language of P.L. 90-370.

In my view, one extreme is unmanageably broad and the other is unnecessarily narrow. That is why the question at the beginning of this article was framed in such a way that it applies to all negotiated contracts where the payment is in part based on cost, but only to such contracts.

Problem Categories

If the group concerned set out to develop all-inclusive cost standards, it would have to cover at least these five contexts:

1. There is the situation I described, where the problem is to measure the total (i.e., "full") costs incurred in performing a contract.

2. There is the problem of defining the costs that company management should weigh in deciding between proposed alternative courses of action. These are often labeled "decision-making" costs. In contrast with the first type, these are not incurred costs, but estimates of future costs. Neither are they necessarily full costs, but differential or incremental costs.

3. There are the costs considered in setting selling prices for other than cost-type contracts. Some persons regard pricing as one type of decision-making problem, while others regard it as a special case in the measurement of costs incurred. In view of this disagreement it would be arbitrary to classify the costs relevant for pricing as coming within either the costs-incurred or the decision-making categories.

4. There are the costs involved in measuring inventory amounts on the balance sheet and cost of sales on the income statement. Perhaps the principles governing measurement of costs for financial statements are so similar to those in the first category that this is not really a separate category. Such a conclusion is, however, premature.

5. There are the costs used as a basis for influencing the actions of managers and measuring their performance. They may be called "management control" costs. They properly involve motivational considerations, so they differ in some respects from those in the other categories. As with the previous category, further analysis may show that these differences are not significant enough to warrant the creation of a separate category.

To summarize this list, there are at least two quite different kinds of costs: total, incurred costs and differential, future costs. There may also be other important categories, depending on whether the principles relevant to costs for pricing, costs for financial statements, and costs for management control are essentially the same as those in one or the other of the categories listed.

Some very broad comments about cost can be made that apply to all these categories. This, for example, is the approach taken in William J. Vatter's *Standards of Cost Analysis.* A study of this excellent report shows, however, that statements made at this level of generality provide only what Vatter himself describes as "first steps" in approaching any of the classes of problems I described.

The cost concepts study sponsored by the American Institute of Certified Public Accountants (AICPA)—described in the February 1969 issue of *The Journal of Accountancy*—appears to take the same broad approach as does Vatter.

Choosing a Category

If the contexts in which cost is used are too diverse to allow tackling them simultaneously, which one should be selected as the focus for a program to develop standards? Of the two main categories—a focus on total costs that have been incurred versus a focus on estimates of differential costs *to be* incurred—the former is clearly the more desirable.

In internal decision making, company management can specify the definition of cost it thinks best. Some cost constructions are more useful than others, and management should welcome advice on what constructions are most useful for purposes of decision making. But it should be free to accept or reject this advice; there is no compelling reason why some outside agency should impose its views on the company in the guise of a set of standards.

On the other hand, A and B, the negotiators in the episode at the beginning of this article, *must* have some standards. Without them, A and B have no practicable way of reaching a meeting of minds as to what the contract means by the word "cost," once the parties have agreed that reimbursement is to be based in part on cost. This area is the one on which the standards-development effort should be focused.

The effort should not be limited to developing cost standards for defense contracts. Those responsible will render a greater service to the business community if they view their job as relating to all cost-type contracts. For what difference is there, in principle, between costs that are relevant to a defense contract and those relevant to a nondefense contract? The defense establishment consumes 8 percent of our gross national product, and its contracts cover nearly every conceivable kind of product and service.

Defense contracts do, however, have a few peculiarities. DOD has rules for reimbursing contractors for some items that may not fit within a general definition of costs incurred on a contract–principally those known as "independent research and development costs" and "bid and proposal costs." Provision in the standards for such items, if they indeed turn out to be exceptions (and it would be premature to so classify them before cost standards have been developed), could easily be treated as special cases, applying only to defense.

A set of standards is useful in most contracts involving payments based on cost. The standards would in no way prevent the parties, whether or not it is a government negotiation, from defining cost in a different way if they mutually agree to do so.

Many construction contracts, for instance, specify the use of 2″ × 4″ lumber. There is a standard for 2″ × 4″ lumber which, among other characteristics, defines it as having dimensions of at least 1½″ × 3½″ under certain circumstances and at least 1⁹⁄₁₆″ × 3⁹⁄₁₆″ under other circumstances. It is normally not done, but the parties can, if they wish, change this definition and require that the lumber actually measure 2″ × 4″, or any other dimension they specify.

The problem of defining cost obviously is vastly more complicated than that of defining the dimensions of lumber. Cost standards would therefore not be anywhere near as specific as those for lumber or those for similar criteria worked out by the U.S.A. Standards Institute. I stress this point because many persons have a mistaken impression about it.

Parameters of Analysis. The question posed in the "A and B negotiate" episode was worded so as to restrict the analysis in certain dimensions. For one, it is deliberately limited to the problem of reimbursable costs.

Costs are used for other purposes in connection with contract work, such as measuring performance while the work is going on. But performance measurement involves several problems that need not be faced in measuring the costs to be reimbursed. For example, in the Defense Department a controversy currently goes on as to the proper timing of material charges for performance measurement purposes: Should they be reported when material is acquired or when it is consumed? This question of timing does not even arise in the cost reimbursement area; if an item of material is used on a contract, it is unquestionably a cost of that contract, regardless of when it is acquired or used.

The question early in the article was stated so as to exclude also the problem of developing standards for cost estimates that are often used by negotiating parties in deciding on the work to be done under a contract. They are important in negotiated fixed-price contracts as well as cost-type contracts.

These cost estimates should be influenced by the standards in the sense that the buyer ought to insist that the cost constructions used in the estimates are consistent with the standards applicable to the measurement of costs incurred. The job of making the estimates, however, involves certain considerations (some of them quite complicated) that are not present in the measurement of costs incurred.

For example, the standards for measuring costs incurred should indicate what kind of effort constitutes direct labor, and what, if any, fringe benefits should be included in the price of each hour of direct labor. *Estimates* of this labor cost should ordinarily be constructed in the same terms; but the estimator must also make certain assumptions about future wage rates, future labor productivity, and the number of hours required to produce the article. It does not appear feasible, as a part of the initial effort to develop standards, to work out standards governing the choice of these assumptions.

The contracting parties may also be involved in change orders, repricing formulas, renegotiation provisions, termination costs, and similar complications. All involve the measurement of costs actually incurred, as distinguished from estimates of costs to be incurred, and therefore the standards should apply to them.

For these reasons, then, the approach suggested at the beginning of this article seems to be the most feasible and the most useful. By limiting the focus to developing standards for costs incurred, we can avoid the complications involved in developing standards for other kinds of cost. By broadening it from defense contracts to all negotiated contracts, we gain in breadth of coverage with no significant increase in effort.

FIRST THINGS FIRST

The formulation of cost standards resembles the efforts of the Accounting Principles Board (APB) of the American Institute of Certified Public Accountants to develop standards for financial accounting. Its experience teaches an important lesson; namely, that the undertaking should consist of two sequential stages:

The development of a few underlying, basic concepts.

The development of standards based on those concepts.

A third possible stage, the development of detailed rules and procedures, is not properly a part of the effort, of course.)

When the APB began its work in 1959, it decided that its opinions should rest on a foundation of broad principles. It therefore encouraged research that could be used as a basis for formulating principles. The work culminated in "A Tentative Set of Broad Accounting Principles for Business Enterprises."

The APB did not accept the principles proposed in that study, but neither could its members agree on any alternative set of principles. So the APB proceeded to formulate standards for specific topics, without the conceptual underpinning that a statement of broad principles would have provided. There was some justification for this approach; certain problems required immediate resolution, and it may not have been feasible to hold up action on them until an agreement on broad principles could be reached.

Whatever justification there was at the time, we know by hindsight that the subsequent APB opinions, and the discussions leading to them, have suffered greatly from the absence of an agreed-on conceptual foundation. As a leading practitioner comments:

> The APB . . . has been so busy "putting out fires" and dealing with a large and ever-increasing backlog of current problems that it has never established an adequate basis upon which to build. This deficiency results not only in the waste of a great deal of time in debating each subject on a more-or-less isolated basis but also in makeshift conclusions which could in the end defeat the entire effort to improve accounting principles. . . . This approach can be compared to building a room for a house without having either a foundation or plans for the house.

In 1968, the APB began another effort to decide on broad concepts, so the importance of doing so is still recognized. In the meantime, whoever is responsible for developing cost accounting standards can learn from the experience. The individual standards must be derived from a conceptual foundation, and the first task is to build it.

BUILDING THE FOUNDATION

What should the conceptual foundation look like? Its general nature is, I believe, quite easy to sketch out. Cost measures the use of resources. To return to my original example:

When B agrees to pay A an amount based on cost incurred, he has in mind that A will use certain resources in the time period covered by the contract, and that this use will be measured by a dollar amount known as cost.

Some of this use of resources can be directly related to the contract, and B expects to pay the cost of these resources. Some are used jointly for contract work and noncontract work, and B expects to pay a "fair share" of the cost of these resources. The sum of these two elements he regards as the cost of performing the contract. (He may specify that he will pay for these costs only to the extent that they are reasonable.)

This suggests that the conceptual foundation should spell out in broad terms the answers to two questions:

1. What are the total costs incurred by an organization in an accounting period?

2. How should this total be divided among the several cost objectives of that period? (A cost objective is anything to which costs are assigned. We are here interested in a contract as one cost objective.)

Costs Incurred in a Period

The concepts governing measurement of the total costs incurred in an accounting period are financial accounting concepts. If the APB had adopted a complete and acceptable set of broad principles, the cost accounting effort would require no further work with respect to this question. It seems highly unlikely that the APB will answer this question in the near future. If it does not, the new group must develop these concepts.

This job involves wrestling with only a relatively few topics. A measure of agreement already exists on at least some of them, and the task is therefore to find words to express the concepts unambiguously. There is general agreement, for example, that the accrual concept should govern measurement of costs, but no generally accepted unambiguous statement exists on what should be meant by the accrual concept. For writing such a statement, the literature can be used as a basis for discussion.

The principal aspects of the main question to be considered are:

The types of resources that are properly included in the costs of an accounting period.

How these resources should be priced.

In regard to resources that provide services to more than one accounting period, how the amount applicable to a single period should be measured.

In addition, attention should be given to the terms "materiality" and "consistency." Moreover, since most cost-type contracts contemplate that reimbursement will be limited to "reasonable" cost, rather than cost in an unqualified sense, "reasonable" needs to be defined.

There is, finally, the special problem of the cost of capital. Although capital has a cost, it is not recognized as such under currently accepted financial accounting principles. Interest, which is the cost of *debt* capital, is recognized for some purposes, but there is no formal recognition in the accounts of the cost of *equity* capital.

This situation has led to confusion and inequity in contract costing. Under ASPR (paragraph 15-305.17), interest is an unallowable cost. If, however, a contractor leases an asset, the lease payment generally includes an allowance for the cost of capital—both debt capital and equity capital—and such a lease payment is often an allowable cost.

The cost of a building constructed by a contractor's own work force may include an allowance for interest, but it rarely includes an allowance for the cost of equity capital. If a third party constructed the building for the contractor's account, the cost would normally include the cost of capital.

It is inappropriate here to suggest a solution to this problem, but it surely is one to which special attention must be given.

Assignment of Costs

The second question, the assignment of total costs to cost objectives, is the province of cost accounting. In this area APB opinions give no substantial guidance. The closest authoritative precedent is ASPR, and this is useful in providing a structure for the conceptual problem. In rough outline this structure is:

Costs are divided into direct costs and indirect costs.

Direct costs are assigned to cost objectives.

Each cost objective is assigned a "fair share" of the indirect costs.

This structure suggests two main considerations, investigation of which can provide the conceptual foundation necessary for the construction of individual standards:

The *first* consideration has to do with how direct costs should be defined. The definition should, I believe, encompass more costs than those that clearly can be traced to a cost objective, because they exclude most kinds of fringe benefits, overtime, labor that is closely but not unequivocally related to a cost objective, many aspects of material cost, and many services.

Some of these cost elements should be included within the definition of direct costs, leaving the indirect cost category as small as possible, for the more costs that reasonably can be assigned directly, the more confidence that the total costs are indeed equitable. So the answer to this question is by no means as simple as it may appear.

The way to approach this problem, I believe, is to break it into: (a) What physical inputs should be costed as direct? (b) How are these inputs to be priced?

The latter is the more difficult. Consider, for example, two pieces of timber of identical size which required an identical amount of effort to grow, harvest, and transport to where they are to be used. Log X is in some significant sense "better" than Log Y; it has fewer defects or a better grain. If Log X is used on Contract A and Log Y on Contract B, it seems reasonable to some persons that more than half the cost of the two logs should be assigned to Contract A. Others believe that the same amount of cost should be assigned to each contract.

This is a basic conceptual disagreement that must be resolved. The treatment of overtime and material waste and spoilage are other topics that have this same characteristic.

The *second* consideration has to do with the concepts governing the assignment of indirect costs to contracts. Although some persons find the idea of "fair share" or "equity" a less than satisfactory basis for approaching this question, no one, as far as I know, has proposed a better one.

If those responsible cannot come up with a better approach (and I doubt that they can), they will presumably use the foundation that is already familiar to cost accountants: costs are initially collected in relatively homogeneous pools, and the total of each of these pools is then divided among the cost objectives on some equitable basis. So there needs to be one set of criteria for specifying what is meant by a "homogeneous pool" and another set for deciding among the possible ways of allocating the total of each pool to cost objectives.

In the report to the comptroller general which I mentioned, Vatter classifies cost pools as people-oriented, payroll-oriented, materials-oriented, machine-oriented, or uncorrelated with any of the others. This classification provides a good starting point in approaching the question of homogeneity. It should not be difficult to frame a general concept of the meaning of homogeneity, together with a *de minimis* qualification that limits the creation of separate pools in situations where the effort to do so is not worthwhile.

A decision on the concepts governing the method of allocating the total cost accumulated in a pool to the relevant cost objectives is much more difficult to reach. The literature suggests a number of alternatives, including benefits received, correlation with individual input elements, correlation with total input cost, correlation with outputs, relative use of facilities, and degree of control by cost objective. These must in some way be sorted out.

There are several possible ways of doing this. One is to arrange the methods of allocation in a hierarchy according to their conceptual desirability and specify that a particular method should be used only when a more desirable one is not feasible.

The concept might state, for example, that the costs in a pool should be allocated to cost objectives in proportion to the benefits received, if it is feasible to do so. If this is not feasible, another criterion should govern, then another, until one is left with a pool of costs for which no logical basis for allocation exists. (Such a pool would contain at least part of the element often labeled "general and administrative costs.")

In the absence of a logical basis for allocating such costs, the method of allocation is necessarily arbitrary. The relevant concept is therefore also arbitrary. But this is nothing to be concealed or be ashamed of; it is simply inherent in the situation.

The set of basic concepts emerging from this analysis should be relatively brief, a few thousand words at most (which is much shorter than Section XV of ASPR). There will nevertheless be much sweat, some tears, and possibly even some blood shed by members of the group responsible for this effort. The job of selecting the best ideas is a formidable exercise in logic tempered by the realities of practice, and the job of expressing those ideas in unambiguous language is almost as difficult.

But unless this job is completed before the work of setting standards on individual elements of cost begins, the undertaking is likely to be a patchwork of loosely related, sometimes conflicting, statements, which is one of the troubles with the present state of affairs.

Approach to Procedure

This is what I have in mind by the term "concepts": they are broad, they are few in number, and they govern the standards to be developed for individual elements of cost—but they do not themselves deal with those elements. Once these concepts have been agreed to, the task of developing cost standards can begin. Probably this work could be divided according to the principal elements of cost, although other methods of breaking it down may turn out to be preferable.

Whatever the basis for selecting topics, the research and analysis leading to a recommendation on each topic should seek to:

Define alternative circumstances that warrant different methods of cost assignment.

State the method (or methods) that is appropriate under each of these circumstances.

Take one of the most difficult problems as an example: the amount of depreciation cost assigned to an accounting period can be determined on a straight-line basis, or an annuity basis. The standard on depreciation should spell out either the circumstances under which each of these methods is appropriate, or, as a minimum, the circumstances under which each is inappropriate.

At best, cost accounting standards are guides to practice; they cannot provide detailed solutions to all problems. They can and must narrow the choice of alternatives, but they cannot eliminate the necessity for making judgments among alternatives according to the circumstances in a specific situation. The real world is too complicated for that.

ORGANIZING FOR THE TASK

Next, there is the question of how to go about it. In other words, what organization should be responsible, and what procedures should it follow? Here are some considerations bearing on these questions:

The organization must be a continuing one, for the formidable task has no foreseeable end. While results in development of the broad cost concepts can be produced in two years or so, devising standards consistent with those concepts is a much more time-consuming job. It has no foreseeable end because any set of standards will doubtless require modification as circumstances change.

One organization should be responsible for both aspects of the undertaking. Otherwise, human nature is such that the standards-setting group would probably start by a reexamination of the cost concepts, which might well take as much time as the concepts formulation in the first place.

The organization must be authoritative. Experience has demonstrated that recommendations of an individual or an ad hoc committee, however brilliant or logical they may be, have little practical impact. Authority can be derived either from legislative fiat or from the prestige of the organization, although each of these sources of authority offers disadvantages.

Authority, incidentally, is a necessary, but not a sufficient, condition. A poor set of standards is unlikely to gain permanent acceptance even though it is promulgated with substantial authority.

Standards can be developed for contracts in general, in which case they could be applied to government contracts as a special case, or to defense contracts as an even more special case. Alternatively, standards can be developed for defense contracts, or for government contracts, and then extended to other types of contracts.

I have given the argument for the first approach: essentially the same standards should apply to most contracts, and it is therefore artificial to select a special category for attention. The argument for the second approach is the practical one that congressional interest, and hence public interest, is aroused about the problem of defense contracts, and this interest might dissipate if the problem were tackled in broader terms.

With respect to defense contracts, there is a basic conflict of interest between the parties. The contractor wants the standards to be few and general, giving him the maximum amount of latitude in choosing the most advantageous cost alternative in a particular circumstance. The government, on the other hand, wants the standards to be specific in order to minimize the judgments required in auditing cost reimbursements.

(Some, by the way, deny the existence of this conflict. They assert that a contractor, even in the absence of standards, will voluntarily measure costs according to what is fair, even when this is inconsistent with his interests. This is a naive point of view, and it is surprising that knowledgeable men appear to expect that other knowledgeable men will give credence to it.)

The task of devising standards is expensive. Counting the work done in the public accounting firms and the salaries of those who spend a substantial amount of time on the effort, the work of the APB costs more than a million dollars a year. The cost concepts effort should be even more expensive per year than that unless it is strung out over an unacceptably long period of time.

The organization must be able to attract competent people. The task requires experts who have a profound understanding not only of accounting, but also of the realities of business—plus an ability to think conceptually and write precisely. Such people are scarce and are well paid in their current jobs. Much thought needs to be given to the inducements that would lead them to undertake this novel and potentially frustrating effort.

If the job of developing standards is carried out under the aegis of a professional organization, it may take a long time. The standard for 2″ × 4″ lumber I mentioned took 7 years to develop. The APB has issued only 15 opinions in the 10 years of its existence. Some of them supersede others, and it has not yet covered all the important topics even once.

Some persons fear that standards developed unilaterally by a government agency might be more restrictive than the situation warrants. The accounting standards developed by the Interstate Commerce Commission, the Civil Aeronautics Board, the Federal Power Commission, and the state public utility regulatory agencies are examples of overly restrictive standards. On the other hand, those of the Securities and Exchange Commission are by no means too restrictive; and the regulations of the Internal Revenue Service, though restrictive, are in my view not *overly* restrictive. This concern is therefore not necessarily justified.

Private or Public?

With these considerations in mind, we are in a better position to weigh the decision whether the work should be carried out under private or public auspices.

A Private-Sector Effort. The business community undoubtedly would like to see this effort undertaken by a group in the private sector analogous to the APB. But the considerations of authoritativeness, permanence, and financing lead me to the reluctant conclusion that such an approach is unlikely to succeed.

The APB, in its work on financial accounting principles, has had two great advantages that no other private organization seems likely to match in developing cost accounting standards:

1. The APB is authoritative. It can enforce its pronouncements through sanctions applicable to all members of the AICPA. The other leading organizations—the National Association of Accountants, the Financial Executives Institute, and the American Accounting Association—have no way whatsoever of ensuring compliance with their pronouncements.

2. The APB can raise substantial sums of money from the profession, since the development of financial accounting standards is now recognized by the public accounting firms to be very much in their own interest. No other private group has corresponding sources of support for the development of cost concepts and standards.

As for the AICPA itself, it is unlikely that it could succeed in this endeavor. It would have no way of obtaining adherence to cost standards comparable to the sanctions it can apply to information on published financial statements, and it has no obvious new source of financial support that would at least double the money it now raises.

Congress, moreover, which will undoubtedly have the final say on how the job gets done, would be unwilling to rely on a private organization unless it was convinced that the group would be permanent, well financed, and authoritative; that it adequately represented the interests of both government and business; and that it had safeguards against dilatory tactics.

I cannot visualize a private-sector effort that would satisfy these conditions. Indeed, the generally negative testimony of trade association representatives before the Senate Banking and Currency Committee in 1968 and negative responses to the General Accounting Office's request for comments on the feasibility of cost standards indicate that substantial segments of the business community are unwilling to meet these conditions.

A Government Effort. It seems likely, therefore, that the organization will be set up within the framework of the federal government. This can be done in either of two ways:

1. Congress could direct the comptroller general to undertake the task. (The Bureau of the Budget, the other possibility among existing organizations, has not been as close to the problem, nor does it have the nucleus of a staff.) The comptroller general might then set up a cost standards board, similar to the APB. He probably would obtain nominations for membership on this board from the accounting profession, business organizations, government organizations, and the academic community.

The board would specify the research that should be undertaken, and it would eventually make recommendations on cost concepts and standards to the comptroller general. The ground rule might be that the comptroller general would normally accept these recommendations, but he could modify or reject them for substantial cause.

2. An independent organization could be created, consisting of a small group of commissioners supported by an appropriate staff. It would be appointed by the president (probably in consultation with the comptroller general as the representative of the legislative branch in these matters) and financed with appropriated funds. Its pronouncements on standards would be authoritative since they presumably would be binding for government contracts, and might well be made applicable to the cost-measurement systems prescribed by various regulatory agencies.

Such a body could easily evolve into the "accounting court" which Leonard Spacek, chairman of Arthur Andersen & Company, has long advocated. After cost standards are developed, questions of interpretation will arise, and the board would provide a logical mechanism for resolving such questions. With such a procedure, there would also be a greater likelihood that the standards are kept in tune with changing circumstances.

The choice between these alternatives is by no means clearcut. An independent commission would give greater status to the effort, and it also would be more acceptable to those segments of the business community that are worried about the impartiality of an effort lodged within the General Accounting Office.

On the other hand, a commission is an unknown quantity. With appointees of the right caliber, it could do a better job than an existing organization, but if its members are second-rate, nothing useful would happen. It will not be easy to find high-salaried men who are willing to risk their careers in a much lower-paying job. Perhaps a part-time commission is the answer, though this device is rarely used in the federal government.

However established, the organization needs an adequate staff both to undertake research and to arrange for outside parties to do research. Such a staff would also operate the mechanism for circulating drafts of proposed concepts and standards for comment, and it would analyze and summarize the comments for the board or commission.

CONCLUDING NOTE

Too often, as I have tried to show, the word "cost" has a vague and ill-defined meaning, which can be troublesome particularly in contracts where cost is part of the reimbursement. An increasing number of persons for whom the meaning of cost is important have come to realize that standardization of meanings is a feasible goal.

These persons—in the business sector, in government agencies, and in Congress—understand that what must be done is to establish an authoritative, well-financed group which is charged with development of cost concepts and standards. So far the activity is just talk, but in the not-distant future the creation by the mutually interested parties of such a body may become a reality.

Inaction would be very disadvantageous to business. Congress might be persuaded to take no action, either on the false premise that there is no problem or on the promise that the business community will do the job in some unspecified way.

If Congress does not act, and if the subsequent voluntary effort is half-hearted and dilatory, in a few years the problem will make the headlines once more, and we will then almost surely see a unilateral government effort, probably with only insignificant participation by business.

15. Statistical Cost Analysis*

WILLIAM A. LONGBRAKE

Statistical techniques provide information useful in making many types of business decisions. For several reasons, however, statistical analysis is seldom used in analyzing production and other costs. Standard costing procedures, such as time and motion studies and direct costing procedures based on past experience and modified by anticipated changes, are sufficient in many decision-making situations.

Data limitations frequently hinder the employment of statistical analysis. To use it, data concerning costs, output, and product characteristics must exist for a sufficient number of time periods in one business firm or, alternatively, these data must be available for one time period for several firms producing essentially the same product. Another impediment is the general lack of knowledge about statistical cost analysis.

This article will demonstrate the use of statistical analysis for product costing, incremental costing, and cost forecasting. While the illustrations are developed specifically for use by commercial banks in making decisions about demand deposit operations, the basic techniques could be modified for cost analysis of products in other industries or products of a single firm.

Detailed cost accounting and production data exist for a sample of nearly 1,000 banks that have voluntarily participated in the Federal Reserve Banks' Functional Cost Analysis (FCA) program. Development of uniform accounting classifications and methods of allocating costs by the FCA has enabled participating banks to compare their performance with the average performance of similarly-sized banks. As a result, the accuracy and consistency of FCA data is excellent. Hence, the data afford a good basis for demonstrating the use of statistical analysis.

METHODOLOGY

Before statistical analysis can take place, it is necessary to construct a cost function that describes accurately all relevant factors. First, cost categories must be defined. For example, three types of costs are incurred

* *Financial Management,* vol. 2, no. 1 (Spring 1973), pp. 49–55.

in providing services to demand deposit customers—fixed maintenance costs, variable maintenance costs, and transactions costs. Fixed maintenance costs arise from routine operations performed on a regular basis for every account, e.g., carrying a master record of an account on a ledger card and preparing and sending monthly statements. Variable maintenance costs, such as FDIC insurance and "free" services, vary with the size of an account. Transactions costs vary directly with the volume of transactions.

Second, measurable variables must be found that explain variations in each general cost category.

Third, other factors that may indirectly influence the costs of providing demand deposit services should be identified, and variables should be defined that explain their effects. For example, to the extent that common production costs exist and cannot be allocated precisely, the level of time deposit operations may have an influence on demand deposit costs. Other factors arise when the cost behavior of several firms is being analyzed. For instance, legal organizational form—unit, branch, or holding company affiliate—may influence the organization of demand deposit operations and, therefore, influence operating costs as well. In addition, wage rates prevailing in local labor markets will have an important effect on demand deposit costs because of the large amount of labor required.

It may be impossible to determine the separate effects of each of these factors because of their complex interrelationships. Moreover, if the volume of output affects the unit cost related to any one of these factors, the accountant's use of standard costs may overlook important variations that occur with changes in the level of output. Thus, a cost function may be a useful alternative to ordinary accounting practices.

Bell and Murphy and Longbrake have demonstrated that a log-linear cost function of the type defined in the following equation is appropriate for commercial banks and explains most of the variation in demand deposit operating costs among banks:

$$\begin{aligned}\log C = \log H &+ \delta_1 \log N + \delta_2 \log S + \psi_1 \log T_1 + \psi_2 \log T_2 \\ &+ \psi_3 \log T_3 + \psi_4 \log T_4 + \psi_5 \log T_5 + \psi_6 \log T_6 \\ &+ \alpha_1 \log B + \alpha_2 \log M + \alpha_3 \log w + \alpha_4 \log I,\end{aligned}$$

where C is total *direct* operating costs allocated by a bank to the demand deposit function. A glossary of the symbols in the equation appears in the inset. The reader is asked to peruse them before proceeding, and refer to them as necessary in company with the following exposition.

Coefficients of the variables in the cost equation shown above—δ_i, ψ_i, and α_i—indicate that percentage change in total cost occurring when a particular variable changes by 1 percent, with all other variables unchanged. The effect on costs of the addition of a new account with characteristics *identical* to the existing "average" account is measured by the

Glossary of Symbols

C	=	total *direct* operating costs allocated by a bank to the demand deposit function
$\log H$	=	cost function constant
N	=	average number of accounts per banking office
S	=	average dollar size of a demand deposit account
T_1	=	average number of home debits (items posted to the debit column in the ledger for each account) per account
T_2	=	average number of deposits per account
T_3	=	average number of transit checks (checks written on banks other than the home bank) deposited per account
T_4	=	average number of official checks issued per account
T_5	=	average number of checks cashed per account
T_6	=	average number of transit checks cashed per account
B	=	number of offices operated by a bank
M	=	ratio of the number of regular checking accounts to the sum of both regular and special accounts
w	=	average annual wage rate per demand deposit employee
I	=	ratio of the dollar volume of demand deposits to the dollar volume of demand and time deposits, measures the effects of time deposit production activities on demand deposit costs
$\delta_i, \psi_i, \alpha_i$		indicate that percentage change in total cost that occurs when a particular variable changes by 1 percent, given that all other variables remain unchanged.

coefficient of $\log N$. The indicated percentage change in costs will include additional fixed maintenance, variable maintenance, and transactions costs. The percentage change in costs caused by an increase in the average size of account S will indicate primarily increases in variable maintenance costs associated with account size. The percentage change in costs caused by an increase in T_1 will show the change in transactions costs due to a large number of home debits per account. Changes in the other transactions variables can be interpreted in a similar fashion.

If a regular account is substituted for a special account, the coefficient of $\log M$ will indicate whether costs increase or decrease. The change in costs may result from differences in either fixed maintenance, variable maintenance, or transactions costs for two accounts which are identical in all respects except that one is a special account and the other is a regular account. The coefficient of $\log w$ indicates the percentage change in costs which occurs when the wage rate changes. Differences in local wage rates or differences in the mix of personnel engaged in demand deposit operations could cause differences in total costs. Therefore, the effects of maintenance, transactions, and other factors on demand deposit costs are contained within the cost function. Although the cost of a specific demand deposit production operation may not be identifiable, the statistical cost function can be used to determine the costs which occur for a given set of production relationships.

Data for estimating the coefficients of the cost equation shown above were obtained from 964 banks that participated in the 1971 FCA program. These banks ranged in size from $5 million to $6 billion in total deposits. Regression analysis was used, to estimate the coefficients; the results are presented in exhibit 1. These results will serve as a base for

EXHIBIT 1
Regression Results for the 1971 Demand Deposit Cost Function*

$$\begin{aligned}
\log C = & -1.7345 + .9503 \log N + .3936 \log S + .0467 \log T_1 \\
& \quad (.1792) \quad (.0127) \qquad\quad (.0248) \qquad\quad (.0268) \\
& + .1427 \log T_2 + .0742 \log T_3 + .0583 \log T_4 + \\
& \quad (.0348) \qquad\quad (.0126) \qquad\quad (.0111) \\
& + .0183 \log T_5 - .0046 \log T_6 + 1.0150 \log B + \\
& \quad (.0105) \qquad\quad (.0124) \qquad\quad (.0092) \\
& - .0626 \log M + .4312 \log w + .0113 \log I \\
& \quad (.0251) \qquad\quad (.0470) \qquad\quad (.0311)
\end{aligned}$$

$\bar{R} = .9630$
Standard Error of Estimate = .0998
F-Ratio = 2087.5

* Numbers in parentheses are standard errors of the regression coefficients.

developing illustrations of product costing, incremental costing, and cost forecasting below.

PRODUCT COSTING

Accountants generally recognize two methods of product costing—job order costing and process costing. In job order costing, each job is an accounting unit to which material, labor, and other costs are assigned. However, in process costing, attention centers on total costs incurred by a department for a given time period in relation to the units processed. Dividing total costs by the quantity of units produced gives the average unit cost. Process costing is usually more appropriate for mass production.

Statistical analysis of costs is more applicable in process than in job order costing. Costs are accumulated over a period of time for a specific department, and data concerning production activities in the department are collected for the same time period. However, rather than employing traditional accounting methods to ascertain average unit costs, average unit costs are estimated through a statistical analysis of the cost-output relationship as defined in a cost function. Traditional accounting methods must assume a rather uncomplicated relationship between output and costs (or various categories of costs); however, if complex interrelationships prevail among the various factors influencing total costs, statistical methods may be more appropriate. It must be remembered that data are required for several time periods or for several firms producing essentially the same product before statistical analysis is feasible. Traditional accounting methods do not have such a requirement.

In many respects, servicing demand deposits in a bank is similar to a continuous production process in manufacturing and thus will serve as a good general illustration. Tellers perform several operations including counting cash, verifying deposit amounts, and issuing receipts. The proof department sorts checks by type and identifies questionable checks. The bookkeeping department posts deposits and checks to appropriate accounts. Furthermore, many other activities, in addition to those mentioned above, occur on a regular and continuing basis.

Two kinds of demand deposit accounts—regular and special—customarily exist in most banks. Special accounts have no minimum balance requirement whereas regular accounts do. As a result of the no minimum balance feature, special accounts tend to be held by individuals rather than businesses and they tend to be less active and have smaller average balances than regular accounts. Thus, regular and special accounts are distinct products; however, production operations for both always occur simultaneously. Consequently, the cost of servicing each type of account is not easily separable.

In exhibit 2, it is shown how the total and average cost per $100 of an average regular and an average special account can be determined from the results of the statistical analysis shown in exhibit 1. For convenience, values of the various account characteristics and bank characteristics have been selected that are approximately equal to the sample geometric means of these characteristics. In the cost computations for regular accounts, it is assumed that no special accounts exist. However, in the cost computations for special accounts, it is assumed that 1 percent of the accounts are regular. This assumption is required because the log of the mix variable (M) is undefined when there are no regular accounts.

The average regular account in exhibit 2 is more than twice as costly to service as the average special account. However, the average regular account is only 29 percent as costly per *dollar* of deposits as the average special account. Product costs developed in this way can be used to develop pricing policy. In the case of banks, this kind of information is useful in establishing service charge schedules. It should be noted that the average unit cost of an account need not be the same for each set of

EXHIBIT 2
Computation of Average Unit Costs for Regular and Special Checking Accounts

	(1)	(2)	(3)	(4)	(5)	(6)	(7)
	Regular Account				Special Account		
	Value	*Log of Value*	*Cost Function Coefficient*	*Product of Columns 2 and 3*	*Value*	*Log of Value*	*Product of Columns 3 and 6*
Characteristics of average account							
S Account size	$2,100	3.32222	.3936	1.30763	$ 300	2.47712	.97499
T_1 Home debits/accounts	230	2.36173	.0467	.11029	100	2.00000	.09340
T_2 Deposits/accounts	40	1.60206	.1427	.22861	25	1.39794	.19949
T_3 Transit checks deposited/accounts	180	2.25527	.0742	.16734	20	1.30103	.09654
T_4 Official checks/accounts	3	.47712	.0583	.02782	2	.30103	.01755
T_5 Checks cashed/accounts	30	1.47712	.0183	.02703	30	1.47712	.02703
T_6 Transit checks cashed/accounts	14	1.14613	−.0046	−.00527	16	1.20412	−.00554
Bank characteristics							
N Number of accounts	3,250	3.51188	.9503	3.33734	3,250	3.51188	3.33734
B Number of offices	3	.47712	1.0150	.48428	3	.47712	.48428
M Regular accounts/all accounts	100%	.00000	−.0626	.00000	1%	−2.00000	.12520
w Annual wage rate	$5,700	3.75587	.4312	1.61953	$5,700	3.75587	1.61953
I Demand deposits/total deposits	40%	−.39794	.0113	−.00450	40%	−.39794	−.00450
H Cost function constant				−1.73447			−1.73447
Total cost (log)				5.53860			5.23084
(antilog)				$345,623.00			$170,054.00
Average cost per account				35.45			17.44
Average cost per $100				1.69			5.81

account characteristic and bank characteristic variables. Any bank which knows its values for the variables in exhibit 2 may determine its average unit costs by following the demonstrated computational procedure.

This method of product costing would be useful in any business enterprise that produces more than one product on a regular and continuing basis using essentially the same types of resources. For example, different types of telephone service—private, party, or commercial—could be costed using the methods described above. Other possible applications might include the manufacture of canned and processed foods, book publishing, manufacture of apparel, manufacture of consumer durable goods such as automobiles, refrigerators, television sets, appliances, lawn mowers, and so on.

INCREMENTAL COSTING

Incremental or differential costs are the increases or decreases in total costs, or the changes in specific elements of cost, that result from some variation in operations. An incremental costing approach to decision making is important when certain costs are fixed and, as such, are not influenced by changes in operations. Ordinarily such a situation occurs in the short run when scale of operations cannot be changed. When the decision is whether or not to accept another order or expand output from a given level, and certain costs are fixed or are relatively inflexible, use of standard costs or average unit costs may lead to the wrong decision. This could happen because the incremental cost of the additional output may differ from the change in total costs indicated by multiplying the additional output by the average unit cost.

Situations in which an incremental cost approach to decision making may be appropriate include: taking on new orders; increasing, decreasing, or eliminating production of certain products; replacing old equipment with new; and so forth. In commercial banks, it may be useful to know the incremental costs of a new demand deposit account, especially if it is tied to a loan arrangement, so that an appropriate pricing strategy can be developed. Incremental costs can also be developed for specific types of demand deposit accounts that differ in various respects from the average account.

The usual accounting approach to differential costing is to identify variable and fixed costs. Then, in a particular situation the affected variable costs can be used to determine the differential cost. However, if variable costs cannot be determined easily, or if variable costs do not remain constant per unit of output at various levels of output, the usual accounting techniques may prove to be insufficient.

Statistical cost analysis may improve the accuracy of incremental cost determination in such circumstances because estimates of incremental (marginal) costs can be derived directly from the cost function for every variation in the basic product that might exist. For example, incremental costs can be determined for each type of transaction that is identified in the demand deposit cost function. Thus, the incremental cost of one additional home debit per account is the change in total cost, C, which results from an increase in home debits per account, T_1, while all other variables in the cost equation shown above remain unchanged. This incremental cost is computed by taking the partial derivative of total cost, C, with respect to home debits per account, T_1. In the present instance, the incremental cost of one additional home debit per account is equal to the cost function coefficient of T_1 (Ψ_1) times total cost (C) divided by T_1. Thus, the incremental cost of an additional home debit per regular demand account is computed in column 3 of exhibit 3 by multiplying the appropriate cost function coefficient in column 1 (.0467) by total cost ($345,623) and then dividing by the number of home debits per regular account (230). Incremental cost per unit, shown in column 4, is obtained by dividing the incremental cost figure in column 3 by the number of regular accounts (9,750). Incremental costs for other variations in the product are calculated in a similar fashion and the results are shown in exhibit 3.

The incremental cost of an additional regular demand deposit account that is *identical* to the average regular account is $33.69. This is less than the average unit cost of $35.45 for an existing regular account as indicated in exhibit 2. However, the incremental cost of an additional special account is slightly larger than the average unit cost of a special account. Thus, increases in the number of regular accounts would reduce average unit cost, but increase in the number of special checking accounts would increase average unit cost. To the extent that unutilized capacity exists, management may wish to promote regular rather than special accounts.

An additional dollar in a special account is more than three times as costly to service as an additional dollar in a regular account. This indicates that the cost of providing extra services to small special checking accounts is greater per dollar than the cost of providing additional services to large regular checking accounts. This also implies that the incremental cost associated with an additional dollar of deposits most likely depends on the size of the deposit, i.e., fixed account maintenance costs can be spread over more dollars in large accounts. Home debits are associated with highly routinized operations which may explain why there is little difference in the incremental costs of home debits in regular and special checking accounts. With the exception of transit checks deposited, incremental costs of changes in other account characteristics are greater for regular accounts than they are for special accounts. There are only one ninth as many transit checks deposited annually in special accounts as in regular accounts. The difference in incremental costs for transit

EXHIBIT 3
Incremental Costs for Various Characteristics of Regular and Special Accounts

		(1)	(2)	(3)	(4)	(5)	(6)	(7)
			Regular Accounts			*Special Accounts*		
	Characteristics	*Cost Function Coefficient*	*Value*	*Incremental Cost*	*Incremental Cost per Unit**	*Value*	*Incremental Cost*	*Incremental Cost per Unit**
N†	Account	$\delta_1 = .9503$	9,750	$ 33.69	$33.6867	9,750	$ 17.67	$17.6664
S	Account size	$\delta_2 = .3936$	$ 2,100	64.78	.0066	$ 300	223.11	.0229
T_1	Home debits/accounts	$\psi_1 = .0467$	230	70.18	.0072	100	79.42	.0081
T_2	Deposits/accounts	$\psi_2 = .1427$	40	1,233.01	.1265	25	970.67	.0996
T_3	Transit checks deposited/accounts	$\psi_3 = .0742$	180	142.47	.0146	20	630.90	.0647
T_4	Official checks/accounts	$\psi_4 = .0583$	3	6,716.61	.6889	2	4,957.07	.5084
$(T_5 - T_6)$‡	Nontransit checks cashed/accounts	$\psi_5 = .0183$	16	210.83	.0216	14	103.73	.0106
T_6	Transit checks cashed/accounts	$\psi_6 = -.0046$	14	97.27	.0100	16	54.84	.0056
		$\alpha_2 = -.0626$						
C	Total costs		$345,623			$170,054		

* Incremental cost per unit is determined by dividing incremental cost by 9,750 accounts.

† The number of accounts variable (N) includes both regular and special accounts. However, the mix variable also contains both regular and special accounts. Let $N = (N_R + N_S)/B$ and $M = N_R/(N_R + N_S)$. Then, the incremental cost of another regular account $= (\delta_1 - \alpha_2)[C/N_R + N_S)] + \alpha_2(C/N_R)$. The incremental cost of another special account $= (\delta_1 - \alpha_2)[C/N_R + N_S)]$.

‡ Nontransit checks cashed per account equals $(T_5 - T_6)$ while transit checks cashed equals T_6. The sum of these two categories is total checks cashed (T_5). The incremental cost of nontransit checks cashed $= \psi_5(C/T_5)$. The incremental cost of transit checks cashed $= \psi_5(C/A_5) + \psi_6(C/T_6)$.

EXHIBIT 4
Computation of the Cost of a Regular Checking Account Which Differs from the Average Regular Checking Account

	Characteristics	(1) Value Example Account	(2) Value Average Account	(3) Difference (1) – (2)	(4) Incremental Cost per Item	(5) Change in Average Cost per Account
S	Account size	$5,000	$2,100	2,900	.0066	$19.14
T_1	Home debits/account	400	230	170	.0072	1.22
T_2	Deposits/account	50	40	10	.1265	1.26
T_3	Transit checks deposited/account	300	180	120	.0146	1.75
T_4	Official checks/account	5	3	2	.6889	1.38
$(T_5 - T_6)$	Nontransit checks cashed/account	20	16	4	.0216	.09
T_6	Transit checks cashed/account	20	14	6	.0100	.04
Total						$24.88
Cost of average regular account						+35.45
Cost of example regular account						$60.33
Cost per $100 of the example regular account						1.21

checks deposited in regular and special accounts may occur if the cost of handling the first few transit checks is high while the cost of handling each additional transit check declines.

Suppose management wishes to know the cost of a specific regular checking account that differs in identifiable ways from the average regular account. Incremental cost analysis can be used to help determine the cost of this *example* regular account. Characteristics of the example regular account to be costed are shown in column 1 of exhibit 4 and characteristics of the average account are contained in column 2. Column 3 is the difference of the first two columns. The incremental cost in column 5 is the product of the figure in column 3 and the incremental cost per item in column 4, which was computed in exhibit 3.

Although the cost of the example regular account in exhibit 4 is considerably greater than the cost of the average regular account, the cost per $100 is lower because of the larger balance. This result suggests that service charge rates should be based on account size and the number of various types of transactions. Knowledge of incremental costs can be used to establish variable rate service charge schedules which reflect the actual cost incurred in servicing a particular account more accurately than using average unit costs or some kind of standard costing procedure.

Such an approach to pricing may be useful in nonfinancial firms that produce a product or service capable of being differentiated or varied in several ways. For example, the incremental costing method may be useful in establishing the cost of selling particular types of merchandise in retailing firms or in determining the cost of handling particular types of customer credit accounts.

COST FORECASTING

When management contemplates or expects some change in operations at a future date, it is important to forecast the effects of this change on costs. The use of statistical analysis in forecasting, especially for forecasting sales, is well established. However, cost forecasts ordinarily are based on a nonstatistical evaluation of the production facilities, equipment, labor, and materials required to produce enough to meet the sales forecast. When statistical methods are used to forecast costs, it usually involves either a simple regression analysis of volume and cost or, in rare cases, a multiple regression analysis.

The principal danger inherent in statistical cost forecasting is that future behavior may differ substantially from past cost behavior, thus making forecasts unreliable. Changes in plant and equipment, materials, products, production techniques, personnel, internal organization, prices paid for materials and labor, and many other factors will tend to impair the reliability of statistical cost forecasts. Nevertheless, in some circumstances statistical cost forecasting may provide helpful information. For example, if prices of materials and labor have varied in the past, this information can be included in the statistical cost function. Then, the effect of expected future changes in these prices on costs can be determined. In a firm that operates several plants or branches, all producing and selling the same product, statistical cost analysis may prove useful in forecasting the costs of *operating* a new plant or branch. Statistical analysis is not as likely to be useful in determining the cost of constructing a new plant. Several illustrations of cost forecasting are given below.

Turning to the banking example, suppose a branch bank is operating three offices with an average of 3,250 demand deposit accounts per office. It is considering opening a new office that it expects to be able to attract 3,250 new demand deposit accounts having characteristics essentially similar to those of existing demand deposits. Management is concerned about the effect of this expansion on its costs of operation for demand deposits. The change in costs can be forecast by making appropriate changes in the statistical cost function shown in the cost equation above:

$$\begin{aligned} \log C_1 &= \log C_0 + \alpha_1 (\log B_1 - \log B_0) \\ &= 5.53860 + 1.0150\ (.60206 - .47712) \\ &= 5.53860 + .12681 \\ &= 5.66541 \end{aligned}$$

Total costs are $345,623 before the addition of the new branch and will be $462,820 afterwards, an increase of $117,197. Average unit cost before expansion is $35.45, but after expansion it will be $35.60. The $.15 increase in average unit cost reflects added costs of coordination associated with the operation of the new branch.

Suppose that this branch bank is not considering opening a new branch but expects the number of demand deposits handled by each branch to increase from 3,250 to 4,333. The change in costs that occurs when 1,083 new demand accounts are added to each of the three existing branches can be computed in the same manner as described above: $5.53860 + .9503(3.63682 - 3.51188) = 5.65733$. Total costs will be $454,289 and average cost per account will be $34.95, a decline of $.50 per account. In both of the cost forecasting examples given here, there will be 13,000 accounts and $27.3 million in deposits (assuming that average account size is $2,100). In one example, though, there are four offices while in the other there are only three. Having one more branch for the same number of accounts and the same amount of deposits causes a difference of $7,531 or nearly 2 percent in total operating costs.

Management can also forecast the effect of an increase in the average annual wage paid per employee. Suppose management expects wages to rise by 10 percent from $5,700 to $6,270. Total costs will be: 5.53860 +

.4312 (3.79727 — 3.75587) = 5.55645 or $360,125. Average unit costs will be $36.94, an increase of $1.49 per account.

The effects of other anticipated changes, in addition to those illustrated above, can be determined in the same way. In fact, the effects of all expected changes on total costs can be forecast simultaneously.

Any business firm able to construct its own cost function can use it to forecast the effects of changes in any or all of its variables. This procedure is legitimate so long as there is no significant change in the production-cost relationship.

CONCLUDING REMARKS

These uses of statistical cost analysis were demonstrated for commercial banks. However, any business enterprise which produces its products on a relatively regular and continuing basis and which maintains detailed records about output, resource prices, product characteristics, and costs can construct its own statistical cost function and use it for product costing, incremental costing, or cost forecasting. Thus, a host of business enterprises have the potential to use some kind of management-oriented statistical cost analysis.

If the production-cost relationship is more complex than that presumed in break-even analysis or variable budgeting, statistical cost analysis may provide useful supplemental information that these more conventional cost accounting techniques are incapable of providing. It is not suggested that information derived from employing statistical techniques should supplant other types of information; rather, it is urged that statistical cost information be used in conjunction with other cost accounting information to help *improve* decision making.

16. The Economies of Scale*

GEORGE J. STIGLER

The theory of the economies of scale is the theory of the relationship between the scale of use of a properly chosen combination of all productive services and the rate of output of the enterprise. In its broadest formulation this theory is a crucial element of the economic theory of social organization, for it underlies every question of market organization and the role (and locus) of governmental control over economic life. Let one ask himself how an economy would be organized if every economic activity were prohibitively inefficient upon alternately a small scale and a large scale, and the answer will convince him that here lies a basic element of the theory of economic organization.

The theory has limped along for a century, collecting large pieces of good reasoning and small chunks of empirical evidence but never achieving scientific prosperity. A large cause of its poverty is that the central concept of the theory—the firm of optimum size—has eluded confident measurement. We have been dangerously close to denying Lincoln, for all economists have been ignorant of the optimum size of firm in almost every industry all of the time, and this ignorance has been an insurmountable barrier between us and the understanding of the forces which govern optimum size. It is almost as if one were trying to measure the nutritive values of goods without knowing whether the consumers who ate them continued to live.

The central thesis of this paper is that the determination of the optimum size is not difficult if one formalizes the logic that sensible men have always employed to judge efficient size. This technique, which I am old-fashioned enough to call the survivor technique, reveals the optimum size in terms of private costs—that is, in terms of the environment in which the enterprise finds itself. After discussing the technique, we turn to the question of how the forces governing optimum size may be isolated.

* *The Journal of Law and Economics,* vol. 1 (October 1958), pp. 54–71.

I. THE SURVIVOR PRINCIPLE

The optimum size (or range of sizes) of enterprises in an industry is now ascertained empirically by one of three methods. The first is that of direct comparison of actual costs of firms of different sizes; the second is the comparison of rates of return on investment; and the third is the calculation of probable costs of enterprises of different sizes in the light of technological information. All three methods are practically objectionable in demanding data which are usually unobtainable and seldom up to date. But this cannot be the root of their difficulties, for there is up-to-date information on many economic concepts which are complex and even basically incapable of precise measurement (such as income). The plain fact is that we have not demanded the data because we have been unable to specify what we wanted.

The comparisons of both actual costs and rates of return are strongly influenced by the valuations which are put on productive services, so that an enterprise which over- or undervalues important productive services, will under- or overstate its efficiency. Historical cost valuations of resources, which are most commonly available, are in principle irrelevant under changed conditions. Valuations based upon expected earnings yield no information on the efficiency of an enterprise—in the limiting case where all resources are so valued, all firms would be of equal efficiency judged by either average costs or rates of return. The ascertainment on any scale of the maximum value of each resource in alternative uses is a task which only the unsophisticated would assume and only the omniscient would discharge. The host of valuation problems are accentuated by the variable role of the capital markets in effecting revaluations and the variable attitudes of the accountants toward the revaluations.

The technological studies of costs of different sizes of plant encounter equally formidable obstacles. These studies are compounded of some fairly precise (although not necessarily very relevant) technical information and some crude guesses on nontechnological aspects such as marketing costs, transportation rate changes, labor relations, etc.—that is, much of the problem is solved only in the unhappy sense of being delegated to a technologist. Even ideal results, moreover, do not tell us the optimum size of firm in industry A in 1958, but rather the optimum size of new plants in the industry, on the assumption that the industry starts *de novo* or that only a small increment of investment is being made.

The survivor technique avoids both the problems of valuation of resources and the hypothetical nature of the technological studies. Its fundamental postulate is that the competition of different sizes of firms sifts out the more efficient enterprises. In the words of Mill, who long ago proposed the technique:

> Whether or not the advantages obtained by operating on a large scale preponderate in any particular case over the more watchful attention, and greater regard to minor gains and losses usually found in small establishments, can be ascertained, in a state of free competition, by an unfailing test. . . . Wherever there are large and small establishments in the same business, that one of the two which in existing circumstances carries on the production at the greater advantage will be able to undersell the other.[1]

Mill was wrong only in suggesting that the technique was inapplicable under oligopoly, for even under oligopoly the drive of maximum profits will lead to the disappearance of relatively inefficient sizes of firms.

The survivor technique proceeds to solve the problem of determining the optimum firm size as follows: Classify the firms in an industry by size, and calculate the share of industry output coming from each class over time. If the share of a given class falls, it is relatively inefficient, and in general is more inefficient the more rapidly the share falls.

An efficient size of firm, on this argument, is one that meets any and all problems the entrepreneur actually faces: strained labor relations, rapid innovation, government regulation, unstable foreign markets, and what not. This is, of course, the decisive meaning of efficiency from the viewpoint of the enterprise. Of course, social efficiency may be a very different thing: the most efficient firm size may arise from possession of monopoly power, undesirable labor practices, discriminatory legislation, etc. The survivor technique is not directly applicable to the determination of the socially optimum size of enterprise, and we do not enter into this question. The socially optimum firm is fundamentally an ethical concept, and we question neither its importance nor its elusiveness.

Not only is the survivor technique more direct and simpler than the alternative techniques for the determination of the optimum size of firm, it is also more authoritative. Suppose that the cost, rate of return, and technological studies all find that in a given industry the optimum size of firm is one which produces 500 to 600 units per day, and that costs per unit are much higher if one goes far outside this range. Suppose also that most of the firms in the industry are three times as large, and that those firms which are in the 500 to 600 unit class are rapidly failing or growing to a larger size. Would we believe that the optimum size was 500 to 600 units? Clearly not: an optimum size that cannot survive in rivalry with other sizes is a contradiction, and some error, we would all say, has been made in the traditional studies. Implicitly

[1] *Principles of Political Economy* (Ashley ed.), p. 134. Marshall states the same argument in Darwinian language: "For as a general rule the law of substitution—which is nothing more than a special and limited application of the law of survival of the fittest—tends to make one method of industrial organization supplant another when it offers a direct and immediate service at a lower price." *Principles of Economics,* p. 597 (8th ed., 1920).

all judgments on economies of scale have always been based directly upon, or at least verified by recourse to, the experience of survivorship.

This is not to say that the findings of the survivor technique are unequivocal. Entrepreneurs may make mistakes in their choice of firm size, and we must seek to eliminate the effects of such errors either by invoking large numbers of firms so errors tend to cancel or by utilizing time periods such that errors are revealed and corrected. Or the optimum size may be changing because of changes in factor prices or technology, so that perhaps the optimum size rises in one period and falls in another. This problem too calls for a close examination of the time periods which should be employed. We face these problems in our statistical work below.

We must also recognize that a single optimum size of firm will exist in an industry only if all firms have (access to) identical resources. Since various firms employ different kinds or qualities of resources, there will tend to develop a frequency distribution of optimum firm sizes. The survivor technique may allow us to estimate this distribution; in the application below we restrict ourselves to the range of optimum sizes.

The measure of the optimum size is only a first step toward the construction of a theory of economies of scale with substantive content, but it is the indispensable first step. We turn in later sections of this paper to the examination of the methods by which hypotheses concerning the determinants of optimum size may be tested.

II. ILLUSTRATIVE SURVIVORSHIP MEASURES

The survivor principle is very general in scope and very flexible in application, and these advantages can best be brought out by making concrete applications of the principle to individual industries. These applications will also serve to display a number of problems of data and interpretation which are encountered in the use of the survivor technique. We begin with the American steel industry.

In order that survivorship of firms of a given size be evidence of comparative efficiency, these firms must compete with firms of other sizes—all of the firms must sell in a common market. We have therefore restricted the analysis to firms making steel ingots by open-hearth or Bessemer processes. Size has perforce been measured by capacity, for production is not reported by individual companies, and capacity is expressed as a percentage of the industry total to eliminate the influence of the secular growth of industry and company size. The geographical extent of the market is especially difficult to determine in steel, for the shifting geographical pattern of consumption has created a linkage between the various regional markets. We treat the market as national, which exaggerates its extent, but probably does less violence to the facts than a sharp regional classification of firms. The basic data are given in table 1.

TABLE 1
Distribution of Output of Steel Ingot Capacity by Relative Size of Company

Company Size (percent of industry total)	*1930*	*1938*	*1951*
1. Percent of Industry Capacity			
Under 0.5	7.16	6.11	4.65
0.5 to 1	5.94	5.08	5.37
1 to 2.5......	13.17	8.30	9.07
2.5 to 5	10.64	16.59	22.21
5 to 10	11.18	14.03	8.12
10 to 25	13.24	13.99	16.10
25 and over	38.67	35.91	34.50
2. Number of Companies			
Under 0.5	39	29	22
0.5 to 1	9	7	7
1 to 2.5......	9	6	6
2.5 to 5	3	4	5
5 to 10	2	2	1
10 to 25	1	1	1
25 and over	1	1	1

Sources: *Directory of Iron and Steel Works of the United States and Canada*, 1930, 1938; *Iron Age*, January 3, 1952.

Over two decades covered by table 1 (and, for that matter, over the last half century) there has been a persistent and fairly rapid decline in the share of the industry's capacity in firms with less than half a percent of the total, so that we may infer that this size of firm is subject to substantial diseconomies of scale.[2] The firms with 0.5 to 2.5 percent of industry capacity showed a moderate decline, and hence were subject to smaller diseconomies of scale. The one firm with more than one fourth of industry capacity declined moderately, so it too had diseconomies of scale. The intervening sizes, from 2.5 to 25 percent of industry capacity, grew or held their share so they constituted the range of optimum size.

The more rapid the rate at which a firm loses its share of the industry's output (or, here, capacity), the higher is its private cost of production relative to the cost of production of firms of the most efficient size. This interpretation should not be reversed, however, to infer that the size class whose share is growing more rapidly is more efficient than

[2] In 1930 the firm with 0.5 percent of the industry capacity had a capacity of 364,000 net tons; in 1951, 485,000 net tons. Of course, we could have employed absolute firm size classes, but they are less appropriate to many uses.

other classes whose shares are growing more slowly; the difference can merely represent differences in the quantities of various qualities of resources. In the light of these considerations we translate the data of table 1 into a long-run average cost curve for the production of steel ingots and display this curve in figure 1. Over a wide range of outputs there is no evidence of net economies or diseconomies of scale.

FIGURE 1

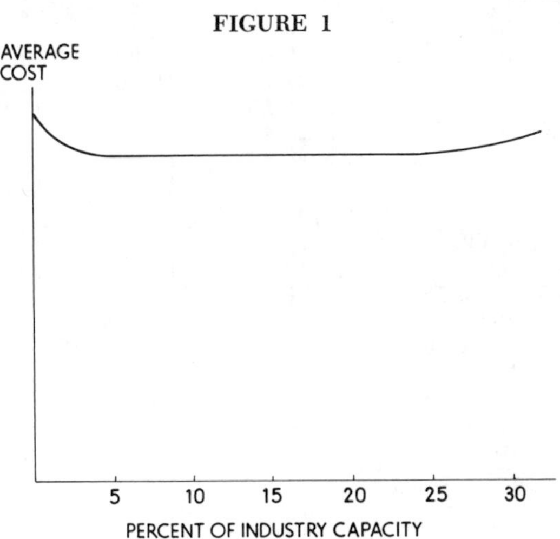

Although the survivor test yields an estimate of the shape of the long-run cost curve, it does not allow an estimate of how much higher than the minimum are the costs of the firm sizes whose shares of industry output are declining. Costs are higher the more rapid the rate at which the firm size loses its share of industry output, but the rate at which a firm size loses a share of industry output will also vary with numerous other factors. This rate of loss of output will be larger, the less durable and specialized the productive resources of the firm, for then exit from the industry is easier. The rate of loss will also be larger, the more nearly perfect the capital and labor markets, so that resources can be obtained to grow quickly to more efficient size. The rate of loss will be smaller, given the degree of inefficiency, the more profitable the industry is, for then the rate of return of all sizes of firms is larger relative to other industries.

By a simple extension of this argument, we may also estimate the most efficient size of *plant* in the steel ingot industry during the same period (table 2). We again find that the smallest plants have a tendency to decline relative to the industry, and indeed this is implied by the company data. There is no systematic tendency toward decline in shares

TABLE 2
Distribution of Output of Steel Ingot Capacity

Plant Size (percent of industry total)	*1930*	*1938*	*1951*
	1. *Percent of Industry Capacity*		
Under 0.25	3.74	3.81	3.25
0.25 to 0.5	6.39	5.81	7.20
0.5 to 0.75......	6.39	4.18	3.82
0.75 to 1	9.42	12.29	10.93
1 to 1.75......	21.78	15.56	20.67
1.75 to 2.5	13.13	16.73	17.01
2.5 to 3.75......	23.49	17.18	8.10
3.75 to 5	8.82	12.07	12.46
5 to 10	6.82	12.37	16.56
	2. *Number of Plants*		
Under 0.25	40	29	23
0.25 to 0.5	20	16	18
0.5 to 0.75......	11	7	6
0.75 to 1	11	14	12
1 to 1.75......	18	13	15
1.75 to 2.5	6	8	8
2.5 to 3.75......	8	6	3
3.75 to 5	2	3	3
5 to 10	1	2	3

Source: Same as Table 1.

held by plants between 0.75 percent and 10 percent of the industry size. We may therefore infer that the tendency of very small plants and companies to decline relative to the industry is due to the diseconomy of a small plant, and the tendency of the largest company (U.S. Steel) to decline has been due to diseconomies of multiplant operation beyond a certain scale.

An equally important and interesting industry, passenger automobiles, uncovers different problems. Here we can use production data instead of capacity, and have no compunctions in treating the market as national in scope. The basic data for the individual firms are given in table 3.

A striking feature of the automobile industry is the small number of firms, and this poses a statistical problem we have glossed over in our discussion of steel: what confidence can be attached to changes in the share of industry output coming from a firm size when that size contains very few firms? For the automobile industry (unlike steel) we possess annual data, and can therefore take into account the steadiness of direction or magnitude of changes in shares of various firm sizes, and to this extent increase our confidence in the estimates. We may also extend the period which is surveyed, although at the risk of combining periods with different sizes of optimum firms. Aside from recourse to related data (the survivorship pattern of the industry in other

TABLE 3
Percentages of Passenger Automobiles Produced in United States by Various Companies 1936–41 and 1946–55

Year	General Motors	Chrys-ler	Ford	Hudson	Nash	Kaiser	Willys Over-land	Packard	Stude-baker	Other
1936........	42.9	23.6	22.6	3.3	1.5	...	0.7	2.2	2.4	0.8
1937........	40.9	24.2	22.6	2.7	2.2	...	2.0	2.8	2.1	0.5
1938........	43.9	23.8	22.3	2.5	1.6	...	0.8	2.5	2.3	0.3
1939........	43.0	22.7	21.8	2.8	2.3	...	0.9	2.6	3.7	0.3
1940........	45.9	25.1	19.0	2.3	1.7	...	0.7	2.1	3.1	0.1
1941........	48.3	23.3	18.3	2.1	2.1	...	0.8	1.8	3.2	0.1
1946........	38.4	25.0	21.2	4.2	4.6	0.6	0.3	1.9	3.6	0.2
1947........	40.4	21.7	21.3	2.8	3.2	4.1	0.9	1.6	3.5	0.5
1948........	40.1	21.2	19.1	3.6	3.1	4.6	0.8	2.5	4.2	0.7
1949........	43.0	21.9	21.0	2.8	2.8	1.2	0.6	2.0	4.5	0.2
1950........	45.7	18.0	23.3	2.1	2.8	2.2	0.6	1.1	4.0	0.1
1951........	42.2	23.1	21.8	1.8	3.0	1.9	0.5	1.4	4.2	0.1
1952........	41.5	22.0	23.2	1.8	3.5	1.7	1.1	1.4	3.7	...
1953........	45.7	20.3	25.2	1.2	2.2	1.0		1.3	3.0	...
1954........	52.2	13.1	30.6	1.7		0.3		0.5	1.6	...
1955........	50.2	17.2	28.2	2.0		0.1		2.3		...

Source: Hard's Automotive Yearbook 1951,1955, 1956.

countries, for example), there is no other method of reducing the uncertainty of findings for small number industries.

The survivorship record in automobiles (summarized in Table 4) is more complicated than that for steel. In the immediate prewar years there was already a tendency for the largest company to produce a rising share and for the 2.5 to 5 percent class to produce a sharply declining share; the smallest and next to largest sizes showed no clear tendency. In a longer span of time, however, the smallest companies reveal a fairly consistently declining share. In the immediate postwar period, the 2.5 to 5 percent size class was strongly favored by the larger companies' need to practice price control in a sensitive political atmosphere, and the same phenomenon reappeared less strongly in the first two years after the outbreak of Korean hostilities. From this record we would infer that there have been diseconomies of large size, at least for the largest size of firm, in inflationary periods with private or public price control, but substantial economies of large scale at other times. The long-run average cost curve is saucer shaped in inflationary times, but shows no tendency to rise at the largest outputs in other times.

TABLE 4
Percentage of Passenger Automobiles Produced by Companies of Various Sizes

	Company Size (as percent of industry)				*Number of Companies*	
	Over 35	*10–35*	*2.5–5*	*Under 2.5*	*2.5–5*	*Under 2.5*
Year	*Percent*	*Percent*	*Percent*	*Percent*	*Percent*	*Percent*
1936	42.9	46.2	3.3	7.6	1	5*
1937	40.9	46.8	5.5	6.8	2	4*
1938	43.9	46.1	5.0	5.0	2	4*
1939	43.0	44.4	9.1	3.5	3	4*
1940	45.9	44.1	3.1	6.9	1	6*
1941	48.4	41.6	3.2	6.8	1	5
1946	38.4	46.2	12.4	3.0	3	4
1947	40.4	43.0	13.6	3.0	4	3
1948	40.1	40.3	18.0	1.5	5	2
1949	43.0	42.9	10.0	4.0	3	4
1950	45.7	41.3	6.8	6.1	2	5
1951	42.2	44.9	7.2	5.7	2	5
1952	41.5	45.2	7.2	6.1	2	5
1953	45.6	45.5	3.0	5.8	1	4
1954	52.2	43.7	0	4.1	0	4
1955	50.2	45.4	0	4.4	0	3

Source: Table 3.
* Or more.

The automobile example suggests the method by which we determine whether changing technology, factor prices, or consumer demands lead to a change in the optimum firm size. We infer an underlying stability in the optimum size in those periods in which the survivorship trends are stable. Indeed it is hard to conceive of an alternative test; one can judge the economic importance, in contrast to technological originality, of an innovation only by the impact it has upon the size distribution of firms.

Before we leave these applications of the survivorship technique we should indicate its flexibility in dealing with other problems which seem inappropriate to our particular examples. For example, a Marshallian may object that firms must begin small and grow to optimum size through time, so that the size structure of the industry in a given period will reflect this historical life pattern as well as the optimum size influences. In an industry such as retail trade this interpretation would be quite plausible. It can be met by studying the survivor experience of firm sizes in the light of the age or rate of growth of the firms. Again, one may argue that firms of different sizes have different comparative advantages at different stages of the business cycle. Such a hypothesis could be dealt with by comparing average survivorship patterns in given cycle stages with those calculated for full cycles.

Let us now turn to the methods by which one may test hypotheses on the determinants of optimum size.

III. INTER-INDUSTRY ANALYSES OF THE DETERMINANTS OF OPTIMUM SIZE

Once the optimum firm size has been ascertained for a variety of industries, the relationship between size and other variables can be explored. This is, in fact, the customary procedure for economists to employ, and the present investigation differs, aside from the method of determining optimum size, only in being more systematic than most such investigations. For example, numerous economists have asserted that advertising is a force making for large firms, and they usually illustrate this relationship by the cigarette industry. Will the relationship still hold when it is tested against a list of industries which has not been chosen to illustrate it? This is essentially the type of inquiry we make here.

Although the survivor method makes lesser demands of data than other methods to determine optimum firm size, it has equally exacting requirements of information on any other variable whose influence is to be studied. In the subsequent investigation of some 48 ("three-digit") manufacturing industries, whose optimum firm size is calculated from data in *Statistics of Income,* we have therefore been compelled to exclude some variables for lack of data and to measure others in a most imperfect manner. The industries we study, and the measures we contrive, are given in table 5; we describe their derivation below.

TABLE 5
Basic Data on Forty-eight Manufacturing Industries

Industry	Optimum Company Size (in thousand dollars of total assets) (1948–51)	Optimum Range Class Limits (in thousand dollars) From	To	Average Establishment Size (in thousand dollars of value added) (1947)	Number of Chemists and Engineers per 100 Employed (1950)	Advertising Expenditure as Percent of Gross Sales (1950)
Motor vehicles, incl. bodies and truck trailers	$827,828	$100,000	$open	$ 3,715	1.5879	0.4395
Petroleum refining	765,716	100,000	open	3,420	6.9171	0.4562
Blast furnaces, steel works, and rolling mills	525,485	100,000	open	8,310	2.0956	0.1321
Dairy products	446,483	100,000	open	110	0.7865	1.5221
Distilled, rectified, and blended liquors	248,424	100,000	open	2,090	0.9041	1.3674
Pulp, paper, and paperboard	203,794	100,000	open	1,645	1.4927	0.3357
Paints, varnishes, lacquers, etc.	175,404	100,000	open	394	6.0431	1.3539
Railroad equipment, incl. locomotives and streetcars	150,217	100,000	open	3,407	2.7171	0.3611
Tires and tubes	141,600	10,000	open	11,406	2.0974*	0.9453
Grain mill products ex. cereals preparations	128,363	100,000	open	210	1.0344	1.2492
Drugs and medicines	123,662	100,000	open	552	6.2599	8.3858
Smelting, refining, rolling, drawing, and alloying of nonferrous metals	100,398	10,000	open	1,658	2.9845†	0.4088
Office and store machines	65,914	10,000	open	1,411	2.5860	1.5812
Bakery products	58,960	50,000	100,000	192	0.2359	2.1335
Yarn and thread	44,375	10,000	open	687	0.4461	0.3238
Carpets and other floor coverings	37,337	10,000	100,000	1,119	1.2391	1.7295
Broadwoven fabrics (wool)	31,265	10,000	open	1,211	0.4461	0.3400
Watches, clocks, and clock work operated devices	31,025	10,000	50,000	705	1.2027	5.3238
Cement	29,554	10,000	100,000	1,600	2.1277‡	0.2726
Malt liquors and malt	28,922	10,000	open	1,750	0.9041	4.7962
Agricultural machinery and tractors	28,291	1,000	open	684	2.1816	0.8956
Structural clay products	24,001	10,000	100,000	253	1.6292	0.4552
Newspapers	23,428	10,000	100,000	168	0.1348§	0.1948
Knit goods	17,918	10,000	100,000	273	0.1244	0.8522
Confectionery	13,524	5,000	50,000	335	0.5950	2.6281
Commercial printing including lithographing	11,939	5,000	50,000	97	0.1348§	0.6474
Furniture—household, office, public building, and professional	11.378	5,000	50,000	209	0.3990‖	0.9152

* Rubber products.
† Primary nonferrous.
‡ Cement, and concrete, gypsum, and plaster products.

TABLE 5 (*continued*)

Industry	*Optimum Company Size (in thousand dollars of total assets) (1948–51)*	*Optimum Range Class Limits (in thousand dollars)*		*Average Establishment Size (in thousand dollars of value added) (1947)*	*Number of Chemists and Engineers per 100 Employed (1950)*	*Advertising Expenditure as Percent of Gross Sales (1950)*
		From	*To*			
Men's clothing	$ 10,077	$ 5,000	$ 50,000	$ 247	0.0456#	0.8795
Dyeing and finishing textiles, excl. knit goods	9,625	5,000	50,000	545	1.1223	0.3472
Canning fruit, vegetables, and seafood	6,536	1,000	open	240	0.9144	1.8462
Broadwoven fabrics (cotton)	5,847	50	open	2,595	0.4461**	0.2822
Footwear, exc. rubber	4,359	1,000	100,000	524	0.1474	1.1619
Paperbags, and paperboard containers and boxes	4,127	1,000	100,000	428	0.6939	0.1854
Cigars	3,753	250	50,000	174	0.2274††	2.3188
Meat products	2,665	500	100,000	322	0.5983	0.4264
Nonferrous foundries	2,365	500	50,000	172	2.9845†	0.2793
Fur goods	1,966	1,000	5,000	55	0.0456#	0.4119
Partitions, shelving, lockers, etc.	1,545	500	50,000	121	0.3990‖	0.8678
Narrow fabrics and other small wares	1,382	500	5,000	226	0.4461**	0.3212
Wines	1,304	500	5,000	227	0.9041‡‡	3.5854
Women's clothing	1,304	500	50,000	150	0.0456#	0.9150
Books	1,137	50	50,000	399	0.1348§	2.8796
Periodicals	1,117	250	10,000	307	0.1348§	0.5245
Leather—tanning, curring, and finishing	764	0	10,000	720	0.8140	0.1813
Concrete, gypsum, and plaster products	762	250	10,000	53	2.1277‡	0.6855
Window and door screens, shades, and venetian blinds	667	100	10,000	110	0.3990‖	1.0581
Nonalcoholic beverages	546	100	50,000	75	0.9041‡‡	4.0740
Millinery	468	250	5,000	108	0.0456#	0.4438

§ Printing, publishing, and allied industries
‖ Furniture and fixtures.
†† Tobacco manufactures.
‡‡ Beverage industries.
# Apparel and accessories.
** Yarn, thread, and fabric mills.

1. *Size of Firm.* The optimum size of firm in each industry is determined by comparing the percentage of the industry's assets possessed by firms in each asset class in 1948 and 1951.[3] Those classes in which the share of the industry's assets was stable or rising were identified, and the average assets of the firms within these sizes was calculated. The range of optimum sizes is also given in Table 5. An industry was excluded if it had a very large noncorporate sector (for which we could not measure firm size) or gave strong evidence of heterogeneity by having two widely separated optimum sizes (as, for example, in "aircraft and parts").

2. *Advertising Expenditures.* We have already remarked that extensive advertising is often mentioned as an explanation for the growth of large firms, especially in consumer goods industries such as cigarettes, liquor, and cosmetics. The argument supporting this view can take one of three directions. First, national advertising may be viewed as more efficient than local advertising, in terms of sales per dollar of advertising at a given price. Second, long-continued advertising may have a cumulative impact. Finally, and closely related to the preceding point, the joint advertising of a series of related products may be more efficient than advertising them individually. We measure the variable by the ratio of advertising expenditures to sales, both taken from *Statistics of Income.*

3. *Technology and Research.* A host of explanations of firm size are related to technological characteristics and research. Complicated production processes may require large companies, or at least large plants. The economies of research are held to be substantial; the outcome of individual projects is uncertain, so small programs are more risky; a balanced research team may be fairly large; and much capital may be required to bring a new process to a commercial stage and to wait for a return upon the outlay.

At present there is no direct measure available for either the importance of research or the intricacy of technology. We use an index, chemists and engineers as a ratio to all employees, that may reflect both influences, but probably very imperfectly. When it becomes possible to make a division of these personnel between research and routine operation, a division which would be very valuable for other purposes also, the interpretation of an index of technical personnel will be less ambiguous.

4. *Plant Size.* Plant size normally sets a minimum to company size, and therefore exerts an obvious influence on the differences among indus-

---

[3] These particular dates were dictated by the data; there were large changes in industry classification in 1948, and no minor industry data were tabulated for 1952. A better, but more laborious, determination of optimum size could have been made if the data for intervening years were utilized.

tries in company size. We are compelled to resort to a measure of plant size—value added per establishment in 1947—which is not directly comparable to company size because the 1947 Census of Manufacturers did not report corporate establishments at the requisite level of detail.

Preliminary analysis revealed that there is no significant relationship between firm size and advertising expenditures, so this variable was omitted from the statistical calculations. The average ratio of advertising expenditures to sales was 1.97 percent in consumer goods industries and 0.57 percent in producer goods industries, but in neither group was there a significant relationship between the ratio and firm size.[4]

A regression analysis confirms the impression one gets from table 5 that the other variables we examine are positively related to optimum firm size:

$$X_1 = -5.092 + \underset{(10.8)}{34.6\ X_2} + \underset{(12.2)}{42.7\ X_3},$$

where

X_1 is firm size, in millions of dollars of assets,
X_2 is plant size, in millions of dollars of value added,
X_3 is engineers and chemists per 100 employees.

The standard errors of the regression coefficients are given below the coefficients.

An examination of table 5 suggests that the correlation would be higher if the data were somewhat more precise. The size of plant is unduly low in motor vehicles, because of the inclusion of suppliers of parts. Moreover the plant sizes have not been estimated by the survivor technique. Technological personnel are exaggerated in nonferrous foundries because we are compelled to use the ratio for a broader class, and the same is true of concrete products. The relatively small size of company in footwear, as compared to plant size, is at least partially due to the fact that the machinery was usually leased, and hence not included in assets. Industries which are "out of line" have not been omitted, however, for similar considerations may have caused other industries to be "in line." Yet the general impression is that the correlation would rise substantially with improved measurements of the variables.

The range of optimum sizes is generally wide, although the width is exaggerated, and our measurements impaired, because the largest asset class (over $100 million) embraces numerous firms of very different sizes—growth and inflation are outmoding the size classes used in *Statistics of Income*. In ten industries only this largest size has had a rising share of industry assets, and in another nine industries it is included in the range of sizes with rising shares. When the upper limit of optimum

---

[4] The respective rank correlation coefficients were —.187 and —.059.

sizes is known, the range of optimum sizes is typically three or four times the average size of the firms in these sizes.

The results of this exploratory inter-industry study are at least suggestive—not only in their specific content but also in pointing out a line of attack on the economies of scale that escapes that confession of failure, the case method. The chief qualifications that attach to the findings are due to the imperfections of the data: the industry categories are rather wide; and the measure of technical personnel is seriously ambiguous. At least one finding—a wide range of optimum firm sizes in each industry—is so general as to deserve to be taken as the standard model in the theory of production.

IV. INTRAINDUSTRY ANALYSIS OF THE DETERMINANTS OF OPTIMUM SIZE

One may also examine the varying fates of individual firms within an industry in the search for explanations of optimum size. If, for example, firms moving to optimum size were vertically integrated and those moving to or remaining in nonoptimum size were not so integrated, we could infer that vertical integration was a requisite of the optimum firm in the industry. This approach has the advantage over the inter-industry approach of not requiring the assumption that a determinant such as advertising or integration works similarly in all industries.

The intraindustry analysis, however, has a heavy disadvantage; it can be applied only to those variables for which we can obtain information on each firm and in industries with numerous firms hardly any interesting variables survive this requirement. Because we could examine so few influences, and because the results were so consistently negative, we shall be very brief in describing our results in the industry—petroleum refining—in which this approach was tried.

The basic survivor experience for companies and plants in petroleum refining is given in tables 6 and 7, for the postwar period 1947–1954. In each case only operating plants are included, and asphalt plants and companies are excluded. Capacities are measured in terms of crude oil; as in the case of steel plants, actual outputs cannot be obtained for all companies.

There is a family resemblance between the data for petroleum and steel companies: in each case there has been a substantial reduction in the share of the largest company. In the petroleum refining industry, the size range from 0.5 percent to 10 percent has contained all the size classes which have stable or rising shares of industry capacity.

The plant survivor data suggest that the disappearance of the smaller companies has been due to the relative inefficiency of the smaller plants,

TABLE 6
Distribution of Petroleum Refining Capacity by Relative Size of Company

Company Size (percent of industry capacity)	*1947*	*1950*	*1954*
1. *Percent of Industry Capacity*			
Under 0.1	5.30	4.57	3.89
0.1 to 0.2	4.86	3.57	3.00
0.2 to 0.3	2.67	2.16	2.74
0.3 to 0.4	2.95	2.92	1.65
0.4 to 0.5	2.20	0	.89
0.5 to 0.75	3.04	4.66	5.05
0.75 to 1.00	.94	0	1.58
1.0 to 2.5	11.70	12.17	10.53
2.5 to 5	9.57	16.70	14.26
5 to 10	45.11	42.15	45.69
10 to 15	11.65	11.06	10.72
2. *Number of Companies*			
Under 0.1	130	108	92
0.1 to 0.2	34	24	22
0.2 to 0.3	11	9	11
0.3 to 0.4	8	8	5
0.4 to 0.5	5	0	2
0.5 to 0.75	5	8	8
0.75 to 1.00	1	0	2
1.0 to 2.5	6	7	6
2.5 to 5.0	3	5	5
5.0 to 10.0	7	6	7
10.0 to 15.0	1	1	1
Total	211	176	161

Source: Bureau of Mines, Petroleum Refineries, including Cracking Plants in the United States, January 1, 1947, January 1, 1950, January 1, 1954, Information Circulars 7455 (March 1948), 7578 (August 1950), and 7963 (July 1954).

for all plant size classes with less than 0.5 percent of the industry's capacity have also declined substantially. The sizes between 0.5 percent and 2.5 percent of industry capacity have all grown relatively, and the top plant size has declined moderately, so that the growth of company sizes beyond 2.5 percent of industry capacity has presumably been due to the economies of multiple plant operation.

It has been claimed that backward integration into crude oil pipelines was necessary to successful operation of a petroleum refinery. We tabulate some of the material bearing on this hypothesis in table 8. There does not appear to be any large difference between the changes in market shares of firms with and without pipelines. Since all firms with more than 0.75 percent of industry refining capacity have some pipelines, a comparison (not reproduced here) was made between changes in their market shares and crude pipeline mileage per 1,000 barrels of daily refining capacity. There was no relationship between the two variables.

TABLE 7
Distribution of Petroleum Refining Capacity by Relative Size of Plant

Plant Size	*1947*	*1950*	*1954*
	1. *Percent of Industry Capacity*		
Under 0.1	8.22	7.39	6.06
0.1 to 0.2.	9.06	7.60	7.13
0.2 to 0.3.	6.86	4.95	3.95
0.3 to 0.4.	5.45	4.99	7.28
0.4 to 0.5.	4.53	6.56	4.06
0.5 to 0.75	9.95	10.47	11.82
0.75 to 1.0.	5.35	7.07	8.33
1.0 to 1.5.	12.11	10.36	13.38
1.5 to 2.5.	17.39	23.64	22.45
2.5 to 4.0.	21.08	16.96	15.54
	2. *Number of Plants*		
Under 0.1	184	158	138
0.1 to 0.2.	64	53	51
0.2 to 0.3.	27	19	16
0.3 to 0.4.	15	14	21
0.4 to 0.5.	10	15	9
0.5 to 0.75	17	16	19
0.75 to 1.0.	6	8	10
1.0 to 1.5.	10	8	11
1.5 to 2.5.	9	12	12
2.5 to 4.0.	7	5	5
Total	349	308	292

Source: Same as table 6.

TABLE 8
Industry Shares of Petroleum Refining Companies with and without Crude Pipelines in 1950

Company Size (average of 1947, 1950, and 1954 percentage of industry capacity)	*Companies with Pipelines*			*Companies without Pipelines*		
	Number 1950	*Share 1947*	*Share 1954*	*Number 1950*	*Share 1947*	*Share 1954*
Under 0.1	25	1.40	1.12	60	2.87	2.18
0.1 to 0.2.	17	2.19	2.50	5	0.77	0.77
0.2 to 0.3.	6	1.48	1.63	2	0.34	0.50
0.3 to 0.4.	5	1.90	1.63	0	. . . .	. . . .
0.4 to 0.5.	1	0.40	0.55	2	0.54	1.22
0.5 to 0.75	7	3.59	4.72	1	0.38	0.61
0.75 to 1.0.	0	. . . . .	. . . . .	0	. . . .	. . . .
1.0 to 2.5.	7	11.54	13.10	0	. . . .	. . . .
2.5 to 5.0.	4	11.11	11.69	0	. . . .	. . . .
5.0 to 10.0.	7	45.11	45.69	0	. . . .	. . . .
10.0 to 15.0.	1	11.65	10.72	0	. . . .	. . . .
Not in existence all years	16	2.30	0.05	79	2.43	1.33
Total.	96	92.67	93.40	149	7.33	6.60

Source: *International Petroleum Register.*

The intraindustry analysis has its chief role, one may conjecture, in providing a systematic framework for the analysis of the data commonly employed in industry studies. A complete analysis of the plausible determinants of firm size requires such extensive information on the individual firms in the industry as to make this an unattractive method of attack on the general theory.

V. CONCLUSION

The survivor technique for determining the range of optimum sizes of a firm seems well adapted to lift the theory of economies of scale to a higher level of substantive content. Although it is prey to the usual frustrations of inadequate information, the determination of optimum sizes avoids the enormously difficult problem of valuing resources properly that is encountered by alternative methods.

Perhaps the most striking finding in our exploratory studies is that there is customarily a fairly wide range of optimum sizes—the long-run marginal and average cost curves of the firm are customarily horizontal over a long range of sizes. This finding could be corroborated, I suspect, by a related investigation: if there were a unique optimum size in an industry, increases in demand would normally be met primarily by near proportional increases in the number of firms, but it appears that much of the increase is usually met by expansion of the existing firms.

The survivor method can be used to test the numerous hypotheses on the factors determining the size of firm which abound in the literature. Our exploratory study suggests that advertising expenditures have no general tendency to lead to large firms, and another experiment (which is not reported above) indicates that fixed capital-sales ratio are also unrelated to the size of firms. The size of plant proves to be an important variable, as is to be expected, and the survivor method should be employed to determine the factors governing plant size. A rather ambiguous variable, the relative share of engineers and chemists in the labor force, also proves to be fairly important, and further data and work is necessary to disentangle research and routine technical operations. The determination of optimum size permits the investigator to examine any possible determinants which his imagination nominates and his data illuminate.

17. Commercial Bank Profitability by Function*

THOMAS J. COYNE

In studying the profitability of commercial banks by function it becomes obvious that they need to know much more about cost of funds and price output behavior if they are to expand service(s) profitably. With the possible exception of university administrators and church leaders, it is highly probable that commercial bankers know less about specific functions within their business than any similar group. Nonetheless, research into this troublesome area has been practically nonexisting. Bell and Murphy studied economies of scale by bank function, but relatively little has been published recently about the cost, price *and* profitability of commercial banks *by function*. Other profitability studies have been done but they overlook profit by function.

This paper is concerned with the cost, price, and profit by function. It estimates the profit for real estate, installment, commercial and agricultural loans, and investments for banks stratified by size of deposit.

Raw data were obtained from the Federal Reserve Bank of Cleveland's functional cost analysis of 41 banks. In addition, a questionnaire sent to the chief executive officer of 510 commerical banks provides insight into the manner in which commercial banks utilize: (1) the degree to which the average cost of funds by function is known to the bank and the method, if any, that is used to make that determination; (2) the degree to which the average price (interest rate) by function is known to the bank and, expressed by a percent, whether it is equal to or greater than the cost of funds by function; and (3) the degree to which the bank is able to determine its profit by function from 1 and 2.

Assuming that the results of the questionnaire are representative of the aggregate commercial banking community, the study concludes by applying cost of funds estimates to average balance sheet entries for the Representative Bank of America (RBA), a hypothetical company created from averages of 41 banks with deposits ranging from $8 million to $50 million.

* *Financial Management,* vol. 2, no. 1 (Spring 1973), pp. 64–73.

FUNCTIONAL COST ANALYSIS

The most serious effort to date to determine profitability by bank function has been made by the Federal Reserve System. Its work is concerned mostly with cost and is confined to relatively few banks, perhaps 1,000 or so.

The Fed's functional cost system is a major attempt to make comparative data available to banks of similar size in terms of total deposits. The data are presented in annual reports and are designed to serve as a basic management tool. These yearly reports are based upon annual data, and contain the usual shortcomings associated with such figures. Balance sheet averages vary, for example, as each institution determines for itself what date to select for calculations. Very few measures of dispersion about the mean are included. In addition, the report concentrates on earnings before taxes and does not calculate "below-the-line adjustments." These below-line adjustments are not included because the major purpose of the annual Functional Cost Analysis (FCA) report is to make possible performance comparisons through time and cross-sectionally.

The cost of funds section of the Fed's functional cost analysis does not include cost of capital statistics. In addition, differences in salaries or other expenses, such as depreciation practices, of the individual bank are not considered. Consequently, a small bank that leases the space that it occupies, for example, must consider this rental expense to be a cost for FCA purposes; but if that same bank owns its premises and is depreciating it over time, its cost of capital figure as presented annually in the FCA report would be distorted. Figures are presented for occupancy costs, of course, but each bank would have to adjust the data to make it usable. In other words, the FCA is not wholly valid without interpretation for comparative purposes.

FCA analyzes and presents explicit costs only. Implicit costs, such as the opportunity cost to the bank of not investing idle funds, are not considered.

Many bankers do not calculate their total costs and/or profits by function. The main object of this study is to determine the degree to which these costs are unknown to the banks and to suggest a method by which they could be determined.

Cost of Funds: Calculation

A survey of 510 commercial banks was conducted, stratifying all banks into five classes of total deposits at the end of 1971. This classification is more detailed than that used by the Fed because of the author's belief that for some analytical purposes FCA data stratifications are too broad.

Class	*Deposit Size*	*Number of Banks*
1	$ 1,000,000–$ 5,000,000	89
2	5,000,000– 15,000,000	194
3	15,000,000– 25,000,000	71
4	25,000,000– 50,000,000	79
5	50,000,000 and over	77
Total		510

The result of this survey reflect the degree to which costs and profits by function are unknown. As a percent of the total number of banks within a class size, Class 5 banks provided the greatest number of responses. The heavier response by Class 5 banks was not unexpected for they are the ones that are better able to employ a highly professional management group.

Exhibit 1 indicates that, when grouped by bank size, the larger banks are somewhat better informed concerning their costs of funds than are the smaller banks. None of the smaller banks, Class 1, had any indication of their cost of funds. When asked to explain specifically how these costs of funds are determined, most of the Class 2, 3 and 4 banks and many of the Class 5 banks responded by saying that they "participate in the Federal Reserve's Functional Cost program." The Fed's FCA program, it should be noted, is designed to produce a weighted rather than marginal or incremental cost-of-funds figure.

In addition to FCA, many of the Class 5 banks use a pool of funds concept of available funds. Therefore, the cost of funds to the using function, i.e., installment loans, is the average of the total costs of providing all functions. In addition, many of these larger banks tend to have their own unique method(s) of calculating the total cost of funds but these methods do not isolate necessarily all costs by type of function. These larger banks, however, do tend to be more "cost center," or "profit center" oriented than are banks that fall within Classes 1 through 4 in size of total deposits. This effort on the part of individual commercial banks that have total deposits of $50 million or more is encouraging but Class 5 banks represent only 15 percent of the total number of commercial banks surveyed. Also, as noted later in this study, even Class 5 banks when viewed in the aggregate have less than what some observers believe to be adequate information concerning their cost of funds.

Cost of Funds: Utilization

The results of the survey indicate that most banks do not have a method of determining their cost of funds. Moreover, a strong association

EXHIBIT 1
Tabulation of Results from Survey of Commercial Banks

Questions	Percent of Banks Responding "No," by Bank Class					
	Class 1	*Class 2*	*Class 3*	*Class 4*	*Class 5*	*All Classes*
(1) Bank has method of determining cost of funds by:						
(a) Demand deposits	100	82	87	59	43	74
(b) Time deposits	89	82	68	52	39	68
(c) Total capital accounts	100	82	79	54	47	73
(2) Bank considers cost of funds in determining the general level of interest rate(s) to charge in a given area, i.e., commercial lending	89	73	81	50	56	69
(3) Bank has method for determining operating expense(s) for each department	94	93	87	58	26	74
(4) Bank knows the total cost of operating each department (cost of funds plus operating costs)	100	88	87	62	45	77
(5) In determining the general level of interest rates to be charged in each department the bank considers:						
(a) Total costs	69	59	39	27	17	38
(b) Cost of funds only	100*	89	100*	66	57	79
(c) Operating costs only	100*	100	100*	79	55	83
(6) Bank can determine net income (gross income minus cost of funds and operating expenses) of each lending department?	94	86	81	65	39	73
Number of banks answering	22	50	18	29	30	149
Percent of total banks answering	24	25	25	36	38	29

* The absolute number of respondents was too small to consider this relative finding significant.

is revealed between banks that have no method of determining their costs of funds and banks that do not *consider* their costs of funds in determining what price (interest rate) must be charged in order to operate profitably. The question, then, becomes: How *does* a bank determine what interest rate(s) it will charge within a given functional area? The response of a Class 1 bank: "charge a higher rate of interest on loans than we are paying for (time deposit) funds used."

Virtually none of the banks queried appear to be following traditional pricing techniques other than, perhaps, the rigid adherence to full-cost pricing, however defined, as followed by some of the smallest firms in the industry. If the typical small bank deviates from this practice, it considers cost of funds on real estate loans only or cost of funds for *one* similar function, i.e., consumer installment loans, and then maintains a system of cost plus fixed markup pricing for that function. In some cases, if the bank knows that it is receiving a "proper" rate of interest in comparison to other portfolio investments available (an opportunity cost concept), plus consideration of the prime rate and compensating balances, it is satisfied.

A few of the Class 4 and most of the Class 5 banks indicate a higher degree of sophistication than implied by the comments above but even they consider cost of funds on a very cursory basis only. One Class 5 bank explained that this consideration amounts often "to little more than saying that interest costs and tax costs are so much, consequently our rates should be so much. We have no formula or formal plan."

Yet, the results reveal isolated examples of bankers who understand fully that the cost of funds should have a direct bearing on interest rates that are charged within a functional area, and as the cost of funds fluctuate the impact on a specific department should be measured in terms of the ultimate profitability that will be obtained from continuing that function. "Firm control over the cost of funds is the only way to predict profitability and establish corporate goals." (This is a quote from a Class 4 bank which acknowledges also that it neither knows nor considers its cost of funds.)

Pricing positions were volunteered by some respondents. Conspicuous by its absence, however, was any mention of full costs plus variable markups, pricing using programmed costs other than full costs, and pricing based upon incremental or marginal costs. No mention is made of first, second, or third degree price discrimination. None of the banks answering stated that they sought a certain target marketshare, nor did any bank say that they priced to achieve a target return on investment. Indeed, most banks establish prices (interest rates) with little reference to costs. They are interested mainly in matching or "meeting competition." Some observers would argue that this behavior is appropriate, and indeed it would be if these banks were operating in competitive product markets. In the words of one Class 5 respondent, not the same bank quoted above, "In these days of high competition and rapid monetary policy changes, less and less attention is paid to the cost of funds in determining rates to be charged for loans. Usually, rates are established in relation to what the market will bear. Cost of funds may indicate that loan rates should be a certain level, but monetary policy and competition can dictate otherwise, regardless of cost of funds."

Operating Expenses: Calculation

Quite clearly, the larger the bank the better the knowledge that it has concerning its total operating expenses. Most banks surveyed, regardless of size, recognize that with bank holding companies becoming a large competitive factor, and with more lenient banking laws a possibility, intelligent identification, planning, and control of operating expenses is mandatory. Yet, many small banks are not departmentalized; and, although salaries often are allocated on a time-study basis and total expenses are reviewed periodically, expenses incurred as a result of operating individual departments are "not real specific," according to a Class 4 bank. This shortcoming is serious because 85 percent of all commercial banks surveyed lie in size Classes 1 through 4.

Some banks in Class 5 are attempting to develop "responsibility accounting." The department(s) responsible for the expense is charged directly for the expense. The majority of explicit costs are coded by the accounting department at the time of payment, entered daily into the computer, printed and distributed to department heads and other members of upper middle management and top management. Other explicit costs, such as employee benefits, personal property tax, and so on, are allocated to applicable departments and are made known to management by the computer print-out. Some of these banks attempt also to assign indirect costs to specific departments. but with somewhat less success.

Two of these large banks assign direct charges to major departments and branches but make no attempt to allocate indirect charges, and another Class 5 bank states "we do not allocate in any manner, any type of expenses." And this observer found that none of the banks responding to the survey attempt to quantify and allocate implicit costs.

NET INCOME DETERMINATION

Commercial bankers seem to agree that they should be able to determine the net income generated by each lending department.

The Class 5 banks that determine net income of each lending department do so in a variety of ways, but the most prevalent method is to deduct total operating expenses from total departmental income and from this figure the cost of money (funds) is deducted to produce net income by function.

The net income figure by function, once obtained, is used in various departmental and branch operations, budgeting, personnel, and expansion proposals. This information is used also by some banks to determine which lending department is to receive the bulk of the available cash. In addition, of course, *ex post* rankings of departments according to profitability is possible, and bank management analyzes these rankings when making decisions that will affect the allocation of resources. It should be noted, however, that several Class 5 banks state that they can and do determine net income in each lending department but that they "do not utilize it very efficiently."

The cost of funds, of course, should be calculated by each bank, regardless of whether it participates in FCA, and the resulting figure(s) should be used by that bank when determining interest rates to be charged by bank function and when measuring net profit after taxes by function.

One approach to illustrate a solution to this problem is to start with the righthand side of a typical bank's balance sheet. Exhibit 2 presents the average balance sheet of 41 commercial banks. For purposes of this presentation, these figures are to be considered those of the Representative Bank of America.

Bank balance sheets must be adjusted in calculating the cost of funds. Two bank balance sheet definitions are: (1) "valuation reserves" and (2) "available funds." Respectively, they are those reserves created to cover potential losses on loans, securities, and other assets and the sum of cash and due from banks, loans, and investments.

Net capital for RBA is as follows:

Capital and valuation reserves	$2,768,312
Plus other liabilities and borrowings	339,688
Net capital subtotal	$3,108,000
Less fixed and other assets	837,679
Net capital funds available	$2,270,321

Net capital funds represents one of three major components of total financing available. The other two components of the bank are demand deposits and time deposits, which amount in the case of RBA to $10,042,581 and $15,149,431, respectively. Taken together, these three components amount to $27,462,333 and represent the total available for lending and investment purposes. This figure differs from total assets by the amount of money invested in bank premises, other real estate, and some miscellaneous assets as presented in exhibit 2. In other words, with reference to exhibit 2, the net capital figure of $2,270,321 is the summation of lines 28, 29, 30, and 31, minus lines 17, 18.

EXHIBIT 2

Representative Bank of America Balance Sheet (average of 41 banks having total deposits ranging from $8 million to $50 million), 1970

1. Cash and due from banks			$ 2,762,199
2. U.S. securities, under 5 years	$3,780,146		
3. U.S. securities, 5 years and over	466,548		
4. Tax exempt loans and investments	4,874,269		
5. Other bonds and stocks	980,395		
6. Liquidity loans	936,990		
7. Subtotal, investments		$11,038,348	
8. Real estate mortgage loans		5,787,707	
9. Direct installment loans	$2,520,006		
10. Indirect installment loans	1,233,759		
11. Floor plan loans	110,193		
12. Subtotal installment loans		3,863,958	
13. Commercial and other loans	$3,798,936		
14. Agricultural loans	211,185		
15. Subtotal comm'l and agricul. loans		4,010,121	
16. Subtotal, loans and investments			24,700,134
17. Bank premises			530,257
18. Other real estate and other assets			307,422
19. Total Assets			$28,300,012
20. Regular checking accounts	$9,077,134		
21. Special checking accounts	393,698		
22. Other demand deposits	571,749		
23. Subtotal demand deposits		$10,042,581	
24. Regular savings accounts	$7,652,552		
25. Club accounts and school savings	103,812		
26. Certificates of deposit and other time	7,393,067		
27. Subtotal, time deposits		15,149,431	
28. Other liabilities and borrowed money		339,688	
29. Capital funds		2,413,959	
30. Valuation reserves		321,257	
31. Preferred stock, notes, and debentures		33,096	
32. Total Liabilities and Capital			$28,300,012

Capital cost includes two elements: one called "net capital expense," an internal cost, and the other, called "cost of common equity," an external cost. The calculation of net capital expense is presented below and calculation of cost of common equity is explained in a subsequent section.

From exhibit 3 one is able to determine the before-tax dollar cost of funds. These costs, of course, need to be compared with the aggregate figures presented in the balance sheet, exhibit 2, as adjusted for changes in net capital funds available, in order to obtain the before-tax cost of funds rate. This before-tax cost of funds figure is simply the ratio of the net cost of funds to total funds available, by component part. Using

EXHIBIT 3
Representative Bank of America Net Dollar Cost of Funds

	Net Capital	*Demand Deposits*	*Time Deposits*	*Available Funds*
Servicing costs and interest expense	$60,106	$308,106	$809,225	$1,177,437
Less service charge and other income	2,433	89,732	1,865	94,030
Net cost of funds	$57,673	$218,374	$807,360	$1,083,407

RBA's component parts, as presented in exhibit 2 and 3, and as elaborated upon in exhibit 5, this calculation reveals before-tax cost of funds rates of 2.54 percent, 2.17 percent, 5.33 percent, and 3.95 percent for net capital, demand deposits, time deposits, and total available funds, respectively. Assuming a 48 percent tax rate, the after-tax equivalents, as revealed in exhibit 5, would be 1.32 percent for net capital; 1.13 percent for demand deposits; 2.77 percent for time deposits; and 2.05 percent for total available funds.

The total cost of net capital expense, $60,106 in exhibit 3, is the summation of officers' salaries, processing salaries and wages, fringe benefits, directors' fees, examinations and audits, fees, legal and so on, and "other" expenses, plus federal fund and borrowing costs, and capital note and debenture interest. All of these costs are deductible for income tax purposes.

The total demand deposit expense, $308,106 in exhibit 3, is the summation of tellers' salaries and wages, transit and bookkeeping wages, fringe benefits, furniture and equipment, computer service expenses, printing and stationery supplies, postage, freight and deliveries, telephone and telegraph, legal and other fees, officers' salaries and supplemental benefits, publicity and advertising, F.D.I.C. insurance, lease (occupancy) costs, and "other" expenses. All of these costs are deductible for income tax purposes.

The composition of the total time deposit costs of $809,225 in exhibit 3 is virtually identical to that of demand deposits and capital funds and, of course, these costs also are tax deductible.

To these cost figures, however, the bank should add the cost of two additional components: (1) the cost of common equity; and (2) implicit cost of holding cash in excess of required reserves.

One method of determining the cost of equity capital is to determine the rate of return that stockholders expect to earn on the bank's common stock. In other words, the bank should solve for k, where k equals the cost of equity capital: $k = D/P_0 + g$, where D equals average 1970 dividends paid of $1.89, g equals the required or anticipated growth rate assumed arbitrarily to be 5 percent and P_0 equals the average price of the bank's common stock in 1970, $54.21. The price per share of RBA is equal to the mean of the 1970 prices of seven banks chosen from the 41 banks comprising RBA's balance sheet. Consequently, the cost of equity capital is 8.5 percent.

The total market value of RBA's stock is equal to $54.21 times the average number of shares outstanding, 45,908, or $2,488,673. At 8.5 percent the dollar cost of RBA's equity capital on this market value is $211,537. The after-tax equivalent of the cost of available funds shown in exhibit 3 is $563,372. When equity cost is added the total is $774,909. The combined after-tax cost of funds rate for RBA is then 2.82 percent, $774,909 divided by total capital, $27,462,333.

The cost of holding cash reserves in excess of required reserves is, of course, an opportunity cost. Required reserves of national banks at the end of 1970 amounted to about 15 percent of demand deposits and 3 percent of time deposits. In total dollars for the RBA that required reserve amounted on average to $1,960,871, as depicted in exhibit 4. There is, of course, an implicit cost associated with required reserves over which the bank has no control. The bank, however, *can* control the use of excess reserves.

Had the excess reserves shown in exhibit 4 been invested in 1970 at a 6 percent federal fund rate, about $48,079 would have been generated. Since the bank chose instead to hold this $801,328 as idle cash and due from banks, this foregone income of $48,079 may be considered as an opportunity cost to the bank.

One could argue that the $801,328 excess cash held by RBA is not all "excess." Since the total dollar reserve figure from RBA, column 5 of exhibit 4, is the average "cash and due from banks" entry for the year 1970, and inasmuch as certain levels of cash must be retained for daily operations, there is no way of determining precisely how much of this

EXHIBIT 4
Excess Reserves, Representative Bank of America, December 1970

	(1) Total Deposits*	(2) Required Reserve Rate*	(3) Required Reserves	(4) Total Required Reserves	(5) Total Dollar Actual Reserves	(6) Excess Reserves
Demand deposits	$10,042,584	15%	$1,506,388			
Time deposits	$15,149,431	3%	$ 454,483	$1,960,871	$2,762,199	$801,328

* Rounded for illustrative purposes. The actual calculation for demand deposits is made by subtracting cash and due from banks from demand deposits to arrive at net demand deposits. Against this net figure apply a 12.5 percent reserve for all deposits up to $5,000,000 and a 13 percent reserve for all net demand deposits in excess of $5,000,000; for time deposits apply a 3 percent required reserve against savings accounts. Three percent for all "other" time deposits up to $5,000,000 and a 5 percent reserve for all monies in excess of $5,000,000.

EXHIBIT 5
Total After-Tax Cost of Funds, Representative Bank of America, 1970
Part I

	(1) Dollar Cost	(2) Capital Component Available	(3) After-Tax Dollar Cost[a]	(4) Before-Tax Cost of Funds	(5) After-Tax Cost of Funds Rate (Col. 3 ÷ Col. 2)
Net capital	$ 57,673	$ 2,270,321	$ 29,990	2.54	1.32
Demand deposits	218,384	10,042,581	113,555	2.17	1.13
Time deposits	807,360	15,149,431	419,827	5.33	2.77
Total	$1,083,407	$27,462,333	$563,372	3.95	2.05

[a] Assumes a 48 percent tax rate.

Part II

	(1) Total Market Value of Equity Capital[b]	(2) Dollar Cost of Equity Capital	(3) Cost of Equity Capital Expressed as Percent[c]
Common stock	$2,488,673	$211,537	8.5

[b] Market value of RBA's stock is equal to its mean value, $54.21 times average number of shares outstanding, 45,908.
[c] The cost, 8.5 percent, represents a combination of dividend yield, 3.5% plus growth, 5%.

Part III

	(1) Excess Reserves	(2) Opportunity Cost	(3) Implicit Dollar Cost	(4) After-Tax Cost of Funds Rate
"Excess cash"	$801,328	.06[d]	$48,079	3.12

[d] Assumed opportunity cost of hoarding excess cash.

Part IV

	(1) Total After-Tax Dollar Cost	(2) Total Available Funds	(3) After-Tax Cost of Funds Rate (Col. 1 ÷ Col. 2)
Summation of Parts I, II, and III	$822,988	$27,462,333	2.99

money is controllable excess. Consequently, this $48,079 opportunity cost of holding excess cash is the maximum. On the other hand, however, the federal funds rate during 1970 averaged over 7 percent. Consequently, this $48,079 opportunity cost might be a little low. Knowing the rationale behind its calculation, individual commercial banks should have no trouble in determining their own opportunity costs, if any, of idle cash.

Calculation of total weighted cost of funds is made by adding the after-tax dollar cost of net capital, demand deposits, and time deposits which total $563,372 to the dollar cost of equity capital, $211,537, and the implicit cost of excess cash reserves, $48,079. These costs are revealed in parts I, II and III, respectively, of exhibit 5. These figures total $822,988 and when divided by the total dollar amount of available funds, $27,462,333, a cost of funds rate of 2.99 percent results.

PROFITABILITY BY FUNCTION: REPRESENTATIVE BANK OF AMERICA

Profitability by function for the RBA is determined by subtracting all direct and allocable indirect expenses from total gross revenue generated by that function. The resulting figure is the net revenue, or yield, exclusive of cost of funds. From the net yield the cost of funds is substracted to determine the net profit of the bank by function. For purposes of this presentation, four major leading functions are presented: investments, real estate mortgage loans, installment loans and commercial and agricultural loans. These four component parts amount to 87 percent of the RBA's total assets.

Profitability by function, expressed as percentage return on available funds, is presented in exhibit 6. Three different assumptions concerning cost of funds are used. The first assumption calculates the cost of funds by function using the after-tax rate on net capital, demand deposits, and time deposits. This after-tax cost of funds rate is 2.05 percent. The second assumption adds the cost of equity to net capital. This after-tax cost of funds is 2.82 percent. And assumption three makes the calculation based upon all of the components of assumption two plus the opportunity cost of holding idle cash. The third version is the total after-tax cost of funds. It amounts to 2.99 percent and is the most valid of the three for decision making purposes.

The advantage of this approach is obvious: the bank can determine its most profitable lending functions, rank them in descending order of profitability, and channel loanable funds into those functional areas that generate the highest percentage and/or dollar return(s) consistent with degree of risk. Of course, banks must attempt to lend in all areas even though some generate more deposits than others, for this lending is necessary to maintain total deposits. Consequently, so long as the rate of

EXHIBIT 6
After-Tax Profitability By Function,

	Installment Loan Function			*Investment Function*		
Total funds employed	$3,863,958			$11,038,348		
Gross revenue	$ 462,143			$ 798,870		
Minus expenses	163,795			15,835		
Income before taxes and cost of funds	$ 298,348			$ 783,035		
Minus tax-exempt securities				411,751		
Income before taxes and cost of funds				$ 371,284		
Minus taxes @ 48 percent	143,207			178,216		
Income after taxes and before cost of funds	$ 155,141			$ 193,068		
Add actual tax-exempt securities*				205,876		
Net income after tax and before cost of funds	$ 155,141	$155,141	$155,141	$ 398,944	$398,944	$398,944
Minus cost of funds	79,211[a]	108,964[b]	115,532[c]	226,286[a]	311,281[b]	330,047[c]
Net profit	$ 75,930	$ 46,177	$ 39,609	$ 172,658	$ 87,663	$ 68,897
After-tax return on funds employed under three assumptions regarding cost of funds:						
Assumption one:		1.96%		1.56%		
Assumption two:		1.19%		0.79%		
Assumption three:		1.02%		0.62%		

[a] assumption one; 2.05%
[b] assumption two; 2.82%
[c] assumption three; 2.99%
* Actual income received by the bank

return within a function is equal to or greater than the cost of funds for that function, loans can be made profitably by the bank. At a minimum, commercial bankers should know these costs and levels of profit by function within their own firms. In the case of RBA, this percentage return on available funds ranking would be: (1) installment loan function; (2) investment function; (3) commercial and agricultural loan function; and (4) real estate and mortgage function.

One could argue that the cost of funds is irrelevant when a pooling of funds is used because the cost is the same for each function. The author uses this method, however, for he is interested in revealing the total *dollar* cost of money allocated to a function and the total *dollar* after-tax profit of that function. Also, it is desirable to have a method of cost calculation for those commercial banks who neither know their total costs of operating each department (function) nor their overall cost of funds. The method is of use also to determine the resulting dollar profit if the gross yield for a function, any function, were high enough to justify allocation of funds but there was only limited absorptive capacity. In such a situation, it would be essential for the bank to know the total *dollar* after-tax yield of a function as well as its after-tax rate of return. Exhibit 6 reveals both pieces of information.

Representative Bank of America, 1970

Commercial and Agricultural Function			*Real Estate Mortgage Function*			*Total Bank Functions*		
$4,010,121			$5,787,707			$24,700,134		
$ 320,302			$ 397,501					
51,046			40,873					
$ 269,256			$ 356,628					
129,243			171,181					
$ 140,013			$ 185,447					
$ 140,013	$140,013	$140,013	$ 185,447	$185,447	$185,447			
82,207[a]	113,085[b]	119,903[c]	118,648[a]	163,213[b]	173,052[c]			
$ 57,806	$ 26,928	$ 20,110	$ 66,829	$ 22,234	$ 12,395	$ 373,223	$183,002	$141,011
1.44%			1.15%			1.51%		
0.67%			0.38%			0.74%		
0.50%			0.21%			0.57%		

CONCLUSION

This study is designed to provide a method of cost and profit calculation to the numerous small and medium-sized banks who indicated in response to the author's survey that they knew little or nothing about their costs by function. To the extent that the results of this survey in general and the profitability of RBA in particular is representative of the entire banking community, this study should be helpful to individual banks as well as being of some value at the policy-making levels of state and national government where questions concerning matters such as usury laws and price (interest rate) controls appear to be taking a disproportionately large amount of time and effort to resolve.

18. Short-Run Cost Functions of a Multiproduct Firm*

RONALD S. KOOT and DAVID A. WALKER

I. INTRODUCTION

In discussions of the neoclassical theory of the firm in economic theory textbooks, short-run average and marginal cost curves of a firm are U-shaped. However, U-shaped curves derived from the principle of diminishing returns is only one of many hypotheses about the forms of cost functions to be subjected to empirical verification. An alternative hypothesis is that of constant short-run marginal cost. In at least four industry studies without critical shortcomings, marginal costs have been found to be constant in the short-run. Three of these are Dean's studies of a furniture factory, a hosiery mill, and a department store. Another study is of a multiproduct food processing firm by J. Johnston. Although the results of these studies differ from what is predicted by the traditional theory of the firm, A. A. Walters concludes that ". . . the evidence in favor of constant marginal cost is not overwhelming. Certainly the revision of theory to include this phenomenon is not an urgent matter."

In this paper, linear, quadratic, and cubic cost functions are tested for a multiproduct manufacturing firm. It is found that the short-run total cost functions are linear for each product and for the firm as a whole. The implication is that marginal and average variable costs are constant over the observed range of outputs.

According to the management of the firm, several observations on output are at more than 90 percent of "full-capacity" output. There are no observations at "full-capacity" output. Marginal and average variable costs do rise at some output level. However, the data employed in this paper do not allow a conclusion as to whether costs rise sharply but smoothly between 90 percent capacity and "full-capacity" or whether the average variable cost curve is L-shaped with costs rising vertically at "full-capacity."

Finding additional evidence to support the conclusion of studies by Dean and Johnston on linear cost functions is not a useless exercise. The

* *Journal of Industrial Economics,* April 1970, vol. 18(2), pp. 118–28.

current interest in optimal decision making for the firm hinges on applications of linear programming. These models rely on maximizing or minimizing a linear function subject to a set of constraints. For the firm that cannot readily influence its demand, as is the case for most manufacturing plants, the goal of the firm is usually to minimize costs. If the firm's total cost function is linear, linear decision models can often be constructed, since there are numerous mathematical approaches to forming an appropriate constraint set.

The data and estimation technique used in this paper are described in section II. The regression results for each product are presented in section III. In section IV, cost interrelationships are discussed. It is shown that the relationship between cost and output for any product is independent of the cost–output relationships for all other products. In section V, two aggregated cost–output relationships are estimated using different indices to find a measure of aggregate output for the firm.

II. THE DATA AND ESTIMATION TECHNIQUE

Data have been obtained from a major American firm engaged in producing ten types of plastic containers. Monthly observations for the period January 1966 to September 1967, are reported on (*a*) physical production of each product and (*b*) direct per-unit costs for labor, machinery, and materials. No attempt is made to allocate indirect or overhead costs among the ten products. Such methods of allocation are arbitrary and, in any case, changes in indirect costs during the 21-month period are not substantial. During the period under study, plant capacity is fixed, and all factor prices are fixed by contract. Furthermore, wide variations in output occur during the observed 21 months. Several observations are over 90 percent of "full-capacity" output level as defined by the management of the firm. Therefore, the cost–output relationship is not observed for only a narrow range of outputs well below the "full-capacity" level.

Ideally, an investigation of the relationship between costs and output should be part of a model which includes a description of the firm's decision to produce at a given level of output. Hence, the econometric problem is one of simultaneous-equation estimation techniques. However, output can be treated as an exogenous variable in the cost function, and the technique of single-equation least squares can be employed if one of two conditions exists: (1) the disturbance terms in the output-determination equations and the cost functions are independent, or (2) the differences between planned and actual output are small and have little effect on the disturbance term in the cost-function. Data are also reported by the multiproduct firm for planned production for each of the 21 months. The differences between planned production and actual production are small. Thus, single-equation least squares is used to test the following three hypotheses about the cost–output relationships for each product and for the firm as a whole:

$$\text{I} \quad C_t = \beta_0 + \beta_1 Y_t + \epsilon_t$$
$$\text{II} \quad C_t = \beta_0{}^1 + \beta_1{}^1 Y_t + \beta_2{}^1 Y_t{}^2 + \epsilon_t{}^1$$
$$\text{III} \quad C_t = \beta_0{}^{11} + \beta_1{}^{11} Y_t + \beta_2{}^{11} Y_t{}^2 + \beta_3{}^{11} Y_t{}^3 + \epsilon_t{}^{11}$$

where Y_t is current output, and C_t is total direct costs and is the sum of labor, machine, and materials costs. Estimates of the coefficients of the variables are tested for statistical significance using the t-test, and tests for autocorrelated disturbances are made using the Durbin–Watson d-statistic.

III. REGRESSION RESULTS FOR PRODUCTS

Table 1 presents regression results of hypotheses I–III for each of the ten products. For each product, the coefficient of variation is calculated to determine if the observations on output have a range great enough to justify regression analysis. The coefficients of variation have a range of 48.7 percent to 131.9 percent. These coefficients compare favorably with other studies. In Table I, b_0 is the estimate of the intercept, and b_1, b_2, and b_3 are the estimates of the coefficients of Y_t, $Y_t{}^2$, and $Y_t{}^3$, respectively. R^2 is the coefficient of determination, and the standard errors of the coefficient estimates are in parentheses.

The d-statistics indicate that there is autocorrelation at the .05 probability level in regressions I–III for Product 6 and regression I for Products 7, 8, and 9. To eliminate the autocorrelated disturbance in any regression, a transformation is applied to the cost and output variables by assuming a first-order autoregressive scheme, ϵ_t as $\rho\epsilon_{t-1} + \mu_t$. An estimate of ρ, $\hat{\rho}$, is found by applying ordinary least squares to this first-order scheme. The value $\hat{\rho}$ is then used to calculate the transformed variables $C_t - \hat{\rho}C_{t-1}$ and $Y_t - \hat{\rho}Y_{t-1}$, $t = 2, 3, \ldots, 21$, and these transformed variables are used to re-run the regressions. Since tests for autocorrelation in regressions II and III for products 7, 8, and 9 are inconclusive, this method of transformation is also applied to the variables in these regressions. The regression results of the transformed variables are given as products 6′, 7′, 8′, and 9′ in Table 1. Also given in Table 1 are the values of $\hat{\rho}$ used intransforming the variables in each regression. The transformations improve the d-statistics for each product except product 7. The tests for autocorrelation in each of the regressions for product 7′ is inconclusive.

Table 1 shows that Hypothesis I, a linear total cost function, can be accepted for each product. The coefficient estimates of $Y_t{}^2$ are significant only for Hypothesis II for Products 2 and 10. In Product 2, the inclusion

TABLE 1
Regression Results for Products

Product	*Hypothesis*	b_0	b_1	b_2	b_3	R^2	*d-Statistic*	$\hat{p}$	*Coefficient of Variation (percent)*
1	I	648.909 (1031.979)	425.938 (10.603)**			.988	1.60		120.1
	II	−403.776 (1117.349)	503.406 (41.507)**	−.403 (.209)		.990	1.59		
	III	123.063 (1122.618)	405.169 (72.342)**	1.157 (.980)	−.0055 (.0034)	.992	1.73		
2	I	−665.256 (746.712)	277.961 (7.681)**			.986	1.81		112.4
	II	364.924 (550.305)	199.407 (17.121)**	.436 (.090)**		.994	2.24		
	III	76.664 (546.585)	258.380 (37.379)**	−.330 (.446)	.0024 (.0013)	.995	2.05		
3	I	2856.548 (3038.692)	420.655 (41.010)**			.847	2.39		64.4
	II	480.967 (3738.013)	538.344 (116.188)**	−.912 (.843)		.856	2.42		
	III	−562.838 (4517.404)	662.324 (309.203)**	−3.088 (5.085)	.0096 (.0220)	.858	2.38		
4	I	318.179 (728.914)	258.084 (5.250)**			.992	1.63		90.7
	II	396.455 (834.334)	255.095 (15.112)**	.012 (.057)		.992	1.61		
	III	−38.490 (874.589)	301.431 (36.933)**	−.407 (.311)	.0009 (.0007)	.993	1.62††		
5	I	−2138.314 (3299.575)	419.421 (26.864)**			.928	1.65		96.6
	II	136.973 (3352.630)	246.706 (97.797)**	.873 (.477)		.939	1.49††		
	III	−40.471 (3576.918)	300.903 (309.280)	.171 (3.821)	.0022 (.0116)	.939	1.49††		

TABLE 1 *(continued)*

Product	*Hypothesis*	b_0	b_1	b_2	b_3	R^2	*d-Statistic*	$\hat{p}$	*Coefficient of Variation (percent)*
	I	6384.367	322.886						
		(8059.923)	(34.903)**			.818	.94†		51.5
6	II	−4184.877	487.871	−.440					
		(9949.536)	(103.847)**	(.262)		.843	.86†		
	III	−508.584	300.425	.828	−.0022				
		(10806.340)	(233.162)	(1.435)	(.0024)	.850	.80†		
	I	−28438.648	316.993						
		(5707.139)**	(23.440)**			.910	1.80	.4730	
6′	II	−34877.798	412.629	−.224					
		(7465.759)**	(76.865)**	(.172)		.919	1.57	.4421	
	III	−2804.474	162.184	1.273	−.0023				
		(8638.585)**	(188.252)	(1.047)	(.0016)	.928	1.65††	.4715	
	I	1752.642	292.316			.926	1.17†		78.5
		(4132.142)	(18.906)**						
7	II	7676.778	164.599	.340					
		(5290.321)	(78.068)*	(.202)		.936	1.39††		
	III	1833.758	443.659	−1.768	.0039				
		(5478.575)	(144.788)**	(.972)	(.0018)*	.951	1.58††		
	I	−643.819	302.151			.918	1.21††	.0757	
		(4337.019)	(20.615)**						
7′	II	6707.732	172.106	.326		.928	1.33††	.0146	
		(6517.810)	(89.557)	(.222)					
	III	−3116.019	511.587	−2.042	.0042	.943	1.54††	.0197	
		(7071.263)	(163.296)**	(1.016)	(.0018)*				
	I	172.060	411.653						
		(2388.007)	(12.211)**			.984	1.18†		48.7
8	II	−804.875	430.477	−.061					
		(3418.820)	(47.763)**	(.150)		.984	1.26††		
	III	790.569	365.045	.448	−.0011				
		(5131.953)	(161.528)*	(1.208)	(.0025)	.984	1.27††		

TABLE 1 *(concluded)*

Product	Hypothesis	b_0	b_1	b_2	b_3	R^2	d-Statistic	$\hat{p}$	Coefficient of Variation (percent)
8′	I	1046.867 (1442.133)	403.568 (11.064)**			.986	1.74	.4009	
	II	1582.522 (2096.132)	387.696 (43.690)**	.055 (.139)		.985	1.61	.3635	
	III	2193.395 (2934.418)	347.517 (138.009)*	.369 (1.027)	−.0007 (.0021)	1.61††	1.61††	.3621	
9	I	645.323 (1345.056)	486.013 (14.948)**			.982	1.11†		87.3
	II	−472.476 (1950.177)	531.914 (59.080)**	−.249 (.310)		.983	1.23††		
	III	342.594 (2541.533)	462.825 (146.842)**	.824 (2.103)	−.0040 (.0078)	.983	1.17††		
9′	I	400.452 (921.523)	480.334 (10.991)**			.990	1.88	.4257	
	II	190.671 (1221.817)	497.441 (49.194)**	−.089 (.261)		.989	1.79	.3594	
	III	1117.046 (1439.237)	363.782 (129.721)**	1.963 (1.885)	−.0077 (.0070)	.989	1.68	.3853	
10	I	1615.229 (1920.127)	351.875 (21.693)**			.966	1.89		131.9
	II	1000.417 (1545.855)	545.735 (49.417)**	−1.010 (.244)**		.966	1.53††		
	III	143.965 (1384.346)	320.789 (91.652)**	1.972 (1.094)	−.0090 (.0033)*	.976	1.66††		

* Indicates significance at the 5 percent level.
** Indicates significance at the 1 percent level.
† Indicates autocorrelation at the 5 percent level.
†† Indicates test for autocorrelation inconclusive at the 5 percent level.

of the variable Y_t^2 explains only an additional .8 percent of the variation in costs, and the coefficient estimate loses significance when the variable Y_t^3 is added. In Product 10, the inclusion of Y_t^2 adds nothing to an explanation of the variation in costs, and again, the coefficient loses significance when the variable Y_t^3 is added. The coefficient estimates of Y_t^3 are significant at the .05 level for Products 7′ and 10, but the inclusion of Y_t^3 explains only an additional 2.5 percent and 1 percent of the variation in costs for Products 7′ and 10, respectively. For all cases except Product 6′, the intercept estimates are not significantly different from zero. This implies that average variable direct cost is constant and equal to the constant marginal costs for the observed range of outputs. For Product 6′, b_0 is not an estimate of β_0, but of $\beta_0(1 - .473)$ because of the transformation employed. However, the transformation of the variables does not destroy any of the relationships found for Product 6, and an intercept coefficient not different from zero can probably be accepted for Product 6′ also.

IV. COST INTERRELATIONSHIPS

In a multiproduct firm, several products are produced simultaneously, and the cost–output relationship for each product might depend upon or be influenced by the levels of output of other products. Such cost interrelationships are likely to have consequences for the conclusion made in the previous section that average variable direct costs are constant and equal to marginal costs. If there are cost interrelationships, the firm is unlikely to be able to operate over wide ranges of output under conditions of constant average variable cost for each product.

If cost interrelationships exist among products, larger outputs of all products but one should increase the cost of producing a given output of that one product. The first-order correlation coefficients, $r_{CI.Y}$ show the relationship between the cost of producing a given level of one product and the output levels of all the other products. None of the values of $r_{CI.Y}$ for Products 1–10 in Table 2 is significant at the .05 level. The simple correlation coefficients, r_{IY}, indicate the relationship between the output of one product and the outputs of all other products. Again, none of these coefficients is significant at the .05 level. The d-statistics indicate that there is autocorrelation in the regressions for products 8 and 9 at the .05 probability level. Although the test for autocorrelation in the regression for product 7 is inconclusive, the d-statistic barely falls into the inconclusive range. When the variables C_t, Y_t, and I_t are transformed by assuming a first-order autoregressive scheme for products 7, 8, and 9, the results are those given as 7′, 8′, and 9′ in Table 2. None of the values of $r_{CI.Y}$ or r_{IY} is significant at the .05 level, and the d-statistics for products 7′, 8′, and 9′ indicate that there is no autocorrelation at the .05 probability

TABLE 2
Cost Interrelationships

Products	$r_{CI.Y}$	*d-Statistic*	$\hat{p}$	r_{IY}
1	−.1509	1.64		−.1984
2	.1105	1.86		.3030
3	.0164	2.31		.0350
4	−.3155	1.32**		−.1080
5	.0254	1.64		.1905
6	−.0715	1.83		.2765
7	−.0854	1.16**		−.0845
7′	−.2184	1.55	.0903	−.0881
8	−.1695	1.10*		−.2002
8′	−.2598	1.64	.4320	.1046
9	−.2777	1.13*		.1774
9′	−.2523	1.74	.4232	.1556
10	.3102	1.96		.3451

* Indicates autocorrelation at the 5 percent level.
** Indicates test for autocorrelation inconclusive at the 5 percent level.

level. Thus, the existence of cost interrelationships among products is ruled out, and the firm can likely operate over wide ranges of output under conditions of constant average variable costs for each product.

V. REGRESSION RESULTS FOR THE AGGREGATE COST–OUTPUT RELATIONSHIPS

Hypotheses I–III are tested for the firm's aggregate cost-output relationship. The cost data art aggregated by summing all product costs in each period. The data on physical output are aggregated by using base period product prices as weights and by finding the sum

$$Q_t = \sum_{j=1}^{10} P_{jo} Y_{jt} \quad t = 1, \ldots, 21$$

for each of the 21 monthly periods. The results of regressing aggregated costs $\sum_{j=1}^{10} C_{jt}$, on aggregated outputs are presented in Table 3.

The coefficient of variation is 28.5 percent and indicates a range of observations great enough to justify applying regression analysis. The d-statistics indicate that there is no autocorrelation at the .05 probability level. The only coefficient estimate that is statistically significant is the coefficient of Q_t, and it is significant at the .01 level. Again, the same hypothesis that is accepted for each of the individual products is accepted for the aggregate cost–output relationship—total direct costs linearly related to output.

TABLE 3
Regression Results for the Aggregate Cost–Output Relationships

Hypothesis	b_0	b_1	b_2	b_3	R^2	*d-Statistic*	*Coefficient of Variation (percent)*
I	56392.870	3.368					
	(27690.867)	(.270)**			.891	1.88	28.5
II	−22343.057	4.993	.0000				
	(99367.413)	(1.992)**			.895	1.92	
III	−80182.433	6.874	.0000	.0000			
	(353436.282)	(11.193)			.895	1.93	

* Indicates significance at the 5 percent level.
** Indicates significance at the 1 percent level.

Following Johnston, an alternative method of aggregating physical outputs is also used. This output index employs average variable costs as weights where average variable costs are taken as the coefficient estimates of b_1 from Hypothesis I for each product in Table 1. The output index is:

$$Q_t' = \sum_{j=1}^{10} b_{1j} Y_{jt} \quad t = 1, \ldots, 21$$

where the subscript j refers to the jth product. Defining Q_t' in this manner permits a joint test of the constancy and independence of the average variable costs of the individual products. Johnston says that Q_t' is

> . . . in fact, an estimate of what aggregate variable costs would be if average variable cost were constant for each product and independent of the outputs of the other products. Correlating the actual aggregate variable cost with this index should then give a correlation coefficient and a regression slope which both approach +1 the more perfectly the two assumptions are realized.

The results from regression aggregate variable costs on Q_t' are:

$$\sum_{i=1}^{10} C_{jt} = \underset{(22270.944)}{5897.821} + \underset{(.058)}{1.026}\, Q_t'.$$

The regression slope does not differ significantly from 1 and r = .971. It is concluded from this test that the average variable costs of the individual products are constant and independent of each other. Similar results are derived from both aggregated relationships even though different sets of weights are used in the aggregation procedure. Also, the results and conclusions that are reached in this section and section IV are the same even though the tests of interrelationships among products are different.

VI. CONCLUSIONS

In this paper, short-run cost functions are estimattd for a multiproduct firm. Contrary to what is expected from the traditional theory of the firm, the average variable cost curves estimated in this paper do not have the familiar U-shape. For each individual product and for the aggregate cost–output relationship, total direct costs are linearly related to current output. Average variable costs are constant and equal to constant marginal costs. No cost interrelationships among products are found, and it is concluded that the constant average variable costs of the individual products are independent of each other. If subsequent short-run cost curve studies arrive at similar results, perhaps the phenomenon of constant marginal cost should be incorporated into the mainstream of neoclassical theory.

part FIVE
Pricing

INTRODUCTION

The relative places of demand and cost in the pricing decisions of firms of the real world—as opposed, presumably, to those of theory—was once a likely topic of debate in the economic journals. The participants arranged themselves mainly into two camps, the "marginalists" and the "full costers," the latter denying virtually any role to demand and some of the former coming dangerously close to denying any role to costs. Not so much is heard about the question nowadays, partly because interest in it has run its course (economics being no less prey to fashion than most disciplines), but mostly because we are coming to realize that the marginalists were talking primarily about *determinants* and the full costers mainly about *mechanics*. But each new generation of students begins with a clean slate, and must be convinced of the practical importance of demand.

Business firms, presumably, are attempting to maximize something. It may be profits, total revenue, position in the community; nonetheless, all firms must sell their product(s) at some price. How is and/or should that price be determined? The survey by Aubrey Silberston is a classic presentation dealing with pricing developments and their impact on the overall theory of the firm. Pricing decisions represent only one of the decisions a firm must make but they are very important ones, by any standard of measurement. Does price determination differ by size of firm? Some economists believe that pricing practices in small firms differ significantly from those policies of larger firms. Warren W. Haynes concludes a form of "partial marginalism" prevails in small business. Demand is very important to them.

The pricing practices of larger firms contrast sharply with Haynes' results. Robert F. Lanzillotti studies large firms that have, one supposes, sophisticated marketing and operations research departments. These companies pay relatively little attention to demand.

Joel Dean's classic article treats the separate issue of transfer pricing.

It is the standard introduction to this subject and directs attention to the main principles of rational pricing policy in any context. This subject is as disturbing as it is important, for Dean states that to be economically effective autonomous divisions of most large companies *must* establish transfer prices. Most existing transfer price systems are inadequate and huge quantities of time and patience are required to install competitive transfer prices. Yet, once a "good" system is obtained, executives should be prepared to meet certain objections which critics always raise.

On the surface, a kilowatt hour of electricity may be considered no different than another kilowatt hour of electricity. But 100 hours of electricity may not have the same value to apartment dwellers on Fifth Avenue in Manhattan at 10 a.m. as 100 hours of electricity would have at 10 p.m. on the same day. Many goods and services, such as electricity, are homogeneous products only if (1) the use to which they are put remains unchanged during the period of time the commodity or service is being used, (2) the value of the product remains unchanged during the same time period. Donald N. DeSalvia demonstrates the applicability of peak-load pricing theory to a typical U.S. electric utility.

Some decision-making procedures are essentially "marginalist" in character and implication; others are "nonmarginalist." James S. Earley studies results obtained from a questionnaire "to test the validity of certain nonmarginalist propositions concerning business behavior . . . and marginalist hypotheses derived from the management literature."

19. Surveys of Applied Economics: Price Behaviour of Firms*

AUBREY SILBERSTON

INTRODUCTION

The determination of prices has played a central part in economic theory for a hundred years or more. It forms the core of microeconomics, and is often the first topic of economics that students are taught. Its role in the allocation of resources is stressed, and—more recently—its role in the process of inflation. Yet it has been, and remains, a subject of considerable controversy. More recently managerial theories of the firm have been put forward in which the pursuit by managers of goals other than profits has been postulated. During the last few years the theory of the firm has particularly emphasized growth as an objective. This is partly an outcome of the attention given to the role of the manager, but it is also linked with the increasing emphasis on growth in economic theory generally.

As yet, the latest developments in the theory of the firm have not been outstanding in their implications for price theory. This is not necessarily a criticism of them. Pricing decisions are only one of the complex of decisions that a firm must take.

THE MEANING OF PRICE

It is important to realise first that price is not an unambiguous concept. Let us consider, for example, what is meant by the price of a car. Anyone who has ever bought a new car knows that the catalogue price is not the price he will eventually pay. There will be all kinds of optional extras that he can buy. Where he is free to specify these there is no problem—the price now refers to a particular type of car, specified more closely than previously. But there may also be an involuntary ele-

* *The Economic Journal,* vol. 80, no. 319 (September 1970), pp. 511–75. Cambridge University Press, London, England.

ment in the choice of optional extras. The intending purchaser may find that he can get a deluxe model, but that it may prove very difficult to get a standard model, which is what he really wants. The deluxe model must, in effect, be bought, and the price of the car is therefore higher than appears at first sight.

It has been assumed that prices are fixed by sellers, i.e., that sellers are "price-makers." Where a unique manufactured product is being sold, or a unique service offered, sellers may indeed have great discretion over price. But where a product is standardised and sold in a commodity market the discretion open to sellers is slight: they are effectively "price-takers." This point does not need labouring: every text-book tells the story of how price determination is affected by the structure of the market. It is important to bear in mind, however, that one of the ways in which competition manifests itself in different market situations is in the amount of scope that these give for competition in the various dimensions of price.

The argument of this section can be put another way. It can be said that it is not "price" which has many dimensions: it is "product." There are far more "products" in the car market, for example, than at first appears, and each of these myriad products has its own unambiguous price. This comes to the same thing, of course, but my personal preference is for laying the stress on the dimensions of *price,* since this seems to me the more helpful and natural way of expressing the point.

PRICE BEHAVIOUR IN THEORY

Later in this survey a good deal of attention will be paid to studies of how firms actually determine prices. It is well known, however, that in this field, as in many others, the answers depend a good deal on the questions, and the questions themselves depend on the theoretical approach of the questioner. It will be appropriate therefore to begin our survey with a consideration of the theory of price.

Price theory is usually formulated in terms of the price charged to the ultimate consumer, although little differentiation, if any, is normally made between prices charged by manufacturers and retail prices. For the sake of clarity, it will be best to think, at this stage of the analysis, in terms of the prices facing the ultimate consumer. Other types of price will be considered later. We will also think at this stage of each firm making a single product, although this is notoriously untrue in manufacturing industry.

It is assumed that the reader is familiar with the theory of price as it is normally expounded. Under conditions of perfect competition, it is argued, firms will push output to the point where their marginal cost equals price, and this price is determined by the market. In the long run price is equal to the average cost of production at the (relatively small) scale of output where long-run average cost is at its minimum. This is not because firms want this: they want maximum profits, but competition ensures that they earn "normal" profits only. Under conditions of imperfect competition the demand curve is not horizontal. The firm is a "price maker," and it maximises profits by choosing that combination of price and output at which marginal revenue equals marginal cost. In the long run firms may earn more than normal profits, but the extent to which they can do this depends on the market situation. In conditions of monopoly there will be no tendency for supernormal profits to be competed away, but where there are many firms in an industry supernormal profits may be eliminated altogether: the firms will, however, typically be below the scale at which long-run average cost is a minimum. The picture is less clear under conditions of oligopoly: with firms selling a homogeneous product (the usual assumption in the simplest case) price may end up anywhere between the competitive and the monopoly price, depending on the assumptions made.

The Full-Cost Attack on Imperfect Competition

Joan Robinson was concerned with what she called "imperfect competition," a state of affairs where one of the many conditions needed for perfect competition to exist was absent. In practice, she was particularly concerned with monopoly and with the "large group" case, and said little about nonprice competition and the small group. Chamberlin, on the other hand, was primarily concerned with what he called "monopolistic competition"—the middle ground between pure competition and monopoly, which was especially characterised by product differentiation. Chamberlin's treatment was more comprehensive, though less intensive, than that of Joan Robinson, and it stimulated much work, by authors such as Bain, on the relationship between the structure of an industry and the conduct and performance of the firms within it. Chamberlin attempted, inter alia, to deal with the small group case, but it is generally agreed that his treatment of his case was one of the least satisfactory parts of his work. The analysis of oligopoly, therefore, was left in a weak state. Apart from this, a well-defined price theory emerged from the work of these two authors, although any detailed consideration of Chamberlin's book made clear the yawning cracks opened up in the theory by the introduction of product differentiation.

Triffin's criticism of Joan Robinson and Chamberlin, apart from its technical aspects, was particularly effective in its attack on the notion of group equilibrium. The essence of the attack was that product differentiation, when taken to its logical conclusion, made nonsense of the idea of an "industry" equilibrium. One had to consider the firm (and its immediate competitors) and then the economy as a whole. Perhaps Triffin was too enamoured of the logic of his argument to give sufficient credit to those instances in the real world where industries or subindustries contain firms in more active competition with each other than with firms outside the "industry." Be that as it may, one of the results of Triffin's book was to reemphasise the gap in the theory of the firm left by the unsatisfactory nature of the theory of the small group. Apart from this, Triffin's analysis was essentially in the imperfect competition tradition. He did not doubt that the object of the firm was to maximize its profits and that marginal analysis was an appropriate tool for attaining this objective.

Hall and Hitch, on the other hand, appeared to many to have mounted a root-and-branch attack on the notion of profit maximization itself. They argued, on the basis of an empirical study of pricing, that firms do not attempt to maximise profits. Instead they base prices on "full" costs, i.e., average direct costs (assumed to be constant over a wide range of output), plus average overhead costs, plus a margin for profit. At the root of this behaviour is the moral principle that there is a price that *ought* to be charged—the "right" price—and this ought to be charged in periods of both good and bad business. To this way of thinking, profit maximisation was the wrong way to approach the question of pricing. As has been pointed out by many critics, including Austin Robinson and Kahn, important elements of profit maximisation, or loss minimisation, entered into the pricing decisions of many of the businessmen investigated by Hall and Hitch. Moreover, Hall and Hitch themselves laid a good deal of stress on the kinked demand curve in cases of oligopoly, with its emphasis on sticky prices in the short run. As they themselves point out, the kink in the subjective demand curve makes the price at this point the profit-maximising price for a wide range of marginal costs, on account of the discontinuity in the marginal revenue curve at this particular price and output.

Of greater interest is the discussion by Hall and Hitch of how price came to be what it is, and how it comes to be changed. They argue, it will be recalled, that a price change is likely to come about as a result of a general change in costs. This is where full costs come back into the picture, but as Kahn has pointed out, the interesting question is—*whose* full costs? Clearly, if an industry is competitive in some sense firms will not each be able to base their prices on their own full costs, regardless of the costs of others. The possibility of price leadership must then be considered, but this subject was not dealt with satisfactorily by Hall and Hitch.

At first sight the work of Andrews appears to follow similar lines to that of Hall and Hitch. On further analysis it contains significant differences, which make it at the same time both more realistic and less satisfactory theoretically. The major difference is inherent in Andrews' use of the concept of the "costing margin." This margin is conceived as an addition to (constant) average direct costs, and "will normally tend to cover the costs of the indirect factors of production and provide a normal level of net profit." In its basic form, therefore, the costing margin gives a similar answer to that suggested by Hall and Hitch, and appears equally, at first sight, to be at variance with profit-maximising ideas. There is a good deal of discussion in Andrews, however, of the circumstances in which there might be some flexibility in the costing margin, in response to competitive and market forces, which brings his theory much closer to a theory of profit maximisation. The characteristics of the type of market with which Andrews is principally concerned—a mature oligopolistic industry, with potential competition limiting the scope for short-run profit-taking—would suggest, even for a firm intent on profit maximisation, a price policy similar to that postulated by him. However, Andrews lays much stress on the costing margin that one *has* to add, and hence on a defensive type of price policy which, it could be argued, is a policy more appropriate to a price *follower* than a price *leader*. "Conventional" maximising theory, on the other hand, is concerned with a firm which, at least in conditions of imperfect competition, has a certain amount of freedom to choose among various policies, including price policies. In this sense conventional theory deals with a price leader, although this is not usually made explicit.

The full-cost, normal-cost debate, and the parallel controversy in the United States, was perhaps more a source of good questions than of useful answers. However, it threw grave doubt on the extent to which businessmen think in the same terms as economists. It also raised the question whether, in many types of market, a policy of maximising profits in a succession of short periods was the best way of maximising profits in the long period. It drew attention to the prevalence in manufacturing industry of price stability, and described the process of price formation more realistically than hitherto. It also raised fundamental questions about the nature of business ethics and motivation generally, questions which are still the subject of vigorous debate.

The Development of the Theory of Oligopoly

While these attacks on the conventional theory of the firm were in progress the theory of oligopoly was being developed by those more in the mainstream of economic thought. Even these writers, however, were led by the nature of the problem to discuss topics far outside those usually treated in orthodox analysis. The fundamental problem of oligopoly is that competition among the few inevitably gives rise to problems of interdependence: no firm can act on the assumption that what it does will not provoke a reaction from its competitors. This reaction cannot be forecast with certainty, although relative costs of production, existing market shares and past history, all help firms to anticipate their rivals' reactions. But other factors, such as the view taken by the entrepreneur of his competitors, his strength of nerve and attitude to risk, have also to be considered before price behaviour can be determined in any particular oligopolistic situation. In the light of this one can appreciate Rothschild's view that to understand oligopoly one needs to understand the rules of war.

The classic approach to oligopoly is via the theory of duopoly. Here formalised models have been constructed in which standard reactions have been assumed by competitors. Cournot's model assumed that each firm would set its own output in the belief that the other firm's output would remain unchanged. Bertrand postulated that a firm would set prices in the belief that the other firm's price would remain unchanged. Stackelberg developed a more realistic model of leadership–followership: the follower behaved as in the Cournot model, while the leader took advantage of the assumed behaviour of the follower. In this model the interesting possibility is raised of both firms wishing to act as leaders, thus giving rise to an aggressive situation, with no determinate outcome.

We return to the more interesting question of the principles on which the price leader, whether one firm or a succession of different firms, fixes price. In general, the models of duopoly together with oligopoly models such as those of Fellner, lead to the conclusion that price will be above that ruling in perfect competition. The greater the number of firms in the group, and the more easily firms can enter it, the nearer the price will be to the competitive level. When the analysis is moved to a more realistic plane it has to be recognised that the perfectly competitive level of price (or costs) may have little meaning in an industry which consists of a few large firms, each enjoying considerable economies of scale. There may still be justification for talking of a departure from competitive price levels, however, in the sense that the price ruling in the industry may yield profits above "normal" to some or all of the firms in the group (i.e., above the level of profits ruling in industry as a whole). This situation may, of course, be compatible with a price level below that which would rule in an industry consisting of small firms in keen competition with each other, because economies of scale may be enjoyed by large firms.

The possibility of entry into a group is clearly very relevant to the level of profits that can be achieved, and hence to the ruling level of price.

Bain formulated his "limit price" theory of entry as early as 1949, some years before his important empirical work on barriers to entry appeared. The "limit price" set by a group of sellers, acting in collusion, is the highest common price which the established sellers believe they can charge without inducing entry into the industry. This price may well be lower than the profit-maximising price in any short period of time, and will depend, inter alia, on the relative costs of "inside" and "outside" firms, and on the conditions of demand in the industry. It may be that, given these relationships, the actual price has to be set above the limit price, thus enabling entry to occur. Or established firms, in order to maximize long-run profits, may choose to set price high enough to induce a limited amount of entry. In other cases it may be possible to maximise profits while setting price below the limit price. The number of possibilities is large, especially when competitive as well as collusive behaviour among established firms, and differences of efficiency between firms, are allowed for. In general, however, opportunities for earning monopoly profits in oligopolistic industries are likely to be closely related to the height of barriers to entry in these industries.

Bain did not set out primarily to formulate a general theory of price equilibrium under conditions of oligopoly. He was concerned with establishing, in a series of notable empirical studies, what factors created barriers to new competition in an industry. His main empirical work was on economics of large-scale production, and he concluded that where such economies were important (and they turned out—in the United States economy, be it conceded—to be a good deal less important than is often thought) they constituted an important barrier to entry. The other main barriers to entry, Bain argued, were product differentiation and absolute cost advantages for existing firms. His view was that the main culprit was product differentiation, and that industries where this was a prominent factor were likely to have high selling costs. He also found that industries with very high barriers to entry tended to have higher profits, and more monopolistic output restrictions, than others. Industries with somewhat lower barriers to entry tended to have lower profits and to be more "workably competitive." Seller concentration alone did not appear to be an adequate criterion of the workability of competition, since it had different effects, depending on the height of the barriers to entry.

Sylos-Labini assumed that if new firms entered the market existing firms would continue to produce as much as before. This would discourage the entry of new firms, since their additional output would depress prices and make the whole market less profitable. New firms could be deterred from entering the market if a large firm in the group set an "entry-preventing" price. The height of this price would depend on the size of the potential entrant, since this would determine his costs (another assumption was that all firms of a given size had the same costs). If price were not changed initially, new entrants would, by increasing the scale of the industry's output, bring down the level of price. They would anticipate such an outcome, because they would realise that existing firms would not reduce their own output. Whether they entered the industry in these circumstances would depend on whether the price level expected to rule after their entry would cover their costs, including their minimum level of required profit. The possibility of entry thus depended on several factors, among these being the relative costs of firms of different sizes, price elasticity of demand in the market and the attitude of the large firms already in the market. These large firms might simply sit there and allow entry; they might fix an entry-preventing price; or they might even adopt an aggressive policy and try to drive out small firms already in the industry. Sylos-Labini considered all these cases and showed how, on his assumptions, determinate solutions could be reached and an equilibrium price arrived at. He also showed that the absolute size of the market was an important consideration which might affect the nature of the final equilibrium. In particular, a large market increased the likelihood of an aggressive price policy on the part of large firms, especially if they acted in agreement with one another. There is no unique solution in the Sylos-Labini model, but the general price tendency is that "the price tends to settle at a level immediately above the entry-preventing price of the least efficient firms which it is to the advantage of the largest and most efficient firms to let live."

Almost the most interesting thing about any model, especially one of price determination, is how it deals with changes in the parameters. In this case changes of costs are obviously of great importance. Sylos-Labini examined this question in the context of the full-cost principle, and argued that, where cost variations are relatively small, the full-cost principle acted as a guide and enabled a new equilibrium to be reached quickly and easily. With large changes in costs, on the other hand, or with changes in the size of the market, in technology, or the quality of products, the upshot was less predictable. He also argued that in the boom the costing margin would tend to fall, partly to discourage entry, while in the slump the margin would tend to rise. But it would fall less and rise more in industries with high entry barriers than in those with low barriers. A fall in the costing margin in the boom was compatible with a rise in the rate of profit on capital because of the rise in output, with contrary results in the slump.

Sylos-Labini's basic thesis, that price tends to settle at the highest entry-preventing price, that this price will be fixed by the large firm and that the full-cost principle will be a useful rule of thumb when costs change, does give a good deal of body to the full-cost story. It also helps to explain how a price may be (honestly) represented by businessmen as having been arrived at by full-cost methods, when the truth is that a whole complex of relevant considerations have actually been taken into account, many of them implicitly only.

Is Bain right, to emphasise the importance of barriers to entry in a world of multiproduct firms, where existing large firms can, as Andrews has argued, probably enter a new "industry" a good deal more easily than completely new firms can be expected to do? Are Bain and Sylos-Labini right to assume that the aim of the large firm will be to maximise its profits in the long run? The meaning and validity of this assumption, and its implications for the behaviour of firms, have occupied a good deal of attention in recent years.

Some Aspects of Monopoly Pricing

Once one has discussed oligopoly, there is in a sense little point in discussing monopoly, since this is equally well treated when considering collusive types of group behaviour. There are, however, one or two topics in this area that are worth referring to briefly. The first is "vintage" pricing, as it is sometimes called, the second is price discrimination, and the third is countervailing power.

Vintage pricing means crudely that higher prices are charged in the early years of the life of a plant because uncertainty about the future makes distant profits too speculative to count on. A similar situation may arise in the early years of the life of a new product. Kaldor has argued, for example, that (except for a minority of exceptional firms) differences in labour and material costs per unit of output mainly reflect the age of equipment. The lowest-cost firms are those with the most recent equipment, while the marginal firms are operating the oldest surviving equipment. The profits earned on new plant will correspond to the required rate of profit on new investment, and the corresponding output price will determine the rate of profit on old equipment. The required rate of profit is very high, Kaldor argues, because "in a world of continual technical progress and obsolescence . . . business firms except the profits derived from today's equipment to be much smaller and more uncertain in the more distant years." Accordingly, they adopt a short "pay-off period" and an appropriate level of price to reflect this. The more dynamic the industry, the shorter the pay-off period and the higher the price.

This analysis is in effect a monopoly analysis, since it envisages a situation where a firm has a monopoly of the latest equipment, even though this monopoly is short-lived. A more obvious example of the same sort of behaviour applies to the introduction of a new product. Here again, there is a likelihood that the monopoly will be limited in time, and there is a consequential need to charge high prices in the early years. The new product may be protected by a patent, and it has frequently been suggested that the price of a patented product falls, sometimes steeply, towards the end of the life of the patent. This inter-temporal price discrimination is not necessarily a simple question of making hay while the sun shines. It may be that heavy research and development costs have been involved, as well as heavy investment, and there is therefore a drive to recoup these while the monopoly lasts. The opportunity to do so may well be there, since demand for a new product is likely to be inelastic in its early years. This is especially likely to be the case if the level of production takes time to build up. In later years output will be greater, newer products will jostle for attention and demand is therefore likely to be a good deal more elastic. This strategy has the added advantage of enabling the firm to make sharp price reductions in later years in response to the challenge of new competitors.

The possibility of price discrimination under conditions of monopoly is, of course, widely known. The argument here, of course, is that a monopolist will take advantage of less elastic demand in markets which can be kept distinct from those in which demand is more elastic. Obvious examples are that of a doctor charging rich patients more than poor patients, or a firm selling abroad at prices lower than on the home market. An important, but perhaps less well-known case, is that of a firm selling part of its production to a manufacturer, for incorporation in his output, and part direct to consumers. This type of behaviour may be found in the motor industry, for example, where prices charged for articles sold to manufacturers as "original equipment" may be very much lower than those charged to wholesalers and retailers for sale to consumers as replacement parts. In so far as price discrimination of this or other types occurs it means, of course, that full-cost policies are certainly not being followed in every market, since the essence of price discrimination is charging on the basis of what the market will bear, subject to the necessity of covering overall costs.

Price discrimination may also in effect occur with uniform prices. For example, two services may sell at the same price, although the cost of supplying them may be different. Price discrimination in this or other forms, however, need not necessarily lead to high profits. It may be that costs could not be covered at all if price discrimination were not practised.

The problem of pricing in a multiproduct firm has analogies with the case just described. Here there are obvious possibilities for setting prices to yield high profit margins on some products and low profit margins on others. The strength of competition in the markets for the products concerned is obviously likely to be an important consideration. The existence of common costs in a multiproduct firm may also encourage a pricing policy which pays particular attention to the market situation of individual products, since the full costs attributable to the production of any particular product may not easily be ascertainable. Even when common costs are not an important factor, however, a multiproduct firm may find it possible to earn high profits in one part of its business with safety, since the firm's financial results, as shown in its published accounts, will not normally reveal the profits earned on different products. The fact that prices are set well above (or below) any plausible "full-cost" level may therefore escape undetected for some considerable time. In the long run the threat (or the fact) of entry from alternative producers may well squeeze profit margins on old products. Products may also be abandoned if they do not cover the full costs attributable to them: from this point of view, as Robertson has pointed out, it is the average cost of producing them which is relevant in the long run. In the long run, however, there will still be opportunities for high profit margins if the firm succeeds in putting new products on the market from time to time.

It has to be remembered, in all these discussions of price discrimination and behaviour similar to it, that "perfect" price discrimination is rarely possible. Incomplete information, and the difficulty of adjusting prices frequently, limit the extent to which "perfect" price discrimination can be practised. Here there are similarities with problems of "satisficing."

It might be appropriate to add a word here about Galbraith's notion of countervailing power. This envisages restraint being placed on the freedom of action of monopolists or oligopolists by the existence of power in the purchasing market, or in the labour market. This is essentially a monopolist versus monopsonist problem. As such it has no determinate solution, although the solution must lie within a range. Countervailing power is undoubtedly an important phenomenon, although it may not always eliminate the danger of monopolistic exploitation of the consumer. Monopoly profits may be shared by the firms on opposite sides of the market, or by a firm and its labour force. Lower prices to the consumer may, however, result from its existence. For example, firms selling to the large vehicle manufacturers have to reckon with the threat that the vehicle manufacturers themselves may make the products concerned, and this exerts pressure on their prices. Similarly, the buying power of retail firms almost certainly limits monopoly pricing on the part of their suppliers. In cases such as this the benefit of lower buying prices is likely to be felt by the final consumer.

Prices, Products, and Selling Costs

Reference has already briefly been made to the problems raised by the introduction of the possibility of competition in product and selling costs. From a theoretical point of view these problems are considerable, but they can be handled analytically without great difficulty. From an empirical point of view their importance is clearly very great. For the moment, however, we confine ourselves to the theoretical aspects.

Chamberlin introduced product variation and selling costs into his price–output model by the simple device of holding two variables (for example, price and selling costs) constant, while altering the other variable in such a way as to obtain maximum profits. He repeated the exercise notionally for all possible values of the other two variables, and thus arrived at a *maximum maximorum*. This was made to appear straightforward in the case of product variation, but with selling expenses the problem arose more explicitly that these elements of cost were incurred to adapt the demand to the product, i.e., to change preferences, rather than the product to the demand. Chamberlin therefore emphasised the shifts in the demand curve of the firm that took place as the amount of selling expenses altered. Having taken account of this effect, however, he was able to arrive at the maximum profit combination without difficulty.

How far firms making similar products are able to get away with dissimilar prices will, of course, depend on whether consumers think that these products are similar or not. Hence the emphasis, by such writers as Bishop, on the importance of cross-elasticities of demand under conditions of differentiated oligopoly. But the measurement, notionally or otherwise, of cross-elasticities of demand does not dispose of the problem. Crosselasticities can be altered by advertising, or by the introduction of new or modified products. Any firm worth its salt is well aware of this and takes advantage of it. But the scope for product differentiation is greater in some situations than others; and price behaviour is likely to be affected by this. Where the scope for product differentiation appears to be small, one would expect prices to be closer together than otherwise, and the industry concerned to be more "workably" competitive. But it is not always easy to say a priori whether the scope for product differentiation is small or not in any particular case—an able entrepreneur can perform miracles of differentiation if he thinks his firm will benefit thereby.

Considerations of this sort lead one in the direction of arguing, as several authors *have* argued, that it is very difficult to generalise about price behaviour, and that a particular industry or group needs to be studied in some detail before useful predictions can be made. There is obviously much truth in this, but it can also be maintained that generalisations which are not entirely vacuous can be made about price behaviour, even in a world of differentiated products.

Profit Maximisation

One of the features of the full-cost theory of price is its stress on "fair" profits and on the influence of this principle on price fixing. What is by no means clear in the literature, however, is whether the full-cost principle is thought to be adhered to—on account of the fair-profits principle—when it is known to reduce profits below the level that could be attained, or whether it is adhered to because it *is* in fact thought to be the most profitable long-run policy. This question becomes involved with that of the length of the price-maker's time horizon. When this is assumed to be a long one it becomes difficult to say exactly what is implied by the notion of profit maximisation, especially when uncertainty about the future is brought into the picture. Arguments also arise, of the type that arose between Robinson and Farrell, about whether maximising profits in a succession of short periods is the same as maximising profits in the long period. An empirical question is involved here—whether consumers react favourably or not to a flexible pricing policy—but the argument involves also a consideration of what is meant by the long period over which profits are assumed to be maximised.

In some sense "long-run" profits will be preferred to "short-run" profits, but what do "long-run" profits mean? Presumably a time-horizon of several years is implied. Five years might be regarded as short, while over 20 years might be regarded as long. But suppose one compromises on 15 years: this still gives an ambiguous guide-line unless one adds something about the relative importance of different future years. In other words, one must specify the rate at which future profits should be discounted. The firm anxious to survive, assuming it has no short-run crises over liquidity, might well think of applying a very low discount rate, i.e., it would be almost equally happy with a given sum in profits whether it were earned next year or in 15 years time. At the other extreme the barrow-boy might apply a discount rate which approached infinity, both because he would be likely to need money today and because he would probably be in a different "industry" tomorrow. Most firms are likely to apply some positive rate of discount, its height varying with the extent to which they are concerned about future survival. If the rate of discount is high this will imply a short time-horizon, since profits many years hence will have a negligible present value. A long time-horizon will imply a low rate of discount on future profits. The difference between the barrow-boy and the large industrial or commercial enterprise can perhaps best be put, therefore, not in terms of the length of their time-horizon but in terms of the rate at which they discount future profits in their particular "industries."

When new investment is being considered the minimum rate of discount that can be applied to future profits, by a profit maximising firm, is the opportunity cost of capital to that firm, i.e., the market rate, or some rate close to it. Any lower rate would imply that new investment was expected to yield a rate of profit below the market rate. Even a firm not intent on long-run profit maximisation would be likely to run into difficulties, with its shareholders, for example, if it discounted future profits at a lower rate than this.

One can differentiate between a profit-maximising and a non-profit-maximising firm from two points of view. From the short-run point of view a profit-maximising firm will aim to maximise the present value of its discounted stream of profits, given its existing assets. It has to choose a subjective rate of discount at which to do this. If its time-horizon is long it will choose a low subjective rate. The lower the subjective rate of discount it chooses, the lower its prices are likely to be, since a low price policy is probably the best policy to adopt if it is desired to safeguard profits many years ahead. A firm will not be a profit-maximiser if, at its chosen subjective discount rate, it makes no attempt to maximise the present value of its profits. If, for example, it has a high subjective rate it will not maximise its profits if it follows a policy which safeguards its markets many years ahead, for example, by charging a low price. A profit maximising policy would in these circumstances imply a relatively high price, yielding high profits in the years immediately ahead.

From the long-run point of view all firms need a rate of return on new investment of at least the market rate. A profit-maximising firm will push its rate of investment to the point where the rate of return on the marginal investment equals the market rate. If the supply curve of funds is rising the firm will maximise its profits at the point where the marginal rate of return on new investment equals the marginal cost of borrowing. A firm will not act as a profit maximiser if it invests beyond this point. Nor will it act as a profit maximiser if it stops short of it, possibly because it is more interested in the maximum rate of return on any given investment project than in maximum total profits.

How does all this connect with the full-cost argument that, in manufacturing industry, firms do not aim to maximise their profits, but aim at "fair" profits only? From the short-run point of view this might simply be taken to imply the choice of a low subjective rate of time discount, with a concomitant low price policy. But this could be a profit-maximising policy, subject to the chosen discount rate. It would not be a profit-maximising policy only if the price policy chosen were not compatible with this discount rate, or if the subjective discount rate itself were set below what would be possible if the stock market were working more perfectly. From the long-run point of view a fair profit policy might imply investing beyond the point where the marginal rate of return on new investment equalled the marginal cost of borrowing. It would be difficult to reconcile a fair profit policy with a low investment policy, calculated to yield a high return at the margin.

It follows from this that it is not at all clear what there is distinctive about a fair profit policy. In so far as high short-run prices are avoided, for example, this may be a profit-maximising policy, subject to a low subjective rate of time discount. Similarly, a firm aiming at fair profits on its new investment may simply be a profit-maximising firm, pushing its investment to the point where the rate of return at the margin just covered the marginal cost of funds. When long-run profit maximisation is correctly interpreted, therefore, it may not differ in any essential respect from a "fair" profit policy. The essential point is not the difference between profit maximisation and nonprofit maximisation but the choice of a long time-horizon—and the low subjective time rate of discount which reflects this.

It is worth referring here to another of the ideas thrown up by the full-cost argument. This is the view, which I was myself guilty of propagating, that firms aim not only at maximising their money profits but also bring into the equation other considerations, e.g., their prestige with the government, with other firms and with their workpeople. On this view, profit maximisation has to be interpreted sufficiently broadly to take these factors into account as well as money profits. The trouble with this line of argument is not that it may not be true—indeed, there is clearly much truth in it—but that it is of no analytical value in this form. As Robertson pointed out, the concept of profit maximisation must not be stretched so far "as to cover all the possible motives that may animate businessmen, thereby robbing the proposition that businessmen normally pursue profit of all empirical content, since profit has now become whatever the businessman pursues." This kind of implicit theorising has generally been avoided by those writers who argue that managers aim to maximise their own utility rather than money profits, in that they specify closely the particular variables that enter into the utility function, and thus give their theories some operational validity.

Behavioural and Managerial Theories of the Firm

Three other theories of the firm need to be considered here. They are the "managerial" theories of Baumol, Williamson, and Marris. They all emphasise the role of the manager and his motivations. Since he is assumed to be motivated by many other considerations than maximising the profits of his firm, the decisions taken are likely to be different in many instances from those to be expected from more conventional theory.

Baumol argues that oligopolistic firms aim to maximise their sales revenue in the long run, subject to a minimum profits level. His reason for adopting this (somewhat unconvincing) model is that, in his experience, managers always emphasise sales rather than profits, and that the prestige of the manager is associated with his firm's sales. Clearly he cannot ignore profits although, since if the firm wishes to continue in existence it must pay acceptable dividends to its shareholders and promise acceptable dividends to those subscribing new capital. Because of this, Baumol argues, each company's minimum rate of profits is set competitively in terms of the current market value of its securities.

One of the implications of Baumol's model is, of course, that profits will be sacrificed for the sake of greater sales. This is likely to lead, *ceteris paribus*, to lower prices than would be charged by a profit-maximising firm, since revenue is maximised when marginal revenue is zero. Another implication is that advertising expenditure would be undertaken if it were thought likely to lead to increased revenue, subject to the minimum profit constraint. Advertising might make it possible to charge a higher price for any given output than would otherwise be the case, and a rise in price is positively desirable, other things equal, since revenue is quantity of sales multiplied by price. But other things might not be equal, since sales may be sensitive to price. In these circumstances the elasticity of sales revenue with regard to advertising expenditure may be such that it is best not to increase price at all. A further implication of Baumol's model is that there may be a conflict between pricing in the long and the short run. In a short-run situation, where output is limited, revenue would often increase if price were raised; but in the long run it might pay to keep price low in order to compete more effectively for a large share of the market. The price policy to be followed in the short run would then depend on the expected repercussions of short-run decisions on long-run revenue.

Williamson's model of "rational managerial behaviour" is based on the assumption that managers conduct the affairs of the firm so as to attend to their own best interests. They will only have real scope to do this when competition is not vigorous: once again therefore an oligopolistic type of market structure is assumed. Williamson argues that managers will operate the firm so as to maximise their utility function. This has as its chief components staff (since the larger his staff, the higher the manager's salary, prestige, etc.), discretionary spending for investments, and management slack absorbed as cost. This last item increases managerial utility by expenditure on luxurious offices and other comparable benefits. Discretionary spending for investment is defined by Williamson as the difference between reported profits and the minimum profits required by shareholders. It reflects investment decisions made by the firm less on the basis of economic necessity (minimum profits include what is needed to raise finance for these investments) than on the success of managers in diverting resources to their own part of the firm, and thus augmenting their prestige. Williamson recognises clearly that the special advantages that insulate a firm from the pressures of competition are often eroded with time, and he argues therefore that this particular model is best restricted to short- and medium-term analysis.

Williamson's model preserves the results of the normal profit-maximising model in conditions of pure or perfect competition. Where competition is weak and demand strong, however, the model predicts that the expansion of staff will exceed that suggested by the normal hypothesis. In addition, expenditure on advertising, managerial luxuries, etc., will grow, and more management slack will be absorbed as cost. When demand weakens these sources of high costs will diminish in size, i.e., they will vary with the business cycle.

It is interesting to contrast the predictions of Baumol's and Williamson's models in the face of an increase in taxation on the firm, and to compare these with the prediction for a profit-maximising firm. If a lump-sum tax is imposed on the firm both Baumol and Williamson predict a reduction in expenditure, since there has in effect been an increase in the minimum profit constraint. In Williamson's case the reduction will be particularly directed towards expenditure on staff. If, however, the increase in taxation is in the rate of profits tax Williamson and Baumol may predict different results. In Williamson's model the firm may increase expenditure on staff, etc., in an effort to reduce "reported" profits, which are less attractive than previously, since they now carry a higher rate of tax. In Baumol's case the firm would reduce these expenditures, since once again the minimum profit constraint has been increased. For a profit-maximising firm, on the other hand, it makes no difference whether a lump-sum tax is levied or the rate of profits tax increased—in both cases output and expenditure will be unaffected, and the firm will take no action.

In spite of their differences from each other and from more conventional models, the models of Baumol and Williamson both resemble the traditional model in that, given their assumptions, a solution can be found analytically.

This is perhaps an appropriate point at which to leave the theoretical analysis of price behaviour and turn to the empirical evidence, such as it is. Only when this has been surveyed will it be possible to draw the threads of the previous analysis together, in an attempt to assess the present state of price theory, and to place price theory in its context as part of the theory of the firm as a whole. At that point it will be appropriate to consider further the quotation from Williamson that has just been given.

PRICE BEHAVIOUR IN PRACTICE

In discussing price theory, empirical studies have from time to time been referred to. There was no avoiding this, especially when dealing with the full-cost school, as exemplified by Hall and Hitch, since the full-cost theory was specifically constructed to explain the findings of the Oxford economists' study of pricing. The empirical findings of Hall and Hitch have been only briefly described, however, and it would be appropriate to start this account of pricing in practice with a further account of them.

Micro Studies of Pricing

Very briefly, since their work is so well known, Hall and Hitch analysed the answers to questionnaires of 38 businessmen, 33 of whom were manufacturers, and the results of the questionnaires were discussed with the businessmen concerned. An overwhelming majority of those questioned thought that a price based on full average costs (including an allowance for profit) was the "right" price to charge. But of the 30 firms adhering to this full-cost principle only 12 adhered "rigidly" to it. Even these 12 firms differed in the way they estimated output for the purpose of calculating the addition to prime costs to be added for overheads: some took "full" output, while most took "actual" or forecast output. The other 18 firms adhered to full-cost "normally" or "in principle," but they would cut prices below the full-cost level if business were very depressed. However, only 2 of the 30 full-cost firms said that they would charge more than full cost in exceptionally prosperous times.

If one takes into account the element of discretion in the treatment of overheads, even in those firms adhering "rigidly" to full cost, it is clear that, taking the 38 firms as a whole, the full-cost principle was interpreted pretty loosely. In particular, the state of the market seems to have played an important part in the prices actually charged. Hall and Hitch's findings threw grave doubts, as was said earlier, on what had appeared to be the previously received doctrine, but the doubts expressed about the validity of the Hall and Hitch findings, by Kahn and others, show how tricky it was (and is) to use empirical work to confirm or deny any particular theory of price.

In spite of the attention focused on the pricing behaviour of firms by Hall and Hitch in Britain, by Machlup and Lester in the United States, and by numerous later writers, there is a paucity of published work of an empirical kind on pricing. Some light has been thrown on the question by what might be called "macro" studies (i.e., statistical or econometric studies: these will be considered later), but studies concentrating on the pricing behaviour of individual firms are rare.

Although many industry studies include a discussion of prices, it is comparatively rare for the *process* of pricing to be investigated in any detail. This is partly because prices are only one of a large number of subjects studied, and partly because many, if not most, industry studies undertaken by economists have deliberately been carried out from the "outside in," so to speak, i.e., they have concentrated on objective data rather than on material derived from interviews, etc. My own work with Maxcy on the British motor industry, for example, discussed prices and price leadership at some length, but it did not investigate the process of pricing, except in a brief reference to General Motors' practice in the early 1920s. Our study did bring out the fact that different firms have to take very different profit margins, even though their cars sell at comparable prices, and to this extent threw doubts on any rigid adherence to the full-cost principle. It also stressed the importance of competition in product in this industry rather than in price. The motor industry may, of course, be held to be so competitive that the market makes it imperative for prices to be similar, but if this can be said of an oligopolistic industry, with pronounced product differentiation, it casts doubt on how extensive the scope can be for full-cost pricing in industry generally.

Joe S. Bain has summarised the pre-war, and immediate post-war, literature in the United States on price and production policies in his chapter on this subject in *A Survey of Contemporary Economics,* published in 1948. He referred there to empirical studies of demand and costs for a number of industries, including automobiles and steel, and then considered "industry" studies for aluminum, steel, newsprint, butter and margarine, motion pictures, cigarettes, oranges, and automobiles, among others. Distinct differences apparently emerged between price behaviour in highly competitive industries with many firms and price behaviour in highly concentrated industries. Barriers to entry, product differentiation, and the number of buyers all affected selling and production costs and, through these, prices. Potential indeterminacy under conditions of oligopoly was often found to be solved in practice by collusive behaviour. Bain pointed out that one of the main achievements of these industry studies was to go behind demand and supply curves to the basic institutional, technological, and other conditions underlying them, and he stressed the complexity of competitive behaviour in actual situations and the need to study the effect of changes through time. He admitted that price theory tended to be "overly general," but he gave a warning (badly needed, if I may say so) that theorising based on empirical studies can easily become "overly specific." One interesting point made by Bain was that businessmen had been reluctant to tell economists how they calculated prices, and to discuss their relations with rival firms. He suggested that the antitrust laws might have been a major barrier here.

Since Bain wrote his survey, a number of other studies of pricing have been published in the United States. The most massive were those carried out by the Subcommittee on Antitrust and Monopoly of the United States Senate Committee on the Judiciary. Hearings on "administered prices" took place over the period 1957–63, and were published in 26 volumes. In addition, reports were published on administered prices in steel, automobiles, bread, and drugs. To attempt to summarise this material other than very briefly would be a labour of Hercules—although admittedly a lesser labour than the original achievement itself. The committee found, in all four of the industries it studied, a pattern of price leadership. Companies in these industries tended to change their prices only after the leader had changed his, even though they might be more efficient then he, with lower costs and higher profit margins. In the drug industry an additional feature was observed. This was that firms, on introducing a new drug, put it on the market at or very near the price charged for an existing drug used to treat the same general type of ailment. This was said by the firms concerned to be "meeting the competition," but it tended to occur even when the new drug might be a good deal cheaper to produce than the existing competitive drug. The result was often high profit margins, which were able to persist because of the "live and let live" attitude of the major firms in the industry, and the patent protection afforded to new drugs. Whether or not margins on new drugs are excessive, in view of the high expenditure of drug companies on research, and the high proportion of failures, is of course still very much a matter of controversy in Britain and other countries, as well as in the United States. It was discussed by the Sainsbury Committee in Britain, and was brought prominently to the fore by the use by the Ministry of Health of the Crown User provisions of the Patent Act to import drugs from abroad more cheaply than they could be obtained from the patent holder. This is not the place to enter into this extensive controversy. All that it is necessary to note here is that the American drug industry undoubtedly displays marked oligopolistic behaviour in its pricing policy, allied with elements of monopolistic behaviour, and that many other drug industries display the same characteristics.

An American study of the A&P company (a grocery chain) by Adelman is of interest because it tells the story of a United States government antitrust suit in which an alleged monopolist was criticised, not for prices which were too high, but for prices which were too low. A&P were accused of lowering the gross margins they aimed for on their products in order to expand their business. In this way they were selling "below cost" and thus indulging in unfair competition. The A&P answer to this was that the greater volume for which they were aiming would bring about lower costs, and hence justify their low prices. So it appeared to have turned out in the event, but apparently the government would have preferred more orthodox costing, i.e., prices based on actual and not on prospective costs. Unfortunately for A&P's own policy many of their local managers were apparently as orthodox in their approach as the government, and the company had the greatest difficulty in persuading its managers to adhere to its policy of low gross margins.

At the other extreme from these studies of oligopolistic industries is a study by Mead of the Douglas-fir lumber industry. Here, in spite of the fact that prices are generally negotiated between buyer and seller, Mead found that conditions prevailed which approximated to those of a perfect market. Prices changed from day to day as market conditions changed. Producers apparently believed that they faced a horizontal demand curve, and had no option but to sell at the market price. There were elements of oligopsony, especially in local purchases by large firms of federal timber, but, by and large, competition prevailed.

Other United States studies have been made of the Midwestern coal industry, copper, food manufacturing, agricultural processing, oil, carpets, electrical machinery, automotive parts, and public utilities such as railroads. One of the major recent studies of pricing in private industry was that carried out by the Brookings Institution and published in 1958 under the authorship of Kaplan, Dirlam and Lanzillotti. Their material was derived from case studies, based on a series of interviews with top management in 1948–51 originally, but subsequently brought up to date. The firms studied were all large ones, and covered a wide variety of industries, including primary production and distribution, as well as manufacturing. General points to emerge were that it was difficult for those interviewed to analyse pricing as a separate process distinct from other policy decisions. It was also found that most of the top executives interviewed did not concern themselves with pricing details: these were delegated to lower levels of management. Large multiproduct companies did not necessarily pursue similar policies in all parts of their business, since circumstances differed from product to product; thus a general policy covering the business as a whole might have to be interpreted differently in different branches of it.

In analysing company pricing policy the authors differentiated between five main types of price policy, giving examples of each. These were pricing to achieve a target return on investment (e.g., General Motors), stabilisation of price and margin (e.g., United States Steel), pricing to maintain or improve market position (e.g., A&P), pricing to meet or follow competition (e.g., Goodyear Tire and Rubber), and pricing related to product differentiation, *i.e.*, different policies for different products (e.g., American Can). These categories were not seen as necessarily being mutually exclusive: they were devised in an attempt to characterise very broadly the predominant policies pursued by firms studied.

In summarising the major influences on the pricing policies of big businesses, Kaplan, Dirlam and Lanzillotti stressed the importance of the character of the product, and the place that a particular product occupied in the product mix. They also emphasised the different pricing objectives of companies, many of which had become traditional. Price and nonprice competition were found to be closely linked, especially in firms relying on service for their products or on product styling. Advertising or style changes were not, however, looked upon as alternatives to price change but as part of the whole competitive "package." Some new products were found to be priced high to begin with, and then lowered in price, while others were found to maintain their initial price (which might be set lower than the initial price under the other policy). In some companies the antitrust laws were found to be an important influence on price, especially if the company had already been involved in antitrust proceedings. Alcoa, American Can and A&P had all been affected this way. The Robinson–Patman Act had tended to reduce discounts for quantity, and the cement antitrust decision had thrown doubts on basing-point systems of pricing. There was even a suggestion that product differentiation had been encouraged as an alternative to policies of price collusion, on the one hand, or "unfair" prices, on the other, both of which could have been vulnerable on antitrust grounds.

Leadership was another factor found to enter into price policy: its responsibilities as well as its market-dominating aspects. "Administered prices" tended to be adopted by large firms to ensure stability in their industry, to avoid price wars in depression and to prevent price rises in booms. Standard-cost systems provide a rationalisation for such pricing policies, although they were only one of the factors involved. However, not all firms, it was found, could always achieve their pricing objectives in difficult times, while others, such as Swift, considered themselves to a considerable extent at the mercy of market forces. What finally emerges from this study of big business, according to its authors,

> is an inability to fit their price policies into a common category . . . in pricing as in other aspects of big business operation, the stable solution is far from having been attained. There is no apparent slackening in the rate of presentation to management of new situations . . . to compel periodic re-thinking and readjustment of company policy and of pricing as an inescapable part thereof.

Finally, mention must be made of a study by Earley, published in 1956, which came to some interesting conclusions. Earley confined his attention to "excellently managed companies," as listed by the American Institute of Management. He got 110 of these companies to complete questionnaires designed to throw light on the extent to which they followed marginalist policies. Marginal accounting and costing principles were found to have a strong hold among these companies, and the bulk followed pricing, marketing, and new product policies that were in essential respects marginalist: as one example, higher profits were normally aimed for in the early years of the life of a new product. Earley reported a widespread distrust of full-cost principles among these firms, and the pursuit of marginalist policies in both the long and the short term. "Marginalism-on-the-wing" is how Earley described their general attitude. The suspicion must arise that Earley simply found what he was looking for, but his study carries conviction, especially as it is widely recognised that sophisticated costing systems are a feature of many large and successful firms—and not only in the United States.

Monopoly and Price Control

This survey has concentrated on the pricing behaviour of private firms in normal market situations. It is not the intention to try to deal here with the very wide area of public control or setting of prices. But it seems desirable to say something briefly on this subject, partly because the official bodies concerned have provided a mass of evidence on pricing, and partly because price behaviour itself may well be affected by public policy in these areas.

Monopoly, or antitrust, policy has, it is generally thought, had an appreciable influence on the nature of competition in many sectors of United States industry. The basic situation is that, following the Sherman, Clayton and other Acts, price collusion is per se illegal, price discrimination is suspect and the collective enforcement of resale price maintenance is forbidden. It is a misdemeanour to attempt to monopolise. Price behaviour has figured prominently in numerous cases brought by the antitrust division of the Department of Justice and by the Federal Trade Commission. These cases comprise a voluminous literature, and cover every conceivable variety of pricing behaviour. In Britain, on the other hand, monopoly policy is of much more recent origin, at least in its present form. Even so, the reports of the Monopolies Commission, and of cases in the Restrictive Practices Court, cover a wide field. The legal situation is different from that in the United States, in that price agreements are not in themselves illegal.

Be that as it may, these monopoly investigations undoubtedly reveal a considerable variety of pricing practices. They also give some insight into what those responsible for carrying out monopoly policy consider to be a justifiable price policy. Put crudely, it is a policy which aims to give no more than a reasonable (i.e., average) return on capital, with a higher target rate being justified for special risk, for special merit in innovation or for some other desirable aspect of performance. In a sense, the impression is given that what is thought desirable is that prices should be based on the full-cost principle, interpreted as including a "fair" profit margin only. The marginal principle is not necessarily objected to—indeed, it may explicitly be commended—for individual pricing decisions, but the end-result should be fair profits only.

The same type of consideration seems to apply to bodies concerned with price control. War-time price controls were almost all based on the notion of price reflecting costs, plus a fair profit margin. The same principle, in broad outline, was espoused in Britain by the National Board for Prices and Incomes, although in a more sophisticated form. However, we are concerned today with a state of affairs where costs and prices are continually moving upwards. Bodies such as the National Board for Price and Incomes were concerned primarily, in their pricing work, with whether price increases were justified in the light of cost increases. This led them (especially in view of their terms of reference) to study how far costs could be brought down as an alternative to prices being raised, and this was considered in all their reports on proposed increases in price.

Where it is suggested that prices should be based on long-run marginal costs, some appropriate rate of return on capital has to be assumed. This is because long-run marginal cost includes the cost of new investment needed in the long-run, and this must earn some minimum rate of return on the capital to be employed. This rate of return must clearly be a "reasonable" one if it is to be approved. The difference between this and the full-cost approach lies in the particular costs to be chosen on which prices are to be based, not on the level of profits assumed. The results may be very different in practice. Where marginal costs are below previous average costs, a price based on marginal costs may imply a very low profit on past capital, and it may even imply a loss.

Public Utility Pricing

In the United States, among many other countries, there has also been a long history of regulation of public utility pricing through the agency of such bodies as the Federal Communications Commission. This whole question is an extensive one, with a large body of literature in North America, France, and elsewhere. This must be regarded as largely "another subject" from the point of view of the present survey, and it cannot be pursued adequately here. It is, however, probably worth mentioning the current orthodoxy in Britain, as laid down by the government in a White Paper published in 1967. The first principle is that nationalised industries should normally set prices so as to cover their accounting costs in full. But cross-subsidisation is not generally desirable, and the consumer should pay the "true costs" of providing the goods and services that he consumes. Where there is spare capacity, however, prices may be set so as to cover escapable costs only. Similarly, in industries with peak-load problems prices should be low off-peak and high on-peak, where this is administratively feasible: two-part tariffs are commended in such cases. Another principle is that prices should be related to costs at the margin, in the long-run as well as the short-run. Long-run marginal costs include provision for the replacement of fixed assets, together with a "satisfactory" rate of return on the new capital employed. This rate of return is expressed as a minimum test of discount on new low-risk projects: the original rate of 8 percent was raised to 10 percent in August 1969. A final principle is that prices may be set below costs for social reasons, but the government would consider granting subsidies in such cases.

These principles are the outcome of the long post-war discussions among economists on the correct pricing principles for publicly owned enterprises. They are not often suggested for private firms, partly perhaps because these are less likely to be natural monopolies, but mainly because it would be difficult to advocate pricing policies which might involve private firms in heavy book losses. Even the principles advocated for public enterprises reflect the debate among economists only crudely. In particular, they ignore almost completely the problem of the second best, although it is obvious that the economy in general is not working in first-best conditions. In advocating first-best solutions, the Government is not, of course, unaware of the second-best problem, but it presumably takes the view that it is better to aim at the first best, and make allowance for exceptions, than to formulate much more complicated principles, or even to admit that in the present state of economic knowledge no clear principles can be formulated at all.

Marginal-cost pricing was not unknown to British public utilities long before the latest set of principles was formulated. The electricity industry in particular has long had a two-part or multi-part tariff, even though extreme types of marginal pricing—for example, the time-of-day tariff advocated by Little—have not generally been adopted. The coal industry, on the other hand, has pursued a policy much closer to average-cost pricing, with high-cost pits subsidising low-cost pits. At the same time, however, it has attempted to lower costs at the margin by its extensive programme of closures of high-cost pits.

The obvious lesson derived from it is that micro studies of pricing must always be treated with the greatest reserve.

Wholesale and Retail Pricing

This is another subject which can be discussed only briefly. It cannot, however, be ignored, since wholesale and retail margins play a large part in the makeup of the prices paid by consumers.

A distinguishing feature of the wholesale and retail trades is that typically the cost of the goods they buy represents a high proportion of their total costs. The common method of pricing is to add a gross margin to the purchase price to arrive at the selling price. This gross margin is usually similar on similar classes of goods, but, as writers like Jefferys have shown, it may vary greatly between classes of goods. The gross-margin method of pricing is used partly because the cost of handling any particular commodity cannot be calculated separately, since distribution is one of the classic cases of joint costs. Margins differ between different classes of goods for several reasons: their price level; the service they require; the length of time they remain in stock; their perishability; and so on. It can be shown that there is a close relationship between these factors, which determine the level of distributive costs on different goods, and the gross margins commonly added.

Much of the empirical work on retail prices and margins has been carried out in the context of the debate on resale price maintenance, but it has proved difficult to arrive at convincing answers in a field where one is principally attempting to come to conclusions about the prevalence of excess capacity. Other empirical work has been carried out in the context of antitrust policy, as was seen in the discussion of the A&P company earlier. The A&P policy, of setting low prices in an attempt to expand volume and to lower costs, has been characteristic of many participants in the supermarket revolution in Britain in recent years. Here again, however, pricing cannot be separated from other competitive strategies, for example, the policy of standardised "own-brand" commodities in firms such as Marks and Spencer and Sainsbury, in clothing and food respectively.

Taxation and Pricing

Another way of investigating the setting of retail prices is to consider the impact on these prices of taxes on commodities. Nearly every textbook contains a discussion on this subject, illustrated usually with the help of demand and supply curves. It is shown that the less elastic the demand and the more elastic the supply, the more likely it is that such a tax will be passed on in full. In a world where the demand and supply curves of retailers are not widely known, even to the retailers themselves, it is far from easy to discover exactly what the effects on prices of particular commodity taxes are. Superficially it would appear that taxes are passed on in full: for example, when the purchase tax is raised prices seem normally to be raised by the full amount of the increase. What is not so evident is how far the increase is fully passed on in the long run. Where it is difficult to sell adequate quantities at the new price, action may be taken to reduce costs and eventually to make some reduction in price. Or a new type of product may be put on the market which costs less to produce, and which retails, including tax, at a lower price than the previous product. Although it seems rare for tax increases not to be passed on in full at the time they are made, this may occur in difficult market situations. Devices may also be adopted to delay the increase, for example, by selling quantities of the commodity in question on which the old lower tax has allegedly been paid.

In the long run, costs may be raised by a tax, in comparison to what they would have been, because economies of scale have not proved possible to achieve. It has even been argued (especially by manufacturers) that the increase in average short-run costs, because taxation has reduced volume, leads to prices being raised in the short run by *more* than the increase in tax, but there is little evidence for this extreme type of full-cost behaviour. In general, it is probable that commodity taxation is less likely to affect prices through costs in the short run than in the long run.

The empirical evidence on this question is neither extensive nor conclusive. The Richardson committee conducted an inquiry among a number of large businesses. Almost all those questioned in manufacturing and distribution denied that they took profits tax into account in pricing, at least in any direct way. One witness thought that an increase in the tax might lead to a hardening of attitude to prices, but that a reduction would not have a symmetrical effect in lowering prices. There was more support for the view that profits tax affected investment policy, and that higher taxes might lead to higher target prices at the planning stage. American studies by Krzyaniak and Musgrave give some support to the suggestion that the reaction to a change in profits tax may not be symmetrical, and that a reduction might not cause a fall in prices in the short run. Gordon, on the other hand, found no effect on prices in either direction in the short run, i.e., he found no shifting. Taking all the arguments and evidence together, the case for concluding that prices are significantly affected by profits tax changes in the short run is not strong, but the long-run effects on pricing, via investment, may be important. A rise in taxation may raise prices in the long run, while a fall may lower them. This effect will not be due to full-cost methods of pricing, but to a parallel effect on the side of investment—taking prospective profits *after* tax as the objective, and raising pretax target rates of profit when taxes go up.

Macro Studies of Pricing

By "macro" studies I mean in this context studies which do not rely on questionnaires and interviews with businessmen but which rely on the analysis of data, usually published data. Essentially these are statistical and econometric studies. In so far as they nearly always have to rely on inadequate data, and in so far as such studies are both difficult to carry out and open to economic and technical criticism, the conclusions drawn from them must be treated with reserve. Indeed, studies of the same problem quite often come to conflicting conclusions. Nevertheless, studies of this sort have an enormous advantage over the interview type, in that they are far more objective. They also make use of the wealth of data that exists on pricing and related subjects, and provide a most valuable check on other types of research.

These macro studies may be crudely divided into three groups. The first group, while it may use time series, is essentially concerned with the general relationship between market structure, profits, and prices. The second is concerned with how different types of market structure may affect changes over time in the behaviour of prices and profits. The third is not concerned with market structure at all but with movements over time in industrial prices, etc., particularly in periods of inflation. All three groups of studies are of interest in throwing light on the price behaviour of firms, but a problem connected with all of them is that the connection between costs and prices is so close that it is difficult to sort out specific price implications. It is easier to draw conclusions about profits, but these, although of course affected by prices, are also sensitive to movements in output and other variables.

The principal American study is that of Bain. He was concerned especially with barriers to entry, and his findings were briefly referred to above. Bain found that industries with very high entry barriers tended more towards high excess profits and monopolistic output restrictions than others. If product differentiation was an important entry barrier there was a tendency towards high sales promotion expenditure. Industries with somewhat lower entry barriers tended to be more workably competitive, but Bain found little difference between this group, which had "substantial" (but not "very high") barriers, and the group where entry barriers were "moderate to low." Seller concentration was found to be of some importance in explaining "good" or "bad" performance with groups with a given height of barrier to entry, but high seller concentration was particularly significant in its effect on performance when associated with high entry barriers. These findings of Bain, which are, of course, consistent with marginalist behaviour, were confirmed by Mann, using later data for 30 industries. Mann found a big difference in the average rate of profit between those industries where the eight largest firms accounted for over 70 percent of output and those where they accounted for less than 70 percent. He confirmed Bain's findings about the importance of barriers to entry, and found that industries with high barriers to entry and high seller concentration earned distinctly more than highly concentrated industries in other categories. High barriers to entry and high concentration tend, however, to be associated, and George, in examining Mann's results, has suggested that the degree of concentration *as such* may not contribute materially to the explanations of high profitability. The main factors, in his view, are barriers to entry and growth.

The importance of seller concentration on profits has also been investigated in the United States by Schwartzman, Weiss, Levinson, Fuchs, Stigler, and Collins and Preston, among others, although some of these studies were primarily concerned with changes over time. Not all the studies confirmed the finding that high seller concentration and high profits were correlated, but it is interesting that Stigler, after throwing some doubt on the connection in one study, found a positive association in a later study. Collins and Preston, in a survey of 32 food-manufacturing industries, found a curvilinear relationship which in their view strongly supported the hypothesis that there was a positive relationship between concentration and price-cost margins (i.e., the average gross margin as a percentage of average price). No systematic increases in margins accompanied increases in concentration at the lower levels of concentration, but beyond a point increasing concentration was associated with successively larger increases in price-cost margins. High capital-output ratios accounted for only part of the differences, and their conclusion—in contrast to studies such as that of George—was that concentration alone accounted for 50 percent of the variations found.

Comanor and Wilson tackled a somewhat different problem: the relationship between advertising, market structure and performance. They found that advertising appeared to be a highly profitable form of investment. Much of the difference found in profit rates between industries appeared to be explainable by high entry barriers, which were closely linked with high concentration. These entry barriers might have been created by advertising itself, but other entry barriers, such as high capital requirements and substantial economies of scale, also seemed to be important. The authors did not think it plausible to argue that high profits led to high advertising, rather than the reverse, and expenditure on advertising was found to be only weakly correlated with aspects of structure other than barriers to entry.

It is worth referring to a description by Bain of pricing behaviour in a number of oligopolistic industries during the 1930s. Bain was principally concerned with how far collusive conduct in these industries indicated the presence or otherwise of monopoly profits, and on this point he concluded that a study of conduct without a study of performance revealed very little. Of interest here, however, is his description of price "shading" (i.e., of selling below published prices) in the slump in such industries as petroleum and steel. This brings out the point that apparent price rigidities in oligopolistic industries over the trade cycle may conceal the truth, since published prices may be more stable than the actual prices charged. What really occurs is perhaps more likely to be brought out in statistical studies of the type we have been describing than in industry studies of the more conventional type.

The third and final group of studies to be considered are those concerned not primarily with market structure but with movements over time in prices, costs, and profits. This is a field less dominated than the last by work done in the United States. There is, however, a substantial National Bureau volume on the subject, written by Hultgren. He found that prices did not regularly rise and fall with sales, although before the Second World War price variations were more common. Profits fluctuated much more than prices, since they were affected not only by price changes but by changes in output, which affected unit costs as well as the volume of sales. Hultgren found that prices continued to rise as long as sales rose, and declined, if at all, towards the end of the contraction in sales. But price movements were less sharp than movements in costs. When price indices rose they did so much more often in the neighborhood of peaks of activity than of troughs. This suggests that demand influences may have played some direct part in influencing price movements.

Taken together, the studies cited in this section give strong support to the view that high barriers to entry and higher than average profitability go together, and that high seller concentration may also play a part. The evidence for differences of price behaviour over the trade cycle between industries with different degrees of seller concentration appears to be weak. Price behaviour over the cycle in manufacturing industry seems to be much more a function of the nature of the product sold and of changes in the level of costs. In the long run there is a strong negative association between movements in prices and in output per head. Any direct connection between prices and demand in a period of general inflation seems to be a weak one, although here there is rather more controversy among different authors. All agree that cost influences are much the most important factor, and it is, of course, well recognised that demand factors may influence costs, both of raw materials and of wages. A rise in costs might, however, be used as an excuse for a rise in profit margins, and some evidence does exist to suggest a direct influence of demand on price in manufacturing industry, although the effect is not a strong one. It has been found that price rises and falls do not occur frequently, and that, even at times of rising costs, the interval between price changes for any one product may be two years or more. The interval may be shorter, however, when costs are rising very steeply. There is no evidence for the general existence of extreme forms of administered pricing, such as the alleged practice of raising prices when costs rise but not reducing them when costs fall.

SUMMING-UP

An attempt must now be made to draw together the theoretical and empirical work on pricing that has been discussed, and to see whether some sort of coherent story emerges. Essentially, this means discussing price behaviour in manufacturing industry, but a little needs to be said about price behaviour in the distributive trades and in publicly owned undertakings.

It might be worth saying first that virtually no doubt has been cast on the fact that several sectors of the economy exist where firms have no real discretion over price. These sectors are not in manufacturing or the distributive trades but in the primary sector. We have seen an example of this in Mead's study of the Douglas-fir lumber industry. In markets such as these sellers have little or no influence over price in the short run. In the long run they influence price through their decisions about whether to remain in the industry or not, i.e., essentially through their investment decisions.

The prices of many primary products are, of course, now influenced by agreements between primary producing countries, for example, in tin and wheat, and also by national governments, so that monopoly elements enter into the pricing process. Also, some prices for primary products, for example, nickel and copper, are greatly influenced by large producing firms. The area in which prices are freely determined by market forces is therefore less wide than might be thought. But when there are a large number of small producers in a market they still have to act as price takers, even when the ruling price may have been influenced by an international commodity agreement. In many ways, also, *exports* of manufactured goods exhibit the same price characteristics as primary products, their prices varying with the state of world demand and supply.

Price behaviour becomes interesting when there is scope for discretion to be exercised by sellers, and this occurs par excellence in manufacturing industry and in public utilities, especially in sales to the home market. In such industries the classic preconditions for perfect competition are never fully satisfied. There are two few firms, products are differentiated, or market is broken up by transport and selling costs. Another problem is caused by the virtual absence of one-product firms, so that an individual firm may operate in several "industries." This makes the notion of some sort of industry equilibrium more difficult to accept than perhaps it once was. Up to a point, these departures from the idea of a perfectly competitive world have occurred because the world has indeed changed—for example, with the growth of large firms, both nationally and internationally. But the main factor is that it has become more and more evident, as analysis and empirical work have developed, that the world was never as simple as it was once represented to be. This last point applies also to some of the early ideas about imperfect competition. It can now be seen that not only is perfectly competitive pricing not widely applicable in manufacturing industry but also that notions of the pricing process derived from the original analysis of imperfect competition leave a great deal to be desired. Few, if any, writers now believe that the pricing behaviour described in Joan Robinson's *Economics of Imperfect Competition,* for example, is a literal description of what occurs in the real world: certainly Joan Robinson herself does not. In the course of time ideas on this whole subject have become more sophisticated, and controversy is now concerned not so much with black and white as with different shades of grey.

Nearly all the evidence supports the view that the home market prices of manufactured products tend to be stable for months or even years at a time. Exceptions occur when a raw material which fluctuates widely in price forms a high proportion of costs, and in such cases the price of the final product may change when that of the raw material changes appreciably. Apart from cases such as this, short-run price stability is the rule, and short-run demand changes do not normally affect price. When demand increases, output tends to be raised and stocks reduced, and if this still does not satisfy demand queues are formed or waiting lists drawn up. Profits rise, not primarily because profit margins are increased but because a given gross margin (i.e., the margin between price and prime costs) yields more and more surplus over prime costs as the quantity sold goes up, while overheads rise relatively little. Even those who argue that some increase in the gross margin is likely to occur at times of high demand would not, I think, deny that it is the increase in the volume of sales which is the prime cause of higher profits.

The evidence also supports the view that the main influence leading to price changes is a change in the level of costs, especially when this is general in its effects. One reason for a change in the level of costs is that the level of demand may change, and in this way demand may indirectly affect price. One of the questions raised in the literature is whether, when an increase in costs is passed on, this leads to an increase in price by the same proportion as the increase in costs or by its absolute amount. If the former occurred this would lead to a larger absolute gross margin than previously, and this would give higher profits (unless overhead costs had risen sufficiently to offset this effect). It has been suggested by Yordon that when wages increase, prices may be raised by the same proportion, but that when raw-material prices increase, prices may be raised by the same absolute amount. In retailing and wholesaling, where percentage gross margins are usual, it would seem to be common for prices to rise in the same proportion as costs. When purchase prices vary greatly over the seasons, or when excise duties are heavy, an absolute rather than a percentage margin may, however, be adopted.

It is at this point that one has to stop recording agreement and enter disputed territory. Indeed, a certain amount of what was said in the last paragraph is in dispute, since some would argue that cost changes are passed on to different degrees at different stages of the trade cycle by changes in percentage gross margins rather by the addition of a constant percentage gross margin to prime costs. The evidence does not support any flamboyant general use of this type of policy, but authors such as Hultgren have found some signs of its existence.

Before exploring such questions further, it is desirable to make some general remarks which are germane to the controversies that remain. It has become increasingly recognised, partly as a result of the work of the managerial and behavioural school of writers, that pricing decisions in manufacturing industry have to be looked at as only one of a set of interlinked policy decisions. Many other aspects of policy have to be considered, including policy towards the introduction of new products, towards advertising, towards actual and potential competitors, towards diversification and mergers, and towards investment and growth. Those taking decisions within the firm must do so in the light of all these considerations, explicitly or implicitly, as well as in the light of the market situation of the firm and the state of trade generally. The less pressing the external competitive situation, and the less the threat of takeover, the greater the degree of freedom open to the firm in coming to decisions on these policy matters, including price policy.

One of the questions that arises in this context is that of the identification of those responsible for policy. Much recent work has emphasised the importance of the manager, and has explored the possibility of his attempting to maximise his utility in a way that may not maximise the utility of his shareholders. Cyert and March have stressed that conflicts may arise within what they call the "organisational coalition," so that the outcome of any particular change in external circumstances may not be easily predictable. To predict what may occur, it may be necessary to know a great deal about the individuals and the circumstances involved. Other recent writers of the managerial school, such as Baumol, Williamson, and Marris, have been more inclined to make generalisations about managerial behaviour which have enabled them to make predictions, but they have all thrown doubt on any simple acceptance of static profit maximisation as an objective. They have stressed the importance of not allowing shareholders to become discontented on account of low profits and dividends, and have recognised that there must be some minimum profit constraint if takeovers, etc., are to be avoided. These and other authors have also emphasised the importance placed on the survival of the firm as an objective, and thus the importance of concentrating on long-run rather than short-run profits. Marris, indeed, has framed his theory in terms of the rate of growth of the firm, and has argued that the objective of managers will be to maximise this rate of growth, subject to a minimum profit constraint.

Several authors, notably Simon, have concentrated attention on uncertainty, and on the costs of obtaining information. Simon has suggested that "satisficing" rather than maximising is the best that one can hope to achieve. Indeed, the very notion of profit maximisation has become an ambiguous one when uncertainty and growth have been brought into the picture. Another consideration stressed by the behavioural and managerial schools has been the extent to which a firm's costs may be discretionary, and can thus be reduced if the need to do so is sufficiently great. The concept of "organisational slack" has been introduced to focus attention on this point.

As Williamson has admitted, the analysis of the behavioural and managerial writers has not produced many detailed implications for price behaviour as opposed to other aspects of the behaviour of the firm. It has, however, drawn attention to the process by which pricing and other decisions are taken, and has stressed the need for decisions which reconcile multiple objectives, including those of the managers of the firm as well as of its shareholders, its labour force and others affected by it.

In the light of the work of these writers, the psychological assumptions of the full-cost school now look almost as naïve as those of the marginalist school. It is also clear that both schools omit many important considerations from their analysis. But, even so, the broad controversy between the full-cost and the marginalist writers has not been rendered irrelevant by the modern theorists of the firm. Whatever one says about internal pressures in the firm, the motivation of those taking decisions in it, and the composition and ownership of its assets, the external situation of a firm still appears to be of great importance.

The evidence certainly suggests that many of the predictions of the marginalist school (supplemented by the work on barriers to entry) are borne out in practice. There is in the first place ample proof (especially arising from antitrust proceedings) of a wide variety of monopolistic pricing practices and of high profit margins in protected situations. Price discrimination is widespread, as is the practice with firms of taking very different margins on different products. A number of writers have also pointed to the prevalence of "vintage" pricing, i.e., the charging of higher prices in the early years of the life of a product than in its later years. Earley has found evidence for marginal influences on the pricing and other policies of his "excellently managed" companies. The studies of Bain and others have strongly suggested higher profit margins when entry barriers and (less certainly) seller concentration are high. Some empirical studies have suggested a widening of profit margins at times of high demand, although this seems to be done with discretion when it is done at all.

As against this, writers such as Barback have argued for the existence of full-cost behaviour, although I think it is true to say that there is now much less support than formerly for full-cost views, except in rather sophisticated forms. But behaviour such as that suggested by Weiss, who found more profit taking in competitive markets than in concentrated markets in the period immediately after the Second World War, is certainly not implausible.

These and other findings suggest that it may be desirable, in any discussion of price behaviour, to make certain important distinctions in addition to those that are usually made. Three in particular suggest themselves. The first is a distinction between different classes of firms, based on the sophistication of their costing systems and of their management generally. This is not necessarily the same as the distinction between large and small firms, though it may approximate very roughly to it. The point of making this distinction is to suggest that the prevalence of otherwise of "marginalist" pricing behaviour may depend to a considerable extent on how good a costing system is employed. As Earley's "excellently managed" firms spread their empires, as they seem likely to do, the sectors where firms think in terms of full costs may become smaller and smaller.

The second distinction concerns the different stages of the life of an industry and the firms within it. In the early days of an industry the competitive situation is likely to be fluid, with high rewards for many firms but considerable instability. As time goes on, the market may well become less buoyant, and the possibility of various types of warfare, including price warfare, more likely. Once the number of firms in the industry has become more or less settled, each will have learned a good deal about the others, and tacit collusion may be practised. It is in this situation of "mature oligopoly" that full-cost behaviour would seem most likely to exist. The situation may not remain stable, however. An existing firm may develop a new product, or may acquire an aggressive manager, or a powerful firm outside the "industry" may enter it. If the situation changes in this fashion price instability may be one of the ways in which the general instability in the industry manifests itself.

The third distinction is that between different historical periods. The studies cited in the present survey have related to three periods of time: the relatively depressed period before the Second World War; the boom that followed the war and lasted until the mid-1950s; and the period of less steady growth, with occasional set-backs, since then. The circumstances and opportunities of these periods have differed widely, and there is some evidence to suggest differences in price behaviour as a result of this.

The prevalence of "marginalist" behaviour may depend therefore on a wide variety of factors, including those just discussed. But the evidence does not give general support to extreme forms of short-run marginalist behaviour in pricing on the home market. There are a number of reasons why this should be so, and why the often superficial impression is given that full-cost methods of pricing are prevalent in manufacturing industry. In part the explanation is administrative: it takes a long time to change a complicated price list, and to make the change known. In part it is the result of uncertainty about the future or the reaction of competitors; of the ambition of managers to keep prices down so that their firms may grow; of the adoption of safer forms of competitive behaviour than price competition, and of a fear of antitrust or other government regulatory activities.

It is important, however, not to forget that competitive forces may sometimes be strong, especially in the long run. A concentration on monopoly or oligopoly situations tends to draw attention away from the many possible sources of competition in western economies. Even under oligopoly, there are many instances of similar prices being charged by firms with very different costs. There is also the possibility of firms entering "industries" other than their traditional ones, either because of the attraction of high profits or because of a desire to diversify in order to grow. Given this threat of entry, many apparently monopolistic firms, or firms which dominate oligopolistic markets, may be restrained in their pricing and profit behaviour. Here Bain's findings that once one departs from industries with high barriers to entry, there is little difference in profitability between groups with "substantial" barriers to entry and groups with "moderate to low" entry barriers, may be of significance. The idea of industry equilibrium in the Chamberlinian sense may now be suspect, but there may still be justification, on the evidence before us, for regarding many sectors of manufacturing industry as "workably" competitive in the long-run.

There is not much that needs to be said here about wholesale and retail pricing. Apart from the fact that the use of gross margins for arriving at selling prices is more prevalent than in manufacturing, the same type of considerations apply. In this sector monopoly is conferred partly by location, but competition between large concerns in town centres and between them and suburban stores sets limits on the extent to which monopoly pricing is practicable. The prevalence of taxes on commodities, with frequent changes in their rates, gives many opportunities for observing price behaviour in response to these changes, but even so, there is much uncertainty about the effect of commodity and other related taxes on retail prices. The study carried out in the Department of Applied Economics at Cambridge on the effects of the selective employment tax has provided useful evidence on this.

Pricing by publicly owned bodies has been mentioned only briefly in this survey as being somewhat outside its scope. The subject of interest in the present context, however, since the pricing rules laid down by governments and other agencies express some sort of pricing ideal as seen by these authorities. These rules, in Britain at least, are a mixture of average and marginal-cost considerations. Much importance is placed on basing prices as far as possible on long-run marginal costs, i.e., on costs of production in a new plant using the most modern techniques. But the rules also say that investment in new plant should be undertaken only if a test rate of discount can be achieved; since this test rate must be earned, it enters into the calculation of long-run marginal cost. Thus pricing policy and investment policy are intimately connected. This is a point of more general application. Joan Robinson has argued that "to behave monopolistically in the long period sense, means to pursue a cautious investment policy, restraining the growth of capacity relatively to demand." As several antitrust cases have shown, such a policy is not unknown, although it is unlikely to be favoured by Marris-type managers.

Among sectors omitted altogether from this survey have been construction, road transport, services other than distribution, and nonproduced goods, such as second-hand cars, existing houses, and land. Nor has much been said about the pricing of "one-of" products, or products made in small quantities to special order. My excuse for these omissions is partly a lack of published evidence and partly the need to keep the survey to a manageable length.

Other gaps in the present survey are due to the fact that future work needs to be done on pricing, of both an empirical and theoretical nature. It will be evident from what has been said earlier that I am no great believer in what I have called "micro" studies of pricing: studies of the Hall and Hitch or the Barback type, for example. My own experience in the steel industry is only one reason why I hold this view. On the other hand, there is, I think, more to be said for inquiries of the type suggested by Baumol and Quant, into "rules of thumb" laid down by firms for arriving at prices, or into other specific instructions, if such can be found, which are used to determine actual rather than "desired" prices. Computer simulations of market behaviour may also yield interesting insights into the forces making for stability or instability in different types of market situation. Most useful would, in my view, be further studies of a "macro" nature, i.e., investigations of a statistical or econometric type into the relationships that can be deduced from movements in costs, prices, profits, and so on. A number of studies of this kind have been quoted, but many have been concerned primarily with the effect of concentration and monopoly on price, and few with the behaviour of prices in conditions of inflation, or in response to changes in taxes on commodities. More work of this latter type would, I think, be very useful. It would also be of considerable interest if it were possible for such work to be carried out at the level of the firm, and of particular products made by the firm. Such studies would not be easy to devise, and could only be undertaken with the help of data produced by firms, whereas "macro" studies of the type normally carried out have referred to large numbers of firms and have relied mainly on published data. These studies have the advantage of objectivity, but too often give a misleading appearance of uniformity to what is in fact a complex reality.

More needs to be done also in the field of price theory and the theory of the firm generally. To a considerable extent the main ingredients are already to hand, but they have not been welded into a coherent whole, even by such authors as Marris and Williamson. The theory of the firm as depicted in the textbooks is not, in my view, as inadequate as it is often alleged to be, but it is nevertheless both incomplete and relatively unsophisticated. This applies particularly to the theory of imperfect competition. The theory of perfect competition can be said to be an intellectual whole, even though it is static and its practical application is disputable. The theory of imperfect competition, on the other hand, is either so schematic as to be of relatively little practical interest or so piecemeal and detailed that no clear picture emerges. Perhaps the task is impossible—as has been seen, the number of variables to be considered is extremely large—but one cannot help feeling that some further progress could be made. Theories of monopolistic competition and oligopoly, of barriers to entry, of multipleproduct output, of managerial motivation and behaviour, of asset holding and stock-market constraints, of technical progress and growth: all these need to be brought into the picture, and their implications for pricing and other aspects of behaviour made clear.

Perhaps it would be appropriate to conclude by considering again the quotation from Williamson given earlier. He said, it may be remembered, that perhaps it was not too great a criticism of managerial models that they could not produce detailed implications for price behaviour, "since price making is surely of subordinate importance to such matters as economic efficiency and equity, on which managerial models yield important . . . implications." Leaving aside the point about managerial models, is Williamson correct in playing down the importance of price making? It may scarcely behoove the author of a survey of price behaviour to say so, but there is much in what Williamson says. As has been frequently stressed here, price policy is one aspect only of the competitive behaviour of the firm, and looked at alone gives a partial picture. It is, of course, of considerable interest and importance in its own right, but since it is only part of the story, it perhaps merits rather less attention than has traditionally been devoted to it. What is most important is to concentrate attention on attempts to study and evaluate the overall performance of firms, and to discover under what conditions, and with the help of which stimuli, their overall economic efficiency is likely to be fostered.

20. Pricing Practices in Small Firms*

W. WARREN HAYNES

An advance in our knowledge of the price mechanism requires research into the pricing practices of individual firms. Recent studies have extended our knowledge of pricing in large firms, though they leave considerable disagreement about the interpretation of the findings. Pricing in small firms is a relatively neglected subject. This article tries to fill in part of this gap by summarizing the main findings of an extensive study of small business pricing.

The study is based on intensive interviews with the officials of 88 small firms. The firms include 26 retailers, 6 wholesalers, 21 service outlets, 28 manufacturers, 5 garden or landscape nurseries, and 2 combined retail and service firms. The study makes use of an interview and case approach, rather than the structural questionnaire technique. It tries to overcome the tendency to accept the initial responses of company officials as valid by follow-up interviews at later dates and by cross-checks on the responses of different officials. Throughout an attempt is made to uncover the deeper reasons for the pricing decisions, rather than to take at face value all of the rationalizations of practice which are likely to show up in interviews.

Earlier studies suggest the central issues requiring investigation, which include: (1) The extent to which measurements of full cost influence pricing; (2) the extent to which demand considerations, including the policies of competitors, influence pricing; (3) the extent to which the observed pricing processes are consistent with the assumptions and tenets of "marginalism"; (4) the extent to which the objective of the firms is maximum profits or, alternatively, a target return or a mixture of other goals; (5) the flexibility of prices or price formulas with changing conditions over time, an issue closely related to that of marginalism but not synonymous with it; (6) the extent of trial and error in pricing; and (7) the appropriate classification of these firms by market structure, including the influence of market structure.

* *The Southern Economic Journal,* vol. 30, no. 4 (April 1964), pp. 315–24.

The procedure in the sections that follow is to start with the simpler issues: ones that can be answered clearly and directly on the basis of the interviews. These include the fairly objective questions about flexibility and the use of full cost. It will then be possible to move on to the more complex and nebulous issues, such as pricing objectives and the relevance of marginalism.

I. FULL-COST PRICING—A VARIETY OF DEFINITIONS

A recent and generally excellent book on managerial economics expresses a widely accepted view that cost-plus pricing (or full-cost pricing) predominates in business.[1] The present study lends no support to this conclusion as far as small business is concerned. In fact, the conclusion is the opposite: full-cost pricing is the exception rather than the rule.

Part of the disagreement on full-cost pricing arises from a general failure to define what it means. At least three different definitions are implicit in the literature, with frequent unannounced shifts from one definition to the next.

(1) An extreme definition restricts full-cost pricing to the addition of a single predetermined markup to full cost for all goods sold. This definition recognizes a variety of measurements of cost, such as the cost accountant's "standard cost" (including unit overhead at some arbitrary percentage of capacity), or recent actual costs, or costs expected in the coming year. In any case the method for determining cost is specified in advance and a predetermined markup is added.

(2) Multi-product firms predominate even in small business; among the 88 firms in our study, 84 produce or sell a variety of products or services. They apply different markups on different segments of their business. A second definition of full-cost pricing recognizes this use of different markups on various sectors of the business. The base for the markup is standard, actual, or estimated cost, and the markups are still predetermined, but the markups vary from sector to sector within the firm. The pricing procedure is mechanical. Some discussions suggest that the markups are based on what is considered "fair" or "reasonable," which may in turn reflect what is customary. Ethical considerations are claimed to compete with profit maximization as an influence on pricing. One of the issues in this article is the extent of such mechanical markups on full costs in small business.

(3) A third definition of full-cost pricing recognizes not only the cross-sectional flexibility of markups just cited but also flexibility over time. Many firms do use full cost as the starting point but vary the markups according to current competitive conditions.

[1] Milton H. Spencer and Louis Siegelman, *Managerial Economics* (Homewood, Ill.: Richard D. Irwin, 1959), p. 292.

The question is whether we can still call the procedure full-cost pricing when such flexibilities appear. It is clear that in such cases pricing is no longer mechanical and that it no longer is in such direct opposition to the usual descriptions of economic theory. The literature on pricing appears to have been caught up in an unusual amount of semantic confusion, with the use of the label "full-cost pricing" to cover a wide variety of behavior.

The findings in the present study include at most six cases of the first variety of full-cost pricing (a single markup on full cost). They include a few additional cases of the second variety (in which several sets of markups are applied to cost with little flexibility over time). They include many more cases in the third category, which permits both cross-sectional flexibility and flexibility over time. And they include still other cases which do not fit into the full-cost framework at all. The findings do not lend much support to the view that full-cost pricing prevails.

Full Cost plus a Single Predetermined Markup

Most of the six companies in this category raise some difficult points of interpretation. The best way to proceed is to cite cases from the study.

Three printing companies represent extreme full-cost pricing. Leading firms and trade associations in the printing industry have long attempted to restrict "cutthroat competition" through a wider adoption of full-cost pricing. Many printers have developed strong ethical objections to "chiseling" by those who shade price. But, as we shall see, it does not follow that all printers, or even a majority of them, avoid flexible pricing practices. The three cases cited here are the ones showing the strictest adherence to formula pricing and the greatest reluctance to make exceptions.

The first of these three printing firms operates on a policy of full cost plus 20 percent. Not all of the costs are determined internally; frequently cost information is obtained from nationally published manuals which provide regional cost data, though these are checked against company experience. The company tries to avoid price differentials, except to the extent that large quantities result in lower unit costs. But even in this extreme case of full-cost pricing, there are exceptions. For example, the markup is only 10 percent on envelopes and letterheads. The management claims that it would lose this business at higher prices and that it must maintain such lines as a service to customers. Thus the elasticity of demand does have an influence on the outcome; cost measurements do not tell the entire story.

Another printing firm follows an even more rigid full-cost policy. Paradoxically, demand conditions appear to account for the ability to apply the cost formula rigidly. The firm has a reputation for high quality and dependability, which protects the firm from competition. The management states that, "We are slightly higher in price and could go even higher because of the quality of work," indicating that in management's view the demand is inelastic.

The last printer in this category is such an extreme full-cost advocate that he insists that he would charge more in poor times because of the higher overhead per unit. So far he has not faced the decline in demand that would test his implausible policy. This printer is not, however, a consistent full-cost pricer, for he lowers markups to secure new customers or in submitting competitive bids.

One furniture company appears to be a rigid practitioner of full-cost pricing. Oddly this company sells its product on a bidding basis that would seem to preclude rigid formulas. But "bidding" in this case does not mean competitive bidding. Certain large customers seek a bid from this single furniture firm and will accept the bid if it is within reason. Again demand conditions (the firm has no difficulty in selling capacity production) help account for the rigid policies, though it is not completely clear why the firm does not try to exploit the favorable demand more fully.

Space limitations preclude outlining the other two cases in detail. It is even doubtful that the last case (a flour mill) belongs in this category, for the management sets prices at full cost (material cost, plus labor cost, plus a percentage for overhead, plus a predetermined percent for profit) only if the resultant price is not more than 5 percent above the general market.

In conclusion, "pure" cases of full-cost pricing are hard to find. Most of the firms cited in this section do make exceptions, though mechanical formulas have an influence on their pricing. Evidence of demand influences appears in even these most extreme cost oriented cases.

Full Cost plus Multiple Predetermined Markups

We are now concerned with a special variety of multiple markups on full cost: predetermined markups which are changed only occasionally over time. We are dealing with cross-sectional flexibility with little flexibility over time. Only five firms fit into this category.

One concrete contractor quotes its prices to builders on a straight full-cost basis. This firm is a member of a cartel and full-cost pricing is apparently a device to limit price competition. In fact, on other lines of business (to homeowners, for example), the firm varies price according to conditions of demand and in slack times even goes below full cost on small jobs to keep employees busy.

A machine shop applies different markups on various categories of work. Its manager makes no price reductions to induce sales or reduce inventories in poor times, nor does he take advantage of the semi-monopoly position in the locality on bronze and stainless steel. The fact that he uses round number prices (20¢, 25¢, and 30¢ per pound rather than 18¢, 23¢, 27¢, etc.) is not a fundamental departure from his cost-plus policy, though it does result in variable markups.

Three of the automobile repair shop managers claim not to adjust markups to temporary demand shifts or to differences in demand elasticities (a fourth case to be discussed later is a clear case of flexibility in markups carefully adjusted to conditions). These officials refer to national manuals on parts prices that provide predetermined markups; they also obtain standard times from such manuals for charging labor time and overhead. We suspect that further research might reveal a more flexible use of price discrimination than the managers indicated in the interviews. But even if we give the benefit of the doubt to full-cost pricing, we still find that cases of mechanical formula pricing are the exception.

Full Cost plus Variable Markups

At least twenty of the cases fall clearly into the third category. These firms compute full costs but are flexible in adapting the markups on these costs to circumstances. Space permits a discussion of only a few cases.

At one end of a continuum of flexibility is a printing company which would prefer to avoid flexibility but which makes exceptions. This firm computes hourly machine rates based on estimated total labor costs and allocated overhead. It combines these rates with time standards to arrive at the cost of the particular job. Management uses "judgment" in modifying these estimates and also in determining the appropriate markup; this judgment reflects demand conditions, including the current volume of business. This firm recognizes five classes of business, each with a different markup, but does not always adhere to this schedule of markups. The managers of this printing firm resist lowering the markups below those appropriate to the class of business. They believe that reduced prices: (1) depress market prices and reduce industry profits; (2) offend regular customers; (3) may, when used to fill in idle times, result in a bunching of business that slows down the flow of regular price business; and (4) represent an unethical form of competition. But the management is perfectly willing to provide extra services (such as free editorial time) at no cost.

Managers of most of the other firms are less hesitant about varying markups as conditions warrant. In several furniture firms, for example, they recognize the need to vary markups as the market shifts or as a particular line loses popularity. One automobile repair shop owner exhibits great ingenuity in varying markups on cost, giving better deals to classes of customers who seek competitive bids and who watch the estimates carefully. A builder charges a lower markup when business is slow, reflecting the lower "opportunity cost" of his time in slack periods. A chemicals manufacturer tries to charge what "the traffic will bear," taking into account the volumes he can sell at various prices. On old established products he follows the prices of his large competitors rather closely. On new products he charges higher prices reflecting his greater monopoly control.

Further illustrations would merely elaborate on the flexible way in which firms use full-cost data. The evidence does not suggest the mechanical use of formulas but instead considerable judgment in determining what markups should be added to the costs.

II. FULL COSTS AS REFERENCE OR RESISTANCE POINTS

The argument so far is clear: The use of full costs may be mechanical in a minority of small firms but permits considerable flexibility in pricing in the great majority of cases. Past literature on the subject has too readily leaped to the conclusion that the mere use of full costs must mean that pricing is cost oriented. The majority of the cases in this study (and, despite the limitations of the sample, no doubt the majority of small firms in the nation) adjust prices to the changing market environment. Can we conclude from these cases that full costs are irrelevant? Such a position is too extreme. Many (probably most) firms are influenced by their measures of full cost. In some firms full costs act as resistance points below which prices are not permitted to fall.

Again a few cases will illustrate. One dry cleaning and laundry firm was willing to cut price to full cost but refused to accept business below that point. The firm had an opportunity to obtain some additional business from motels in the slow summer months at prices below full cost but above incremental cost. Incremental reasoning indicated to the research worker that the business would add profits, without any undesiraable repercussions in the future. But management believed that accepting business below full cost was unsound, though it could give no reasons for this position.

Similarly, a sheet metal and air conditioning contractor lost a large order (one that management agreed on incremental grounds would add to profits), because of a refusal to go below full cost. The management is willing to shade the markup and even lower salaries to get business, but is not willing to extend flexibility below the full cost limit.

The interviews suggest that even when full cost is not a rigid floor, as it is in the two cases just cited, it exerts an influence on pricing.

The fact that firms so frequently refer to full costs, that they claim to price on the basis of those costs even when follow-up interviews suggest other, perhaps more powerful, influences must mean that the cost estimates have an influence on the final outcome.

It should be mentioned that a firm with hundreds of pricing decisions may find reference to full cost a convenient simplification. The manager may use a great deal of analysis or judgment in determining the markup on one class of goods, but once he has made the decision on markup he can apply it mechanically to individual items. Much of the confusion about pricing results from a failure to recognize two steps in pricing: (1) Determination of a schedule of markups with attention to market forces as well as tradition. (2) Application of full-cost formulas to individual items.

The difficulty in much of the literature on pricing is an insistence on a black-or-white dichotomy between firms that use full costs mechanically and those that follow the precepts of marginalism. The majority of small firms undoubtedly fall somewhere between, demonstrating flexibility when the penalties of rigidity are great but finding it "comfortable" to lean back on a simple formula when the pressure is off. Furthermore, even the mechanical use of full costs may not be in conflict with marginalism when it represents a reasonable adaptation to the market structure or to uncertainty.

III. PRICING WITH NO REFERENCE TO FULL COST

Almost half of the companies made no use of full-cost computations at all. While the nature of the sample would warn against taking the exact number of such firms too seriously, there can be no doubt that a wide segment of small business lies completely outside the scope of the full-cost pricing category.

The most important reason for ignoring costs in these firms is that "cost" is sometimes difficult to determine. Five garden and landscaping firms illustrate this point. What is the cost of growing a particular shrub? An answer would require an estimate of the rental on the land, some way of dealing with the uncertainties of the weather and growing conditions, methods for allocating not only the fixed costs but also most of the labor cost (most small nurseries do not keep records of times spent on different products). There is a problem of determining the opportunity cost of funds tied up in plants with different growth rates. Such complications explain the usual nurseryman's skepticism of cost accounting.

How do nurserymen actually price their product? The small sample of firms in this study suggests that they are influenced by pricing in nearby regions, but only in a loose way. They do not make a systematic study of competitive prices but do become concerned if their prices get too far out of line with competition. They give attention to the rate at which items are selling, raising prices (usually once a year) when supplies appear to be short and reducing prices on items no longer in great demand by the public.

Similarly, the owner of a radio and television repair firm pays little attention to costs, either full or incremental, in his pricing. He charges a flat $3.00 per service call (plus transportation) and a flat $6.50 as a "bench charge" (for work done in the shop), with only rare modifications. The owner apparently believes that higher prices would lead to substantial losses of goodwill and volume. He believes that variations in charges according to time would also lead to reductions in goodwill and volume.

Other cases support this picture of managers with only rough conceptions of demands and costs, who as a result price on a trial-and-error basis. Many such firms give their primary quantitative attention to the income statement, which apparently plays a homeostatic role in motivating price changes. If profits are "unsatisfactory" according to some predetermined profit expectations or aspirations, the managers seek price changes that will improve profits. But the accounting data in such firms provide little help in determining which prices should be changed or the direction of price change.

The cases of retailers and wholesalers are consistent with the preceding discussion. As is well known, retailers use wholesale costs rather than full costs as reference points in pricing. Information on such costs is readily available, which suggests that the convenience of data sources is a major influence on pricing. But small retailers usually do not apply single markups. They vary markups according to demand and competitive conditions, with some unsystematic attention to turnover and the relative costs of storing and selling different items. Some retailers are more rigid than others about varying markups over time. One firm in the study never marks down goods, but sometimes "gives a price" on an item that has occupied shelf space too long. More frequently, however, retailers resort to special sales and variations in price to meet changing conditions.

Retailers are heavily influenced by the price suggestions of manufacturers or wholesalers, indicating that they prefer to escape decision making on prices when that is possible. Such practices do not mean that market conditions are ignored but rather that the analysis of those conditions is made by the manufacturers or wholesalers rather than by the individual retailers.

Our limited sample suggests that stores catering to low or medium income customers pay more attention to price policy and are more flexible in pricing. Any fuller discussion of retailers would take us beyond the scope of the present article. The main point here is that the behavior of both retailers and wholesalers clearly contradicts generalizations about the prevalence of full-cost pricing.

IV. SYSTEMATIC SURVEYS AND USES OF TRIAL AND ERROR

Among the firms that ignore full costs are a few that make systematic studies of cost-volume-profit relationships before embarking on price changes. A new bowling alley, for example, selected prices that had succeeded in similar size alleys in other towns of the same size. The owners made a careful study of rates and volumes in other firms and did not make their decision until they completed a thorough study. They selected rates on the high side of the range in the belief that the trend of feasible prices was upward. In view of the thoroughness of their market analysis, it is not surprising that the actual revenues came close to the forecasts.

Some firms use their trial-and-error experiences with past price changes as guides to future pricing. A billboard firm with branches in several towns has learned from experience the point at which the customers rebel against high prices and curtail their advertising. The owners of this firm believe that other billboard firms are unnecessarily cautious in raising prices; they have found that prices above the "going rate" are viable.

Most small firms do not study past experience systematically. But many of them are influenced by the results of past experience, through direct observation of effects of price changes or by noting the results on the income statements. It would be difficult to quantify the influence of trial and error and past experience, for this influence is subtle and gradual. Most managers would assert that they have learned from past experience, but they are understandably inarticulate on the details of the learning process.

V. MARGINALISM IN PRICING

We are now ready to discuss a central issue on pricing. We have rejected the full-cost theory most strongly antithetical to the traditional marginalist theory. But does this means that our firms are careful practitioners of marginalism? The answer depends on one's definition of marginalism.

Machlup's definition of marginalism—one which is widely accepted by economists—is broad enough to encompass most of the behavior found in this study. Machlup quite correctly notes that subjective estimates of cost and revenues, guesses and hunches, and trial and error, are perfectly consistent with marginalism. A business man who follows the precepts of marginalism does not mathematically determine the exact point at which marginal revenue equals marginal cost. He will take into account the long run as well as the immediate effects of his pricing decisions. Marginalism is even consistent with the temporary application of mechanical markups to full costs if the costs of the flexible adaptation to market forces are too large. Thus this study is generally consistent with Machlup's views.

Unless we define marginalism so broadly as to include nonpecuniary considerations as well as profit maximization and to rationalize any attention to full costs as merely a convenient shortcut, we must conclude that some of the evidence is inconsistent with the complete adherence to marginalism. In some of the cases, ethical considerations come into conflict with the attainment of greater profits. In other cases, the reference to full costs seems clearly to interfere with the application of full-scale marginal reasoning. Some managers are confused by overhead allocations in making decisions which appear inconsistent with marginalism.

Several economists have critized Machlup's definition as too broad—almost so broad as to rationalize any kind of behavior. Machlup's views are correct if we are interested in "certain strong tendencies in a representative sector of business." But if we wish to study individual firm decisions we must be interested in the divergencies in behavior as well as in its general tendencies. The findings in this study suggest that most managers do price in the direction indicated by marginalism up to a point, but that they do let full costs and inertia deflect them from a full application of marginal reasoning. Thus the study supports the conclusion that most small business pricing practices are characterized by "partial marginalism."

The use of modern marginalist methods of accounting might be taken as evidence of marginalism in pricing. Such methods are rare in small business. The closest our cases come to this is the use of projected income statements and break-even charts in the billboard and bowling alley firms. In most small firms there is little formal attention to formal breakdowns of fixed and variable costs. No firms in the sample make any quantitative estimates of "marginal revenue" or "elasticity of demand."

The findings are in contrast to Earley's conclusions on large firms. Earley concluded that his special sample of "excellently managed" large firms did use cost breakdowns and marginal accounting in the direction suggested by theory. In our small firms most of the marginalist behavior that exists is instead a result of subjective evaluations based on past experience.

The evidence favorable to the partial or subjective marginalism position is: (1) the approach of some managers by trial and error to prices that lead to higher profits; (2) the widespread practice of varying markups on different demand elasticities; (3) the flexibility of markups over time, with apparent adjustments to changing market conditions; and (4) the probability that imitative pricing and the adherence to suggested prices permit firms to apply prices which outsiders have found consistent with demand conditions. Such evidence does not support a conclusion that marginalism is applied precisely or consistently; it does suggest that a great deal of pricing behavior is working in a marginalist direction.

VI. PROFIT OBJECTIVES

The traditional assumption in economics is that the objective of pricing is profit maximization. Some economists assert that this assumption was never intended as a description of actual behavior but rather as a useful simplification permitting prediction. A somewhat different view in a recent empirical study is that firms establish profit targets and administer their prices to achieve such targets. The extent of profit maximization in actual pricing is still unknown.

Small firm managers do not refer to "target returns" to the extent observers have found in big business. The management of one furniture firm does stress a profit target, but this is expressed as a percentage of *revenue* rather than of *investment*. Most managers who indicate the influence of targets appear to think in terms of absolute income rather than percentages.

On the other hand, many of the managers express views that indicate that profit maximization is not their sole aim. A college-owned retail store which limited profits out of respect to the financial needs of students is hardly representative, since it has special reasons for placing itself in a "public utility" category. But other cases suggest a wide variation in the drive for profits, with some managers expressing a strong sense of responsibility to the community and ethical objections to charging what the market will bear, and other managers demonstrating an intense striving for higher profits. The cynic may rationalize all limitations on short run profit taking as aimed at building up good will that will contribute to long-run profits; but the interviews suggest that many managers are directly influenced by ethical considerations and by their desire to retain a position of respect in their communities. The manager of one gift shop, for example, would certainly have found it difficult to apply the rather subtle techniques of price discrimination found in an auto repair shop. She would have retired from business rather than resort to such practices. The personal ethics and objectives of individuals are influential in pricing, blunting the force of profit maximization.

VII. CONCLUSIONS

Space does not permit a full discussion of all of the findings of this study. For example, it is possible to give only a hint of the conclusions on the influence of market structures on the pricing behavior of these firms. Economic theory indicates that the pricing behavior of firms depends on the structure of competition; policies that would be appropriate in a highly competitive industry would not, for example, be suitable in oligopoly or monopoly. The present study finds considerable evidence of adaptation to the market structure. The findings indicate that oligopoly is rather common in small business. The cases also include examples of local market monopoly and collusion. It is inappropriate to assume that small business necessarily reflects either pure competition or monopolistic competition of the multi-firm variety.

Much of the stress on full cost is an attempt in oligopolistic industries to reduce the risks of price competition. If competitors can agree on similar accounting systems based on full costs, they may achieve flexibility of prices with changing costs without the danger that competitors will not follow. Some of our cases illustrate such a pattern of pricing. It is strange, however, that the printing industry, which seems so clearly *not* to be an oligpoly (over 80 firms in one locality covered by the study), should place so much stress on full costs. The attempt to limit price competition through adoption of common accounting and pricing formulas would appear to be doomed in such an industry in which the rewards of price shading would often exceed any possible dangers of direct price retaliation.

The major conclusion of this study is that partial marginalism prevails in small business. There is little evidence of the rigid adherence to mechanical full-cost pricing indicated by some previous studies, but costs do serve as resistance or reference points. In general, markups are flexible, with variations among products and variations over time. Inertia and the desire to reduce the volume of decision making reduces the frequency of changes in prices.

The fact that small firm pricing behavior falls between the extremes of mechanical full-cost formulas and the exact application of the precepts of marginalism is not surprising. It would be strange if managers consistently ignored opportunities for increased profits afforded by varying margins from product to product and from time to time. But, in view of uncertainties and the obstacles to measurement, it is impossible for these managers to determine the precise point at which marginal revenues equal marginal costs. Some managers are motivated not only by the desire for profits but also by other personal goals, including maintenance of their status in their communities. The result is a complex pattern of considerable inertia, unsystematic experimentation, widespread price discrimination or at least the tailoring of markups to demand, subjective estimates of market conditions, imitation of the pricing behavior of other firms, and the acceptance of the suggested prices of manufacturers, spotted with a few cases of collusion and a few cases of careful market analysis. The theorist of course prefers a simple explanation of behavior to such a description of diversity and variability. It remains to be seen whether simple generalizations based on the assumption of profit maximization and complete certainty at one extreme or based on the assumption of mechanical full-cost formulas at the other extreme can take the place of more eclectic explanations that come closer to the diversity of observed pricing practices.

21. Pricing Objectives in Large Companies*

ROBERT F. LANZILLOTTI

The sharpened interest in administered prices and inflation has focused attention once again on the inadequate state of knowledge of the price-making process. In particular, more empirical information is needed with respect to (a) the motivational hypothesis of the firm, i.e., the specific objectives upon which business firms base pricing decisions, and (b) the mechanics of price formulation. This article is addressed to the first problem; it will present some data on pricing objectives of the firm which have been developed in the course of a general study of pricing policies and practices of large industrial corporations.

I. SCOPE OF PRESENT STUDY

The procedure followed involved the postprandial variety of research. Lengthy interviews were undertaken with officials of twenty companies over periods ranging up to about one week in most cases.[1] A second set of interviews was undertaken several years later to fill in gaps in the data and to ascertain if any changes had been made in price policy since the original interviews. Pricing obviously being a sensitive area, some officials did not care to discuss their policies except in general terms, but these persons paved the way to individuals who were more willing and, in some cases, more aware of the practices employed and reasons for them.

The questions were designed to elicit information concerning: (1) whether any formal or informal commercial goals had been adopted by the corporation; (2) the procedures employed for implementing and

* *The American Economic Review,* vol. 48, no. 5 (December 1958), pp. 921–40.

[1] The companies were selected from among the largest corporations on the basis of the willingness of management to cooperate by permitting extensive interviews with top company officials: Aluminum Company of America, American Can, A & P Tea Company, du Pont, General Electric, General Foods, General Motors, Goodyear, Gulf, International Harvester, Johns-Manville, Kennecott Copper, Kroger, National Steel, Sears, Standard of Indiana, Standard Oil Company of New Jersey (ESSO), Swift, Union Carbide, and U.S. Steel.

evaluating the goal; (3) the techniques of price determination (i.e., the mechanics of pricing); and (4) the functions of pricing executives (individuals, committees, special divisions, etc.)—including extent of authority on price matters, kinds of materials utilized by them in setting prices, and relative weights given to various price-influencing factors. The portion of the information presented in this paper concerns, for each of the twenty companies, the principal and collateral objectives which are regarded as guiding pricing decisions.

The twenty corporations have one feature in common—each of them is among the 200 largest industrial corporations, and over one half fall within the 100 largest industrials, in terms of assets. But they differ in a wide variety of ways from each other. Some, like Johns-Manville, U.S. Steel, International Harvester, and Union Carbide, dominate a whole industry and are price leaders. At the other extreme, there are companies like Swift and A & P which face so many competitors of various sizes and abilities that in spite of their absolute size they are very far from being able to make decisions for the market, and do not think of competition in terms of actions of one or a few competitors. The other companies fall between these extremes.

II. COMPANY GOALS: RATIONALIZATIONS OF PRICING METHODS

It is important to recognize at the outset that a company statement of policy is not necessarily an accurate representation of what that policy is.[2] Also, company rationalizations of pricing do not always represent the first step in planning price policy, and not all pricing of a given company is determined by the general company objective.

In a few cases officials insisted that there was little latitude in selecting a policy. However, for the most part, the prominence of each of the corporations in their respective industries makes most of them masters, to a significant degree, of their fates; hence, they are able to adjust pricing to the company's general goal.

Table 1 presents a summary of the principal and collateral pricing goals of the twenty companies as determined from interviews with their respective officials. The most typical pricing objectives cited were: (1) pricing to achieve a target return on investment; (2) stabilization of price and margin; (3) pricing to realize a target market share; and (4) pricing to meet or prevent competition. In most of the companies, one of the goals predominates, but as the listing of collateral objectives

[2] The following analysis is based upon the author's interpretations of views expressed orally by officials of the corporations concerned. Of course, neither the companies nor the author wish these views to be interpreted as necessarily the official views of the companies.

indicates, price making by any one firm was not always ruled by a single policy objective.[3]

III. PRICING TO ACHIEVE A TARGET RETURN ON INVESTMENT

Target return on investment was perhaps the most frequently mentioned of pricing goals.[4] About one half of the companies explicitly indicated that their pricing policies were based mainly upon the objective of realizing a particular rate of return on investment, in a given year, over the long haul, or both; but in most cases the target was regarded as a long-run objective. The average of the targets mentioned was 14 percent (after taxes); only one was below 10 percent; and the highest was 20 percent.

Under this pricing system both costs and profit goals are based not upon the volume level which is necessarily expected over a short period, but rather on standard volume; and the margins added to standard costs are designed to produce the target profit rate on investment, assuming standard volume to be the long-run average rate of plant utilization. In effect, the procedure is designed to prevent cyclical or shorter-run changes in volume or product-mix from unduly affecting price, with the expectation that the averaging of fluctuations in cost and demand over the business cycle will produce a particular rate of return on investment.

[3] To illustrate, in U.S. Steel out of a variety of divergent views mentioned, three rationales can be distinguished. (1) The first is the "ideal" price, i.e., pricing that is believed to be "just, fair, and economic," with reference to a general target of about 8 percent after taxes on stockholders' investment plus long-term debt. This strand is colored by the management's concept of the corporation as the industry leader vested with the responsibilities and subject to the inhibitions of a public utility. In fact, one official said he was "unable to understand or properly describe the Corporation's pricing policy except as something like the approach of the public utilities." (2) The second rationale centers on the difference between the "ideal" system and what officials regard as the "practical exigencies of steel price-making," i.e., limitations imposed upon price policy "by followers who are disloyal and prices of competitive products that get out of hand." (3) A third policy objective is essentially a target market share and is embodied in the motto: "to obtain as a minimum that share of all markets for the products sold, product by product, and territory by territory, to which the corporation's capacity in relation to the industry as the whole entitles it, and to accomplish this participation ratio through the exercise of judgment so as to insure the maximum continuing return on investment to the Corporation."

[4] Target-return pricing is defined as the building up of a price structure designed to provide such a return on capital employed for specific products, product groups, and divisions, as to yield a predetermined corporate average return. In most cases managements referred to stockholders' equity (net worth) plus long-term debt. Usually a standard cost system is used as a means of allocating fixed cost to various product divisions, with the standards premised on an assumed rate of production, typically about 70 percent to 80 percent of capacity, and an assumed product-mix as "normal."

Firms that were conscious of shooting for a particular target return on investment in their price policies were those that sold products in a market or markets more or less protected and in which the companies were leaders in their respective industries. In Alcoa, du Pont, Esso, General Electric, General Motors, International Harvester, Johns-Manville, Union Carbide, and U.S. Steel, the pricing of many products was hinged to this particular objective, and with the expectation of being able to reach the target return. Target-return pricing was usually tied in with a long-run view of prices, especially on new products where an "orderly" stepping down ("cascading") of prices was followed by du Pont, Union Carbide, and Alcoa.

A distinction should be made, however, between those companies that use target return on investment as a rigid and primary guide to pricing and those to whom it is more useful as a benchmark in an area where prices otherwise might be subject to wide and dangerous variations.[5]

Columns 4 and 5 of Table 1 show the average and range of the profit rates realized by the 20 companies over the 1947–1955 period. It will be noted that the target figures are *less* than the actual returns: for the nine-year period, the target-return companies earned on the average slightly more to substantially more than their indicated profit objective (International Harvester being the only exception). Also, there is a rather wide range in the profit rates for each company.

The actual profit rates may be higher than the targets for several possible reasons: (a) the targets may only be nominal or minimal goals; (b) the generally prosperous nature of the period in question in which company operations exceeded "Normal" or average percentage of capacity upon which costs and prices were determined; and (c) some of the companies have found that pricing on an historical-cost basis using the

[5] To illustrate, the use of rate-of-return pricing by U.S. Steel (likened by its officials to a public utility's "fair return"), apparently has not always been consistently followed. Under market pressure, U.S. Steel has at times had to accept much less than this return; when desperate for business, as in 1938, its competitors offered substantial concessions below published prices on almost every type of business. A very different situation shows up in the discussions of the target return by officials of General Motors. Instead of vainly attempting to realize its target in good years and bad, General Motors takes a long-run view and has sufficient assurance of its retention of a minimum market share to accept a diminished profit rate in years when diminished output bears a heavy unallocated overhead. Du Pont seems to assume its ability to realize a target return, especially in connection with new products. The same could be said for Union Carbide, the other chemical producer in the sample. International Harvester, although as vulnerable as U.S. Steel to wide swings in volume of business, appeared to be less worried by competitors' ability to jeopardize its prices based on long-run normal cost and return. Harvester was not able to maintain its prices during the great depression, and there is no evidence that such reductions as it made correspond merely to changes in direct cost. But in spite of frank admission by Harvester's management that the company was faced by tough competition, company officials appeared to be much more independent in their pricing policy than U.S. Steel.

TABLE 1
Pricing Goals of Twenty Large Industrial Corporations

Company	Principal Pricing Goal	Collateral Pricing Goals	*Rate of Return on Investment (After Taxes) 1947–1955*[a]		*Average Market Share*[b]
			Avg.	*Range*	
Alcoa	20 percent on investment (before taxes); higher on new products [about 10 percent effective rate after taxes]	(a) "Promotive" policy on new products (b) Price stabilization	13.8	7.8–18.7	Pig & ingot, 37 percent; sheet, 46 percent; other fabrications, 62 percent[c]
American Can	Maintenance of market share	(a) "Meeting" competition (using cost of substitute product to determine price) (b) Price stabilization	11.6	9.6–14.7	Approx. 55 percent of all types of cans[d]
A & P	Increasing market share	"General promotive" (low-margin policy)	13.0	9.7–18.8	n.a.
du Pont	Target return on investment—no specific figure given	(a) Charging what traffic will bear over long run (b) Maximum return for new products—"life cycle" pricing	25.9	19.6–34.1	n.a.
Esso (Standard Oil of N.J.)	"Fair-return" target—no specific figure given	(a) Maintaining market share (b) Price stabilization	16.0	12.0–18.9	n.a.
General Electric	20 percent on investment (after taxes); 7 percent on sales (after taxes)	(a) Promotive policy on new products (b) Price stabilization on nationally advertised products	21.4	18.4–26.6	—[e]

General Foods	33⅓ percent gross margin: ("⅓ to make, ⅓ to sell, and ⅓ for profit"); expectation of realizing target only on new products	(a) Full line of food products and novelties (b) Maintaining market share	12.2	8.9–15.7	n.a.
General Motors	20 percent on investment (after taxes)	Maintaining market share	26.0	19.9–37.0	50 percent of passenger automobiles[f]
Goodyear	"Meeting competitors"	(a) Maintain "position" (b) Price stabilization	13.3	9.2–16.1	n.a.
Gulf	Follow price of most important marketer in each area	(a) Maintain market share (b) Price stabilization	12.6	10.7–16.7	n.a.
International Harvester	10 percent on investment (after taxes)	Market share: ceiling of "less than a dominant share of any market"	8.9	4.9–11.9	Farm tractors, 28–30 percent; combines, cornpickers, tractor plows, cultivators, mowers, 20–30 percent; cotton pickers, 65 percent; light & light-heavy trucks, 5–18 percent; medium-heavy to heavy-heavy, 12–30 percent
Johns-Manville	Return on investment greater than last 15-year average (about 15 percent after taxes); higher target for new products	(a) Market share not greater than 20% (b) Stabilization of prices	14.9	10.7–19.6	n.a.
Kennecott	Stabilization of prices		16.0	9.3–20.9	n.a.

[a] Federal Trade Commission, *Rates of Return (After Taxes) for Identical Companies in Selected Manufacturing Industries, 1940, 1947–55*, Washington [1957], pp. 28–30, except for the following companies whose rates were computed by the author using the methods outlined in the Commission Report: A & P, General Foods, Gulf, International Harvester, Kroger, National Steel, Sears Roebuck, and Swift.

[b] As of 1955, unless otherwise indicated. Source of data is company mentioned unless noted otherwise.

[c] *U.S.* v. *Alcoa et al.*, "Stipulation Concerning Extension of Tables III–X," dated May 31, 1956, U.S. District Court for the Southern District of New York.

[d] As of 1939, U.S. Department of Justice, *Western Steel Plants and the Tin Plate Industry*, 79th Cong., 1st Sess., Doc. No. 95, p. L 1.

[e] The company states that on the average it aims at not more than 22 to 25 percent of any given market. Percentages for individual markets or products were not made available, but it is estimated that in some markets, e.g., electrical turbines, General Electric has 60 percent of the total market. *Cf.* Standard and Poor's, *Industry Surveys*, "Electrical-Electronic-Basic Analysis," Aug. 9, 1956, p. E 21.

[f] Federal Trade Commission, *Industrial Concentration and Product Diversification in the 1000 Largest Manufacturing Companies: 1950*, Washington, January 1957, p. 113.

TABLE 1
(Continued)

Company	*Principal Pricing Goal*	*Collateral Pricing Goals*	*Rate of Return on Investment (After Taxes) 1947–1955*[a]		*Average Market Share*[b]
			Avg.	*Range*	
Kroger	Maintaining market share	Target return of 20 percent on investment before taxes[g]	12.1	9.7–16.1	n.a.
National Steel	Matching the market—price follower	Increase market share	12.1	7.0–17.4	5 percent
Sears Roebuck	Increasing market share (8–10 percent regarded as satisfactory share)	(a) Realization of traditional return on investment of 10–15 percent (after taxes) (b) General promotive (low margin) policy	5.4	1.6–10.7	5–10 percent average (twice as large a share in hard goods v. soft goods)
Standard Oil (Indiana)	Maintain market share	(a) Stabilize prices (b) Target-return on investment (none specified)	10.4	7.9–14.4	n.a.
Swift	Maintenance of market share in livestock buying and meat packing		6.9	3.9–11.1	Approximately 10 percent nationally[h]

Union Carbide	Target return on investment[i]	Promotive policy on new products; "life cycle" pricing on chemicals generally	19.2	13.5–24.3	—[j]
U.S. Steel	8 percent on investment (after taxes)	(a) Target market share of 30 percent (b) Stable price (c) Stable margin	10.3	7.6–14.8	Ingots and steel, 30 percent; blast furnaces, 34 percent; finished hot-rolled products, 35 percent; other steel mill products, 37 percent[k]

[g] Target return on investment evidently characterizes company policy as much as target market share. In making investment decisions the company is quoted as follows: "The Kroger Co. normally expected a return on investment of at least 20 percent before taxes." See McNair, Burnham, and Hersum, *Cases in Retail Management*, New York 1957, pp. 205 ff.

[h] This represents the average share of total industry shipments of the four largest firms in 1954. *Cf. Concentration in American Industry*, Report of Subcommittee on the Judiciary, U.S. Senate, 85th Cong., 1st Sess., Washington 1957, p. 315.

[i] In discussions with management officials various profit-return figures were mentioned, with considerable variation among divisions of the company. No official profit target percentage was given, but the author estimates the *average* profit objective for the corporation to be approximately 35 percent before taxes, or an effective rate after taxes of about 18 percent.

[j] Chemicals account for 30 percent of Carbide's sales, most of which are petrochemicals, a field that the company opened 30 years ago and still dominates; plastics account for 18%—the company sells 40% of the two most important plastics (vinyl and polyethylene); alloys and metals account for 26 percent of sales—top U.S. supplier of ferroalloys (e.g., chrome, silicon, manganese), and the biggest U.S. titanium producer; gases account for 14 percent of sales—estimated to sell 50 percent of oxygen in the U.S.; carbon, electrodes, and batteries account for 12 percent of sales—leading U.S. producer of electrodes, refractory carbon, and flashlights and batteries; and miscellaneous—leading operator of atomic energy plants, a leading producer of uranium, the largest U.S. producer of tungsten, and a major supplier of vanadium. *Cf.* "Union Carbide Enriches the Formula," *Fortune*, February, 1957, pp. 123 ff.; Standard and Poor's, *Industry Surveys*, "Chemicals-Basic Analysis," Dec. 20, 1956, p. C44; and "Annual Report for 1955 of the Union Carbide and Carbon Corporation."

[k] The range of the corporation's capacity as a percentage of total industry capacity varies from 15 percent to 54 percent, as of January 1957. For more detail see *Administered Prices, Hearings Before the Subcommittee on Antitrust and Monopoly of the Senate Committee on the Judiciary*, 85th Cong., 1st Sess., Pt. 2, *Steel*, Washington 1958, pp. 335–36.

company's traditional objective does not provide adequate capital for replacement and expansion at current costs, and accordingly have made allowance for this factor in their pricing formulas. Thus, if actual profit rates were "adjusted" for changes in the price level, the actual profits would more closely approximate the stated targets.

Whichever of the foregoing may be the most plausible explanation of the differences between actual and target profit rates, the findings indicate that a distinction must be made between year-to-year and secular profits objectives. The evidence on actual profit rates, taken in conjunction with the targets mentioned, raises serious questions whether these companies are attempting to "maximize" profits on a year-to-year basis. Moreover, to construe the actual profit rates (as against target rates) as evidence of a long-run maximization policy would require the demonstration that the prices charged were based not upon the targets but on what the firms believed they could get as a maximum. In any event, for this sample of firms and for this time period, there are limitations upon profit maximization as an adequate explanation of the relationships between profit targets and actual profit rates.

It is perhaps significant that there has been an increasing tendency in recent years for the companies in the sample to adopt some form of target-return pricing, either across-the-board or at least for particular products. In a few cases it was found that managements had developed a target-return policy between the time of the first interviews with the company and subsequent interviews several years later. The reasons for this movement toward greater use of a target-return approach are varied, but the major influences seem to have been: (a) an increasing awareness of and concern by managements for profit-capital-investment planning and capital budgeting, especially in the conglomerate company within which there is keen competition for capital funds by many units; (b) the desire for a good common denominator for evaluating the performance of divisions and product groups; (c) the wartime experiences of most of the companies with "cost-plus," "cost plus fixed fee," and other contractual arrangements with the government which focused attention on the return on investment; and (d) the emulation, by competitors and others, of successful large companies which have followed a target-return policy for many years (several companies in the sample mentioned that they had patterned their general target-return policy after that of du Pont or General Motors).

It is not surprising that new products above all are singled out for target-return pricing. Since they have no close rivals, new products are usually expected to produce a predetermined level of profit return on the investment represented.[6] No rigid length of time after the introduc-

---

[6] A good example of the kinds of data utilized in determining which new products will be added or which existing facilities will be expanded is one company's procedure

tion of the product was mentioned in which the target is supposed to be achieved. However, the time horizon is more short range vis-à-vis established products in the sense that the target payout is delineated from the start. Accordingly, pricing may take the form of "skimming" the market by exploiting the inelasticity of demand in different markets (maintaining a selected price as long as actual or potential competition permits), or a "penetration" price policy designed to develop mass markets via relatively low prices, provided a rapid expansion of the market and higher returns may be obtained later. This approach is most typical of du Pont, Union Carbide, Alcoa, International Harvester, and General Foods. The prescribed target for new products is usually higher than on established products, at least initially. But the target approach is not limited to unique products; it is also typical of low-unit-profit high-volume commodities (e.g., steel, aluminum, and chemicals).

Minimum target profit figures also are used by most of the companies as a basis for sloughing off products and in arriving at "make-or-buy" decisions. An exact minimum target figure was rarely mentioned, but good justifications were required of operating divisions or product departments when returns consistently fell below the corporate average. Not infrequently, officers made statements along the following lines: "If the average corporate return were, say, 20 percent and the return on investment for a particular item kept falling below 10 percent, it would be dropped unless (a) a good customer needs it in order to keep a full line, or (b) it is a by-product anyhow, and anything it brings in is really gravy."

A variety of explanations was given by the companies to justify the

---

for capital investment decisions. The request by a division for new funds shows (a) estimated new commitment (new fixed investment, working capital, and noncapital expenditures); (b) estimated total utilized investment (the new investment plus transfer of existing investment); (c) estimated annual operating income (i.e., income before depreciation, amortization, depletion, other income and income taxes); and (d) estimated return on investment income, which is shown both as a ratio to the new commitment and the total utilized investment. No figure was mentioned as a minimum return; normally new products were expected to return better than the corporate average, but expansions of existing facilities have been made on a projected return of no greater than 20 to 25 percent before taxes.

An elaborate check-off list is designed to insure attention to various aspects of projected demand, supply, costs, and competition. Of particular interest are such items as: capacities, captive requirements and future expansion plans of competitors; company's estimated market share before and after expansion; degree of diversity of customers; extent to which success of venture depends upon short- or long-term contracts; the effects of changes in tariff rates on competition from abroad; selling prices used for sales to other units of the company; shape of short-run unit cost curve; comparative cost position of competitors; the degree to which an alternative exists of either making or buying important intermediates; flexibility of proposed facilities for production of other products; the probabilities of obsolescence of the process or products; and the relative position of the company with respect to research and development, technical knowledge, labor supply, patents, and raw materials.

particular size of the profit target used as a guide in pricing decisions. The most frequently mentioned rationalizations included: (a) fair or reasonable return, (b) the traditional industry concept of fair return in relation to risk factors, (c) desire to equal or better the corporation average return over a recent period, (d) what the company felt it could get as a long-run matter, and (e) use of a specific profit target as a means of stabilizing industry prices. At least one of the foregoing, and most frequently the first, was mentioned by the companies interviewed, and in a few cases the entire list was offered as justification for the company profit goal.

This reinforces the observation made earlier that no one single objective or policy rules all price making in any given company. In fact, in many companies a close interrelationship exists among target-return pricing, desire to stabilize prices, and target market share (either a minimum or maximum objective); this is especially true of U.S. Steel, Union Carbide, and Johns-Manville. It would seem, however, that a target-return approach is ordinarily incompatible with a market-share policy; that is, if a company desires to expand its share of the market, it will be inclined to place less emphasis on rigid adherence to a predetermined target.

IV. STABILIZATION OF PRICE AND MARGIN

The drive for stabilized prices by companies like U.S. Steel, Alcoa, International Harvester, Johns-Manville, du Pont, and Union Carbide involves both expectation of proper reward for duty done, i.e., "proper" prices, and a sense of *noblesse oblige*. Having earned what is necessary during poor times to provide an adequate return, they will refrain from upping the price as high as the traffic will bear in prosperity. Likewise, in pricing different items in the product line, there will be an effort (sustained in individual cases by the pricing executive's conscience) to refrain from exploiting any item beyond the limit set by cost plus.

The distinction between target return on investment as a pricing philosophy and cost-plus pricing in the companies surveyed is difficult to define. Some of the companies that clearly employ the target-return-on-investment procedure in pricing new products—the area of most frequent use of target-return pricing—use cost-plus pricing for other products. The difference between the two rationalizations lies in the extent to which the company is willing to push beyond the limits of a pricing method to some average-return philosophy. According to a General Motors executive, the target plays a prominent role in the formulation of the cost-plus method. But in the case of International Harvester, U.S. Steel, A & P, Johns-Manville, Alcoa, or Union Carbide, it seems fair to say that the pricing executive sets the prices of many products on a cost-plus basis (except where competition precludes such action) without questioning the appropriateness of the traditional mark-up.

Cost plus, therefore, may be viewed as one step on the road to return-on-investment as a guide, or precept for price policy. But some firms never go any farther. The standard can be accepted as self-sufficient; just as the target return perhaps needs no modification to make it accord with profit maximization (with all the necessary qualifications). Pricing executives seldom look beyond the particular formula with which they are accustomed to justify their decisions. They differentiate between price policies according to the degree of control they exercise; but not by the gap between the price policy and an ideal of profit maximization. They appear as ready to accept cost plus at a reasonable volume as an ultimate standard for pricing as any other principle.

V. TARGET MARKET SHARE

A maximum or minimum share of the market as a determinant of pricing policy was listed almost as frequently, and seemed to govern policy almost to the same extent as target return on investment. Share of the market was ordinarily thought of in terms of a maximum, bearing witness to the power of the corporations interviewed. Being giants, they were careful to limit themselves; they apparently did not wish to gobble up any market they entered, unless it was one which they had created, like nylon, asbestos pipe, aluminum screen wire, cable products, or some synthetic chemical.

Hence, the target share of the market as a guide to pricing tended to be used for those products in which the firm did not, at the outset, enjoy a patent or innovative monopoly. Du Pont made no mention of shooting for a given share of the cellophane or nylon market, nor did Union Carbide in the Prestone market; Johns-Manville set no limit to its market share in specialized insulation materials; American Can was not thinking in terms of winning against stiff competition a moderate share of the market for vacuum packed cans; nor was Alcoa in the wire and cable market. But a General Electric official spoke at length of the company's policy of not exceeding 50 percent of any given market because it then would become too vulnerable to competition. Johns-Manville officials likewise indicated that product and sales development are geared to attaining a given percentage of the market for a product line. The company endeavors, executives indicated, to maintain the offensive, rather than to be subject to attack because of their large product share. The company felt strongly that 20 percent of competitive markets was the maximum share in which it was interested. This policy ruled in those areas where Johns-Manville was *not* the price leader. It stresses sales, service, and superior quality of its product in order to maintain its prices somewhat above those of its competitors. Apparently the program of reaching no more than a given market share and of moving ahead against competition does not find expression in price reductions.

It is not possible to reach any general conclusions from comparisons of target market-shares and actual share of business realized by the companies mentioning this as a policy for pricing purposes. This is due on the one hand to the unwillingness of the companies to specify in detail particular target-share percentages, and on the other to the lack of sufficiently detailed information for the companies in question, especially for the highly diversified firms. Patently, most of these companies have very significant proportions of national markets.[7]

VI. "MEETING OR MATCHING COMPETITION"

To some of the officials interviewed, the requirement that the product price "meet competition" appeared, at first glance, to preclude the existence of any pricing policy at all. Meeting competition according to their view cannot be regarded as a rationalization of action; it is the action itself.

The rationalization of this policy of meeting competition is far from elaborate; at first blush it is perhaps unnecessary. How can "meeting competition" be dignified as one out of several alternative guides to action? In chemicals, du Pont seems to apply a rule of thumb of adopting the going price in the markets for many standardized products where it never had or else had lost the leadership—e.g., carbon tetrachloride, hydrogen peroxide, disodium phosphate, nitric acid, hydrochloric acid, and various rubber chemicals. Moreover, in the case of many products selling on a freight-equalization basis, prices were not set at a high executive level; the pricing in many cases had not been reviewed for years, having been established beyond the ken of anyone now in the

[7] One interesting example of the connection between pricing (livestock bidding), market share, and investment policy is found in Swift. An analysis of livestock buying raises the question whether there is something of an understanding by the major packers of what constitutes their "normal share" of the animals sold in given public stockyards, which was the essence of the Department of Justice's complaint (1948) against Armour, Swift, Cudahy, and Wilson (since dismissed). It would seem that the relative constancy of the proportions of livestock purchased by the principal meat packers is traceable in large part to the short-run fixity of plant capacity, the desire to keep that plant operating at least up to a specific minimum level of utilization (governed partly by labor commitments), and the ever present threat that another packer may secure a larger share of the animals and the market for dressed meats. In view of these considerations, the percentages of animals purchased by the major packers would logically evidence substantial constancy over periods of weeks or months in given markets. But, unless this same approach is carried over into the planning of plant sizes in new locations (or enlargement of established plants), as well as the rate of utilization of these facilities, this would seem to be an insufficient explanation for the long-run stability of shares.

organization. Yet, even here there is perhaps more discretion than the officials are willing or accustomed to admit. In the pricing of neozone, du Pont was forced—though it had introduced the chemical—to change its price policy because of the tactics of competitors, who shifted the basing point. But need the matter have stopped there? Was there not a decision by du Pont to go no further than matching the Akron-based price? In many other cases du Pont undoubtedly could, if it chose, have altered the basing points or other features of the marketing of chemicals of which it produced more than an inconsequential market share.

In many cases the policy of meeting competition appears to be materially influenced by market-share psychology. Esso Standard, while going to great lengths to devise a cost-plus theory, has modified it when and where it seemed necessary or desirable. Standard of Indiana was even more specific in basing its policies on "meeting"—or forestalling—competition. Esso and, to a much lesser extent, Standard of Indiana refrained from publishing or trying to reduce to definiteness the details of the policy. A number of questions related to the companies' rationalizations are basic to understanding the functioning of the policy, for clearly neither company changed prices instantaneously when facing "competition": Did they meet the exact price charged, at the refinery or to the retail dealer? How long did a substandard price have to prevail before it could undermine a cost-plus price? Whose competitive price brought action? How were competitors rated in effectiveness? Answers to these questions are basic to an understanding of the policy. But the oil companies have not divulged the facts that would permit full and consistent treatment of the theory of "meeting competition" as seen by their managements.

It seems also that in some cases the companies are not simply meeting competition—they are preventing it. This appears to have been the purpose of A & P in localizing price cuts to make matters difficult for a competitive store on its opening day, or General Foods in reducing the price of Certo and Sur-Jell in the Northwest where rival pectins were strong. Standard of Indiana, a dominant seller not overfond of price wars, may easily justify meeting competition locally on the basis that the policy offers a permanent threat to potential price cutters.

In other cases, the companies are aware of specific competitive products whose prices must be matched by their own if volume is to be expanded. Union Carbide knew that its synthetic organic chemicals, like the various alcohols, had to meet or undersell the price of the natural products if the investment was ever to be returned. In other cases, where a standardized commodity—e.g., bakery flour, livestock feeds, and frozen fish sold by General Foods, flour by General Mills, or wholesale meat by Swift—is simply marketed at a price over which no firm, or even small group of firms, can have control, then pricing policy ceases to have meaning. The phrase "meeting competition" is either inapplicable or inaccurate, since there is no specific competition to meet—only the market price.

VII. OTHER RATIONALIZATIONS

There are other pegs on which managements hang pricing decisions. In view of American Can's undisputed (at least until 1954) leadership in the metal container industry, and its bargaining power vis-à-vis both its suppliers and customers, it is somewhat surprising that the company should not have set out an explicit pricing goal in terms of return on investment. The management seems to be more concerned with the assurance of funds for innovating research than any particular target return on investment, although the maintenance of its market share through its closing-machine leasing policy indirectly accomplishes the same objective. The company's pricing policy could be construed as "marginal" in the sense that it automatically (via its contracts) transmits to its customers increases or decreases in costs of materials (tin plate) or labor in the can factories. In turn, this adjustability in price seems to have had the effect of stabilizing American Can's margin, the price of its services as the owner of can-closing equipment and engineering services, and, at the same time, the price of cans throughout the canning season.

The companies cited many instances involving the need for resolution of conflicts of interest between integrated and nonintegrated firms and between established giants and newcomers, which displaced the usual bases for their pricing decisions. The Robinson-Patman and Sherman Acts, even when they have not been the basis for actions against the companies, were used as fundamental rationalizations of policy.

VIII. A COMPOSITE VIEW OF PRICING OBJECTIVES

Because it is big the large firm envisages itself as a part of a socially integrated group, with responsibilities for the whole pipeline and production (including full-line offerings) and associated distribution. They see themselves in a continuing relationship not only with their own distributors, but even with dealers and ultimate customers, and with their suppliers—even when the latter lacked, or especially when they lacked, the bargaining power of a larger firm. The market, in effect, is regarded as a creature of the firm, and the firm has the responsibility for preserving these relationships and perpetuating its own position.

The size of these firms also makes them an obvious target for antitrust suits, legislation, Congressional investigation, and similar restraining forces. To a certain extent, size thus entails a vulnerability and generates a sense of *noblesse oblige*. This is reinforced by the disposition of the government and the community generally to look on and appeal to these firms as "pattern setters" for industry generally; and in pricing they are expected to avoid taking full advantage of immediate profit opportunities. This attitude is perhaps most clearly expressed in the *Economic Report of the President* of January 1957, which stated:

> Specifically, business and labor leadership have the responsibility to reach agreements on wages and other labor benefits that are fair to the rest of the community as well as to those persons immediately involved. . . . *And business must recognize the broad public interest in price set on their products and services.* (p. 3, italics added.)

From this point, it is an easy step to the position taken by the typical large firm that it is entitled to a "just price" and "fair return" on investment. In the case of some companies, like U.S. Steel, the resolution of conflicts of interest between integrated and nonintegrated firms, between established giants and newcomers, and between the pattern setter and the community generally, has modified company price policy to a point where even the managements have come to refer to it as akin to that of a public utility. This may be a logical development in cases where unpleasant experiences of cutthroat competition—especially in fairly standardized products like steel, copper, gasoline, and aluminum—have generated a disposition by management to avoid price changes except through periodic, thoroughly considered, and well-publicized alterations in recognized base prices. By relating price revisions to changes in direct costs (especially increases in wage costs), the firm avoids the annoyance to itself and its customers (who they claim vastly prefer stable prices) of frequent changes in price structure.

This desire for stabilized pricing, oftentimes described with a blanket adjective as "administered," usually implies that the company or companies set some kind of target to which their price policies conform. The price, according to this view, is under the control of one firm acting as the price leader of a group of firms that make policy for the industry. The contention of the business executives themselves is that an administered price, like the tank-wagon price of gasoline, far from being an independent creation of the price leader, is merely a device for approximating a market equilibrium. According to this view, there are so many possibilities of substitution of one product for another, or an off-brand for a name brand, that the limits of discretion are much narrower than is generally supposed. Administration of prices, officials contend, thus merely avoids the decision to use cutthroat competition—which itself would be another form of administered pricing; it also avoids temporary exploitation of shortages. Refraining from raising prices when a higher price is necessary to equate supply with demand, is also justified by management on the grounds that over the long run higher prices would disturb equilibrium by bringing unneeded capacity into the industry. But it is impossible to accept the conventional justification for leadership. It can masquerade as resulting in a genuine "equilibrium" only if the word is made equivalent to whatever is the decision of the leading firms.

The foregoing data, above all, make it clear that management's approach to pricing is based upon *planned* profits. The company proceeds on the assumption of the need for a certain amount of capital to undertake the investment in plant expansion and new facilities which are envisaged for the long haul in order to maintain and/or improve market position. In some cases, quite in contrast to the thinking of management before the second world war, this desire to hold position and to penetrate wider markets requires that capital investment should be planned with built-in excess capacity (this is best illustrated by the fact that prices are premised on the assumption of operating at a rate of 75 or 80 percent of capacity, which is assumed to be the long-run normal). In deciding upon which products and productive facilities will be added or expanded, the top-level corporation appropriations committee relies upon estimates of returns on utilized investment. The only way in which price policy can be viewed in such companies as these, with their wide variety of products and selling in a large number of different markets, is in terms of profits-investment ratios. This criterion serves as an effective guide for pricing decisions at divisional and departmental levels. If we are to speak of "administered" decisions in the large firm, it is perhaps more accurate to speak of administered *profits* rather than administered *prices.*

IX. CONCLUSIONS

The principal purpose of this paper has been to contribute to our knowledge of the actual process by which prices are formed in industry, with the expectation that the data will help in constructing a more realistic theory of the firm capable of yielding useful predictions of industrial price behavior. The general hypothesis which emerges is that (a) the large company has a fairly well-defined pricing goal that is related to a long-range profit horizon; (b) its management seeks—especially in multiproduct multimarket operations—a simultaneous decision with respect to price, cost, and product characteristics; and (c) its pricing formulas are handy devices for checking the internal consistency of the separate decisions as against the general company objective. Under this hypothesis no single theory of the firm—and certainly no single motivational hypothesis such as profit maximization—is likely to impose an unambiguous course of action for the firm for any given situation; nor will it provide a satisfactory basis for valid and useful predictions of price behavior.

In pursuit of price policies that will yield the maximum satisfaction of the company's community of interests, the findings show that one company will prefer stability, another will seek to expand its market share, or to engage in continuous discovery and preemption of new fields, while others will be content to meet competition, to satisfy a set target, or to aim at combinations and variations of these goals. It seems reasonable to conclude that the pricing policies are in almost every case equivalent to a company policy that represents an order of priorities and choice from among competing objectives rather than policies tested by any simple concept of profits maximization. Managerial specialists down the line are given a framework of requirements that must be met, while managers at the top, of course, are free to and do change these requirements to meet particular situations.

Another relevant aspect of the data for theoretical analysis is the conception of the market held by managements of large corporations. Individual products, markets, and pricing are not considered in isolation; the unit of decision making is the enterprise, and pricing and marketing strategies are viewed in this global context. Because of the tremendously complex joint-cost problems and the lack of knowledge of actual relationships between costs and output or sales, on the one hand, and the joint-revenue aspects of multiproduct companies, on the other, pricing is frequently done for product groups with an eye to the overall profit position of the company. This means that costing of products ends up as a result of price policy rather than the reverse. In view of the various external pressures on the company and the nature of the strategy of the enterprise, however, it is doubtful if prices would bear any closer relationship to actual costs were detailed cost data available to management. The incentive to realize target rates of profits for the long haul better suits the objectives of management-controlled companies than any desire to profiteer or to seek windfall profits.

It might appear that there are conflicts between the objectives of price leaders and price followers, e.g., between such companies as U.S. Steel and National Steel. Actually, however, it is a matter of leaders having fairly well-defined target objectives, whereas price followers evidently do not have independent targets. Their objective, especially where undifferentiated products make up the bulk of the product line, will be determined by the target set by the price leader. If the target is acceptable, the follower is content to hold a market share and will adjust price policy accordingly.

In more general cases, including differentiated product markets as well as undifferentiated, the extent to which companies—with the dimensions and diversification of those under discussion—serve as leaders or followers on individual products or product groups depends upon the profit-importance of a particular product in a given company's line, the nature of the product—whether a producer or a consumer good—and the size and degree of diversification of companies with which there are product overlaps. Moreover, the manner in which interfirm policies will be coordinated will depend upon the above factors as they bear upon particular products, plus the overall objectives of the enterprise as a unit and its general market strategy.

A further implication of the findings for the theory of the firm is the relationship found between price and investment decisions. The information on this aspect is limited, but nevertheless the setting of and attempt to follow specific target returns on investment are manifest at two separate levels of operations: short-run pricing and investment decisions. The investment decision presupposes a price (and usually a market-share) assumption, which, in turn, determines short-run price decisions thereafter. Thus, investment decisions in effect are themselves a form of pricing decision, and over time become an inherent part of price policy.

Finally, the general approach of these large corporations to price policy, and the attendant price behavior, raise some important issues for public policy. Their very size—both absolutely and relatively—permits the managements to select from among various alternative courses of action. This is a fairly clear manifestation of economic or market power. In partial reflection of this power, plus a variety of other reasons related to their size, vulnerability to public criticism, and potential antitrust action, these corporations tend to behave more and more like public utilities, especially the target-return-minded companies. To complicate the issue further, target-return pricing implies a policy of stable or rigid pricing, even though exceptions are found within particular product lines.

A crucial question raised by these facets of policy is: What is the net impact on economic growth and stability? More specifically, do target-return pricing, profits planning, and the attendant price behavior, tend to promote or inhibit stability and growth? Much more adequate empirical data on corporation objectives and detailed study of individual company pricing, profits, and investment planning over the course of economic fluctuations are needed before answers can be given to this question.

22. Decentralization and Intracompany Pricing*

JOEL DEAN

A fist fight determined the intracompany transfer price policy that is in effect today in a major oil company. The issue was the price at which gasoline would be transferred from the company's refinery to its marketing division.

The present heads of the marketing and refining divisions had witnessed, as loyal but appalled lieutenants, the contentious negotiations that culminated in the fight. When these two men came to power, they vowed that their interdivisional bliss would not be marred by any arguments over intracompany pricing as had their predecessors'.

They finally found a way to abolish all disagreements about transfer prices. They simply abolished transfer prices, thereby neatly tossing out the baby with the bath.

This story—now a legend in the company—is probably exaggerated, and other events certainly contributed to the outcome. It does show, however, that the subject of this article is as disturbing as it is important: how and where to set prices for products that are transferred between divisions (or between different stages of processing and distribution) inside the company.

Our industrial system today is made up of many large, multiple-product, multiple-process companies. As these companies have expanded, it has become generally recognized that the best pattern for their managerial organization is one of decentralization, i.e., the setting up of more or less autonomous operating divisions within a company. But as more and more large companies have adopted divisional management, they are finding that splitting up the enterprise and exhorting the divisional managers to go out and set new records for sales or production does not always accomplish the hoped-for profit results.

For an autonomous division to be an economically effective operation it has to follow the same basic rules of behavior as any independent firm competing with other independent firms, and this implies the same

* *Harvard Business Review*, vol. 33, no. 4 (July–August 1955), pp. 65–74.

standards of economic performance—profits. But how can it be held to such competitive standards if there is no sound way to price the products transferred to it or from it in dealings with other divisions of the same company? In that question lies the reason for this article.

In the course of the discussion I shall set forth these propositions:

1. Transfer prices are necessary for almost all large companies. Trying to do without them sacrifices so much that it is no solution at all.

2. Intracompany price discrimination is not good business, either for the individual firm or for private enterprise in general.

3. There is need of a new system of transfer prices featuring: (a) profit centers with operational independence, access to sources and markets, separable costs and revenues, and profit intent; and (b) competitive pricing among these centers.

4. Such a system has many advantages. It brings the division manager's interests closer to those of top management, provides a more accurate basis for evaluating his performance, bulwarks his independence, and gives him sound guides in purchasing and marketing decisions.

5. Most present systems for setting transfer prices, by contrast, are inadequate. They employ economically indefensible methods, keep many losses hidden, and have a negative value in the making of management decisions.

6. It takes time and patience to install competitive transfer prices. Top management will find it easier to make the change-over if it follows eight rules drawn from experience. Executives should also be prepared to meet certain objections which critics are likely to raise.

Here are the key terms which will be used in this article:

1. *Transfers* mean movement of product between operating units within the largest policy-making unit, regardless of corporate entities; for example, transfers within the family of companies represented by the Cities Service Oil Company or among the divisions of E. I. du Pont de Nemours & Company.

2. *Product* should be broadly interpreted to include raw materials, components, and intermediate products and services as well as finished products in the ordinary sense of the word.

3. *Transfer price* refers to the net value per unit that records the transaction for the purposes of operating statements.

NEED FOR SOUND PRICING

Why not do the same as the oil company referred to at the start of this article and dispose of the problem altogether by doing without transfer prices?

For most large firms this solution sacrifices too much. Our peace-loving oil company, for example, now has no knowledge of the cost and value of gasoline, heating oil, and other petroleum products at various stages of refining and distribution. Abolition of transfer prices prevents meaningful measurement of the profits of individual operating units, such as refineries, bulk stations, and service stations. It also prevents accurate estimates of the earnings on proposed capital projects. Basic decisions about market penetration, pricing, and capital expenditures are cut adrift from cost or profit moorings. And there is no way to assure that the product will be directed where it will produce the highest dollar return, either as among alternative processes or as among alternative channels and levels of distribution. The river of crude oil suddenly goes underground, disappearing from cost and profit sight, and comes up again at the consumers' doors, millions of processing dollars away.

So abolition is not the right answer. In fact, it is no solution at all. For most large companies the problem remains one of learning how to live with and use some system of internal transfer pricing. Sound transfer prices give division managers both the economic basis and the incentives for correct decisions. They also provide top management with profit and loss information indispensable for evaluation of the results of complex combinations of managerial skills and diverse facilities. Thus correct transfer prices are the basis for attaining the managerial decentralization sought by virtually every large American enterprise today.

One reason this has been such a problem for executives is that no systematic analysis of transfer pricing principles and policies has, so far as I can learn, heretofore been available.

Transfer prices have significance for public policy as well as for private policy. Criticism of vertical integration has focused on pricing of intracompany transfers. It is alleged that discrimination within the company hurts competition. For example, oil refineries are supposed to gain an advantage by charging their marketing affiliates lower prices than their independent customers, and aluminum and copper producers are supposed to benefit similarly in favoring their fabricating affiliates. Actually, shoving the profits around inside the company and into safe corners serves no useful purpose and succeeds only in confusing both operating managers and top management. But the fact that intracompany price discrimination is not the good business that many companies think it is hardly makes public criticism less damaging.

Fortunately, the correct economic solution for the company's managerial problem—transfer prices determined competitively—also solves this public policy problem.

NEW CONCEPT

How can the hodgepodge of intracompany pricing methods that is found in many large companies today be avoided? What is an economically realistic basis for intracompany pricing applied uniformly throughout the whole company? The answer lies in a new system of executive control which has the two intermeshed features of profit centers and competitive transfer prices.

Profit Centers

Before responsibility for profits or losses can be assigned, it is necessary that the management of the particular operation be in fact made primarily responsible for its economic performance. Four characteristics distinguish this type of autonomous unit from service functions.

1. ***Operational Independence.*** Each profit center must be an independent operating unit, and its manager must have a large measure of control over most if not all operational decisions that affect his profits. This means that he must have considerable discretion in determining the volume of production, methods of operation, product mix, and so forth, subject only to broad policy discretion from top management. The areas of the company where this independence of action cannot exist should properly be considered as service centers. For them, the volume and character of services rendered are to a large extent determined by decisions originating outside their divisions; an example is the public relations department.

2. ***Access to Sources and Markets.*** The profit-center manager must have control over all decisions relating to sources and markets. He must be genuinely free to buy and sell in alternative markets both outside the company and inside. For example, the manager of the canned meat division of an integrated meat packer must know that it is just as respectable to buy uncured hams outside the company as to buy from the company's own pork division.

Freedom to trade is essential to the new concept because it dissolves alibis. Brother buyer and seller have ample incentive to reach agreement on prices if neither is restricted to a particular source or market. They have almost no incentive, and everybody feels cheated, if these channels are predetermined.

The required access to sources and markets cannot be created by edict; outside sources or markets must either be there or be capable of creation. To illustrate, crank shaft and other major components of an automobile engine require highly specialized machine tools already in the possession of the supplying division. It is impracticable to get a sound figure on what it would cost to supplant the intracompany manufacturing source, since an outside supplier will not make a realistic bid unless the company signifies its willingness to make a long-run commitment sufficient to cover his installation of major facilities. Without this commitment, freedom to trade in such cases is meaningless.

3. *Separable Costs and Revenues.* A profit center must be able to split off its costs and find an economically realistic price of the end products; otherwise measurement of its profit performance is impossible. This requirement eliminates service-type staff activities from consideration.

4. *Management Intent.* A distinction between a profit center and a service center can also be drawn in terms of management's intention. Only if the basic goal is profits should the operation be treated as a profit center.

A service activity may contribute as much or more *in fact* to the company's profitability as an operating division, but still not qualify because top management does not and should not judge its performance solely on the basis of profitability. For example, the legal department could be run as a captive law firm and be judged by its performance in producing profits by chasing ambulances inside the company. But despite its ability to meet the requirements of operational independence, access to outside customers and talent, and separable costs and revenues, the legal department should not be made a profit center because individual decisions cannot be controlled by the profit motive.

In surveying operations within the company to determine which should be profit centers, management may want to restudy the fundamental objectives of each operation. The proclivity to view many activities as service center lean-tos for major divisions or the company as a whole should not lead top executives to ignore the advantages of conducting every possible operation as a profit center. Particular care should be taken in marginal cases like this one—

A captive steel mill that produces a substantial part of the requirements of a large manufacturer of equipment turns in a poor profit performance. This is due in part to the fact that it is not judged by profits alone; management's intent is to meet the requirements and specifications of the fabricating divisions at the expense of efficient scheduling and profitable product mix. Under these circumstances, the mill is viewed as a service function. It could, however, be operated as a profit center. While the difficulties of negotiating price premiums for special steels and special scheduling would be great, a price on the mill's unique services to the fabricating divisions would lead to correct allocation and remove the wasteful illusion that these special services are free.

To summarize, the modern integrated, multiple-product firm functions best if it is made into a sort of miniature of the competitive, free-enterprise economic system. The firm should be comprised of independent operating units that act like economic entities, free to trade outside the company as well as inside. Each such entity or profit center will, in seeking to maximize its own profits, do what will also maximize the profits of the entire company, just as individual firms in a private-enterprise society, by seeking their selfish advancement, generate the high productivity and well-being of a competitive economy.

Competitive Pricing

The underlying requisite for profit-center controls is competitive prices negotiated in arm's length bargaining by division managers who are free to go outside the company if unhappy with prices paid by or to brother division managers.

Small differences in the unit price of transferred products can make big differences in the division's profits and executive bonuses. Intracompany pricing must preserve the profit-making autonomy of the division manager so that his selfish interests will be identical with the interests of the company as a whole. This can be accomplished by following three simple principles:

1. Prices of all transfers in and out of a profit center should be determined by negotiation between buyers and sellers.
2. Negotiators should have access to full data on alternative sources and markets and to public and private information about market prices.
3. Buyers and sellers should be completely free to deal outside the company.

The practical benefits of sound transfer pricing for profit-center control are not always obvious. Many companies—especially if they are decentralized—seem to get along fine without it, never knowing what they are missing. This is because decentralization "digs gold with a pickax." In the flush of gratification for this great improvement over old authoritarian ways management may neglect the tools to get the most out of it.

In a big company there is danger that interest in making profits will be diluted as a result of managerial specialization and the separation of operation from ownership. The parochial ambitions of operating managers need to be held in check; performance should be judged in terms of alibi-proof, objectively measured profits. When transfer prices are economically correct and profit centers are properly established, top management can delegate and still have peace of mind, because the division manager's targets and incentives will be so set up that his interests are identical to those of top management.

How to protect the independence of operating divisions against the insidious encroachment of staff advice, the restrictions of policy rules, and the fettering effect of top-level supervision is an ever present problem. The fact that top management finds it necessary to protest so much about the independence of its division managers often shows how limited this independence is in reality. Competitively negotiated transfer prices bulwark the independence of operating divisions by making possible meaningful measurement of economic performance.

The harm that can be done by arbitrary and authoritative pricing of intracompany transfers is hidden. Such prices lead to sins of omission as well as sins of commission. They fail to give definitive indication of the profitability of added volume. They rob management of an economically correct basis for evaluating various profit figures. They provide a distorted and incorrect measure of the economic desirability of different channels of distribution. Bad transfer prices can also misdirect capital investment and cause friction and dissension among executives.

But negotiated competitive transfer prices can prevent these losses. They can make the division's procurement, processing, pricing, and distribution sensitive to market requirements and responsive to competitive alternatives. They provide sound guidance in making purchasing decisions, indicate the extent to which additional processing will be profitable, and direct the flow of products so as to make the greatest net profit for the company. Furthermore, the very process of negotiation avoids arbitrariness and tends to create agreement. This eliminates the cause of much friction and ill feeling.

OTHER PRICING SYSTEMS

What about existing systems of setting transfer prices? How adequate or inadequate are they? Various bases are now in use, such as:

1. *Published market prices.* Example: uncured hams priced to the canning division at prices reported in the *National Provisioner.*

2. *Marginal cost.* Example: electric motors transferred to the refrigerator division at cost of materials plus direct labor.

3. *Full Cost Plus.* Example: gasoline transferred to the transportation division at the refineries' full costs plus a "fair" profit markup.

4. *Sales Minus.* Example: transfers of gasoline from the refinery at the retail price minus an allowance for the marketing department's services in getting it from the refinery to the customer.

5. *Traditional Prices.* Example: the transfer price of financing service, a customary 6 percent.

The choice among the different transfer pricing systems depends both on the kinds of information that are available and on the objectives that the management hopes to accomplish through the system.

If no measurement of the competitive market price exists for the intermediate product, some type of cost basis may have to be used, unless a negotiated price can be based on indirect alternatives of buying and selling units. But choice among cost bases may be narrowed by the kind of cost records used.

In the event that available information does permit a free choice, then what management wishes to accomplish by intracompany pricing should determine the system to be followed. For example, if a company wishes to use intracompany pricing as the primary means for controlling costs and profits, for measuring operational results, and for directing the product flow in the most profitable ways, some sort of market price system is clearly indicated.

Now let us examine the relative advantages and disadvantages of the different systems used today for setting transfer prices, so that we can see how they compare with the competitive pricing method advocated here.

Published Market Prices

Basing intracompany transfers on published statistical reports of market price has much merit. It often approximates the ideal of a competitive transfer pricing system. But practical difficulties arise from three sources:

1. *Conditions may make published statistics an inaccurate statement of the market price for the size, quality, timing, and location of the intracompany transaction.* Market price statistics often have systematic time lags which make them an inaccurate picture of the true market at near turning points. Also, they may represent a different quantity, grade, type of package, or duration from the intracompany transaction.

For example, published prices of intermediate products and services usually pertain to the spot price, whereas the intracompany transfer calls for a long-term contract price, which is usually lower and more stable. Thus, rates for chartered oil tankers, which fluctuate wildly, are not an adequate basis for pricing stable intracompany water transport.

Some of these deficiencies in the published market price can be partly remedied by market-determined price spreads for term contracts as opposed to spot prices, carload lots as opposed to small lots, and bulk as opposed to packaged products. But if these spreads are large, it is likely that they cannot be established objectively in a manner that will be satisfactory to buyer and seller without negotiation.

2. *The market place may not offer a real alternative for the intracompany buyer or seller.* The volume traded on the market may be so small compared with intracompany transactions that an attempt to get supplies there would drive up the price. Or the quality standards of its market plan may be lower than those of the company or fail to meet the peculiarities of design and appeal of the company's own brand, so that price comparisons are futile.

3. *It may be difficult to distinguish between nominal price quotations and real ones.* No matter how honestly and carefully prices are reported,

there are times when a very few strategically placed transactions can make a big difference in the published price. When these published prices affect the divisional manager's promotion and pay, he cannot be expected to be blind to opportunities to "make" the market. Cunning maneuvers of this sort are hardly in the company's interest.

Marginal Cost

Next to negotiated transfer pricing, marginal-cost pricing is most defensible economically. Under this plan transfer prices are based on the additional cost caused by the production of an additional unit of the product. Moderately close approximation to marginal cost can be made by confining costs to those that vary with volume and are traceable—i.e., direct costs. This is the best of the authoritarian pricing schemes for these reasons: (1) it determines cost of underlying processes in terms that are relevant for short-run operating decisions on pricing, promotion, and product policy; (2) the buying division has a guide as to when it is in the company's interest to acquire a product or material from outside sources so long as it knows the short-run marginal cost of producing the product inside the company; and (3) troublesome and contentious problems of assigning overhead costs to joint product operations and changing overhead loadings as a result of variations in operating rates are avoided.

Marginal-cost pricing has, however, several distinct disadvantages:

(1) Divisional profit and loss statements are made meaningless as a measure of economic performance. All contributions to profits are passed along to the final operation, and therefore no profits appear for earlier divisions. This gives the last division, frequently the sales division, a big cushion for maneuvering. No wonder sales divisions like marginal-cost transfer pricing!

(2) Where many divisions handle products in succession, operating management may overlook profitable changes in methods or product flows because the inefficiencies of one division are covered up by the low costs of more efficient divisions that worked on the product in earlier stages.

(3) Commercial abilities that are so desirable in a well-rounded division manager are stunted under marginal-cost transfer pricing. He is isolated from the pitfalls and opportunities of the market and is confined to the role of a service division manager.

Full Cost Plus

Cost-plus pricing sets intracompany prices on the basis of the complete costs of the producing unit plus some allowance for profit. Many variations of the system, both as to the cost base and the add-on, are possible.

The commonest cost base is orthodox accounting costs for the latest period. Normal cost and standard cost are sometimes used. The add-on or profit ranges from a niggardly coverage of overheads to a markup on sales which produces a handsome return on investment. The standard for the amount of profit takes two principal forms: (a) a margin on sales and (b) a rate of return on investment. In practice, partly because of the difficulty of determining profit margins on reasonably similar operations, the margin is usually set arbitrarily.

Bare costs with no add-on were more common in the past than now. They are frequently justified on moral grounds: that it is wrong to take profit out of the hide of a brother division. Today, full cost plus a "reasonable" rate of return on the investment of the selling division appears to be gaining wider acceptance.

Supporters of full cost-plus pricing of transfers claim these conflicting virtues of the system:

(1) That the company is assured of an adequate profit on the entire process if transfer prices at each stage force the addition of a profit.

(2) That no company can make money by selling things to itself and allowing divisions to exploit each other; therefore prices limited to costs plus a fair margin should be used to prevent conflict and promote cooperation.

(3) That cost-plus pricing assures that the economic benefits of integration will be achieved and will be passed on to the company's customers.

(4) That cost-plus pricing makes the producing and supplying units attend to the business of producing cheaply without being diverted by concern about commercial problems of pricing sharply.

None of these virtues, however, minimize the fact that cost-plus pricing is arbitrary and authoritarian. As such, it provides a poor basis for evaluating division performance, it beclouds profits, and it inevitably diverts production into uneconomic channels.

Sales Minus

Basing intracompany transfer prices on what the customers pay has considerable vogue, particularly in organizations which are strongly market oriented. Transfer prices are geared to final selling prices by subtracting allowances that more or less completely provide for the costs and profits of intervening operations. For example, retail price lines of sheets and pillow cases once governed transfer prices for the textile mill subsidiary of a merchandising organization. Similarly, in the case of an integrated wholesale distribution unit, $4 was subtracted from the price paid by the retailer on a certain kind of canned food to get the transfer price from the canning factory to the distribution department. The factory allowed $2 a case for direct costs (transportation, promotion, etc.) and another $2 a case for overhead and profits.

This system has the virtue of being oriented toward the market value of the final product. However, it shifts the full impact of fluctuations in final price to the basic production units of an integrated firm, with the intermediate processing and marketing operations sheltered by an assured margin. In a buyer's market like that recently experienced in textiles, sales-minus pricing for gray goods would come close to what outside textile mills, hungry for business, could be forced to sell at. Under these supply and demand conditions, transfer prices that would approximate competitive market prices and realistically negotiated prices would result from sales-minus pricing. In a seller's market, by contrast, sales-minus pricing will undershoot the market; a division will not be able to get from intracompany transfers what it could get from outsiders or what it could negotiate at arm's length with brother divisions.

Traditional Prices

A weird throwback to medieval times when the concept of "just" price prevailed is occasionally encountered in modern business. The use of traditional prices in transfer pricing belongs in this category. An example is the costing of financial services at 6% in intracompany charges; such a rate has borne no relationship to the market place within the memory of today's executives.

It is hard to see any advantages in this method, beyond the fact that it is as convenient and consistent as most of the concepts of feudalism. But the other methods now in vogue are not much more useful. All have serious shortcomings; none can be relied on to produce profit-oriented decisions by division managers.

INSTALLATION AND OPERATION

We turn now to the more mundane problems of what needs to be done to install and operate competitive transfer pricing.

Comprehensive Study

A practical starting point is a systematic, impartial study of the intracompany pricing methods the company is now using, and the facts that can be marshaled concerning market prices and market price relationships. The next thing to do is to lay the foundation of understanding of the economic and management philosophy, the benefits, and the problems of this new concept of competitively negotiated intracompany dealings.

Managers of profit centers and of service centers need a new orientation—one that is pointed toward the economics of their operation rather than exclusively toward the technology of the operation. When they become managers of profit centers rather than merely managers of factories, they need a new set of ideas, values, and facts, with dimensions broad enough to embrace marketplace choices and competitive return on capital expenditures. All this takes time as well as education. Overnight installation by a presidential decree of the new transfer-price and profit-center policy is not likely to succeed or last.

Gradual Progress

After the research and educational foundation has been laid, a program of gradual installation can be tailored to the company's needs. The following rules should prove helpful:

1. *Widen the coverage gradually.* Start with areas where competitively negotiated pricing is easiest and take on the tougher ones as know-how improves.

2. *Apply first to basic volume.* Start with negotiated prices on the minimum basic quantities needed for planned future production. Negotiate term contracts for the distant future, so that both buyer and seller will have maximum fluidity and alternatives. Then gradually move toward arrangements for the fluctuating sector of volume for which real alternative outside sources get quite restricted. For these negotiations the trading experience and regard for long-term interests gained in previous dealings will help to steady the bargaining by curbing temptations toward exploitation in the short run.

3. *Establish pricing guides through research.* For products and components where the producing division has had no occasion to study market prices and outside trading opportunities, a foundation of knowledge must be laid so that neither brother division will be handicapped by ignorance in negotiating a competitive price. It takes time to dig this information up and to familiarize operating executives with its use.

4. *Set pricing limits temporarily.* These initial limits on the range of prices over which bargaining can take place will become as vestigial as the hip bone of a whale when the system gets into operation. But they provide assurance and prevent undue exploitation of ignorance at the outset. For example, a lower limit on price might be set by an estimate of the marginal cost, and the upper limit might be the commercial price charged outsiders plus 5 percent.

5. *Limit the volume of outside trading initially.* The freedom to trade outside can be temporarily restricted by setting volume limits as, for instance, 75 percent inside the company, 25 percent outside the company. Those who fear that the advantages of integration will be dissipated are reassured by this expedient.

Price Mediator

One executive is needed to (a) pull together the transfer-price and profit-center investigations, (b) organize the conferences and training sessions, and (c) supervise the gradual installation of the new system of economic controls. To ease the transition, both emotionally and economically, this executive also can temporarily undertake to mediate the negotiation of some transfer prices.

Note that the price mediator should not attempt to arbitrate. The experience with price arbitration is almost universally bad. It is expensive and time consuming, and the results do not satisfy either party. Everyone feels cheated, and everyone has an alibi for his profit and volume results. Instead the mediator should aim at securing agreement by keeping the negotiations going, by supplying information, and by exercising business judgment on issues of fact as well as on commercial alternatives. For example, one transfer-price mediator in a meat packing firm reviewed and substantially deflated cost information which was burdened with fictitious charges for packaging and shipping sausage material at successive stages of processing. Up to this time the selling division had been using these costs in good faith for internal decisions as well as in transfer-price bargaining with other divisions. The delusion that these were rock-bottom incremental costs led the selling division to set its refusal price at a level which was above the market. Such a price would have led to idle facilities and would have sacrificed incremental profits if the buying division had been forced to go outside to get the supplies.

One of the functions of the mediator, particularly in the early stages of installation, is to distill the truth from conflicting, misguided, exaggerated, and prejudiced pricing facts which the negotiating parties often bring to a mediation conference. To illustrate again—in negotiating transfer prices for a pharmaceutical firm, the participants faced two major common problems: (a) the outside market was very thin, with a wide spread resulting between highest and lowest prices at which sales were made; and (b) the transactions covered by this range differed from the intracompany transactions in volume, packaging, location, and so on. Quite naturally, each party came to the negotiations with a highly biased sample of market transactions to support its point of view. The triumph of the transfer-price mediator was to demonstrate to both parties that extreme prices, ranging from $.50 a pound to $1.50 a pound, were inapplicable; he managed to narrow the range within which both parties agreed that the real market lay for the transactions in question.

As profit-center managers gain experience in using the competitive pricing system and grow to appreciate its value, the effective mediator will work himself out of a job.

Term Contracts

The period over which the transfer prices are to be negotiated should be at least as long as the planning period required to design and schedule production, or to dig up satisfactory alternative outside sources, whichever time period is longer. For example, the planning and design period for automobiles is so long that in the short run, say over the next quarter, the divisions which make basic engine components have no real alternative market for their product. Similarly, the vehicle divisions could not on short notice dig up alternative outside sources for properly designed engine parts. Many operations are characterized by short-run inflexibility of alternatives especially where design, quality, and packaging must conform to rigid and publicized specifications. A product made to such specifications has passed the point of no return.

In such cases, *short*-run negotiations (less than three or four months for the automobile manufacturer) concerning transfer prices have the hallmark of bilateral monopoly; they are similar to wage-rate negotiations. They generate heat, bad temper, and rarely produce economic transfer prices that are gauged and policed by outside alternatives and freedom to use them.

But over a long period even a branded product like an automobile can properly be subject to transfer prices that have the virtues and characteristics of a free-enterprise system. If long-term specifications contracts are negotiated, the buying unit will generally be able to get outsiders to bid on products made to its requirements, and a producing unit will have a real choice—either to adapt its output to other uses or to again assume the commitments on design, volume, and productive facilities which are tied to the branded product.

Good Businessmen

Successful operation of a profit center under a miniature free-enterprise system within the corporate fold calls for talents and experience often summed up by the tag, "He is a good businessman."

These abilities need to be systematically cultivated because they are not likely to have survived in a big corporate bureaucracy where transfer prices have been authoritarian. Executives of highly centralized companies are likely to have been reared as if they were in one big happy family, in which each child has an assigned set of chores and emphasis is on cooperation and the subordination of individual desires to group interests. Some executives may have forgotten how to make independent decisions. They will need help in taking responsibility for decisions in a profit-center controlled company where anything that affects their profit is their business, where performance is judged by how much profit they can make, and where right, independent opinions quickly improve the executives' profit and loss statements.

ANSWERING OBJECTIONS

Any new system of transfer prices will be criticized, and this one particularly because it removes needed alibis and may blemish careers by exposing executives' inadequacies. In addition, it may appear to be fundamentally opposed to the reason for existence of a large multi-product corporation. Therefore anyone who is considering this new system of intracompany pricing and profit control needs to give some thought to the objections that are likely to be viewed as most telling by those who doubt. The following questions are ones which I have encountered constantly in work in the field.

"Why can't our company get along without transfer prices?" Some companies can. There is no need for management coordination through an apparatus of economic transfer prices and profit achievement measures if all complicated managerial functions can be competently exercised by one small, closely knit group of men. This was found to be true of a regional grocery chain. But very few large companies have such an administrative setup.

In some situations it may be possible to devise mathematical models which can solve empirically all the problems of allocating facilities, materials, and intermediate and finished products without continued exercise of managerial judgment and know-how. In these cases transfer prices are not essential, either. In using the new computers that are here and on the horizon management is handicapped, however, by the shortage of analytical ability and judgment needed to set up models which will adequately reflect fluid and changing alternatives at every stage.

"Why worry, since we already have that kind of transfer price?" Many companies think they have competitive transfer prices, but most of them do not. The consequences of noncompetitive transfer prices are present, but they seem to spring from such other causes as selfishness and lack of team spirit. There are two clear symptoms of noncompetitive pricing which cannot be explained away: (a) a continuous awareness of a conflict between the interest of the operating unit and what appears to its managers to be the interest of the company as a whole, reflected in self-congratulation for putting the company's interest before that of the division; and (b) the prevalence of exhortations not to let transfer prices prevent the company from making money.

"Will the benefits of integration be lost?" Integration which is actually economically justified has such great and clear benefits to both buying and selling divisions that competitive transfer pricing is not a threat. Only integration which does not produce economies—which does not

profit both the buying and the selling division—will be eliminated by virtue of division buyers and sellers going outside the company. This assumes that the division managers are alert to the possible conflict between their short-run and long-run interests, both in maintaining customer relations and in having a stable and sure source of supply.

"Will cooperation be undermined?" Measuring profit-center performance on a competitive economic basis motivates each unit to do what is in its own best profit interest. These interests, if the transfer prices are determined economically and the profit centers properly defined, are identical with the interests of the company. Rivalry to make the best profit showing will certainly encourage shrewd, hard-headed negotiations, but the promotion of mutual economic interests will, as always, stimulate cooperation.

"Does perishability of a product rule out negotiable transfer pricing?" Physical perishability does not create a new kind of problem. Physical perishability causes price sacrifices, and it is this economic perishability alone that matters. Negotiated prices have proved practical for perishable products; indeed, they have been used for them in the market place for thousands of years.

"Will the system work if there is no true market price?" This does not matter. Sometimes the negotiated price will be above the general market average, sometimes below. So long as buyers and sellers are free to know and to choose competitive alternatives, the price will be mutually agreeable and will be determined by supply and demand forces for that particular kind of transaction.

Published data on market prices are likely to be too fragmentary and too unreliable to determine transfer prices; they should be used as a guide only. Sometimes negotiation leads to agreement to use the particular published price as a bench mark. However, this is not because the figure is published but because the negotiating parties agree to its economic validity.

"Will profit centers be shortsighted in their quest for gain?" No system of transfer prices and performance measurement makes judgment unnecessary in appraising the value of hanging on to a customer and in balancing long-run and short-run interests. Shortsightedness is no more likely with good transfer prices than with bad. Profit-center managers have a big stake in their long-run future, and good supervision can clarify this stake and induce a long view when short-run profits conflict.

"Will the sales organization sell too cheaply?" The rather general mistrust of the business acumen of the marketing organization is a peculiarity of the big bureaucracy. From it stem the practices of kidding the sales organization about costs, pushing products down its throat, and rigging transfer prices to make marketing operations look like losers. The result is that atrophy of commercial instincts sometimes associated with sales specialization.

Under the proposed system the sales organization will control factors that determine its profits, will be held responsible for the profits, and will have its profit performance measured. Given this encouragement, there is no reason to expect that salesmen should be any less capable of acting like businessmen than are engineers or accountants.

The company's interests require, not simply top price or top volume, but top profit. Sometimes a larger profit contribution comes from a bigger volume at lower price; sometimes it is the other way around. With this method, sales units will have the knowledge, the authority, and the incentive to sell the product at prices that will produce the greatest profits for themselves and therefore for the company. These advantages in turn will put the units in a better position to develop and attract men who are competent merchandisers.

CONCLUSION

Difficulties of installation and operation *can* be overcome; questions of criticism and skepticism *can* be met. Management will do well to make the necessary effort in view of the deficiencies of existing transfer pricing systems:

1. Economically indefensible methods of intracompany pricing are widely used in American industry.

2. Losses sustained from bad transfer prices do not show up on any set of books, because what would have happened under economically correct transfer prices will never be known. Anyone who has tried to restate in terms of correct transfer prices what has been reported in terms of wrong ones will testify to the practical impossibility of measuring the foregone profits. In other words, whatever losses result from noneconomic transfer prices are well and forever hidden.

3. Bad transfer prices do not necessarily lead to losses; but if they do not, it is because no attention is paid to them in making decisions. In some companies the critical decisions concerning flow of product, degree of processing, and channels and geography of distribution can be made without reference to any internal costs or prices. In such companies bad transfer prices may do no harm—they also do no good. And if the operations of these companies do not require an economically correct system of transfer prices, they probably require no intracompany pricing at all.

As a practical matter the chances are strong that an unsound system of transfer pricing *will* cause harm. For a large integrated organization with a diversified product line which is sold to a variety of industrial, commercial, and consumer market levels, the only system which will accomplish the needs of management is one based on negotiated competitive prices.

23. An Application of Peak-Load Pricing*

DONALD N. DE SALVIA

INTRODUCTION

In 1960 an article dealing, in general, with a theory of pricing for nonstorable products and, in particular, with the pricing of electricity appeared in this *Journal*.[1] It introduced at a theoretical level a novel approach to pricing pioneered by the French. Subsequently, other papers on the theory of peak-load pricing have appeared. All have been largely concerned with theory and there has been no empirical application in the United States.

The purpose of this paper is to demonstrate the applicability of peak-load pricing to a typical U.S. electric utility. The paper will also isolate problems which will require further investigation if the theory is to be made generally applicable. In addition, it will be argued that existing rate structures do not adequately reflect resource costs and thus result in poor utilization of resources. The firm studied is considered to be typical of private owned electric utilities in the United States. All cost data are for the year 1963, which was the latest year for which complete information was available when the project was undertaken.

Before presenting the empirical study, the theory of peak-load pricing and events leading to its development will be reviewed. Treatment of the theory necessarily will be brief and those interested in a more complete development may refer to the original articles.

In a classic article published in 1938, Hotelling proposed the use of marginal cost pricing for utilities. This system, he believed, would produce a welfare optimum in the Paretian sense. In the ensuing debate it was shown that marginal cost pricing in the case of decreasing-cost industries cannot be proven optimal without resorting to interpersonal comparisons. Since in decreasing-cost industries average cost is greater than marginal cost, pricing at marginal cost must produce a deficit. No feasible method of

* *The Journal of Business,* vol. 42, no. 4 (October 1969), pp. 458–476.

[1] Marcel Boiteux, "Peak-Load Pricing," *The Journal of Business,* vol. 33 (April 1960), pp. 157–79.

FIGURE 2
Long-Run Total Cost Curve

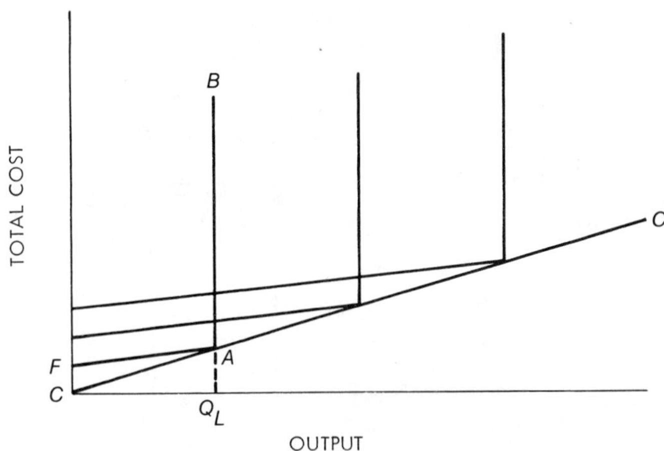

tional capacity and according to the French should bear a charge equal to the long-run marginal cost of owning and operating an additional unit of capacity. Long-run marginal costs would be equal to the slope of an envelope curve (CC') touching the elbows of total cost curves for plants of different capacities.

Assuming that fixed costs vary linearly with plant capacity and are zero at a capacity of zero, long-run total cost will equal fixed costs plus variable cost per unit (b) times plant capacity. That is, $C = F\ (Q_L) + bQ_L$. Long-run marginal cost is given by $\partial c/\partial Q_L$ of $f'\ (Q_L) + b$, but $f'\ (Q_L) = \partial F/\partial Q_L$, and under these conditions $\partial F/\partial Q_L$ will be a constant (ϕ) which is equal to average fixed cost per period. Long-run fixed costs will therefore equal $\phi + b$.

The pricing problem then becomes one of dividing the daily load curve into intervals in which demand is fairly uniform and recurrent, and applying a charge of b to off-peak periods and a charge equal to long-run marginal costs to peak periods. If the daily load curve is divided into n equal periods and fixed cost is defined in terms of a period of length $24/n$, the long-run marginal cost will be $n\phi + b$.

If demand is sufficiently price elastic, this type of price structure would serve to expand off-peak consumption and diminish peak consumption. Consider the load curve shown in figure 3 which is based on prices uniform in time. A plant of capacity $q(A)$ is required to meet peak demand at current prices, and a total cost of $n\phi\ q(A) + b\ \Sigma\ q$ is incurred. If a price of $n\phi + b$ is applied to demand in period A and a price of b is charged in all other periods, demand in period A is likely to be depressed. As long as the new demand in period A exceeds all other demands at a

FIGURE 3
Load Curve

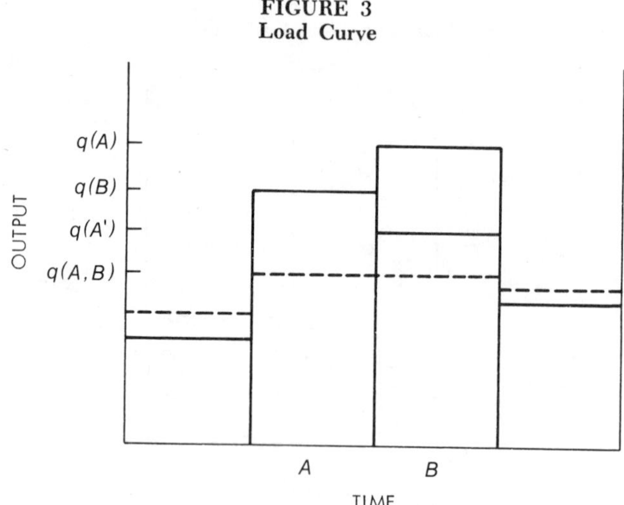

price equal to $n\phi + b$, there is no problem and the price structure is sound. If, however, demand in period A changes to $q(A')$, it will exceed demand in another period (B). The peak will have shifted and period A should no longer be priced as before. This problem could be avoided by assigning a price less than $n\phi + b$ to period A and a price greater than b to period B, in such a way that their respective demands are equal. At this point, however, peak price must be less than marginal peak-production costs for a plant of a scale equal to the changed required capacity. The prices charged do not justify a capacity equal to demand. A reduced capacity will result in a lower peak charge (i.e., $n\phi + b$ will be smaller), but if demand in period A and B is to be depressed to the smaller capacity, prices in period A and B must be further increased. Ultimately, a point will be reached where the price charged in the new peak period just equals the now diminished long-run marginal cost. All other periods still will be priced at short-run marginal costs. Ideally, a daily load curve similar to the dashed line figure 3 will be achieved. Boiteux and Drèze have shown that the revenues resulting from the above charges will just equal the costs of production.

To make efficient use of multiple generating stations, a grid or transmission network connecting all stations is required. In addition, each consumer is connected to the grid through a system of distribution lines. If deficits are to be avoided, the costs of transmission and distribution also must be recovered by service charges.

The principles of peak-load pricing can be applied to transmission as well as production costs. Off-peak transmission loads can be serviced at very low marginal costs equivalent to line losses incurred in transmitting an additional unit of power. Peak loads give rise to a need for additional capacity and in theory should be charged the costs of owning and operating an additional unit of capacity.

Distribution costs include not only line expenses but also such administrative expenses as metering and billing. Although a complete and practical theory of pricing for distribution costs has not been developed, an approach to the problem has been suggested.

EMPIRICAL PRODUCTION COSTS

Demand and Capacity Requirements

Applying the French theory to American utilities poses some difficulties due to differences in the nature of the industry in each country. In France the industry is nationalized and one agency controls production and distribution of virtually the total amount of electrical energy generated and consumed. The utility selected for this study is one of several suppliers in its section of the country. It engages in transactions with many utilities in the surrounding area. The French could study a closed system while this study centers on an open system. This difference will necessitate special treatment of interfirm transactions.

In France, methods of data collection were developed along with the theory. The information available to an independent researcher is much more limited. Since the utility studied had never considered peak-load pricing, data necessary for its implementation had not been collected. In many cases, only total cost data were available. In some instances, individual costs could be derived from the aggregate data. In others, lack of data precluded full implementation of peak-load pricing. The results, however, provide a first approximation and serve to demonstrate the feasibility of applying the French system in this country.

The first step in the analysis involves a consideration of daily load patterns in order to isolate peak and off-peak intervals. Selection of the number of intervals is largely arbitrary. Many small intervals would be more accurate but fewer large intervals yield a more administrable regimen of prices.

Figure 1 shows the firm's daily load curve for December 19, 1963. A yearly peak was reached at 5:00 P.M. on this date. Similar information is presented in a more conveninent form in figures 4 and 5, where an average load model is depicted. In this model, average demand in a given hour for each month is expressed as a percentage of the system peak demand for the year. The model is based on data from 1957 through 1961.

Examination of the curves reveals some interesting differences. The November through February curves give evidence of an early evening peak greater than demand during the rest of the day. The remaining

FIGURE 4
Average Load Model Selected Winter Months

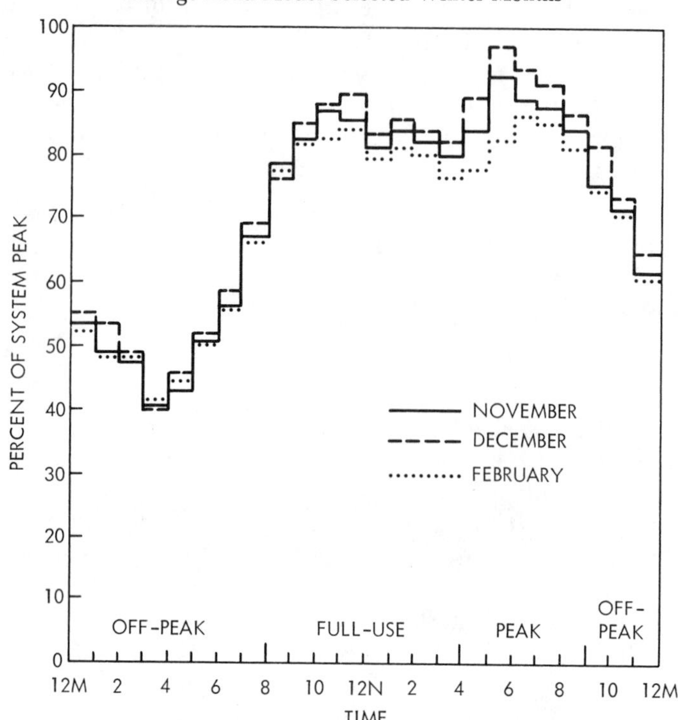

months show a less marked peak occurring in late morning. This suggests separate winter (November–February) and summer rate schedules.

Patterns of demand in the winter months suggest three daily intervals—peak, full-use, and off-peak. The off-peak interval runs from 9:00 P.M. through 7:00 A.M. and is followed by full-use hours from 8:00 A.M. through 3:00 P.M. The interval from 4:00 P.M. through 8:00 P.M. will be taken as the peak period.

The remaining months, which will be loosely termed summer months, do not experience an evening peak. They will be divided into full-use (8:00 A.M.–8:00 P.M.) and off-peak (9:00 P.M.–7:00 A.M.) periods.

The curves just examined include only weekdays. Load curves for Saturday and Sunday are distinctly different. Rather than complicate the rate structure with special rates for weekends, Saturday rates will be based on summer schedules and Sunday demands, which are always low, will be billed at off-peak rates.

Translating the average-load model into absolute demands for the rate periods derived above yields the required capacity for each period. The capacity requirements are summarized in table 2.

FIGURE 5
Average Load Model Selected Summer Months

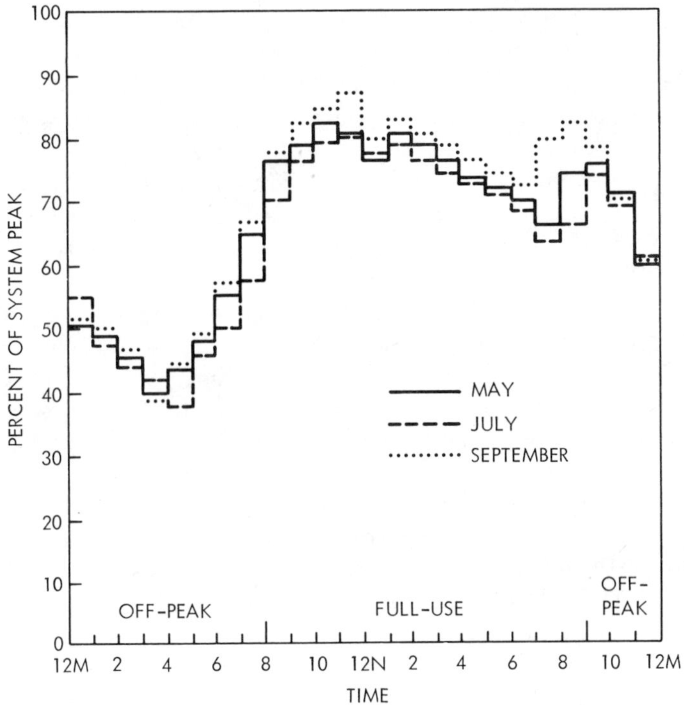

TABLE 2
Capacity Requirements

Period	*Winter Requirements* Percent of Peak	*Winter Requirements* Megawatts	*Summer Requirements* Percent of Peak	*Summer Requirements* Megawatts
Peak	100	3,321.7	—	—
Full-use	83	2,757.0	78	2,590.9
Off-peak	57	1,893.4	57	1,893.4

In meeting output requirements the utility has available both hydraulic and thermal generating capacity. In addition, utilities often make use of power generated by other producers. Each source has different cost and use characteristics and will be treated separately.

Purchased power is employed whenever its costs are less than the incremental cost of internal generation. In 1963 the utility studied had firm purchase contracts for 1,412.5 megawatts of electricity. This abnormally large usage of purchased power is a consequence of a peculiar relationship with a governmental producer in which the purchased power is costed for consumer pricing purposes as if produced internally. Since this is not a common procedure and since the power is priced as if produced internally, purchases from this source will not be included in the study. Purchases from other producers will be considered, since such purchases are typical of utility operations.

Power is purchased at varying rates of use. For this analysis, however, aggregate purchased power will be assumed to be used at a constant rate. For 1963 this would yield an equivalent continuous capacity of 129.5 megawatts.

The fixed costs of hydraulic generation of electricity generally are much greater than the fixed costs of thermal generation. The variable costs of hydraulic generation, however, are quite small in relation to thermal generation. The short-run marginal cost of hydraulic output, therefore, is extremely low in comparison to steam output. Thus, it would seem appropriate to make use of available hydro output resorting to steam generated output. Other characteristics of hydraulic generation, however, must be considered. It is relatively simple to bring a hydraulic generator "on-line." In comparison the start-up time and costs of thermal generation are substantially higher. For this reason the pond storage portion of hydraulic capacity often is employed during peak periods. Surplus or nonstorable water is used whenever it is available and in any given year total hydraulic capacity is always used.

Determination of an optimal schedule for the use of hydraulic capacity in itself would be a major study involving estimates of demand patterns, production, distribution, and shortage costs, and the probabilities of all possible water conditions. Lacking data on the availability of hydro power in different time periods, it will be assumed that hydraulic capacity is used at a constant rate. This is at variance with actual practice and will result in a slight distortion of the end results. In an actual application where more data would be available, this possible error could be avoided.

Hydraulic capacity, of course, is subject to uncertainties. It is influenced by the amount of water available, which varies with climatic conditions. Capacity in a dry year may be much less than in a wet year. In arriving at a dependable hydraulic capacity, the most adverse conditions on record for each month were employed. Under the worst conditions experienced, the total amount of hydro energy available for a year is 2,073,585 kwh. Assuming this energy is to be used at a constant rate, under adverse conditions a continuous hydraulic capacity of approximately 250 megawatts is available.

Combining purchased and hydraulic power sources yields a capacity of 379.5 megawatts. Remaining output requirements must be met from

TABLE 3
Thermal Capacity Requirements

Daily Period	*Winter Requirements (megawatts)*	*Summer Requirements (megawatts)*
Peak	2942.2	—
Full-use	2377.5	2221.4
Off-peak	1513.9	1513.9

steam generation. Table 3 summarizes the required steam-generated output.

Short-Run Marginal Production Costs

It now remains to determine the short-run marginal cost of the required steam output for peak, full-use and off-peak periods. The primary variable cost factor in the firm's steam-generating facilities is coal. In order to increase the output of a generator, there must be greater input. Increments of energy input in terms of fuel costs for a given output level are readily determined.

The operation of a generating system is highly mechanized and requires little labor input. Labor is required mainly to control rather than to operate facilities. Given that a unit is to be operated rather than remain idle, a certain amount of labor input is required for control functions. This basic labor input is sufficient for a wide range of operating outputs. Although no detailed studies have been undertaken, it is agreed by utility engineers that marginal laber costs are nonexistent or extremely low.

As generators are operated at higher capacities, greater wear is to be expected. Thus one would expect a relationship between output and maintenance costs. In practice, however, most maintenance activity is programmed. Generators, for instance, are scheduled for overhaul every four years while boilers are overhauled every two years. Despite maintenance procedures, it is logical to assume that maintenance costs increase with output.

Following standard practice, the utility examined increases its incremental fuel costs by 15 percent to reflect incremental maintenance costs. This figure is not based on any particular study. Rather, its use is justified by the firm on grounds that it is standard practice in the industry.

The proper determination of incremental maintenance costs would require a detailed study. New cost accounting procedures would have to be installed to isolate data not currently recorded by the firm. This type of study will not be undertaken here. Rather, the incremental fuel cost with a 15 percent allowance for maintenance costs which is used by utilities in scheduling generator units will be employed. The error introduced by a failure to consider all costs will be an underestimation of marginal costs. Conversely, errors which overestimate the quantity of required steam-generated output will produce an overestimation of marginal costs. The use of adverse water conditions in determining hydraulic capacities leads to such an error, since costs are based on the use of more steam-generated output than will be required in most years. It is not suggested that the errors are necessarily balancing. They will, however, tend to be offsetting.

Incremental fuel cost data were obtained by setting the generators to operate at various outputs and then measuring the BTU input required to maintain the output. The required BTU inputs were then converted to fuel requirements and finally fuel costs, and the resulting data plotted on graph paper. The data are summarized in table 4.

Notice that incremental costs for generators 11 and 12 range from 3.18 mills per kilowatt hour at an output range of 0–35 megawatts to 4.60 mills per kilowatt hour for outputs of 75–95 megawatts. A 40 percent increase in incremental costs occurs over an output range of 90 megawatts. In this case, incremental cost increases sharply over a limited output

TABLE 4
Incremental Fuel Cost by Generating Units

Unit or Units	*Maximum Capacity (megawatts)*	*Output Range (megawatts)*	*Incremental Fuel Costs (mills/kwh)*
1	90	0– 35	3.06
		35– 90	3.47
2	98	0– 40	2.78
		40– 75	3.09
		78– 98	3.66
3	102	0– 65	2.55
		65–102	2.96
4	102	0– 65	2.71
		65–102	3.12
5, 6	210	0–110	2.45
		110–205	2.84
7, 8	102	0– 65	2.58
		65–102	3.00
9, 10	205	0–110	2.47
		110–205	2.87
11, 12	95	0– 35	3.18
		35– 75	3.65
		75– 95	4.60
13	98	0– 55	3.04
		55– 98	3.68
14	102	0– 65	2.80
		65–102	3.31
15, 16, 17, 18	102	0– 65	2.86
		65–102	3.27

range. This is at variance with the French assumption of constancy of marginal costs. However, on the newer units, such as numbers five and six, incremental cost is approximately constant from 0 to 100 megawatts, a range greater than the maximum output of units 11 and 12. The incremental cost of outputs from 110 to 205 megawatts increases by only about 15 percent. This suggests that the French assumption is reasonably valid for modern generating units.

In table 5, the incremental cost data have been rearranged to permit

TABLE 5
Cumulative Capacity in Order of Incremental Fuel Cost

Unit or Units	*Maximum Output (megawatts)*	*Cumulative Output (megawatts)*	*Incremental Fuel Costs (mills/kwh)*
5	110	110	2.45
6	110	220	2.45
9	110	330	2.47
10	110	440	2.47
3	65	505	2.55
7	65	570	2.58
8	65	635	2.58
4	65	700	2.58
2	40	740	2.71
14	65	805	2.80
5	95	900	2.84
6	95	995	2.84
15	65	1060	2.86
16	65	1125	2.86
17	65	1190	2.86
18	65	1255	2.86
9	95	1350	2.87
10	95	1445	2.87
3	37	1482	2.96
7	37	1519	3.00
8	37	1556	3.00
13	55	1611	3.04
1	35	1646	3.06
2	35	1681	3.09
4	37	1718	3.12
11	35	1753	3.18
12	35	1788	3.18
15	37	1825	3.27
16	37	1862	3.27
17	37	1899	3.27
18	37	1936	3.27
14	37	1973	3.31
1	55	2028	3.47
11	40	2068	3.65
12	40	2108	3.65
2	23	2131	3.66
13	43	2174	3.68
11	20	2194	4.60
12	20	2214	4.60

ready determination of incremental costs for various levels of output. It shows that the off-peak steam-generating requirement of 1513.9 megawatts could be produced with an incremental cost of 3.00 mills per kilowatt hour. The winter peak output and full-use hours for winter and summer would require the use of all steam-generating capacity plus additional purchased power. The incremental cost for the last steam-generating unit employed is 4.60 mills per kilowatt hour. These costs will be used as an approximation of short-run marginal costs.

Long-Run Marginal Costs of Production

In theory, long-run marginal production cost is defined as the cost of providing and using an additional unit of capacity. Its calculation would require a forecast of future construction and operating costs. As previously indicated, the French have demonstrated that for plants of the appropriate capacity relative to demand, long-run marginal costs equal the short-run marginal cost b plus $n\phi$, the marginal plant charge. The short-run marginal production cost b has been estimated, and a first approximation of the marginal plant charge may be obtained from an examination of the fixed costs of operating existing equipment.

An estimate of the marginal plant charge should include all fixed operating expenses. This includes the cost of supervision, maintenance, taxes, and depreciation. In addition, an interest charge reflecting the allowed rate of return on investment should be included.

Total fixed operating costs for the last installed generating unit amount to $9,920,471 per year. This is equivalent to $22.75 per year per kilowatt of steam-generating capacity. This figure will be used as an approximation of the yearly marginal plant charge. As an estimate, it is subject to two possible errors. Improvements in technology may reduce the investment cost per unit of capacity. On the other hand, rising construction and fixed operating costs will tend to increase the marginal plant charge. Together these changes will be partially offsetting. Moreover, it will be shown that even a greatly reduced marginal plant charge still would support peak off-peak price differentials.

A peak demand of 3,321,700 kw would require total charges of $75,568,675 ($22.75 × 3,321,700) per year. This total is to be levied against consumption during the peak period through some specified regime of prices. When the charges are levied, however, it is quite possible that the load curve will shift. Consumption during off-peak and full-use hours may be substituted for peak consumption. What is required is a set of prices for different periods which will result in a broad flat peak.

As a first approximation, the above charges will be applied to the current demand pattern, assuming that it will not be altered. This procedure will allow a direct comparison of existing prices and peak costs. If peak costs exceed current prices, overcapacity will be confirmed.

Accordingly, the yearly plant charge of $75,568,675 will be allocated to current consumption during the peak period. The peak, however, occurs only on weekdays during four winter months, and then only for a four-hour-a-day period. The total number of peak hours in a year is 348. Electricity is consumed at an average rate of 2,860,000 kw during peak periods. Total peak consumption, therefore, amounts to 995,280,000 kwh for the year. This consumption is to bear the entire plant charge of $0.07593 per kilowatt hour. Adding the short-run marginal production cost to this figure yields a peak charge of $0.0805.

TRANSMISSION AND DISTRIBUTION COSTS

Long-Run Transmission Costs

Long-run transmission costs are determined in a similar manner. Transmission, however, is subject to sharply increasing returns. Strict marginal cost pricing would result in less revenues than costs.

In France, capacity is almost equally divided between thermal and hydraulic generation. By basing all production prices on costs of production in dry years, which implies use of more expensive thermal production, a surplus is achieved which can then be applied to the recovery of the excess of average transmission costs over marginal transmission costs. This is not possible in the firm under study where hydraulic generation is a small fraction of total output.

Since it is unlikely that a system of subsidies for electric utilities would be seriously considered in the United States, a departure from peak-load pricing as planned by the French will be necessary. Nonetheless, it is obvious that consumption at the peak determines transmission capacity requirements. Therefore, the problem will be handled by allocating total (rather than marginal) fixed costs of transmission to peak consumption. This approach will insure complete recovery of fixed transmission costs and will reflect the capacity costs of peak consumption. At the same time, it forces a departure from marginal costs which, as noted earlier, will preclude proving the system Pareto optimal.

The costs to be recovered include the costs of operating and maintaining the transmission plant. The total investment in transmission equipment amounts to $279,592,748. A 6 percent return is allowed on the investment and an additional 5 percent allowance is made for taxes. In addition, depreciation is to be included in the fixed charges. Total fixed transmission charges applicable to the franchise area amount to $30,386,615. Following the same procedures as employed for long-run production costs leads to a peak transmission charge of $0.0305.

Short-Run Transmission Costs

During off-peak periods, the marginal costs of transmission consist solely of transmission losses. In the French system, they are accounted for by the manner in which production costs are propagated from the marginal production center under study to all other locations in the network. Rate differences are established for all centers of consumption.

The regulatory body of the utility under study has adopted a philosophy of complete equalization of charges within customer classifications, and differentiation by regions has been discouraged. Under these circumstances it is not surprising that the firm does not record data on transmission losses. Transmission losses increase required output, but since they cannot be traced to particular locations they are in effect allocated to all consumers regardless of location. While the author is opposed to this approach, a lack of data forces its adoption.

Total Production and Transmission Costs

Total charges, including long- and short-run marginal production costs and fixed transmission charges, are summarized in table 6.

TABLE 6
Production and Transmission Costs: Inelastic Case

Daily Period	*Winter Charges (cents per kwh)*	*Summer Charges (cents per kwh)*
Peak	11.11	—
Full-use	0.46	0.46
Off-peak	0.30	0.30

Peak marginal costs greatly exceed current prices while off-peak marginal costs are significantly less than current prices (see table 1). This divergence provides direct evidence of excess capacity resulting from current pricing methods. A comparison of peak and off-peak costs provides further evidence.

The assumption that current demand patterns will remain constant produces a peak transmission and production charge 24 times the full-use charge and 37 times the off-peak charge. The surprising magnitude of the price ratios is a result of demand patterns arising from uniform prices rather than from some failure of theoretical principles. Capacity must be made available to service peak demands. Peak demand occurs, however, only during four months and for a relatively brief period of time—only 348 hours out of the entire year. The average demand could be serviced with a much smaller plant. Thus, a considerable portion of the firm's capacity with its concomitant investment and operating costs is directly attributable to peak consumption. Even if the marginal charges were incorrectly estimated, the peak to off-peak price ratio would remain significant. Suppose, for instance, that the marginal plant charge were overstated by a factor of 2. The peak/off-peak ratio of production and transmission charges would be 25 to 1. The brief duration of the peak then is the primary factor which accounts for the large price differentials. Current pricing procedures produce a pattern of demand which requires excessive capacity which necessarily is inefficiently utilized. Clearly an alternative system of pricing is warranted.

The prices calculated above assume that demand patterns will remain constant even after the new price schedule is put into effect. Despite the rather widespread belief among utility managers that demand is inelastic, a large price change could be expected to alter the pattern of demand. Direct comparison of current quantity-differentiated prices with the proposed time-differentiated price is not possible, but as a rough measure average revenue per kilowatt hour sold to residential consumers (2.40 cents/kilowatt hour) can be compared with the calculated peak rate of 11.11 cents/kilowatt hour. Even though prices still would be low relative to other goods and expenditures on electricity in most cases will remain a small fraction of consumers' budgets, changes in monthly bills are likely to be rather substantial. Industrial, commercial, and residential consumers may seek means of avoiding peak consumption. Demand is more likely to be shifted to off-peak periods than to be reduced in total. Residential consumers, for instance, might schedule the use of major appliances during off-peak periods and will more carefully monitor consumption at the time of the peak. Industrial consumers will give greater thought to the use of off-peak shifts. Commercial users might consider expanding week-end hours and limiting evening hours. In the long-run, other adjustments which would make more use of off-peak periods or alternative sources of power are possible. More widespread employment of off-peak electric water heating and auxilliary space heaters would be likely. Industrial firms might alter methods of production. On balance, some shifting of the load curve is to be expected.

In this case a decrease in average peak consumption of only 5 percent would lower the average peak demand to the level of average winter full-use demand. A 5 percent increase in the summer full-use demand would raise it to the same level. With the price differentials just determined, a shift of this magnitude or more is likely to occur. If peak demand is depressed to or below the level of winter full-use demand, an allocation of the plant charge to full-use as well as peak hours would be warranted.

In other words, immediate application of the calculated price differentials based on current marginal costs is likely to result in a changed demand pattern. A changed demand pattern would require a different capacity and, therefore, would result in a different set of marginal costs and prices.

The likelihood of a shift in consumption patterns poses a difficult operational problem. Exact calculation of a set of time-differentiated prices for peak and full-use hours which would produce a broad flat peak would not only require knowledge of the influence of price in a period on that period's demand but also the impact of prices charged in all other periods. That is, direct and cross-price elasticities would have to be found for all periods. The cross-elasticities would be of particular relevance since a considerable portion of demand adjustment is likely to consist of changes in the time of consumption. Since elasticities are not known, an interim allocation of the marginal plant change over full-use and peak periods based on the French experience will be proposed. It will yield a winter to summer full-use price ratio of 1.1:10 and a peak to summer full-use price ratio of 1.4:10. While the resulting price schedule may not be entirely stable, it will be self-correcting. Any shift in the load curve as a result of the new price schedule will provide additional data on elasticities, which will then allow computation of more appropriate prices. Hopefully, after some period of time, a set of prices which produce a relatively flat and stable peak will be determined.

Based on this interim proposal, the plant charge and fixed transmission charges are to be allocated over the 348 peak hours and 3,408 full-use hours with the peak period bearing a proportionately larger share. The resulting price schedule, including long- and short-run production costs and fixed transmission costs, is shown in table 7. It can only be interpreted as a first step in the introduction of time-differentiated prices.

TABLE 7
Proposed Initial Production and Transmission Charges

Period	*Winter Charges (cents per kwh)*	*Summer Charges (cents per kwh)*
Peak	2.04	—
Full-use	1.60	1.45
Off-peak	0.30	0.30

Distribution

In addition to transmission and production cost, the costs of distribution must be recovered if subsidies are to be avoided. As noted, distribution costs include the expenses of owning and operating lines and other equipment which serve to connect individual consumers to the main transmission network as well as administrative expenses such as billing costs.

The cost of an individual's connection depends solely on the consumption behavior of the customer and, in theory, he should be charged accordingly. In practice, this would require up to as many different rates as there are customers. Such a complex rate structure might be constructed at great expense, but it would be difficult to administer. Small cost differences would give rise to a plethora of rates. There is a limit to the amount of cost differentiation that is administratively feasible. Minor differentials should be ignored in order to preserve the allowable degree of rate complexity for essential cost parameters. Thus, main types of customers within which cost parameters are roughly equal will be separated. The classification will be based on that used by the Federal Power Commission which includes residential (nonfarm), commercial, industrial, farm, and street lighting and traffic systems. Within consumer classifications, distribution charges will be equalized.

The same comments apply to individual responsibilities for collective distribution lines. Cost responsibility has been shown to be in some way related to average consumption at the time of the collective peak, variation in consumption, and correlation of individual consumption with the collective peak. By a sampling procedure, it might be possible to determine approximately a relationship among these variables and costs. The firm has not, however, undertaken such a study and one is unlikely to be undertaken in the absence of pressure from regulatory bodies. It will be assumed, therefore, that within consumer classifications individual cost responsibilities are approximately the same.

The distribution costs to be allocated to consumer classifications include such things as maintenance, general supervision, and accounting. In some cases allocation of costs is quite simple. The cost of maintaining street lighting systems in a given area clearly can be allocated to street-lighting customers, usually municipalities. Allocation of joint costs, however, is necessarily arbitrary. Two bases for allocating these costs are available. They may be allocated to customer classifications by the number of consumers in each class or according to amount of consumption in each class. The costs of operating and maintaining distribution switching stations logically may be allocated by consumption. Accounting costs, on the hand, are better allocated by the number of consumers in each class. The costs and methods of allocation employed are shown in table 8.

In the absence of detailed studies of distribution costs, all such allocations are judgmental. However, they are unlikely to be less satisfactory than the allocations implicit in existing charges, which for the most part are based on historical accident.

The allocation of distribution costs results in a fixed monthly share

TABLE 8
Allocation of Costs of Distribution and General Administration to Consumer Classes

Costs	Total (N = 1,142,000)	Consumer Class: Residential (N = 935,402)	Commercial (N = 122,133)	Farm (N = 49,874)	Industrial (N = 3,235)	Street Lighting (N = 1,257)	Method of Allocation
Operations:							
General supervision and engineering	174,623	146,893	19,174	7,841	506	192	By consumers
Station	1,233,155	243,054	247,494	32,555	69,340	13,565	By kwh
Overhead lines	1,472,781	589,113	147,278	589,113	147,278	—	40%, 10%, 40%, 10%
Underground lines	264,308	26,431	237,877	—	—	—	10%, 90%
Street lighting	—	—	—	—	—	867,186	Direct
Meter expenses	1,648,309	1,386,558	180,984	74,009	4,780	1,813	By consumers
Installations	596,455	501,738	65,491	26,781	1,730	656	By consumers
Miscellaneous	1,638,495	322,947	328,846	43,256	921,326	18,023	By kwh
Maintenance:							
Supervision and engineering	359,709	80,935	80,935	80,935	80,935	35,971	22.5%, 22.5%, 10%
Station equipment	1,129,524	254,143	254,143	254,143	254,143	112,952	22.5%, 22.5%, 22.5%, 22.5%, 10%
Overhead lines	7,639,388	3,055,755	763,939	3,055,755	763,939	—	See operations
Underground lines	758,205	75,821	682,385	—	—	—	See operations
Transformers	514,902	433,136	156,536	23,119	14,939	1,566	Consumers
Street lighting	927,271	—	—	—	—	927,271	Direct
Meters	353,969	297,759	38,866	15,893	1,027	389	By consumers
Accounting, general administration, sales and general maintenance, and general expense (91.5%)	31,510,845	26,506,923	3,459,891	1,414,837	91,381	34,622	By consumers
Depreciation, allowed return and taxes	40,899,426	20,449,713	8,179,885	4,089,943	4,089,943	4,089,943	50%, 20%, 10%, 10% 10%
Total	89,314,666	54,370,919	14,704,858	9,708,180	6,440,761	4,089,943	
Per consumer per year	78.21	58.13	120.40	194.65	1,990.96	7,856.00	
Per consumer per month	6.52	4.84	10.03	16.22	165.91	404.67	

for residential consumers of $4.84. Fixed charges for commercial, farm, and industrial consumers would be $10.03 per month, $16.22 per month, and $169.51 per month, respectively. For purposes of comparison, an equal distribution among all classes of consumers would result in a monthly charge of $6.52. These charges do not reflect the increased costs of metering which would be necessitated by time-differentiated rates. Determination of the costs of time metering will have to await further study. However, even if it were to be twice current metering costs, the monthly charge for residential consumers would only increase by approximately 15 cents. Moreover, the monthly fixed charge would not have a significant influence on either the timing of consumption or quantity consumed.

TOTAL CHARGES

The final rate schedule consists of a monthly fixed charge differentiated by customer classification and a consumption charge differentiated by season and time of use. Residential consumers would be charged $4.84 per month plus 2.04 cents per kilowatt hour for peak consumption, 1.60 cents per kilowatt hour for winter full-use periods, 1.45 cents per kilowatt hour for summer full-use periods, and 0.30 cents per kilowatt hour for off-peak consumption.

EVALUATION AND CONCLUSION

Short- and long-run production and transmission costs and distribution costs have been estimated. It remains to comment on the adequacy of the estimates and to suggest areas which should be strengthened.

Greater accuracy in analysis of production cost was possible because more adequate cost data was available. Energy charges based on estimates of short-run marginal costs and capital charges based on an estimate of long-run marginal production costs appear to be reasonable in a relative, if not absolute sense. It is not suggested that the empirical results equal true marginal production costs, but the possibility of reflecting the marginal costs of production in a rate structure has been demonstrated.

The treatment of some distribution costs necessarily was arbitrary. Nonetheless, the procedure employed yields distribution differentials at least as reasonable as those implicit in current rate schedules. A completely satisfactory treatment of distribution costs may never be feasible, but rate structures could be improved by studies designed to determine improved methods of cost allocation.

Two principal defects of the empirical investigation should be noted. Transmission losses have not been directly considered. An absence of information on energy flows and losses precludes discrimination by geographical areas. If the principles underlining peak-load pricing are accepted by regulatory commissions, steps should be taken to remedy this defect. Differentiation by communities would be justified on economic grounds. In this area, improvements in application of peak-load pricing could be readily accomplished.

Another weakness stems from the necessity of making an implicit judgment on price elasticities.

Not only are the actual direct and cross-price elasticities unknown, but the elasticities implied by the procedure employed are indeterminate. Elasticity calculations would require determination of percentage changes in price and consumption. In order to determine a percentage price change a single initial or current price would have to be stated. Current prices, however, are related to quantity consumed, which varies from consumer to consumer. Use of a crude approximation will allow this problem to be overcome. Since average consumption is in excess of 200 kwh/month, it may be assumed that consumers purchase power at a marginal rate of 1.57 cents/kilowatt hour (refer to table 1). Proposed peak rates are 30 percent greater.

Measurement of the percentage change in quantity consumed poses further difficulties. Peak consumption has been assumed to decrease by about 5 percent. In practice this change would be due to changes in the full-use period price as well as the new peak-period price. The proposed full-use price (1.60 cents/kwh), however, is quite close to the existing marginal rate (1.57 cents/kilowatt hour). If it is assumed that the entire variation in demand is due to the change in peak-period price (in effect neglecting the important cross-price elasticities) a direct price elasticity of 0.17 is implied.[2] Under the assumptions employed, a proportionately greater direct price elasticity would require a proportionately smaller price change to achieve a flattening of the load curve.

Although problems in determining elasticities subject the proposed initial rates to suspicion, they do not negate the possibility of practical application of peak-load pricing principles since the system will tend to be self-correcting. The proposed rate structure will give rise to additional information which will permit subsequent improvements in the initial rates.

After an initial period of experimentation, a reasonably stable system of prices might be achieved, but a peak-load pricing scheme cannot be expected to be as stable as rates which ignore peaking problems. In the

[2] Considering the assumptions this calculation requires, particularly regarding cross-price elasticities, little certainty can be attached to the end result. In addition it should be noted that knowledge of direct and cross-price elasticities alone might not guarantee that appropriate prices could be determined. What is needed is a measure that incorporates price differentials. Such a measure should relate percentage changes in quantity consumed to changes in the ratio of prices in each period as well as the absolute price.

last decade many utilities have experienced pronounced shifts in the timing of peaks as a result of expanded use of air-conditioning. Similar changes in consumer behavior are likely to occur in the future. Changes of this nature tend to be unique and there is little evidence to suggest that future developments will produce rapid and frequent changes. As long as changes are gradual, application of the principles of peak-load pricing would be feasible.

Technological developments in production and distribution of electricity also may influence the treatment of peak loads. The trend toward increased interconnection among major utilities warrants more detailed study of patterns of use of purchased power and its effect on production costs. Widespread interconnection may assist in smoothing out peaks. Development of more efficient methods of servicing peak demands such as pumped storage and gas-turbine generation, may be expected. Technological innovations, however, are more likely to reduce short-term marginal production costs than to eliminate peak loads or significantly reduce long-term peak marginal costs of producing and distributing power.

Notwithstanding the above areas of potential improvement, the illustrative rate structure is based on economic reasoning and is considered a reasonable approximation of the theoretical ideal pioneered by the French. It demonstrates the feasibility of applying peak-load pricing principles. In addition, acceptance of its underlying philosophy would make possible additional research to increase the absolute accuracy of the rates.

Like current price structures, the proposed pricing scheme cannot be shown to be optimal in the Paretian sense. No practical method of meeting all marginal conditions in a decreasing-cost industry has been found. Moreover, if the marginal conditions were met, changing from current prices to a new regime would involve gains for some and losses for others, thereby precluding a welfare judgment, without interpersonal comparisons. In spite of this, decisions on pricing systems must be made. If the proposed system is to be economically compared with existing rates, value judgments must be admitted. On this basis is it suggested that a change to peak-load pricing would be desirable.

From a practical standpoint, total costs must be recovered by the set of prices employed. Economically, total cost coverage is not a sufficient requirement. Consumption at the time of the peak directly determines capacity and, therefore, the amount of resources devoted to electricity production. Uniform rates based on an implicit averaging of total costs do not reflect differences in resource costs between peak and off-peak consumption and, therefore, fail to rationally influence consumer behavior. Specifically, uniform rates encourage high peak consumption and, therefore, capacities which are not efficiently utilized in other periods. In the utility studied, residential consumers are charged a rate as low as 1.57 cents per kilowatt hour, depending on the quantity consumed. This rate is applicable to all periods. There is no incentive for consumers to avoid consumption during the peak period and no stimulation of consumption during off-peak periods. Peak consumption under the proposed rate system would be billed at a rate of 2.04 cents per kilowatt hour. If demand is at all elastic, charging this rate, which more accurately reflects resource costs, would reduce peak consumption and, therefore, reduce capacity requirements and the quantity of resources allocated to the production of electricity. Effects of off-peak consumption are likely to be even more significant. A reduction of the charge per kilowatt hour for off-peak consumption from the current low of 1.57 cents per kilowatt hour to the proposed 0.30 cents per kilowatt hour would result in an increase in demand. Since this increase requires no additional capital investment, existing capital resources would be more effectively employed. It is concluded that under elastic demand conditions, the results in regard to both peak and off-peak consumption are socially desirable.

In the unlikely case that demand is completely inelastic, the above economic benefits would not be achieved. Nonetheless, the proposed rate system would be an improvement when judged by the "cost of service" standard used by regulatory bodies since rates would more nearly reflect actual costs. In both the elastic and inelastic case, peak-load pricing is judged to be more socially desirable than current rate structures.

The level of rates, or more specifically, the return on investment achieved under current pricing systems, could readily be achieved with peak-load pricing. The proposed rates as applied to electricity consumption in 1963 would result in approximately 4 percent greater revenues than under existing rates. Adjustment to any desired rate of return could always be achieved by changes in the fixed charges.

In brief, peak-load pricing based on economic principles offers a practical solution to the problem of supplying peak loads. As opposed to uniform rates, it would act to depress peak demands and thereby reduce the total amount of resources which need be devoted to the industry. In addition, it would stimulate off-peak consumption, thereby allowing more efficient utilization of existing resources. Finally, the rate structure would be more in line with the costs of providing service. Despite initial resistances which might be encountered, the adoption of peak-load pricing principles would be an important step toward improving the organization of the industry.

24. Marginal Policies of "Excellently Managed" Companies*

JAMES S. EARLEY

In another article I presented evidence from management literature that leading cost accountants and management consultants are currently advocating principles of accounting analysis and decision making that are essentially "marginalist" in character and implications. The present article reports on a questionnaire survey designed to test empirically the acceptance and influence of these new principles among leading American manufacturing firms. It seeks to ascertain what relationships there are between organizational and accounting practices and the policies of the firms employing them. It seeks above all to test the validity of certain "nonmarginalist" propositions concerning business behavior found in recent economics literature, and the "marginalist" hypotheses derived from the management literature.

The survey does not purport to cover a cross-section of American business by size and type. It is deliberately restricted to a type of firm taken as "representative," in something akin to the Marshallian sense. These firms are leading firms, and are presumably in the vanguard in the use of the newer management techniques. Through diffusion, direct imitation, and the competitive pressures they create, they are likely to set the dominant patterns of *future* business practice. Inquiry is also directed especially towards multi-product and multi-market companies, both because marginal accounting has most applicability in these cases and because such firms appear to be becoming increasingly representative of American business. It is confined to fairly large companies for similar reasons.

The basic list of companies to which the questionnaire was sent is that of the entire group of 217 manufacturing companies rated as "excellently managed" by the American Institute of Management; 110 useable replies were received.

* *American Economic Review,* vol. 46, no. 1 (March 1956), pp. 44–70.

More than most empirical studies of business policies, this one relies upon inference from indirect evidence. Only a few direct questions concerning policies were asked. Most of the evidence refers to organizational structure, accounting practice, and certain oblique judgments of management, from which inferences as to behavior are drawn. This strategy was deliberately chosen in the belief that it would yield more reliable evidence of wider theoretical value than more direct questioning. The inferential approach is fortified by two special features of the analysis—the search for *patterns* of responses, and *tests of consistency* of the patterns.

It is suggested by many recent theoretical and empirical studies in economics that the modern business firm behaves nonmarginally in at least two essential respects: in having predominantly a long-run and defensive viewpoint in its pricing, production, and investment policies (rather than an alert attitude towards its near-at-hand profit opportunities); and in using, in the main, a full-cost rather than incremental-cost calculus in its pricing, production, and investment decisions. These are the major nonmarginalist hypotheses tested in this survey.

The major hypotheses from the management literature, which run counter to those above, and in this respect and others are considered to be "marginalist" in their implications, are the following:

1. Among well-managed multi-product companies there will be found a substantial amount of what I call marginal accounting. The essential characteristic of such accounting is systematic (1) segmentation and (2) differentiation of costs (and, where appropriate, also revenues). By segmentation is meant the separate calculation of the costs and revenues of each of the firm's operations and prospective actions (so-called "segments")—e.g., each process, product, or product group, market area, "function," division, plant or contemplated action. Cost differentiation, which is as far as possible carried out for each segment, takes two forms: (1) the breaking apart of fixed and variable costs to obtain a variable cost function; and (2) differentiation between those fixed costs that can be specifically assigned to a segment and those that must be considered common to the enterprise as a whole.

Such accounting is "marginal" in two essential respects: first, it provides discrete data for considering each segment as an alternative field of management action; and second, in place of average cost information it provides data for estimating the *differences* in costs (and in revenues) that any action would entail.

2. In multi-product, multi-process enterprise, marginal accounting (and the basing of policies upon it) will be associated with, and facilitated by, an organizational structure differentiated, administratively and technically, along lines of major segments, such as product lines, functions, and market areas. This facilitates the above-mentioned segmentation and differentiation of costs and revenues and helps management focus upon each major sector of the enterprise as a profit-making entity.

3. Marginal accounting data will be found useful in a wide range of managerial problems, including (1) evaluation and control of operating efficiency; (2) minimizing costs (as by proper selection of processes and methods); (3) determination of the relative stress that should be placed among products and markets in selling; (4) pricing decisions, both short-range and long-range; (5) selecting, adding, or dropping products or market segments; and (6) product- and market-related investment (including disinvestment).

4. Marginal accounting analysis will lead firms to employ marginal techniques of planning and decision making (called by the National Association of Cost Accountants "cost-volume-profit analysis" and "marginal income analysis"), and to adopt marginalist viewpoints and policies. The basic principle of such marginalism being to concentrate upon the differences in costs, revenues, and profit that decisions involve and to neglect "inescapable" costs not affected by them, special attention will be given to ratios between price and variable costs ("marginal income ratios" in NACA terminology), and to differences between revenues and variable-plus-separable costs (so-called contribution margins). Overhead allocations and full-cost computations will tend to fall into disuse for decision-making purposes.

Specific policies likely to flow from marginal accounting analysis are: much reference to variable costs in short-range pricing decisions and in "selective selling"; attention to both variable and separable fixed costs in choices among markets and products and in product-related investment decisions; and differential pricing and other forms of "market segmentation" according to estimates of differing variable/fixed cost compositions, competitive pressures, and demand elasticities.

5. Such analyses and policies, especially if accompanied by budgeting and "profit planning," will be associated with a short-dated time horizon (at least as far as pricing and other product-related decisions are concerned), and a fairly keen and short-dated search for increased profit.

6. Pricing, product, and investment decisions will be made with a lively sense of impending innovation and obsolescence; hence the possible long-run reactions of rivals to the profits currently being made will not greatly influence these decisions. This is in contrast to full-cost theories in particular, which implicitly assume that firms make their decisions within the horizon of a given production function.

These are the major hypotheses to be tested. The following sections present a summary of major results to date.

I. COMPANY ORGANIZATION

Proper organization and procedures are considered important for securing marginal accounting data and using them effectively. Three such aspects of organization were inquired into: the administrative and technical differentiation of activity by products and market areas; management reports of variable/fixed cost breakdowns by segments; and the participation of different enterprise functions in planning and decision-making. Only the returns bearing on organization structure and cost reporting are analyzed in this article, although the responses on functional participation are tallied in Appendix A.

Most of the companies show that their organization is conducive to cost and revenue differentiation by product groups and market areas (see table 1). In these matters 78 percent of the respondents are aided

TABLE 1
Suitability of Company Organization to Marginal Accounting Analysis (questions 1, 2, and 3)

	Number of Companies	*Percent of Responses*
A. Product lines differentiated by:		
1. Wholly or mainly specialized plants (Q. 1)	58	54
2. Organization into product divisions (Q. 2a)	76	70
3. Either (1) or (2)	84	78
4. Neither (1) nor (2)	24	22
B. Selling activities differentiated by:		
1. Product-division selling organization (Q. 2b)	83	79
2. Market-area selling organization (Q. 3)	93	85
3. Either (1) or (2)	103	99
4. Both (1) and (2)	69	66
Component index 1: Suitability of Organization[a]	*Number of Companies*	*Percent of Total*
(+2) Strong marginalist evidence—product costs differentiable by either specialized plants or product divisions; selling costs by both products and market areas (A3 and B4)	59	56
(+1) Substantial marginalism—product costs differentiable by either plants or divisions; and selling by *one* of products or markets	24	22
(−2) Strong nonmarginal evidence—product costs differentiable by neither specialized plants nor divisions; selling by neither products nor markets	1	1
(−1) Substantial nonmarginal evidence—product costs differentiable by neither plants nor divisions; selling by only *one* of products or markets	13	12
(0) Ambiguous evidence—patterns other than those above	10	9
Average of component index: = +1.2		

[a] The figures to the left are the assigned positive and negative values of each category.

either by having their plants mainly or wholly specialized by product lines, or by being organized administratively into product divisions (item A-3). Selling activities are even more highly differentiated, and along both product and market-area lines. Only one company does not organize its selling activities by either products or markets, and approximately two thirds of them differentiate their selling activities in both these respects (item B-4).

An index of the marginal or nonmarginal organizational characteristics of the respondents is presented in the lower portion of table 1. This is the first of six component indexes of this type by which, in part, the questionnaire evidence has been analyzed and evaluated. It will be observed that the average value of this index, secured by the algebraic weighting shown in the table, works out at somewhat above the level of "substantial" marginalism. These organizational characteristics cannot, of course, be taken by themselves as impressive evidence as to policy or behavior; they will later, however, be correlated with indexes covering other evidence to establish patterns and test consistencies and hypotheses.

II. VARIABLE/FIXED COST BREAKDOWNS AND THEIR TRANSMISSION TO MANAGEMENT

The practice of making variable/fixed (V/F) cost breakdowns and putting them into management's hands in connection with planning and decision making is overwhelmingly followed by these "excellently managed" companies, as table 2 reveals. Such V/F breakdowns are, moreover, preponderantly carried through for the separate functions of the enterprise, and by major products and product groups. Such *segmented* V/F cost analysis, recent cost accounting literature shows, is the hallmark of marginal accounting and marginal income analysis, as distinct from the mere use of break-even charts. Especially when taken in conjunction with responses concerning the uses to which these breakdowns are put (section III), this data is strongly evidential of a "marginal" approach to management problems.

It is also significant that most of the companies make these segmented V/F breakdowns available as regular reports, not only as special analyses. One can reasonably assume that with these companies reference to segmented variable cost functions is an established working rule of management.

For the component index covering this portion of the questionnaire, the availability of V/F breakdowns for major products or product-groups is used as the criterion, and the three major types of costs—production, selling, and total—are included in the index.[1] On this basis virtually four fifths of the companies can be classified as showing strong marginalism, and only six companies evidence nonmarginalism. The average of all companies is extremely high.

[1] Because of the large number of matters covered by some portions of the questionnaire, it was not considered advisable in most cases to include responses to all questions in the component indexes. Those selected are those which seem to be most relevant and important in connection with each characteristic being measured.

TABLE 2
Availability of Variable/Fixed Cost Breakdowns for Management Planning and Decision Making
(question 5)

	Companies Making V/F Cost Breakdowns Available (percent)			*Companies Not Making V/F Cost Breakdowns Available (number)*	
Types of Costs	*As Regular Reports*	*As Special Analyses*	*Total**	*Not Practi- cable*	*Not Useful*
A. Overall company costs:					
1. Total	61	28	91	2	7
2. Production	72	19	23	3	4
3. Selling	68	17	88	6	7
4. Design, engineering, and research	52	28	85	10	7
5. Administrative	63	19	85	9	7
6. By territorial divisions	51	21	76	7	17
B. Costs by major products or product groups:					
1. Total (T)	63	25	90	5	5
2. Production (P)	70	23	95	4	0
3. Selling (S)	54	29	86	12	4
4. Design, engineering, and research	42	31	76	19	6
5. Administrative	47	26	76	16	9
All of (1) to (5)	33	12	72	—	—

Component index 2: Availability of product V/F breakdowns	*Number of Com- panies*	*Percent*
Strong marginalist evidence: total (T), production (P), and selling (S) breakdowns all made available by products	83	79
Substantial marginalist evidence: *two* of T, P, or S product breakdowns made available	12	11
Strong nonmarginalist evidence: none of T, P, or S made available	4	4
Substantial nonmarginalist evidence: only *one* of T, P, or S made available	2	2
Ambiguous evidence: only two of three items answered and one of these made available	4	4
Average of component index: +1.6		

* Includes small numbers of companies, varying from two to five, responding "Planned but not Available."

III. USES OF VARIABLE/FIXED COST BREAKDOWNS

The responses to question 6 strongly support the claim that variable cost functions are becoming a widely used multipurpose management tool. (See table 3.) All but three respondents make use of them in at least one of the problems listed in the questionnaire, and most of them use them in connection with problems stretching from control of efficiency

TABLE 3
Uses of Variable Costing: Percent of Responding Companies Considering V/F Cost Breakdowns Helpful in Specified Problems
(question 6)

	Number of Responses	*Percent Responding "Helpful"*
Management problem		
1. Judging and controlling sector efficiency (6a)	106	89
2. Determining cost effects of volume variations (6c)	107	94
3. Pricing: (P)		
Estimating advantages of price reductions (6d)	106	83
Deciding on prices of multiple products (Q. 9)	104	61
One (or both) of these	110	89
4. Selective marketing: (M)		
Deciding which products to stress (6e)	105	66
Deciding which markets to stress (6f)	105	49
One (or both) of these	105	66
5. Product selection: (S)		
Whether to drop products (6g)	106	84
Deciding types of products to add (6h)	107	71
One (or both) of these	107	89
6. Methods selection:		
Choosing best production methods (6i)	107	71
Choosing best distribution methods (6j)	107	48
One (or both) of these	108	73
Component index 3: "Variable costing"	*Number of Companies*	*Percent*
Strong marginalist evidence—V/F considered helpful in pricing (P), marketing (M), and product selection (S)	63	59
Substantial marginal evidence—V/F considered helpful in two of P, M and S	31	29
Strong nonmarginalist evidence—V/F not considered helpful in any of P, M or S	4	4
Mild or ambiguous evidence—V/F considered helpful in one of P, M or S	9	8
Average of component index: +1.5		

and selecting best production methods to pricing and product selection. In distribution problems other than pricing the incidence is considerably lower, but still high enough to demonstrate that their value extends throughout the whole spectrum of production, pricing and selling problems. Since management tends to look upon variable cost as a close approximation to the economist's short-run marginal cost, this is impressive evidence of marginalist viewpoints and behavior among leading companies.

IV. USE OF "SEPARABLE" FIXED COSTING

Marginal accounting analysis can be brought to bear on many longer-range problems by combining V/F breakdowns with the identification of the separable fixed costs of segments or actions—here called S/C (separable/common) or separable costing. When combined with calculations or estimates of segment revenue, these combined operations lead to marginal accounting's measurement of long-range profitability—the segment or action's "contribution margin." This is a marginal (incremental) measurement in two respects: it shows the amount of fixed cost directly attributable to the segment or action independent of the common and average fixed costs of the enterprise; and it retains the variable cost function relating levels of production to differences in variable and hence in total costs.

While such measurements may be retrospective, they are especially useful in forward-looking decisions entailing additions or reductions in fixed charges. Accordingly, question 7 inquired whether, in contemplating a number of such actions, fixed cost calculations were made on an incremental or an allocation basis.

The incidence of S/C costing, while lower than that of V/F costing,

TABLE 4
Use of Separable Fixed Costs in Long-Range Management Problems (question 7)

	Percent Using:	
	Incremental or Separable Costs	*Allocation or Other Bases*
Management problem		
Deciding whether to drop products (7a) (D)	72	28
Closing plant or division (7b)	81	19
Both 7a and 7b	69	16
Adding production capacity for existing products (7c) (I)	86	14
Choosing new product types (7d)	68	32
Opening new sales office or territory (7f)	52	48
Introducing (and pricing) a new product (7e) (estimating price and volume required to make its introduction profitable) (N)	71	29
One or more of 7a to 7f	91	
All of 7a to 7e	48	
Component index 4: Separable costing	*Number of Companies*	*Percent*
Strong marginalist evidence: separable fixed costs used in dropping products (D), adding product capacity (I), and introducing new products (N)	57	56
Substantial marginal evidence: separable fixed costs used in two of D, I or N	27	26
Strong nonmarginal evidence: separable fixed costs used in none of D, I or N	10	10
Substantial nonmarginal evidence: separable fixed costs used in only one of D, I or N	8	8
Average of component index: +1.08		

is impressively high (see table 4). Over nine out of ten of the respondents use the S/C method in one or more of the listed problems, and almost half use it in all of them except the opening up of new sales offices or territories. Even in such problems as adding to existing product capacities and introducing new products, where the conventional canons of making decisions turn on net profitabilities after "due allocation of overheads" would have strong traditional backing, the large majority of the respondents look rather to the specific additions to their total fixed charges. As in the case of V/F breakdowns, S/C costing is less prevalently used in distribution decisions.

On the three criteria selected for our index of marginalism in long-range costing principles, 82 percent of the companies provide at least substantial evidence of marginalist practice and only one out of ten companies give evidence of strong addiction to full-costing principles.

V. COMBINED USE OF V/F AND S/C COSTING

Table 5 tests the use of both (and neither) of these complementary types of cost differentiation. Even by this rigorous test, the marginal approach has a high incidence, ranging from 54 percent to 83 percent of the respondents except in distribution decisions. On the other hand,

TABLE 5
Use of Both (and neither) V/F and S/C Costing in Long-Range Management Problems (questions 6 and 7)

	Number of Responding Companies	*Number of Companies Using:* Both	*Number of Companies Using:* Neither	*Ratio of Both to Neither*
1. Adding production capacity for existing products				
(a) 7c, plus reference to variables in cost/volume analysis (6c)	101	83	2	42:1
(b) 7c, plus reference to variables in volume/price estimates (6d)	100	72	4	18:1
2. Dropping products or product-groups: 7a, plus reference to variables in dropping products (6g)	100	65	8	8:1
3. Choosing new product types: 7d, plus reference to variables in choosing product types (6h)	100	54	16	3.4:1
4. Adding (and pricing) new products: 7e, plus reference to variables in cost/volume analysis (6c)	100	68	3	23:1
7e, plus reference to variables in price/volume estimates (6d)	99	59	6	10:1
5. Adding distribution facilities: 7f, plus reference to variables in volume/price estimates (6j)	99	35	33	1:1

with this last exception the number using neither type of marginal costing is very small. An interesting measure of marginal vs. nonmarginal costing is provided by the ratios of companies using both V/F and S/C costing to those using neither, shown in the right-hand column. With the exception of the distribution facilities problem, these ratios are high.

VI. DIRECT EVIDENCE ON PRICE POLICY

Table 6 analyzes the responses to four direct questions on pricing policy (8–11). Although of special significance when related to other portions of the questionnaire, these responses in themselves provide important evidence that most multi-product companies do not base their prices on full-costs, but instead differentiate cost-price ratios to reflect major factors recognized in the marginal analysis. The questions were phrased and ordered to try to secure evidence on the companies' normal policies, as distinct from what might be done in exigent circumstances, although this interpretation could not be relied upon independently of other evidence.

The first question (8) concerned the company's general pricing objective. A full-cost pricing philosophy could be expected to lead management to try at least to maintain more or less equal margins between prices and full costs on its various product and market segments. Yet almost three quarters of the companies responded that this was not their policy. Most of these companies apparently either consciously pursue the advantages of price-cost differentiation or make so many exceptions to uniform full-cost-plus pricing that it has ceased to be recognized as an objective.

There followed questions on three factors that, if frequently made the basis of modifications of price-cost ratios among multiple products, would indicate either marginal policy or marginalist behavior regardless of policy: differing V/F cost compositions of products; differing buyer sensitivity to price; and differences in expected competitive pressures.

Of these, the highest proportion (84 percent) of the companies declared they modify their relative price-cost relationships to "reflect differences in the degree of competitive pressure" expected from other companies. While the full-cost theory recognizes, and even emphasizes, that business will pay close heed to threats of market invasion in its pricing, this response strongly suggests: (a) that in most cases invasion expectations differ considerably among the products and market areas of the same company; and (b) that full-costs are not generally considered a reliable measure of what prices it is safe to charge in different cases.

These latter inferences, which contradict the central tenet of full-cost pricing theory as developed by Andrews, Harrod, et al., are strengthened when responses to this and to question 8 on pricing objectives are paired and their patterns tested, as is done in item 2a of

TABLE 6
Adherence to marginal and Full-Cost Pricing Policies: Responses on Pricing of Multiple Products
(questions 8–11)

	Responses and "Patterns" (percent of total)	
	Marginal[a] *Responses*	*Full-Cost*[b] *Responses*
1. Is company policy to try to maintain roughly equal price-full cost ratios among its products and markets? (Q. 8) (106 companies)	73	27
2. Are price-cost ratios modified for differences in expected competitive pressures? (Q. 11) (106)	84	16
(a) "Patterned" responses to Q. 8 and 11 (105)	63	8
3. Are they modified for differing buyer sensitivity to price?[c] (Q. 10 *or* 15) (105)	77	23
(a) Patterned responses to 8 and 10 *or* 15 (104)	58	9
4. Modified for differing V/F cost compositions? (Q. 9) (104)	61	39
(a) Patterned response to 8 and 9 (104)	44	10
5. Price-cost ratios modified for both (or neither) differing competitive pressures and buyer sensitivity. (Q. 10 *or* 15, and 11) (104)	69	9
Component index 5: Pricing policies	*Number of Companies*	*Percent*
Strong marginalist evidence—do not try to maintain equal cost-price ratios (Q. 8), and modify prices for differing V/F compositions (Q. 9), buyer sensitivity to price (Q. 10 *or* 15), and expected competitive pressures (Q. 11)	34	33
Substantial marginalist evidence—differential pricing objective (Q. 8), modify price-cost ratios for either or both of V/F composition and buyer sensitivity to price	35	34
Strong nonmarginalist evidence—have equal cost-price objective and prices modified for none of above factors	1	1
Substantial nonmarginalist evidence—equal price-cost objective, and prices modified for one or two of above factors but not both V/F and buyer sensitivity	18	17
Ambiguous evidence—patterns other than above	16	15
Average of component index: +.81		

[a] Includes responses of "No" to question 8 and "Yes" to questions 9, 10 and 11, and such response patterns.
[b] Includes responses of "Yes" to question 8 and "No" to questions 9, 10 and 11, and such patterns.
[c] Question 10 was inadvertently omitted from first mailing of the questionnaire, and only 43 responses were secured. Where 10 was unanswered, response to question 15 was substituted.

table 6. Sixty-three percent of the respondents answered both questions in a "marginalist" manner, while only 8 percent showed consistent full-cost responses. The companies making marginal responses to both questions were 86 percent of those which stated a marginal pricing objective, whereas the "consistent" response pattern is only 30 percent for companies stating a full-cost objective.

Question 10 sought to ascertain whether estimates of differences in elasticity of demand among buyers is given any systematic recognition in modifying price-cost relationships of multiple products. The percentage of companies indicating that this is done is somewhat lower than that of those who pay attention to differing competitive pressures, but is still very high. The proportion of consistent "marginal" patterned responses is also very impressive in comparison with that of consistent full-cost responses, being 79 percent as compared with only 33 percent.

The proportion of companies that "take into consideration the extent to which costs of different products are made up of variable as against fixed costs" (61 percent) is appreciably lower than those modifying price-cost ratios for the other two factors investigated. And only 60 percent of the companies whose responses to question 8 indicate a differential pricing objective explicitly recognize differing V/F ratios as a basis for such differentiation. These lower percentages indicate that the implications of differing V/F cost ratios, in situations in which competitive pressures and market elasticities differ among products, is less well understood in connection with general pricing policy than in connection with short-run price adjustments, product selection, and possibly pricing new products.

Certain questions not included in table 6 bear inferentially on the companies' pricing policies, and reinforce the above evidence that marginal pricing is the norm for the type of company being studied. Thus the fact that 73 percent of the respondents stated that in pricing their new products they give primary attention to expected demand elasticities over the "first few years" of introduction rather than over longer periods (Q. 15), tends to gainsay the basic rationale of the full- or average-cost pricing theory that companies give primary consideration to the danger that if they price above present normal costs, including "reasonable overhead allocations" they will open themselves to competitive market invasion. In the same direction points the fact that 58 percent of the companies state their new products can "usually command a higher price in relation to their costs than [their] well-established products" (Q. 14). Presumably these companies, at least, recognize the "life cycle" of many products from distinctiveness to comparative obsolescence that results from gradual market saturation and the appearance of new products and methods, and differentiate price-cost ratios between their new and older products accordingly.

Impressive evidence of "marginalism" and of distrust of "full-cost" pricing is also provided by the very high proportion (89 percent) of the companies stating in response to the final question (20) that they consider the speed with which they improve their products and production and selling processes more important to their profitability and growth over the years than "close pricing of products in relation to costs." This evidence will be referred to again below.

VII. TIME PERSPECTIVES AND INNOVATION RECOGNITION

The latter portion of the questionnaire sought primarily to secure evidence regarding the time horizons of these companies, and the extent to which prospective innovative changes influence their pricing and product-related policies. A short horizon and keen innovation-awareness is taken to be evidence of marginalist attitudes and behavior, and an opposite posture indicative of nonmarginalism. The responses to the most relevant questions are summarized in table 7.

TABLE 7
Management's Time Perspective and Views Regarding Innovation

	Percent
1. Percent of (105) companies feeling profit and growth more dependent upon speed of innovation than on close cost-pricing (Q. 20)	89
2. Percent of (100) companies giving more importance in pricing new products to buyer price sensitivity over first few years than over longer periods. (Q. 15)	73
3. Percent of (107) companies considering present (process) costs of their established products reliable measures of their own or stronger competitors' costs of these (or competitive) products:	
(a) not even "2 or 3 years ahead" (Q. 17a)	20
(b) not more than "2 or 3 years ahead" (Q. 17b)	70
(c) not more than "5 or 10 years ahead" (Q. 17c)	83
4. Percent of (100) companies stating new products can usually command higher price-cost ratios than well-established products (Q. 14)	58
5. Percent of (104) companies stating most new products requiring substantial capital outlay must promise "pay out" during their first few years (Q. 16)	52

Component index 6: Time perspective and recognition of innovation	*Number of Companies*	*Percent*
Strong marginalist evidence—give primary attention to short-range demand (Q. 15), cannot project costs more than two to three years ahead (Q. 17b), and speed of innovation considered more important than close cost-pricing (Q. 20)	45	44
Substantial marginalist evidence—two of above three responses	44	43
Strong nonmarginalist evidence—negation of above three responses	0	0
Substantial nonmarginalist evidence—only one of above responses	13	13
Average of component index: +1.2		

The responses show a definite preponderance of short-range over long-range horizons, a preponderantly rapid pace of innovation, and prevailing sharp recognition of its implications. This is especially notable in the view, expressed by almost nine tenths of the respondents, that staying abreast or out ahead in the innovative race is more important to their long-range business success than a "defensive" policy of basing prices closely on costs. In addition, as already noted, almost three quarters of the companies state they give more importance, in pricing new products, to estimates of short-range than of long-range buyer elasticities (Q. 15). A short horizon and innovation-sensitivity are implicit also in the responses of the 58 percent stating that their new products can usually command higher price-cost ratios than their established products (Q. 14). The evidence of rapid innovation and its effect upon policy is less impressive with respect to "payouts" expected on substantial capital outlays entailed in producing a new product.

The prevalence of these "short-run" views is, of course, highly consonant with the earlier testimony: only 27 percent of the companies try to follow a policy of uniform pricing in relation to full accounting costs; 61 percent of them explicitly take variable cost functions into consideration in their multiple-product pricing policies; and variable cost functions are almost universally considered "helpful" in a wide range of management problems, both short-range and long-range in character (see table 3).

VIII. COMPOSITE EVIDENCE; INTERRELATIONS AMONG COMPONENTS

Judged either by responses to individual questions or the foregoing component indexes, the evidence of overall marginalism among these companies is very strong. The unweighted composite average of the six indexes is +1.23, or considerably above "substantial." When the plus and minus scores in each component are added algebraically,[3] for each of the 88 companies ratable uniformly in this manner (see table 8), not a single company presents nonmarginalist evidence on balance, and all but 10 companies show more than negligible marginal characteristics. Approximately 60 percent of them show what can be considered from "substantial" to "very strong" marginalism.

In short, the hypotheses taken from the management literature appear to be generally supported by the questionnaire returns. Most of these companies do employ marginal accounting extensively, including segmented variable-fixed cost differentiation and the determination of separable fixed costs in most relevant contexts (Hypothesis 1). Most of them are organized, as to product and market, in a manner condusive to such accounting (2). They use variable-fixed and separable-common cost differentiation in a wide variety of important problems of planning and decision making (3). Most of them follow essentially marginal principles, and eschew or subordinate cost allocations and

[2] "Strong" and "substantial" marginalism (and nonmarginalism) are given weights of +2, +1 (−2 and −1) respectively, and mild or ambiguous evidence is given a weight of zero.

TABLE 8
Number of Companies Having Various Algebraically Summed Scores in the Six Component Indexes Combined[a]

Algebraic Score	*Number of Companies*	*Algebraic Score*	*Number of Companies*
+12	7	+6	13
+11	12	+5	6
+10	10	+4	7
Very strong marginalism	*29*	Moderate to substantial	*26*
+ 9	5	+3	3
+ 8	6	+2	6
+ 7	12	+1	1
Substantial to strong	*23*	Negligible	*10*
		Zero	None
		Negative scores	None

[a] Confined to the 88 companies whose responses permitted inclusion in all of the six component indexes.

full-costing, in their product selection, product investment, and both short- and long-range pricing decisions (4). (They apparently employ these principles to a lesser degree in problems of selective marketing.) The companies also have preponderantly a short time perspective (5) and a keen awareness of innovative implications in their pricing and related policies (6).

It remains to test systematically the hypotheses, embedded in the others, that marginalism (and nonmarginalism) in some of these characteristics will be associated with marginalism (and nonmarginalism) in others. Operationally, the hypotheses would run: (1) marginalism in organization and accounting analysis, and a short-time horizon and innovation sensitivity, can be taken as evidence of essential marginalism in business behavior; and (2) the growth of marginal accounting and associated techniques is likely to impart more marginalism to business behavior as time goes on.

The requirements of the study as a whole, plus the high degree to which the other hypotheses were substantiated, unfortunately impair the value of the evidence for testing these hypotheses. Marginalism is so prevalent among these companies that the number of nonmarginal cases is in most cases uncomfortably small for statistical testing. Secondly, some of the questions and components are ambiguous for this purpose. Finally, several variables that may affect the relationships—such as company size, nature of products and processes, and industry structure—have not yet been introduced. Nevertheless, although the results are only partial and suggestive, some relationships of significance emerge.

To secure rigorous tests of significant relationships, χ^2 tests were run on a number of intercomponent relationships that the literature of management economics would suggest. The formal results are presented in table 9.

The first hypothesis tested, that enterprise organization differentiated by product-line and market area will stimulate marginal accounting and marginal policies, is partially sustained and partially unconfirmed (section A of table 9). There is a strong relationship, with a chance probability of less than 1 percent, between differentiated organization and

TABLE 9
χ^2 Tests of Relationships Among Components[a]

Related Components	Number of Companies	χ^2 Values	Degrees of Freedom	Chance Probability (percent)
A. *Organization (1) and:*				
V/F availability (2)	102	10.278	1	Less than 1
Variable costing (3)	104	2.598	2	20–30
Separable costing (4)	93	3.002	2	20–30
Pricing (5)	101	2.979	4	50–70
B. *V/F availability (2) and:*				
Variable costing (3)	103	8.032	1	Less than 1
Separable costing (4)	97	0.949	1	30–50
Pricing (5)	99	6.358	2	2–5
C. *Organization plus V/F availability (1 + 2) and:*				
Variable costing (3)	100	5.478	2	5–10
Separable costing (4)	96	2.054	2	30–50
(3) and (4) combined	96	1.602	2	30–50
Pricing (5)	96	2.171	4	70–80
D. *Regularity of reporting*[b] *and:*				
Variable costing (3)	60	0.361	1	50–70
Pricing (5)	58	0.000	2	100
E. *Variable costing (3) and:*				
Separable costing (4)	101	12.232	2	Less than 1
Pricing (5)	101	6.014	2	2–5
F. *Separable costing (4) and:*				
Pricing (5)	100	6.038	4	10–20
G. *Variable plus separable costing (3 + 4) and:*				
Pricing (5)	97	11.112	4	2–5[c]
H. *Perspective (6) and:*				
Variable costing (3)	99	0.191	2	90–95
Separable costing (4)	96	0.769	2	50–70
Pricing (5)	100	7.088	2	2–5[d]
I. *Perspective plus variable costing (3 + 6) and:*				
Pricing (5)	97	21.661	4	Less than 1

[a] In all cases negative and zero component scores were combined. Degrees of freedom were then reduced, by combining "substantial" marginalist with ambiguous and nonmarginal cases where necessary, to the points required to secure five or more cases in each expected frequency. Numbers in parentheses signify the components related in each case.

[b] For these tests two groups of companies were segregated; those making total, production, and selling V/F product breakdowns available as regular reports, and those making them all available but only as special analyses.

[c] At 2° of freedom the χ^2 value has a probability of less than 1%.

[d] At 1° of freedom χ^2 value has probability of less than 1%.

the availability to management of product V/F breakdowns for major cost components. On the other hand only relationships so moderate as to be of no clear significance are found between organization on the one hand, and use of V/F breakdowns in selective marketing, product selection and price adjustment, the employment of S/C fixed cost breakdowns, and differentiated pricing policies, on the other.

The second hypothesis tested is that the availability of variable cost functions of products will lead management to give this marginal cost element greater weight in its pricing, marketing, and product selection decisions than in the absence of such accounting data. This seems definitely to be the case, the relationship between components (2), V/F Availability, and (3), Variable Costing, having a chance probability of less than 1 percent (section B). In this connection it should be recalled that component (2) measures merely the extent to which product V/F breakdowns are "available," regardless of their purpose; while (3) records whether they are found useful in the specific problems of selective marketing, product selection, and pricing. Historically, such product breakdowns were used primarily for cost budgeting and control. This strong relationship indicates that they are also strongly associated with marginal attitudes in these important areas of business decision making.

On the other hand, the mere availability of product V/F cost breakdowns does not appear to increase significantly the use of separable rather than allocated fixed costs in the longer-range problems included in component 4 (section B, second item).

Two supplementary possibilities regarding the influence of organization structure and product variable cost availability upon the costing practices of management were also tested. The first was that a combination of differentiated organization *plus* product V/F differentiation might tend more strongly toward marginal costing principles in decision making than would either of these conditions alone. The second hypothesis was that the transmission of V/F breakdowns to management via regular reporting, rather than only sporadically as special analyses, might be especially conducive to variable costing. Neither of these hypotheses, however, receives significant support from the χ^2 tests (sections C and D).

The next hypothesis tested, a very interesting one, received strong confirmation. The positive correlation between variable costing and separable costing is so strong as to have a chance occurrence of less than 1 percent (section E). It appears from this that alertness to variable cost functions in marketing, pricing, and selecting products will make management look at long-run costs too in a more "marginal" manner.

The hypothesis that a short-time perspective will tend in itself toward marginal (variable and separable) costing is not substantiated by the intercomponent relationships, the χ^2 tests between (6) on the one hand and variable and separable costing on the other yielding results of very low reliability (section H). The significance of these seemingly anomalous results will be commented upon below.

In view of the prominence given to pricing in the literature surrounding the marginalist controversy, and the claims of advocates of marginal accounting that its use will engender more marginalist pricing, the relations between the other components and Pricing (5) are of special interest. These are shown in the bottom items of each section of the table.

Some of the interrelationships are negligible. Thus neither organization nor the regularity of reporting product V/F breakdowns seem in themselves to influence pricing policies significantly (sections A and D). Nor does the relationship between pricing and separable costing seem to be close enough to be clearly statistically significant (section F).

On the other hand there are several key relationships that are statistically significant. Both V/F availability (2) and the use of such breakdowns in decision making (3) appear to be quite strongly related to marginalism in standard pricing policies (sections B and E). Those companies using both variable and separable costing also appear to be especially marginalist in their pricing (G). So too do companies having short-time horizons and keen innovation sensitivity (H). In short, the hypotheses that (a) use of marginal accounting techniques and (b) short views will each evoke marginalist behavior in pricing receive statistically significant support.

A pattern that is somewhat perplexing appears when some of the key tests are juxtaposed. The most notable apparent anomaly is that although both variable costing and short perspective seem to be associated wth marginal pricing, there is no significant cross-relationship between short perspective on the one hand and variable costing on the other (section H). This seems strange inasmuch as close attention to variable cost functions might itself seem evidential of short views toward a company's needs and opportunities.

To throw some light on this apparent anomaly, each company's scores in variable costing (3) and perspective (6) were combined and related to its score in the pricing component. Significantly, the already quite strong relationships between each of these components and pricing becomes even stronger in this text, the χ^2 value becoming the highest of all those tested (section I).

IX. CONCLUSIONS

A reasonable inference would seem to be that the use of marginal accounting techniques and a short-time perspective and innovation sensitivity are each *independent* influences tending toward marginalist pricing. The kind of costing which is appropriate to something akin to conventional theory's short run is itself sufficient to incline companies toward pricing on essentially marginalist lines. The addition of other conditions that may lead management to take especially short views of their needs and opportunities simply increases this tendency.

When combined with other results of the survey, this conclusion has, it seems to the author, interesting theoretical and practical implications. The significant pattern of results can be summarized as follows: (1) short views, innovative sensitivity, marginal costing, and marginal pricing are all preponderant among the responding companies; (2) where considerable segmented variable cost data are brought to management's attention, the companies' short-range policies (inferred from the substantial attention given to variable cost functions in the various problems covered in question 6) are consistent with their longer-range costing, pricing, and other product-related policies; (3) with such companies marginalism is apparently not dependent upon—though it is increased by—a short time perspective.

It appears reasonable to conclude from this pattern that the bulk of these "excellently managed" companies do not conceive of short-run vs. long-run profitability as alternative and inconsistent goals, and that they seek to "maximize" their long-run welfare by alertly trying to maintain and increase their current profits within their practicable horizons. With regard to such companies, there arises a serious question whether it is valid to build our analytical models on theoretical time periods, short or long, as presently conceived. What seems to be typical of these companies is not "marginalism sitting," short or long run, but "marginalism-on-the-wing."

In any case the major messages seem to be fairly clear: (1) Marginal accounting and costing principles have a strong hold among these companies, and the bulk of them also follow pricing, marketing, new product, and product-investment policies that are in essential respects marginalist. (2) Whether interested in short-run profits or long-run health, very few of these companies give any evidence of ignoring the opportunities and/or necessities of practicing marginalism in the above range of problems.

Whether the same will be found true of most American firms only further study—and perhaps the passage of time—can tell. "In the long run," it is safe to say, the influence of firms such as these is bound to be substantial. At least as long as a reasonable amount of company autonomy and rapid innovation prevail, their influence is likely to be strongly in the direction of growing "marginalism" in American enterprise.

APPENDIX A

Questionnaire on Costing and Market Analysis
(with tally of responses)

Name of Company ______________________

1. Are plants specialized by product lines? Wholly 18 Mainly 40 Partly 44 None 6
2. Is your company organized into product-divisions?
   (a) Production activities Yes 76 No 32
   (b) Selling activities Yes 83 No 22
3. Are selling activities administered on a market area or territorial basis? Yes 93 No 16
4. Please indicate by "yes" or "no" in the following spaces, whether representives of the following functions of your company participate in the following types of major decisions:

In major decisions of the following types, there is participation by officials representing:

	Production Function	*Selling Function*	*Engineering Design or Research*	*Accounting and Finance*
(a) Sales planning and budgeting	77	110	49	97
(b) Product pricing	58	110	36	89
(c) Altering or dropping products	99	108	93	77
(d) Introducing new products	100	109	102	74
(e) Changing production methods	108	78	91	58
(f) Changing distribution methods	27	107	18	67
(g) Investment decisions	55	48	45	106
(h) Research programs	79	96	108	61

Questionnaire on Costing and Market Analysis *(continued)*

5. Are breakdowns of costs into their variable* and fixed components made available to your management, for *planning and decision-making purposes,* along the following lines? Please check appropriate spaces:

	(1)	(2)	(3)	(4)	(5)
	Are Available		*Are Not Available Because*		
The following breakdowns of costs into Variable and Fixed components:	*As Regular Reports to Management*	*As Special Analyses*	*Not Considered Practicable*	*Not Considered Useful*	*Planned but Not Available*
(a) Total Company Costs:					
1. Total Costs	62	29	2	7	2
2. Total Production Costs	78	21	3	4	2
3. Total Selling Costs	73	19	6	7	3
4. Total Design, Engineering and Research Costs	55	30	10	7	5
5. Total Administrative Costs	67	21	9	7	3
6. By Territorial Divisions	52	21	8	17	4
(b) By Major Products or Product Groups:					
1. Total Costs	62	25	5	5	2
2. Production Costs	75	24	12	4	2
3. Selling Costs	56	30	12	4	3
4. Design, Engineering and Research Costs	43	32	19	6	3
5. Administrative Costs	49	27	16	9	3

* By "variable" cost is meant those types (or portions) of costs that vary *in total amount* (*not* per unit) with variations in levels of activity or output—sometimes called "direct" or "volume" costs. (Examples are direct materials and labor, sales commissions, and ordinarily portions of indirect expense and power costs.) "Fixed" costs are those which remain much the same *in total amount* during a period, regardless of variations in levels of activity—sometimes called "overheads" or "period charges." (Examples are rents, general offices, salaries, most depreciation, and a portion of branch office sales expense.)

6. In which if any of the following problems do you consider *fixed versus variable cost* breakdowns helpful to management?

(a) Judging and controlling the efficiency of operations in various sectors of a company?	Yes 94	No 12
(b) Determining "break-even points" for:		
(1) Total company operations?	Yes 81	No 26
(2) Individual divisions or sectors?	Yes 87	No 20
(3) Major products or product groups?	Yes 81	No 23
(c) Determining the effects upon costs of changes in volume?	Yes 101	No 6
(d) Estimating the advantages of possible increases in sales that might accompany price decreases?	Yes 88	No 18
(e) Deciding which *products* to stress in selling efforts?	Yes 69	No 36
(f) Deciding which *markets* to stress in selling efforts?	Yes 52	No 53
(g) Deciding whether to drop a product or product-group?	Yes 89	No 17
(h) Deciding what types of product to *add* to a line?	Yes 76	No 31
(i) Choosing the best methods of production?	Yes 76	No 31
(j) Choosing the best methods of distribution and selling?	Yes 52	No 55

Questionnaire on Costing and Market Analysis *(continued)*

7. In the following *planning and decision-making problems,* does the cost analysis you use "break out" and consider as the fixed cost involved the *addition* (or *reduction*) in your total fixed charges that the change would entail? (Or are these problems analysed in some other manner, such as by calculating "full costs," including *all* overhead allocations?)*

(a)	Deciding whether to *drop* a product or product-group?	Yes 73	No 28
(b)	Deciding whether to *close down* a plant or division?	Yes 82	No 19
(c)	Deciding whether to *add to capacity* to produce an existing product?	Yes 88	No 14
(d)	Deciding what types of product to *add* to a line?	Yes 68	No 33
(e)	Estimating the price and volume at which a new product must sell to make its introduction profitable?	Yes 72	No 30
(f)	Deciding whether to open up a new sales office or a new sales territory?	Yes 52	No 49

* The distinction in costing involved here is that sometimes made in accounting literature between those fixed costs that are "separable" or "specific" to an operation or sector, as against those that are "inseparable" or "common." For example, if the new machinery required to make a new product would add $50,000 a year in fixed charges, and that were the only *added* fixed charge involved, the $50,000 would be the "separable" or "specific" fixed cost of introducing the product. On the other hand, if a part of the fixed charges on the building in which the machinery was to be installed were allocated to the new product, that would be an example of ascribing "common" fixed costs to its introduction.

8.	Is it your policy to try to maintain, as among your various products and market areas, more or less equal percentage margins between prices and "full costs?" (Note: Full cost includes allocation of all overheads.)	Yes 29	No. 77
9.	In pricing decisions on your various products, do you take into consideration the extent to which costs of different products are made up of *variable* as against *fixed* costs?	Yes 63	No 41
10.	Do you modify price-cost relationships, as among your various products, to reflect differences in buyer sensitivity to price—that is, how much more or less buyers would take if the price were lower or higher?	Yes 34	No 9
11.	Do you modify price-cost relationships among your various products to reflect differences in the degree of *competitive pressure* you expect from other companies?	Yes 89	No 17
12.	*In pricing a new product* do you employ formal market research to ascertain buyers' sensitivity and/or probable *competitive pressure* from other companies?	Yes 60	No 47
13.	In the case of *already established products* do you employ formal market research to keep informed as to *buyer sensitivity* and/or *competitive pressure?*	Yes 56	No 51
14.	Can your new products usually command a higher price in relation to their costs than your well-established products?	Yes 56	No 47
15.	In introducing a *new product,* is estimated sensitivity of buyers to price over the first few years of its introduction given *more* or *less* importance in fixing its price, than estimated buyers' sensitivity looking a long period (say ten to fifteen years) ahead?	More 73	Less 29
16.	Are prospective rates of obsolescence of products and/or processes in your industry such that most of your *new products* that require substantial capital outlay must give strong promise of "paying out" on their capital outlay during their first few years?	Yes 54	No 50
17.	Aside from possible changes in wages and material prices, do you consider the *present* cost of your *established products* reliable measures of the costs at which you (or your stronger competitors) will be able to produce these (or competitive) products:		
	(a) 2 to 3 years ahead?	Yes 85	No 22

(b) 5 to 10 years ahead? Yes 32 No 74
(c) 10 to 15 years ahead? Yes 18 No 88

18. *In introducing new products,* do you consider that setting their prices in close relation to their "full costs" plus a normal profit is an effective means of avoiding competitive invasion of their markets? Yes 48 No 56
19. Do you consider that maintaining prices in close relation to "full costs" plus "normal profit" is an effective means of avoiding market invasion of your *established products?* Yes 46 No 61
20. Do you feel that the profitability and growth of your company over the years depends *more* or *less* upon close pricing of your products in relation to costs *than* upon the speed with which you improve your products and your production and your production and selling processes? More 12 Less 93

APPENDIX B

Industrial Classification of Circularized and Responding Companies

		Number Circularized		
Census Code	*Industry*	*Total*	*Net of "Non-applicable"*	*Number of Useable Responses*
2000	Food and kindred products	17	15	10
2100	Tobacco manufacture	2	2	0
2200	Textile mill products	6	6	4
2300	Apparel	1	1	0
2400	Lumber and wood products	2	2	0
2500	Furniture	2	2	2
2600	Paper and allied products	20	18	9
2700	Printing (publishing excluded)	1	1	1
2800	Chemicals and allied products	36	30	16
2900	Coal and petroleum products	19	15	7
3000	Rubber products	4	4	2
3100	Leather and leather products	1	1	0
3200	Stone, clay and glass	14	13	5
3300	Primary metals	20	18	10
3400	Fabricated metals	9	9	5
3500	Machinery, except electrical	34	33	23
3600	Electrical machinery	13	13	5
3700	Transportation equipment	16	11	5
3800	Instruments and related products	9	7	4
3900	Miscellaneous manufactures	2	2	2
		228	203	110

part SIX

Capital Budgeting

INTRODUCTION

Capital budgeting is a major topic in many managerial economics texts. Capital budgeting procedures and techniques are utilized by companies planning long-term investment projects. It is a process which requires an understanding of the time value of money and, simultaneously, the cost of capital; also, its use assumes one's ability to predict net cash inflows and outflows from a specific investment.

Known also as investment decision making, equipment replacement analysis, and the analysis of capital expenditures, it is concerned with choices among the investment alternatives available to the firm, with the goal of accepting the most profitable alternatives and rejecting the others.

Main parts of capital budgeting include (1) the cost of capital, (2) replacement policy and the estimation of useful life, (3) ranking criteria, and (4) uncertainty. Work on the cost of capital has grown so technical in recent years as to be largely inaccessible on the introductory level. Until the results and controversies associated with the names of Modigliani and Miller are synthesized, they must be ignored here.

In economics, it is not uncommon for wide disparities to exist between theory and practice. Capital budgeting does not differ in this regard. The theory of capital budgeting assumes the existence and application of sophisticated analytical techniques; in practice, executives may ignore results of the analysis. James C. T. Mao surveys this condition and suggests ways in which current theory may be modified to make it more operationally useful.

The part of capital budgeting literature not concerned with the cost of capital and uncertainty tends to dwell on ranking criteria, especially the "theoretically correct" methods of present value and internal rate of return. But there appears to be little evidence that actual firms are influenced much by the results. Warren Haynes and Martin Solomon argue that capital budgeting theory fails to cover enough of the decision-making process. The struggle for continued existence by small firms in highly competitive markets, for example, may be more important than the refinements of theoretically sound budgeting techniques.

The problem of uncertainty is in many ways the most interesting part of capital budgeting and has received some of the best work in the field. But attacks on it take such a multitude of approaches that the form of a new synthesis, if it ever occurs, cannot be foreseen. That the problem is so serious as to raise doubts about the attention paid to refined ranking criteria based on certainty assumptions is shown in the article by Martin Solomon.

Joel Dean's article is concerned with the extension of capital budgeting into the field of advertising. It argues that so long as responses to advertising occur with a delay, advertising expenditures are a form of capital investment and should be treated as such.

25. Survey of Capital Budgeting: Theory and Practice*

JAMES C. T. MAO

I. INTRODUCTION

There exists a wide disparity between the theory and practice of capital budgeting. During the past 15 years, the theory of capital budgeting has been characterized by the increased application of such analytical techniques as utility analysis, mathematical programming, probability, and statistical theory. The practice of capital budgeting has no doubt changed at the same time, but business executives do not appear to have adopted many of the new techniques. The purpose of this paper is to compare current theory with practice: (1) to discuss the nature of the gap and the reason for its existence, and (2) to try to lessen this disparity by suggesting ways of modifying theory to make it more operationally meaningful. To aid discussion, this paper is divided into four sections: objective of financial management, risk analysis in investment decisions, profitability criteria for investment selection, and conclusions.

It is difficult, if not impossible, to characterize the current theory of capital budgeting in a few words. By current theory, I shall mean the type of work on capital budgeting that appears in journals such as *Management Science, Journal of Finance, Journal of Financial and Quantitative Analysis*, and *Engineering Economist*. These theories generally make use of modern quantitative tools. By current practice, I shall present the findings of case studies I conducted during the summer of 1969. In all, I interviewed eight medium and large companies in the following industries: electronics, aerospace, petroleum, household equipment, and office equipment. I held full-day discussions in each company interviewed. Because of the small sample I do not wish to put forward any statistical generalizations about current practice. However, since the companies studied were chosen for the efficiency of their management, they do give a preliminary view of current capital budgeting practices in firms with progressive management.

* *Journal of Finance,* vol. 25, no. 2 (May 1970) pp. 349–60.

II. OBJECTIVE OF FINANCIAL MANAGEMENT

Theory

Any theory of optimal investment decisions is premised on the existence of an objective function which the firm maximizes. Current financial theory generally assumes that the firm should maximize the market value of its common shares. There is a growing body of literature that explains how share values are determined under conditions of uncertainty. For example, according to John Lintner, a perfect capital market with homogeneous investor expectations, the risk of a security in a portfolio is measured by the weighted average of the variance of its return and the covariances between its return and other returns. The price of a share, then, is a function of its expected earnings, the pure rate of interest, the price of risk, and risk measured in this way.

Before discussing what financial executives regard as their objective, let us examine the objective of maximizing share value from an operational viewpoint. In order to implement this objective, the financial executive needs criteria for choosing between alternative time patterns of share prices within his planning horizon. Current theory does not provide this. Of course, this issue will not arise under conditions of certainty and perfect capital market, since the action which maximizes share value at the end of the firm's horizon also maximizes share prices throughout the horizon. (See figure 1A.) Since curve I dominates curve II,

FIGURE 1

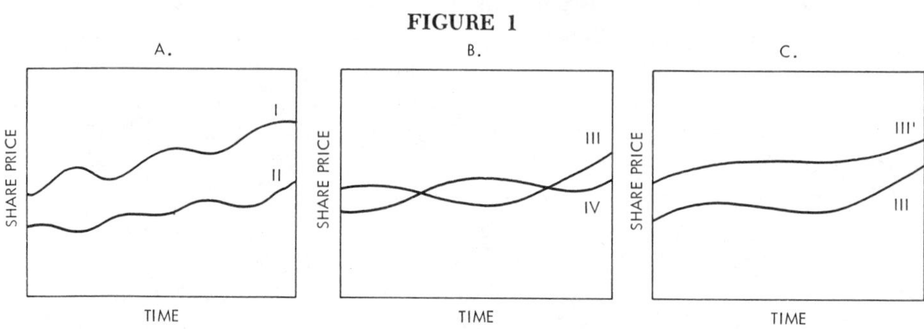

it is clearly preferable. However, under conditions of uncertainty and imperfect capital market, the relative share prices at the end of the horizon do not necessarily determine the relationship between the prices during the time span. Two possible courses of action could thus easily result in time patterns of share prices with multiple crossings. (See figure 1B). In the latter case, the objective of maximizing share value has no operational meaning until there are criteria for choosing between criss-crossing price patterns. To make this choice, we may wish to consider the duration for which one pattern exceeds the other, as well as the timing and size of the difference. One formula which incorporates these considerations is the following:

$$\phi = \int_0^T (P_t - P_t')e^{-rt}\,dt \tag{1}$$

where P_t and P_t' stand for share prices as depicted by curves III and IV respectively, r stands for the rate of discount, and T stands for the time horizon. A simple rule would be to choose time pattern III if $\phi \geq 0$, and to select time pattern IV otherwise. It should be noted that this problem is quite similar to choosing between criss-crossing loss functions in decision theory, and perhaps some of its criteria could be used to choose alternatives here.

Let us suppose that time pattern III is preferred. How is it possible to improve curve III further so that the share price will be raised at every point along the time pattern? (See figure 1C.) To put it differently, if there is an earnings per share (eps) series that corresponds to price pattern III, how should the eps series be modified to raise share prices from curve III to curve III′? B. G. Malkiel has shown that under conditions of certainty the price-earnings ratio of any stock is equal to the price-earnings ratio of a standard reference stock, adjusted for the difference in growth rates and the duration of this difference. Although he applied his model to conditions of uncertainty, the complexities involved prevented him from constructing a full uncertainty model. Here, we shall make a simple extension of Malkiel's certainty model by introducing the risk factor. Risk is to be measured by the standard deviation to the eps series, calculated with regard to its trend. An eps series with a higher trend and less risk would result in a uniformly higher price.

To illustrate how this risk measure can be implemented, let us say that eps at any time t, denoted as $x(t)$, is the sum of three components:

$$x(t) = a + bt + c \sum_{h \epsilon H} \sin \frac{t}{h} + u \tag{2}$$

where a, b, c are constants, h is an element of a set of incommensurate real numbers and t stands for time. Component $a + bt$ is the trend, component $\sum_{h \epsilon H} \sin \frac{t}{h}$ is the sum of a set of sine functions with incommensurate periods, which results in nonperiodic oscillations; and component u is the source of random fluctuations. If we denote $x^*(t)$ as the trend value of $x(t)$, then our risk measure, the standard deviation about the trend, is given by the formula:

$$\sigma = \left\{\frac{1}{N} \sum [x(t) - x^*(t)]^2\right\}^{1/2} \tag{3}$$

where N stands for the number of observations. It should be noted that the concept of risk presented here is the risk of a security considered by itself. This risk concept needs to be modified if investors have sufficient resources to diversify their portfolios. In that case, the distinction made by some financial writers between diversifiable and nondiversifiable risks is relevant. It is the nondiversifiable component that determines the risk of a security in a portfolio context.

Practice

The executives interviewed were asked what they regarded as the objective of financial management. More specifically, they were asked whether they chose between alternative courses of action so as to maximize the value of the firm. Here is a sample of the answers given:

> Our objective is to finance the high growth rate of this company. Since we do not use debt, we have to make sure that we earn enough profit to finance the growth. It may be that share value is maximized as well, but we don't think about that.
>
> We have a goal of earnings per share which we manage astutely every quarter. Because this is a young, growing company, it is important in terms of future financing that we do not disappoint the investing public.
>
> The thing that means the most to the stockholder is the value of their stock. In determining the value of stock, the most critical factor is probably the earnings per share, but it also involves the fact that you are not static but moving forward and increasing your earnings per share. To increase earnings, you have to have sales growth which is the life blood of any business.
>
> The goal of the financial manager is to have his company produce a record that will enable it to raise capital at the lowest possible cost. To accomplish this goal, he needs a proper concept of stability and a proper concept of growth. In this company, we try to achieve a growth rate of 15 to 18 percent, compounded annually, in both sales and earnings.

Although most of the comments are self-explanatory, three points should be noted. First, while some executives did not explicitly state that the maximization of the value of the firm was their goal, this reason was implicit in all their answers. Since the management is operationally oriented, the goal of maximizing share value is translated into operating targets of growth and stability in the earnings stream. Second, the executives tend to view the value of their company independently of the effect of diversification by the investing public. From a practical standpoint, this approach has the advantage of being simple. Theoretically, this approach to valuation is adequate if the nondiversifiable risk represents a substantially large proportion of the total risk. Third, if the maximization of share value depends upon consistent growth, then it becomes vital for executives to have a constant flow of new ideas.

Although the executives may search continually for new ideas, financial theorists have not contributed much to understanding how new ideas can be generated.

III. RISK ANALYSIS IN INVESTMENT DECISIONS

Concept of Risk

Theory. A central aspect of any theory of capital budgeting is the concept of risk. Most financial writers argue that firms should choose portfolios rather than projects, and they measure the risk of a portfolio by the variance of its return.[1] This approach to the analysis of risk is a straightforward adaptation of Markowitz's quadratic programming model of portfolio selection. Although the variance is easy to manipulate mathematically, financial writers have not been completely satisfied with the concept of risk. In fact, Markowitz himself had reservations about choosing variance as a measure of risk. Beside variance, he considered five other alternative measures of risk: the expected value of loss; the probability of loss; the expected absolute deviation; the maximum expected loss; and the semi-variance. The first four measures were rejected for one reason or another as unsuitable. For the remaining two measures, variance and semi-variance, Markowitz preferred the latter for theoretical reasons, but chose the former because of its familiarity and ease of computation.

Why is semi-variance a better measure of risk than ordinary variance? Consider investment return, R, as a random variable with known probability distribution. If h stands for a critical value against which the actual values of R are compared, and $(R - h)^-$ if $(R - h) \leq 0$ and for zero if $(R - h) > 0$, then S_h (semi-variance with h as the reference point) is given by the formula:

$$S_h = E[(R - h)^-]^2 \tag{4}$$

where E is the expectation operator. In words, semi-variance is the expected value of the squared negative deviations of the possible outcomes from an arbitrarily chosen point of reference. In contrast, variance is the expected value of the squared deviations (whether positive or negative) of the possible outcomes from the mean of the random variable. This means that semi-variance evaluates the risks associated with different distributions by reference to a fixed point which is designated by the investor. The variance measure introduces no such refinement, but uses the means of the distributions, which may vary widely, to make the

[1] Return could refer to either internal rate of return, net present value, payback period, or some other measure. We are purposefully leaving the term "return" undefined, so that we can proceed with the discussion of risk.

judgments. Also, in computing semi-variance, positive and negative deviations contribute differently to risk, whereas in computing variance, a positive and a negative deviation of the same magnitude contribute equally to risk. In essence, then, since capital has an opportunity cost, the risk of an investment decision is measured primarily by the prospect of failure to earn the return foregone. Semi-variance is more consistent with this concept of investment risk than ordinary variance.

Practice. The business executives interviewed were asked what they understood by the term "investment risk":

> Risk is the prospect of not meeting the target rate of return. That is the risk, isn't it? If you are one hundred percent sure of making the target return, then it is a zero risk proposition.
>
> Risk is financial in nature. It is primarily concerned with downside deviations from the target rate of return. However, if there is a good chance of coming out better than you forcast, that is negative risk (a sweetener) which is taken into account in determining the security of an investment.
>
> There are three things that concern me in evaluating the risk of an investment: the chances of losses exceeding a certain percent of my total equity, the chances of earning the required rate of return, and the chances of breaking even on a cash flow basis. Cash break-even is kind of a survival point. [The investment decisions in this company are few, but large in size.]
>
> There are some projects in the company which I don't think are going to pay off, and I disagree with the fellows who are running the show. These projects are the risky investments. Also, I never worry about the project return going above the target return. Risk is what might happen when the return is going to be less.

These statements give rise to two observations. First, when the investment decision involves only a small portion of the resources of the company, risk is primarily considered to be the prospect of not meeting some target rate of return. However, when the investment concerns a large proportion of the company's resources, risk also involves the danger of insolvency. Second, the executives' emphasis on downside risk indicates that their concept of risk is better described by semi-variance than by ordinary variance.

To verify further the empirical relevance of semi-variance as a risk measure, a test was designed in which the business executives were asked to choose between two hypothetical distributions of investment returns. Each investment is assumed to cost x dollars now, and after one year to return the cost of x dollars plus the profit (or loss) as given by the probability distributions in figure 2. In this figure, each asterisk represents one possible investment outcome, and hence distribution A has a mean of 3, variance of 4 and a semivariance of 1, whereas distribution B has a mean of 3, variance of 4, and a semi-variance of zero.[2] For this test, it

[2] For this example, the critical value h in the definition of semi-variance is taken to be zero.

FIGURE 2

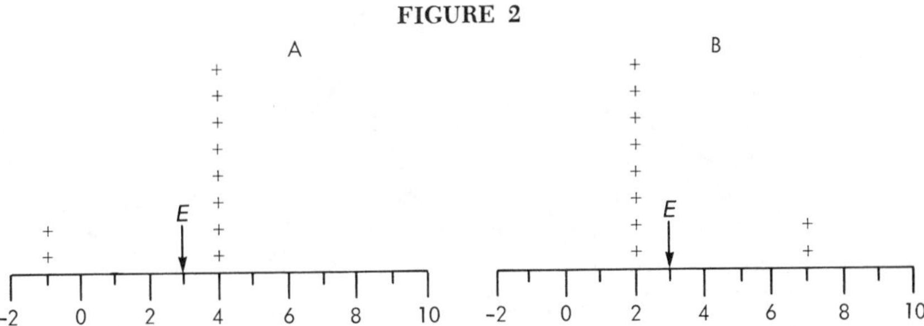

is necessary to use a cost figure that the executive is familiar with, and which produces a rate of return that is reasonably close to his target rate of return as to call for considerable deliberation before arriving at a decision. Although both the target rate of return and the assumed cost of investment varied from company to company, for the sake of discussion we shall assume this cost to be $100,000 and the target rate of return 20 percent. The executives were asked to assume a position of capital rationing in which they had to choose either A or B. About one third of the executives chose A, another third chose B, and the remaining third indicated that their choice would depend on circumstances.

The reasons given for the decisions vary from company to company, but the following quotes summarize the major viewpoints:

> Why do I pick A? Well, I am going to earn a profit of 4 in eight out of ten times and suffer a loss of 1 in the other times. Sure, the investment is risky, but that is part of the game. I would be very much surprised that anyone in our industry wouldn't pick A because we face this kind of risk all the time.
>
> Because of the current tight money situation, I am worried about capital replacement in the event of loss. If we were in a period when capital could be easily replaced at a reasonable cost, then I would have an enhanced willingness to take on risky investments. In any case, I would never pick A unless I could get a reasonable repetition of the projects to enable the averages to come home.
>
> Our present portfolio has a sufficient number of high risk-high return projects in it, so I would probably select B. But at another point in time I might look at those projects in terms of the portfolio aspect and pick A.
>
> Project B has an 80 percent chance of returning 20 percent on my investment. Since my target return is 20 percent, I would probably play safe and accept B. Also, I prefer B because I have seen more heads roll as a result of negative returns.

Executives seemed more likely to choose A if their businesses accustomed them to that degree of risk, if they personally preferred risky ventures, and if they could control the loss possibility in A through diversification.

When these conditions are absent, the executive is more likely to pick B because the absence of loss possibility makes it a more secure investment.

The previous analysis was concerned with a choice between two individual investments. It is equally important to examine the risk concept from the portfolio viewpoint. The executives were asked to imagine the same alternatives on a larger scale, where x represented the total company investment, and questioned as to which portfolio they would select. The answer was unanimously B, and their reasons were most succinctly voiced by the statement of one executive:

> The key is survival. We will take a chance on evaluating individual projects rather optimistically, but we will not take a chance on the main company. One of our obligations is to sustain this company in life and every time we put it in a minus position, it dies a little bit if not in total.

This evidence is consistent with semi-variance as a concept of risk. If semi-variance is used by the business executives, there is a possibility that it may also be the risk concept used by security investors. If so, the definition of the risk of individual securities within a portfolio needs to be adjusted, with corresponding alterations to the existing theory of share valuation under uncertainty.

Method of Incorporating Risk

Theory. For the present, let us accept variance as a measure of risk. How does current theory incorporate risk into investment analysis such that, given two investments with different returns and different risks, the factors can be adjusted to reach a single figure with which to compare the investments? Two methods can be distinguished: the certainty equivalent approach and the risk-adjusted discount rate approach. When the method of certainty equivalent is used, the value of an investment is calculated by discounting the random cash flows at the pure rate of interest. The resulting expected value and variance are converted into their certainty equivalent with the risk eliminated. This certainty equivalent figure determines the profitability of the investment. Under the method of risk-adjusted discount rate, the value of an investment is calculated by discounting the expected cash flow at a rate that allows for the time value of money and also for the risk present in the cash flow. The investment is profitable if the resulting value is positive.

Whichever approach is used, the investor must also decide between the single project or the portfolio framework of investment selection. This distinction can be illustrated most easily by using the certainty equivalent approach to risk analysis. In current theory, the single project approach is justified if the firm contemplates only one investment during its planning horizon. A good example of this analysis is the work of Frederick

S. Hillier who derived formulas for calculating the expected value and variance of NPV from the cash flow distributions associated with an investment. However, when more than one investment may be taken, the firm's optimal selection of investments must be based on an examination of all possible combinations of investments, rather than the examination of single investments. When the portfolio approach is used, the model is generally an adaptation of the Markowitz portfolio selection model with 0–1 conditions imposed on the decision variables to reflect project indivisibility. A different model which also employs the portfolio approach is the chance-constrained model of R. Byrne, A. Charnes, W. W. Cooper, and K. Kortanek in which they imposed a probabilistic payback constraint over all investments simultaneously. The objective is to pick those projects which satisfy the constraints while maximizing expected net present value.

Practice. The executives' method of incorporating risk is primarily the risk-adjusted discount rate approach. In all companies interviewed, although the executives talked about the concept of probability, none used an explicit probabilistic framework for investment analysis. The operating division proposing a project has the responsibility of forecasting the incremental cash flows associated with the investment. In some companies, three sets of figures are forecast: optimistic, pessimistic, and most likely. The optimistic and pessimistic figures denote the range of possibilities. The "most likely" figure does not mean the mode: it is a conservative estimate which the executives consider as having a probability of about .75 of being attained or exceeded. In fact, one executive requires a minimum probability of .80 from his staff.

In most instances, the chief financial executive will receive the analysis of an investment based upon the most likely figure, and containing all the underlying assumptions. The executives were questioned as to what particular aspects of a report were most instrumental in their decisions:

> The project justification may run into volumes, but I am still going to ask my project manager one question: Why do you believe we can get a 5, or 10, or 15 percent share of the market against our competition. If he sells me on this and on the accuracy of his cost estimate, then it is a worthwhile risk venture.
>
> Before committing myself, I ask what else can we use the investments for, if things should go wrong. A project may have a fast payout, but it is not a good investment if we can't hedge our risk of failure.
>
> Sometimes I make a decision truly on the basis that I have enthusiastic support from the people that are going to implement it. I also look at their track record.

In essence, the executive is trying to check the accuracy of the most likely figure. He is modifying the projected outcome by considering the human factor and by introducing a contingency plan. His dilemma is the uncertain nature of his forecasts. The real difficulty is the search for a reliable probability distribution of cash flows to base the decision upon. Thus, if a theorist begins his analysis with an assumed probability distribution, he has assumed away one critical aspect of the problem involved.

Next, although the firms do use the portfolio approach to investment, the method of implementation and the reasons for its use differ from current theory. Current theory visualizes the investor in a portfolio framework as follows. He obtains the cash flows for the set of investments, and derives from them the means, variances, and covariances of the returns. He then chooses that portfolio of investments which gives the best combination of risk and return. But in reality, since these project analyses are submitted independently by separate divisions, no allowance is made in the risk assessment for the covariances between projects. In other words, the proposals top management receive do not contain the figures necessary for evaluating project risks on a portfolio basis in the manner presented by current theory.

The executives were asked how they introduced the portfolio approach in their investment decisions, and more specifically what was the objective and method of diversification. Diversification is thought of in terms of major activities, not with regard to every piece of capital expenditure. In practice, this involves a long-range plan (usually five years) which sets out broad guidelines for the operating divisions. The plan may call for changing, or adhering to the emphasis placed on existing activities, or for incorporating brand new ideas or products. This is where critical decisions regarding diversification are made. In formulating this plan, the executives group the many activities of the company into larger, global areas of concern, not into particular, isolated investments. Details of variances and covariances are generally left in the background. Theoretically, diversification is concerned with stabilizing the earnings stream; but, in practice, the executive is often more concerned with growth.

IV. CRITERIA FOR INVESTMENT SELECTION

Theory. In the above discussion of return and risk, we purposefully used the term "return" in its generic sense, without defining it as internal rate of return (IRR), net present value (NPV), payback period, or accounting profit, so that we could focus on the concept of risk. Current theory generally regards IRR, or its equivalent NPV, as a better measure of return than either the payback period or the accounting profit. The reason for this preference is that under conditions of certainty, of two investments of equal size, the one which has a higher IRR results in higher value for the firm. This preference has been carried over to conditions of uncertainty without sufficient critical analysis. Both the payback period and accounting profit have been regarded as inferior, because at best they can only be used to approximate the IRR. However, since the payback period is usually justified as a method of incorporating risk, a much more pertinent criticism is the limited applicability of the payback period as a method of risk analysis. Also, since reported earnings do affect share prices, investment decisions must consider the effect on accounting profit, if the goal is to maximize share values.

Although theorists have advocated IRR and NPV for measuring return, they are aware that the majority of business still use the payback period and/or the accounting profit criterion. Two reasons have been advanced to explain the relatively slow acceptance of the IRR and NPV criteria. One explanation focuses on the failure of IRR and NPV criteria to consider the effect of an investment on reported earnings. Thus, in choosing between two investments, the application of the IRR (or NPV) criterion may result in the acceptance of those investments which have a higher level of earnings, but which also produce an erratic eps pattern. Since the price-earnings ratio tends to vary inversely with the stability of earnings, the strict application of IRR criterion does not guarantee the maximum value for the firm. The other approach shows how the payback period can incorporate factors which the IRR does not pay full attention to. In their paper, Byrne, Charnes, Cooper, and Kortanek attempted to explain the common use of the payback period as a way of minimizing the risk of lost opportunities. More recently, H. Martin Weingartner tries to explain the payback method as a measure of the "liquidity" of an asset and as a simple device for "the resolution of uncertainty." In the next subsection, we shall look at the practice to determine which measure is actually used and why.

Practice. Of the eight companies questioned about investment criterion, two make primary use of the IRR, four use IRR together with accounting profit and payback, and two use accounting profit, payback, and an "exposure index," which measures the probability that the maximum investment loss will exceed a specified percentage of the firm's total equity. The two companies using primarily IRR are growth companies with closely held stock which finance growth through internal generation of funds, and whose typical investments are small in relation to the total resources of the firm. The four companies which use IRR together with accounting profit and payback are publicly held companies which rely heavily on external sources to finance growth, and whose businesses are fairly risky and competitive. The remaining two companies are similar to the above four in terms of stock ownership and in their reliance on outside capital. However, they differ in one major aspect. Their investments are more risky because of strong industry competition and because of their few, but large, investments.

These findings suggest that the payback period is primarily a risk measure. Accounting profit, since this is what the financial community focuses on, is especially important if the company is widely held and relies on external sources of financing. IRR is most likely to be the major criterion in closely held firms which are less worried by erratic patterns in their per share earnings, which finance themselves, and which make many small investments so that the risk in any one investment is not critical.

V. CONCLUSIONS

In making these case studies, I have focused on the essential points of disparity between the theory and practice of capital budgeting. The evidence suggests that there are at least six ways in which current theory can be modified to make it more operationally meaningful:

1. If we accept the objective of investment decisions to be maximizing the value of the firm, then we must provide the financial executive with a criterion for choosing between criss-crossing time patterns of share prices. The choice criteria in decision theory may be relevant to this analysis.

2. Current theory generally explains the equilibrium value of a firm in a static model. However, the financial executives need a dynamic model which explains how investors appraise eps series which exhibit different patterns over time.

3. Variance is the generally accepted measure of investment risk in current capital budgeting theory. There are theoretical reasons for preferring semi-variance and the evidence is more consistent with semi-variance than variance.

4. Accurate estimates of cash flows are crucial to the investment decision process. To date, theorists have emphasized the analysis of investments with assumed cash flow distributions. Theorists can contribute even more by developing concepts and techniques which will enable the executives to make more reliable cash flow forecasts.

5. Current theory views diversification as a means to stabilize earnings. In fact, the executive may be more concerned with the objective of stable growth. More emphasis by theorists on ways to search for new and profitable growth opportunities seem appropriate.

6. While theorists recommened the IRR (or NPV) criterion of investment appraisal, this study confirms the prevalence of the payback period and the accounting profit criteria in practice. The theorists must identify the reason why financial executives prefer these alternative criteria and modify the IRR (or NPV) method to make it more generally applicable.

26. A Misplaced Emphasis in Capital Budgeting*

W. WARREN HAYNES and MARTIN B. SOLOMON, JR.

This article is based on detailed research on small business investments. Our findings are somewhat opposed to the usual emphasis in the literature on capital budgeting. We believe that the three most promising areas for the improvement of managerial performance, especially in small firms, are the search for investment opportunities, the search for information about each of the discovered alternatives, and the careful estimation of the incremental gains and costs that will result from investments. The literature, however, stresses an entirely different step in the decision-making process: the precise computation of the relative worth of investment alternatives. It is contended here that management would be mistaken to devote so much attention to refinements of computation that it neglects the really important, more basic steps in the investment process. Perhaps such a neglect is less likely in large firms which have definite procedures for finding investment opportunities and developing information. But the evidence in this study is that small firms often do neglect the early stages of the decision-making process.

One case in the study illustrates a main theme of this article. The owner of a small, two-year-old chemicals firm was neglecting the refinements of investment analysis. His funds were in short supply. His investment opportunities were numerous. His problem was one of keeping up with his most urgent needs, to keep his operation going, and to make as full use of his plant as possible. He believed he knew what the most urgent investment needs were; he relied on a subjective evaluation, sometimes supported by a rough payback computation.

This chemical manufacturer was unusual among our managers in that he was somewhat familiar with the theory of investment. He knew about the discounted rate of return and present value. He was somewhat confused by this knowledge. He was apologetic for his crude decision-making

* *The Quarterly Review of Economics and Business,* vol. 2, no. 1 (February 1962), pp. 39–46.

processes and claimed that "as soon as things settled down" he would use more refined criteria.

We believe that this manager would be mistaken to devote much attention to the usual refinements of investment theory. His time (and the time of his staff) is more valuable in other occupations, such as improving the working capital position and stimulating sales. We shall present other case illustrations to support this viewpoint and to indicate important improvements some managers can make in investment decision making.

THE EMPHASIS IN CURRENT LITERATURE

Three recent publications are representative of current capital budgeting literature: *The Management of Corporate Capital,* edited by Ezra Solomon; *The Capital Budgeting Decision,* by Harold Bierman and Seymour Smidt; and George Terborgh's *Business Investment Policy: A MAPI Study and Manual.* The Ezra Solomon volume is a collection of somewhat technical articles, written primarily by economists concerned with the investment problem. Of the 22 articles, 8 are concerned with measuring investment worth, giving attention to present value and rate of return computations. Six articles are concerned with the difficult problem of measuring the cost of capital. Only two short articles devote much attention to the administrative and organizational aspects of decision making, though there are passing references to such matters in other parts of the volume.

The Bierman-Smidt volume is similar in its relative emphasis, devoting the majority of its space to measures of investment worth and to the cost of capital. The MAPI volume quite naturally is also concerned primarily with the arithmetic of evaluating and ranking projects, with a great deal of technical explanation of the MAPI formula. Somewhat surprisingly the MAPI volume gives proportionately greater attention than is usual to the other steps in the investment decision-making process. It gives attention to organizational and informational problems, including the maintenance of records, the systematic use of the records already in existence, and the need for "enlightened judgment" in addition to formulas. But the major stress in the MAPI volume is on the computation and use of formulas.

The refinements of analysis contained in these and similar books obviously represent an advance in knowledge. We now know more about the implicit assumptions underlying each formula. We know the conditions under which the payback reciprocal will give a close estimate of the discounted rate of return. We know how little we know about the cost of capital. Further advances in the computation of investment worth are desirable, but not to the neglect of the other steps in investment decision making.

WEAKNESSES OF THEORETICALLY CORRECT METHODS

Two formulas are generally accepted as "theoretically correct" when dealing with investment decisions. In spite of controversy about which of the two is superior, there is general agreement that one or the other is the standard by which all other formulas are to be judged. The two methods are present value analysis and computation of the discounted rate of return.

These formulas will not be discussed in great detail. They appear in most discussions of capital budgeting and even in elementary textbooks.[1] The main point to stress here is that while these methods may be theoretically correct, they are not widely used in actual investment decisions. Not one of the 50 small firms included in this study used either of these methods; and other surveys suggest that their use is exceptional even in large firms. This raises the question of whether management is remiss in failing to apply refinements that have received attention for over a decade. Can management justify its continued use of qualitative and crude quantitative methods?

A further development of this issue requires a discussion of the weaknesses of the theoretically correct methods so far as practice is concerned. Four central weaknesses receive attention here: (1) the reduced productivity of refinement in the face of the uncertainty involved in investment

[1] The simplest formula for the present value is

$$V = \frac{Q_1}{1+i} + \frac{Q_2}{(1+i)^2} + \cdots + \frac{Q_n}{(1+i)^n} + \frac{S}{(1+i)^n}$$

where V = present value,
Q_t = after-tax cash flow in year t (t is the year in which the cash is received),
S = terminal salvage value,
i = rate of interest, and
n = useful life of asset.

The formula for the discounted rate of return is closely related to that for the present value. The discounted rate of return is the rate of discount which when applied to the future cash inflows will equate them to the supply price of the investment. The formula is

$$C = \frac{Q_1}{(1+r)} + \frac{Q_2}{(1+r)^2} + \cdots + \frac{Q_n + S}{(1+r)^n}$$

where C = the supply price or installed cost of the asset, and

r = the discounted rate of return.

decisions; (2) conceptual difficulties in determining what the actual theoretically correct criterion is; (3) the difficulty of educating management in the use of the refined methods; and (4) the misdirection of managerial attention that the stress on refined calculations may entail.

The Problem of Uncertainty

While traditional managerial and economic literature has recognized the usefulness of the present value method under conditions of certainty, it has generally neglected to point out its limitations under conditions of uncertainty. The businessman cannot assume conditions of certainty when he is faced with the problem of ranking a set of investment proposals in order of profitability. He is uncertain about the annual costs and revenues resulting from each proposal, the length of life of each proposal, the possible salvage values, the opportunity cost of capital, competitors' retaliatory actions, availability of capital, actual interest rates, reinvestment opportunities, and the supply price of the proposal under consideration. The uncertainty involved in each of these categories is a matter of degree. Usually the investor is not completely ignorant of what the future holds but at the same time he cannot derive mathematical probability distributions concerning these variables.

One case is selected to illustrate the uncertainty connected with capital investments. A diversified investor was considering a proposal to open a coin-operated laundry. The total investment was estimated at about $40,000. He was highly uncertain about annual revenues. After months of careful study he estimated that revenues would range from $30,000 to $60,000 annually. He was also uncertain about the life of the equipment involved; estimates ranged from two to six years. The discounted rate of return for this investment ranged from negative figures to more than 60 percent. When he narrowed down the possible revenues-life combinations that he thought were most likely the discounted rate of return ranged from negative figures to about 30 percent.

How could refined investment formulas help such a businessman? They would probably confuse him rather than aid in a logical decision-making process.

As mentioned before, most businessmen do not use the theoretically correct methods. They prefer alternative methods that are simpler, more direct, and involve fewer hidden assumptions. Alternative methods deserve greater attention in investment literature than they have usually been given and are more useful than has been generally recognized. In many cases these alternative methods provide close estimates of the discounted rate of return and, what is more important, they seem to have the ability to rank investments in about the same order as theoretically correct methods.

To illustrate the use of an alternative method, we return to the laundry case discussed earlier. This businessman simplified his decision-making problem by using the payback criterion. While losses were possible, he was pretty certain that the investment would pay off in one year and much more certain that it would pay off in less than two years.

Since estimates about years beyond the second became extremely uncertain, it is not surprising that this investor should focus on the payback criterion. If profitability depends heavily on returns beyond the payback period, there is a natural unwillingness to take chances on the investment. The payback criterion acts as a "go-no-go" gauge which may at first seem crude but which may actually be a sensible way of dealing with the problem of uncertainty.

In this respect, payback analysis is analogous to break-even analysis. Both are simplified treatments of the outcomes of decision making. Both may represent reasonable compromises with uncertainty. In break-even analysis, the manager can concentrate on the probability that sales and output will exceed the break-even point, without having to specify the exact level of future output. In payback analysis, the manager can focus attention on the probability that the life of the investment will exceed the payback period, without having to make exact estimates of how profitable the investment will be. Both methods provide the manager with shortcuts to decision making that are often satisfactory substitutes for refined analysis.

Conceptual Difficulties

It is often assumed that discounted rate of return and present value are theoretically correct criteria for evaluating alternative formulas. The two methods may, however, give a somewhat different ranking of investment proposals. The difference between the present value method and the discounted rate of return arises from a difference in the implicit assumptions about the reinvestment of the returns from the initial investment. Present value analysis assumes that earnings will be reinvested at the discount rate used. The discounted rate of return rests on the assumption that returns can be reinvested at the same rate as the proposed investment.

A purist on investment theory might insist on the "chain of machines" formulation. It seems certain that most firms that *do* use the present value or discounted rate of return do not make use of this refinement. Managers normally make a rough estimate of length of life. In some cases they include an estimate of the salvage value at the end of this life, but they avoid the problem of explicitly determining how the inflow of funds will be reinvested. The theoretical issues at that point are too abstract and complex for most managers.

The Problem of Education and Communication

Even if it were clear that the use of theoretically correct methods is helpful under conditions of uncertainty, it is unlikely that managers of small firms will take the time to understand the formulas and their interpretation. No doubt the difficulty of communicating the meaning of the refined methods is a major reason for their unpopularity. Even for large firms it would be a mistake to conclude that the answer is to delegate investment decisions to the specialists; general management normally has much to contribute to the evaluation of investments that the specialists may overlook.

A Possible Misdirection of Managerial Attention

The obvious reply to the position just taken about the difficulty of communicating with managers unfamiliar with the refined formulas is that they should *take* time to learn and to apply these methods. But this depends on whether management can afford the time required. To use the language of economics, there must be a comparison of the marginal product of refinement in measuring investment worth with the marginal product of other allocations of management time. The argument so far has been that in many cases, and almost always in small firms, the marginal product of refinement is low, especially under conditions of uncertainty. The remainder of this article is concerned with demonstrating that other uses of management time, even in the sphere of investment decision making, are likely to be more productive.

OPPORTUNITIES FOR IMPROVEMENT OF CAPITAL BUDGETING

Capital budgeting involves much more than the careful computation of the worth of a project and its comparison with a norm. Capital budgeting requires, first of all, the search for and discovery of investment opportunities. Second, it requires the collection of information about alternatives, such as estimates of the resultant changes in revenues and costs. Third, it requires the application of incremental reasoning to the collected information, to ensure that the relevant estimates are used and irrelevant considerations are ignored. In our opinion, these are the areas in which a great improvement in practice is possible, especially in the small businesses which are the object of our research. Each of these opportunities for the improvement of capital budgeting deserves special attention.

The Search for Alternatives

The best way to indicate the importance of the search for alternatives is to cite some cases from our study.

A wholesale liquor dealer devotes most of his time to the search for and evaluation of alternatives. After years of routine work, he decided he was not moving forward. He hired a sales manager to relieve him of routine work and turned to larger issues. He built up a file of ideas for investment which he reviewed periodically with the addition of new schemes. He now keeps his time free to search for new and better investments. He applies unsophisticated methods to his selections.

The backlog of investment opportunities built up in this firm helps assure that unprofitable alternatives will not be selected. The backlog contributes to a high "aspiration level," leading to rejection of less profitable proposals without a refined evaluation of the relative profitability of alternatives.

As a contrast to this case of the active search for investment opportunities, take the case of a wearing apparel firm. The president admits that "only one investment opportunity seems to come up at a time." No search for alternatives is undertaken. As a result, when a proposal is evaluated, the president has few if any other investment opportunities with which to compare it. It seems likely that the engineering department of this company could discover internal improvement in such areas as materials handling and purchasing. The failure to seek such alternatives appears to reduce the profit potential of this firm.

Other cases in the study reveal a similar inattention to new investment opportunities. They also illustrate a failure of management to set aside time for search activity. It is our impression that the distinction between firms that are actively engaged in search and those that are not is a major factor in determining small firms' success or failure in sound, imaginative investment programs.

The Search for Information

Great differences exist among firms in the devotion of managerial time to the search for information about alternatives, once these alternatives are discovered. Again two cases illustrate these differences.

One successful manager and his associates were considering investment in a bowling alley. They had opportunities to invest in other activities: an expansion of their manufacturing activities (the production of wooden parts), or of the advertising business in which several of them were engaged. The outstanding feature of the decision-making process in this case was the long period of time devoted to the collection of information about the alternatives. The manager and his associates interviewed the owners of bowling alleys in other parts of the country; they collected operating statements for bowling alleys of a size similar to that of the one under consideration; they obtained statistics from a national accounting firm on bowling alley financial results. In addition, they sought the opinions of business associates. They made estimates of volumes of business that could be expected and of potential costs. They projected income statements and source and application of funds statements for three years of bowling alley operation. They made up break-even charts based on several sets of assumptions and considered the probabilities of being above the break-even point and the prospective profits at various volumes. They compared their estimates and had business associates make independent estimates.

In the meantime these businessmen were gathering similar information on the advertising alternative. It seems highly unlikely that they would invest in an unprofitable venture after such careful collection and evaluation of information; the information and the existence of alternatives were more certain guarantees of profitable decisions than any mechanical formulas could be.

In contrast to this case are the firms that make investments on the basis of "hunches" or extremely limited information. Some managers fail to take advantage of investment opportunities because of inadequate information or the pressure of routine duties.

The president of a small tire company was thinking of opening a branch retail store. Because he was busy with more routine work he neglected the collection of information about this opportunity; he let the idea drop. A little study on the part of the interviewer revealed that the president had probably passed up an extremely lucrative opportunity. The president, at the request of the interviewer, estimated that revenues (in a particular location) would range from about $48,000 to $80,000. An analysis of *incremental* costs indicated that annual pretax profits of from $750 to $12,000 were likely. The entire investment amounted to only $2,000. The careful collection of data about this alternative would have revealed its hidden potential.

The accumulation of information must take priority over refinement in computation. It is not particularly helpful to apply a theoretically correct formula to the wrong information.

Correct Incremental Reasoning

The collection of information is not enough. It is necessary to separate relevant information from the irrelevant and to organize the data in a meaningful form. For example, many managers are confused about the costs that should be considered in an investment decision. In particular, they are not clear on the treatment of overhead costs.

One case from a large firm illustrates this type of confusion. A manufacturer of rubber and plastic products utilized more elaborate decision-making procedures than the firms cited so far. The firm required a 30 percent return on investment despite the fact that it was in a highly liquid position, with a current ratio of 7 to 1 and several million dollars of low-yield government bonds. The rate of return was based on first year performance. But in obtaining the first year performance the firm not only charged depreciation against the new investment, it also charged depreciation on a "capital corollary," which was considered to be 70 percent of the investment. This analysis was based on the assumption that each new machine required space involving an average investment of 70 percent of the machine cost. The analysis ignored the possibility of idle space. It neglected the probability that some labor-saving or capital-saving equipment might not take up additional space or might even save space.

Similarly this firm charged overhead and selling and administrative expenses against the returns on a new investment. Again predetermined averages were used. It appears that the overhead allocation duplicated the depreciation charges already mentioned. In addition, it is not at all clear that each new investment would result in the same proportional change in selling and administrative expense.

The method used by this rubber and plastics firm violates the canons of incremental reasoning in several ways. It ignores the fact that each investment will affect overhead costs in a different way, so that overall averages are inappropriate. It fails to recognize that many overhead costs may be "fixed" for a particular decision. This company substitutes predetermined allocations for "tailor-made" estimates of the impact of investments on costs.

Other cases in this study reveal a similar confusion about the correct treatment of depreciation and overhead costs. The result may be a 50 percent or even 100 percent error in the estimates of cash inflows. No formula can overcome fundamental errors in the collection and evaluation of data. If there is to be education of managers for improved decision making, it might be best to concentrate on the incremental reasoning that will help them make correct estimates of cash inflows and outflows.

CONCLUSION

The need, especially in small business, is not for further refinement in the application of formulas for investment worth, but for greater attention to the other steps in the decision-making process.

Capital budgeting consists of at least five managerial functions: (1) continuous and creative search for investment opportunities; (2) forecasting the supply and cost of funds for investment purposes; (3) estimating each project's cash flows and other benefits; (4) ranking and choosing among competing projects; and (5) post-auditing already committed investments.

The literature has devoted primary attention to the fourth function (ranking and choosing) and considerable attention to the second (forecasting the cost of funds), but has usually neglected the others. Our case studies suggest that the highest priorities should be assigned to the search for alternatives, the search for information, and the correct processing of the available data *before* ranking formulas are applied. Precise computations applied to the wrong information cannot result in correct measurements of investment worth.

We do not consider our position to be antitheoretical. Advances in the theory of capital budgeting are to be welcomed. The difficulty is that the currently publicized theory is too narrow to cover the entire decision-making process. As is natural, the theory has concentrated on those phases that are most amenable to systematic analysis and to quantification. The theory has stressed the fine points that require clarification when one constructs a precise model. The need is not for less theory but for more and broader theory. Important phases of capital budgeting cry for research and for theoretical generalization. For example, there are questions of motivation involved in investment decisions: why are some managers and some subordinates more effective in the search for alternatives? There are problems of measuring the productivity of search. There is a need for the empirical measurement of the increased profits resulting from refinement in ranking. It is interesting that the literature stressing the quantification of evaluations of investment worth is so vague on the rate of return on refinement itself.

Thus, Walker's stress on managerial judgment that goes beyond the technical computations of investment worth is welcome.[2] But, as Simon has stated, the word "judgment" is a challenge to the scientist, who must feel the urge to identify the characteristics of sound judgment. We have suggested that judgment on investment decisions may frequently require more attention to the less developed phases of decision making, even if this requires reduced attention given to the refinements of ranking and measurement of investment worth.

---

[2] Ross G. Walker, "The Judgment Factor in Investment Decisions," *Harvard Business Review,* vol. 39, no. 2 (March–April 1961), pp. 93–99.

27. Uncertainty and Its Effect on Capital Investment Analysis*

MARTIN B. SOLOMON, JR.

This article is concerned with one specialized aspect of capital budgeting: the usefulness of "theoretically correct" choice criteria[1] in real-world investment decisions.

There are other areas of capital budgeting that are surely much more important; but this one deserves special attention because so many recommendations, explicit and implicit, based on these criteria have bombarded the businessman. Before we assail the business practitioner for his crude and unscientific methods, we should be sure that our theory will provide better total results than his unsophisticated decision rules.

There is general agreement that if investment parameters such as costs, revenues, salvage values, and interest rates were amenable to accurate prediction, theoretically correct methods could be used to great advantage in most firms. But all capital investments involve uncertainty in one form or another. The contention of this article is that theoretically correct choice criteria have *limited practical value due to the uncertainty involved in the estimates required for the analysis.*

A GENERAL ANALYSIS OF ESTIMATING ERRORS

Two types of investments are considered: investments with constant annual returns and investments with declining annual returns. The discussion centers on two hypothetical illustrations that have been purposely framed for easy calibration of errors. We ignore errors in salvage values.

Proposals with Constant Annual Returns

Suppose we estimate that an investment will yield $1,000 annual pretax returns[2] for seven years. Assuming the supply price of the asset

* *Management Science,* vol. 12, no. 8 (April 1966), pp. B334–B339.

[1] Without entering into a unnecessary debate, present value and the discounted rate of return are simple defined for the purposes of this article as "theoretically correct" criteria.

[2] Returns is used here to mean the excess of revenue over out-of-pocket cost.

is $4,000, a 32 percent tax rate, straight-line depreciation over the life of the asset, and no terminal salvage value, the posttax discounted rate of return would be 11.6 percent. Now if the proposal lasts only six years, all else remaining equal, the discounted rate of return is 9.1 percent. This means that the actual return is 2.5 percentage points less. On the other hand if the proposal lasts for the predicted seven years but returns $800 per year (before taxes) instead of $1,000 the discounted rate of return falls to 6.5 percent which is 5.1 percentage points less than the estimate. There is a plethora of possible combinations of returns, lives and rates of return. The simplest way to illustrate these relationships is to graph them as in figure 1. Shown are lines connecting the discounted rates of return for proposals with the same life and different pretax annual returns. The line labeled "7 years" shows the discounted rates of return for all investments with a life of 7 years. As the pretax returns decrease, the discounted rate of return declines. For this reason the lines slope downward to the left.

In evaluating the effect of uncertainty, we can use figure 1 to determine the possible variations in the discounted rate of return when uncertainty exists. (The data used to construct figure 1 are shown in table 1.)

How much variation then in the discounted rate of return could we

FIGURE 1
Constant Annual Pretax Returns

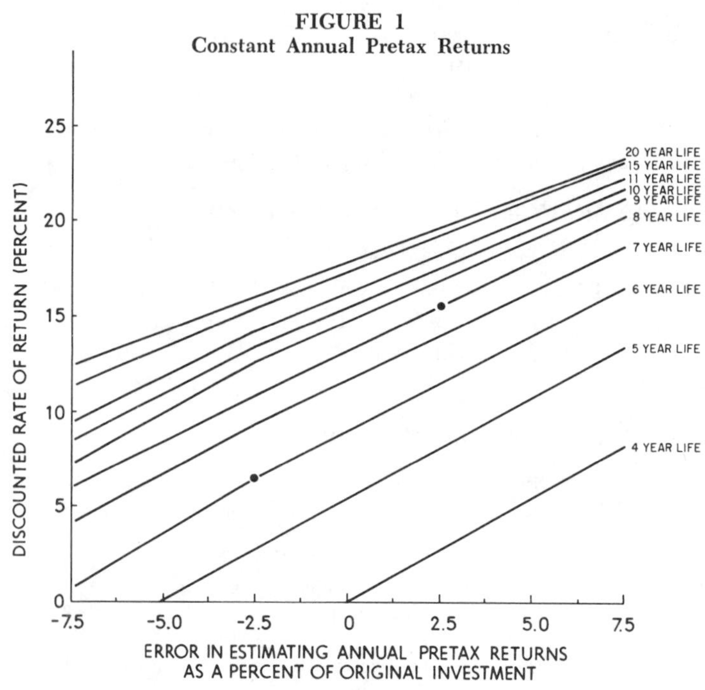

TABLE 1
The Effect of Estimating Errors on the Discounted Rate of Return—Constant Annual Pretax Returns

Life of the Proposal (years)	*Annual Pretax Return*												
	$700	*$750*	*$800*	*$850*	*$900*	*$950*	*$1000*	*$1050*	*$1100*	*$1150*	*$1200*	*$1250*	*$1300*
20.	.122	.132	.142	.151	.161	.170	.180	.189	.198	.207	.216	.225	.234
15.	.112	.123	.134	.144	.154	.165	.175	.184	.194	.204	.213	.223	.232
11.	.092	.104	.116	.127	.139	.150	.161	.172	.182	.193	.203	.213	.223
10.	.083	.096	.108	.120	.131	.143	.154	.165	.176	.187	.197	.208	.218
9.	.072	.085	.097	.110	.122	.134	.145	.156	.168	.179	.190	.200	.211
8.	.057	.071	.083	.096	.109	.121	.133	.145	.156	.168	.179	.190	.201
7.	.037	.051	.065	.078	.091	.103	.116	.128	.140	.152	.163	.175	.186
6.	.010	.024	.038	.052	.065	.078	.091	.104	.116	.129	.141	.153	.165
5.	*	*	.010	.015	.028	.042	.055	.068	.081	.094	.107	.119	.131
4.			*	*	*	*	.010	.014	.027	.041	.054	.066	.079
3.							*	*	*	*	*	*	*

* Indicates negative discounted rate of return.

expect with this amount of error? If the returns of this estimated 7-year $1,000 per year investment are subject to an error of plus or minus 2.5 percent and plus or minus one year, the maximum and minimum rates of return are 15.6 percent and 6.5 percent (as shown in figure 1 by the X's).[3] This is a variation of about 9 percentage points. If we extended the possible error to plus or minus two years, the maximum and minimum rates are 16.8 percent and 2.8 percent, a variation of 14 percentage points. Errors in estimates of these magnitudes do not appear at all unlikely. This much uncertainty would seem to discourage the use of theoretically correct rationing methods for ranking investment proposals. There may be no significant difference among proposals' rates of return if they are nearly equally profitable; and if one or more proposals are obviously more profitable than the others, "alternative" methods[4] provide the same information with less cost.

Another interesting feature of figure 1 is that it provides some insight into the effect of errors in length of life versus error in returns. The relationship between annual pretax return and the discounted rate of return is close to linear with a slope of about .02 to .03. This means that an estimating error of about 1 percent results in an error of about

[3] In figure 1, —7.5 percent represents annual pretax returns of $700; —5.0 percent represents returns of $800; —2.5 percent represents returns of $900, etc. The percentage errors are percentages of the original investment. ($4,000). That is,

$$(\$700–\$1000)/\$4000 = -7.5 \text{ percent}$$
$$(\$800–\$1000)/\$4000 = -5.0 \text{ percent}$$
$$(\$900–\$1000)/\$4000 = -2.5 \text{ percent}$$

[4] Alternative methods such as the payback period, rate of income on investment, or MAPI urgency rating.

2 to 3 percentage points in the discounted rate of return. This relationship is fairly constant throughout. On the other hand, the relationship between discounted rate of return and length of life is not stable. As the life becomes shorter, an error of one year in the estimated life becomes more critical; the relationship is curvilinear. The difference in the rate of return between a life of 20 years and 15 years is only about one half of 1 percentage point when pretax profits = $1,000 (zero or horizontal axis). The difference of only 2 years between a life of 4 and 6 years (with $1,000 returns) results in a change of more than 6 percentage points in the discounted rate of return. Perhaps this is a good reason for businessmen being particularly cautious about making length of life estimates.

The conclusions here are that standard formulations of theoretically correct rationing methods have limited usefulness when dealing with uncertainty.

Proposal with Declining Annual Returns

To make the analysis more complete, the case of declining annual returns is included.[5]

The results are shown in figure 2. There is much similarity between figures 1 and 2 as most everything that has been said applies to both. The conclusions about uncertainty seem to apply equally to both constant and declining return investments.

Unless an investment will continue for a long period, a relatively small positive miscalculation in the estimate of length of life (two to three years) can result in a serious overstatement of profitability.

[5] An investment's estimated pretax returns are: $2500 the first year, $2400 the second year, $2300, $2200, $2100, $2000, $1900. The estimated life of the investment is therefore seven years. Errors in length of life are handled the same as before, that is, if the estimated life overstates actual life by one year, the actual investment would return $2500, $2400, $2300, $2200, $2100, $2000, or an actual life of six years insteȧd of the estimated seven years. This estimate, although in error as far as length of the life is concerned, is correct concerning the returns (0 on the horizontal axis). Errors in pretax returns indicate an error in the initial annual returns. For example, a —2.5 percent error in estimating returns represents an investment that actually returns $2300 the first year instead of the estimated $2500. The annual decline in returns ($100 per year) remains constant. Thus an investment whose life was correctly estimated as seven years but whose returns were overstated by 2.5 percent would return $2300, $2200, $2100, $2000, $1900, $1800, $1700 (before taxes). In figure 3, zero on the horizontal axis represents an investment with an actual initial return of $2500 and a $100 annual decline in pre-tax returns. A +3 year error in length of life (ten-year life) and a —8.75 percent error in estimated pretax returns would designate an investment that actually returns $1800 the first year, $1700 the second year, $1600, . . . , $1000. The cost of the investment is $8000, the tax rate is 32 percent, and straight-line depreciation is used over the life of the asset with no terminal salvage value assumed. As before, errors are computed as a percentage of the original investment ($800 in this case).

FIGURE 2
Declining Annual Pretax Returns

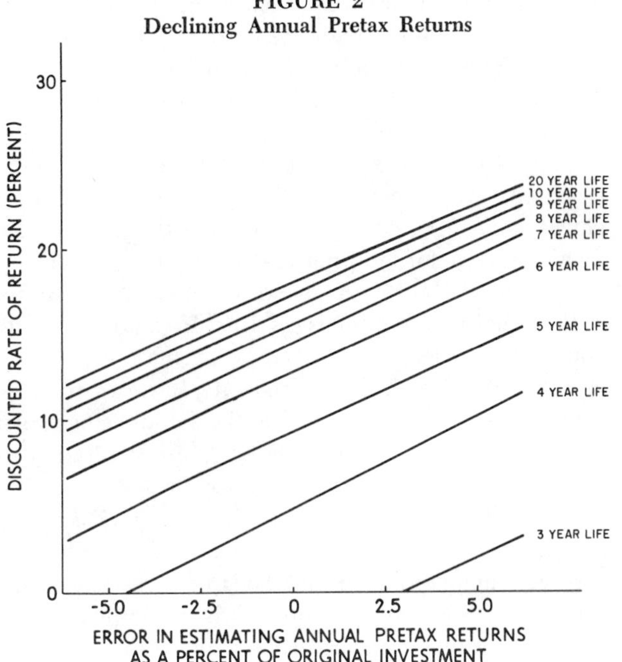

The Effect of Technological Change

Because errors in returns are linear and errors in life are curvilinear, errors in estimating annual returns may average out over a large number of investments, whereas errors in length of life will not. Proposals that last less than the estimated life lower the average discounted rate of return for the firm more than proposals lasting longer than the estimated life raise the average.[6]

Today, with technological advancement so rapid and innovation so frequent, it seems logical to assume that many capital investments will be subject to extremely high rates of obsolescence. Businessmen do not usually know which of their investments will become obsolete soon; they are understandably worried about proposals that require ten years to pay for themselves. The farther into the future one predicts, the more uncertainty of obsolescence he is subjected to and the more unsure he is of the prediction.

[6] This curvilinear phenomenon occurs whether we plot present values or discounted rates of return. It may, however, be more apparent than real. It stems from an assumption underlying the discounted rate of return: proceeds are assumed to be reinvested at the rate of return for the original project; there is a cumulative effect of a high return project. If proceeds are not reinvested at this high rate but placed into low yield investments, this assumption does not hold and the curvilinear phenomenon is not operative.

By insisting upon proposals that pay back quickly, or by using a higher discount rate, within the realm of feasible prediction, the businessman is providing greater flexibility for himself and, in a rough way, taking into account the effects of uncertainty. He is in a better position to maneuver and change his plans when necessary but will accept fewer projects. His hope is that those projects that are rejected (that otherwise might be accepted) will become obsolete before earning a return.

Technological change is one difficulty in estimating length of life. Businessmen can search for information about the expected annual returns from a proposal, but it is generally much more difficult to do research on the length of a proposal's life. In addition, figures 1 and 2 suggest that errors in length of life may be more serious. Use of the short payback period or higher discount rate tends to reduce errors of this type. The old saying about one in the hand being worth two in the bush is quite descriptive of business behavior in relation to projects in danger of obsolescence. It may be more worthwhile to invest, receiving a small quick return, than to take a chance on a larger return or obsolescence.

Simple (or even simple-minded) methods of investment ranking may not be as absurd as some of the literature would lead us to believe if used in a careful way by clever people; and although no one claims superiority for a payback method, it appears that in investment decisions confounded by large amounts of uncertainty, the present value and discounted rate of return rankings are so sensitive to estimating errors that the payback criterion may provide results that are about as good as any. The main point of this paper is to point out the sensitivity of discounted rate of return results and not to recommend alternative methods.

28. Measuring the Productivity of Investment in Persuasion*

JOEL DEAN

I. PROLOGUE

My starting point in this article is ten propositions, which are debatable, at least as boldly stated here:

1. Much advertising (and other corporate persuasion) is in economic reality partly an investment. The investment mix varies over a wide spectrum.
2. Investments in promotion are different from conventional capital expenditures, but their peculiar traits do not disqualify promotion from investment treatment.
3. Profitability must be the basic measurement of the productivity of capital invested in promotion. Despite the multiplicity of conflicting corporate goals, the overriding objective for decisions on investment of corporate capital should be to make money.
4. The main determinants of profitability of an advertising investment that need to be estimated are the amount and timing of added investment and of added earnings, the duration of advertising effects, and risks.
5. The measurement concepts of capital productivity that must be estimated are future, time-spotted, incremental, after-tax cash flows of investment outlays and of added profits from added sales.
6. Discounted cash-flow analysis (DCF) supplies the yardstick of investment worth which is most appropriate for promotional investments. By comparison, payback period, though widely used, has no merit.
7. Advertising belongs in the capital budget. Promotional investments should be made to compete for funds on the basis of profitability, i.e., DCF rate of return.
8. The criterion for rationing scarce capital among competing investment proposals should be the DCF rate of return. The minimum acceptable return should be the corporation's cost of capital—outside market cost or internal opportunity cost, whichever is higher.

* *Journal of Industrial Economics,* vol. 15, no. 2 (April 1967), pp. 81–108.

9. Plopping advertising into the corporation's capital budget will not perform a miracle. The most that it can do is to open the way for a research approach which is oriented to the kind of estimates that are relevant and that will permit investment in promotion to fight for funds on the basis of financial merit rather than on the basis of personal persuasiveness of its sponsor. Judgment cannot be displaced by DCF analysis and computers. But judgment can be economized and improved.

10. To make this investment approach produce practical benefits will require an open mind, fresh concepts, substantial research spending, and great patience.

Readers who find these propositions unacceptable as a point of departure should stop here. Right-thinking readers who persist are warned that the analysis is necessarily technical, studded with charts and culminated by mathematics.

My paper has two interrelated parts: theory and measurement. It is primarily concerned with the conceptual framework for deciding how much to invest in promotion. Measurement problems are examined only incidentally and mechanics of application not at all. The analysis is presented in terms of advertising; but is equally applicable to all forms of promotion. Advertising is used because it is the purest and most indisputable form of persuasion cost and for many firms also the largest. For clarity, the analysis is narrowed to one product and one medium. In principle, however, it is extensible to all forms of corporate persuasion. Allocation of the advertising budget among media and among products is not formally tackled but the decision-making apparatus could be logically extended to these problems. The interplay of promotion with other ways of getting business such as product improvement and pricing is, for simplicity, bypassed.

My approach, blushingly labeled "profitometrics," can be previewed thus: because most advertising is in economic essence a capital expenditure, the question of how much to invest in advertising (and other forms of persuasion) is a problem of investment economics. A new approach is therefore required: economic and financial analysis of futurities. This approach focuses on future aftertax cash flows, centers on the profit productivity of capital and relies on quantitative estimates.

II. THEORY OF OPTIMUM PROMOTIONAL OUTLAY

A. Two Time Horizons

Strictly and elegantly, all promotion can be viewed as investment, since there is some time lag in its benefits, even though short. Nevertheless, the problem of determining optimum persuasion outlay can, in principle, be solved in two separate time-horizon settings: (1) immediate-impact promotion, where most of the benefits come soon; and (2) delayed-impact promotion, where benefits are deferred and often cumulative.

Pure forms of either are rare or nonexistent. Most promotion brings about some benefits quickly and others spread out into the future. The proportion accounted for by either kind depends on the product, the nature of the promotional benefit, and perhaps the character of the media. The controlling determinant is the anatomy of the purchasing decision, which differs greatly among products.

Pure types are nevertheless notoriously appealing for developing principles. As a first approximation, therefore, we shall examine each category separately. The immediate-impact case will be studied first.

B. Two Decision Increments

Two kinds of decision increments in promotional investment need to be distinguished: (1) intensity increments and (2) project increments.

The first kind, intensity increments, are small increments of additional depth of investment in a single advertising submedium. The intensity increment of investment is pertinent (*a*) when outlays can be varied by small additions, and (*b*) when the decision is to select, by examining this growing edge, that amount of advertising outlay which would maximize the rate of return from this investment project.

The second kind, project increments, are pertinent when the incremental unit of decision is the entire advertising project. The choice (because of indivisibility or other restraints) is to take it or leave it. Under these circumstances, we do not have the choice of a panorama of outlay amounts. Consequently, optimization of the advertising amount is not the problem. Instead, what is at issue is acceptance versus rejection of the entire project. The total advertising outlay of the project is, therefore, in this case, the pertinent increment of investment. And the question is whether the added profits from resultant sales as they spread through time will or will not produce a rate of return greater than the cost of capital.

In both situations the basic concept is incremental. In the intensity-increment case, we use profitometrics analysis at the margin to select, from a gradation of alternative outlays, that investment amount which is optimum. Hence, small increments are the vehicle of decision for optimizing the size of this investment project. In the project-increment case, lacking this fluidity of choice, we use the profitometrics method to stack the entire project against alternative uses of capital, so as to make it fight for funds in rate-of-return rationing of the corporation's scarce capital.

Both kinds of increments are normally needed. Optimization of some sort (within the restraints) may be presumed to have taken place before a project of the all-or-none sort comes for capital-rationing decision. The intensity-increment analysis leads us to an optimum depth of advertising investment. But the entire project might nevertheless fall short of the minimum profitability requirement, e.g. cost of capital. To find this out we need to estimate the capital productivity of the project increment.

The two kinds of decision increments are, for illustrative purposes, examined separately for the two kinds of time horizons in the analysis which follows. For the first time-horizon, namely immediate-impact advertising, intensity increments are alone used. For the second time-horizon, namely delayed-impact promotion (investments), both kinds of decision increments are needed. For one-shot investments, intensity increments are examined for one treatment and project increments for another. For spread-out investments, both are needed, but the analysis is in terms of project increments only.

C. Immediate Impact Promotion

The basic tenet of the profitometrics approach to decisions on immediate-impact advertising outlay is simple common sense: advertising expenditures are justified to the extent that they cause increases in sales which add enough to corporate profits to warrant the outlay. To determine if this is the case, we must measure two things: (1) the effect of advertising on sales, (2) the effect of sales on profits.

To illustrate these ideas in simple terms, I have a series of charts and tables relating to direct-mail promotion of a book. In our example, we have assumed that the price will remain the same at all rates of sale considered, and, further, that the added cost of production and physical distribution per copy—which we call the incremental production cost—will also not change. These assumptions are realistic for a surprisingly wide range of commodities.

Exhibit 1 shows the kind of relationship we can reasonably believe exists between advertising and sales and which in fact has been found to exist when measurements have actually been made. You will observe that the increase in sales attributable to advertising becomes less and less as more and more advertising is used. That is, the increase in sales resulting from spending \$9000 on advertising rather than \$8000 is less than the increase in sales attributed to the expenditure of \$2000 rather than \$1000. This conforms to common sense: initial advertising attracts the most susceptible customers and subsequent advertising must be more and more intense to induce the less susceptible to become customers.

As an example, consider the response to successive mailings of adver-

EXHIBIT 1
Effect of Advertising on Sales

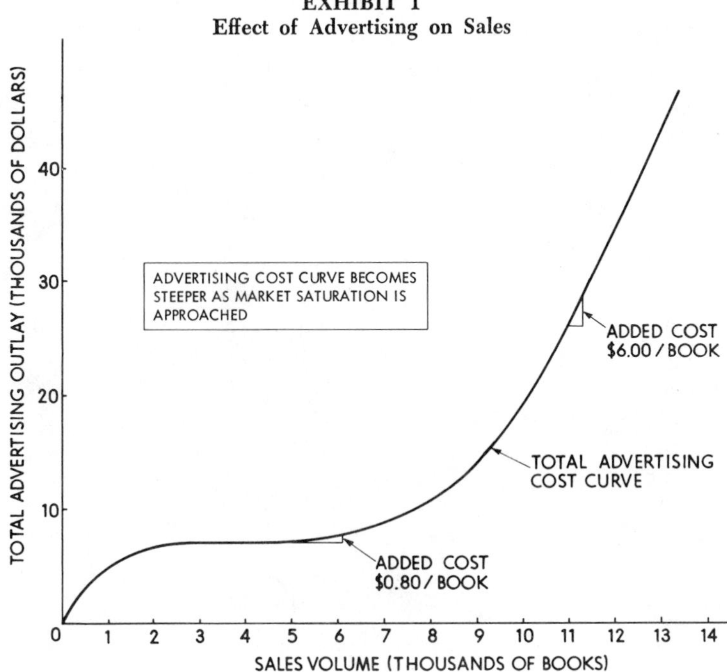

tisements for the book. The initial mailing will bring in the customers while subsequent and more intense persuasion may be required to induce recipients of other mailings to become customers. As a result, the added advertising outlays required to sell one more copy increases from $.80 to $6.00 in our example. (The curve in Exhibit 1 traces total costs. The slope of this curve, that is the rate of climb, indicates added cost of selling one more book.) The same form of relationship is found when single mailings are made to lists that differ in susceptibility.

Exhibit 2 shows the same basic relationship restated in terms of the added advertising outlay required to produce added units of sale—a relationship that might be called the incremental advertising cost curve.

The second measurement that this approach requires is the relationship between sales and profits. Exhibit 3 shows the relationship following from our assumptions that the price is independent of promotional outlays and that incremental production costs remain the same over the range of variation in sales that it seems relevant to consider. Because price stays the same and incremental production cost is constant, the incremental prepromotional profit remains constant. That is, leaving advertising costs aside for the moment, each additional book that is sold results in a constant increase in profits—$6.00 in our example.

EXHIBIT 2
Added Advertising Cost Necessary to Make An Added Sale

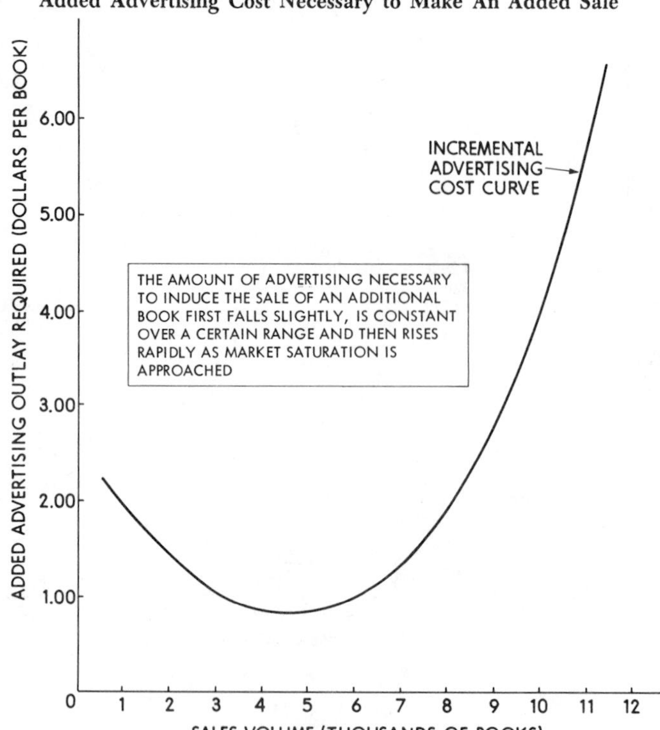

We can now combine the two measurements to see how large the advertising outlay should be. In exhibit 4 we superimpose the curve representing the relationship between advertising and sales of Exhibit 2 on the chart representing the relationship between sales and profit. We can see that advertising beyond the intersection of these two lines results in an absolute reduction in profits. That is, beyond the point of intersection it costs more than $6.00 to increase sales by one book whereas the increase in sales by one book adds only $6.00 to our profits.

Exhibit 5 summarizes in a table the analysis of immediate-impact one-shot advertising outlays charted in Exhibits 1, 2, 3, and 4.

D. Delayed Impact Advertising

Most advertising is an investment, in essence, since it has delayed as well as immediate impacts. This kind of advertising requires a different kind of economic analysis from that described above. The appropriate analysis is directed at the productivity of the capital tied up in a promotional investment measured in terms of rate of return.

EXHIBIT 3
Effect of Sales on Profit

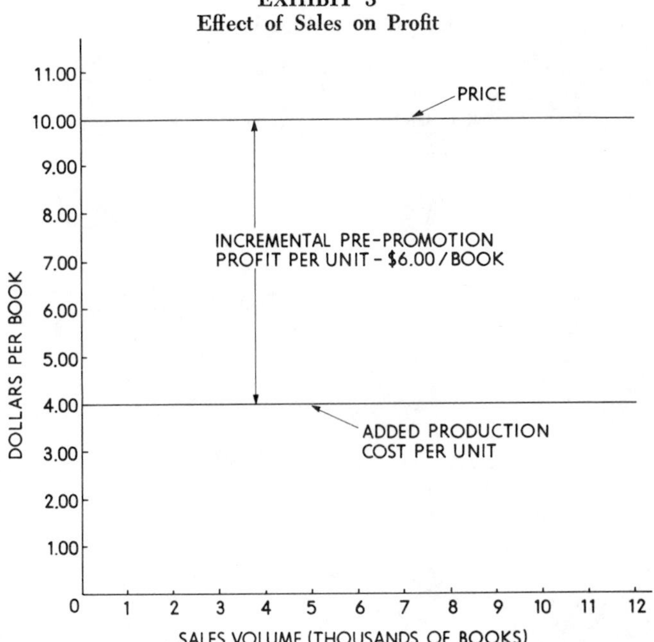

In measuring capital productivity it is convenient to classify promotional investments into two categories: (1) one-shot promotions, where all or most of the outlay is made all at once; and (2) spread-out investments, where outlays are sprinkled over a period of years.

1. *One-Shot Investments.* For one-shot investments in advertising there are two alternative attacks. One is a simple extension of the preceding analysis of immediate-impact advertising. The second is a pure-investment approach which, though compatible with the first, gets at the problem in a different way, namely through DCF measurements of capital productivity. Incidentally, this second attack is alone suitable for spread-out investments.

(*a*) *Patch-on Analysis.* Exhibit 6 illustrates how the analysis of immediate-impact advertising which is summarized in Exhibits 1, 2, 3, and 4 can be patched up to account for the follow-on effects of a one-shot advertising investment. Essentially the process is: (1) estimate the incremental per-unit profits (or other benefits) from follow-on sales in each follow-on year; (2) find the present value at the corporation's cost of capital of each year's profits; (3) sum them as a single figure of present worth of incremental profit from follow-on sales; and (4) add this sum to the incremental prepromotion profit from immediate sales. This present-value sum in our illustration is **$14.24** a unit. The

EXHIBIT 4
Effect of Advertising on Profits

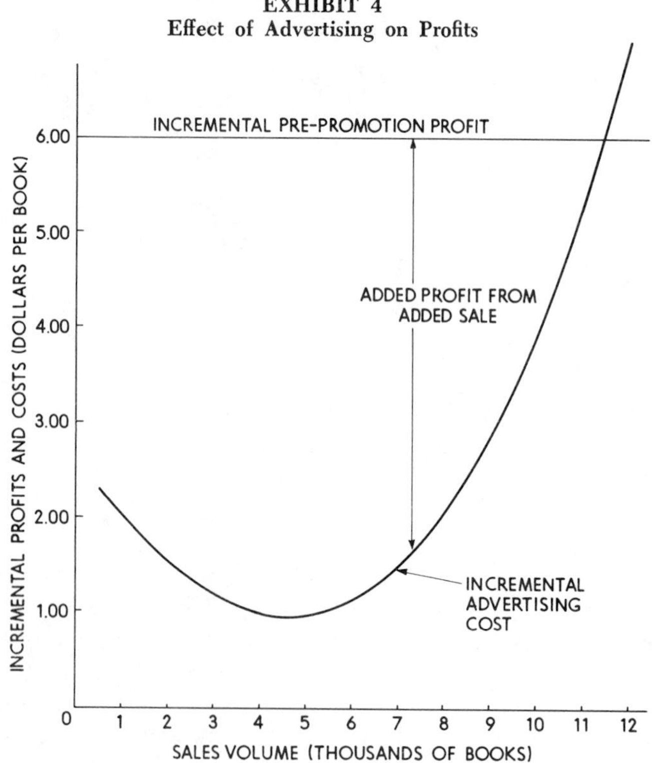

resulting aggregate of incremental profit from immediate plus follow-on sales supplies a cutoff criterion identical in concept to that illustrated in Exhibit 4.

Exhibit 6 indicates quite plausibly that the amount that it is economic to spend on a one-shot advertising outlay is greater when it has follow-on effects than when it does not.

This simplified solution presumes that the corporation's overall cost of capital has been measured, that it is used as a cutoff for rate-of-return rationing of funds for other capital expenditure, and that the corporation's internal opportunity cost of funds is not significantly higher than this market cost.

How the add-on for follow-on sales that is diagrammed in Exhibit 6 is computed is shown in Exhibits 7 and 8. Exhibit 7, like Exhibit 5, examines six alternative levels of advertising outlay. It goes further by also considering the effects upon sales and profits in the second year. Exhibit 8 is derived by extending Exhibit 7 in that it shows several follow-on years. Exhibit 8a shows how we calculate the present value of immediate and follow-on effects of the sale of one additional book.

EXHIBIT 5
One-Shot Advertising Outlay with no Follow-on Effect

	Advertising Outlays ($1000)		*Effect on Sales (1000 units)*		*Effect on Prepromotion Profits ($1000)*		*Effect on Net Profit per Unit of Added Sales ($ per unit)*		
	Altern. Total Advt'g Outlays	*Differential Advt'g Outlays*	*Total Sales*	*Differential Sales*	*Total Profits*	*Differential Profits*	*Increm. Pre-prom. Profits*	*Increm. Advt'g Cost*	*Added Net Profit from Added Sales*
A	5	5	1.7	1.7	10.2	10.2	6.00	2.94	3.06
B	10	5	7.8	6.1	46.8	36.6	6.00	.82	5.18
C	15	5	9.0	1.2	54.0	7.2	6.00	4.17	1.83
D	20	5	10.0	1.0	60.0	6.0	6.00	5.00	1.00
E	25	5	10.9	.9	65.4	5.4	6.00	5.56	.44
F	30	5	11.6	.7	69.6	4.2	6.00	7.14	–1.14

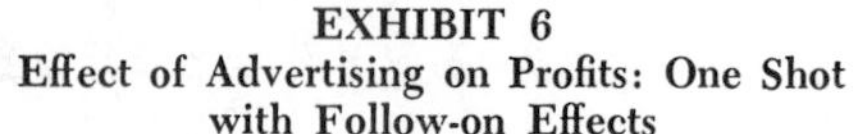

EXHIBIT 6
Effect of Advertising on Profits: One Shot with Follow-on Effects

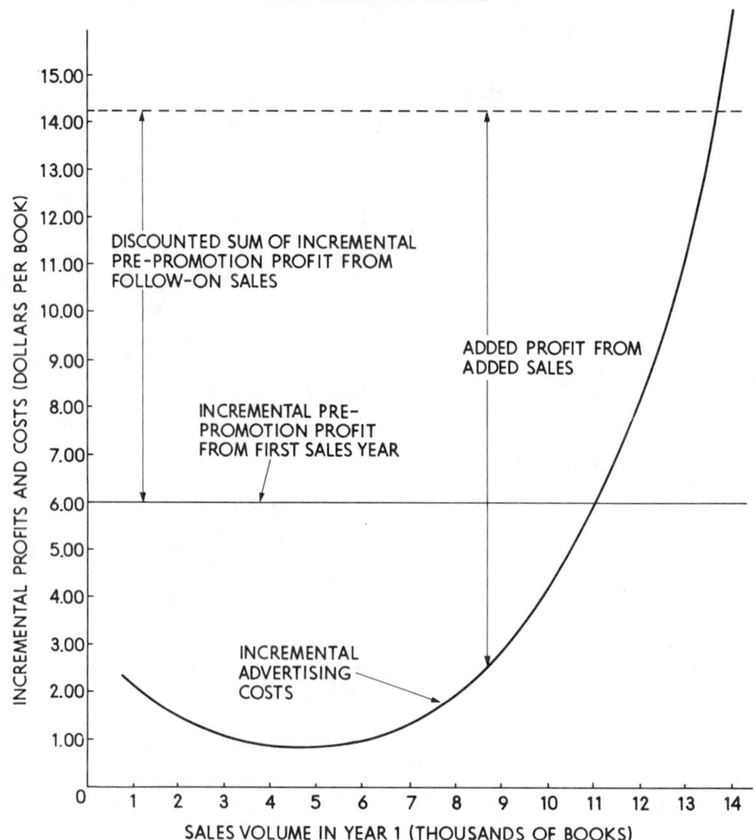

Follow-on profits are discounted to a present value at 10 percent and then added to the immediate profit to give a total present value of $14.24. Exhibit 8b shows this present value stacked up against incremental advertising costs to provide a net incremental profit figure.

(*b*) *New-Cloth Analysis.* There is an alternative but intellectually compatible attack on the problem of a one-shot advertising outlay with follow-on effects. It is to treat the entire outlay as an investment by starting anew and measuring directly the capital productivity of the immediate, together with the follow-on, benefits. The investment profile of a one-shot advertising outlay which has follow-on effects is diagrammed in Exhibit 9. The outlay is portrayed in the negative section of the chart as a down-bar. The whole-life incremental prepromotion profits are depicted for each year in the positive section of the diagram as bars of diminishing length. This illustrates the kind of timetable used for DCF calculation of the rate of return for such an investment.

EXHIBIT 7
One-Shot Advertising Outlay with Follow-on Effects

	Alternative Advertising Outlays ($1000)		*Sales (1000 units)*				*Profits ($1000)*				
			First Year		*Second Year*		*First Year*		*Second Year*		*Face Value of Differential Profit Sum*
	Total	*Differential*	*Total*	*Differential*	*Total*	*Differential*	*Total*	*Differential*	*Total*	*Differential*	
A	5	5	1.7	1.7	1.1	1.1	10.2	10.2	6.6	6.6	16.8
B	10	5	7.8	6.1	5.2	4.1	46.8	36.6	31.2	24.6	61.2
C	15	5	9.0	1.2	6.0	.8	54.0	7.2	36.0	4.8	12.0
D	20	5	10.0	1.0	6.7	.7	60.0	6.0	40.2	4.2	10.2
E	25	5	10.9	.9	7.3	.6	65.4	5.4	43.8	3.6	9.0
F	30	5	11.6	.7	7.7	.4	69.6	4.2	46.2	2.4	6.6

EXHIBIT 8A
Follow-on Effects Due to One-Shot Advertising Outlay

Year	*Incremental Prepromotion Profit**	*Present Value at 10 percent*
1	6.00	5.71
2	3.99	3.44
3	2.65	2.06
4	1.76	1.24
5	1.17	.75
6–10	2.02	1.04
		Total 14.24

* Assumes that quantity sold during year n due to promotional outlay at time o is $Q\ (.665)^{n-1}$ where Q is quantity sold during year 1.

EXHIBIT 8B
Added Net Profit Per Book from Added Sale Due to One-Shot Advertising Outlay with Follow-on Effects

Alternative Advertising Outlays			
Total ($1000)	*Incremental per Book*	*Present Value of Incremental Pre-promotion Profit per Book from 8a ($)*	*Added Net Profit per Book from Added Sale ($)*
5	2.94	14.24	11.30
10	.82	14.24	13.42
15	4.17	14.24	10.07
20	5.00	14.24	9.24
25	5.56	14.24	8.68
30	7.14	14.24	7.10
35	10.00	14.24	4.24

The calculation format is illustrated in Exhibit 10. The investment amount ($200,000) is shown as a negative value. For convenience it is put in the column entitled *Incremental Prepromotion Profits,* where the incremental prepromotion profits estimated for each year are shown as positive amounts. In the next four columns these face-value amounts are translated into present value by discounting each at four trial rates of return: 30, 20, 18, and 17 percent.

The mechanics of the DCF method of measuring the productivity of capital consists essentially of finding that interest rate which discounts the future earnings of an advertising investment to a present value precisely equal to the investment outlay. This rate (roughly 18 percent

EXHIBIT 9
Investment Profile of One-Shot Advertising Outlay with Follow-on Effects

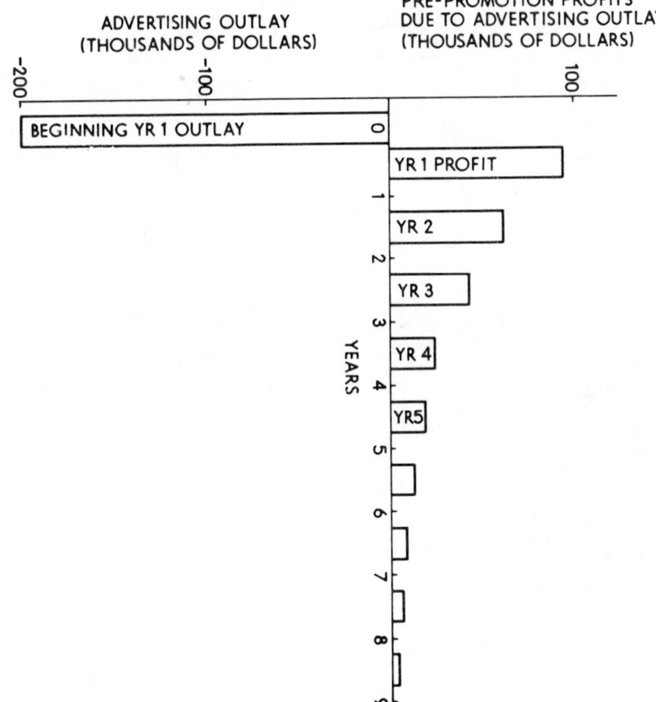

EXHIBIT 10
Discounted Cash-Flow Method of Computing Rate of Return from One-Shot Advertising Investment with Follow-on Effects

Year	*Added Pre-promotion Profits (face value) ($1000)*	*Present Value Discounted at*			
		30 percent	*20 percent*	*17 percent*	*18 percent*
0.	(200)	(200)	(200)	(200)	(200)
1.	96	83	87	88	88
2.	64	41	47	50	49
3.	43	20	26	28	27
4.	29	10	15	16	15
5.	19	5	8	9	8
6.	13	2	4	5	5
7.	9	1	2	3	3
8.	6	1	1	2	2
9.	4	—	1	1	1
10.	3	—	—	—	—
	Net present value	(37)	(9)	3	(1)

in our illustration) is the true rate of return on that investment. It is the highest rate of interest that could be paid to an outsider to whom you turn over all the earnings of the project to pay back the loan and still come out with a zero balance at the end of the project's economic life (i.e. its stream of incremental earnings).

The source of the typical time shape of follow-on incremental profits is shown in Exhibit 11, which charts profiles of follow-on incremental sales obtained by an added dollar of advertising. Plausible profiles of

EXHIBIT 11
Profiles of Follow-on Incremental Sales from an Added Dollar of Advertising Outlay at Beginning of Year 1

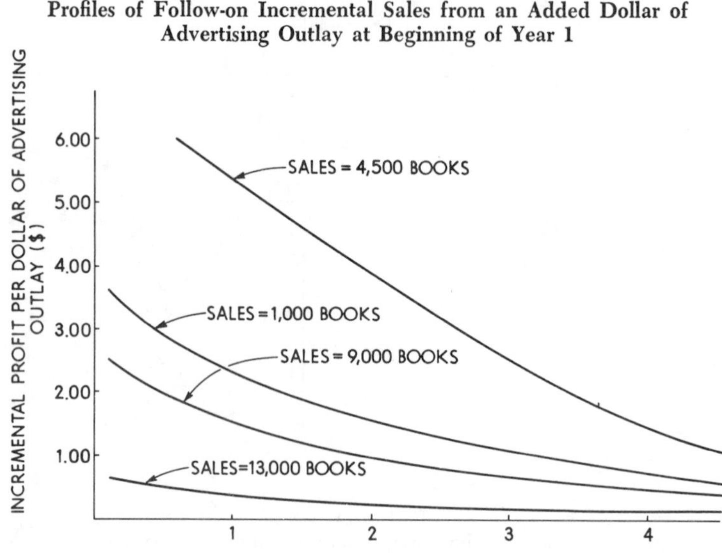

follow-on incremental sales from an added dollar of advertising indicate that the impact of a one-shot promotional outlay does not die—it just fades away. If, as we have assumed, marginal production costs are constant with output rate and if prices are independent of promotion, then incremental prepromotion profits would follow the same pattern. Exhibit 7 shows how these would be derived, and Exhibit 8 shows their time shape.

The present-value variant of DCF analysis provides an alternative route to measurement of investment profitability. Instead of computing the individual rate of return for the promotional project it applies a "go, no-go" gauge to promotional investments. It does so by merely computing the present value of time-spotted incremental profits discounted at the corporation's cost of capital. If this present value is greater than the face value of the one-shot advertising outlay, then the promotional investment should be made (assuming an adequate allowance in the estimates for any above-average risk this particular project may entail). Unless the corporation's opportunity cost of capital is significantly higher than its market cost, the promotion investment should be made, since the productivity of capital exceeds its price.

This DCF variant is illustrated in Exhibit 8, where the present value of incremental prepromotion profits is stacked up against the incremental advertising outlay to produce a net present increment profit per book. This net present value decreases as the level of output increases and will eventually become zero at the maximum-profit advertising outlay.

To summarize, in measuring the productivity of one-shot promotional investments (i.e. outlays which have follow-on effects), we can use three kinds of economic techniques:

1. Patch-on analysis: graft a summary figure of the present value of follow-on benefits on to the value of first-year incremental profits, which is the criterion of optimum outlay for immediate-impact advertising.

2. New-cloth analysis of the DCF rate of return: treat the initial year of benefits as earnings of the advertising investment as well as all the follow-on years. Compute DCF project rate of return, after allowing for any unusual risks of the advertising investment as compared with rival corporate investments. If its DCF return is higher than the

EXHIBIT 12
Investment Profile of Spread-out Advertising with Follow-on Effects

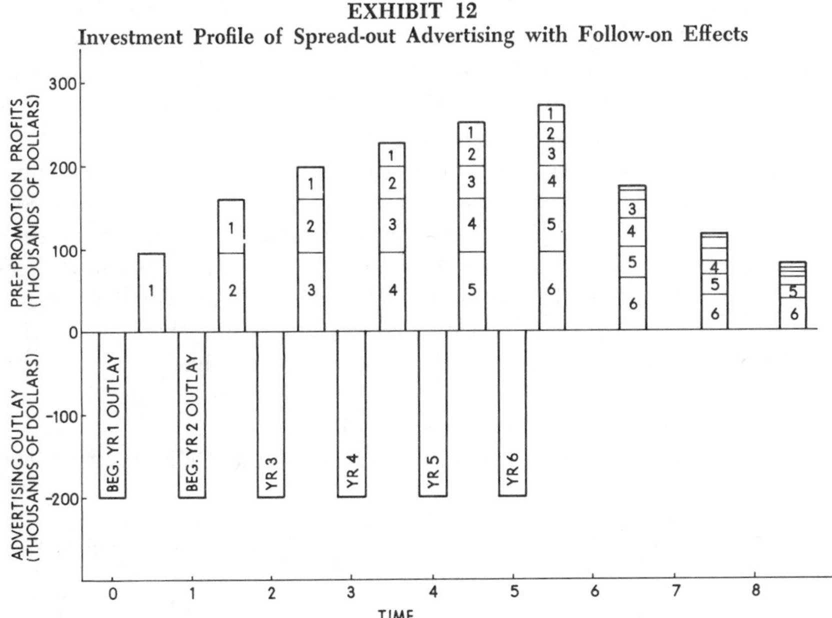

corporation's market or opportunity cost of capital, the project should be accepted.

3. Present-value version of DCF analysis: simply find the present worth of the entire stream of incremental prepromotion profits (adjusted for risk) using a single discount rate, namely, the corporation's cost of capital. If this is bigger than the outlay, accept the project.

2. *Spread-Out Investments.* So much for one-shot outlays. Now we turn to the second and more common category of promotional investments, namely those spread out over a number of years. For spread-out investments, several analytical treatments are possible; modern investment-economics practice has, however, narrowed them to the two variants of DCF analysis: (1) individual project return, and (2) present value at cost of capital.

The investment profile of a spread-out advertising investment is shown in Exhibit 12. Diagrammed by down-bars in the negative section is the advertising investment of $200,000 each year for six years and then none for four years. The incremental prepromotion profits caused by each year's advertising trail off over a six-year period following the pattern suggested in Exhibit 9. For each year they are identified with numbers corresponding to the year of advertising outlay which caused them.[1] Profit bars are slightly offset, primarily for clarity, but also to indicate some time lag.

The net balance of cash flows from spread-out advertising investment with follow-on effects is illustrated in Exhibit 13. It is derived from Exhibit 12 in a manner diagrammed for the first year where the down-column is the net balance of an advertising outlay of $200,000 and an incremental profit of $96,000. This balance each year is shown in black and traced by a solid line. It is this net balance which is fed into the DCF computation to save arithmetic.

Exhibit 13 also shows the cumulative balance of outlay and inflow for each year. This cumulative balance is shown by crosshatched columns. The dotted line which hooks up these columns indicates that after the fifth year, in terms of face (not discounted) value cash flows, the advertiser has got his bait back in incremental profits. But he has not yet any return on his investment, and the only thing that matters for such a return is what happens after he gets his bait back. Productivity of capital is *not* measured or even indicated by how *soon* he gets back his advertising investment (payback period).

The mechanics of applying both variants of the DCF measurement

---

[1] The cumulative impact of this time pattern can be seen most clearly by tracing the effects of year 1, diagrammed at the pinnacle of the profit bar for successive years. By year 7 the effects of the first year's advertising have disappeared; by year 8 the effects of the second year's advertising have, too, and so on. After advertising ceases at the end of year 6, the follow-on benefits of this and previous years continue for several years but trail off in aggregate.

EXHIBIT 13
Profile of Net Balance of Cash Flows from Advertising Outlays Spread Over Six Years

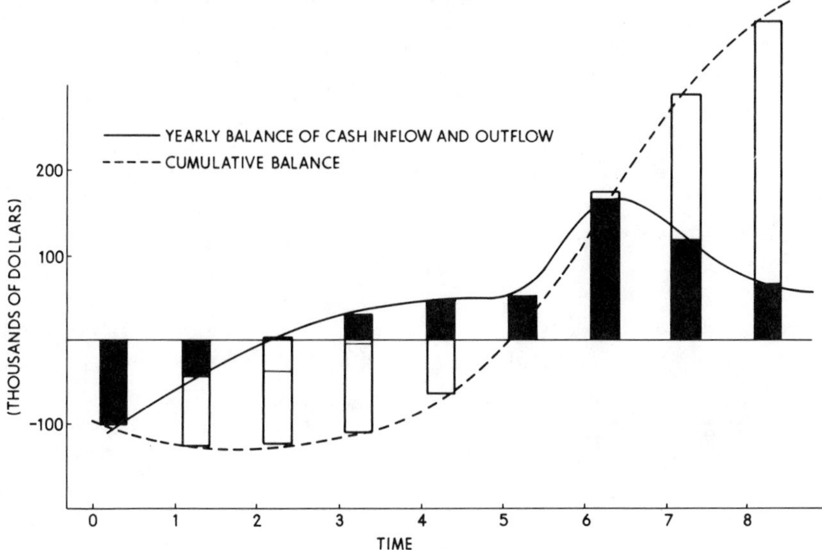

of the productivity of a promotional investment are illustrated in Exhibit 14. For each year the advertising outlay and the prepromotion incremental profits of Exhibit 12 are shown and are netted as in Exhibit 13. The DCF project rate of return is computed from continuous discount tables; it is found to be 18 percent. The present-value variant of DCF is also applied, with cost of capital assumed to be 10 percent. With this value of money the advertising investment promises plus values, since discounted incremental profits when summed are bigger than the present value of the advertising outlays by $1140.

Hence we see that for promotional investments of the spread-out type, DCF measurement of the productivity of the capital that is tied up gives management an engine of analysis which can cope with a stream of future investment outlays forecasted to produce a fluctuating, delayed, and cumulative stream of prepromotional incremental profits. This analysis makes it possible for promotional investments to compete for corporate funds on an objective rate-of-return basis of economic merit, and for investments in persuasion to become an integral part of the firm's planning and rationing of capital.

Thus, there are at least two decision edges for each medium. For example, in direct-mail advertising of a book one decision is where to cut off in working down candidate mail lists which have been laddered as to productiveness. The other decision is where to stop in progressively more intensive promotions of each mail list thus selected.

For immediate-impact advertising the criterion is the same for deci-

EXHIBIT 14
Discounted Cash Flow Method of Computing Return for Spread-out Investment

Year	Net Cash Flow ($1000)	Present Values* at 10 percent	Present Values* at 18 percent
1.	(104)	(109.0)	(112.0)
2.	(40)	(41.0)	(45.0)
3.	5	(7.7)	(12.0)
4.	30	4.0	6.2
5.	50	25.0	17.7
6.	65	32.0	18.0
7.	175	91.4	54.0
8.	115	54.3	30.0
9.	75	32.1	16.3
10.	50	19.3	9.1
11.	25	8.8	1.3
12.	15	4.8	.6
	Net present value	114.0	(6.0)

* Since continuous discount tables are used, each year's net cash flow must be separated into beginning year outlay and "through year" inflow before being discounted.

sion edges. It is the point where incremental costs of advertising equal incremental profits.

For delayed-impact advertising, the investment decision can be all or none, in which case the cutoff criterion is where the rate of return equals the cost of capital.

The concept that a corporation's investments in promotion should be made to compete with traditional capital expenditure proposals for scarce investable funds is illustrated in Exhibit 15, where the rate-of-return ladder for capital rationing is portrayed.

The idea is simple and plausible. Investment proposals should be ranked on the basis of productivity of capital. In rationing capital, the corporation should work down the rate-of-return ladder until its investable funds are exhausted, if it is unwilling to go to market for additional capital and if the rate of return on the least profitable project thereby accepted is higher than the corporation's market cost of capital. If, on the other hand, the corporation is willing to secure additional capital which can be profitably invested then it should work down the rate-of-return ladder to its market cost of capital (e.g. 10 percent,) accepting all projects above that cutoff and rejecting all below it.

DCF analysis has three variants. The project rate-of-return variant is that illustrated in Exhibit 15. The present-worth variant has also been discussed and used in the preceding analysis. By computing the

EXHIBIT 15
Rate-of-Return Ladder for Capital Rationing

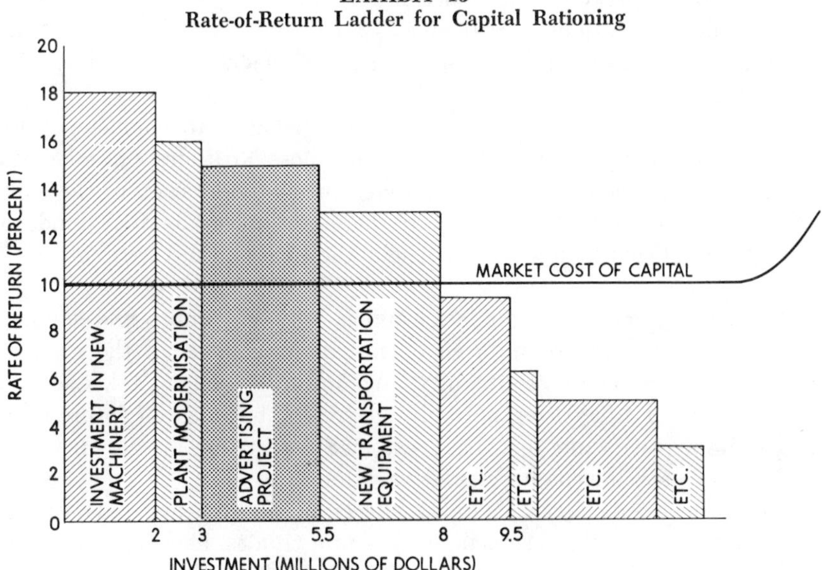

present worth of the benefits of a project at the corporation's cost of capital, all projects on the rate-of-return ladder whose profitability is greater than cost of capital are implicitly accepted by this "go, no-go" gauge and all below it rejected. The third variant, labeled "profitability index," is simply the ratio of the present-worth variant to the amount of capital tied up. If this profitability ratio is greater than 1, the project has a DCF return which beats cost of capital and is implicitly accepted. The profitability-index variant differs from the present-worth variant only in expressing results as a ratio rather than in terms of subtraction.

III. MEASURING THE EFFECTIVENESS OF PROMOTION

Measuring effectiveness of advertising is a big subject, contentious and technical. It would go beyond the scope and space limitations of this paper to do more than touch on a few aspects of it which relate most closely to measuring the productivity of investments in persuasion.

Measurement of the effects of advertising has two dimensions: kinds of effects, and techniques of measurement.

A. Kinds of Advertising Effects

There are basically four kinds of advertising effects that can be measured: (1) effects on behavior (sales), (2) effects on attitudes (usually brand preferences, but sometimes attitudes toward the company), (3) effects on intentions to buy, and (4) effects on the level of knowledge (usually brand awareness, but sometimes knowledge of product characteristics or uses).

Sometimes the explicit purpose of advertising is to change people's attitudes quite apart from the effect of those attitudes on sales and profits. This paper is, however, restricted to a consideration of the effect of advertising on profits. We shall therefore judge the four kinds of advertising effects in terms of the light they cast on advertising's effect on profits.

Clearly the most direct relationship is between profits and sales. If we can measure advertising's effect on sales, we have all the material necessary to measure profitability. We must, of course, take account of the effect of advertising not only on present but also on future sales. For example, the value of a new customer depends on his "loyalty-life" expectancy as well as on his emulation value.

To measure all *other* kinds of effects of advertising, it is usually necessary to translate observed changes in attitudes, intentions, or levels of knowledge into changes in sales. This is usually difficult. The translation can be avoided only when the findings are negative. Sales could not have been favorably affected by advertising if there was no improvement in brand preferences, intentions to buy, brand awareness, etc.

To interpret positive findings, however, it is necessary to know how much sales will increase because of a given improvement in consumer attitudes, intentions, or knowledge. Although the relationship between changes in these indirect effects and changes in sales can sometimes be estimated at given points in time by making both direct and indirect measurements, there is no assurance that the relationship will be stable through time. This basic fact limits the usefulness of measurements of these indirect effects in determining the optimum size of the advertising budget. Therefore, direct measurement of the effect of advertising on sales is usually the only firm basis for the application of the profitometrics approach.

B. Measurement Techniques

Just as there are different kinds of effects that can be measured so there are different techniques for measuring them. Techniques can be put in two groups: (1) controlled experiments, and (2) nonexperimental techniques.

1. *Controlled Experiments.* By far the most powerful technique available for measuring the effect of anything—be it chemical compounds or advertising—is the designed experiment. No other technique provides such precise information with so little ambiguity. Controlled experiments deserve to be better understood. There is ample evidence that businessmen have failed to appreciate and utilize fully this very powerful technique for providing useful information.

These are three basic principles to designed experiments: (1) The factor being investigated—whether it be advertising or penicillin—must be administered to identifiable subgroups of the entire group in which you are interested. If you are interested in all consumers in the United States, you must administer your advertising to only a portion of these consumers. (2) The subgroup exposed to the facts being investigated must be representative of the entire group which is of interest. (This means that the subgroup must be selected by some random process, defined in its technical, statistical sense.) (3) The difference between changes in the subgroup and the rest of the group (or some portion of it) must be measured before and after the factor being investigated is administered. (This means that controlled experiments on the effects of advertising would involve measuring the rates of sale before and after the advertising in groups which had been exposed to the advertising and groups which had not.)

Many businessmen fail to realize that experimentation, which has been so productive in the natural sciences, can be used with equal validity in business and advertising research even though the subject investigated is the uncontrollable behavior of people. The designing and interpretation of experiments is a technical process to be performed by trained statisticians, but businessmen should understand the potential value of such experiments to all executives responsible for the control of substantial discretionary expenditures.

It is much easier to carry out controlled experiments of this sort in some advertising media than in others. For example, it is very hard to conduct a controlled experiment for a promotion that uses mass media like television or radio, since we cannot isolate randomly selected groups only one of which was exposed to the promotion. Radio and TV promotions have an impact on all households in a specifiable geographic area that own receiving equipment. Thus, it is necessary to match up groups of geographic areas rather than groups of individual households, and random selection is not usually feasible.

In contrast, a promotional campaign conducted by mail is ideally suited for a carefully controlled scientific experiment aimed at gauging the effectiveness of the promotion quickly and accurately. A process of selecting every *nth* household or of sampling candidate mailing lists presumably produces a random group within the mailing-list population. And two such groups constitute a matched pair of random samples with all the characteristics required for comparison. Thus, the main problem with measuring the effectiveness of a mail promotion is obtaining data on sales to individual households in each of the matched groups.

Even for mass media, where matched random-sampled groups cannot in general be obtained, there are statistical procedures capable, in principle, of producing reliable results. Instead of comparing sales in perfectly matched (randomly selected) groups, one can compare sales in areas exposed to the promotion with sales in areas not exposed, adjusting the comparison statistically for whatever differences exist between buyers in the two areas. That is, while the groups are not matched in the sense of being the same in all respects except exposure to the promotion, the effect of the differences between the groups on sales can sometimes be independently estimated, and consequently we can estimate the net effects of the promotion. Whether this procedure will produce reliable results depends on the adequacy of the adjustments for differences.[2]

Painful experience with the practical difficulties of developing controlled experiments in this area make me recognize that competitors can sometimes, without making the outlays, learn much about research findings and even, under some circumstances, distort results. I am aware that the variables that determine a product's sales are numerous and hence that it is impossible to control all variables except the one under study. But this impossibility exists in the physical sciences, too, and it has not prevented the enormous productivity of the controlled experiment here. The variation caused by factors other than the one examined is usually greater in the social sciences. But because we know it is bigger we can sometimes design the experiment so as to show us how much of the variation comes from these irrelevant factors.

2. *Nonexperimental Techniques.* When the measurements ideally called for in the profitometrics approach are not feasible, it is sometimes possible to obtain, by inferior means, suggestive indications of the effect of advertising. Information about changes in consumer attitudes, buying intentions, and levels of product and brand knowledge can sometimes provide valuable negative information about advertising effects. However, for positive usefulness it is necessary to measure the relation between sales behavior and these indications of buying conditioners. Bridging this gap metrically is difficult indeed.

An inferior technique of measurement is that involving information gathered in a nonexperimental situation. Data can often be obtained

[2] Ideally, if we know that two areas are matched in all critical respects except that household income is higher in one area (the one receiving the promotion) than in the other, and if we know the true relationship between household income and sales, we can obtain an accurate estimate of the promotion's influence on sales by a simple comparison of sales adjusted for the known income difference. But in the real world, groups of people in "matched" areas differ in a variety of subtle ways that we do not fully understand and cannot adequately measure. As a consequence, we can only approximate the true effects of a promotion on sales, and the measurement is subject to a good deal of uncertainty.

with less planning, cost, and technical knowledge than is required for experimentation. The basic and inevitable deficiency of nonexperimental data is that it is never possible to be sure what they mean. There is an inherent ambiguity in all nonexperimental data which makes it impossible to identify and measure causal relationships with certainty and precision. If you are interested in measuring the effect of advertising on sales with the use of historical data relating to advertising and sales, you will always run the research risk that any observed correspondence between increases in sales and advertising is the result of something other than the effect of advertising on sales. For example, when the advertising budget is set as a fixed percentage of sales, the research risk is that sales have determined advertising rather than vice versa. Or conceivably, both advertising and sales increased during periods of rising national income and prosperity and decreased during periods of declining national income, correlation being partly spurious. Under these circumstances, it would be hard to isolate and measure the effect of advertising on sales. The picture gets even more confused when one recognizes the important effects of concurrent changes in competitors' advertising and product policies during the period.

No amount of data can prevent the possibility of several different and perhaps equally plausible interpretations of the results. Under such circumstances the interpretation often chosen is one which conforms to preconceptions or prejudice. This, of course, largely destroys the function of the measurement.

To sum up, profitometrics requires the measurement of the effects of advertising on sales and the effects of sales on profits. These effects ideally should be measured by means of controlled experiments. Delayed and cumulative impacts should be analyzed in terms of the investment return produced by the stream of incremental profits over the loyalty-life expectancy of the customers acquired by the advertising investment.

IV. SOME IMPLICATIONS

There are some interesting implications of this analysis and its underlying postulates:

1. Most promotional outlays are in economic reality (even though not for bookkeeping, for taxpaying, or for conversation) largely investments.

2. Although most companies have multiple objectives the overriding corporate goal for the decisions on investment of corporate capital should be to make money. The basic measurement of the productivity of capital invested in promotion must therefore be profitability.

3. For immediate-impact advertising in principle, profits can be maximized by pushing spending up to the point where the added adver-

tising cost of increasing sales by one unit just equals the incremental prepromotion profit which the additional sale will create. For advertising whose significant effects are "quick and dead," the incremental profit obtained from the sale adequately measures worth.

4. For advertising whose impact is delayed and cumulative and whose results may create a stream of repeat sales, a more complex measure of worth is needed. Because such advertising is really an investment, purchasing customers by promotion is like purchasing annuities. The value of a customer, like the value of an annuity, is the present worth of the stream of future profits he will produce. How long this stream will last has a profound effect on customer worth. It is partly determined by gestation period, partly by the new customer's loyalty life.

5. The investment-profitability yardstick that is realistic and economically appropriate for promotional investments derives from discounted cash-flow analysis (DCF). It has three variants: (*a*) project rate of return, (*b*) present worth at cost of capital, and (*c*) profitability index.

6. Because much promotion is really an investment (happily expensable for tax purposes), it should compete for funds with alternative ways of investing them. This rivalry for capital should be on the basis of profitability. The present worth of the stream of profits which the promotion can yield should be compared with the cost of funds and with the present worth of the stream of profits which could be obtained by the best alternative use of funds.

7. In rationing scarce capital among competing investment proposals, the cutoff or minimum acceptable rate of return should be the corporation's cost of capital—outside market cost or internal opportunity cost, whichever is higher.

8. The estimates necessary for practical application of discounted cash flow analysis *can* be made:

(*a*) Incremental production cost and prepromotion profit per unit can be predicted cheaply with adequate precision for most mass-produced products.

(*b*) The effect of advertising on sales is far more difficult to estimate. Yet progress must be and is being made here. Of the various kinds of estimating techniques, the controlled experiment is by far the most precise and powerful means of measuring advertising's effect on sales.

(*c*) The cost of its equity capital can, with modern techniques, be measured and predicted with sufficient precision so that no corporation is today justified in refusing to use it in sourcing and rationing its capital.

(*d*) The cost of direct-debt capital is easy to measure with precision. The cost of indirect debt, such as lease debt and oil payments debt, is harder to measure, but workable approximations can be made.

(*e*) The mix of equity and debt capital that is economic for each corporation can be estimated with adequate accuracy. The mix that is probable for the future (which often differs from the existing mix) is all that is needed to complete the estimate of the corporation's combined cost of capital.

9. There are a number of reasons why the profitometrics approach has not been widely used in determining the advertising appropriation. The basic explanations for this oversight are, I think (1) lack of a determined desire to find the most scientific solution for this intricate management problem, (2) ignorance of the potentialities of modern research techniques for this problem, and (3) quite normal distrust of practically any sort of analysis which is not easily understood by the untrained layman. Economic analysis, even in its most managerial applications, sounds academic, and a DCF investment approach to the advertising budget sounds formidable as well as being unfamiliar.